D1407299

By the same author

MILITARY HISTORY
Wolfe at Quebec
The Destruction of Lord Raglan: A Tragedy of the Crimean War
Corunna
The Battle of Arnhem
Agincourt
Redcoats and Rebels: The War for America, 1770–1781
Cavaliers and Roundheads: The English at War, 1642–1649

HISTORY
King Mob: Lord George Gordon and the Riots of 1780
The Roots of Evil: A Social History of Crime and Punishment
The Court at Windsor: A Domestic History
The Grand Tour
London: The Biography of a City
The Dragon Wakes: China and the West, 1793–1911
The Rise and Fall of the House of Medici
The Great Mutiny: India 1857
The French Revolution
Rome: The Biography of a City
The English: A Social History 1066–1945
Venice: The Biography of a City

BIOGRAPHIES
Benito Mussolini: The Rise and Fall of Il Duce
*Garibaldi and His Enemies: The Clash of Arms
    and Personalities in the Making of Italy*
The Making of Charles Dickens
Charles I
The Personal History of Samuel Johnson
George IV: Prince of Wales, 1762–1811
George IV: Regent and King, 1811–1830
Edward VII: A Portrait
Queen Victoria in Her Letters and Journals
The Virgin Queen: The Personal History of Elizabeth I

Christopher Hibbert

FLORENCE

THE BIOGRAPHY
OF A CITY

VIKING

VIKING

Published by the Penguin Group
Penguin Books Ltd, 27 Wrights Lane, London W8 5TZ, England
Penguin Books USA Inc., 375 Hudson Street, New York, New York 10014, USA
Penguin Books Australia Ltd, Ringwood, Victoria, Australia
Penguin Books Canada Ltd, 10 Alcorn Avenue, Toronto, Ontario, Canada M4V 3B2
Penguin Books (NZ) Ltd, 182–190 Wairau Road, Auckland 10, New Zealand

Penguin Books Ltd, Registered Offices: Harmondsworth, Middlesex, England

First published 1993

10 9 8 7 6 5 4 3 2 1
First edition

Line drawings by Ursula Sieger
Maps by Reginald Piggott

Filmset in Bembo by Selwood Systems, Midsomer Norton
Printed in Great Britain by Butler and Tanner Ltd, Frome, Somerset

A CIP catalogue record of this book is available from the British Library

ISBN 0-670-842974

For Bruce Hunter with gratitude and affection

CONTENTS

ACKNOWLEDGEMENTS   ix

ILLUSTRATION ACKNOWLEDGEMENTS   x

AUTHOR'S NOTE   xi

MAPS   xiii

1. The Roman City, 59 BC–AD 405   I

2. Marauders, Emperors and Margraves, 405–1115   5

3. Merchants, Guelphs and Ghibellines, 1115–1280   13

4. Blacks and Whites, 1280–1302   27

5. Life in Dante's Florence, 1265–1348   35

6. Strikes and Riots, 1348–1420   61

7. The Rise of the House of Medici, 1420–39   74

8. Artists of the Medici, 1439–64   92

9. Father of the Country, 1455–64   97

10. Wives and Weddings, 1464–72   109

11. The Pazzi Conspiracy, 1478   131

12. Lorenzo the Magnificent, 1478–92   136

13. The Bonfire of the Vanities, 1492–8   150

14. Conspirators and Cardinals, 1498–1527   164

15. Siege and Murder, 1527–37   173

16. The Grand Duke Cosimo I, 1537–74   179

17. Pageants and Pleasures, 1560–1765   186

18. Tourists and Tuft-hunters, 1740–88   208

19. The Grand Duke Peter Leopold, 1765–91   220

20. Napoleonic Interlude, 1796–1827   226

21. Risorgimento, 1814–59   237

22. The Capital of Italy 250

23. 'Ville Toute Anglaise' 260

24. Residents and Visitors 277

25. 'Firenze Fascistissima', 1919–40 285

26. War and Peace, 1940–66 294

27. Flood and Restoration, 1966–92 305

NOTES ON BUILDINGS AND WORKS OF ART 314

TABLE OF PRINCIPAL EVENTS 370

THE MEDICI FAMILY 372

BIBLIOGRAPHY 376

INDEX 384

ACKNOWLEDGEMENTS

We are most grateful to the authors, editors, translators and publishers of these books for the use of the extracts quoted in the following pages:

Harold Acton, *The Last Medici* (Methuen) and *More Memoirs of an Aesthete* (Hamish Hamilton); Glenn Andres, John M. Hunisan and A. Richard Turner, *The Art of Florence* (Cross River Press); Pietro Bargellini, *La splendida storia di Firenze* (Vallechi); Eric Cochrane, *Florence in the Forgotten Centuries* (University of Chicago Press); Leon Edel, *The Life of Henry James* (Penguin Books); Richard Ellmann, *Oscar Wilde* (Hamish Hamilton); Carlo Francovich, *La Resistenza a Firenze* (La Nuova Italia); Richard A. Goldthwaite, *The Building of Renaissance Florence* (Johns Hopkins University Press); Frederick Hartt, *Florentine Art under Fire* (Princeton University Press); 'Lawrence H. Davison' [D. H. Lawrence], *Movements in European History* (Oxford University Press); Eric Linklater, *The Art of Adventure* (Macmillan); Franco Nencini, *Firenze: I giorni del diluvio* (HarperCollins); Harold Nicolson, *Diaries and Letters* (Collins): Ugo Pesci, *Firenze capitale* (Bempored e Figlio); Mark Phillips, *The Memoir of Marco Parenti* (Heinemann); John Pope-Hennessy, *Learning to Look* (Heinemann); Osbert Sitwell, *Great Morning* (Macmillan); Giorgio Spini and Antonio Casali, *Firenze* (Laterza); Lina Waterfield, *Castle in Italy* (John Murray).

The translations of Giovanni Villani's *Cronica fiorentina* are by Rose E. Selfe, of Giorgio Vasari's *Vite* by George Bull, of J. Lucas-Dubreton's *La Vie quotidienne à Florence au temps des Médicis* by A. Lytton Sells, of Luca Landucci's *Diario fiorentino* by Alice de Rosen Jervis. The translations of Antonio Pucci's poem on the Mercato Vecchio is by Nicholas Havely, of Galeazzo Sforza's account of his meeting with Cosimo de' Medici by Rab Hatfield, and of Benozzo Gozzoli's letter to Piero de' Medici, of Boccaccio's description of the Black Death and of Giovanni Rucellai's of his son's wedding by Edward Chaney.

ILLUSTRATION ACKNOWLEDGEMENTS

Alinari, 37, 75, 87, 90, 145, 148, 151, 193, 198, 261, 263; Associated Press, 309, 311; Bridgeman Art Library, 55, 94, 119, 140, 187, 209, 231, 267, 274; Browning Collection, Mills College Library, California (on permanent loan to the Armstrong-Browning Library, Baylor University), 264; Fitzwilliam Museum, Cambridge, 211; Kunsthistorisches Museum, Vienna, 184; Magnum Photos, 312–13; Mansell Collection, xviii, 16–17, 66, 77, 80–81, 81, 103, 244; Mondadori, 49; National Gallery, London, 162; National Gallery of Ireland, Dublin, 126; National Portrait Gallery, London, 266, 282 (left); New York Public Library, 282 (right); Parker Library, Corpus Christi College, Cambridge, 10; Rijksmuseum, Amsterdam, 54; Royal Academy of Arts, London, 278; Scala, 3, 29, 39, 44, 45, 52, 56, 59, 62, 78, 101, 105, 117, 124, 125, 133, 142, 183, 194–5, 203; Wim Swaan, 72, 85, 165; Topham Picture Library, 289; Vatican Library, 11; Wallace Collection, 235.

All colour illustrations are reproduced by courtesy of Scala with the exception of (second inset) pages 4 (bottom), Royal Albert Memorial Museum, Exeter; 5, Royal Collection, St James's © H.M. The Queen; 8 (bottom), Mary Evans Picture Library.

AUTHOR'S NOTE

Although this book is intended as a well-illustrated introduction to the history of Florence and of the social life of its people from the days of the Roman Empire to those of Mussolini and the flood of 1966, I have tried at the same time to make it, in some sense, a guidebook. It cannot pretend to be a comprehensive one, but the notes at the back contain some information about the places, buildings and treasures which are mentioned in the text; and I believe that none of the principal sights and delights of Florence has been omitted. I have also attempted to describe the city as it appeared to foreign visitors and residents, generation after generation, century after century, from the time of Dante to that of the Brownings, the Trollopes and Henry James. The book will, therefore, I hope be of practical use to all those who intend one day to visit or revisit Florence, as well as providing an outline of its varied past and character sketches both of the men and women who have played their parts in its long history and of the many strangers who have come under its peculiar spell, so many of them English or American that to the Goncourt brothers it seemed in the 1850s 'une ville toute anglaise'.

For her help in writing the notes I am most grateful to my daughter, Kate. She, assisted by my wife, by Bruce Hunter and Belinda Hollyer, has also helped me in checking these notes while we were working in Florence to ensure that the information given is as up to date as may be.

Once again I owe a particular debt of gratitude to the Hon. Edmund Howard, who has assisted me so much with my research, particularly with Italian books and articles not available in English. The translations of the quotations from these, and from his brother Hubert's account of his entry into Florence in August 1944, which originally appeared in *Il Ponte*, are mostly his. I am most grateful also to John Guest; to Eleo Gordon and Peter Carson of Viking; to Ursula Hibbert for having read the proofs; to Josine Meijer, who found the pictures for the book; to Esther Sidwell, who edited it; to Ursula Sieger, who drew the pictures for the Notes on Buildings, and to Reginald Piggott, who drew the maps; to Claire Smith of Harold Ober Associates and Eric Swenson of W. W. Norton, New York; to my wife for having made the index; and, for their help in a variety of ways, to Margaret Lewendon, Val Goodier, Alison Riley, Caroline Elam, Maria Orsini, Sophia Carducci-Loredan, Marcello Camelloni and Sir Harold Acton. As when I was working on my similar books on Rome and Venice, the staffs of the British Library, the London Library and the Italian Institute of Culture have all been unfailingly helpful. So, too, have the staffs of the Biblioteca Nazionale in Florence and the Museo di Firenze com' era.

Finally I must thank Jacques Braun, Derek Bond and Leo Derrick-Jehu for having read various chapters of the book and given me so much useful information; and Dr Edward Chaney, sometime research fellow in the history of architecture at Lincoln College, Oxford, former resident of Florence and co-editor of *Florence: A Travellers' Companion*, for having read the whole of the typescript and suggested so many improvements.

CHRISTOPHER HIBBERT

MAPS

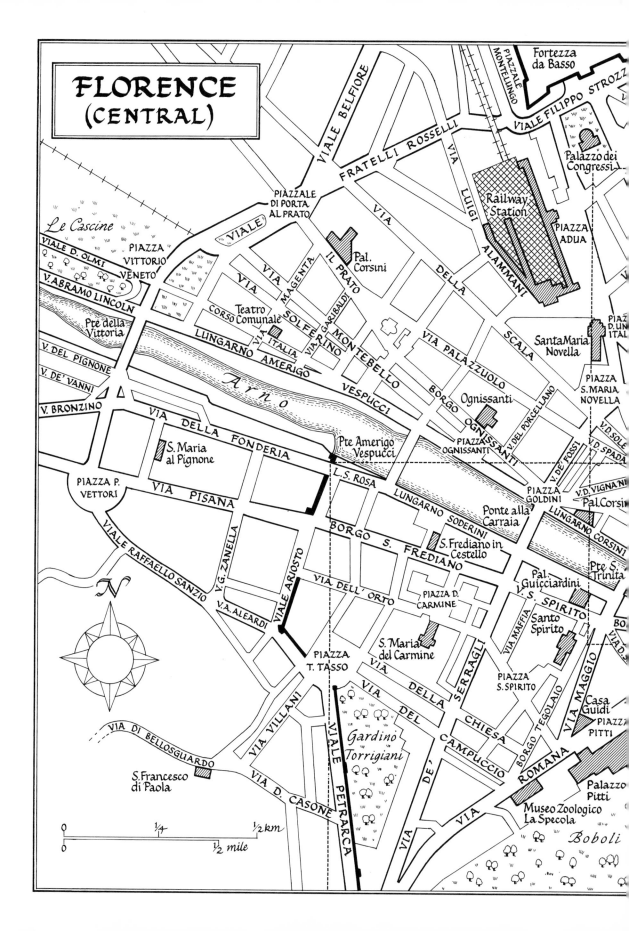

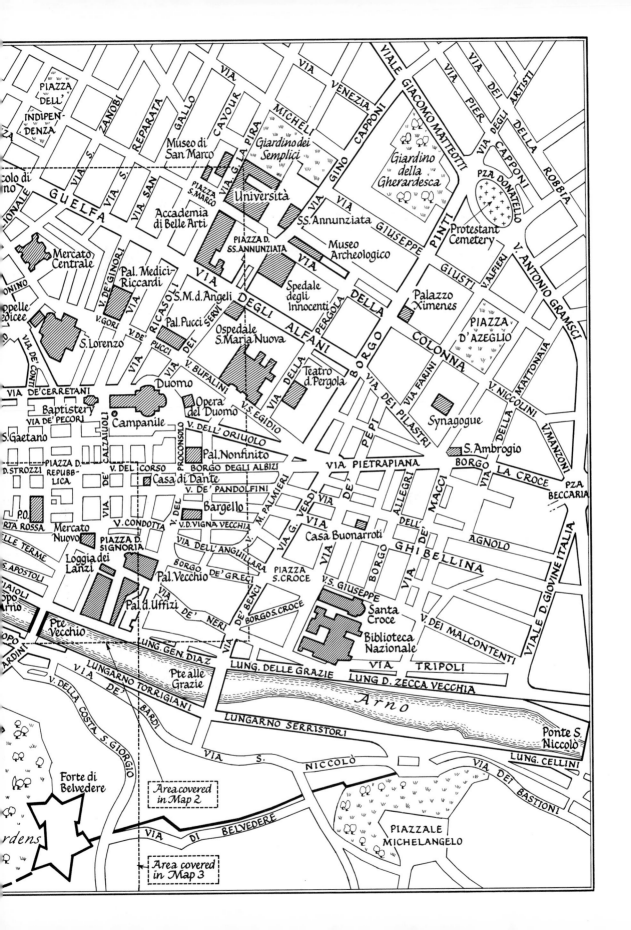

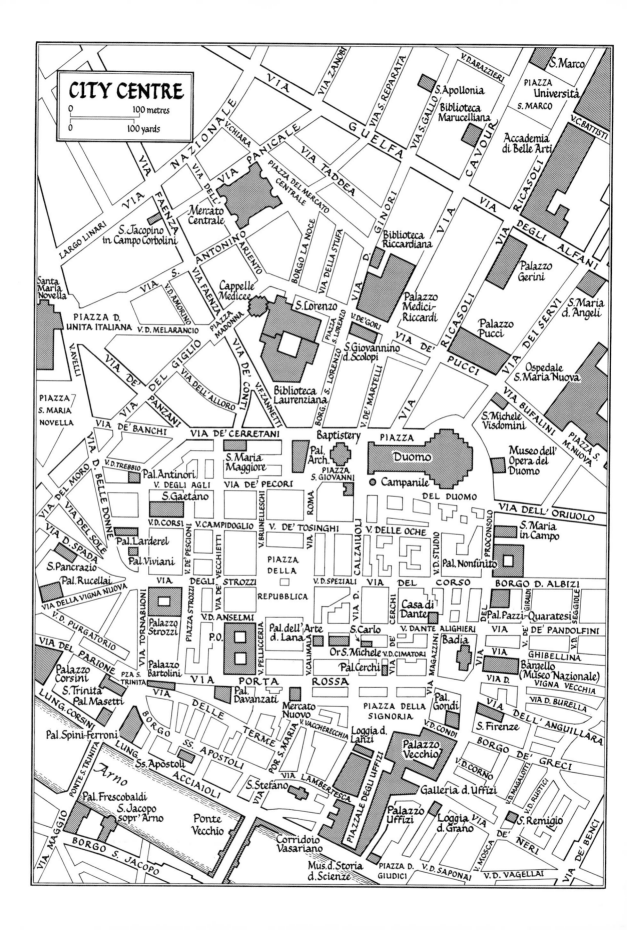

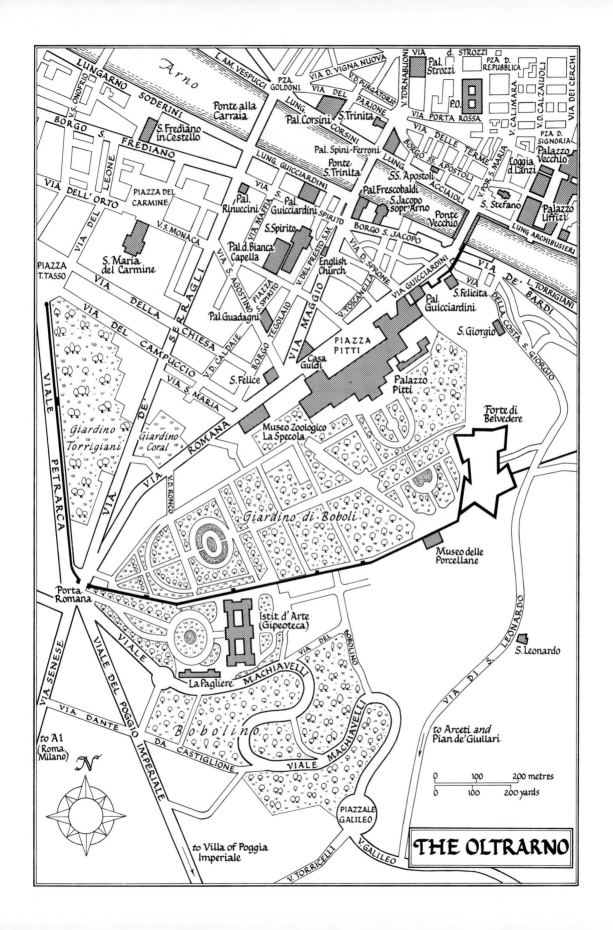

THE OLTRARNO

THE ROMAN CITY
59 BC —AD 405

———————

'Municipium splendidissimum.'
LUCIUS ANNAEUS FLORUS

High above Florence, on the south bank of the River Arno, stands the beautiful church of San Miniato al Monte. Hereabouts, towards the middle of the third century, were laid to rest the bones of Florence's one and only martyr. A Greek by birth, he had been decapitated, so tradition has it, during the persecutions of the Emperor Decius.

By the beginning of the eleventh century St Miniato was all but forgotten and his grave had long since been lost. But neither the decline of the martyr's reputation nor the disappearance of his remains deterred the then Bishop of Florence, Hildebrand, from choosing Miniato as the patron saint of a monastery which he had made up his mind to build on this hill overlooking Florence. So, ignoring a well-founded story that the saint's bones had been removed years ago to Metz by a relic-hunting German, the Bishop announced that they had been discovered on the very spot where the church of San Miniato al Monte still commands its magnificent panorama.[1]

The first abbot of the monastery adjoining the church was named Drogo. Instructed by Bishop Hildebrand to write a biography of the saint to whom his monastery was dedicated, Drogo evidently set to work with a will; but, finding the scattered references to him in ancient histories of little use in such an enterprise, he produced a splendidly romantic hagiography in the final scenes of which Miniato is presented as having his head cut off outside one of Florence's gates, and then flying with it across the Arno to place it upon the hillside where he wished it to be buried with his body.

The origins of the city of Florence itself, as recorded in its earliest histories, are no less fanciful than Abbot Drogo's biography of his patron saint; and it is largely through archaeological excavations that the outlines of the Roman town can be discerned as it came into existence at a time

The interior of the eleventh-century church of San Miniato al Monte. The raised choir above the crypt is approached by steps on either side of Michelozzo's tabernacle (c. 1448). Several of the capitals of the columns in the aisle were taken from Roman buildings in the city below the church.

when the Etruscan kings were a distant memory and before its stones disappeared into the mists of the dark ages which followed the fall of the Roman Empire.

The Etruscans were a mysterious people who seem to have arrived in Europe either by sea from the Balkans or Asia Minor or overland from the north, and to have established themselves in the Po valley and along the Tyrrhenian coast in what was to become Tuscany. Known to the Greeks as *Tyrrhenoi*, they were experts in metalwork and in pottery as well as farmers and merchants carrying on a thriving trade with the Greek cities of southern Italy. Extending their own empire to the south, they eventually seized control of Rome. Their kings had ruled the city for almost a hundred years when, in about 507 BC, the populace rose up in arms against them and the days of the Roman Republic began.

In the years that followed, the armies of the Republic subdued the towns of Etruria one by one, including the fortified hill-town of Fiesole, which had been established above the Arno, then a broad river flowing deeply westwards to the Ligurian sea; and about 200 BC, so it used to be generally believed, the Etruscan people of Fiesole, taking advantage of the peace which the Republic had imposed upon Etruria, came down into the valley to build a town by the banks of the river. Recent discoveries, however, have suggested that Florence may not have been an Etruscan foundation, and that it may, indeed, not have come into existence before 59 BC, the year in which Julius Caesar was appointed consul. Certainly the provincial town which arose on the north bank of the Arno, despite its name, Florentia, 'the flourishing town', was neither in the days of the Roman Republic nor in those of the Empire a large or exceptionally important place.[2] The gate in its eastern wall was less than half a mile from its counterpart in the west. The southern wall, a hundred paces or so from the river bank at its nearest point, roughly following the course of today's Via Porta Rossa[3] and Via Condotta,[4] was also less than half a mile from the northern wall which, extending along the line of Via de' Cerretani,[5] just enclosed the present site of the Piazza del Duomo. The western wall ran roughly along what is now Via Tornabuoni,[6] the eastern along Via del Proconsolo.[7] If the Bargello had then existed it would have been outside the wall on this side; Santa Maria Novella would have been well beyond it on the other.

Yet in this small place, its streets neatly laid out at right angles to each other in the customary Roman way, there were, as in other towns of the Empire, baths and temples, a theatre, a Capitol and a Forum which occupied part of the present Piazza della Repubblica. Most of the buildings were built of brick; some had marble facings and, in imperial times, were decorated with polychrome ornamentation. There was an aqueduct some eight miles long which carried water on high arches from the abundant springs of Monte Morello; and in the Forum there was a deep well

Giorgio Vasari's Foundation of Florence, *painted for the ceiling of the Salone dei Cinquecento in the Palazzo della Signoria in 1563–5.*

filled with filtered water from the Arno. A bridge, which spanned the Arno where the Ponte Vecchio was to be built in the early Middle Ages, carried the Via Cassia from Rome across the river and through Florentia's southern gate; and in the suburbs, which had soon spread beyond the town's walls, there was an amphitheatre, a modest version of the Colosseum in Rome, whose arena, in which gladiators fought and wild beasts charged their tormentors, has long since disappeared beneath the pavements of the Piazza Peruzzi.[8]

The Capitol, raised on a platform about fifteen feet high, was crowned by an impressive white marble temple enclosed by Corinthian columns. It was dedicated to Jupiter, Juno and Minerva, statues of whom were displayed in imposing tabernacles. There were other temples dedicated to the Emperor Augustus, revered after his death in AD 14 as Augustus the Divine; and by the third century, to Isis, goddess of the Nile. In early times the market was held in the Forum, where drinking troughs for beasts of burden were supplied from the well; but in the days of the Empire the market was transferred to the suburbs, and the Forum, by then paved with marble slabs, was being used for political and social gatherings.

Scarcely anything of this Roman town is now to be seen, except the scattered stones which were used in the construction of later buildings, like the Corinthian capitals of the columns in San Miniato al Monte. Beneath the Baptistery of San Giovanni is part of a black and white Roman mosaic pavement, perhaps that of a bakery. But the Baptistery itself, for centuries supposed to have been originally a Roman temple dedicated to Mars in honour of a Florentine victory over the Etruscan city of Fiesole, is, in fact, a Romanesque building begun perhaps in the sixth or seventh century.[9] Yet there are street names in Florence to remind us that a Roman town once stood here – Via delle Terme, for example, the 'street of the baths',[10] Via del Campidoglio, 'street of the Capitol', near the Piazza della Repubblica, where the Forum once stood,[11] Via Capaccio, supposed to be a corruption of *caput aquae*[12] and Via Calimala, which took its name from the *cardo major*, the street that ran from south to north through the centre of Florentia.[13]

By the time of the Emperor Hadrian, who reigned from AD 117 to 138 and who seems to have been commemorated by a statue raised in his honour in the Forum, Florentia had become a prosperous commercial town.

Soon to be the seat of the Governor of Tuscany and Umbria, it was already becoming well known for its copper vessels and woollen goods, which were taken by road and river to Pisa for onward transmission by sea, as well as for the timber cut down in the surrounding forests and embarked at Pisa for delivery to the builders' merchants in Rome. In former times Florence had been encircled by forests, but these were gradually giving way to cornfields, olive groves, orchards and vineyards, and to the gardens of handsome villas with marble colonnades, mosaic floors and courtyards adorned with statuary imported from Greece or Rome.

For generation after generation the people of Roman Florence, and of the lovely *contado* which surrounded it, seem to have lived in pleasant and peaceful obscurity, rarely appearing in such chronicles of the time as have come down to us. But darker days were soon to come as the Empire crumbled into ruins under the persistent invasions of the barbarians from the north and as the population of Florence fell from an estimated 10,000 in the second century to little more than 1,000 in the sixth.

2

MARAUDERS, EMPERORS AND MARGRAVES
405–1115

'No longer Pope but false monk.'
EMPEROR HENRY IV

In AD 405 a host of marauding Ostrogoths besieging Florentia were defeated and massacred outside Fiesole by Flavius Stilicho, a skilful professional general, half-Vandal by birth, in command of an army of mercenaries in Roman pay. But this was the last decisive defeat which Roman forces were able to inflict upon the barbarian invaders.

By now the Roman Empire had been divided into two by the Emperor Diocletian, who had decided that Rome could no longer serve as the capital, being too far removed from the Empire's eastern and northern borders. The greatest of Diocletian's successors, the Emperor Constantine, who had been born in what was to be called Yugoslavia and had spent most of his youth in the eastern part of the Empire, removed his court from Rome to Byzantium and there founded a new capital which was to become known as Constantinople. For a time the Emperor Constantine was able to maintain his rule over the whole of the Empire, East and West; but after his death the Empire of the West began to disintegrate. The invasions of the Germanic Ostrogoths and Visigoths were followed by those of the Huns under the restless, savage-tempered Attila, 'Scourge of God', and the Vandals, fierce Germanic warriors who attacked by night, blackening their faces and their shields. When the boy Emperor Romulus Augustulus was deposed in 476, the German warlord, Odoacer, became King of Italy, establishing his capital at Ravenna. After the death of Odoacer's successor as King of Italy, the Ostrogoth Theodoric, there were further catastrophic upheavals in the land. The Byzantine Emperor, Justinian I, resolved to drive the Ostrogoths out of the peninsula once and for all, and to re-establish direct imperial rule; but, once the Ostrogoths had been finally defeated, another Germanic people, the Lombards, invaded Italy in 568 and settled down in that part of the country to which they have given their name.

Although no longer in control of Italy, the Byzantine Emperors in Constantinople still claimed to rule it, keeping their hold over much of its coastal area through the power of their fleet and maintaining a presence in the persons of their viceroys or exarchs living in Byzantine splendour in Ravenna. In 751, however, the Lombard king, Aistulf, captured Ravenna, thus ending Byzantine dominion in northern and central Italy; and, two years later, when Rome itself was threatened, the Pope, Stephen II, travelled north across the Alps and made his way to St-Denis near Paris to the Christian ruler of the Franks, a Germanic people who had established their rule over a vast territory between the Pyrenees and the Rhine, including the land named after them, France. At St-Denis, the Pope, in return for a promise of support against the Lombards, anointed the Frankish leader, Pepin the Short, King of the Franks. Soon afterwards the Lombards were defeated and forced to restore to Rome the patrimony of St Peter, those extensive tracts of land in central Italy which they had seized from the Church and which, together with former Byzantine territory, were to be known as the Papal States.

In 800, Pepin's son and successor, Charlemagne, arrived in Rome where, on Christmas Day, the Pope placed a crown upon his head and the congregation rose to acclaim him with shouts that rang round the walls: 'Long life and victory to Charles Augustus, crowned by God, the great and pacific Emperor of the Romans!' The Roman Empire of the West had been revived and with it a rivalry between Pope and Emperor which was to last for centuries, bedevilling the early history of Florence.

The Empire was not now just a Roman Empire: under Charlemagne's successors it was to become known as a Holy Roman Empire. For Christianity had, generation by generation, been gaining converts all over the world that Charlemagne knew. Long before 325 when Constantine the Great, the first of the Roman Emperors to profess Christianity, had presided over a General Council of the Church at Nicaea, merchants and traders from the eastern Mediterranean, Greeks and Syrians and Jews, had been riding into Florence not only with pack-animals laden with goods for sale and barter but also with the gospel of Jesus of Nazareth. The Christian faith had spread slowly in Florence at first; yet by the time that Ambrose, a leading churchman and former Governor of Aemilia-Liguria, had come to the town in 393 as an exile from Milan, Christianity had gained a hold over the people which was to prove unbreakable. It was Bishop Ambrose who dedicated a small church in the northern suburbs of the city to San Lorenzo and who traditionally installed in this church a man named Zenobius as Bishop of Florence.[1] Zenobius was still bishop when the Ostrogoths were defeated outside Fiesole in 405, a mercy which he took care to proclaim as being due to the intervention of the Christians' God. He died in 433; and as his body was being taken for burial, so legend has it, the coffin knocked against a dead elm tree which thereupon burst into life, a miracle commemorated by the column which still stands in the Piazza San Giovanni.[2]

Soon afterwards the seat of the Bishop of Florence was moved inside the Roman walls to the church of San Giovanni and from there to a larger nearby church dedicated to Santa Reparata, an obscure early martyr from Asia Minor upon whose feast day victories had been won over invading barbarian armies. Many years later, towards the end of the thirteenth century, Santa Reparata in Florence was re-dedicated to Santa Maria del Fiore and as such it remains the cathedral of Florence today.[3]

In these days of the early Middle Ages, when so little is known about Florence for sure, it is at least certain that monasteries such as the Benedictine house of San Miniato al Monte – both within and outside the town's walls – helped to preserve the old culture of Florence when the town was intermittently under the jurisdiction of various foreign masters, Lombard dukes and Frankish counts or margraves of Tuscany. Yet, as the lands of these monasteries were extended and their riches increased, the more worldly of their abbots became almost indistinguishable in their ways of life from the self-indulgent bishops, whose behaviour in turn resembled that of the great landowning nobles, the owners of the castles which could be seen on every eminence between Florence and Bologna.

The growing impiety and materialism of the Church deeply distressed many Christians, whose disapproval was voiced by evangelists such as St Romuald, who travelled from town to town denouncing the wickedness of those who should have been guiding their flocks away from the paths of wickedness. The son of a nobleman from Ravenna, Romuald had entered a monastery of which he was soon appointed abbot; but, finding the rules of the order insufficiently severe, he had wandered off into the countryside where he had led a life of the most extreme asceticism, spending hours on end in prayer interspersed with bouts of self-flagellation. Having purified himself to the best of his ability, he set out upon his travels, preaching against the wickedness of the clergy and urging the foundation of monasteries and hermitages as a means of reviving Christian zeal. And in this work he created a deep impression upon the mother of the Margrave of Tuscany.

This Margrave, 'il gran barone' as Dante was to call him, was named Ugo. His mother, Willa, was evidently persuaded by Romuald to found an abbey within the walls of Florence. She did so in 978; and to this abbey, La Badia, her son Ugo gave much wealth and property, decreeing that he should be buried there when the time came, as indeed he was, near the church's altar in a Roman sarcophagus, which was later replaced by a tomb created in his honour by Mino da Fiesole.[4]

In Ugo's days the seat of the Margrave of Tuscany was at Lucca, not being officially moved to Florence until the middle of the next century.

Ugo, however, frequently visited Florence, of which he was clearly fond, staying in his palace on the site of the present-day Palazzo Arcivescovile.[5] When he was in Lucca or elsewhere on the Emperor's business in Tuscany, the Margrave's authority was left largely in the hands of the Bishop of Florence, an arrangement far from satisfactory when most bishops seemed more intent upon the personal appropriation of their episcopal estates than upon the discharge of their lay and ecclesiastical duties.

Even Bishop Hildebrand, who founded San Miniato al Monte and certainly took some interest in church reform, was said to have lived in unseemly luxury, having obtained his bishopric by bribery, and to have attended upon the Emperor accompanied by numerous retainers. He did not surround himself with concubines as many of the higher clergy in Tuscany were alleged to have done; but he had a mistress whom he eventually married, an extremely bossy woman, the mother of his many children, named Alberga who, so a medieval chronicler assures us, sat by her husband when he was called upon to receive petitioners or pronounce judgement, and did not hesitate to speak in his name.

> Guarinus [abbot of a monastery at Settimo in the Florentine diocese] made a practice of speaking openly against simoniacs [clergy who sold or bought ecclesiastical preferments, as Hildebrand had done]. On one occasion, having some business in hand, he sought the presence of the Bishop of Florence and, having presented his case, awaited the episcopal decision. Thereupon the wife of the Bishop, Alberga, who was seated at his side, made answer, 'My Lord Abbot, concerning this business you have brought forward, my Lord the Bishop has not yet been advised. He will take council with his *fideles* and inform you of his pleasure.' At these words the Abbot, fired with the zeal of God, poured out vehement maledictions upon her, saying, 'You accursed, sinful Jezebel, how do you dare open your mouth before this assembly of chosen representatives and priests? You ought to be burned at the stake for having presumed to speak thus to a priest of God.'

After this outburst Guarinus thought it as well to go immediately to Rome to explain himself personally to the Pope, who agreed to remove his abbey from the control of Hildebrand's diocese and place it directly under papal jurisdiction, although it was only about five miles from Florence.

It was against such worldly prelates as Bishop Hildebrand that Giovanni Gualberto now began to preach in the manner of St Romuald. Giovanni Gualberto, born about 990, was the son of a nobleman from the Tuscan countryside south of Florence. Trained as a soldier, he seems to have spent a youth characteristic of his class and time, but was persuaded to take the cowl when, having the murderer of his brother at his mercy, he was moved to spare the man's life by a vision of Christ on the Cross. He sought admittance to the monastery of San Miniato al Monte; but no sooner had he been accepted there than he denounced both his abbot for having given the usual presents to the Bishop of Florence on being appointed to the abbacy and the bishop for having accepted them. Not content with condemning them in the hearing of his brother monks, Giovanni Gualberto castigated them in the Mercato Vecchio in Florence and· wherever else crowds gathered to listen to him, until he was beaten up by a gang of the bishop's supporters and driven from the town. He sought safety at Camaldoli, where St Romuald had founded his monastery some twenty years before, and then moved on to the place later known as Vallombrosa, about twenty miles east of Florence, where he founded a monastery of his own.

Giovanni Gualberto continued to preach against simony and corruption; and when it became known that the new Bishop of Florence, Peter Mezzabarba, had acknowledged his appointment by the Emperor with the usual presents, he came down from Vallombrosa with his monks to continue his campaign against corruption in the Church in the streets of Florence, demanding that the bishop should prove his worthiness to remain in office by submitting himself to the judgement of God, that was to say to an ordeal by fire.

The bishop naturally declined to undergo any such test, so Giovanni Gualberto, unabashed, declared that the ordeal would take place anyway on 13 February 1068, that one of his monks would walk through fire and that if he did so unharmed then surely this must be taken as God's sign that the bishop was unworthy of taking his seat in Santa Reparata ever again.

Faggots were lit; the watching crowds waited expectantly; the monk chosen to walk through the fire prepared himself for the ordeal; he moved forward into the smoke. The chroniclers record how he came through the experience unharmed; how the onlookers rushed upon him and mobbed him almost to death; how he later became a cardinal and was revered as a saint; how Giovanni Gualberto, his abbot, did become a saint; and how, having had the satisfaction of seeing Bishop Peter deposed by papal decree, and having founded Santa Trinita, the mother church of the Vallombrosian Order in Florence,[6] Giovanni died in 1073, the year in which that great Church reformer, his fellow Tuscan, Gregory VII, was consecrated Pope in St Peter's.

At the time of Pope Gregory's election, the throne of St Peter had been occupied by a succession of inconceivably disreputable pontiffs. Yet when an attempt was made to elect a Pope sympathetic to the growing movement of reform which was spreading throughout Tuscany, imperial troops intervened and installed the Emperor's own candidate by force.

The reformers' quarrel with the Emperor was still unresolved when Gregory VII became Pope in 1073. The bright son of a Tuscan labourer, he had been taken to Rome for his education and had become an influential figure among the reformers, whose programme was being extended from attacks on abuses in the Church to demands for complete freedom from political and foreign interference and for the right of the Church to be solely responsible for the election of popes and the investiture of bishops. Indeed, soon after his election, Gregory, a brave and uncompromising man, went so far as to claim that the Pope had not only the right to overrule Church councils but to depose emperors and to wear a papal tiara as a symbol of his government of the world by ordinance of God. Such assertions· were bound to anger the Emperor, who considered that he himself held office 'by the pious ordination of God'.

Pope Gregory VII's rival, the Holy Roman Emperor, Henry IV (1050–1106) from an illuminated manuscript of c. 1113.

The Emperor at this time was Henry IV, an impulsive, mercurial young man, twenty-three years old when Gregory became Pope. Provoking Gregory by nominating his court chaplain as Archbishop of Milan, he then announced that Gregory, 'no longer Pope but false monk', was deposed and called upon an assembly of bishops convened at Worms to refuse obedience to Rome. Gregory promptly responded to this provocation by excommunicating the Emperor and releasing his subjects from their oaths of allegiance, so alarming clergy and laity alike that the Emperor began to fear he had gone too far and decided he must make a gesture of submission.

Matilda, Countess of Tuscany,
a detail of a miniature from a
twelfth-century life of La Gran
Contessa by Donizo of
Canossa.

Pope Gregory had a warm supporter in his quarrel with the Emperor in
the person of Matilda, Countess of Tuscany, *La Gran Contessa,* who had
been born in 1046 at Lucca, where her forebears had long held sway over
Tuscany in the name of the Emperor. Her father, head of the powerful
Canossa family, whose great castle stood behind triple walls in the foothills
of the Apennines, had been appointed Margrave of Tuscany by Henry IV's
grandfather. He had been assassinated when she was a young girl; her elder
brother had since died; and she herself had come into possession of the vast
estates of her family as well as the margravate of Tuscany. Her brief and

unhappy marriage to an ugly hunchback, the heir to a French dukedom, ended abruptly when her husband was assassinated, and Matilda returned to Italy, where she became a celebrated figure, renowned for her bravery in the hunting field, the glittering armour which she wore when inspecting her troops and the subservience with which her inferiors addressed her on their bended knees. She was by all accounts revered in Florence: Dante was to praise her virtues in his *Divina Commedia*. It was in her time that the Margrave's official residence was moved here from Lucca; and it was in her family castle at Canossa that the Pope, as her guest, accepted the submission of the Emperor who, after waiting for three cold January days outside the walls, was admitted to receive absolution on condition that he gave up his crown into Gregory's hands, and that if he were restored to the throne, he would swear obedience to the Pope's will.

The submission, however, was not a lasting one; the quarrel was far from over; and the violent disputes between the faction which supported the Emperor, the Ghibellines – most of whose leaders were descendants of feudal lords – and the popular faction which supported the Pope, the Guelphs – led generally by the descendants of rich merchants – were to convulse Florentine society for generations to come, drawing into the age-long dispute members of rival families and rival groups, many of whom had little idea, had never known or had long forgotten what the supposed reasons for their rivalry were.[7]

3

MERCHANTS, GUELPHS AND GHIBELLINES
1115–1280

*'If he does not obey you well, beat him
like a dog, as if he were your own.'*
LAPO MAZZEI

When Matilda, *La Gran Contessa*, died at the beginning of the twelfth century, Florence was becoming recognized as one of the pearls of Tuscany, a town much favoured by the Countess and one whose reputation had been greatly enhanced by the part which it had played in the movement for Church reform and by its support of the Pope and Matilda in their defiance of the Emperor. Once more a flourishing centre on important trade routes, as it had been in the time of the Roman Empire, the days were long since gone when visitors travelling across the lovely valley of the Arno would pass through crumbling walls into a town whose creeper-covered Roman buildings were tumbling into ruins and sinking below such mean shops and habitations as satisfied the needs of a dwindling population. From the 1,000 or so people living here in the sixth century, after a probable decline in the seventh, numbers had risen to about 2,500 in the eighth and to about 20,000 by the middle of the eleventh.

A new town, enclosed by walls reconstructed in 1078, had been built on a level up to ten feet above the old remains. Most of its inhabitants still lived in houses constructed largely of wood, as poky, dark and primitive as others in Europe; but rising above them, all over the town, were tall stone towers, most of them owned by those rich families who now spent as much time in Florence as they did in their castles in the surrounding countryside, the *contado*. These towers, built as defensive strongholds and entered by means of bridges, had living quarters on the upper floors, into which families and their dependants could withdraw in times of trouble, and wooden balconies supported on beams. By the time of the *Gran Contessa's* death there were over a hundred of them in Florence, clusters of them allied together for mutual protection in tower societies, their high walls looming over the roofs of the surrounding buildings, like the surviving Torre dei Donati[1] opposite the church of Santa Margherita in Santa Maria de' Ricci.[2] The river below them was still spanned by the Ponte Vecchio, rebuilt in the twelfth century;[3] but this single bridge was soon to be joined by three others, the Ponte alla Carraia, built about 1220; the Ponte Rubaconte, constructed entirely of stone in 1227, and later known as the Ponte alle Grazie; and the Ponte Santa Trinita,[4] paid for by a member of the rich Frescobaldi family in 1252.[5]

It was families such as the Frescobaldi which now effectively ruled the city. Since the decline of feudalism and of the unquestionable power of the great lords in their forbidding stone castles in the still heavily wooded *contado*, the leading families of Florence had been slowly evolving a commune to organize its civic and mercantile affairs. They had even on occasions raised troops to attack castles occupied by nobles who were antagonistic to the development and growing influence of the town and who arbitrarily imposed tolls and duties on wagons and pack-horses carrying goods in and out of the city. In 1107 a small army marched out of Florence to destroy the castle of Monte Gualandi, which belonged to a branch of the ancient Alberti family; seven years later, in 1114, another small army attacked the nearby castle of Monte Cascioli, whose feudal chatelain was a proclaimed enemy of Florence's commercial prosperity; in 1135 Monte Buoni was assaulted; in 1146 Quoria. Other castles were voluntarily submitted to the commune and their land sold to it. The infantry of the makeshift armies was composed of workers who were summoned to such arms as could be mustered by the ringing of a bell. They marched to battle in their ordinary clothes behind more affluent citizens who could afford a horse, weapons and armour, and thus qualified as cavalrymen. With them, drawn by white oxen, was their Carroccio, a war chariot from whose tall mast flew the flags of the commune. In command were those leading men of the town, the consuls, who were deemed most skilled in military affairs.

Although it seems that the election of these consuls had to be approved by a general meeting of the townspeople – a *parlamentum* assembled in the church of Santa Reparata – in fact the consuls invariably came from one or other of the leading families of the town, either lesser nobles, who now usually lived within the walls but continued to own land outside it, or successful merchants whose riches enabled them to find husbands for their daughters among the young sons of the nobility. In time the family trees of these prosperous merchants became so entwined with those of the nobles that there emerged a composite ruling class in which trade was no dishonourable occupation. Privileged members of this oligarchy supervised Florence's system of weights and measures, in existence well before the end of the eleventh century; they filled the higher offices in the merchant and craft guilds, the *arti*, already coming into existence to regulate the trade in hides and cloth, dyes and spices for which Florence was celebrated; and it was they who directed the foreign policy of the town, so far as there could yet be a policy independent of the Emperor and his representative, the Margrave.

Upon the Countess Matilda's death, the new Emperor, Henry V, appointed to the margravate a man of German rather than Italian birth, a man who immediately removed his official residence from Florence to San Miniato, a town several miles to the west overlooking the road to Pisa, which consequently became known as San Miniato del Tedesco, the German San Miniato. In an effort to assert his authority over the Florentines, this German Margrave occupied the castle of Monte Cascioli, which they had recently taken over from its feudal overlord. The Florentines promptly responded by raising an army. They marched out to the fortress, retook it and killed the Margrave in the process.

Despite representations from Florence, the Emperor appointed another German as Margrave and, after his departure, yet other Germans were sent to fill his place. The Florentines, however, paid them as little attention or respect as they had paid the Countess Matilda's immediate successor; and it was only when an imperial army marched into Tuscany that the Emperor was able to enforce his will upon his supposed subjects.

In the days of the Emperor Henry V and of his two immediate successors, Lothar III and Conrad III, imperial troops were rarely to be seen in Italy; and the commune of Florence, like other communes in Tuscany, was able to increase its influence at the expense of those feudal families who were the Emperor's natural allies and who still possessed numerous castles throughout the Florentine *contado* and beyond. One after the other, these once powerful families were brought to heel by the Florentine commune and were required to make a token of submission to the cathedral church of Florence, through whose doors they were asked to parade in solemn procession, with lighted candles in their hands, on the annual festival of St John the Baptist.

As well as these feudal lords, the Florentine commune was anxious to bring to submission those Tuscan towns which were seen as rivals or impediments to the expansion of Florentine trade. The small town of Prato was attacked and almost destroyed before it was recognized as a useful ally in Florence's rivalry with the growing town of Pistoia, which in those days commanded the road to Bologna. Then Fiesole was besieged and captured in 1125, when most of its walls were pulled down and many of its buildings destroyed, apart from its Romanesque cathedral.[6] And, four years later, the Florentines turned upon Siena in quarrels over the limits of their respective *contadi*, and over rival commercial interests, which were to last for centuries.

Florence's conflicts with her neighbours and rivals continued more or less unchecked throughout the first half of the twelfth century until in 1154

a recently crowned Emperor marched into Italy to reassert his rights in the peninsula. This was Frederick I of the House of Hohenstaufen, who, because of the luxuriance of his red beard, came to be known and feared in Italy as Barbarossa.

Determined to accept neither the rights of investiture of bishops and abbots which the Pope had won in the reigns of his predecessors, nor the growing independences of the Italian communes, the Emperor Frederick, autocratic, energetic and a firm believer in the feudal system, crossed the Alps into Lombardy, ravaged Milan, whose commune had dared to resist him, and, advancing south, engineered the election in Rome of an anti-Pope as a rival to Pope Alexander III, a dedicated exponent of papal authority. Pope Alexander, however, proved a formidable opponent. Organizing a Lombard League of several cities, including Milan and Venice, he brought about the decisive defeat of the Emperor Frederick at Legnano in 1176; and in Venice the next year he sat in state in St Mark's Basilica and, in the words of a German prelate who was present, received the homage of the Emperor who 'threw off the red cloak he was wearing and prostrated himself before the Pope and kissed his feet and then his knees'.

The success of the Lombard towns in gaining for themselves a large

A fresco by Spinello Aretino (fl. 1373–1410), a painter who was probably trained in Florence. His cycle of frescoes in the Palazzo Pubblico, Siena, is devoted to the Sienese Pope Alexander III, a stern advocate of papal supremacy, here shown being escorted by the Emperor Frederick Barbarossa, who was obliged to pay homage to him after the Pope's defeat of imperial forces at Legnano in 1176.

measure of self-government by the subsequent Peace of Constance induced the towns of Tuscany to assert similar rights; and when the Emperor Frederick, by then over sixty years old, travelled through the area on his way to marry his son to the daughter of the King of Sicily, he was dismayed to discover that several Tuscan towns, including Florence, were arrogating to themselves privileges which it was not their right to assume but his to bestow. Indeed, Florence, ignoring imperial authority, pursued a policy entirely her own, subjugating several smaller towns in the *contado*, including Figline and Certaldo; completely wiped out another, Semifonte; and, after a brief alliance with Pisa, quarrelled with that town also, while making overtures to Pisa's traditional enemy, Lucca.

Turbulent as were her relations with her neighbours, Florence continued to grow and to flourish, contriving to diminish the uproar which generally accompanied the election of consuls and the violent vendettas which frequently erupted upon their taking office, and to limit the fights between families, factions and tower associations by inviting a foreigner from a city at least fifty miles distant from Florence to become Podestà. This foreigner, preferably with some legal training, was to combine the offices of chief of police and governing magistrate and would, it was hoped, be more effective in the administration of justice than the naturally partial native officials he was to replace.

The town over which the Podestà presided had grown considerably in size over the past century. The suburbs, the *borghi* beyond the old Roman walls, had become so crowded with buildings that they constituted a threat not only to public health but also to the safety of the town should it come under attack from an enemy determined to set it alight. In the 1170s therefore, when the population had risen to about 30,000, new walls, pierced by several gates and overlooked by watch-towers, were built to encompass these suburbs, circumscribing an area well over twice the size of the Roman town and divided into six neighbourhoods, known as *sestieri*, each with a militia responsible for guarding its own section of the fortifications. These walls included within their boundaries the church of San Lorenzo in the north and extended southwards to take under their protection the area now occupied by the Piazza Pitti and the Piazza Santo Spirito on the far bank of the Arno. By the middle of the following century the Order of Augustinian Canons had established the church and convent of Santo Spirito in this part of the Oltrarno beyond the Ponte Santa Trinita.[7] By then two other religious orders had also founded monasteries and churches just outside the new walls. Friars of the order established by St Francis, son of a rich cloth merchant from Assisi, who was said to have often preached in Florence, began to build their church of Santa Croce in 1228 beyond the eastern gates, in a swampy, slummy area where many wool-workers lived.[8] The Dominicans, an order founded by the severe Spaniard, Domingo de Guzman, which had been granted an old church and lands just outside the western gates, started in 1246 to build their church of Santa Maria Novella, known at first as Santa Maria tra le Vigne, St Mary among the Vineyards.[9]

Both the Dominicans – in particular Fra Pietro da Verona, later St Peter Martyr, who came to Florence in 1243 – and the Franciscans were warm in their support of the papacy against the pretensions of the Emperor, whom they denounced in their sermons in the streets of Florence, as well as from the pulpits of their churches, as a heretic, even as the anti-Christ. When the Dominicans began to build their church of Santa Maria Novella in Florence, Frederick Barbarossa's grandson, Frederick II, had been Emperor for a quarter of a century. A forceful, highly intelligent and contradictory man, at once sensual and pious, by turns cruel and forgiving, he was twice excommunicated by Pope Gregory IX, a close friend of St Francis of Assisi, and then not only excommunicated but also deposed by Gregory's successor, the forthright Genoese, Innocent IV.

In defiance of papal objections, the Emperor advanced into Italy in 1237 intent upon putting an end to what he took to be the increasing insubordination of the Italian communes. After overwhelming the forces of the Lombard League at Cortenuova, he appointed one of his illegitimate sons, Frederick of Antioch, Viceroy of Tuscany and Podestà of Florence, with instructions to take up residence in the town rather than in the old imperial headquarters at San Miniato del Tedesco.

The arrival of this imperial bastard naturally provoked renewed quarrels and disturbances among the leading families of Florence, savage arguments between the pro-imperial party of the Ghibellines and the papal party of the Guelphs. Already in 1216 there had been a ferocious altercation involving several rival families, which the fourteenth-century chronicler, Giovanni Villani, described as marking the beginning of 'that accursed division of Florence into Guelph and Ghibelline... and much evil and ruination befell our city as a consequence'.

This altercation, if not actually inaugurating the 'accursed division', was certainly characteristic of the quarrels which divided the old aristocratic houses of feudal tradition from those more closely connected with the commercial life of the city, and of its claim to independence from the Emperor with the support of the Pope. The trouble began during a feast at a rich man's country house five or six miles beyond the city walls. As was the custom then, the dishes were presented so that two guests shared one dish between them, helping themselves to the food piled upon it as fancy dictated. One of the pairs of guests happened unfortunately to consist of two members of rival families, one a young man of the Buondelmonti and the other from the Uberti. When a jester with reckless joviality snatched their dish away, there was an immediate uproar in which the Uberti youth was hit over the head with a plate and Buondelmonte de' Buondelmonti wounded another guest with a knife. After order had been restored and the guests had returned to their homes, it was decided that to prevent yet another prolonged vendetta, Buondelmonte de' Buondelmonti should marry a girl from the Amidei family, with which the Uberti were closely connected. 'Thereupon,' so an anonymous chronicler related,

> Madonna Gualnada, the wife of Messer Forese Donati, sent secretly for Messer Buondelmonte and when he came spoke to him as follows: 'You will for ever be disgraced by taking a wife through fear of the Uberti. Abandon her and take instead [my own daughter] and your honour will be restored.' As soon as he heard this he resolved to do as he was told without consulting his own family. And when on the following day the guests of both parties had assembled, Messer Buondelmonte passed through the gate of Santa Maria and he went to pledge troth to the girl of the Donati family; and her of the Amidei he left waiting at the church door.
>
> The insult enraged [the Amidei and their relations and supporters] and thus it came about that when Messer Buondelmonte, in doublet of silk and mantle, came riding over the bridge, Messer Schiatta degli Uberti rushed upon him and striking him on the head with his mace brought him to the ground. At once [another of the Amidei's friends] was on top of him and opened his veins with a knife and having killed him they fled . . . Immediately there was a tremendous tumult. The body of the murdered man was placed on a bier and the bride took her place on the seat of the bier, holding his head in her lap and weeping aloud; and in this manner the procession moved through all Florence.

For generations thereafter the vendetta between the families involved was intermittently resumed; other feuds were pursued with equally virulent animosity; quarrels erupted; fights broke out in the streets and on the bridges between families and factions; cries of '*Guelfi!*' and '*Ghibellini!*' echoed round the grey stone walls as the partisans of the opposing factions took shelter behind the massive gates of their tall towers. Even those who would have been hard put to it to explain why they were of one party or the other took to wearing the cut of clothes by which a Guelph or a Ghibelline could be recognized, to sporting a Guelph or Ghibelline feather in their hats, and acknowledging a fellow supporter by a Guelph or Ghibelline sign or watchword.

So long as the Emperor's son, Frederick of Antioch, was established as Podestà in Florence, the leading Ghibelline families, the Uberti, the Amidei, the Lamberti and their friends, were in the ascendant; and in February 1248, after a peculiarly savage fight, those Guelphs who had castles to which they could retire retreated into the *contado*, abandoning their houses in the city to the Ghibellines, who pulled down no fewer than thirty-six towers, one of which was the exceptionally high tower of the Adimari family, known as *il Guardamorto* because it stood as though on watch above the graveyard next to the Baptistery. This tower, sent crashing to the ground, would have landed upon the roof of the precious building, so awestruck bystanders reported, had not St John the Baptist himself miraculously appeared to deflect the falling masonry.

After the death in 1250 of the Emperor Frederick II, whose sudden fatal illness overtook him in Apulia, at Fiorentino – thus almost fulfilling a court astrologer's prophecy that he would die in Florence, a warning that had led him to avoid that city as though it were infested by the plague – his illegitimate son, the Podestà, left Florence for good, and the exiled Guelphs, having defeated a Ghibelline force at Figline, south of the city, returned to it to take control, driving the Ghibellines into exile in their turn and afterwards demolishing their houses and towers as thoroughly as their own had been destroyed, leaving the tumbled ruins uncleared as a warning to other erstwhile supporters and as 'a memorial to their perfidy'.

No sooner had the weight of imperial power been lifted from their shoulders than the Florentines set about establishing a Guelph government of their own, a government acclaimed by the people who paraded through the streets to shouts of '*Viva il popolo!*'. A Capitano del Popolo, a neutral foreigner like the Podestà, was appointed to command the newly formed militia of twenty companies and to act in conjunction with the Podestà in keeping order in the city. A council of twelve *anziani* (elders) was elected, two from each of the six districts into which the city was divided; a new badge was devised for Florence, a red lily on a white field, as well as an emblem for the militia, the Marzocco, the heraldic lion, whose image was to appear on several buildings in Florence and in the public squares of towns brought under Florentine rule.[10] And, as a suitably imposing palace for the Capitano del Popolo, the new government ordered the construction of the Palazzo del Popolo, soon to be renamed the Palazzo del Podestà, and later to be known as the Bargello.[11]

Ostensibly democratic, this government, known as *il Primo Popolo*, was influenced if not directly controlled by the merchant families which had never been far from the centre of power. Its foreign policy consequently continued to be aggressive and expansionist, designed to bring the whole of Tuscany under Florence's control, in particular to force Pisa to allow Florentine goods to pass down the Arno and out to sea free from all customs duties, to compel the smaller towns between Florence and Siena – Volterra, Poggibonsi and San Gimignano – to accept a Florentine citizen as their Podestà and to submit either to having their walls demolished or to having a fortress built for Florentine troops to keep an eye on them. As for Siena itself, this perverse town, the *soi-disant* City of the Virgin, which had welcomed the exiled Ghibellines from Florence under the leadership of Farinata degli Uberti, this must be crushed once and for all.

The Florentines spared no efforts in raising an army for war against the Sienese. Not only were their own men between the ages of fifteen and seventy, with few exceptions, told to hold themselves ready to fight, but envoys were sent to all their subject towns with requisitions for troops and even to towns beyond the borders of Tuscany – to Bologna and Orvieto among others – with requests for support. By the end of August 1260 an army of about 70,000 men had been assembled and equipped with pikes and arquebuses, crossbows and swords, thousands of pack-animals and wagons.

Florence's own companies, 16,000 strong, marched out of one of the city's southern gates confident of victory, their white banners and standards, emblazoned with the red lily, fluttering in the summer sunlight. Joined by the companies provided by their allies, by forces from other Tuscan towns, from Prato and Pistoia, Lucca and Arezzo, San Miniato del Tedesco, San Gimignano and Volterra, all under their separate banners, they assembled on the afternoon of 3 September around the castle of Montaperti within sight of the red-brick walls of Siena.

The Sienese were greatly outnumbered. A few companies had joined them from their own small subject towns, but they had been unable to enlist help from any other Ghibelline city, even from Pisa, which would have welcomed a Florentine defeat. To support them in the battle now imminent, the Sienese were forced to rely upon some mercenaries who had been sent from Germany and the south of Italy by the Emperor Frederick's illegitimate son, Manfred, the self-proclaimed King of Sicily, and the Florentine Ghibelline exiles under Farinata degli Uberti.

Small as their army was, the Sienese did not hesitate to attack the host drawn up outside their walls. They marched down to the banks of the river Arbia, waded through the shallow stream and advanced towards the Florentine ranks, which were not yet ready to receive them. According to the Florentine chronicler, Giovanni Villani, whose version of the subsequent battle is wildly at variance with those of the Sienese annalists, their unpreparedness was largely due to Ghibelline traitors in Florence's army who,

when they saw the enemy approach took to flight, as had been agreed beforehand ... Moreover, they did not permit the Florentines and their allies to form rank and join battle.

And just as the squadron of German mercenaries violently struck the Florentine knights, their banner-bearer, Jacopo del Nacca of the [pro-Guelph] family of the Pazzi, and a man of great valour, was violently struck by that vile traitor, Messer Bocca degli Abbati, who rode close to his side and, hitting him with his sword, cut off the hand which supported the Florentine banner. And immediately Bocca was set on and killed. Seeing the banner on the ground and themselves betrayed at the very moment when they were powerfully assaulted by the Germans, the Florentine knights and foot soldiers were soon put to flight.

Whether or not there was treachery within the Florentine ranks, the Sienese victory was certainly quick and decisive. It appears that the foot soldiers both of Florence and of Lucca stood their ground for a time after the more highly born cavalry had galloped off the field. But their resistance was brief and even Villani admitted that 'a great butchery ensued of the Florentine infantry as well as of the Lucchese and Orvietans who had shut themselves up in the castle of Montaperti. And such as were not killed were taken.'

It has since been estimated that as many as ten thousand men were killed and that some twenty thousand Florentines and allied prisoners were led away to be crammed into the cellars and dungeons of Siena.

Once again the Ghibellines, accompanied by the German mercenaries from Montaperti, rode into Florence, and the defeated Guelph leaders slunk away, first to Lucca, and then – driven from there – to seek the protection of the Guelphs of the Romagna, abandoning their houses and towers to the fate which was then becoming all too familiar in the city: over a hundred Guelph *palazzi* were demolished, and almost six hundred houses, nearly ninety towers and numerous workshops, foundries, mills and cloth-drying sheds. The ten-year-old government of *il Primo Popolo* collapsed, and the Palazzo del Popolo, by then nearing completion, became the headquarters of the Ghibelline leader, Farinata degli Uberti, and of King Manfred's newly appointed Ghibelline Viceroy in Tuscany, Count Guido Novello. He was the husband of an illegitimate daughter of the late Emperor Frederick II and member of an ancient Tuscan family, several of whose members were Guelphs and one of whom, Count Guido's brother, had fought on the Guelph side at Montaperti.

Count Guido Novello seems to have owed his appointment to his family connections rather than to his efficiency and character: his prompt response to demonstrations against the German mercenaries by the people of Florence was to ride out of the city taking the Germans with him. The Ghibellines remained, however; and, in an effort to bring an abiding peace to the city, they asked the exiled Guelphs, as fellow Florentines, to come back. This overture was, however, roundly condemned by the Pope, who wanted no *rapprochement* between the two factions but rather the complete discomfiture of the Ghibellines.

The Pope was now Clement IV, a strong-willed, decisive Frenchman, as intent upon the destruction of Hohenstaufen influence in Italy as he was upon the extinction of the Hohenstaufens' friends, the Ghibellines.

Declining to recognize the Hohenstaufen Manfred as King of Sicily, the Pope supported the rival claims to the Sicilian throne of the King of France's brother, Charles of Anjou, who marched into Italy, gave battle to Manfred near Benevento, defeated and killed him, and had himself crowned king in his place. Then, with the Pope's encouragement, Charles of Anjou sent several troops of his French knights north into Tuscany; and, accompanied by numerous Florentine Guelphs riding beside them, these knights entered Florence in the Easter week of 1267. Once more the Ghibellines fled, never again to wrest control of the city from their rivals.

For a time the Ghibellines maintained their ascendancy elsewhere in Italy; but after Charles of Anjou's defeat of the Emperor Frederick's grandson, Conradin, the last of the Hohenstaufens, at Tagliacozzi in the Abruzzi, east of Rome, in August 1268, they were no longer a power in Tuscany. Following a mock trial, Conradin was beheaded in the market square at Naples; the next summer a Guelph army of Florentines and French knights defeated the Sienese and their Ghibelline allies outside the small town of Colle di Val d'Elsa near Poggibonsi; and in 1270 Pisa, as well as Siena, accepted the inevitability of Guelph supremacy, both towns agreeing to the appointment of a Guelph Podestà.

In Florence the Guelphs now organized themselves into a party, the Parte Guelfa, which, with Charles of Anjou's representative as Podestà, successfully excluded all outsiders from office, filling the city's councils with their own nominees and directing the domestic policies of the government, while content to leave the formulation of its foreign policy in the hands of Charles of Anjou. The six *capitani* comprising the executive committee of the government were all from old Guelph families; so were the fourteen members of the *Credentia*, the advisory body to which the *capitani* brought matters for consideration. There were government departments, notably the treasury, to which were admitted such merchants as had influenced the policies of *il Primo Popolo*; but these were invariably rich merchants. The Parte Guelfa, like Charles of Anjou himself, regarded men of the people, however talented, as inferiors to be kept in their place. They also, like Charles, regarded former Ghibellines and crypto-Ghibellines with hatred and suspicion. One of the principal officials of the Parte Guelfa, the head of its secret police, was known as the Accuser of the Ghibellines. In the near future he had much work to do in rooting out troublesome Ghibellines and in ensuring that they were sent into and remained in exile as *confinati*, and that their properties and possessions were sold for the benefit of the commune, of those Guelph families which had previously suffered at their hands and, of course, of the Parte Guelfa.[12]

Under the government of the Guelphs, Florence grew and prospered. All its main streets, formerly of brick, had been paved in the time of a Milanese Podestà, Rubaconte da Mandello, and were now, in the words of a contemporary chronicler, 'more clean, more beautiful and more healthy'. By the end of the thirteenth century the city's population, spreading into new suburbs beyond the walls of the previous century, seems to have increased to about 45,000, considerably more than London's and some eight times that of Oxford, even though the university there was by that time well established. The city's banking houses were making immense profits through their dealings with foreign powers, in particular with the Kings of France and Sicily and with the Pope; and the trade of the city was increasing in volume year by year. Merchants dealt in spices and dyes, hides and silks, sendal and taffeta, gold brocades and braid, and above all in wool. Vast quantities of woollen cloth and bales of raw wool were imported from northern Europe, mainly from France, the Low Countries, the Algarve, Spain and, by the end of the thirteenth century, from England. The wool was refined and dyed in the numerous workshops of Florence, the finished bolts of cloth being sold through so many agents beyond Tuscany's borders, in French fairs and English markets, Flemish towns and Mediterranean ports, that Pope Boniface VIII was to say that the Florentines had become a kind of fifth element: wherever earth, air, fire and water were to be found there were sure to be Florentines as well. In all weathers flat-bottomed barges piled high with cloth could be seen drifting down towards Pisa on the Arno, whose waters – polluted with dyestuffs, tannin and rubbish, when not dried up – drove the workshops' mills and filled the tanks in which the wool was washed and dyed. The dyes used were faster, and of purer, brighter colour, than any to be found elsewhere in Europe. Some were of local origin: yellow dyes came from the crocus fields near San Gimignano; but the ingredients for others had to be transported from far away, insects for cochineal from the shores of the Mediterranean, lichen for the red dye known as *oricello* from Majorca, cinnabar for vermilion from the Holy Land. The bitter juice of aloes which made the dyes fast came from Alexandria and the Levant.

Throughout the year, thousands of ill-paid men were hard at work in the city's shops, in wash-houses and stretching-sheds, as well as in their own cramped houses, undertaking the numerous processes through which the imported wool had to pass, the fulling, spinning and carding, the combing, weaving, stretching and trimming, as well as the washing and dyeing and drying. Nor was it only textiles that left Florence by river or on the backs of pack-horses which made their slow way to the coast or ambled north across the Apennines to Venice for shipment to the ports of the eastern Mediterranean; grain was exported, too, oil and livestock, timber and the fine wines of Tuscany.

In this commerce the banks of Florence played an essential part, not only in supplying capital and in the investment of money for their clients, but in all manner of other activities, including the insuring of ships and cargoes. As inventors of double-entry bookkeeping and of the forerunner of the cheque, and as creators of the gold florin, and lire, soldi and denari, later the LSD of British capitalism, the Florentines were already regarded as the world's leading experts in international commerce; and their banks had the reputation of being safer and more solid business houses than any others.

These banks, operating on their own or in associations of *compagni*, were in the hands of Florence's great families such as the Albizzi and the Bardi, the Baroncelli, Peruzzi, Pulci and Strozzi; and it was rarely that young men less well connected who worked for them as salaried employees, *fattori*, were able to rise to senior partnerships.

The training of a banker was an arduous one. Care was taken to ensure that a boy destined for a commercial career was not indulged in his earliest years. A handbook written for the guidance of parents enjoined them to be strict in the upbringing of their children, to ensure that they did not speak to adults unless spoken to, that they knelt down upon entering a room where grown-ups were gathered and knelt again when leaving it. Mothers must refrain from combing small children's hair too often, from 'making them embroidered little hats and silvered capes and little berib-boned skirts, carved cradles, painted slippers or soled hose, from giving them little wooden horses, pretty cymbals, toy birds or gilded drums... from holding them in [their] arms, kissing them, licking them, singing them songs or telling them fairy stories'.

At the age of seven, boys were expected to be able to read and write, to speak a little Latin and to count with an abacus, and at the age of ten, they would be sent to a *scuola d'abaco* for specialist training in arithmetic and bookkeeping. Then, when they were thirteen or fourteen, they would be apprenticed to a merchant in Florence and would probably be beaten for laziness or disobedience. 'If he does not obey you well,' wrote Lapo Mazzei to the manager of the firm in which his son was learning the business, 'beat him like a dog, as if he were your own.'

Before he was twenty the trainee banker would probably be sent to work abroad in one or other of his company's branches in a foreign city.[13] Here he would be expected to learn the language of the country and the manners and customs of the people with whom he was to transact business, as well as to inform himself of all that he needed to know about local markets, exchange and interest rates, trade routes and customs duties, government regulations and local business practices. Some Florentine merchants, like Bernardo Davanzati, who worked in Venice for forty-five years, spent most of their life abroad; and it was not an easy life, as they were always ready to point out. 'We can do nothing at present,' runs one characteristic letter of grievance from a merchant at the mercy of often antagonistic local auth-orities. 'Foreigners have to endure ill treatment every day. I am one of those who have to suffer constantly at the hands of marshals, captains and anyone disposed to inflict such punishment. There is always someone ready to make trouble for us poor foreigners.'

Despite the habitual grumbles of merchants, late-thirteenth-century Flor-ence flourished so healthily under the Guelphs that they felt justified in relaxing the penalties imposed upon the Ghibellines. Under pressure from the new Pope, Gregory X, a Visconti from Piacenza, and from his successor, the Roman-born noble, Nicholas III, both of whom were anxious to weaken Charles of Anjou's influence over the Guelph towns of Italy, the Guelphs in Florence agreed to allow certain Ghibellines to return to the city, knowing that they were, as they proved to be, too weakened and impoverished to offer any resistance to the power of the Parte Guelfa in the organization of Florentine government and society, a society in which the guilds or *arti* were assuming an authority which was to eclipse that of Ghibellines and Guelphs alike.

4

BLACKS AND WHITES
1280–1302

*'One party began to scoff at the other, and to urge their
horses one against the other, whence arose a great conflict . . . and
all the city was moved with apprehension and flew to arms.'*
GIOVANNI VILLANI

There were at this time seven major guilds, the *arti maggiori*, and a large
though uncertain number of *arti minori*, later reduced to fourteen. The
guild of greatest esteem was that of the judges and lawyers, the Arte dei
Giudici e Notai. Then came the guilds of the city's principal industries,
those of the wool, silk and foreign cloth merchants. The headquarters of
the wool merchants' guild, the Palazzo dell'Arte della Lana, which was
built on the site of a tower house belonging to the Compiobesi family, still
stands in Via Calimala.[1] This was the street in which the cloth merchants'
warehouses were to be found and which gave its name to their guild, the
Arte di Calimala. The silk merchants' guild, the Arte di Por Santa Maria,
also took its name from a street, the shopping street which led, and still
leads, into the city from the Ponte Vecchio and which in turn took its
name from the ancient gate in the city wall, the Por Santa Maria.[2] The
other two major merchants' guilds were the Arte dei Vaccai e Pellicciai,
which looked after the interests of both dealers and craftsmen in animal
skins and furs, and the Arte dei Medici e Speziali, the guild of the doctors
and apothecaries and of merchants dealing in medicine, dyes and con-
diments, whose scales of all sizes, for the weighing of every kind of
spice and powder, were regularly checked against the official scales of the
commune. This was also the guild of certain craftsmen such as painters and
gilders who, buying their materials from members of the guild, were
themselves considered eligible for membership of it. Indeed, as time passed,
guilds admitted to their membership men whose occupations were far
removed from those for whom the guild had originally been established.
The Arte di Por Santa Maria, for example, as well as silk merchants,
had among its members upholsterers and embroiderers, mercers, feather
merchants and even goldsmiths.

Also, many citizens sought membership of guilds purely as a means of becoming eligible for the privileges and rights which membership afforded. Dante, for example, was admitted to the Arte dei Medici e Speziali as a preliminary to his political career; and men like Dante kept up their guild membership for both political and social reasons, whether or not they had ever been involved in the trade with which their guild was connected.

Members of the lesser guilds were regarded with a certain disdain by the richer merchants of the *arti maggiori*; but five of the *arti minori*, those of the Beccai, the butchers,[3] the shoemakers, builders, blacksmiths and *rigattieri*, dealers in second-hand goods, were acknowledged as being somewhat superior to the others, and were sometimes referred to as the *arti medie*. These were granted some of the appearance of power, if not the actual exercise of it, for the major guilds were now arrogating it to themselves. Probably the largest of all the guilds was the Arte dei Maestri di Pietre e di Legname, whose membership included workers in all manner of building crafts besides those in stone and wood.

The major guilds maintained their authority by electing representatives from their number, known as *priori*. These *priori* were each to serve for two months, and towards the end of this period they were to appoint their successors with the help of the senior members of the privileged guilds and a council of *sapientes*, wise men from the city's six districts who might or might not be members of a guild but who were certainly sympathetic towards the guild system.

The self-perpetuating oligarchy thus created, and the militia which was established to safeguard its interests, were not altogether unwelcome to those few of the Parte Guelfa's old guard who belonged to *arti maggiori* or to those, more numerous, who, while not members themselves, were related by marriage to rich merchants who were. But the old noble families as a whole naturally did not take kindly to the new system of government which the merchants of the guilds were formulating. At first there were mere rumblings of discontent, then rowdy altercations in the street, followed by attacks on citizens by young nobles returning home from wars against the Ghibellines of Arezzo and, later, from an inconclusive campaign against a Pisan army led by Guido da Montefeltro, a skilful commander from an old Ghibelline family of Urbino. The arrogant, violent behaviour of the young Guelph cavalry officers provoked a leading official of the Arte di Calimala, Giano della Bella, himself of noble descent, to recruit a new militia from among the members of those *arti minori* which till now had not been permitted any part in the government of the city, including the tanners and armourers, the woodworkers and girdle-makers, the innkeepers and wine merchants, the cheesemongers and dealers in salt and oil, and the workers in wood and iron.

Bas-relief panels by Andrea Pisano (c. 1270–1349) made for the lower part of the cathedral campanile, which was begun by Giotto in 1334. The originals are now in the Museo dell'Opera, the frames in the Campanile being occupied by casts.

Painting

Sculpture

Architecture

Weaving

Astronomy

Medicine

Grammar

With the backing of this militia, of the militia already formed by the major guilds and of the citizens' militia, which had long existed, the *priori* elected by the guilds in 1293, prompted by the popular leader, Giano della Bella, promulgated the celebrated Ordinances of Justice which set down the principles and practice of the new constitution and instituted the office of a senior *priore*, the Gonfaloniere di Giustizia, as standard-bearer of the city republic. The Ordinances of Justice thus effectively destroyed the power of the old, once-feudal families, though they did not transfer this power to the ordinary people of Florence, the families designated as *popolani* generally being quite as rich and often as socially distinguished as the *magnati*.

By the Ordinances all male members of families referred to as *magnati* or *grandi* were required to swear an oath of loyalty to the *priori* and to pay over large sums of money as surety for their future good behaviour. While they were allowed to be members of the guilds, they could not hold positions of responsibility within them, nor were they to be eligible for election as *priori*. As many as 150 families were thus penalized; and as an early demonstration of the punishments which they might expect were they to breach the provisions of the Ordinances of Justice, the new Gon-faloniere, on receiving information that a member of one of these families had murdered two citizens, marched out with his militia, his white silk flag emblazoned with a red cross flying above his head, to the guilty family's house in Via Por Santa Maria, and, to the sound of trumpets, demolished it on the spot.

Disunited though they were by family squabbles, the *grandi* did not, of course, accept the Ordinances of Justice without protest; and regarding the popular leader, Giano della Bella, as being largely responsible for them, they consulted among themselves as to how to bring about his downfall. He was no longer a *priore* and, in accordance with one of the provisions of the Ordinances, he was not eligible for election again for two years after he had left office; but he still exercised great influence in the priorate and it was hoped that his disgrace might eventually lead to the repeal of the Ordinances which he had inspired. A campaign of slander and vilification was accordingly mounted not only by the *grandi* but also by various lawyers in the Arte dei Giudici e Notai, the most conservative of the guilds and one with several members connected by marriage to the older families. It was a member of one of these families, the Donati, who was to be indirectly responsible for Giano della Bella's fall.

Corso Donati was a brash, hearty, quarrelsome soldier, gregarious and bombastic. He had fought bravely at Campaldino as a cavalry commander against the Ghibellines of Arezzo; and, with some of the more impression-able citizens, he had achieved a popularity which he liked to cultivate, riding fully armed through the streets with a clatter of hooves to shouts of '*Viva il Barone!*'

One day towards the end of 1294 he was trotting along when he came by chance upon a cousin, Simone, with whom he had a long-standing quarrel. There was an argument which soon became a fight. Simone was wounded and one of his grooms was killed. The matter was brought to the jurisdiction of the Podestà, who, to the public astonishment, found in favour of the blustering Corso Donati and sentenced his injured cousin, Simone, not merely to the loss of his property but to death. When this extraordinary judgement became known, friends of the murdered groom, crowds of *popolani* and their supporters among the working people, armed with sticks, knives and spears, marched angrily to the Palazzo del Podestà. Finding the great doors locked against them, they burned them down, burst inside and ransacked the building as the Podestà clambered up into a garret and escaped across the roofs of the adjoining houses.

At the subsequent inquiry it transpired, or was at least alleged, that Giano della Bella's brother, a noted demagogue, had encouraged the mob in their attack upon the Palazzo del Podestà. Other witnesses maintained that Giano himself had appeared on the scene, not however to incite the crowd but rather in an attempt to prevent trouble. The mob had, however, as mobs will, turned upon the interloper and threatened to kill him as well as the Podestà. Encouraged by this display of antagonism towards him, his rivals in the priorate ordered Giano's arrest. Rather than face the consequences, he fled from Florence and went to live in France, where he abandoned politics for the more rewarding occupation of commerce.

Now that the *popolani* had lost their most prominent leader, Corso Donati and his like-minded friends among the *grandi* supposed that they could soon dispose of his impertinent Ordinances. They were quickly disillusioned. An ill-planned uprising against the new constitution was promptly put down by the militia of the *priori*, assisted by working men; and when Corso's associates endeavoured to gain support for their views among the rich merchants of the guilds, they found that even those who had previously been covertly sympathetic to the complaints and aspirations of the *grandi* were now inclining to the majority view that attempts to get rid of the Ordinances were a waste of time and doomed to failure so long as the *popolani* and the workers were prepared to fight for their retention. This was certainly the opinion of one of Corso Donati's fellow *grandi*, Vieri de' Cerchi, who had also fought bravely in the cavalry action at Campaldino, and who, although a soldier, was also a banker, the director indeed of one of the most successful and prosperous banking houses in Florence. Corso Donati naturally despised him for this close connection with commerce and despised him also because the Cerchi were not even a Florentine family by origin, but *nouveaux riches* interlopers from Acone in the Sieve valley whose riches had been based not upon land but upon trade.

Scorned though he was by such proud and ancient families as the Donati, Vieri de' Cerchi had widespread influence in Florence, particularly in the Arte dei Giudici e Notai; and although excluded as a *grande* from the priorate by the Ordinances of Justice, he knew well enough how to manipulate their members without being one of their number. By the end of 1295 a powerful Cerchi faction had emerged in Florence in opposition to the faction led by the Donati, and before the following year was out the two sides were at loggerheads. A former *priore* and friend of the exiled Giano della Bella recorded a characteristic fracas between them:

> One day [in December 1296] many citizens gathered in the Piazza de' Fre-scobaldi [named after the family whose palace dominated the northern end of the Ponte Santa Trinita] to attend the funeral of a woman, it being the custom of the country on such occasions for the men of title to sit on wooden benches while the ordinary people sat on the ground on straw mats. With the Cerchi partisans on one side and the Donati supporters on the other, someone stood up either to smooth his dress or for some other reason. Immediately suspicious, the men opposite stood up, their hands upon their swords. The opposing party did the same and fighting broke out until stopped by those who took neither side. Then many people rushed to the Cerchi's palace demanding to be led against the Donati. But the Cerchi refused.

Soon afterwards, however, Corso Donati's enemies did attack him. The attack was led by Guido Cavalcanti, a gifted poet, 'courteous and brave', in Dino Compagni's words, 'but contemptuous of the common people and given to solitude and study'. Knowing how much Guido disliked him, Corso planned to have him murdered while he was on a pilgrimage to Santiago de Compostella. Learning of the plot, Guido returned to Florence

> and incited many youths against Corso, pledging them to come to his aid. And being one day in company with some youths of the house of Cerchi, mounted and armed with javelins, Guido spurred his horse against messer Corso [and threw his javelin at him] but missed. Then Corso and his companions, all armed with swords, pursued Guido; but unable to reach him, they threw stones at him and wounded him in the hands.

Incidents such as these became ever more commonplace in the growing hatred between the rival factions until Corso Donati overreached himself: he used his influence to have one of his pliant friends appointed Podestà and then persuaded this creature of his to find against his mother-in-law in an action which he had brought against her, declaring her property forfeit. This went far beyond the tolerance of *priori* and *popolani* alike: the Podestà was dismissed and Corso Donati fined and sent into exile.

No sooner had he left, however, than his fellow exiles, his remaining friends in the city and the old reactionaries in the Parte Guelfa turned to the Pope to help them dislodge the Cerchi, who were now in unrivalled command of the city.

Pope Boniface VIII was more than inclined to help them. Born into an old Roman family, the Caetani, he was anxious to establish the absolute authority of the Pope in Europe. He was also anxious to do as much for the Caetani as Pope Nicholas III had done for his own family, the Orsini, and as several members of the Colonna family were vainly to hope that their relative Pope Martin V would do for them. So, just as Gregory X had induced Rudolf of Habsburg, heir to the Holy Roman Empire, to allow the Romagna to become part of the Papal States, so Boniface VIII hoped to be able to incorporate Tuscany into them also. With this end in view he listened attentively to the overtures of the Donati, whom he considered less likely to stand in his way than the Cerchi, instructing the leaders of the Cerchi party to come to terms with the Donati and to readmit them to the Florentine government. At the same time Pope Boniface decided to send a trusted cardinal to the Florentines to enlist their support in his quarrel with the powerful anti-papal Roman family, the Colonna; and he entered into negotiations with the French King, Philip IV, with the intention of securing the help of the King's brother, Charles of Valois, in the furtherance of his designs in Italy.

When reports of these complicated negotiations reached Florence the quarrel between the Cerchi and the Donati became more bitter than ever; and the two factions and their respective supporters came to blows as frequently and as violently, and often for as trivial reasons, as had the Guelphs and the Ghibellines in the past. Florence, indeed, became a battleground in which the partisans of the Cerchi, who became known as the Whites, were in perpetual conflict with the Donati and their allies, the Blacks. On one typical occasion, a group of Whites were watching some girls dancing in the Piazza Santa Trinita when they were suddenly set upon by a gang of Blacks, and in the ensuing fight one of the Blacks cut off the nose of Ricoverino de' Cerchi with his sword. Fights like this had become commonplace by the time that Charles of Valois arrived with his French knights outside the walls of Florence in the supposed role of peacemaker.

No one could doubt that Charles had really come to Florence as an emissary of the Pope, who considered the Blacks his natural allies rather than the Whites, nor that the French were not so much peacemakers as predators. Yet, even so, the leaders of the Whites, notably the rich banker, Vieri de' Cerchi, persuaded themselves that it would be wiser to appease the visitors rather than offend them. The gates were opened and the French marched in.

They were very soon followed by Corso Donati and other exiled Blacks, who rode into the town as though they had won it by right of victory in battle. Gathering support from their fellow Blacks within the city, they strolled and trotted about the streets as though to give notice that they were now the party of power. This, indeed, they shortly became. Beginning by entering and ransacking the houses of their intimidated enemies, and by releasing several of their supporters who had been imprisoned by the Whites, together with a number of common criminals to add to the confusion, they then forcibly removed the Podestà and the *priori* from office, replacing them with their own nominees. For several days Florence was in uproar. Witnesses sympathetic to the Whites afterwards described scenes of pillage, kidnapping and rape which might have been witnessed in a town at the mercy of enemy troops at the end of a long and bitter siege.

This outcome the Pope had neither wanted nor expected. Certainly he had hoped to see the Blacks in control of Florence; but not at the cost of forcing the Whites to seek safety and help among the Ghibellines and other rivals of the papacy elsewhere in Italy. His orders to Charles of Valois had been to oversee a change in the balance of power, not to preside over a bloody revolution. Yet Charles was powerless to prevent the complete rout of the Whites, most of whose leaders, summoned to stand trial, fled into exile. Those who remained received little mercy after Charles's departure. Sentenced to death either by hanging, decapitation or burning at the stake, a few actually suffered one or other of these fates. Most chose to leave Florence and join the other Whites in their exile. One of these was the thirty-six-year-old scholar and poet who had once been a White *priore*, Dante Alighieri.

LIFE IN DANTE'S FLORENCE
1265–1348

'And when the time comes for fruit to be sold at fairs
Girls from the country pack their baskets high
With ripe round figs and grapes, peaches and pears.
If you try repartee with them, they won't be shy,
And some of them, brighter than florins, shine
With flowers from gardens that they tend near by.
No garden, though, ever looked half as fine
As the Mercato Vecchio does when spring is here.
It feeds the eye and taste of every Florentine . . . '
ANTONIO PUCCI

Durante Alighieri, whose first name was later contracted to Dante, 'that singular splendour of the Italian race', as his fellow Tuscan writer, Boccaccio, was to call him, was born in Florence in 1265[1] and baptized in the Baptistery, '*il mio bel San Giovanni*' as he called it, a building still surrounded by graves and by the sarcophagi in which many of the older families of Florence chose to bury their dead. His great-great-grandfather, who had died on the Second Crusade, could trace his ancestry, so Dante himself proudly claimed, to the days when Florence was a Roman city. His family was certainly old, but by no means rich, owning no more than a few scattered properties in the *contado*. His grandfather was a moneylender with a counting-house in Florence and a branch in Prato; and his father carried on this family business. Dante himself was drawn to study rather than to commerce and from an early age he fell under the influence of Brunetto Latini, an elderly scholar and notary who had been exiled from Florence as a Guelph in 1260 and had not returned until the year after Dante's birth. Brunetto was a much respected figure in Florentine politics and a master of rhetoric and of both verse and prose written in vernacular Italian rather than in the Latin more usually adopted for such exercises. Later, in the *Divina Commedia*, a vision 'of purgatory, hell and heaven' as well as a work of moral edification full of symbolism and of philosophical and historical allusions, Dante wrote affectionately of Brunetto:

> The dear, benign, paternal image, such
> As thine was, when so lately thou didst teach me
> The way for man to win eternity:
> And how I prized the lesson, it behoves
> That . . . my tongue should speak.

The young Dante also revered the merchant and chronicler, Dino Compagni, who was several years older than himself, and the poet, Guido Cavalcanti, much of whose verse, written in what Dante called the '*dolce stil nuove*', the sweet new style, seems so at variance with the character of the militant Guelph who had thrown his javelin at Corso Donati.

It was at the age of about nine that Dante first set eyes upon 'the glorious lady of his heart, Beatrice', for whom he conceived a passion that was to remain unquenched throughout his life, outliving his marriage to a girl to whom he had been betrothed when a boy and Beatrice's own death in 1290, when this angelic creature, of whom he could ask nothing but to praise her beauty, 'soared to heaven on high, to the kingdom where the angels have peace'.

The year before her death, Dante had fought as a cavalryman against the Ghibellines of Arezzo at Campaldino and had subsequently served in the army sent against the Pisans; but for over two years after Beatrice died he devoted himself to study before being admitted to the Arte dei Medici e Speziali. By then a committed Guelph, he was elected to the priorate in 1300; and by 1301, when Charles of Valois entered Florence, he had been sent on a diplomatic mission to the Pope and never returned to the city. One of the first of the Whites to be condemned to exile by the triumphant Blacks, he was accused of all manner of offences, including misappropriation of public funds, and in his absence was condemned to be burned alive.

His departure from Florence may have been welcomed by some of its inhabitants. His near contemporary, the poet Franco Sacchetti, recounted the story of how Dante, passing by the Porta di San Piero one day, 'saw a smith at work upon his anvil singing one of Dante's poems, but so muddling up the verses, cutting bits here and adding words there, that he seemed to Dante to be doing him much harm'. Dante entered the shop, picked up a hammer and threw it into the street. Then he took up a pair of scales and threw them into the street, too, followed by many of the smith's other tools. The smith cried, 'What the devil are you doing? Are you mad?'

'What are *you* doing?' Dante asked him.

'I am trying to do my job. But you are spoiling my tools and throwing them into the street.'

'Well,' said Dante, 'if you don't like me spoiling your things, don't spoil mine.'

A detail from Paradise *in the chapel of the Podestà in the Bargello, attributed to Giotto. The portrait is a likeness of Dante, who was born in Florence in 1265.*

'What am I spoiling of yours?'

'You are singing out of my book, and not singing it as I wrote it. I have no other trade but this, and you are ruining it for me.'

For the rest of his life, moving in poverty from city to city, refusing to take up arms against the city of his birth, proclaiming his innocence of the charges which the Blacks had brought against him, Dante endeavoured to explain to others as well as to himself the reasons why Florence was rent by so many factions, quarrels within families, quarrels between neighbourhoods and guilds, political parties and social groups. In the *Inferno* he has Brunetto Latini find an explanation in the evil seeds sown by 'that ungrateful race who, in old times, came down from Fiesole':

> Ay and still smack of their rough mountain flint
> Will for thy good deeds show thee enmity.
> Nor wonder, for amongst ill-savour'd crabs
> It suits not the sweet fig tree lay her fruit.
> Old fame reports them in the world for blind,
> Covetous, envious, proud. Look to it well,
> Take heed thou cleanse thee of their ways . . .

Brunetto himself, recognizing factional discord as a universal problem, believed that it might be overcome in communes everywhere provided that officials were impartial and uncorrupt, and the people were trained in obedience to just laws. For his part, Dino Campagni could see little hope for Florence so long as those citizens who held office were governed by self-interest and by the demands of friends and families, and failed to earn either the obedience or the respect of the *popolani*. For Dante, Guelph though he had been, the only hope for the city − where 'avarice, envy, pride, those fatal sparks [had] set the hearts of all on fire' − was firm autocratic rule. The people, he was convinced, must submit to imperial government; and in his *Purgatorio* he begged the German rulers to return to claim their just inheritance:

> Come and behold thy people, how they love!
> And if no pity our distress inspires
> Let blushes for thyself thy pity move.

'Rejoice, oh, Italy,' he wrote when it was announced that the Count of Luxembourg − who had been chosen King by the German electoral princes and who was to become the Emperor Henry VII − had decided to lead an expedition across the Alps. 'Thy bridegroom cometh, the hope of the world, the glory of the people, the ever-clement Henry, who is Caesar and Augustus.'

On his arrival in Italy, Henry was acclaimed not only by the Ghibelline towns of the north but also by the Guelphs, since his coming had been approved by the French Pope, Clement V, who, having removed the papal

QVI COELVM CECINIT MEDIVMQVE IMVMQVE TRIBVNALS   LVSTRAVIT QVE ANIMO CVNCTA POETA SVO   DOCTVS ADEST DANTES SVA QVEM FLORENTIA SAEPE
SENSIT CONSILIIS AC PIETATE PATREM   NIL POTVIT TANTO MORS SAEVA NOCERE POETAE   QVEM VIVVM VIRTVS CARMEN IMAGO FACIT

Dante holding a copy of his Divina Commedia, which throws light on Florence. A painting in the Duomo by Domenico di Michelino, 1465.

residence from Rome to Avignon, was anxious not to become a mere dependant of the French court. Welcomed as a liberator in Piedmont and Lombardy, Henry was crowned King in Milan in January 1311.

The Florentine government, however, firmly declined to take part in the general submission. Their spokesman announced that his countrymen had never yet bowed their sharp horns to any master, and did not intend to do so now; and true to his word, the Florentines began to prepare their defences to resist the man whom they regarded, not as their saviour as the exiled Dante did, but as a German interloper. Orders were issued for the new city walls, begun some years before, to be completed as soon as possible, for missions to be sent to other Tuscan towns to enlist support for resistance, for pardons to be issued to such White exiles in these towns whose return to Florence on the payment of reasonable fines would not endanger the security of the priorate, and, as a gesture of defiance, for representations of the German imperial eagle, whether in paintwork or in stone, to be removed from all buildings in Florence both public and private.

Henry responded by declaring the Florentine people to be outlaws, their goods and lands throughout Italy to be forfeit, and a fine amounting to 5,000 pounds of gold to be levied upon them. In September 1312, having been crowned Emperor in Rome by a delegation of cardinals nominated by the Pope for that purpose, he marched on Florence intent upon its submission to his will.

The Florentines were ready to defy him. They had dispatched further diplomatic missions to towns from which help might be expected; they had also sent a delegation to France; they had brought military stores into the city, had taken over buildings as barracks, and built towers overlooking the walls, which now stretched as far to the south as the present Porta Romana at the west end of the Boboli Gardens and as far north as the Fortezza da Basso between the Porta al Prato and the Porta San Gallo.

Well supplied and armed, the Florentine army was far better placed to defend the city than the Emperor Henry was to take it. The imperial forces, heavily outnumbered, had suffered severe losses from disease; while scavenging parties, sent for miles into the countryside on either side of the flooded Arno, brought back to their camp around the monastery of San Salvi[2] scarcely enough to feed the horses, let alone the men. When Henry himself contracted malaria, he decided not to risk an assault but to withdraw his forces to Pisa. Soon afterwards he died at Buonconvento on his way south towards Naples.

No sooner had the Florentines been released from the attentions of one enemy than they were subjected to those of another. In Pisa an ambitious Ghibelline nobleman, Ugoccione della Faggiuola, whose wide military experience included command in the recent wars, had made himself master of the city after the death of the Emperor Henry VII. He had also taken over Lucca; and, in command of forces from both cities, he had attacked Pistoia as a preliminary to an assault upon Florence. At Montecatini in August 1315 he had decisively defeated an alliance of Tuscan Guelphs. Fortunately for Florence, though, disputes had broken out at Ugoccione's headquarters, where one of his commanders, an equally ambitious young soldier from Lucca, Castruccio Castracani, having made up his mind to take over the control of his city from his general, contrived Ugoccione's downfall.

Once firmly established in Lucca, Castruccio made it plain that he was determined to conquer Florence. First he took Pistoia; and the Florentines could have no doubt that his army would soon appear before their own walls.

The days of Florence's citizen army were now past. Men who had formerly made up the ranks of the infantry were more and more disinclined to leave their work and their homes for the camp and the battlefield, while the decline of the *grandi* had made it more difficult to raise competent cavalry. Richer citizens were traditionally obliged to maintain a horse and buy armour; but the well-to-do merchants of the *arti medie*, the *popolani grassi*, were no more willing to leave their counting-houses than their social inferiors were to leave their workshops, and few of them looked in the least warlike when they did so. Accordingly, as elsewhere in Tuscany, reliance was increasingly being placed upon mercenaries and upon professional soldiers, *condottieri*, usually of noble birth, who were paid to lead them and who had to be carefully watched lest their ambitions led them into political as well as military fields.

When Castruccio's army threatened Florence, the priorate appointed a *Capitano di Guerra* to take over from the Podestà as commander of their army. This *Capitano*, a Spaniard, Raymond of Cardona, enlisted a polyglot force of cavalry from his own country and from Italy, as well as from Germany, France and England. These cavalry companies numbered 2,500 men, of whom fewer than 400 were Florentines. There were, however, far more Florentine citizens among the infantry when Raymond of Cardona's army marched out of the city in June 1325 to face the enemy on the slopes of Altopascio. All the church bells of Florence rang loudly to wish them well, so a chronicler recorded, and a replica of the old war chariot, the Carroccio, the original having been captured at Montaperti, rattled along beside the soldiers, the city's standard flying from its mast, its own bell, the Martinella, clanging in the din.

A few weeks later the whole army was in flight, leaving the Carroccio a trophy in the hands of Castruccio, whose men pursued Florence's defeated army back towards the city. Those who had escaped slaughter outside Altopascio and in the retreat across the Arno's tributaries reached safety within the now completed walls of the city. Yet, so insecure did the priorate feel that they decided to seek the assistance of a protector. When under threat from the Emperor Henry VII they had tentatively turned to Robert I, the King of Naples. Now they sought the help of King Robert's son, the Duke of Calabria, who, for an extremely large allowance and for the right to appoint not only the Podestà but also the *priori*, agreed to garrison the city with a thousand knights. He arrived in July 1326 and established himself in the Palazzo del Podestà renamed in his honour the Palazzo Ducale.

He did not, however, remain there long. Recalled to the south by a threat to his birthright, he died in Naples in November 1328, two months after the death in Lucca of Florence's enemy, Castruccio.

Freed from both predator and protector, the Florentines resumed their old, slightly modified system of government, which, with further modifications in later years, was to survive until the fall of the republic. The names of all guild members eligible for office were placed in leather bags, known as *borse*, which were kept in the sacristy of the Franciscan church of Santa Croce. Every two months they were taken from the church for a public ceremony in which names were drawn out at random. The names of men who had served a recent term were thrown aside; so were those of members of families already drawn; so were debtors. When the names of nine satisfactory men had been extracted from the *borse*, six of them from the *arti maggiori*, two from the *arti minori* and the ninth to serve as Gonfaloniere, the election of the priorate, or, as it became known, the Signoria, was completed. For their two months of office, the *priori* were required to live as well as to deliberate together, consulting as needs be the members of two other elected councils known as *Collegi*, the twelve members of the *Dodici Buonomini* or the sixteen of the *Sedici Gonfalonieri*. When necessary, the *priori* took advice also from such occasionally summoned bodies as the Six of Commerce, the Eight of Security or the Ten of War and, more often, from the advisory council known as the *Pratica*. They were paid a very modest salary but were provided with the services of green-liveried attendants, an excellent cook and a jester to sing to them and to tell them funny stories at their meals. They wore crimson cloaks lined with ermine, the Gonfaloniere's being embroidered with golden stars.

When danger threatened, an emergency committee, a Balìa, was chosen and granted dictatorial powers until the crisis was passed; but a Balìa could only be formed, according to the theory of the constitution, with the agreement of all the male citizens of Florence over the age of fourteen who were summoned by a bell to gather in a *Parlamento*. At the ringing of this bell the men of the city, by now divided into four *quartieri* of four wards each, were expected to march behind their banners and their heraldic beasts to signify their approval of the emergency measures, having first acknowledged that at least two thirds of their total number were present.

The Florentine constitution was acclaimed by those whom it favoured as uniquely just and equitable, much to be preferred to the systems of government of other Italian states which were in the hands of despots or, in the case of Venice, a so-called republic ruled by an oligarchy of rich nobles, only those of impeccable parentage being eligible for membership of the Great Council. In fact, Florence, too, was an oligarchy. Just as, in Venice, the names of the older families, the Foscari, the Morosini, the Grimani and the Loredan, appear constantly in the lists of *consigli*, so do the names of the old merchant families of Florence in the lists of *priori*: the Peruzzi and the Soderini, the Strozzi, the Albizzi and the Acciaiuoli. In Florence, though, the people were more restless than they were in Venice, less ready to allow power to rest with those who assumed authority as a matter of right, particularly, of course, in times of hardship and want.

The decades which followed upon the deaths of Castruccio Castracani and the Duke of Calabria were, however, exceptionally prosperous in

Florence; and they are years in which the form and life of the medieval city can first be clearly seen, thanks to the curiosity and industry of its most assiduous chronicler.

Giovanni Villani was born in Florence about 1275. His father was a partner in the great mercantile house of the Cerchi family, and Giovanni himself became a partner in the banking firm of the Peruzzi, for whom he travelled widely in Italy as well as in France, Switzerland and Flanders. On his return to Florence he left the Peruzzi for another firm, the Buonaccorsi; and, as a senior member of the Arte di Calimala, he was three times elected to the Signoria. In 1308 he began writing his great book, a history of events from the earliest times until his own day, spending much of his time upon it for the next forty years, until his death in 1348.

It is a story of disasters as well as triumphs and prosperity. In its pages there are glimpses of a city racked by feuds and faction, of fighting in the streets, of murders such as that of the *grande*, Betto de' Brunelleschi, stabbed to death by two youths of the Donati family as he was playing chess in his own house, of the bankruptcies of unfortunate merchants, of hunger after poor harvests in the *contado*, when wagons sent to fetch grain from other towns were plundered by marauding bands of discharged mercenaries or sank into the mud by the banks of flooded rivers.

There were disastrous floods from time to time in Florence when the waters of the Arno cascaded down from the east, 'so that a great part of the city became a lake... in which many persons were drowned and many houses ruined'. In November 1333, after four days and nights of rain, the swollen waters, dammed by the high city wall

covered the whole plain of San Salvi to a depth of from ten to fifteen feet... wherefore everyone was filled with great fear and all the church bells throughout the city were rung continuously as an invocation to heaven that the water rise no higher. And in the houses they beat kettles and brass basins, raising loud cries to God of '*misericordia, misericordia*', the while those in peril fled from roof to roof and house to house on improvised bridges. And so great was the human din and tumult that it almost drowned out the crash of the thunder... And at the first sleep of night [on 4 November] the water washed away the city wall above the Corso de' Tintori... In the Baptistery of St John the water rose above the altar and reached to more than half the height of the columns of porphyry before the entrance. And in [the Bargello] it rose in the courtyard to a height of ten feet.

The Ponte Carraia fell with the exception of two arches. And immediately after, the Trinita bridge except for one pier and one arch... It was now the turn of the Ponte Vecchio. When it was choked by the boughs of the fallen trees brought down by the Arno, the water surged over the arches and, rushing upon the shops on the bridge, swept everything away except the two central

Scenes of Florentine life in the middle of the fourteenth century as depicted in frescoes by Andrea di Bonaiuto and his pupils in the Spanish Chapel at Santa Maria Novella.

piers. And at the Rubaconte bridge [the Ponte alle Grazie] the water rushed over the top and destroyed the parapet in several places ... To look at this scene was to stare at chaos.

Three hundred people lost their lives and incalculable damage was done to buildings and stores. Yet even so, the devastation was not so appalling as that caused by the fires that swept through the city, most of whose buildings were still constructed wholly or largely of wood. Fires are, indeed, regular incidents in Villani's chronicle. In the course of a single year, 1331, he recorded a fierce fire on the Ponte Vecchio, which destroyed all its shops 'with heavy loss to many craftsmen, and two apprentices perished'; an even worse conflagration near the church of Santa Trinita 'in certain lowly structures housing some carpenters and a blacksmith whereby six persons perished'; and a fire which attacked the Palazzo del Podestà 'and burned the roof of the old building ... on which account the government ordered rebuilding in stone all the way to the roof'.

Some years before, an

accursed fire fanned by a strong north wind ... burned the houses of the Abati and of the Macci; of the Amieri and Toschi ... the Lamberti and Bachini ... and the whole street of Calimala. And then, attacking the houses of the

Cavalcanti, it travelled round the Mercato Nuovo and consumed the church of Santa Maria as far as the Ponte Vecchio . . . In fact, it destroyed much of the city of Florence, consuming a total of 1,700 palaces, towers and houses. The loss in furniture, possessions and goods of every kind was incalculable . . . And what was not burned in the fire was carried off by robbers.

To avoid such losses, Paolo da Certaldo recommended that every house-holder should make sure his property was well supplied with sacks so that he could carry away his possessions when fire threatened them and with ropes so that he and his family could make their own way to safety.

Tragedy was likely to strike on the happiest occasions, particularly on May Day, when the celebrations drew large crowds into the small squares and narrow streets. One May Day at the beginning of the century the authorities responsible for public spectacles decided to have a representation of hell on the banks of the Arno and on the surface of the river itself. The city's crier went about the streets announcing the forthcoming event and inviting all who wanted to have 'news of the nether world' to go down to the Arno by the Ponte Carraia. 'And on barges and boats moored in the Arno,' so Villani recorded,

> they erected platforms and upon them represented hell with its fires and punishments and sufferings. There were men in the likeness of demons horrible to see, and others acting the part of naked souls. The demons tortured their victims in the most terrible ways amidst a cacophony of shrieks and cries, terrible to hear. And so many people crowded together to view the spectacle that the Ponte Carraia, [at that time] constructed of wooden planks laid from pier to pier, became so overloaded that it broke in several places and crashed into the river with its load. Thus many people were injured and many others were drowned, so play turned to earnest and just as the public crier had announced, many indeed went to get news of the other world, with great lamentation and sorrow to all the city.

While rich and poor alike had to face the possibility of a violent death, it was the poor alone who suffered in times of scarcity when the dealers in the corn market – evading the regulations of the *Sei della Biada*, the Six of Commerce – contrived to profit from the problems caused by the rapidly increasing population.

The grain market was held in the piazza outside the building known as Orsanmichele. This had been constructed on the site of the ninth-century oratory of San Michele in Orto, St Michael in the Garden, which had been destroyed in 1239.[3] Under its roofed loggia, where the standard prices of grain were marked up on boards, moneylenders and money-changers could be found as well as grain merchants; and, in times of famine, as a warning to any customers who felt disposed to attack the merchants or the officials of the *Sei della Biada*, guards with axes stood beside an executioner's block.

Here also, until largely destroyed by fire, there had once been a Madonna painted in fresco on one of the pillars of the loggia, an image believed to have miraculous properties and consequently surrounded by burning tapers and entrusted to the watchful care of the Confraternity of the Laudesi.[4] When orders were given for the reconstruction of the loggia, with two floors above it for the storage of grain, the Florentine painter, Bernardo Daddi, was commissioned to portray a new Madonna and so highly was his picture regarded that one of the city's leading artists, Andrea di Cione, nicknamed Orcagna (local slang for archangel), painter and architect as well as sculptor, was approached to create for it the magnificent tabernacle which is there today.[5] This in its turn was considered far too fine to be kept in a mere grain market; so the market was moved elsewhere; the spaces between the pillars of the open loggia were walled up and Orsanmichele was dedicated as a church.

The ill-nourished beggars who were usually to be found wandering about the Orsanmichele were, so Villani said, the first to fall victim to the outbreaks of plague which visited Florence at frequent intervals, as it did all other overcrowded medieval cities with a contaminated water supply, the most primitive methods of sewerage and drainage, and a population perfectly content to throw their household rubbish into the street to be pushed about and snuffled over by scavenging animals; and for want of the privies and cesspools of the rich men's palaces, people would make use of the ditches by the city walls or the ruins of some convenient tower. The epidemics which plagued Florence were evidently on occasion of a peculiarly virulent kind: the word influenza, not known in English until 1743, was being used in Florence in Villani's time.

In describing one 'great pestilence', that of 1340, Villani estimated that a sixth of the citizens of Florence, that was to say about 15,000 people, perished,

> wherefore the city was full of grief and lamentation and people attended to scarcely anything other than the burying of the dead ... And on account of this great pestilence the bishop and the clergy advised the holding of a great procession. This took place on 18 June and almost the whole body of citizens, men and women, followed the relics of the body of Christ, which are preserved at Sant'Ambrogio,[6] and marched through the city till nones [3 o'clock in the afternoon] carrying more than 150 lighted candles as large as torches.

Despite plague and famine, fire and flood, throughout Villani's lifetime and for the rest of the century, the appearance of Florence was gradually being transformed. In his father's day there were few public buildings of stone and those were of little architectural merit. But as Villani himself grew to manhood there began to appear in the city those great edifices which were to help give it its distinction, buildings lay and ecclesiastical, palaces for guilds and political parties such as the Palazzo dell'Arte della Lana and the Palazzo di Parte Guelfa, and family palaces like the Palazzo degli Acciaiuoli.[7]

In 1296 work had begun on a new cathedral church, probably under the direction of Arnolfo di Cambio, not a native of Florence but a sculptor and architect who had worked in Siena, Rome and Orvieto. He then settled in Florence to undertake his most important commission, which he was instructed to carry out 'with the greatest lavishness and magnificence possible'.

> The foundation stone was laid with much solemnity on the day of St Mary [8 September] by the Cardinal Legate of the Pope and many bishops. And there were present also the Podestà and the *Capitano del Popolo* and the *priori* and all the officials of Florence. And the church was consecrated to the honour of God and Saint Mary and given the name of Santa Maria del Fiore, although the people continued to call it by its former name of Santa Reparata.[8]

Some years later a new campanile was started 'close to the front of the church on the piazza of San Giovanni...and as superintendent of the works,' Villani wrote with pride, 'the commune appointed our fellow citizen, Giotto, the most sovereign master of painting of our time, who drew all his figures and their postures according to nature. And he was given a salary by the commune in virtue of his talents and excellence.'[9]

Appointed *capomaestro* of all the cathedral works in 1334, Giotto di Bondone, who was born at Vespignano near Florence, is believed to have been a pupil of Cenni de Peppe, commonly known as Cimabue, the mosaicist and painter who, as Dante said, held the field in painting until Giotto had 'the cry, and then the fame of Cimabue [was] obscured'. Like Cimabue, Giotto endeavoured to break free from the stylized traditions of medieval art, to revive classical ideals and naturalism, to abandon the bright colours and strong lines of Byzantine and Sienese painting and adopt a more realistic and human approach. Indeed, the sixteenth-century author of *Lives of the Most Eminent Italian Painters, Sculptors and Architects*, Giorgio Vasari, gives Giotto, 'the son of a poor peasant farmer', credit for originating 'the good modern manner'.

A most even-tempered man, in striking contrast to the architect who was later to crown the cathedral with its great dome, Giotto was also

> very sharp-witted and light-hearted, always ready with a witty remark, as is well remembered in Florence. Apart from what Giovanni Boccaccio wrote, Franco Sacchetti records many of Giotto's best sayings... There is a story that when he was still a young man in Cimabue's workshop, he painted on the nose of one of the figures Cimabue had executed a fly that was so lifelike that when Cimabue returned to carry on with his work he tried several times to brush it off with his hand.

Some years before Giotto's appointment as *capomaestro* of the cathedral works, building had begun – about 400 yards south towards the river – on an imposing palace for the *priori*. The site chosen was close by the ruins of the houses of the disgraced family of the Uberti,

> rebels of Florence and Ghibellines. And the ground whereon the houses had stood was converted into a public piazza [the Piazza della Signoria] to make sure that the houses would never be rebuilt.[10] And the commune bought the houses of other citizens as, for instance, those of the Foraboschi, and raised the new palace on the purchased ground. And for the tower of the palace of the priors they used the tower of the palace of the Foraboschi, which was almost one hundred feet high and was called La Vacca. And, so that the palace was not built on land formerly belonging to the Uberti, the committee responsible had it built askew, which was a great imperfection, inasmuch as the palace should have been given a square or rectangular shape and should not have been carried so close to the church of San Pier Scheraggio.[11]

Opposite this church, which had to be demolished in the sixteenth century for the building of the Uffizi, there appeared, after Villani's death, a covered loggia for the reception of ambassadors and the presentation of *priori* for formal election, ceremonies which had previously taken place in the open on a platform, or *ringhiera*, erected in front of the palace. Built on the site of several small houses pulled down for the purpose, this loggia, the Loggia dei Priori, was later to be used as a guardhouse for the *Landsknechte*, the Swiss mercenaries of the Grand Dukes of Tuscany, known in Florence as Lanzi. It survives as an open-air sculpture gallery, the Loggia dei Lanzi.[12]

By the time this loggia was completed, several of Florence's older buildings had been transformed. The church of Santa Croce had been largely rebuilt; so had Santa Maria Novella, by Dominican monks trained as architects. The Umiliati had moved into the convent beside the church of Ognissanti,[13] the Servites, an order founded by seven rich Florentines who had devoted themselves to the service of the Blessed Virgin, into the convent of Santissima Annunziata,[14] and the Carmelites, the severe order known as Whitefriars, into Santa Maria del Carmine.[15] The church of the Badia had been restored; and, although this was completely reconstructed yet again in the seventeenth century, the campanile of the 1330s was spared. In the Baptistery the last of the magnificent mosaics, some by Florentines, some by a master mosaicist from Venice, had been finished, in about 1300, when Andrea Pisano, a sculptor from Pontedera, who was to succeed Giotto as *capomaestro* of the Campanile, was commissioned by the rich Arte di Calimala to provide wax models from which the bronze doors for the south side of the Baptistery might be cast.[16]

Since the floods of 1333 the bridges across the Arno had all been repaired or rebuilt, with the exception of the Ponte alle Grazie, which, although

upstream from the others, had survived. The new Ponte Vecchio, completed in 1345, had been rebuilt in stone a good eight feet wider than its predecessor, with forty-three shops, each sixteen feet square.

Precise as Villani was in describing the measurements of the Ponte Vecchio, he was even more so when he came to write about the city's walls. These, he assured his readers, were some five miles long, nearly six feet thick and forty feet high to the top of the battlements, enclosing large areas of gardens and orchards to allow for an increase in the size of the city. There were fifteen gates and seventy-two towers at regular intervals, overlooking a deep and insanitary moat.[17]

Within this wall, Villani continued with his passion for statistics, there were, in 1328, 90,000 people; and the population was growing year by year, reaching perhaps 100,000 in 1338, the birth of boys slightly outnumbering that of girls according to the officials who examined the beans which were dropped into a box, a black bean for a male child, a white bean for a female. According to Villani's calculations, in the 1320s, about 1,500 people were foreigners, traders, pilgrims and travellers, some 10,000 were children

A detail from the Pianta della Catena, *a woodcut from c. 1490, giving the earliest view of Florence, and showing the four bridges, the Ponte alle Grazie, Ponte Vecchio, Ponte Santa Trinita and the Ponte alla Carraia, which linked the two areas of the city. The woodcut is attributed to Francesco Rosselli.*

in elementary schools, and 600 were boys under instruction in Latin, mathematics, logic and dialectics. There were 600 notaries, 60 physicians and surgeons, 100 apothecaries, 80 banking houses and firms of money-lenders large and small. There were 146 bakers and confectioners and a very large though uncertain number of men in the dyeing, building and clothing trades, 30,000 of them working in 200 wool workshops. There were also many slaves, the importation of which had been authorized in 1336 after an outbreak of plague had severely reduced the numbers of native servants. These slaves, many of them young girls under twelve years of age bought cheaply in the markets of Genoa and Naples, were for the most part Greeks, Russians, Turks, Circassians or Tartars. The Tartars were said to be the most conscientious workers, but the Circassians better natured and better looking, many of these becoming pregnant by their masters and having to take bundles of swarthy babies to the doors of the city's foundling hospitals. Considered as chattels to be worked at full stretch so that they did not 'waste time leaning out of the window', slaves were at the mercy of their owners, who could in theory 'hold, sell, alienate, exchange, enjoy, dispose of by will and do with in perpetuity whatsoever' they liked with them. They were punished cruelly for their misdemeanours. In 1379 a female slave who had put nitrate of silver into an enema which she had administered to her master was tortured in public with red-hot pincers before being burned alive. Yet obedient and docile slaves were generally well treated and in time became accepted as members of their masters' families. They were nearly all freed before their death and were usually given a pension.

Continuing his survey of Florence, Villani noted there were 30 hospitals with 1,000 beds in all, 110 churches, 57 of them parish churches, the rest belonging to religious houses, as well as innumerable fine private houses upon which their owners spent 'a sinful' amount of money. The Palazzo Davanzati was a characteristic example.[18] This tall house in the Via Porta Rossa was built towards the middle of the fourteenth century by the Davizzi family, passing in the sixteenth to the Davanzati, the old merchant family of Bernardo di Antonfrancesco Davanzati, historian and translator of Tacitus, whose large, elaborate coat of arms decorates a façade otherwise unre-markable, except for the long poles supported on brackets between the windows, upon which were hung birdcages, festive banners and, more prosaically, washing. There are also hooks for awnings to protect the principal rooms from the hot summer sun.

At ground-floor level is a large vaulted entrance-hall which was once an open loggia and was used for family gatherings and later as shops. Behind this is an interior courtyard which could be cut off from the street in times of trouble, when water could be obtained from the deep well sunk beneath the floor in the courtyard and provisions from storerooms which were replenished as necessary through doors leading to the narrow streets at the back. Intruders in the entrance-hall were in danger of having blocks of stone thrown on their heads through holes in the floor of the room above. A staircase leads up to galleries on three upper floors, each of which has one large room at the front with a few, a very few, smaller rooms at the back. Few as these smaller rooms, mostly bedrooms, are, however, the Palazzo Davanzati was a comparatively grand house at a time when a house with ten rooms was considered palatial, when families lived in a communal way, sharing accommodation in a manner which later generations would deem distressing.

The Palazzo Davanzati was also unusual in that several of the rooms had fireplaces, a rare convenience when the heating of rooms was more commonly entrusted to portable braziers, the smoke from which had to escape through doors or windows. By the fifteenth century, some of the Davanzati windows may well have been of glass, though it was still customary to tack sheets of oiled cotton to the window frames. The Davanzati kitchen, as was also customary, was on the top floor; above it there was a roof terrace which was replaced in the sixteenth century by the present loggia.

As in other fourteenth-century *palazzi* in Florence, the walls of the principal rooms were covered with bright and charming frescoes, lively patterns and pictures of trees and plants and birds; the wooden ceilings were painted, too, and tapestries hung from hooks beneath the cornices; and, while furniture, though massive in construction, was sparse in such palaces, the painted chests known as *cassoni* were a pleasure to the eye in nearly every bedroom. These *cassoni* were often covered with paintings, the lids decorated both inside and out. Sometimes commissioned from the leading artists of the city, who undertook to supervise the carpentry and gilding as

Painting on a chest of 1417 in the Bargello, showing horsemen taking pali – *costly banners attached to poles – in procession to the Baptistery as part of the celebrations of the feast day of St John the Baptist.*

well as to do the painting, they formed an essential part of a bride's trousseau. The one provided for Caterina Strozzi on her marriage to Marco Parenti came, at a cost of 50 florins, from the workshop of Domenico Veneziano.

Beds were also often of great value, the headboards painted or decorated with intarsia. Some were huge and canopied, twelve feet wide, big enough for four people or even more to sleep side by side, lying naked beneath linen sheets and coverlets filled with goose feathers, breathing air made sweet by scent or by herbs burning slowly in pierced globes hanging from the ceiling.

Architects paid unusual attention to the sanitation of their buildings, ensuring that the larger houses not only had a good supply of fresh water from their own wells, but also sinks and latrines and a satisfactory drainage system, with tile piping to carry waste to cesspools and rainwater to the gutters of streets which were, so Goro Dati said, 'paved with flat stones of equal size so that they were always clean and neat, more so than in any other place'.

Dante condemned his countrymen and countrywomen for their ostentation, complaining of women's dresses sewn with pearls and jewels and precious stones, of their long trains, their wide sleeves which upset goblets at table, their breasts padded or exposed. But, compared with men and women of a later age, most dressed quite simply, the standard dress for all but the richest male citizens being the *lucco*, a dark, ankle-length gown with buttons down the front and a hood hanging down the back like a monk's cowl; hoods remained in fashion until the 1530s, when caps or hats began to take their place and the long hair of former times was cut short. Men wore pouches hanging from their belts, there being no pockets until the sixteenth century; women of high rank, so Villani said, 'were content with a narrow skirt of plain scarlet', while the 'common women were dressed in plain Cambrai green'. Certainly, Villani admitted, young men were more ostentatious, with tunics growing shorter and shorter, legs displayed in highly coloured hose that went right up to the groin, codpieces boldly prominent.

The interiors of Florentine houses were simple, too, the walls being generally whitewashed or, in the houses of the richer families, painted like those of the Palazzo Davanzati, the floors of uncovered stone; tapestries and matting, together with silverware and majolica or glass ornaments, were unpacked from chests only on special occasions. The houses in the crooked, spindly streets were generally narrow and tall, growing taller as the size of the family increased, with further rooms being built on the roof and wooden extensions containing kitchens overhanging the street. The ground floor was usually a shop or a storehouse, or was devoted to the

Right: A still life of game birds by Jacopo Chimenti da Empoli (1551–1640) in the Uffizi.

work in which the family were engaged; above was a room, covering the same floor area, in which they slept and spent their leisure time. Those parts used occasionally as bedrooms might be separated from the living quarters by screens or curtains or partitions, but the rooms were more often undivided. In poorer homes furniture was crude and sparse, limited in most to tables, benches, stools and beds, and these frequently not owned by the family but hired from second-hand-furniture dealers.

In winter the dark and crowded rooms were often extremely cold, the only comfort to be had coming from warming-pans or *scaldini*, earthenware jars filled with hot charcoal. Meals were generally quite simple, too, excessive indulgence being forbidden by sumptuary laws; and, while the richer families paid little attention to these regulations, the ordinary citizen appears to have contented himself with an evening meal of freshly baked bread complemented by such unpretentious dishes as *lasagne* or *pasta* in *savore sanguino* – a red sauce containing meat, wine and raisins – liver sausage with spinach or carrots, goats' milk cheese with beetroot, and, on special occasions, *pinocchiato*, a pudding made from pine kernels. According to Giovanni Villani, as many as 30,000 pigs were brought from the *contado* into the city every year, together with 70,000 sheep, 20,000 goats and 4,000 oxen and calves. This could have provided every person in Florence with over a pound and a half of meat a week; but most of the butchers' supplies went, of course, to the houses of the well-to-do.

Opposite: A painting by Francesco Ubertini, known as Il Bachiacca, showing a Florentine street scene, c. 1530.

The Mercato Vecchio with, in the foreground, the Colonna dell'Abbondanza, which was first set up here in 1428. The old market was demolished to make way for the present Piazza della Repubblica.

A row of shops with canopied roofs near the Ponte Santa Trinita, from a fresco of about 1560 by Giovanni Stradano in the Palazzo Vecchio.

Food was highly seasoned, as it was elsewhere in Europe. Chicken soups and fish pies were spiced with ginger and nutmeg as well as cloves, saffron, powdered bay leaves, marjoram and parsley; strong grated cheese was sprinkled on most savoury dishes as indeed, occasionally, was sugar; *savore sanguino*, as well as its more usual constituents, might contain sandalwood oil and sumach, the dried leaves of a shrub now used only in tanning.

Travellers arriving in Florence in the fourteenth century could not fail to be struck by the evident prosperity of the city: the dealers and traders hurrying in and out of the banks, the bustle of a wool industry that produced every year some 80,000 rolls of cloth worth almost a million and a quarter gold florins, the handsome coins with an image of John the Baptist on one side and a lily on the other, which, first minted a hundred years before in the city that gave them their name, had now become a common currency throughout western Europe. There was a teeming market in the Mercato Vecchio,[19] in which the granite Roman column, the Colonna dell'Abbondanza, was soon to be raised above the stalls and counters.[20] Here clothes dealers and cloth merchants put their wares on show beside the apothecaries and grocers, the traders in kitchenware and jugs, the money-changers, the sellers of hawks and falcons, partridges and pheasants, wild boars and goats, the market gardeners, the vendors of corn and macaroni, of dried fruit and chestnuts, of onion and garlic tarts and herbs fried in batter, and the butchers displaying the skins and heads of the animals from which the meat had just been cut. Through the crowds of dealers and buyers, hawkers made their way crying their wares, shouting above the din, while the heralds of the commune rode from one end of the market to the other calling out news and notices. Ladies were carried in litters from stall to stall, and prostitutes walked about wearing gloves in accordance with the law and with little bells on their heads.

The city's bell-ringer and town-crier, Antonio Pucci, in one of his poems described the noise and bustle of the fourteenth-century market, 'our chief source of life – no other square gives such delight':

> Craftsmen and dealers of all sorts have stands
> Stocked with all kinds of things I'll let you know
> About, now, as this scene of ours expands.
> Sovereign remedies for all ills here below
> Can be obtained; wool and cloth dealers abound;
> Apothecaries and grocers put their wares on show;
> Traders in pots and pitchers can be found –
> As well as those who offer bed and board
> To tramps who'd otherwise doss on the ground.
> Near by stand massive vaults, where goods are stored,
> And splendid butchers' stalls, where they display
> What are the primest cuts in Florence we're assured . . .

The women who sell fruit here might give some fright.
Tough as they are, they surely know their parts
And, just for two dried chestnuts, morning to night
They'll bawl and brawl and call each other tarts –
Though you'll still find as much fruit as you please
(If it's in season) piled up on their carts.
Other women here sell eggs and cheese
For making vegetable flans and pies
Or ravioli or any dish like these.
Next to them, keeping close watch on who buys
What, are women selling herbs and mustard-seeds
To charm the nose or else bring water to the eyes.
   Thus women from the farms as each new day succeeds
Bring fresh supplies in, and the good cook bears
Home again all that the kitchen needs.
And when the time comes for fruit to be sold at fairs
Girls from the country pack their baskets high
With ripe round figs and grapes, peaches and pears.
If you try repartee with them, they won't be shy,
And some of them, brighter than florins, shine
With flowers from gardens that they tend near by.
No garden, though, ever looked half as fine
As the Mercato Vecchio does when spring is here.
It feeds the eye and taste of every Florentine
And in this world it can't be matched – that's clear
To all who care to read this verse of mine
And all who've eyes to see or ears to hear.

In times of plague, of course, the scene in the market was far more sombre. And no plague was more devastating than that of the Black Death – perhaps bubonic plague, perhaps anthrax – which seems to have originated in the East, whence it was brought to the shores of the Black Sea by Tartar horsemen who infected Genoese traders, who, in turn, brought it to Europe. Coming to Florence in the spring of 1348, it was 'greater here than in Pistoia and Prato, in Bologna and in the Romagna . . . It was a disease in which there appeared certain swellings in the groin and under the armpit and the victims spat blood and in three days they were dead . . . And this plague lasted until . . . ' Villani's narrative breaks off here as he waited until he could insert the appropriate date. He never did insert it; he himself died of the Black Death that year.

Those who could do so fled from the city, in which the bodies of victims, to whom frightened priests had not dared administer the last rites, lay in rotting heaps awaiting burial in the summer heat. Most of those who remained in Florence joined the unnumbered dead.

'The deadly pestilence did not manifest itself in the worthy city of

Florence, the most noble in all Italy, as it had done in the East, where whoever started to bleed from the nose would inevitably die,' wrote Giovanni Boccaccio ten years later in his introduction to the *Decameron*:

Here the deadly swellings in groin or armpit which the common people called *gavociolli* would spread at random to every part, the disease soon altering its quality, manifesting itself in black or bruise-like blotches which appeared on the arms and thighs, in some cases large but sparsely distributed, in others very small but frequent . . .

And what made this plague even more virulent was that the afflicted had only to be in the company of the healthy for the latter to become infected in the same way, as fire consumes dry or oily substances when they are near by. Still more evil was the fact that not merely speaking to or treating the infected gave healthy people the disease or caused their death, but the mere touching of the clothes or of any other thing which had been touched by those with the disease seemed to infect one with it. It is extraordinary to hear what I have to say, so much so that if it had not been witnessed by my own and many others' eyes I would hardly believe it let alone record it in writing even if I had heard it from a trustworthy person . . .

I witnessed it, as I have said, with my own eyes. I saw one day that the rags of a pauper who had died of the disease had been thrown out into the public street, where they were discovered by two pigs. As they are wont to, the pigs, first with their snouts and then with their teeth, took them and shook them against their cheeks. In no time, after rolling over as if they had been poisoned, they were dead, lying stretched out on the evil rags.

Such things and worse provoked various fears and fantasies in those who remained alive and almost all reacted rather cruelly by fleeing in disgust from the infected and their possessions, believing they would thus preserve their own health. And there were some, who warned that a moderate lifestyle and the avoidance of every excess would give considerable protection. These formed little groups and lived apart from everyone else, enclosing themselves in houses in which there were no infected persons and, so as to live healthily and temperately, consumed the most delicate foods and best wines, avoiding every luxury and refraining from speaking with outsiders or from hearing any news of the dead or diseased and diverting themselves with music and whatever other pleasures they could conjure up. Others, taking an opposite view, that the surest medicine for so much evil was to drink heavily and enjoy things, went around singing and making merry and satisfying every appetite they could, laughing and ridiculing whatever might happen.

A portrait by Andrea del Castagno of Giovanni Boccaccio, who spent his early childhood in Florence and returned to the city in 1340, writing the Decameron *in the subsequent years. Detail of a fresco in the Uffizi.*

By the time the last victim had been thrown into a communal grave, almost half the inhabitants of Florence had perished. The population fell to no more than 50,000; and several of the city's great families suffered so severely that their political influence was never regained.

Although one consequence of the Black Death was a rise in wages, the years immediately following the plague were miserable ones for Florence.

'The cost of labour and of the products of every trade and craft more than doubled in disorderly fashion,' wrote Matteo Villani, who continued his brother's chronicle. Lawsuits were commonplace because of disputed legacies and successions. Riots broke out everywhere. Sermons at once gloomy and terrifying on the shortness of human life and the eternity of hell were preached in the churches; artists devoted themselves to scenes of suffering; flagellants paraded through the streets whipping their bare backs with knotted cords, chanting psalms as they splashed blood around them: the end of the world was near.

Nor was all as well as it seemed in the economy of the city, even when the first evil consequences of the Black Death had been overcome.

Thanks mainly to the *gabella*, an indirect tax on foodstuffs, salt and wine, and on goods passing through the city gates, the government enjoyed a healthy enough income; but a large part of this was swallowed up by an extremely expensive foreign policy directed towards the control of Tuscany and involving the maintenance of garrisons in the towns which came under Florence's control as well as a standing army of up to a thousand cavalry.

6

STRIKES AND RIOTS
1348–1420

'Every vile craftsman of the city [now aspired] to
reach the priorate and the great offices of the commune.'
MATTEO VILLANI

The man appointed to command Florence's army in 1342 was a Frenchman, Count Gauthier di Brienne, a small, clever, swarthy soldier with a straggling beard whose father had been lord of the Duchy of Athens, a state created by knights who had taken the cross on the Fourth Crusade. Count Gauthier accordingly styled himself Duke of Athens; and it was to him that the rich families of Florence turned when faced by a serious financial and social crisis, largely brought about by the failure of several banks, including those of the Bardi, the Peruzzi and the Acciaiuoli, whose managers had invested unwisely in foreign capitals, lending money to monarchs, including King Edward III of England, whose immensely expensive military adventures made repayment impossible.

Persuaded to believe that a firm outsider might well resolve the crisis into which the greed of the rich had drawn them, the *popolani*, when called to a *Parlamento* in the Piazza della Signoria to confirm the Duke of Athens as the Lord of Florence for a year, cried out *'A vita! A vita!'*, 'For life! For life!'

As a reward for their support the Duke called upon various leaders of the *popolani* to take up office as *priori*. Yet, while this naturally enraged the rich, who had come to regard these appointments as exclusively their own, it did not long placate the *popolani*, who turned against the dictator as soon as it became clear that he was quite incapable of bringing the city, which he was taxing mercilessly, out of its deep depression. Surrounded by enemies of all classes, the Duke withdrew with some four hundred troops into the Palazzo della Signoria (then known as the Palazzo del Popolo) which, as with several other public buildings in Florence, he had plastered with his coat of arms. 'Every citizen was armed,' Villani recorded. 'All were out in the streets, either mounted or on foot. They gathered in their respective neighbourhoods, bringing out their flags and shouting, "Death to the Duke

and his men! Long live the people! Long live the Commune and liberty!"'
To placate an angry mob howling for blood beneath the windows of the
Palazzo, the Duke ordered his soldiers to release various prisoners he had
held in custody without trial and to push out with them the man he had
appointed his chief of police, together with this detested man's young son.
The mob then 'dismembered the son in the presence of his father, cutting
him into little pieces, and after this they did the same to his father. And
one of them speared a bit of flesh on to a lance and another stuck a bit on
to his sword, and in this manner they made the rounds of the city. Some of
them were so cruel and possessed of such bestial fury that they ate the raw
flesh.' Their thirst for blood thus temporarily satisfied, the mob allowed
the Duke and his other officials to escape from Florence.

*Emblem of the Arte della Lana
by Luca della Robbia, in the
Museo dell'Opera del Duomo.*

During his brief time in office the Duke of Athens had allowed it to be
supposed that he would permit the poorly paid proletarian labouring classes
of Florence – the spinners and dyers, the carders and weavers of the wool
industry, many of whom were former peasants who had left the *contado* to
find work in the city – to form their own guilds. Hitherto any attempt at
organization of their labour had been regarded as a crime and punished as
such. The statutes of the Arte della Lana, for example, declared that
meetings of more than ten men employed in the industry for any purpose
was illegal and that the transgressors would be punished by having their
names added to a list of proscribed workers, a sentence, in effect, to virtual
starvation for the men and their families. Other guilds had similar rules and
offences against their regulations were punished with the utmost severity.

When Ciuto Brandini, a wool-carder, attempted to organize his fellow workers in a guild, he was dragged from his bed in the middle of the night and taken into custody. A deputation of his friends in the Santa Croce quarter then 'went to the *priori* and urged them to restore Ciuto safe and sound,' a diarist recorded at the time. 'They said they also wished to be better paid. Ciuto was then hanged by the neck.' And when later the dyers dared to go on strike after the high price of bread had led to riots in the grain market and to the plundering of sacks of wheat, the striking workers were immediately locked out of their workshops and obliged either to abandon their strike or return to their families with no bread at all.

The increase in wages following the Black Death proved to be short-lived, since workers coming in from the countryside to take advantage of the labour shortage soon filled all the vacancies and wages fell again; the population of the city, devastated by the horrors of 1348, increased with such rapidity that it rose by about 30,000 – to 70,000 – in thirty years.

The working day began early with the ringing of bells and the shouts of men calling the hour; and the week was long, Saturday being a full working day, though on that day an indulgent foreman might allow his men to knock off rather earlier than usual. But there were many religious holidays, apart from Sundays, on average about one a week, so that, with his morning break for a meal, the worker had almost as much time off as his modern counterpart, although there were no paid holidays and if he were ill he had to look to charity, not to his employer, to survive.

As well as the food for his morning meal, he was expected to carry his tools to work. Sometimes he might be provided with wine and, on special occasions, with a meal. At Santo Spirito, for example, when the last column had been erected in the nave, the stonecutters were given a dinner of bread, sausages and wine; and at the Palazzo da Gagliano, when the roof of the loggia was finished, they were served with macaroni, cheese and fruit. Some institutions paid part of their workers' wages in kind, but most paid cash, gold florins and lesser silver and copper coins, usually lire and soldi, a few by drafts which could be cashed at one or other of the city's banks. A full-time, experienced and responsible foreman overseeing the construction of a palace in the fifteenth century might expect to receive about 400 lire or 80 florins a year, as compared with the 150 florins which a senior government official could expect. But ordinary stonecutters or wool-workers were, of course, paid far less than this, 200 lire at the most and this only if they were working full time throughout the year as few workers were able to do. The average wage of the poorest families was barely enough to keep them in food, let alone rent or clothing. However, an industrious man, skilled at his work, could contrive to live quite comfortably, paying modest amounts for his rent and clothing, possibly saving up enough to provide his daughters with small dowries, and treating his family, on occasions, to meals which would not have disgraced the tables of palaces.

It was rarely in ordinary times that meat was eaten on days other than Sundays, or that black pudding or the liver sausages known as *fegatelli* would be served as well as pasta. On these special occasions, however, there would be veal or chicken, pigeon and trout, melons and *berlingozzi*, rich and sweet cakes made with plenty of sugar and eggs, cheese and fruit, and, if the women of the household were up to it, one of those exotic confections served at the suppers of the artists' club known as the Company of the Saucepan, representations of subjects taken from *La Divina Commedia* – the *Inferno* perhaps, complete with suffering souls sculpted in marzipan and with devils made of spiced cherries.

While the labouring classes still struggled to make a satisfactory living at the bottom of the social scale, the members of the lesser guilds did manage to improve their lot, despite the continuing economic crisis, after the departure from Florence of the Duke of Athens. Many contemporary observers, from the chronicler Marchionne di Coppo Stefani to Giovanni Boccaccio, the son of a well-to-do merchant, who returned to Florence from a course of business studies in Naples in 1340, lamented the influence that mere shopkeepers and others of the petite bourgeoisie were now exercising in the government. Matteo Villani, who continued the *Cronica fiorentina* after his brother's death, complained that 'every vile craftsman of the city [now aspired] to reach the priorate and the great offices of the commune'.

This presumption on the part of such people naturally aroused the anger of the rich merchants and in particular those who were members of the Parte Guelfa, which, since it had in the past taken over so much property from the exiled Ghibellines, was by now inordinately rich as well as staunchly conservative. Having decided that the ambitions of the minor guilds must be thwarted as firmly as the workers' demands for higher wages, the Parte Guelfa resolved to inspire a series of measures to combat them. First they persuaded the *priori* to enact legislation that made it unlawful for any citizen to hold office unless his father and he himself had both been born in Florence. This would deal satisfactorily with any ambitious trouble-maker who came to the city from the surrounding countryside to find work. They then decided to take measures against importunate upstarts in Florence by a law which declared that those of Ghibelline sympathies were also ineligible for office. Since they themselves were to decide who was and who was not a Ghibelline, this meant in effect that anyone suspected of democratic sympathies could be debarred from the priorate; and since the original differences between Guelphs and Ghibellines had, for all practical purposes, long ago been resolved, it might have been supposed that to condemn a man for Ghibellinism was no longer relevant. But the word had taken on so sinister a meaning that to be accused of Ghibelline sentiments was to be charged with holding views and condoning behaviour of the most disgraceful kind, rather as in our own day the extreme left will condemn certain attitudes as 'Fascist' with little regard to what Fascism originally meant. In any event the campaign against supposed Ghibellines served its purpose, in that hundreds of men considered unsuitable for the priorate were held to be ineligible for election. It also, however, had the effect of creating a large body of dissidents strongly opposed to the continuance of the regime.

In peaceful and prosperous times this opposition might well have been contained. But the peace of Florence was disrupted in 1375 when a band of mercenaries, dismissed from service in the Papal States, invaded Florentine territory with the intention of extracting large bribes for refraining from plunder or of plundering if bribes were not forthcoming.

They were commanded by Sir John Hawkwood, an Englishman, the son of an Essex landowner who had been in a good way of business as a tanner. Sir John had fought in France as well as in Italy, and had achieved fame as the commander of a band of several hundred freelances known as the White Company, a marauding force of cavalry and infantry heavily armed with lances, swords and daggers, and with long bows of yew slung across their backs. They also carried ladders which, tied together, could reach the top of all but the highest walls, over which they would scramble by night into towns foolhardy enough to refuse them ransom money, and would then punish the inhabitants by killing men, raping women and carrying off anything that took their fancy. In Piedmont and Lombardy, in the Papal States and in Tuscany, Hawkwood's White Company had become a dreaded army, sometimes in the pay of government, sometimes acting on their own account. Later to be appointed captain-general by the Florentines – whose interests he was to serve faithfully in exchange for a lavish salary – Hawkwood now appeared to them as a brigand.[1] Convinced that he had invaded their territory at the instigation of the Pope's representative in the Papal States, Florence declared war on the Papacy.

The war – warmly supported by the Florentine dissidents who hoped it might bring about the fall of the Pope's friends, the Parte Guelfa – was fought with neither skill nor enthusiasm by Florence's mercenary army, several troops of which were evidently much perturbed when the Pope placed their paymasters under interdict. Yet, far from bringing the Florentines to heel, the Pope's interdict merely provoked them to further efforts: an emergency war committee of eight military advisers was appointed, the Eight of War, soon referred to by the enthusiastic citizens as *I Otto Santi*. Ecclesiastical property was appropriated and sold; Florence's clergy were ordered to ignore the Pope's ban and celebrate mass as in the past.

IOANNES·ACVTVS·EQVES·BRITANNICVS·DVX·AETATIS·S
VAE·CAVTISSIMVS·ET·REI·MILITARIS·PERITISSIMVS·HABITVS·EST

·PAVLI·VCCELLI·OPVS·

It was not long, however, before the rising costs of the war, and the sacrifices which the people were called upon to make for its prosecution, led to revulsion. Long before peace was signed, the Parte Guelfa concluded that the changing mood of the citizens, fickle as always, justified them in mounting a counter-offensive against their opponents. But their plans to gain direct control of the government by a *coup d'état* soon became known to their enemies, who thereupon decided to make the first strike themselves.

It so happened that the Gonfaloniere di Giustizia at this time was Salvestro de' Medici, a member of one of Florence's older families. Forebears of his had been elected Gonfaloniere in the thirteenth and early fourteenth centuries; but in more recent years the family had suffered a decline, a decline much lamented by a cousin of Salvestro, Filigno de' Medici, who, while thankful at least that they were still quite well off, complained that their social position 'ought to have been higher'. Gone were the days when 'it used to be said, "You are like one of the Medici", and every man feared them'. In those days it was held that the Medici were descended from a brave knight, one Averardo, who had fought under the banner of Charlemagne. Riding one day through the district north of Florence known as the Mugello, this knight had come upon a ferocious giant. He had fought the monster on behalf of the peasants of the neighbourhood, and slain him. In the battle his shield had been dented in several places by the giant's mace. Charlemagne had rewarded his courage by allowing him to commemorate his victory by representing the dents by red balls, or *palle*, on a field of gold, thereafter the insignia of the Medici, which were in the distant future to appear on so many buildings in Florence.[2]

When Salvestro became Gonfaloniere in 1378 the Medici still owned 'half a *palazzo* with houses round it' at Cafaggiolo in the Mugello, where the fight with the giant had taken place; they also had two modest *palazzi* in Florence and several smaller houses. But their name and reputation were not such as to rival those of the Gianfigliazzi, the Soderini and the Albizzi who, discrediting the story of Averardo and the giant, maintained that the balls represented pills or cupping glasses – the Medici, as their name suggested, having originally been mere doctors or apothecaries, descendants of a charcoal burner who had moved into Florence from the Mugello. Or if not pills, the Medici's *palle* no doubt represented coins, the traditional emblems of pawnbrokers.

Whatever his origins, Salvestro de' Medici was known to be sympathetic towards the *popolo minuto* and, as an opponent of the diehard conservatives in the Parte Guelfa, towards the men whom that party had contrived to exclude from office. As a demonstration of their support for him, and in the hopes of what might be done for them while he was Gonfaloniere, a large crowd of the poorer people of Florence gathered outside the Palazzo della Signoria on 18 June 1378 to loud shouts of '*Viva il popolo! Viva il*

Muralled cenotaph in the Duomo by Paolo Uccello of Sir John Hawkwood, the English mercenary who became Captain-General of Florence and died in the city in 1394.

popolo!' Soon afterwards they made a direct attack upon the palaces and houses of the leading members of the Parte Guelfa and its officials, setting them on fire and forcing their occupants to flee for their lives. In submission to the demands of the mob, Salvestro de' Medici and the other *priori* now exiled the Parte Guelfa leaders, released their victims from the restrictions imposed upon them and rescinded all the laws which the Guelphs had recently inspired. They would, it seems, have been content to do no more; but the *popolo minuto*, mostly wool-workers, were determined to bring about a more radical revolution.

For some years now the workers in Florence's wool industry, and by later extension the great mass of the *popolo minuto*, had been known as *ciompi*, a word derived from the French, *compère*, pal or mate, which the Duke of Athens's French soldiers had used when addressing the people they encountered in the city. It was these so-called *ciompi* who in July took the revolt in Florence into its second stage. By then Salvestro de' Medici had been replaced as Gonfaloniere by Luigi Guicciardini; and so it was he and his fellow *priori* who on 21 July had to face a forceful demonstration in the Piazza della Signoria of huge crowds of *ciompi* demanding the right to form a guild and thus be eligible for election to the priorate. Bursting out of the piazza, the demonstrators, who had already burned down the Palazzo dell'Arte della Lana, the headquarters of the wool guild, and hanged the Podestà, rampaged through the streets, and then streamed once more towards the Palazzo della Signoria, shouting their demands as they burst through the gates, driving out the *priori*, their guards and councillors, and acclaiming as the Gonfaloniere a wool-comber by the name of Michele di Lando who, standing in the hall of the palace in a torn shirt and with sandals on his otherwise bare legs, held aloft the banner of the republic.

Confirmed in office by a *Parlamento* summoned to the piazza by the great, booming bell in the tower of the Palazzo della Signoria, the proletarian Gonfaloniere and his chosen *priori* immediately set about the creation of three new guilds, the *tintori*, the dyers, the *farsettai*, the doublet makers, and the guild of the *popolo minuto*, commonly known as the guild of the *ciompi*, since most of its members were workers in the clothing industry.

Determined not to allow so potentially ruinous a revolution in the organization of the city's workforce, the merchants immediately had their premises locked up. Turning to their Gonfaloniere, the former wool-comber, for support, the *ciompi* once more streamed into the Piazza della Signoria, demanding firm action against their employers; and, when Michele di Lando hesitated to accept their demands, a caucus of the more extreme of them marched off to the Piazza Santa Maria Novella where they set up an alternative government and sent two messengers back to the Palazzo della Signoria demanding that power should be shared between the two rival factions.

The Gonfaloniere, bent upon retaining power in his own hands, brandished a sword in the face of the messengers, chased them out of the palace and, leaping astride a horse, called upon all true Florentines to follow him in driving the usurpers out of the city.

This was soon done. But the more moderate lesser guilds were by now becoming alarmed by the revolutionary activities of the *ciompi*; and when the term of office of the wool-comber, Michele di Lando, and his fellow *priori* had run its two months' course, the newly elected government felt strong enough to dissolve the radical guild of the *popolo minuto*, while allowing the two other recently created and more amenable guilds of the *tintori* and the *farsettai* to remain in existence. Thereafter, though there were disturbances and plots enough in Florence throughout the remaining years of the century, the triumph of the oligarchy was assured, much to the relief of respectable merchants, one of whom had feared that the triumph of the *ciompi* would have meant that 'every good citizen would have been kicked out of his home, and the cloth worker would have taken everything he had'. Secure as the oligarchy now was in Florence, however, there were enemies to be faced abroad.

The first of these enemies was the clever, scheming Gian Galeazzo Visconti, Duke of Milan and Count of Pavia, who was well on the way to becoming master of all northern Italy. Brushing aside Florence's declaration of war as a matter of little importance, he gained control of Pisa and Siena in 1399 and of Perugia in 1400. Having annexed Bologna in 1402, he was on the point of mounting an assault on Florence three months later when he died of the plague at Melegnano.

Saved as they had been before and were to be again by a sudden, unexpected death in their enemy's camp, the Florentines now turned upon Pisa, which Gian Galeazzo had bequeathed to one of his illegitimate sons, the heartily disliked Gabriele Maria Visconti, to whom they paid 200,000 florins for the title. Outraged by this commercial transaction, the Pisans refused to recognize it, turned away the Florentine commissioners who came to take possession of their purchase and prepared their city for siege. But so thoroughly did the Florentine army prevent all supplies from entering the city that the population were soon on the verge of starvation; and at the end of the first week of October 1346, Pisa was forced to surrender, leaving Florence in possession not only of this important city on the lower Arno but also of the harbour of Porto Pisano, which the Pisans had built further downstream. The Florentines' later purchase of Livorno from Genoa strengthened their hold on the Tuscan coast and provided them with another port through which goods could pass to and from the Mediterranean world, Constantinople and the countries of the East.

The war with the King of Naples which followed had no such successful conclusion, and might well have ended in a catastrophic defeat had not Florence been saved by the death of the young and energetic Neapolitan King as she had been saved twelve years before by the death of the Duke of Milan. But now as one enemy died, another, in the person of the fat and ugly, dirty and almost blind heir to the Duke of Milan, Filippo Maria Visconti, rose to take his place.

Filippo Maria, younger son of Gian Galeazzo, succeeded to the dukedom after the assassination of his foolish and insanely cruel brother. He himself was eccentric to the verge of madness, stripping the rich clothes from his fat and dirty body on summer days and rolling naked among the flowers in his garden, or suddenly producing a snake from his sleeve when talking to an unsuspecting courtier. Suspicious, secretive and suggestible, he was terrified of death and was known to scream in alarm at the sight of a sword removed from its scabbard. He was frightened of lightning, too, and hid under his bedclothes during thunderstorms, moving to another bed as soon as the storm was over, moving, indeed, at least three times every night from one bedchamber to another for fear of assassination, calling for a page since his legs were so weak that he could not walk on his deformed feet without support. But he was cunning and very clever.

On their own the Florentines could make little headway against the Duke of Milan's mercenaries, led as they were by one of the most skilful *condottieri* of the day, the stumpy Niccolò Piccinino, a butcher's son who had been a weaver. He had begun his military career in the company of the Perugian soldier of fortune, Braccio da Montone, whose daughter he married and whose soldiers he took with him, after Braccio's death, into the service of the Milanese. Another talented and forceful *condottiere* was also at this time in the Duke of Milan's service. This was Francesco Sforza, the illegitimate son of a mercenary. He had fought with his father for the King of Naples and, when his father was drowned in battle, had come north to try his fortunes in Lombardy, where he was to marry Bianca, the illegitimate daughter of Duke Filippo Maria Visconti, and to become Duke of Milan himself, thus founding a dynasty which was to rule in Lombardy for almost a hundred years.

To combat these formidable enemies, Florence entered into alliance with her fellow republic Venice; and to meet the extraordinary costs of equipping and maintaining an army strong enough to defeat the Milanese, the Florentine Signoria introduced a tax to supplement the *gabella*, the tax known as the *catasto*, a direct tax based on a citizen's estimated wealth and, therefore, strongly opposed by those rich merchants who would necessarily have to find the largest part of it.

The year after this tax was imposed, Duke Filippo Maria was at last induced to make peace with Venice and Florence, to allow Venice to extend her territories almost as far west as Lake Como and to confirm Florence in possession of the various fortresses which she had lost in six years of intermittent warfare. Yet no sooner had peace with Milan been concluded than Florence, in continuing pursuit of her dominion over Tuscany, was at war again, intent upon acquiring Lucca. It was a war of undisguised aggression and aroused opposition in Florence itself and anger in Siena, where the people and government alike were well aware that, once the Florentines had taken Lucca, it would not be long before they marched upon their own city, the one free city left in Tuscany. To forestall a Florentine attack, the Sienese turned to the Duke of Milan, who immediately sent an army to Lucca's defence, an army which soon overwhelmed the incompetently led mercenary forces which Florence's committee of war had dispatched to Lucca, in the sanguine belief that that small town would not be able to offer them much resistance.

Having successfully thwarted Florence's bid to extend her dominion, the Duke of Milan now renewed his efforts to expand his own; and in 1440 he paid the crafty Piccinino to lead a powerful army south into Tuscany. On 29 June 1440 Piccinino came upon the Florentine army in the valley of the upper Arno at Anghiari, where, in the subsequent battle, the Milanese army was utterly defeated.

Some years earlier, according to a cynical contemporary chronicler, the advisability of declaring war had been discussed in one of those councils to which the *priori* turned in times of crisis. As the members of the council discussed the problem in detail, elaborating first the possible advantages, then the dangers and expense of further conflict, it was noticed that one man, who had appeared to be taking no notice whatsoever of the opposing arguments, fell asleep. Woken by the man sitting next to him when his opinion was called for, he roused himself to speak a word or two in favour of war. Without further ado the other councillors all agreed that war was the answer; and this was the advice they offered.

The councillor whose words had been decisive was Niccolò da Uzzano; and nothing better illustrates the hold which men such as he had now established over the government of Florence than this anecdote about him.

Niccolò da Uzzano, whose marvellously human bust by Donatello is in the Bargello, was an immensely rich patrician merchant who lived in a palace, now the Palazzo Capponi, in the Via de' Bardi.[3] He was regarded in Florence as one of the main upholders of the by now accepted doctrine that no merchant, however rich and munificent he might be and however ancient the family into which he might have married, could gain the greatest esteem in the city unless there were a tradition of family service to the republic. Indeed, a family whose name did not appear on the parchment lists of former *priori*, which had been meticulously preserved since 1282, was almost beyond the pale. Niccolò da Uzzano kept a copy of these lists

Bust by Donatello of Niccolò da Uzzano, the rich and highly respected early-fifteenth-century Florentine statesman.

hanging on the wall of his study so that, if asked to support the candidature of someone unknown to him, he could satisfy himself that the man was not a parvenu.

For many years Niccolò was at the centre of Florentine affairs. *Priori* might come and go, Gonfalonieri take office for two months before returning to their counting-houses; but all the time the most influential citizens of Florence would meet in the palaces of Niccolò and his friends, and there take the decisions which would govern the home and foreign policies of the state. Among these friends were Gino Capponi, head of a family whose members were to play important parts in the later history of Florence, and Maso degli Albizzi, whose family, having settled in the Borgo di Por San Pietro, now the Borgo degli Albizzi, in the thirteenth century, were to produce nearly a hundred *priori* and thirteen Gonfalonieri.[4]

In the early years of the fifteenth century it was this family, the Albizzi, advised when necessary by Gino Capponi and Niccolò da Uzzano, who exercised control of the government of Florence through their friends and nominees in the Signoria and by the manipulation of the advisory commissions, the *pratiche*. It was during their ascendancy that the Florentines had opened up their passage to the sea by capturing Pisa and Porto Pisano, and had launched the first Florentine armed galley; it was in their time that they had gained possession of Arezzo and had bought Livorno from the Genoese. Theirs was also an age of prosperity so that, although the Albizzi's rule was a harsh one, in which opposition was ruthlessly crushed, it was not an unpopular one; and when the capable Maso degli Albizzi died it was accepted that his son, Rinaldo, although an arrogant, impulsive and vengeful man, should be recognized as the leader of the faction which effectively ruled Florence.

Under Rinaldo degli Albizzi, however, the rule of the oligarchy was neither so successful nor so widely tolerated as it had been under that of his more moderate father. The people began to grumble about the government's conduct of the wars against Milan and Lucca, and about Rinaldo's reported determination to maintain it in power if necessary by halving the number of the lesser guilds and thus hamstringing most of the troublemakers. And the more the people grumbled about the Albizzi the more often the name of a rival family was mentioned, a family which had produced the Gonfaloniere who had shown his sympathy towards the *popolo minuto* at the time of the *ciompi* riots. This was the family of a banker, discreet and modest, a tall, thin man with a hooked nose and sallow skin, who could be seen walking about the city, never with more than one servant in attendance and always quietly dressed, careful to give the wall to older citizens – the family of Cosimo de' Medici.

THE RISE OF
THE HOUSE OF MEDICI
1420–39

'Always keep out of the public eye.'
GIOVANNI DI BICCI DE' MEDICI

Cosimo de' Medici was born on 27 September 1389, the day upon which are commemorated the early Christian martyrs Cosmas and Damian, the patron saints of physicians. By appropriate extension, they also became patron saints of the Medici family and as such appear in several works of art commissioned by Cosimo or created in his honour, in Fra Angelico's *Dream of the Deacon Justinian* in San Marco, for example, and in Donatello's arched reliefs over the doors of the Old Sacristy in San Lorenzo.

Cosimo's father was Giovanni di Bicci de' Medici whose shrewd, attractive face, with its kindly, hooded eyes, and thin, expressive mouth above a determined chin stares out apprehensively from his posthumous portrait by Bronzino. Giovanni had not been born to great riches. From his own father, Averardo detto Bicci, whose money had had to be divided among a widow and five sons, he had inherited little. He started work in the Roman branch of a company largely owned by a relative, soon being appointed manager of the company's office. Then he formed a company of his own. In 1397 he returned to Florence to open a bank, and over the years he astutely developed the family business until his two wool workshops and the bank in Via Porta Rossa were among the most successful enterprises in the city. He was a leading member of the Arte della Lana and, as a banker, of the Arte del Cambio; and he had accepted office three times as *priore* and once as Gonfaloniere; but he had done so reluctantly and only because, as one of his grandsons was to say, merchants did not prosper in Florence without taking their share in the city's government.

He was believed to share the sympathetic feelings towards the *popolo minuto* which Salvestro de' Medici, a member of another branch of the family, had displayed at the time of the *ciompi* revolt. Certainly, Giovanni was well regarded by the ordinary people of Florence, who responded

Posthumous portrait by Bronzino of Giovanni di Bicci de' Medici (1360–1429), father of Cosimo de' Medici, Pater Patriae.

warmly to his humanity and honesty, his quiet humour enhanced by the solemnity of his manner. But he was careful never to offend the ruling oligarchy either by playing upon his popularity with the labouring classes or by the least ostentation in his style of life. He had lived in a quite modest house in Via Larga before moving to a slightly larger but still unpretentious house in the Piazza del Duomo, a far less imposing place than his large income, and the generous dowry which his father-in-law had provided for his wife, would have allowed him to buy. 'If you wish to live in safety,' he advised his two sons, 'take no more from the state than man and the law allow.'

Giovanni also told his sons that, while it behoved them to remain rich, and if possible to become richer, they must remember that a leading Florentine merchant in a respectable way of business was not worthy of honour only because of his riches. He also had a duty to honour the city of his birth. Giovanni himself was one of the donors of the North Doors of the Baptistery which were commissioned as a votive offering in 1402, a year of plague, as a plea to God not to repeat the dreadful visitation of the Black Death.

An open competition was held for these bronze doors, which were to complement those completed by Andrea Pisano sixty-five years earlier. Seven of Italy's leading artists were invited to submit designs for a bronze panel representing Abraham about to sacrifice Isaac. When all the designs were handed in, a panel of judges – of whom Giovanni seems to have been one – were asked to consider the works of three of the artists: Jacopo della Quercia, a young native of Siena, who was later to work on the Baptistery there and on the reliefs on the portal of San Petronio, Bologna; Filippo Brunelleschi, a Florentine, then a goldsmith and sculptor in his early twenties, of whom much was to be later heard; and Lorenzo Ghiberti, also a Florentine who had been trained as a goldsmith and sculptor. He was twenty-three, a few months younger than Brunelleschi, and was then working, not yet a member of a guild, in his stepfather's shop.

Much impressed by the designs of the two Florentines and unable to decide which they preferred, the judges suggested that they collaborate on the work, a proposition which apparently so exasperated the short-tempered Brunelleschi that he stormed out of Florence and seems to have gone off to study architecture in Rome, giving the bronze he had done to the Medici.

Left to work on the doors by himself, Ghiberti set to work with a will in a large room he had rented opposite Santa Maria Novella, building a huge furnace there, and casting and recasting panel after panel until he was satisfied that he had succeeded in his determination to 'imitate nature to the utmost'. It was not for twenty-two years, not until he had moved to a larger foundry in Via Bufalini opposite the hospital of Santa Maria Nuova, that the work was finished at last. The completion of Ghiberti's masterpiece was celebrated by a suitably splendid ceremony in which the *priori*, permitted for once to leave the confines of the Palazzo della Signoria, marched in process to congratulate the artist upon his work.[1]

By then it had been decided to commission new doors for the east side of the Baptistery, the side facing Santa Maria del Fiore; and for this work, which was to take a further twenty-seven years to complete and was to cost some 22,000 florins, there was never any doubt that Ghiberti should be

The East Doors of the Baptistery, on which Lorenzo Ghiberti worked from 1426 to 1452. The porphyry columns from Majorca on either side were given to Florence by the Pisans in 1117. The marble Baptism of Christ (1502–5) above is by Andrea Sansovino and was finished by Vincenzo Danti in 1564.

One of the panels of Ghiberti's East Doors, depicting Joseph sold and recognized by his brethren.

chosen. He devoted himself to it with the assiduity and devotion which he had bestowed upon the doors on the northern side, meticulously depicting in gilded bronze panels scenes from stories in the Old Testament. 'I conducted this work,' Ghiberti himself acknowledged, 'with the greatest diligence and the greatest love.'

The doors were finished at last in 1452; and Michelangelo was said to have stood transfixed in wonderment before them, declaring them 'fit to be the gates of Paradise'.[2] Three years later Ghiberti died. Giovanni di Bicci de' Medici, who had helped to obtain his first commission for him, had long since been buried beside his wife in the sarcophagus by Buggiano which lies beneath the table in San Lorenzo's Old Sacristy.[3]

Before his death Giovanni had benefited Florence by far more than his share of the Baptistery's doors. It was he who, heading a committee of seven other parishioners, had persuaded the Commune to restore the ancient edifice of San Lorenzo, which was by now collapsing into ruins. The seven parishioners, Giovanni suggested, would each build a family chapel in the church, while he himself would not only pay for a family chapel but also for the sacristy, if the commune would undertake the cost of the rest. It was agreed: as architect for the sacristy, Giovanni chose the young, cantankerous architect, Filippo Brunelleschi, who was soon afterwards entrusted with the construction of the whole church, one of the great masterpieces of the early Renaissance.[4] Brunelleschi was also entrusted with the design of the Ospedale degli Innocenti, the foundling hospital in the Piazza Santissima Annunziata, which was established in 1419 by the Arte della Lana and was generously endowed by Giovanni.[5]

Giovanni saw to it that his two sons, Cosimo and Lorenzo, received an excellent education, first at the school of the Camaldolese monastery of Santa Maria degli Angeli, which stood on the site of the present hospital of Santa Maria Nuova, a hospital founded in 1286 by Folco Portinari, the father of the young woman whom Boccaccio identified as Dante's Beatrice.[6] Thereafter the two boys attended the lectures and seminars of Roberto de' Rossi and were brought into contact with the great intellectuals of Florence, with men sharing that reverence for classical learning and classical ideals, combined with a deep interest in man's life on earth, which was to characterize those who were to become known as humanists.

Among these humanists in Florence, whose ideas had so profound an influence upon the culture of the Renaissance city, were Carlo Marsuppini, a lecturer in rhetoric and poetry at the Studio Fiorentino,[7] a scholar whose learning was so extensive that in the course of a single lecture he was said to have contrived to quote from every known Greek and Latin author; Marsuppini's rival, the tirelessly energetic, conceited and spiteful polymath, Francesco Filelfo, who rushed about the Studio Fiorentino lecturing and talking endlessly, finding time to write prolifically in verse and prose, and to give a public discourse in Santa Maria del Fiore once a week on Dante; and Leonardo Bruni, also known as Aretino (from Arezzo). Leonardo Bruni was intense, earnest and strait-laced, a civic official as well as a scholar, Chancellor of the Republic of Florence for seventeen years from 1427, historian of the city and biographer of its greatest writers; his books on Dante, Boccaccio and Petrarch helped to stimulate the humanists' growing appreciation of Italian poetry.

Also in this circle of Florentine humanists of the first half of the fourteenth century – who were often to be found talking eagerly together in Vespasiano da Bisticci's bookshop near the Badia – was Ambrogio Traversari, the small, ascetic and kindly vicar-general of the Camaldolese Order, whose rooms in the monastery of Santa Maria degli Angeli were always littered with Greek and Latin manuscripts, which he translated with astonishing facility and speed. Two others, of comparable learning but far less abstemious, were Poggio Bracciolini, the son of a poor apothecary, a charming, amusing, gregarious man who had studied law at the Studio Fiorentino and made occasional forays from Florence into France, Germany, Switzerland and even Britain in search of texts for his friends, and Niccolò Niccoli, who, having inherited a fortune from his father, an extremely rich wool merchant, spent most of it amassing not only manuscripts but also medals and coins, cameos and intaglios, crystal cups and antique vases.

A most fastidiously aesthetic man, Niccolò spent all his long life in Florence, and, in his later years, became one of the sights of the city as he walked in his stately way about the streets, beautifully dressed, aloof, disdainful, so sensitive that even the squeaking of a trapped mouse was intolerable to him, and so imperious that it was difficult to believe that he had a virago of a mistress of whom he was much in awe. In his fine house he had a library of over eight hundred books, the largest collection of his day, and would have liked to have added to their number by a composition of his own, but he could never finish a passage that reached the impossibly high standards he set for himself. He did, however, develop a most polished *antica corsiva* script which enabled his scribes to copy manuscripts neatly and quickly, and strongly influenced the early Italian printers in the development of italic type. Indirectly, Niccolò was also responsible for the printers' use of Roman type, since his friend Poggio Bracciolini, when unable to buy a manuscript for him on his travels, would make a copy of it in a clear hand based on the eleventh-century Carolingian script, rather than in the clumsy Gothic handwriting which had superseded it.

Deeply impressed by Niccolò's collections, Cosimo de' Medici, twenty-five years his junior, determined to have such a library of his own and began to buy books at an early age. His father, who had no such interest – who, indeed, according to an inventory of 1418, had only three books altogether – became alarmed that his son's friendships with the scholars and intellectuals of Florence would seduce him from the family business; and when it was proposed that Cosimo and Niccolò should go to the Holy Land together in search of Greek manuscripts, Giovanni put his foot down. Cosimo was set to work in the bank before he became as much of a dilettante as Niccolò himself.

Giovanni had good cause to take pride in the Medici bank. There were over seventy other bankers and bill-brokers in Florence, most of them with counting-houses in the area of the Mercato Vecchio. But Giovanni had ensured that the Medici bank was the most successful. He had contrived to do so largely by his good relations with the Papacy. In the past the Curia had dealt mostly with other Florentine banking houses, mainly with the Alberti, the Spini and the Ricci; but after the election of Cardinal Baldassarre Cossa as one of three rival Popes, the improbable friendship between this restless, sensual Neapolitan adventurer, who became Pope John XXIII, and the cautious, reserved Florentine banker, Giovanni di

Right: Cosimo di Giovanni de' Medici, Pater Patriae *(1389–1464) from the portrait by Pontormo in the Uffizi's Tribuna.*

Above: A painting by Giusto Utens of Cosimo's favourite villa, the Villa Cafaggiolo.

Bicci de' Medici, helped to ensure that more and more business came the Medici way, until the two Rome branches of their bank accounted for well over half the astonishing profits of the family's business.

Unfortunately John XXIII was not Pope for long, since this former pirate, whose cardinal's hat, so it was rumoured, had been bought with money provided by the Medici, was deposed in 1415 after being accused of all manner of crimes, including heresy, the murder of one of his rival Popes, Alexander V, and the seduction, while papal representative in Bologna, of no fewer than two hundred ladies of that city. Imprisoned in Germany, he was released after a large ransom had been paid by the Medici bank's Venetian branch, and came to spend the rest of his life in Florence, where the Medici found him a house and commissioned Donatello and Michelozzo to design a splendid monument to his memory which can be seen in the Baptistery.[8]

His successor, Pope Martin V, who lived in Florence for a time in apartments specially prepared for him at Santa Maria Novella, was not as kindly disposed to the Medici, preferring to deal with the Spini; but within a few weeks of Martin V's departure for Rome in a grand procession through the Porta di San Pier Gattolini, the Spini were suddenly forced into bankruptcy. Gradually the Medici regained their old standing with the Curia, and when Giovanni died in 1429 leaving the business to his two sons, Cosimo, then aged forty, and Lorenzo, who was thirty-four, the Medici bank was the most profitable family business in Europe, with branches not only in Italy, in Florence, Rome, Venice, Genoa, Naples and Gaeta, but also in Bruges, Geneva and London.

During his early years in the bank Cosimo travelled widely between these various branches, leaving his young wife at home apparently without regret. She was Contessina de' Bardi, a house-proud, fussy woman, much occupied with servants and cheese moulds, daughter of one of his father's partners, a member of the old Florentine family whose own banking business had been ruined by the insolvency of the English King Edward III.[9] As part of her dowry she brought to Cosimo the Palazzo Bardi in Via de' Bardi,[10] which winds up from the Ponte Vecchio towards the Porta San Miniato and Piazzale Michelangelo.[11] It had formerly been known as the Borgo Pidiglioso (full of fleas), because the poorest of the poor lived there, but later became filled with houses belonging to the Bardi family.

In the Palazzo Bardi, Cosimo's two sons, Piero and Giovanni, were born, and these boys were soon joined there by Carlo, the son of Cosimo's mistress, a dark slave girl – 'a sound virgin, free from disease and aged about twenty-one' – who had been bought for him by one of his agents in Venice to act as his housekeeper while he was manager in Rome. After his father's death Cosimo moved into the Medici family palace near Santa Maria del Fiore; and year by year his influence in Florence grew more marked.

Jealous of this growing authority, the Albizzi family,[12] who had for long exercised control of the government through their friends and nominees in the Signoria, contrived to have him arrested and imprisoned in a small cell in the bell tower of the Palazzo della Signoria. The head of the family, the arrogant and reactionary Rinaldo di Messer Maso degli Albizzi, who succeeded in bringing a charge of treason against him by having two of his associates tortured by the city rackmaster, would have liked to engineer his execution. But there were protests from foreign governments, customers of the Medici bank; there were representations, too, from the Pope; there were protests from Medici supporters in Florence; there were reports of Medici money being used to raise troops in the Mugello and to secure the services of one of Italy's most experienced *condottieri*, Niccolò da Tolentino.[13] The elder statesman, Niccolò da Uzzano, had already advised caution: if it came to a contest between the two families it was doubtful that the Albizzi would win, for the Medici enjoyed wide support among the *popolo minuto*, who were grateful for past favours, while there was equally widespread apprehension that the Albizzi, once all rivals had been destroyed, might become tyrants like the Visconti of Milan. Besides, it was not only the ordinary people upon whom the Medici could rely for support. Several of Florence's leading families were on their side, either through business associations or through marriage: the Portinari and the Malespini, the Bardi, the Cavalcanti and the Tornabuoni. And then there were the humanists of Florence, proponents of what was already being spoken of as the *Rinascimento*, men reviled by the bigoted Rinaldo degli Albizzi as enemies of the Christian faith, yet men of ever-growing influence in the city, among them Ambrogio Traversari, the vicar-general of the Camaldolese Order, whose protests, it was believed, had the strong backing of the Pope.

In his cell in the Palazzo della Signoria, Cosimo himself put his riches to work. He bribed his gaoler; he bribed the impoverished Gonfaloniere, whom the Albizzi had hoped to win to their side by paying his debts; he bribed several of the *priori*, whose election they had manipulated. In the end Rinaldo degli Albizzi was forced to conclude that he would have to be content with a sentence of exile.

So Cosimo left for Venice by way of Ferrara and Padua. Having prudently arranged for the transfer of large sums from Florence shortly before his arrest, he was almost as rich as ever and had lost none of his cunning. Kept fully informed of the changing situation in Florence, avoiding involvement in plots against the Albizzi and awaiting his opportunity, he learned with pleasure that the banishment of one of the Albizzi's formidable critics, Agnolo Acciaiuoli, the respected head of an old family which owned many houses in the Borgo Santi Apostoli,[14] had caused much resentment and that, subsequently, a number of known Medici adherents had been elected to the Signoria, one of them as Gonfaloniere.

While Rinaldo degli Albizzi was away from Florence on business, this Signoria invited Cosimo to return to the city. Rinaldo, upon his own return a few days later, rallied his supporters to keep the Medici out, occupying positions around the beleaguered *priori* in the Palazzo della Signoria, offering the guard on the palace door as many ducats as he could get into his helmet to leave it unlocked, and ordering the five hundred men of his bodyguard to occupy the church of San Pier Scheraggio.

But one by one Rinaldo's adherents, never very trustworthy, began to show signs of deserting him. Ridolfo Peruzzi, head of the banking family, began to waver. So did the inordinately rich Palla Strozzi, who had been the most influential of Florence's elder statesmen since the recent death of Niccolò da Uzzano. So also did Giovanni Guicciardini, whose family palace still stands in the Oltrarno at the south-east end of Via Guicciardini between the Palazzo Pitti and the Ponte Vecchio.[15] For the moment, however, Rinaldo's other principal supporter, Niccolò Barbadori, remained staunch.

Summoned by the Pope to Santa Maria Novella, Rinaldo rode there accompanied by Niccolò Barbadori and an apparently reluctant Ridolfo Peruzzi. The Pope urged them to abandon their opposition to the Signoria, undertaking to do all he could to protect the Albizzi from the vengeance of their opponents. Two days later, on 28 September 1434, the great bell in the tower of the Palazzo della Signoria was tolled to call the people to a meeting in the piazza where, in the time-honoured way, the *Notaio delle Riformagioni*, the official who promulgated the decrees of the Signoria, called out from the *ringhiera*, 'Citizens of Florence! Are you content that a Balìa should be appointed to reform the city for the good of the people?'

The people signified their assent; a Balìa was elected; and the sentence of exile imposed upon the Medici was revoked, while their enemies, the Albizzi, together with numerous members of the Peruzzi, Guasconi, Strozzi, Guadagni, Guicciardini and other families were banished from Florence. Indeed, sentences of exile were imposed upon so many of Florence's leading citizens that when Cosimo de' Medici returned to the city, entering quietly by night through a small gateway near the Bargello, someone observed that it had been almost emptied of its most prominent names. Cosimo replied with one of those sardonic observations for which he was already celebrated, 'Two yards of rose-coloured cloth will make a new gentleman.'

He quickly resumed his authority while contriving to appear no more than an extremely prosperous banker, happier in his counting-house than in the council chamber, though ready to give advice on the political and financial problems of the state when approached, allowing it to seem that the flamboyant, ambitious and talkative Luca Pitti, a rich entrepreneur in the French cloth trade, was of more consequence than himself, persuading others to put forward suggestions and take initiatives. According to his friend, the bookseller Vespasiano da Bisticci, he paraded his virtue by paying

The pietra serena *interior of San Lorenzo looking west. This church, the church of the Medici, was rebuilt to the designs of Filippo Brunelleschi between 1425 and 1446.*

more taxes than anyone else in Florence, while concealing his true wealth by greatly exaggerating bad debts in his accounts; at the same time he attracted esteem by his continued patronage of such institutions as the Studio Fiorentino, by his magnificent gifts to the monasteries and churches of San Marco and San Lorenzo, and by his support of the scholars, artists and craftsmen so busily at work in the libraries, studios and workshops of the city. Regarded as an expert in such matters, he was consulted by other patrons about works they had it in mind to commission – and was depicted in a poem by Giovanni Avogrado strolling about a building site followed closely by a mason scribbling down everything he said.

Soon after his return from Venice, a proposal was made for the creation of a piazza in Cosimo's honour opposite Brunelleschi's church of San Lorenzo. It was in this area, on the corner of Via Larga and Via de' Gori, close by the church of San Giovannino degli Scolopi,[16] that Cosimo had already contemplated building a new palace for his family. Brunelleschi's church was then partially built; and it was considered appropriate that the same architect should design both the piazza and the palace which was to enhance it. When he saw Brunelleschi's designs and wooden model, however, Cosimo shrank from so ambitious and pretentious an architectural scheme, expressing the opinion that they were far too 'grand and sumptuous'. On his deathbed his father had warned him against just such extravagance as this. Be inoffensive to the rich and strong, he had advised him, while being consistently charitable to the poor and weak. 'Do not appear to give advice, but put your views forward discreetly in conversation. Be wary of going to the Palazzo della Signoria; wait to be summoned; and when you are summoned, do what you are asked to do; never display any pride should you receive a lot of votes ... Always keep out of the public eye.'

Cosimo, as though remembering these words and true to his own maxim that envy is a weed that should not be watered, rejected Brunelleschi's designs, later turning instead to a younger Florentine, Michelozzo di Bartolommeo Michelozzi, a slight which so annoyed the touchy Brunelleschi, so Giorgio Vasari said, that he lost his temper 'and smashed his model into smithereens'.

Michelozzo was born in Florence in 1396, the son of a tailor whose family had come from France. He was a sculptor as well as an architect, as was to be expected at a time when few if any distinguished architects did not also have experience in carving stone or wood or in painting pictures or as goldsmiths. He was in his late forties when work began on the Palazzo Medici, and had already worked both as sculptor and architect on numerous buildings and works of art in his native city. He had rebuilt the courtyard of the Palazzo della Signoria, assisted Donatello with the tomb of Pope John XXIII in the Baptistery and worked on the great silver altar frontal now in the Museo dell'Opera del Duomo. He had probably designed the Chapel of Onofrio Strozzi[17] in the church of Santa Trinita and had certainly designed a new church and convent for both San Marco and Santissima Annunziata. He was responsible for the two tabernacles on either side of the chancel in Santa Maria dell'Impruneta[18] and was soon to start work on the Noviziata, the Novices' Chapel,[19] in Santa Croce, and on two new villas for the Medici outside Florence, one, Cafaggiolo,[20] in the Mugello, the other, Belcanto, at Fiesole.[21]

The Palazzo Medici in Florence was, as Cosimo intended, quite modest in size for so rich a family and considerably smaller than the later palace, which was altered and enlarged by his descendants and by the Riccardi family into whose hands it passed in 1659. But it was certainly an imposing building. The ground floor was faced with massive rough-hewn blocks giving the effect known as rustication, in which the stone is either left rough as it came from the quarry or is cut to give variety to the surface, so that light and shadow can play on it in the glare of the sun. The lower floors of most large houses in Florence were rusticated in this way, but the Palazzo Medici was unusual in that all three floors were faced with dressed

An engraving by Giuseppe Zocchi of the Palazzo Medici, which was built for Cosimo de' Medici by Michelozzo in the 1440s. This engraving was done in the eighteenth century after the palace had been extended by the Riccardi family, into whose hands it passed in 1659. The church in the foreground is San Giovannino degli Scolopi.

stone, the strong rustication of the ground floor giving way to less emphatic rustication on the floors above. Originally there were no windows at ground-floor level on the Via Larga front but on the upper floors, above the huge gateway, there were rows of arched windows flanked by Doric columns on the first floor and by Corinthian columns on the second. Above them was a massive cornice eight feet high overhanging the façade so as to cast a welcome shadow down the walls when the sun was at its highest.

On the Via de' Gori front there was an open loggia, the arches of which were later filled in and the walls pierced by windows designed by Michelangelo when the Medici, no longer pretending to be ordinary citizens, greeted guests and celebrated family occasions in the privacy of the palace courtyard.[22] The young Galeazzo Maria Sforza, while on a visit there, told his father that it was the 'most beautiful house' he had ever seen. He was entranced by its

> ceilings, the height of its walls, the fineness of the doors and windows, the number and quality of the books there, the pleasantness and purity of the gardens; and likewise the tapestries with which it is decorated, the chests of incomparable workmanship and inestimable value, masterly works of sculpture and pictures of infinite kinds and even of the most exquisite silver.
>
> I went to visit the magnificent Cosimo whom I found in his chapel. He embraced me most gently and tenderly; and said that at his age nothing could have happened to him that pleased him more; for, since it was his desire above all else to see Your Excellency, seeing me in this way made it seem almost as if he were face to face with yourself. And I, in the best manner I knew how, made my reply – only in generalities, however, and I did not speak of anything else. Afterwards, having returned to my room and stayed there a while, I returned to him a second time. He was still in the same chapel, indeed he could not have gone out during the time I was away from him. I found him there with two of his little ones, who were made to deliver two speeches, one in prose, the other in verse, in a most worthy manner and almost unbelievable coming from the mouths of boys at the age I imagine them to be (for both are most tender in years). Both the speeches were in praise of Your Excellency.

Handsome as the Palazzo Medici undoubtedly was, it scarcely deserved the attacks which were made upon it by Cosimo's enemies, one of whom wrote maliciously, 'He has begun a palace which throws even the Colosseum at Rome into the shade. Who would not build magnificently if he could do so with other people's money?'

Cosimo, hard as he tried to avoid it, could not hope to escape such criticism as his influence in Florence increased. It was held to be understandable that he should wish to place on the corner of his new *palazzo*, above a finely wrought iron lamp by Niccolò Grosso,[23] the Medici arms carved in stone with Cosimo's personal device of three peacocks' feathers signifying the three virtues he most admired, temperance, prudence and fortitude, sprouting from the shield. But it was considered to be hubristic to insist upon the Medici *palle* being displayed upon the public buildings, even though he had contributed so large a proportion of their cost. At San Marco, for instance, where he provided the funds for Michelozzo's rebuilding, he had, so one of his rivals complained, emblazoned 'even the monks' privies with his balls'. He had also presented the friars with vestments, chalices and illustrated missals, and when the aesthetic connoisseur Niccolò Niccoli died, much in his debt, and Cosimo had acquired eight hundred of his books, he gave all the religious volumes to San Marco, retaining the rest for his own library, which, open to all his friends who wished to study there, was to become one of the great libraries of the world.[24]

As well as San Marco, the monasteries of Santa Croce and Santissima Annunziata, the library of the now demolished church of San Bartolommeo and the monastery known as La Badia at San Domenico di Fiesole[25] all seem to have benefited from Cosimo's generosity, as did Orsanmichele, where he paid more than his share for a statue of St Matthew, patron saint of bankers, which his guild, the Arte del Cambio, had commissioned from Lorenzo Ghiberti for one of the fourteen niches on the outside walls, each of which was to contain a statue by a leading sculptor.[26]

Soon after the first of the marvellous collection of statues for Orsanmichele had been placed in its appropriate niche, work had begun on a task which some experts had declared impossible, the crowning of Santa Maria del Fiore with a dome 138 feet in diameter. This had been entrusted to Filippo Brunelleschi, by now the most notable architect in Florence.

With a characteristic combination of petulance and arrogance, Brunelleschi declared that the construction of the dome was really quite simple and could easily be done without scaffolding, though he declined to say how he intended to set about it. Pressed to do so, he remained steadfast in his refusal, becoming so argumentative and insolent that the committee appointed by the masons' guild to supervise the work ordered him to be removed from their presence. Attendants accordingly seized him, carried him out of the room and dropped him on his back in the piazza. This happened twice, according to Antonio Manetti, Brunelleschi's biographer: and 'as a consequence he was later often wont to say that during the period in which that occurred (some days elapsed between the first and second occasion) he was ashamed to go about Florence. He had the feeling that behind his back they were saying, "Look at that madman who utters such nonsense." '

Vasari tells the story of how Brunelleschi asked for an egg and pronounced that anyone who could make it stand upright would be clever enough to build the dome. 'So an egg was produced and they all in turn tried to make it stand on end; but none of them could do so. Then Filippo took the egg and cracked its bottom and made it stay upright. The others complained that they could have done as much, and Filippo retorted that they would also have known how to vault the cupola if they had seen his model and plans.'

A relief in the south aisle of the Duomo of the cantankerous genius Filippo Brunelleschi by his adopted son, Buggiano, probably taken from the architect's death-mask in 1446.

Having decided to accept Brunelleschi as the only man capable of realizing the project satisfactorily, the committee declined to leave him in sole charge, making it clear that he must work under the general supervision of Lorenzo Ghiberti, who was at that time architectural consultant to the cathedral authorities. As the work progressed, Brunelleschi found what he deemed to be Ghiberti's incompetent interference intolerable, and pretended to be too ill to carry on, leaving his superior to supervise the work. This Ghiberti could not do, not being a skilled engineer; and soon some of the members of the committee went to see Brunelleschi to sympathize 'with him over his illness', in Vasari's words, and to tell him 'what great confusion the building had fallen into and what awful trouble his illness had brought upon them'.

'Oh, isn't that fellow Lorenzo there?' Brunelleschi asked. 'Can he do nothing?'

'He will do nothing without you.'

Filippo retorted, 'I would do it well enough without him.'

So Brunelleschi was allowed to continue with the work on his own as *capomaestro* while Ghiberti, though later protesting that he had been responsible for much more of the design than his rival would allow, gradually disappeared from the scene. For over fifteen years the work continued, as Brunelleschi's roof – dispensing with the traditional armature of scaffolding by building up the brickwork in a herringbone pattern between a framework of stone beams in the manner of the ancient Romans – slowly took shape. Immense blocks of stone were brought into Florence from quarries devoted exclusively to the Duomo's needs, bluish-grey sandstone known as *macigno* from Trassinare near Settignano, white Carrara marble by ox-cart from the docks at Porto Pisano, bricks from kilns kept alight by night and day. 'The building had now grown so high that it called for great exertions to climb to the top and down again,' Vasari recorded,

> and the builders were losing a great deal of time in going to eat or drink, as well as suffering intensely from the heat of the day. So Filippo arranged for canteens equipped with kitchens and serving wine to be provided on the cupola itself... Filippo... never took any rest; he would often visit the kilns where the bricks were being shaped and demand to see and handle the clay, insisting... on selecting them very carefully with his own hands. He also inspected the stones being used by the stonecutters to see if they were hard and unflawed, and he would give them models for the joints and the turnings made of wood or wax, or cut from a turnip... he made iron tools for the smiths. He also invented hinges with heads and pivots.

In 1436 the dome was at last completed and on the Feast of the Annunciation, 25 March, the first day of the year according to the Florentine calendar, there was a consecration ceremony in the most splendid tradition of the city. A raised wooden pathway was built between the papal apartments in Santa Maria Novella to the door of the cathedral and 'hung with draperies of blue and white, the colours of the Pope,' Vespasiano da Bisticci recorded. 'And the woodwork which supported these draperies was adorned with myrtle, laurel, pine and cypress... Heavy curtains were stretched all the way between the churches, carpets also and benches on both sides, a marvellous sight to behold.' The Pope 'in full pontificals and mitre, and all the cardinals in damask mitres... and the whole court of Rome duly arrayed' were attended by the Gonfaloniere, the *priori* and all the principal officials of the city.

The Pope was Eugenius IV, the austere son of a Venetian merchant, who, having quarrelled with the powerful Colonna family to which his predecessor, Martin V, had belonged, had been driven from Rome to seek shelter in Florence. He was an imposing figure as he moved slowly along the raised pathway beneath a scarlet canopy, wearing a white and jewelled tiara, walking past banners and garlands, streamers and trophies, and rows of soldiers to keep back the crowds, with a choir singing hymns of praise.

8

ARTISTS
OF THE MEDICI
1439–64

*'Artists of genius are to be
treated with respect.'*
COSIMO DE' MEDICI

Three years after the grand ceremony of consecration in Santa Maria del Fiore, there was an even more splendid pageant when, in the summer of 1439, the leaders of the Greek Orthodox and Roman Catholic churches decided to hold their General Council in Florence. It was an acknowledgement, so a contemporary Florentine observed, of the high regard in which the city was held not only in Italy but throughout Europe.

The Eastern Emperor, John VIII Paleologus, had called for help in the name of Christ to save Byzantium from the Ottoman Turks, who had been threatening it for generations and were now almost at the gates of Constantinople. The Pope, the Venetian-born Eugenius IV, recognizing in the Emperor's plight an opportunity to settle the differences which had kept the two great churches of Christendom apart for so long, responded to the plea and called for a General Council.

The deliberations began at first in Ferrara; but when plague broke out in that city a Florentine delegation urged the Pope and the Patriarch – and the more than seven hundred scholars, theologians, interpreters and officials whom they had brought with them – to transfer their discussions to the more healthy city on the Arno, where they would be welcomed as honoured guests, and, furthermore, granted a generous loan of 1,500 florins a month for as long as the Council lasted.

Although well aware that the Florentines were prompted to make their offer not so much by a desire to see a reconciliation between the two churches as by the financial and political advantages of acting as host, Pope and Emperor both agreed to move south to Florence; and so, in an inauspiciously torrential rainstorm, the delegates and their numerous servants and attendants rode into the city, the Patriarch moving into the

Palazzo Ferranti in the Borgo Pinti, the Eastern Emperor into the houses of the Peruzzi family, the Pope into his apartments at Santa Maria Novella.

The discussions began on a sour note, to the accompaniment of pouring rain and blustering wind; but, as the days went by and the arguments about such doctrinal matters as the nature of the Holy Ghost grew less heated, a compromise seemed possible. At the beginning of July it was reached. 'Let the heavens rejoice and the earth exult,' one of the cardinals declared at a ceremony in the cathedral on 5 July, his words being repeated in Greek by the Archbishop of Nicaea. 'The wall which divided the Western and Eastern Churches has fallen. Peace and concord have returned.'

They did not return for long. The agreement was soon abandoned; the Emperor waited in vain in Constantinople for the help which the West had promised him; and within little more than a decade eighty thousand Turks were laying siege to his capital. They burst through the gates, massacred the inhabitants in a riot of pillage that lasted three days, and displayed the severed head of his successor, the last of the Eastern Emperors, on a column of porphyry.

Yet, while the General Council achieved little for Christendom and did nothing to prevent the collapse of the Empire of the East, for Florence it had served not only as an impetus to trade but also as an inspiration. For the Florentines who watched them pass by in the streets, the sight of the luxuriantly bearded delegates from the East, their gorgeous clothes and astonishing head-dresses, their Moorish and Mongol servants, the strange animals they had brought with them, were never to be forgotten. Certainly there were artists in Florence at the time whose memories of those days were to be reflected years later in their canvases. Benozzo Gozzoli, for example, was nineteen years old then, apprenticed to a Florentine gold-smith; and it is probable that, as well as being influenced by the *Adoration of the Magi* painted for the altar of the Chapel of Onofrio Strozzi at Santa Trinita by Gentile da Fabriano and by the pageants of the Three Kings which traditionally took place in Florence on the Feast of Epiphany – and in which members of the Medici family habitually took part – Gozzoli's wall-paintings in the chapel of the Medici Palace carry echoes of the spectacles witnessed in Florence in 1439. Lorenzo Ghiberti, too, may well have had memories of these scenes in mind when working on the panel depicting Solomon and the Queen of Sheba for the eastern doors of the Baptistery.

Moreover, the presence of so many Greek scholars in Florence had quickened the growing interest in classical texts and classical history, classical art and philosophy, and particularly the study of Plato, the great hero of the humanists, who had so long been overshadowed by his pupil Aristotle. Some of these Greeks, including Giorgios Gemistos Plethon, the Byzantine philosopher and Neoplatonist scholar, were persuaded to remain for a time in Florence, and Cosimo de' Medici, who took particular pleasure in their company, conceived the idea of forming an academy devoted to Platonic studies. This ambition was later realized, when Cosimo adopted the son of one of his physicians, a young medical student named Marsilio Ficino, and installed him in the villa known as Montevecchio (now Le Fontanelle) where the clever, ugly little protégé was to translate all Plato's works into Latin and to become head of the Platonic Academy of Florence at the nearby Medici villa at Careggi.[1]

For the occasion of the General Council's meeting, which he had helped to bring to Florence through his friendship with Pope Eugenius IV, Cosimo de' Medici had been elected Gonfaloniere. He was now fifty years old, richer and more influential than ever, and as concerned as always to be recognized as a discerning patron of architecture, painting and sculpture. In his own palace he provided rooms for both Donato di Niccolò de Betto di Bardi, known as Donatello, the son of a Florentine wool carder, and Fra Filippo Lippi.

Although Donatello was three years older than Cosimo, his patron treated him rather as though he were a favourite child, buying him smart clothes, which he was rather reluctant to wear, and taking proprietorial pride in his successes: in his bronze of Pope John XXIII for the Baptistery, his *St George* for Orsanmichele, his pulpits for San Lorenzo,[2] his enigmatic and erotic bronze *David*, which once stood in the courtyard of the Medici Palace,[3] his *Judith Slaying Holofernes*, which was once a fountain figure in the garden there,[4] and the many other works which graced or still grace the city.

When he was too old to work, Donatello was given a small farm on the Medici estates near Cafaggiolo; but he was not happy in the country and so he was brought back to Florence and given a pension instead. He was 'more than satisfied with this arrangement,' so Vasari said,

> and, as a friend and servant of the Medici family, he lived carefree and happy all the rest of his life . . .
>
> Donatello's death plunged into mourning the citizens and artists of Florence and all who had known him . . . they buried him honourably in San Lorenzo, and all the painters, architects, sculptors, and goldsmiths, the whole city almost, assisted at his funeral . . . The world remained so full of Donatello's works that it may be said with confidence that no artist has ever produced more than he did. He delighted in everything, and so he tried his hand at everything . . . He devoted his life to art.

Tiresome as he could be on occasions as a member of the Medici household, the homosexual Donatello did not cause as much trouble as the extremely heterosexual Filippo Lippi, who was also born in Florence, some twenty years after Donatello and, having taken the vows of a Carmelite monk upon the death of his father, a butcher, was living at the monastery

Donatello's David *(c. 1430) was moved from the Palazzo Medici to the Palazzo della Signoria on the expulsion of the Medici from Florence in 1495. It is now in the Bargello.*

of Santa Maria del Carmine when Masaccio was working there on his marvellous frescoes for the Brancacci Chapel.[5] Lippi himself was far happier with a paintbrush in his hand than a missal, and soon developed a distinctive style of his own which led Bernard Berenson to place him among the 'painters of genius'.

He entered the Medici household in the late 1430s after his great gifts had been recognized by Cosimo. But he immediately proved himself as difficult as a guest as he had been as a monk at Santa Maria del Carmine, where his superiors had been intensely relieved when he abandoned his vows and left the convent. It was generally agreed that he was a most fanciful liar, a cheat, a drunkard and a compulsive lecher. Frequently, when painting in the studio allotted to him at the Medici Palace, 'his lust was so violent that when it took hold of him he could never concentrate on his work' and he would throw down his brush and hurry out in search of some compliant girl; and because of this, when he was working on a picture for the Medici, Cosimo would have him locked in. But after he had been confined for a few days, Fra Filippo's 'animal desires drove him ... to seize a pair of scissors, make a rope from his bed-sheets and escape through a window to pursue his own pleasure for days on end'. When Cosimo discovered that he had gone, he searched for him and eventually got him back to work. 'And after that he always allowed him to come and go as he liked, having regretted the way he had shut him up before and realizing how dangerous it was for such a madman to be confined.' Cosimo determined for the future to keep a hold on him by affection and kindness, and, being served all the more readily, he used to say that 'artists of genius are to be treated with respect', an attitude not common in those days when painters and sculptors, even of the highest distinction, were, like architects, still generally considered to be at best highly skilled craftsmen, as they had been in the earliest Middle Ages.

One day while working on an altarpiece, Fra Filippo asked the nuns who had commissioned it if he could use one of their young novices, Lucrezia Buti, as a model for the Blessed Virgin. Innocently, the nuns agreed; Fra Filippo seduced her and carried her off. She bore him several children including Filippino Lippi, who was also later to work for the Medici.

Despite the constraints to which he had earlier been subjected in the Medici Palace, it was here that several of the greatest of Fra Filippo's earlier works were painted.[6]

Also working for the Medici in the 1440s was a friar of a very different nature, Guido di Pietro, later known as Fra Giovanni da Fiesole, or Fra Angelico, a saintly man who was said to have knelt in prayer before taking up his brush and to have painted scenes of the Crucifixion with tears pouring down his cheeks. 'When any work was required of him he would answer with singular goodness of heart that they must go and ask the prior, and if the prior wished it he would not fail them.' Born at Vicchio near Florence about 1400, he became a Dominican monk some twenty years later at the monastery of San Domenico di Fiesole, where his murals of the *Crucifixion* and the *Madonna and Child* are still to be seen.

Remaining at Fiesole for almost twenty years, he undertook various commissions for Florentine patrons, including the *Deposition* for Santa Trinita, before coming down to live at the monastery of San Marco, where his *Annunciation* and *Crucifixion* and the vibrant, delicate paintings on the walls of the cells, some by himself, others by assistants, are a reflection of a personality which inspired the name by which he became known, Beato Angelico.[7]

The subject of Fra Angelico's painting on the wall of the cell at San Marco to which Cosimo de' Medici liked to retreat from the cares of business and politics was chosen by Cosimo himself. It was a picture of the Adoration of the Magi, an image of rich men laying down their crowns before the manger in Bethlehem, which was always a popular subject with Florentine merchants and which Cosimo liked it to be supposed he always had before his eyes for his guidance as a ruler.

9

FATHER OF
THE COUNTRY
1455–64

'His life was full of honour.
His honour extended beyond his own city to Italy,
indeed to the whole world.'
POPE PIUS II

By the time of Fra Angelico's death in 1455, Cosimo de' Medici, 'more lettered than merchants are wont to be', in the words of the clever, articulate Pope Pius II, had become 'master of the country'. 'Political questions are settled at his house,' Pope Pius said. 'The man he chooses holds office... He it is who decides peace and war, and controls the laws... His mind is keen and alert [though] he often passes whole nights without sleep. Nothing goes on in Italy that he does not know about... He is king in everything but name.' Official correspondence was conducted through the Signoria as it always had been; but no important decision was ever reached without reference to the Medici Palace, through whose gates on Via Larga could be seen arriving foreign ambassadors to offer their respects and Florentine ambassadors to make reports upon returning home from service abroad. As the Florentine historian, Francesco Guicciardini, observed, Cosimo had 'a reputation such as probably no private citizen has ever enjoyed from the fall of Rome to our own day'.

Continuing to avoid the limelight, he depended upon the Medici party to maintain the status quo. They did so with the utmost efficiency, though not with the most scrupulous honesty. When critics became troublesome, Florence's taxation system was used to ruin them and its laws used to banish them, their estates being bought at bargain prices by the party managers, men such as the crafty Puccio Pucci, a brilliant politician who, raised by Cosimo from the artisan class, made a fortune buying and selling government stock, and Luca Pitti who, as a reward for his services to the Medicean party, received 20,000 florins from Cosimo as a contribution towards the cost of his huge new palace in the Oltrarno.

The constitutional institutions and offices of the state remained largely as before, with certain minor modifications like the establishment of a new council, the Consiglio Maggiore, later the Council of One Hundred, the *Cento*, with responsibility for national security and taxation. Yet opponents of the regime could, when necessary, be quickly excluded from election to the Signoria by entrusting the selection of candidates to commissioners known as *accoppiatori*, most of whom happened to be members of or to have close links with the Medici party.

From time to time efforts were made to widen the base of the party and to make less obvious the great chasm between the rich and the poor – according to the records of the *catasto* of 1427, the hundred richest families owned a quarter of the wealth of Florence, while 1,500 heads of households owned no property at all.

Occasionally, very occasionally, opponents of the regime made serious trouble. In 1458, at a time of economic recession, discontent ran so high that Luca Pitti thought it necessary to stage a demonstration to overawe the party's opponents. Summoning mercenaries and armed Mediceans into the Piazza della Signoria, he called for a *Parlamento*. As in times past, the assembled citizens, or those of them who were admitted to the piazza as appearing likely to give the required answer, were asked to approve the appointment of a Balìa. And this they did when the nervous *Notaio delle Riformagioni* had raised his voice sufficiently for them to be able to hear him. The Signoria then returned to the palace, the citizens to their workshops and the mercenaries to their quarters. As supporters of the Medici paraded through the streets, waving banners and shouting slogans, the Balìa passed a series of measures modifying the constitution, intended unobtrusively to strengthen the hold of the Medici party upon the government.

For the rest of Cosimo's life, this hold was not relaxed, although when Filippo Maria Visconti, the gifted, unbalanced Duke of Milan, died in 1447 and his son-in-law, the *condottiere* Francesco Sforza, laid claim to the succession, Cosimo's unremitting support of Sforza's claims and the financial burdens this support imposed upon the Florentine people almost brought about his downfall. Francesco Sforza's claim to the Duchy of Milan was contested not only by Alfonso, the King of Naples, to whom Visconti had bequeathed it, in breach of a promise made to Sforza, but also by the German Emperor, in assertion of his ancient rights, by the republic of Venice, which made it clear that no infringement of her own claims in Lombardy would be tolerated, and by the Duke of Orleans, whose mother was a Visconti. Cosimo's strong backing of Francesco Sforza, which raised up so many enemies against Florence and entailed immense loans from the Medici bank as well as huge subsidies from Florentine taxpayers, was widely condemned in the city. People grumbled that Cosimo's determination to help Sforza was dictated by selfish motives, by his fear of losing the huge sums of money he had lent him and by his expectations of having a more profitable and stable relationship with a powerful despot than he could hope to have either with any of his rivals or with the Milanese people, who had declared themselves a republic upon Visconti's death.

'The citizens have raised a great clamour about the new taxes, and, as never before, have uttered abusive words against Cosimo,' the Venetian ambassador reported.

> Two hundred respected families, who lived on the revenues of their possessions, are in a bad way, their properties having been sold in order to enable them to pay their taxes. When this imposition was levied Cosimo had to announce that no one need complain because he would advance the money required and would not ask for it back until it suited everyone concerned. In order to retain popular favour, Cosimo has had to distribute many bushels of corn every day amongst the poor, who were crying out and grumbling because of the rise in prices.

Two of Florence's leading citizens joined their voices to the protest, Cosimo's former friend, the greatly respected and staunchly republican Neri Capponi, and Gianozzo Manetti, a rich and scholarly merchant and master of that grandiloquent rhetoric so relished by connoisseurs of Renaissance diplomacy, who had frequently been employed on foreign missions for the Signoria. Both these men argued that it was outrageous that Florentines should be taxed for the sake of an upstart *condottiere* and self-proclaimed duke, the declared enemy of the Venetian republic, Florence's traditional ally.

Cosimo de' Medici countered their arguments by maintaining that Venice could no longer be considered a natural ally. Indeed her interests in the Levant and her powerful fleet made her more of a rival than a friend: her territorial possessions in the eastern Mediterranean made her an enemy of Turkey, while Florence enjoyed a mutually profitable trade with the Turkish empire.

Cosimo had his way: Florence's alliance with Milan was signed in August 1450. But provoked by this, and by a subsequent alliance with France arranged by Cosimo's disarming friend, Agnolo Acciaiuoli of the old banking family, Venice declared war on Florence. So did King Alfonso of Naples, enraged by Florence's undertaking to stand aside if the King of France, reviving Angevin claims to his kingdom, decided to invade Italy.

King Alfonso's illegitimate son, Don Ferrante, marched north towards Tuscany, causing such alarm in Florence that crowds gathered round the Palazzo Medici demanding to be told what steps were being taken for the defence of the city. One highly agitated merchant burst into Cosimo's room, crying, 'Rencine has fallen! Rencine has fallen!'

Cosimo, pretending not to have heard of this small town just inside the Tuscan border, softly replied, 'Rencine? Rencine? Where is Rencine?' His assumed calm was justified. Alarmed by the prospect of a marauding French army invading Italy and by the growing Turkish menace after the fall of Constantinople, the Italian states cautiously withdrew from conflict; and in the summer of 1454 Florence, Milan, Venice and the Papal States all joined a Most Holy League formed to guarantee the status quo in Italy and to withstand aggression from without.

Cosimo's policy was thus vindicated: Venice, too concerned with the Turks to pose any further threat to Tuscany, had been checked; Francesco Sforza, a trusted ally of Florence, was recognized as Duke of Milan; Naples was a signatory to the general peace.

There were to be no more foreign entanglements so long as Cosimo lived. When Pope Pius II asked him to supply two Florentine galleys for a crusade against the Turks, Cosimo made the disingenuous excuse which his descendants were to find useful in similar circumstances: 'You write to me as though I were a reigning prince rather than a private man who is satisfied with the moderate dignity of a private citizen ... And you will know how limited is the power of a private citizen in a free state under democratic government.'

The peace which came to Florence after so many years of expensive, intermittent warfare, and the political stability which the Medicean party was able to impose upon the city after centuries of feuding, allowed several of Florence's great families, in addition to the Medici themselves, to build grand new palaces. In the recent past such extravagance and display of wealth would have been considered most unwise. 'Never show your wealth,' Giovanni Morelli, the rich merchant and diarist, had advised. 'Keep it hidden, and always by words and acts make people believe that you possess only half as much as you really do possess.' 'Spending a lot and making a big impression,' another merchant warned in the late fourteenth century, 'are in themselves too dangerous.'

But now attitudes had changed. It was not only that the city was no longer rent by faction, not only that a softening attitude towards usury had made those involved in banking less wary of flaunting wealth acquired by means frowned upon by the Church, there was also a strong self-congratulatory feeling: Florence which, from such modest beginnings, had become one of the greatest cities of Europe, with a model constitution and a flourishing commercial life, surely deserved buildings on the grandest scale.

An account of the city's prosperity was given by a Medici agent who witnessed it, Benedetto Dei, whose passion for statistics rivalled that of the fourteenth-century Giovanni Villani. In his *Cronaca fiorentina* of 1472, Benedetto Dei estimated that the population of the city was 70,000, almost 20,000 more than it was to be a hundred years later. There were 180

A painting of a goldsmith's workshop by Alessandro Fei del Barbiere (1543–92) in the Studiolo di Francesco I in the Palazzo Vecchio.

churches, 50 piazze, 270 woollen-goods shops, 83 shops belonging to members of the silk guild, 66 apothecaries' shops, 84 shops kept by wood-workers, 54 by sculptors and stonecutters, 70 butchers' shops, 8 shops belonging to poulterers and dealers in game, 44 to goldsmiths, silversmiths and jewellers, 30 to workers in gold leaf and silver wire, as well as 33 banks, whose cashiers dealt with their customers sitting outside their premises behind counters on which their quills and inkwells, ledgers and abacuses were laid upon expensive carpets, tokens of their worth and distinction.

Yet Florence was not only distinguished because of its commercial prosperity: it was a city in which the greatest artists of the time from the days of Cimabue and Giotto had lived and worked, in which Dante and Boccaccio had spent their formative years, which Petrarch's parents had left with regret and from which the ideas of the *Rinascimento* were to spread across Europe. Such a city was surely worthy of the honour that great private buildings and public monuments could bestow upon it.

Moreover, the rich now had more money to spend – the *gabella* had been reduced to such an extent that a man like Filippo Strozzi, although twenty times as rich as his father, was required to pay far less in tax – and they were anxious to build palaces which would be not merely a demonstration of their owners' personal distinction and 'bring considerable honour, being more visible than all one's possessions', as Michelangelo was to say, but would also be aesthetically pleasing in themselves. Most of these rich merchants and bankers who built family palaces in the fifteenth century had served on an *opera*, a building committee formed for the erection or maintenance of a church or a hospital, the headquarters of a guild or a state institution; and, during their term of office, for which they were paid not with a salary but with presents such as spices at the Ospedale degli Innocenti or a goose every week at Santo Spirito, they had acquired some knowledge of architecture. They knew what they wanted and often knew also the architect whom they wished to employ to carry out their ideas and with whom, provided he were not a Brunelleschi, they hoped to cooperate.

Having chosen and acquired a suitable site, usually at the expense of existing houses – over twenty had had to make way for the Medici Palace – the next step, after approval of the plans, was to consult an astrologer as to the most propitious time for building to begin. Accuracy was important in this; and since it frequently happened that when several astrologers were consulted the answers varied considerably, there were often lengthy disputes as to the ideal day. When the date had been finally agreed upon, there was just as often a dispute as to the exact moment at which the foundation stone should be laid in place. This also being settled, the stone was laid with appropriate ceremony: coins and medals and other mementoes, together with portraits of the family perhaps, were thrown on top of the stone; and often a mass was said and hymns were sung. When the foundation stone of the Strozzi Palace was set in place, on 6 August 1489, a man who happened to be passing by was asked if he would like to throw in a coin. He ran off to fetch his children and his son was allowed to throw in a coin, too, together with a bunch of flowers. 'I took Guarnieri [my son, then four years old] in my arms and told him to look down there [wrote Tribaldo de' Rossi, a friend of the Medici]. I gave him a coin with a lily to throw

The Strozzi Palace was begun in 1489 for Filippo Strozzi, who contrived to obtain Lorenzo de' Medici's approval for an even larger edifice than was at first proposed.

down, also a bunch of little damask roses which I had in my hand. I said to him, "Will you remember this?" "Yes," he said. The other children then came with our servant, Tita.'

The huge Palazzo Strozzi, on the corner of Via Strozzi and Via Tornabuoni, was designed by Giuliano da Sangallo and built under the supervision of a fellow Florentine, Simone del Pollaiuolo, known, because of his enthusiastic accounts of Rome, as Il Cronaca, the Chronicler, who seems also to have created the decorative details.[1] As well as these two men, Filippo Strozzi, as was common practice, employed a *provveditore*, or purveyor, to take care of the financial arrangements and the supply of building materials, and a foreman to supervise the one hundred or so craftsmen and labourers, stonecutters, carpenters and smiths working on the site. The annoyance to those who lived in the vicinity of the building operations was at times insupportable. 'A great number of overseers and workmen were employed,' complained Luca Landucci, whose shop was opposite, 'and all the streets around were filled with heaps of stones and rubbish, and with mules and donkeys carrying away the refuse and bringing gravel, making it difficult for anyone to pass along. We shopkeepers were continually exasperated by the dust and the crowds of people who collected to watch the progress of the work and by those who could not pass by with their beasts of burden.'

Provided the money was available – and Filippo Strozzi was very rich indeed – there was rarely difficulty in Florence in acquiring building materials as and when they were needed at short notice, while for finished details, like capitals and mouldings, the *provveditore* merely had to look into the small workshops and masons' yards with which the city abounded.

The limy sandstone known as *pietra forte*, with which so many of the city's buildings are faced, came from several quarries just outside the city gates as well as from one inside them, a deep quarry in what are now the Boboli Gardens. In earlier times *pietra forte* was used in the form of very roughly cut blocks; but when the Florentines developed a taste for rustication in the manner of the walls of the Palazzo della Signoria there was an increasing demand for dressed stone and for craftsmen with the skills to produce it.

'The refinement of this taste for stonework through the fourteenth and fifteenth centuries', Professor Goldthwaite has written,

implies a considerable development of the stone industry. More and higher-skilled stoneworkers were needed, and stylistic innovations opened up new possibilities for the development of their skills that obviously had consequences of inestimable value to the craft traditions of the city. There was probably not another city in all Europe with such a large number of highly skilled stone-workers as were found in Florence by the fifteenth century, and in fact the emigration of them throughout Italy was of considerable importance for the diffusion of Renaissance taste.

As well as *pietra forte*, the softer grey sandstone known as *pietra serena* – a favourite stone of Brunelleschi, who used it extensively in San Lorenzo, Santo Spirito and elsewhere – was also required for the Strozzi Palace and this, too, was to be found in large quantities not far away, especially on the hillside between Fiesole and Settignano, where the quarries, so Michelangelo said, were 'continually worked by sculptors and stonecutters for the most part born there'. Nor was timber difficult to come by, since Tuscany was still densely wooded in parts, as indeed it was to remain until the middle of the nineteenth century; nor were supplies of sand and gravel, brought down from the Arno valley in carts which returned with waste from the building sites; nor was iron ore, which came from mines on the island of Elba; nor was glass, though this was not yet widely used for windows, translucent oiled cloth still generally taking its place; nor were bricks, which were used far more extensively in Florence than the appearance of the city suggests, though not until the Palazzo Grifoni[2] was built, after the middle of the sixteenth century, was brick used on the façade of a

The Pazzi family emblem of two dolphins, from a spandrel in the Pazzi Chapel at Santa Croce.

building in Florence as it had been elsewhere in Italy, Renaissance architects in the city preferring to conceal brick walls behind stone. The great number of bricks used in building construction came from numerous kilns just outside the city walls, as, for instance, those beside the road leading out of Porta San Niccolò, still called Via della Fornace, and from a few kilns just inside the walls, these being frowned upon by the authorities because of the danger of fire.

Just as Cosimo de' Medici had had his family emblem as well as his personal insignia prominently displayed upon his palace, so Filippo Strozzi ordered that the emblem of his family, the crescent, and his own insignia, the sheep and the falcon, should be displayed upon his. Indeed, these emblems and insignia can be seen in all manner of places on and in the Palazzo Strozzi, on spandrels, corbels and lanterns. Yet, while the Strozzi laid themselves open to mockery because of the display of their emblems, other families were quite as determined to mark their palaces with their own insignia, the Pazzi with their dolphins, the Ricasoli with their roses,[3] the Rucellai with their Sails of Fortune,[4] the Alberti with their crossed chains,[5] the Bartolini with their poppies.[6] Matteo Palmieri, a philosopher of old merchant stock, outdid them all by having a bust of himself placed on his façade.

While many fine palaces were built to grace Florence in the fifteenth century – it has been estimated that over a hundred were begun in the second half of the century alone – the city had losses to count as well as gains. Many smaller houses were destroyed in the process and whole neighbourhoods changed their characters. Streets which had formerly contained craftsmen's shops and studios were now occupied entirely by buildings on a far more monumental scale, earlier legislation controlling the size of new structures being abandoned in favour of a Florence worthy of what was considered its heroic Roman past or of a new Athens on the Arno.

The first of these Florentine palaces to be built in the second half of the fifteenth century was the Palazzo Rucellai, in Via della Vigna Nuova. The Rucellai family, whose great wealth was based on the famous Florentine red dye, the *oricello*, from which their name (originally Oricellari) was derived, were one of the city's oldest and most respected merchant families, even more proud of having 'spent money well, above all on building', as Giovanni Rucellai put it, than of having earned it. Their family chapel[7] is in Santa Maria Novella, whose façade, decorated with both the name and the emblem of the Rucellai, was commissioned by Giovanni from Leon Battista Alberti, architect also of the Rucellai Chapel[8] adjoining the church of San Pancrazio[9] and of the Rucellai palace.

Alberti, born into a Florentine family far older than the Rucellai, was the ideal of Renaissance versatility, philosopher, poet, painter, musician,

mathematician, architect, athlete and composer of erotic verse. He had a
high regard for birth and for riches. No one who was poor, he said, would
ever 'find it easy to acquire honour and fame by means of his virtues', since
poverty 'threw virtue into the shadows' and subjected it 'to hidden and
obscure misery'. It was natural that Giovanni Rucellai, versatile, too, in his
own way, a poet and dramatist as well as a merchant, and a man who shared
his views and greatly admired his talents, should turn to Alberti for his
palace to grace the city of his birth and 'the sweetest country of the
universe'. For his own part Alberti was anxious to create such a house as
would suit such a city, a house 'easy of access, beautifully adorned, delicate
and polite rather than proud and stately'.

Alberti, who had spent several years in Rome as a secretary in the Papal
Chancery, offered Giovanni Rucellai a far more classically inspired design
than Michelozzo's for the Palazzo Medici. Beneath a classical cornice, the
façade, reminiscent of the Roman Colosseum in its use of the three orders,
was to be divided horizontally and vertically by entablatures and pilasters
marking the heights of the three storeys. Along the whole of the façade
there was, as at the Palazzo Medici, to be a long seat intended for the
convenience of servants awaiting the emergence of their masters and mistresses but more often to be used by shoppers and idle passers-by; and the
stone back to this seat was to be carved in the Roman diamond pattern
derived from *opus reticulatum*.

Although classically inspired, the palace was to be clearly identified as
the property of the family that brought it into existence: the friezes were
to be carved with Rucellai badges rather than the usual decorative motifs
of a classical order, while above the doors at first-floor level were to be
prominently displayed Rucellai coats of arms. Later there were to be
references to other families to which Giovanni Rucellai was connected and
whose eminence cast added distinction upon his own: the Medici into
which his son married and the Strozzi from which his own wife came.

While the Palazzo Rucellai was nearing completion in the 1450s, equally
imposing palaces were being planned or taking shape in other parts of
Florence. In Via del Proconsolo, Jacopo de' Pazzi – whose father had
commissioned the lovely Pazzi chapel next to Santa Croce from Brunelleschi[10] – began to build the palace later known as the Palazzo Pazzi-
Quaratesi.[11] To the north of the Palazzo della Signoria, the Palazzo Gondi[12]
was built for Giuliano Gondi, head of a family whose history could be
traced back to the days of Charlemagne. The design by Giuliano da
Sangallo – the oldest of a large and distinguished family of Florentine
architects who was also responsible for the Medici villa at Poggio a
Caiano[13] – is reminiscent of that of the Palazzo Medici, although the
rusticated stone blocks of Michelozzo's building are here replaced by
smoothly rounded stones, which were also a feature of the Palazzo Strozzi.

When work began on the Palazzo Gondi, about 1490, a far larger palace, the Pitti Palace, was almost finished on the other bank of the Arno. This was designed, possibly by Luca Fancelli, one of Alberti's assistants, for Luca Pitti, the vain, avaricious and garrulous busybody who fancied himself as the panjandrum of the Medicean party and who high-handedly dispossessed the owners of the properties on his chosen site and made little effort to rehouse the families who had lived there. The Pitti Palace was much extended in later years after it had been acquired by the Medici, but even in Luca Pitti's day it was overpoweringly grandiose, with strongly rusticated storeys forty feet high. It was built of vast blocks of *pietra forte*, some nearly four tons in weight, quarried from what were to become the Boboli Gardens – not so much stones, in the words of Hippolyte Taine, as 'chunks of rock and almost sections of mountains'. Never before, Niccolò Machiavelli was later to remark, had a private citizen of Florence built a palace for himself in isolation from his neighbours on the slopes of a hill.[14]

While the Pitti Palace was still being built, Cosimo de' Medici was already living in the Palazzo Medici. He had become an old man, often crippled by arthritis and by gout, a complaint with which his two sons, Piero and Giovanni, were also afflicted. One day the Milanese ambassador called at the Medici Palace and found the three men in bed, all suffering from gout and each one as bad-tempered as the other.

Cosimo was devoted to the younger of his two sons, Giovanni, a shrewd and ugly man, generally most cheerful and always extremely fat; and he was devoted also to Giovanni's son, Cosimino. And when this little boy died and, shortly afterwards, Giovanni died too, from a heart attack, Cosimo never recovered from his grief. As his servants carried their gouty old master through the rooms of the palace which had once contained a household of fifty people, he was heard repeatedly to murmur, 'Too large a house now for so small a family.'

He had lost none of his sardonic humour. His wife, the stout, managing, unimaginative Contessina, upbraided him for crying out every time he was carried in his chair towards a doorway as though his painful foot had already been knocked against the jamb. 'Why do you scream so?' she asked him. 'Nothing has happened.'

'If anything had happened,' he replied, 'there wouldn't be any use crying out.'

When it was proposed to him that a measure should be introduced making it illegal for priests to gamble, he had suggested that it would be better to begin by forbidding them loaded dice; and when his wife asked him why he sat so long with his eyes shut, he answered her sadly, 'To get them used to it.'

He closed them for the last time on 1 August 1464, 'aged a little less than seventy-six years in his villa called Careggi'. It was afterwards maintained in Machiavelli's *Istorie fiorentine* that the funeral, which took place the next day, was 'conducted with the utmost pomp and solemnity, the whole city following his corpse to the tomb'. In fact, in accordance with his own wishes, there was little display. His contemporary, the silk merchant Marco Parenti, said that his body was 'accompanied only by the priests of San Lorenzo and the friars of San Marco and the Abbey of Fiesole (churches he had built), and a few citizens who were relatives and friends'. The Signoria, which had already described him as *Capo della Repubblica*, later issued a public decree conferring upon him the title *Pater Patriae*; and these words were inscribed on his marble memorial directly above his tomb in the chancel at San Lorenzo, a memorial designed by Andrea del Verrocchio, the only one ever to be placed there.[15]

'His life was full of honour,' commented Pope Pius II by way of epitaph. 'His honour extended beyond his own city to Italy, indeed to the whole world.'

WIVES AND WEDDINGS
1464–72

*'I always kept my papers not loose in my sleeve,
but locked up in my study, into which I never
allowed my wife to enter, either alone or with me.'*
LEON BATTISTA ALBERTI

'Since he died, things continue smoothly,' wrote one Florentine citizen in the month of Cosimo's death, 'and I believe that those who have been in power will continue to be so. May God keep them united and let them manage well.' There were others, however, who were hoping for a change of regime. 'It appeared to the Florentines,' commented the silk merchant, Marco Parenti, 'that from Cosimo's way of governing they had experienced a certain subjection and servitude from which they believed his death would liberate them.' Certainly, long before Cosimo died several of his leading rivals had been considering how best to take over the government of Florence once his invalid son, Piero, became head of the Medici family. One of the most influential of the enemies of the Medici was Niccolò Soderini, a gifted orator from an old family which produced no fewer than sixteen Gonfalonieri, an idealist with an almost mystical reverence for the city's constitution as it had existed in the time of his forebears. He abhorred the system whereby *accoppiatori* had been allowed to take over the selection of the *priori* and vehemently pressed for the reinstitution of election by lot so that no single family such as the Medici would henceforth be able to pack the Signoria with their friends and allies. Within less than a year of Cosimo's death, Niccolò Soderini had managed to enlist sufficient support to get the *accoppiatori* temporarily abolished; and on 1 November 1465 he himself walked in solemn procession in his new red robes of office to the Palazzo della Signoria as the duly elected Gonfaloniere, while his admirers shouted their approval and placed a crown of olive leaves upon his head.

Once in office, however, he showed himself to be a philosopher rather than a politician. His speeches, not always entirely coherent, were much admired for their passionate sincerity; but when he proposed some measure which, in pursuit of the revival of an imagined past, seemed to threaten the oligarchy, all those whose fortunes depended upon its continuance, whether Mediceans or not, combined to defeat him. After his two months' office was over he led his fellow *priori* out of the Palazzo – on which was posted a large placard reading 'Nine Fools are Out' – as determined as ever to loosen the grip of the Medici family upon the government of Florence, but more ready to listen to those who believed that it would have to be broken by force.

These proponents of forceful action became known as the 'Party of the Hill', since they centred round Cosimo's former henchman, the rich, ambitious Luca Pitti, whose vast palace on the rising ground of the Oltrarno was now nearing completion. Two other leading members of the Party of the Hill were Cosimo's erstwhile friend Agnolo Acciaiuoli, the loquacious and highly cultivated former Florentine ambassador in Paris who, from being one of Cosimo's closest friends, had become one of his severest critics, and Diotisalvi Neroni, also a diplomat, who had served as ambassador in both Venice and Milan.[1]

The Party of the Hill seized their opportunity to act against the Party of the Plain when the Medici's principal foreign ally, Francesco Sforza, died in Milan, to be succeeded by his son, Galeazzo Maria, a sinister young man with a reputation for acts of appalling cruelty. Luca Pitti and his friends argued that the alliance with Milan must now be broken and that Florence should return instead to its old close friendship with her sister republic, Venice. Piero de' Medici maintained, as his father Cosimo had done, that the Milanese alliance was essential to Florence's prosperity.

Piero was a far more able man than his critics allowed, scrupulous, methodical and resolute, as well as patient and courteous. His portrait bust carved when he was thirty-seven by Mino da Fiesole gives an authentic impression of power and authority.[2] Known as Il Gottoso, Piero was often incapacitated by illness, by arthritis as well as gout, and was constantly plagued by eczema, yet he had been elected a *priore* in 1548, was Gonfalionere a few years later, the last Medici to serve in that office, and had been Florentine ambassador in Venice, Milan and Paris where King Louis XI, impressed by his qualities, had granted him permission to decorate one of the balls of the Medici arms with three of the lilies of the House of Valois.

He was clearly determined that the Medici should maintain their position as the leading family in the republic of Florence, the position which they had so unquestionably held in the time of his father. He adopted the word *Semper* as his motto; while on Donatello's *Judith Slaying Holofernes* he had this inscription incised: 'Kingdoms fall through luxury, cities rise through virtues. Behold the neck of pride severed by humility. Piero, son of Cosimo de' Medici, has dedicated the statue of this woman to the liberty and fortitude bestowed on the Republic by the invincible and constant spirit of its citizens.'

Opposite above: Florence in 1352. The earliest known view of the city from a fresco, Madonna della Misericordia, *in the Bigallo. The campanile to the left of the Baptistery is that of San Pier Maggiore, since destroyed.*

Opposite below: A feasting scene painted on one of the large chests known as cassoni.

Opposite above: A fresco of about 1365 in the Spanish Chapel, Santa Maria Novella, by Andrea di Bonaiuto. Beneath the artist's conception of the completed Duomo are the Pope and Emperor and dignitaries of the Church Militant.

Opposite below: A relief of sculptors at work on the Orsanmichele tabernacle of the Maestri di Pietra e di Legname by Nanni di Banco, c. 1415.

Right: Early-fourteenth-century grain merchants selling their goods in a shop and in the market; from a codex in the Biblioteca Laurenziana.

Below: Bankers sitting behind their counter, or banco, *which is covered by a carpet, a symbol of their distinction as members of the Arte del Cambio.*

Right: The first realistic depiction of Florence, showing it enclosed by the walls built between 1299 and 1333. This painting is a faithful nineteenth-century copy of a woodcut map of the late fifteenth century.

Below: Fifteenth-century costumes, the ladies' dresses with long trains in defiance of the sumptuary laws, as depicted on the Adimari cassone in the Accademia.

FIORENZA

A visit to a sick mother, who is being attended to by a doctor. From a fresco by the school of Domenico Ghirlandaio.

Below: Part of a mural by Domenico Ghirlandaio (1449–94) in the Sassetti Chapel in Santa Trinita showing Lorenzo the Magnificent with Francesco Sassetti, the general manager of the Medici Bank, on his left and Antonio Pucci on his right. The boy is Sassetti's son, Federico.

Opposite above: The dining-room of the Palazzo Davanzati, the house of a rich merchant built in the middle of the fourteenth century and acquired by Bernardo Davanzati in 1578. It takes its name, the Sala dei pappagalli, from the parrot motif of the lower part of the wall decorations.

Opposite below: Ghirlandaio's fresco in the Sassetti Chapel at Santa Trinita shows the Loggia dei Lanzi in the background and, to the left, the Palazzo della Signoria as it was in the fifteenth century, before the present stairway replaced the dais.

Piero's qualities were complemented by those of his wife, the mother of his five healthy children, the charming and gifted Lucrezia Tornabuoni, whose rich father was owner of a fine palace in one of Florence's principal streets.[3] Lucrezia was a clever as well as a delightful and affectionate woman, a poet of more than average ability, a capable businesswoman and something of a scholar. This was not so unusual in a Florentine woman then as it would have been a hundred years earlier.

In the Middle Ages few women were taught to perform other than domestic tasks, and few could read or write unless they were nuns. They were subservient first to their fathers, then to their husbands or the mother superior of their convent. At home submissive, when walking abroad they were expected to be discreet and demure, taking care not to meet men's eyes, perhaps to wear a topaz, a precious stone that quelled passion and desire. Not all that much had changed. Most women were still largely valued for their dowries and their capacity for child-bearing. They still enjoyed little legal independence; the ancient rite of *morgenabio* emphasized the tradition that a husband bought his wife. When the daughter of a house agreed to accept a suitor's hand, the bridegroom presented her family with six rings in token of his purchase, two when his offer for her was accepted, two on the day of the wedding, and two on the following morning. Once a marriage had taken place it was generally understood that there were matters in which the wife should not presume to interfere, rooms which she might not enter. Lucrezia de' Medici's daughter-in-law was to complain that a dress she wanted to wear was kept in a cupboard to which her husband had the only key. 'Never touch the box or purse or other place in which he keeps his money,' one Florentine mother advised her daughter. 'And if it so happens that for any reason you do touch it . . . put it back carefully . . . Also, I command you to be discreet, and not to desire to know too much . . . for it is most unseemly for women to know as much as men about masculine affairs.'

Cosimo de' Medici's friend, Vespasiano da Bisticci, went so far as to say that women should consider nothing but God and their own husbands; and Cosimo himself never allowed his wife into his study, in obedience to a custom which Leon Battista Alberti's experience suggested was quite usual: 'I always kept my papers not loose in my sleeve, but locked up in my study, into which I never allowed my wife to enter, either alone or with me.'

Upper-class wives, however, had become much more independent in Lucrezia Tornabuoni's time, not least in their determination not to be dictated to in matters of dress. They paraded about the streets in all manner of styles and colours, with painted lips and plucked eyebrows, in dresses of silk and velvet adorned with sparkling jewels and silver buttons, trains trailing behind long and pointed shoes. Marco Parenti's *libro di ricordanze,* listing the clothes and materials which formed part of his wife's dowry, gives a good idea of the sumptuousness of a lady's attire. As well as embroidered handkerchiefs, pairs of hose, shoes and slippers, linen collars and belts, the bride's mother provided her with gowns trimmed with fur, woollen dresses, a white and blue silk dress with green velvet sleeves, yard upon yard of rich red damask, seventeen embroidered shirts, twenty-four bonnets.

The bride was also provided by her future husband with a cloak, which had 120 spangles on the front and a further 100 smaller ones on the embroidered sleeves, with furs and braids, 'a garland of peacock tails embellished with silver and pearls', enamelled flowers and gold leaf, corals and eight hundred peacock feathers. 'When she goes out,' her mother proudly wrote to the bride's brother in Naples, 'she will be wearing more than 400 florins.'

Earlier in the century, St Bernardino of Siena, the Franciscan preacher, had roundly condemned such extravagance in one of his Lenten sermons: 'I know some women who have more heads than the devil. Each day they put on a new one . . . I see some who wear hats like pieces of tripe and some like pancakes, others like trenchers or flaps, some folded up, some turned down. Some like castles with towers carrying the Devil's own banners . . . Oh, women! Do take them off! You have made gods of your heads . . . You look like barn owls!'

But they would not take them off; and the officials appointed to compel obedience to the sumptuary laws found their task almost impossible except with regard to slaves, who were strictly enjoined to wear 'neither coats, nor dresses, nor sleeves of any kind in any bright colours', and to limit their head-dresses to linen towels and their footwear to wooden clogs.

With other women, however, the frustrated officials seem to have experienced constant trouble. 'In obedience to the orders you gave me,' reported one of them,

I went out to look for forbidden ornaments on the women and was met with arguments such as are not to be found in any book of laws. There was one woman with the edge of her hood fringed out in lace and twined round her head. My assistant said to her, 'What is your name? You have a hood with lace fringes.' But the woman removed the lace fringe which was attached to the hood with a pin, and said it was merely a wreath. Further along we met a woman with many buttons in front of her dress; and my assistant said to her, 'You are not allowed to wear buttons.' But she replied, 'These are not buttons. They are studs. Look, they have no loops, and there are no buttonholes.' Then my assistant, supposing he had caught a culprit at last, went up to another woman and said to her, 'You are wearing ermine.' And he took out his book to write down her name. 'You cannot take down my name,' the woman protested. 'This is not ermine. It is the fur of a suckling.' 'What do you mean, suckling?' 'A kind of animal.'

Florentine women were as celebrated for the care they took over their make-up and their hair as they were for the splendour of their clothes. If their skins were too sallow they bleached them, if too rosy they powdered them. If their hair was too dark they dyed it or wore a wig of white or yellow silk or sat on their roof terraces wearing straw hats with the crowns cut out and their hair spread over the brim to bleach their tresses in the sun. Ludovico Ariosto complained of the paraphernalia they needed to present themselves to the world with the required degree of elegance:

> How many little knives and scissors for the nails; and little cakes of soap, and slices of lemon for the hands! They need an hour to wash them and another hour to anoint and rub them until they are perfect. And how many powders and how much work are needed to clean the teeth! I could not count the number of boxes, phials, little bottles and other trifles that they use. One could fit out a ship from stem to stern in less time.

Other writers lamented the passing of the days when an unmarried girl of good family was kept at home, forbidden to walk the streets except on the way to Mass and then heavily veiled, or even not allowed out at all without a chaperone beyond the limits of the family loggia or garden.

Lucrezia Tornabuoni allowed her own three daughters more freedom than this. She saw to it that they were as well educated as she was herself and that they not only had the grace of manner to attract husbands from good families, as all three of them did – a Rossi, a Pazzi and a Rucellai – but that they could hold their own in intelligent conversation. 'I should never have believed,' exclaimed a Florentine lawyer upon hearing such wives talk, 'that the ladies of Florence were so conversant with moral and natural philosophy, and with logic and rhetoric.'

Helped and encouraged by a wife of strong character and by his two young sons, now approaching manhood, Piero de' Medici, ill as he was and worried by the declining fortunes of his bank, and consequently often irritable, faced the crisis precipitated by the death of his ally, the Duke of Milan, with confidence and resolution. He was ill at his villa at Careggi when news reached him that his enemies in Florence had come to terms with the Duke of Ferrara and that troops were on the march across the Tuscan frontier with orders to seize him and his sons and have them all executed upon some trumped up charge. Sending the elder of his sons, the sixteen-year-old Lorenzo, galloping ahead of him, Piero had himself immediately carried back in a litter to Florence where, according to Marco Parenti, 'those citizens who were his partisans armed themselves and rushed to defend his house'. Finding himself 'in financial disorder', Piero borrowed 10,000 florins from his extremely rich cousin, Pierfrancesco de' Medici, who 'did not know how to refuse'; and 'with this money Piero demonstrated great liberality, spending freely for all [his supporters'] needs. First of all he purchased all the bread in Florence's bakeries and had it sent to his house.' Then he emptied the wine shops and sent his men to buy up all the weapons they could lay their hands on. The Palazzo Medici was surrounded by armed guards, fortified with planks and scaffolding, and 'furnished with many stones and other stores for battle'. All the gates leading into the city were seized, with the single exception of the Porta San Gallo, which was held open for Medici adherents on the march from the *contado*.

The Party of the Hill, alarmed by Piero's swift reaction to the crisis, and his urgent call for help from Milan, were thrown into disarray. Niccolò Soderini, galloping up to Luca Pitti's palace, urged his associates there to act immediately to call the people to arms and to treat all who did not respond to the call as enemies. He himself, he proposed, would ride through the city shouting 'Liberty!', collecting support, and attack the Medici Palace. But the others held back, fearing that this arousal of the lower orders might endanger their own standing in the city as well as Piero de' Medici's, and lead to an uprising such as that of the *ciompi* in 1378.

Believing their cause to be already as good as lost, Luca Pitti now came to terms with Piero. Approached by Francesco Sassetti, Piero's business partner, he agreed to abandon his confederates on condition that he and his brother should be appointed to important government offices and that his daughter should be married to Piero's son, Lorenzo. Piero agreed to the first condition; as to the second, he undertook to see that the little girl was married 'to someone he held most dear'. Choosing to suppose that this someone was Lorenzo, Luca Pitti agreed to the terms.

By now Piero had made arrangements for the election of a strongly Medicean Signoria. In time-honoured fashion this Signoria called for a *Parlamento*, which, under the eyes of three thousand troops and of the young Lorenzo de' Medici riding up and down in front of them, obediently authorized a Balìa, which, in its turn, confirmed the authority of the *accoppiatori* to supervise the appointment of *priori* in future, rejecting elections by lot.

The uprising was thus crushed before it had taken shape; the conspirators either fled or were forced into exile, with the exception of the disgraced and humiliated Luca Pitti, whose daughter was married to Piero's brother-in-law, Giovanni di Francesco Tornabuoni, the young and well-respected manager of the Roman branch of the Medici bank.

'Therefore M. Luca could not complain of having such a son-in-law with such excellent qualities, even though he was not the one he had in mind,' Marco Parenti commented. 'Nevertheless he was not left in the position he had thought.' Both he and his brother were given the offices they sought but neither of them was consulted by their colleagues or by anyone else. 'M. Luca remained cold and alone at home,' Marco Parenti continued, 'and no one visited him to talk about political affairs – he whose house was formerly filled with every kind of person. Occasionally he ventured out but he could find hardly anyone in the street who would speak a word to him.'

Congratulated by both the King of France, who wrote to say, 'It pleases me greatly that the lilies have come out victorious for my fine cousin, Piero de' Cosimo,' and by the new Duke of Milan, who was thanked for his help in 'putting an end to all civil discord', Piero found his position in Florence more secure than it had ever been and his reputation so much enhanced that when the exiles, plotting in Venice, succeeded in enlisting the help of the *condottiere* Bartolomeo Colleoni, Captain-General of the Most Serene Republic, Piero had no difficulty in raising a strong army to oppose the Venetians' advance, which was brought to a sudden halt at Imola.

His authority secure in Florence, Piero was able to turn once more to his great pleasure in life, his activities as connoisseur, collector and patron. In his father's lifetime he had often dealt with artists and their commissions on Cosimo's behalf, nurturing Donatello and Fra Filippo Lippi, encouraging Domenico Veneziano and Michelozzo and taking a close interest in the work of Luca della Robbia, founder of the Della Robbia's Florentine studio.[4]

Another Florentine artist working for the Medici at this time was Paolo di Doni, whose passion for birds earned him the nickname Uccello. Born at Pratovecchio just outside Florence in 1397, Uccello was an apprentice in Ghiberti's workshop by the age of ten and was not yet eighteen when he became a member of the Arte dei Medici e Speziali. 'He always loved painting animals and in order to do them well he studied them very carefully,' Vasari said, 'even keeping his house full of pictures of birds, cats, dogs and every kind of strange beast whose likeness he could obtain, since he was too poor to keep the animals themselves.' A shy, retiring man, he abandoned a commission at San Miniato al Monte rather than tell the abbot he was fed up with the cheese soups and cheese pies he was always given for his meals, and thereafter he ran away whenever he saw a friar in the streets of Florence.

Uccello had already painted some of the Old Testament scenes in the Chiostro Verde at Santa Maria Novella, designed stained-glass windows for the Duomo and completed the huge heads of prophets around the immense clock there, when he was commissioned by Piero to paint three scenes of the Florentine victory over the Sienese at San Romano in 1432. These three panels, now dispersed, all used to hang in Lorenzo de' Medici's bedroom in the Medici Palace, together with two other Uccellos, a scene from the legend of Paris and a picture of lions fighting dragons.[5] Uccello's last work, according to Vasari, was a fresco over the door of the church of

San Tommaso in the Mercato Vecchio around which he placed a screen of planks so that none should see the painting until he had finished it.

'What kind of work is that you've hidden behind a screen?' Donatello asked him one day.

'You'll just have to wait and see.'

Then one morning, so Vasari recorded,

> Donatello happened to be buying some fruit in the Mercato Vecchio when he saw that Paolo was uncovering his work ... Paolo, anxious to have his opinion, asked him what he thought of the painting. After he had closely scrutinized it, Donatello commented, 'Well now Paolo, now that it ought to be covered up, you're showing it to the whole world.'
>
> Paolo ... felt so humiliated that he no longer had the heart to go out of doors, and he shut himself up in his house and devoted all his time to perspective, which kept him poor and secluded till the day he died. He lived to a ripe but disgruntled old age.

Also working for the Medici in Uccello's time were two other leading Florentine artists, Benozzo Gozzoli and Antonio di Jacopo Benzi, who was known as Pollaiuolo because his father was a poulterer.

Gozzoli, born in Florence in 1420, had worked under Ghiberti on one of the Baptistery doors and with Fra Angelico at San Marco, before starting work on his masterpiece, the fresco cycle in the chapel of the Palazzo Medici. Piero took the greatest interest in this painting, which the artist began in 1459, asking him to use the brightest colours and to make the clothes as rich as possible. Gozzoli agreed but, less timid than Uccello, asked for payment in advance to cover the cost of the gold and ultramarine paint which would be needed. He also let it be known that Piero's criticisms of his work were not always well founded:

> This morning I received a letter from your Magnificence through Roberto Martegli and I understand that the seraphims I have done do not seem appropriate to you. I have done one in a corner among certain clouds owing to which one only sees bits of the wing and he is so well-hidden and covered by the clouds that far from deforming anything he rather gives beauty. I have done another on the other side of the altar also hidden in the same way. Roberto Martegli has seen them and said there is nothing to make a fuss about. All the same I will do whatever you command me to do: two clouds will make them vanish. I would have come to speak with you myself but I began to apply the blue this morning and the task cannot be abandoned. The heat is great and from one moment to the next the glue might stop working.

A detail of Benozzo Gozzoli's Procession of the Magi (1459–60) in the chapel of the Medici Palace. The figure riding the richly caparisoned horse above the black man's bow is supposed to represent Cosimo de' Medici. Between the two bearded figures behind him, Gozzoli has painted himself, with his name on his hat.

When the work was finished, Piero had no cause for complaint about the painting, in which several members of his family were depicted and, so that there should be no mistaking his own identity, the artist included a portrait of himself with his name on his hat.

Piero's father is shown with the trappings of his horse decorated with the Medici arms and his own emblem of three feathers; near by is Piero himself; and in front of them may be the gorgeously clothed young Lorenzo, ten or eleven years old when the picture was painted, the trappings of his horse too bearing the Medici insignia. Piero's younger son, Giuliano, is perhaps also depicted, riding behind a black page carrying a bow; and Giuliano's three sisters are also here, good-looking girls dressed alike with tall plumes in their hats.[6]

Soon after Gozzoli's work in the chapel of the Medici Palace was finished, Antonio Pollaiuolo set to work for the Medici on his bronze of *Hercules and Antaeus*, now in the Bargello; and it was two of the other twelve labours of Hercules, the slaying of the Nemean Lion and the destruction of the Hydra of Lerna, which Piero de' Medici chose as subjects for paintings commissioned from Pollaiuolo for the audience hall of the palace.

Trained as a goldsmith, as so many Florentine artists were, Pollaiuolo was also a sculptor, engraver, enameller and jeweller, as well as a painter. He had worked on the silver altar frontal now in the Museo dell'Opera del Duomo and in Ghiberti's bronze foundry. After years of exacting study and hours spent in the dissection of corpses, he had become renowned for his skill in portraying the naked figure, particularly the naked figure in movement, as his murals of nude dancers in the Villa La Gallina at Arcetri, once owned by the Lanfredini family, well illustrate.

The work of Antonio Pollaiuolo and of his brother, Piero, evidently had a strong influence upon an artist about twelve years younger than Antonio, Sandro Botticelli, whose diaphanously robed dancers in his early work, *Primavera*, painted for Lorenzo di Pierfrancesco de' Medici's *palazzo* in Florence, are the very epitome of graceful movement.[7]

Alessandro di Mariano Filipepi was the son of a Florentine tanner in a modest way of business in Via Nuova Borg'Ognissanti. He seems to have derived his nickname, Botticelli, which means little barrel, from an elder brother, a pawnbroker who was also a *batiloro* – a beater of the gold leaf used for picture frames – who took him off his impoverished father's hands. A sickly child, Botticelli remained at school until he was thirteen, and was then sent to work in a goldsmith's shop before being apprenticed to Fra Filippo Lippi. Soon afterwards, apparently, he was taken into the Medici household, and by 1470, though he was not yet twenty-six, he had his own workshop, which Filippo's son Filippino Lippi joined as an apprentice two years later.

Already Botticelli, recommended by the Pollaiuolo brothers, had painted *Fortitude* for the hall of the Arte di Mercanzia and had been commissioned by the Vespucci family to work in the church of Ognissanti, for which he was later to paint his *Saint Augustine*. It was evidently the Vespucci who recommended him to Lorenzo di Pierfrancesco de' Medici, for whose

Botticelli's Adoration of the Magi, *commissioned for the church of Santa Maria Novella, is now in the Uffizi. According to Giorgio Vasari, the king holding out his hands towards the Holy Child's feet is Cosimo; the kneeling figure in the white robe is Giuliano, Lorenzo's brother; and the man behind him, 'shown gratefully adoring the child', is Cosimo's second son, Giovanni. The man on his knees in the centre foreground has been identified as Piero de' Medici; and the man on the extreme right in the saffron gown is Botticelli himself. The figure in the black gown with a red stripe down the shoulder may be an idealized portrait of Lorenzo il Magnifico.*

palazzo in Florence not only the *Primavera* but also the *Birth of Venus* were painted; and in both these pictures Botticelli is said to have represented members of the family in whose palace he lived. The lovely features of Giuliano's inamorata, the consumptive Simonetta Cattaneo, wife of Marco Vespucci, were recognized in those of Venus, while Giuliano himself was said to be represented by the figure of Mercury to the left of the three dancing graces. Members of the family were later to be identified in the *Profile Portrait of a Lady in a Brown Dress*,[8] in the *Madonna of the Magnificat*[9] and in the *Adoration of the Magi*, which, commissioned by Piero's friend, Gaspare di Zanobi del Lama for the church of Santa Maria Novella, contains supposed portraits of Piero, his father, brother and sons, as well as of Botticelli himself standing on the extreme right in a saffron gown.[10] And, if the youth in the *Portrait of a Young Man with a Medal*, now in the Uffizi, is not a member of the family, the face on the medal is certainly that of Cosimo de' Medici.[11]

After his *Primavera* was finished, Botticelli was kept as busily occupied as any painter in Florence. His work was to be seen in most of Florence's principal churches, in the Ospedale degli Innocenti and in the Palazzo della Signoria. And Piero de' Medici, who encouraged Botticelli in his adaptation of classical mythology to celebrate the virtues and triumphs of Florence and her rulers, remained throughout his life the artist's champion, friend and patron.

Towards the beginning of the last year of Piero's life, on 7 February 1469, a spectacular tournament was held in Florence in the Piazza Santa Croce.[12] Eighteen young men from Florence's oldest and most distinguished families, wearing magnificent clothes over armour made especially for the occasion, paraded round the square, attended by pages and men-at-arms as gorgeously clothed as themselves, applauded and cheered by spectators crowded on to the roofs and balconies, and peering down from every window.

In many cities of northern Europe the tournament that followed might well have developed into a violent conflict, with much blood spilled and even lives lost. Indeed, it was at Urbino, in a tournament held to celebrate the accession of his friend Francesco Sforza as Duke of Milan, that Federigo da Montefeltro, Duke of Urbino, lost his right eye and the bridge of his nose, wounds which led to subsequent portraits of him, such as that by Piero della Francesca, being painted in profile.[13] But in Florence the tournament was essentially an extravagant display of colour and beauty, noisy and exuberant, with trumpets blaring, drums beating and standards flying as the Queen of the Tournament, on this occasion the delicious Lucrezia Donati, was escorted to her panoplied throne.

This tournament of 1469, which cost 10,000 ducats, was to celebrate the betrothal of Piero de' Medici's elder son, Lorenzo, to the sixteen-year-old Roman heiress, Clarice Orsini. It was not a popular match in Florence, and no doubt the Medici felt that the lavish festivities to which the citizens were treated might reconcile them to it. Customarily even the grandest families looked for wives from families within the city, immense care being taken, and great sums of money being spent, to ensure the selection of a suitable bride, with a satisfactory dowry and a healthy body, from a family preferably as high if not higher in the Florentine social scale, but certainly no lower. The Medici's decision to ally themselves with one of the greatest of Rome's families, possessor of immense estates within the Kingdom of Naples as well as in the Patrimony of St Peter, was seen in some quarters as aggrandizement of a peculiarly unacceptable kind.

Lorenzo's mother had been to Rome to see the girl covertly for herself, giving as her excuse for the journey a wish to visit her two brothers who worked in the Medici bank in Rome. Soon after her arrival in the city, she caught sight of Clarice on the way to St Peter's but neither upon that nor upon a second occasion was she able to inspect her properly, since Roman women, as she reported, were 'always entirely covered up'. She saw enough, however, beneath the folds of the girl's *lenzuolo* to be reasonably well satisfied. Her hair was reddish rather than properly fair, she told her husband, and she did not carry her head elegantly as their own daughters did but poked it forward awkwardly; she also seemed to be rather shy. She was fairly tall, however, had a well-shaped bosom, a good complexion and 'long, slim hands'.

The negotiations completed and the amount of the dowry settled, Clarice Orsini arrived in Florence in June to find that the husband to whom she had been married by proxy in Rome was a young man of almost startling ugliness. The prominent nose in his sallow and already deeply lined face was long and flattened; his heavy jaw jutted forward so far that his lower lip almost enclosed the upper; his eyebrows, black, thick and irregular, spread sideways to touch the long, lank hair, parted in the middle, which almost reached his shoulders. He spoke in a high-pitched voice, cracked and nasal; he was short-sighted and had no sense of smell. Yet Lorenzo de' Medici was a far from unattractive man. Virile, animated, clever and amusing, his company was as eagerly sought by men as by women. Like most of his contemporaries, he took what seems to modern sensibilities a most unappealing pleasure in practical jokes; he also took delight in stories of the most obscene bawdy; he was intensely competitive, determined to win or be on the winning side in the many games, from a kind of football to a sort of fives, both of which he played with great skill. Angry when he lost, he was just as disagreeable when defeated in some intellectual exercise. Yet his numerous friends, in praising what Marsilio Ficino called his 'natural happy nature', his *joie de vivre*, his limitless and infectious enthusiasm, spoke also of his essential kindliness, his capacity for deep affection. A scholar as well as a sportsman, a poet of extraordinary diversity and marvellous verve, a talented musician, a gifted amateur architect and highly perceptive connoisseur, he devoted as much energy and interest to the planning of his garden at Careggi and the rearing of his pheasants at Poggio a Caiano as he did to the study of Plato or the artistry of making love.

When it came to planning the celebration of his marriage in Florence, he brought to these arrangements, too, the application of his eager, quick and restless mind. It was understood that there must be no cheese-paring. Weddings in Florence among the rich merchant classes were expected to be public spectacles, not merely family celebrations. Several hundred guests would be entertained over a period of two or three days, and food would be provided for many more citizens who were not invited to the splendid banquets. At the grandest of these banquets the guests would be offered basins of rose-water for washing their hands before settling down to a first course comprising some exotic dish such as capons in white sauce with gilded pomegranate seeds or minced goat's liver flavoured with ginger. The tables would be covered with three or four tablecloths which, together with the used drinking cups, would be removed one by one as course succeeded course, as peacocks and pheasants were brought in to a flourish of trumpets, roebucks and sucking pigs, geese, gilded bread and silvered eels, aniseed and petal syrup, sturgeons and almond soup, jellies and coated almonds and ornate confections of sugar and marzipan in the shape of palaces and churches, family emblems and coats of arms. From time to time servants would appear with towels and more bowls of rose-water or lemon-water; and throughout the meal there would be musical interludes.

The expense of such banquets was naturally enormous: the celebrations attendant upon the marriage of Lorenzo's sister, Lucrezia, to Bernardo Rucellai cost 6,000 florins and necessitated the employment of over fifty cooks and the building of a special kitchen adjoining the Rucellai's palace. The banquet, Giovanni Rucellai declared,

> was held out of doors on a platform – which filled the entire piazza opposite our house. It was hung with very beautiful cloths and tapestries – and a ceiling above to keep off the sun made of turquoise cloths turned inside out adorned across the entire width with garlands of green foliage with roses in their midst and green festoons surrounding them with four escutcheons (half with the Medici arms and half with those of the Rucellai) and with many other adornments and above all a sideboard richly loaded with silver plate.
>
> The whole thing was generally considered to be the most beautiful and impressive display that had ever been prepared for a wedding feast and on the said platform people danced, celebrated and laid out tables for both lunch and dinner. There were present at the said festivities fifty smart and richly dressed ladies and likewise thirty young men well turned out for the occasion. Between friends and neighbours, about fifty of the most important citizens were invited to each meal so that at the first table one hundred and seventy people sat down to dine, and at the second, third and fourth tables... five hundred were fed.

For guests, too, weddings were an expensive business. Special clothes had to be made and costly presents bought. Rich as her husband was, Filippo Strozzi's wife pretended to be ill so that she would not have to go to a grand wedding which was to be celebrated over several days. Presents brought by guests to the Rucellai wedding included all kinds of exotic fruits and sweetmeats, baskets of pomegranates and marzipan as well as quails and hares, wine and a pair of calves.

Attempts were occasionally made to enforce obedience to sumptuary laws; but with families of good standing in the city there seems to have been little interference. Most banquets were conducted with decorum. Francesco Sforza caused some surprise when at a feast given in his honour in Florence in 1445 he strolled about from table to table picking bits he fancied from the plates of other guests, accompanied by a page reciting verses in praise of his achievements; but this, those disconcerted by his behaviour were assured, was quite usual in Milan 'among lords and great masters'.

To celebrate Lorenzo's marriage to Clarice Orsini there were to be no fewer than five banquets at the Medici Palace over a period of three days. Cartloads of food were brought in from the *contado*, game and poultry, fish and meat, 250 calves, 2,000 brace of capons, as well as immense casks of wine, Trebbiano and Vernaccia, sugared almonds and all kinds of fruit from the Mugello. Confectioners and cooks at the Medici Palace worked far into the night on the preparation of fanciful dishes to impress the Roman guests, while long tables were set out in the hall, on the balcony above the loggia, in the garden and in the courtyard. Following Florentine custom the guests were to be separated at these tables in accordance with their sex and age, young women at one, young men at another, the older women at the table presided over by the bridegroom's mother, the older men at his father's table in the courtyard where large copper coolers stood full of Tuscan wine. Between the banquets there were to be musical entertainments and dances, theatricals performed on a specially erected stage hung with tapestries and enclosed by curtains embroidered with the Medici and Orsini arms. There were to be speeches and songs and allegorical masques.

The bride, followed by a long procession of maids of honour and attendants, arrived on a white charger which had been given to the bridegroom by the King of Naples. She was wearing a dress of white and gold brocade; and, as she entered through the gateway, a wreath of olive leaves – traditionally hung over Florentine doorways and in windows when a wedding was to take place – was placed upon her auburn hair.

She behaved with due modesty, an onlooker conceded, overcoming her inborn Roman hauteur; but it was clear that she was nervous and ill at ease. And, as the days passed, it also became clear that she would find it difficult to accustom herself to Florentine ways. She remained a Roman at heart, haughty and petulant when she was unsure of herself, excessively proud of her ancient lineage. Yet her husband grew fond of her and she of him, though at the time of his marriage he had written dismissively, 'I have taken a wife, or rather she was given to me.' She bore him ten children, and seems to have accepted with equanimity both Lorenzo's romantic attachment to Lucrezia Donati and his infidelities with other young ladies, only to be expected in a man who was, in Francesco Guicciardini's words, 'very licentious and very amorous'.

Lucrezia Donati had been 'Queen of the Tournament' in that spectacular display in Piazza Santa Croce four months before Clarice Orsini's arrival in Florence, when Lorenzo – in armour presented to him by the Duke of

A procession in the Piazza San Giovanni. The Duomo on the left lacks the façade which, designed by Emilio De Fabris, was to be built between 1871 and 1887.

Milan, riding a horse given by the Marquis of Mantua, and wearing jewel-encrusted outer garments replete with symbolic devices – had been awarded the first prize, 'a helmet inlaid with silver and a figure of Mars on the crest', although, as Lorenzo himself confessed in his diary, the award was by way of compliment to him as the host rather than in recognition of any unsurpassed prowess, since he had not been 'a vigorous warrior, nor a hard hitter'.

Lucrezia Donati was also 'Queen of the Tournament' a few years later when another and even more expensive *giostra* was held in the Piazza Santa Croce in honour of Lorenzo's brother, Giuliano, who appeared before the excited crowds in a series of costumes made specially for the occasion, carrying a standard designed by Botticelli and, in a *coup de spectacle*, wearing a helmet created by Verrocchio in expectation of his victory. Lorenzo's earlier victory was celebrated in a charming poem, Luigi Pulci's '*La Giostra di Lorenzo de' Medici*'; Giuliano's by the '*Stanze della Giostra di Giuliano de' Medici*', the first masterpiece by Angelo Ambrogini, known from his birthplace as Poliziano, the finest Italian poet since Boccaccio.

The months after Clarice's wedding were afterwards renowned in Florence, already famous all over Europe for its marvellous spectacles, for *giostre* like these, for carnivals and festivals, for parades and revels, and firework displays, for fancy-dress parties in the Mercato Vecchio, for mock battles in

the Piazza Santa Croce, for naumachia on the Arno and *fêtes champêtres* on its banks, for circuses in the Piazza della Signoria – where, once, a mare was set loose among rampant stallions, 'a most splendid entertainment for girls to behold' though it 'much displeased decent and well-behaved people' – and for parties on the bridges where couples and lines of dancers leaped and jumped about in the energetic Florentine manner.

On St John the Baptist's Day, the day of the city's patron saint, the workshops were closed and the shops decorated with banners and wreaths of foliage. In the Piazza della Signoria gilded castles, symbolizing the towns subject to Florence, were carried on wagons past the *ringhiera* of the Palazzo. Processions of priests and choristers, of citizens dressed as saints and of their wives as nuns, passed down the streets carrying candles, as many as twenty thousand of which were sold for this day's celebration alone. The processions on foot were followed by decorated chariots bearing the Duomo's most sacred relics, among them a nail of the Holy Cross, a thorn of the Holy Crown and the thumb of the Baptist. The Piazza del Duomo was covered with blue canopies emblazoned with silver stars; beneath it votive offerings of painted wax were taken to the Baptistery; and from the Porta al Prato down Via della Vigna Nuova, through the Mercato Vecchio and the Corso to Porta alla Croce, riderless horses, with spiked balls hanging at their sides, were sent racing helter-skelter through the city. In the afternoon there was another horse-race, like the one still held at Siena; the winner was presented with a *palio*, an expensive silk banner attached to a pole.

On May Day it was the custom for young men to hang branches of flowering shrubs, *maii*, decorated with ribbons and sugared nuts, on the doors of their sweethearts' houses, and for young girls to wear their best frocks to go dancing the *rigoletto* to the music of lutes in the Piazza Santa Trinita.

At night the streets were crowded with young men strolling up and down in clothes which would have horrified Dante, in 'beautiful rose colour,' so Marco Parenti said, 'in violet or black, and every colour of silk and rich linings', in pink capes and satin jackets, white stockings with silver lace, velvet caps with feathers in the brim. Carrying flaming torches, singing, shouting, blowing trumpets, they called up to the windows of their inamoratas' houses. One winter's night when the snow lay thick underfoot, a crowd of them gathered outside the palace of Marietta Strozzi, the pretty, wayward granddaughter of the great Palla Strozzi, and began to hurl snowballs at her window. 'And what a triumph it was when one of the besiegers succeeded in flinging snow upon the maiden's face,' a friend of Lorenzo de' Medici reported. 'Moreover Marietta herself, so graceful and so skilled in the game, and beautiful, as everyone knows, acquitted herself with great honour.'

The Return from the Palio by Giovanni Maria Butteri (c. 1540 – 1606). The winning horse, 'Il Seicento', is paraded through the streets of the city.

★

Piero de' Medici was too ill now to take part in any of Florence's pageants. He spent most of his days indoors either at his villa at Careggi or in the large, cool rooms of the Palazzo Medici, supervising, in his meticulous way, the affairs of the bank, arranging commissions for his protégés, going over progress reports for the works he had commissioned himself, the tabernacles at San Miniato al Monte and Santissima Annunziata,[14] and the rebuilding of the Badia Fiesolana, examining the coins he had collected and studying the books he had bought for the family library 'as if they were a pile of gold'. 'One day he may simply let his eye pass along these volumes to while away the time and give recreation to the eye,' Antonio di Pietro Averlino Filarete, the Florentine architect and sculptor was told.

> The next day, then, so I am informed, he will take out some of the effigies and images of all the emperors and worthies of the past, some made of gold, some of silver, some of bronze, of precious stones or of marble and other materials which are wonderful to behold... The next day he would look at his jewels and precious stones of which he had a marvellous quantity of great value, some engraved, others not. He takes great pleasure and delight in looking at these and in discussing their various excellencies. The next day, perhaps, he will inspect his vases of gold and silver and other precious material, and praise their noble worth and the skill of the masters who wrought them. All in all, when it is a matter of acquiring worthy or strange objects he does not look at the price.[15]

Piero died at Careggi on 2 December 1469. He was buried next to his brother, Giovanni, in the Old Sacristy at San Lorenzo. His sons called upon Andrea del Verrocchio, who had designed their grandfather's memorial, to create the tomb of porphyry, marble and bronze which honours their father's remains.

The day after Piero's death some seven hundred members and supporters of the Medicean party gathered at the convent of Sant'Antonino. It was decided at this meeting that his son, Lorenzo, although not yet twenty-one years old, should be asked to assume the leadership of the party and of the government of Florence. A delegation accordingly called at the Palazzo Medici and asked Lorenzo to take upon himself the task of 'looking after the city and the government as [his] father and grandfather had done'.

Lorenzo had already written to the Duke of Milan, 'You have been the bulwark of our government and our greatness. May you now assure my protection and preservation.' He was, however, anxious not to appear unduly eager to assume the responsibilities which his acceptance of the leadership of the party would entail; and, indeed, he seems to have been genuinely reluctant to undertake duties which would hinder his enjoyment of a less demanding life. 'Their proposal was naturally against my youthful instincts,' he wrote, 'and, considering that the burden and danger were great, I consented to it unwillingly. But I did so in order to protect our friends and property, since it fares ill in Florence with anyone who is rich but does not have any share in government.'

With his sensible mother to guide him, as well as the heads of such influential families as the Soderini and the Pitti, now anxious to make amends for their part in the attempted coup against Piero, Lorenzo proceeded cautiously in his moves to establish himself as what Francesco Guicciardini was to describe as 'a benevolent tyrant in a constitutional republic'.

Although officially debarred by his youth from membership, he had himself elected to such councils of state as his new authority required; and important matters of both foreign and domestic policy were brought for discussion and decision to the Palazzo Medici. Yet both he and the Signoria were anxious that Florence should be seen not only by its citizens but also by the world at large as a democratic republic. When Francesco della Rovere became Pope Sixtus IV in 1471 and a delegation was sent to Rome to offer the city's congratulations, Lorenzo de' Medici accompanied the delegation but was accorded no higher rank in it than any of its other members.

He had, however, no sooner assumed his responsibilities as head of his house than he demonstrated a firmness and decisiveness that was to mark his future rule, although in this case his resolution was to lead to disaster. On his return from Rome there was trouble in Volterra, where the authority of the Florentine *Capitano* had been threatened in a violent dispute over the working of an alum mine. Alum was essential to the Florentine textile industry, being used in the dyeing of wool and silk; and when the dispute threatened to get out of hand, with unforeseeable consequences in other Tuscan towns, Lorenzo, contrary to the advice of both a majority in the Signoria and the Bishop of Volterra, decided to use force. An army of 5,000 mercenaries was raised and the *condottiere*, Federigo da Montefeltro, was employed as its commander.

As Federigo marched towards the turbulent town, the Volterrans issued pleas for help to governments all over Italy, going so far as to offer the town to the King of Naples in exchange for his support. No effective help was forthcoming, however, and after a month's siege Volterra surrendered. Lorenzo wrote to the Florentine observers attached to the mercenary army to express his satisfaction that the city had been regained without suffering damage.

But, as it happened, the city had already been ransacked unmercifully. No one knew how it had happened. Some said the mercenaries employed by Florence had entered the town after the peace negotiations had been concluded, perhaps let in by Volterra's mercenaries to share in the plunder. In any case the subsequent pillage had been appalling. After several hours of murder, rape and looting, and a landslip caused by torrential rain, much of the town lay in ruins. Lorenzo rode over from Florence to convey the city's profound regret for what had happened, and to distribute compensation to the surviving victims. But he was never to be forgiven in Volterra; and in Florence, his impetuous decision to use force, when patient negotiations might well have concluded in a peaceful settlement, brought his judgement and his capacity to undertake the responsibilities which had so recently been bestowed upon him sharply into question. He knew that he must not make such an error again; he handled the next crisis, which was soon to threaten, much more skilfully.

THE PAZZI CONSPIRACY
1478

'My Lords, beware of what you do.
Florence is a big affair.'
GIAN BATTISTA DA MONTESECCO

Soon after the sack of Volterra, the Medici bank in Rome received an embarrassing request: would the bank advance 40,000 ducats for the purchase of Imola, the strategically placed small town on the Santerno river in the Romagna. The request came from the Pope, Sixtus IV, the son of a poor fisherman from Liguria, a big, blunt, toothless man whose two principal aims in life were the aggrandizement of the Papal States and the advancement of the fortunes of his family. Six of his nephews were, or were to become, cardinals, one of them also Archbishop of Florence and one Pope Julius II; another nephew, appointed Prefect of Rome and Lord of Mondovi in Piedmont, was married off to the eldest daughter of Federigo da Montefeltro, now Duke of Urbino, thus transferring one of Italy's most talented *condottieri* from the service of Florence to that of the Pope; and it was for yet another nephew, who was perhaps really a son, a rough and rowdy young man, Girolamo Riario, that the Pope wanted to buy the town of Imola and thus establish a base from which his family could extend their power in the Romagna.

The request for the loan troubled Lorenzo deeply. He was anxious not to offend the Pope, with whom his relations up to now had been perfectly friendly; but Imola was a strategically placed town dominating the road from Rimini to Bologna, and Lorenzo had had thoughts of arranging its purchase for Florence, well aware that a Romagna in control of an unfriendly power would threaten Florence's trade routes to the Adriatic coast. So when the application for the loan was referred to him he told his manager in Rome to prevaricate. Impatient of delay, the Pope turned to another Florentine banking house, that of the Pazzi, a family for long commercial rivals of the Medici, the manager of whose branch in Rome, Francesco de' Pazzi, a small, fidgety young man of 'great arrogance and pretensions', saw an opportunity not only of obtaining the coveted curial account but perhaps even, with the Pope's help, of displacing the Medici as the leading house in Florence. The required loan was authorized by the Pazzi bank without hesitation.

The Pazzi were an ancient family, owning much property in what is now the Borgo degli Albizzi. One of their forebears, Pazzo di Ranieri, had been among the first to enter Jerusalem on the First Crusade in 1088 and had returned to Florence with some flints from the altar of the Holy Sepulchre, which were placed in the church of Santi Apostoli[1] and subsequently used in an annual ceremony, the *Scoppio del Carro*, performed in the cathedral at midnight mass on Easter Saturday.[2] For long disdaining commerce, the family had eventually become extremely successful bankers and by the time of the *sommario* (the list of taxpayers) of 1457 they had become the richest family in Florence after the Medici, well able to afford to build the lovely chapel at Santa Croce which they had commissioned from Brunelleschi, as well as their palace in Via del Proconsolo.

This palace, which discreetly but clearly declared itself a Pazzi building, has the same strongly rusticated ground floor as the Palazzo Medici; but above this floor the wall is stuccoed, an unusual feature in Florence at this time except where the stucco was decorated with *sgraffito*. The Palazzo Pazzi also differed from the Medici in the form of its windows, which in the Palazzo Pazzi are highly decorative, with vines and pruned branches elaborately carved in stone, with wreaths and the Pazzi emblem of sails billowing fully in a strong wind. There are further Pazzi emblems in the courtyard, sails in the spandrels and dolphins on the capitals of the columns, the columns also being carved with vegetation and with urns pouring forth flames, an allusion to the *Scoppio del Carro*. And in the design of the building itself, so Professor Andres has suggested, there may be an overt reference to the family's anti-Medicean politics:

The series of *oculi* [round windows] beneath the eaves of the main façade is an unusual motif in Florentine domestic architecture. Nevertheless, the *oculus* and the framed roundel were favourite devices of Brunelleschi, ones he used above arched windows in the Pazzi Chapel and in the great hall that he began, probably in the early 1420s, for the Palazzo di Parte Guelfa. This palace, a monumental symbol of the city's mercantile oligarchy and traditional alliance with the papacy, had been left unfinished, deprived of funding and attention as a result of Medicean politics. It is interesting to see the motif of its distinctive façade echoed in two separate projects of the Pazzi family. In the Pazzi Chapel one would be inclined to explain the reappearance of the *oculus* and framed roundels merely as a favourite motif of Brunelleschi. On the much later palace, however, so public an invocation of Guelph-associated imagery seems charged with political significance, especially given the fact that the upper façade was not by Brunelleschi, and may well have been constructed after the Pazzi had aligned themselves with Sixtus IV in opposition to Lorenzo.

Roundels in the Pazzi Chapel, probably designed by Brunelleschi and glazed by Luca della Robbia, depicting the evangelists, Matthew, Mark, Luke and John.

The head of the family when the Pazzi Palace was nearing completion was Jacopo de' Pazzi, a mean and ill-tempered old man who was 'colder than ice' when his young relative Francesco, the manager of the Rome branch of the bank, came to Florence to tell him what he was planning to do. Francesco told him that, having approved the loan to the papacy for the purchase of Imola, he was preparing an anti-Medicean conspiracy in which he had already enlisted not only the Pope's nephew, Girolamo Riario, the new Lord of Imola, but also Francesco Salviati, the Pope's nominee as Archbishop of Pisa, whom Lorenzo de' Medici – not having been consulted in the appointment as custom required – declined to admit into Tuscany. Jacopo de' Pazzi listened to Francesco with evident disapproval. Even when he was told that the conspirators had the support of a trustworthy *condottiere*, Gian Battista da Montesecco – who could be relied upon to enlist good troops to back the proposed *coup d'état* – he held back. 'They are going to break their necks,' he told the *condottiere*. 'I understand what is going on here better than you do. I don't want to listen to you. I don't want to hear any more about it.'

The *condottiere* himself had been reluctant to involve himself in the affair at first, even though the conspirators had assured him that Medici rule was detested by the Florentines and that they would rise up in arms against their present rulers at the slightest encouragement. 'My Lords,' he had said dubiously, according to his own account, 'beware of what you do. Florence is a big affair.' But after an audience with the Pope, who, while refusing specifically to authorize a violent attack upon the Medici, gave the impression that he would condone murder if murder were done, Gian Battista da Montesecco agreed to help the conspirators, provided he were not required to strike a blow himself against Lorenzo, whom he liked. When informed of the Pope's attitude, Jacopo de' Pazzi also changed his mind and, from being an opponent of the coup, soon became an enthusiastic conspirator himself.

It was planned that the attack on the Medici should take place in the cathedral during High Mass on Sunday 26 April 1478. Upon the ringing of the sanctuary bell at the elevation of the Host, when the eyes of the congregation would be cast down reverently, two embittered priests, one a Volterran, the other tutor to Jacopo de' Pazzi's illegitimate daughter, were to snatch daggers from their robes and stab Lorenzo de' Medici to death, while two further assassins, Bernardo Bandini Baroncelli, an adventurer deep in debt to the Pazzi, and Francesco de' Pazzi, the banker from Rome, would at the same time dispose of Lorenzo's brother, Giuliano.

These last two murderers were all too successful. At the agreed signal, Bernardo Bandini Baroncelli, crying, 'Take that, traitor!' brought his dagger down in so ferocious a blow that Giuliano's skull was almost split in two. At the same time Francesco de' Pazzi stabbed their victim so ferociously and wildly that he drove the blade of his dagger through his own thigh and went on stabbing relentlessly until Giuliano's corpse was rent with nineteen wounds.

Lorenzo, however, contrived to escape with a cut in the neck from his two less competent attackers, who were driven off as their intended victim leapt away from them. Drawing his sword, Lorenzo then vaulted over the altar rail and made a dash for the north sacristy, the heavy bronze doors of which were slammed shut behind him by several of his quick-witted friends, one of whom sucked the wound in his neck in case the priests' daggers had been poisoned. 'Giuliano? Is he safe? Where is Giuliano?' Lorenzo kept repeating; but no one answered him.

Someone clambered up the ladder into Luca della Robbia's choir loft to look down into the cathedral, where Giuliano's blood-splashed, mutilated body lay sprawled by the door that leads into Via de' Servi. All around it the congregation was in uproar, as shouts rang round the walls that Brunelleschi's dome had collapsed. The priests who had attacked Lorenzo, as well as Giuliano's assassins, appeared to have escaped in the confusion. Lorenzo was hurried away by his friends to the Medici Palace.

The city too was in uproar. Members of the Pazzi family and their supporters were riding through the streets, shouting, '*Libertà! Libertà! Abasso i Medici! Abasso le palle! Libertà! Libertà!*' Other, larger groups of Medici supporters were riding and running about, crying, '*Vivano le palle! Vivano le palle! Palle! Palle! Palle!*'

As previously planned, Archbishop Salviati and the other conspirators, with a large party of armed supporters, mostly Perugian mercenaries, had already marched to the Palazzo della Signoria to seize it in the name of the insurgents, intending to kill any *priori* who might attempt to resist them. But the Gonfaloniere was too quick for them. Having admitted both conspirators and mercenaries, he contrived to have the Perugians led into rooms behind doors with special catches which could not be operated from the inside; then, grabbing an iron cooking-spit as the nearest weapon to hand, and calling upon the *priori* to follow him, he lashed out at the Archbishop and his companions, who were soon beaten to the ground.

As the great bell boomed above their heads, a large party of Medici supporters burst through the palace gates. Joined by the palace guard, they fell upon the Perugians, massacred them all and bore their heads out into the piazza transfixed on pikes and swords.

The punishments inflicted upon the leading conspirators were exceptionally savage. Francesco de' Pazzi, found in his family's palace still bleeding from the wound in his thigh, was stripped naked and, with a rope tied round his neck, was hurled from one of the windows of the Palazzo della Signoria. Archbishop Salviati was also thrown out. So were three other victims. All five bodies were left dangling beneath the machicolations of the northern wall, where, in a kind of grisly *danse macabre*, the Archbishop, struggling at the end of his rope, fixed his teeth into Francesco de' Pazzi's bare flesh.

The elderly Jacopo de' Pazzi, having succeeded in escaping from Florence to a nearby village, was recognized, brought back to the city, tortured, stripped and also strung from a window of the palace. His body was later dug from its grave and dragged through the streets by the mob before being propped up against his palace door, where, to shouts of 'Open! Your master wishes to enter!', his decomposing head was used as a knocker. At last the corpse was thrown into the Arno, from whose murky waters it was dragged by a gang of children; before tossing it back again and watching it drift down the river, they tied it to the branches of a willow tree and flogged it with sticks.

The *condottiere*, Gian Battista da Montesecco, was beheaded in the courtyard of the Bargello; so, too, was Bernardo Bandini Baroncelli, Giuliano's assassin, who, having escaped to Constantinople, was apprehended there and brought back to Florence in chains. The two priests who had tried to kill Lorenzo were castrated before being hanged. Jacopo de' Pazzi's brother, Renato, whose guilt was never established, was also hanged. Several other members of his family were thrown into prison in Volterra. The rest were utterly disgraced: orders were given for their properties to be confiscated; for their palaces to be given other names, their coats of arms and their family symbols to be obliterated, and their papers to be destroyed. No Pazzi was ever to be allowed to hold office in Florence again; nor was any man who married a woman of the Pazzi family. Representations of the Pazzi traitors, and of those of the other conspirators, were painted by Botticelli on the walls of the Bargello, and beneath each portrait was inscribed a suitable verse composed by Lorenzo.

At the height of the uproar which followed the attempted coup – while gangs roamed through the streets searching for victims, for alleged conspirators and for unpopular citizens who could be accused of complicity – Lorenzo had come out to stand before a window of the Medici Palace, his brocade waistcoat covered with blood, his neck bandaged, as he was to appear in three life-size wax figures subsequently made of him under the direction of Verrocchio. He told the people not to wreak further vengeance, to save their energies for the enemies of the state who had engineered the conspiracy and would now undoubtedly seek to attack the Florentines not only for having thwarted it but also for having taken it upon themselves to punish its perpetrators so mercilessly. His fears were only too well justified.

LORENZO
THE MAGNIFICENT
1478–92

*'Michelangelo always ate at Lorenzo's table
with the sons of the family … and
Lorenzo always treated him with great respect.'*
GIORGIO VASARI

The Pope's anger was, indeed, fearful, so one of his secretaries said. The Vatican rang with his curses. Lorenzo de' Medici, that 'son of iniquity and foster-child of perdition', and all the citizens of Florence who supported him, were 'anathematized, infamous, sacrilegious, culpable'. Their houses were to be levelled to the ground, their 'habitations made desolate so that none may dwell therein'; all their property was to revert to the Church. A furious Bull of Excommunication declared that 'everlasting ruin' would witness their 'everlasting disgrace'. War was declared upon them; Siena and Lucca were induced to declare war too; Federigo da Montefeltro was employed as commander of the papal forces, and the King of Naples encouraged to send his son Alfonso, Duke of Calabria, marching towards the Tuscan frontier with a large army and a further instalment of papal curses.

The Florentines were defiant. 'Remember your high office as Vicar of Christ,' the Signoria admonished the Pope in replying to his fulminations.

Remember that the Keys of St Peter's were not given you to abuse in this way … You say that Lorenzo is a tyrant and command us to expel him. But most Florentines call him their defender … Florence will resolutely defend her liberties, trusting in Christ, who knows the justice of her cause … trusting in her allies, who regard her cause as their own, trusting especially in the most Christian King, Louis of France, who has always been the patron and protector of the Florentine state.

To Philippe de Commines, Louis XI's envoy in Italy, the Florentines' defiance seemed admirable but foolhardy. The French might lend their moral support but there was no French army to defend Florentine liberties, while Florence's other traditional allies, the Milanese, were too preoccupied with their own troubles since the murder of their Duke, Galeazzo Maria Sforza, to concern themselves with the problems of the Medici. Lorenzo's friend, Giovanni Bentivoglio, offered what help he could from Bologna; the Medici's Orsini relatives raised what troops they could on their estates and offered the services of mercenaries; and the experienced Ercole d'Este, Duke of Ferrara, was employed as Florentine commander. But even when his troops had been augmented by a small contingent sent reluctantly from Milan under Gian Giacomo Trivulzio, the Duke of Ferrara did not apparently reckon his chances of success to be very high.

Certainly, cautious as usual, he did all he could, in those marches and countermarches, those plundering forays and circuitous retreats so dear to Renaissance military commanders, to avoid a confrontation with the Duke of Calabria, who was his brother-in-law. Florence's war committee, the Ten of War, reproached him for his reluctance to fight; but he loftily brushed aside objections like these from 'mere mechanics who [knew] nothing of war'.

Soon afterwards he gave up his command and rode away, leaving his men to fend for themselves as best they could. They were poorly placed to do so. The wily, cynical Lodovico Sforza – known as Il Moro because one of his Christian names was Mauro and he had a very dark skin – having established himself in power in Milan, had come to the conclusion that Florence was a lost cause. Not only were her forces in disarray, still threatened by the Duke of Calabria, who, having taken the town of Colle, less than thirty miles south of Florence, was resting his forces in Siena; not only were gangs of brigands plundering the Tuscan countryside, but plague had broken out in Florence, where the citizens, already suffering from the effects of an economy in decline, were becoming restlessly discontented under the weight of the heavy taxes occasioned by the war.

Lorenzo, encouraged by the Tuscan bishops, who had responded to the papal Bull of Excommunication by excommunicating the Pope – and heartened also by the unanimous support of the Ten of War – had established himself as undisputed master of Florence's destiny; and by the end of 1479 he had made up his mind that he could save the city only by going to Naples and personally negotiating peace. 'I have decided, with your approval, to sail for Naples immediately,' he wrote to the Signoria after he had already left Florence for Pisa.

> I believe that I am the person against whom the activities of our enemies are mainly directed. I hope, by delivering myself into their hands, I may be the means of restoring peace to our fellow citizens... Perhaps God wills that this war, which began in the blood of my brother and of myself, should be ended by my means... As I have had more honour and responsibility among you than any private citizen has had in our day, I am more bound than any other person

to serve our country, even at the risk of my life ... I go, praying to God to give me grace to perform what every citizen should at all times be ready to perform for his country. I commend myself humbly to your Excellencies of the Signoria. Laurentius de Medici.

According to Filippo Valori, all the *priori* without exception were in tears by the time the end of his letter had been read out to them. It was known that the King of Naples was an unpredictable man, devious and vindictive; it was even rumoured that he kept the bodies of his defeated enemies embalmed in a private gallery where he could relish their downfall. But what was not so well known was that King Ferrante's second son, Federigo, and Federigo's sister-in-law, the Duchess of Calabria, were both friends of Lorenzo. Nor was it widely known that one of the King's principal advisers, Diomede Carafa, was deeply in debt to the Medici bank, nor that King Ferrante himself, despite his reputation, was a cultivated man, with whom Lorenzo might be expected to have much in common, with whom, indeed, Lorenzo had been in secret correspondence for some time. The ship in which Lorenzo was to sail had actually been sent from Naples to fetch him.

As it happened, the negotiations in Naples were far longer and more difficult than Lorenzo might have hoped. For weeks on end King Ferrante remained by turns intractable and evasive. It seemed that the immense amount of money which Lorenzo had brought with him, and which he lavished in Naples with apparently carefree generosity, was to be spent in vain. But in the end the King's concern about the Turks, whose ships were sailing ever more closely up the Apulian coast, and about the King of France, whose claims to the throne of Naples were being frequently repeated, weighed upon him to reduce the number of his enemies. The terms of a settlement were agreed; and although these terms − not altogether favourable to Florence − came in for some criticism there, Lorenzo returned to the city in triumph.

His opportunity had now come to strengthen the hold of the Medicean party over its affairs. He and his advisers did so without appearing to do so. Using the financial difficulties and economic problems of the time as an excuse, they arranged for the summoning of a Balìa, which authorized the creation of a Council of Seventy with powers superseding those of the Signoria. This new council, whose members were to hold office for five years, became, in effect, Florence's governing body. It was authorized to assume the right to elect the *priori*, which had formerly been exercised by the *accoppiatori*, and to appoint from its own members two new government departments, the *Dodici Procuratori*, who were to direct home and economic affairs, and the *Otto di Pratica*, the formulators of foreign policy.

Although it was understood that Lorenzo de' Medici was head of state, no such title was bestowed upon him; nor could he always get his own way with the Council of Seventy, nor overrule the directions of its members.

He was not *Signore* of Florence, he used to say – as his grandfather had done when asked to initiate some unwelcome policy or do something he did not want to do – he was merely a citizen of Florence. Yet his influence was, in fact, extensive and usually decisive, and, in foreign affairs at least, largely unquestioned. He came to be accepted in Florence as the arbiter of the state's foreign policy and in the peninsula generally as 'the needle of the Italian compass'; and, if it is now accepted that his reputation as a master of diplomacy is not entirely deserved, that he was often rash and short-sighted, taking great risks for trivial gains, he did undoubtedly serve Florence well and displayed in his correspondence with the republic's ambassadors a remarkable understanding of international affairs.

On his return from Naples he was faced by many problems: the Pope's nephew, Girolamo Riario, had bought the town of Forlì, thus adding to his possessions in the Romagna close to the Tuscan border; the Pope himself, angered by Florence's treaty with Naples, had become more furious with Lorenzo than ever, while the Duke of Calabria had taken advantage of an uprising there to become Lord of Siena. But then help had come from an unexpected quarter: a Turkish army landed at Otranto and threatened to march across the peninsula to Naples, then north to Rome. Alarmed by this threat, which brought the Duke of Calabria rushing home from Siena, the Pope made it clear that he was prepared to forgive Florence for the sake of Christendom. Amity was thus restored; and for the rest of Lorenzo's life, after the withdrawal of Turkish troops from Italy upon the death of the sultan, Mahomet the Conqueror, there was peace in Italy. It was broken but twice, and on both occasions was soon restored by Lorenzo's intervention.

On 12 August 1484 Pope Sixtus died in Rome after an all-too-familiar outburst of rage and was succeeded by the Genoese Giovanni Battista Cibò, who chose to be known as Innocent VIII. An amiable, agreeable man, he allowed himself to be guided by Lorenzo to such an extent that a disgruntled Ferrarese ambassador complained that 'the Pope sleeps with the eyes of the Magnificent Lorenzo'. Lorenzo cultivated him assiduously, constantly sending him presents, writing him long letters full of flattery and discreet advice, arranging the marriage of his daughter, Maddalena, to one of the Pope's several sons and, incidentally, finding it difficult to raise the money for the girl's dowry, there being, as he confessed, so many other 'holes to fill up'.

Lorenzo was constantly in financial straits, and he did not hesitate to take money that did not belong to him, both from family trusts and from the public treasury, in order to make up for the rapidly falling profits from the Medici bank. In his grandfather's day, when the bank had been the most profitable organization in Europe, there had been Medici representatives in almost every capital and important commercial centre in Europe. As well

VIRTVTVM
OMNIVM
VAS

VITIAVIRT
VTI SVBIA
CENT

as looking after the affairs of the bank, importing and exporting all manner of spices, fabrics, dyes, furs, fruit and jewellery, supplying their customers with everything from sacred relics and wild animals to slaves and choirboys, the branch managers were also political agents of the Florentine republic; and Cosimo had supervised their activities with the greatest care, reading the long and detailed reports they were required to submit regularly to Florence, sometimes working all through the night.

Lorenzo had no such interest in business. Lacking his grandfather's flair and application, and his father's attention to detail, he allowed the branch managers to conduct their affairs without the close supervision to which they had been subjected in the past. He also relied far too heavily upon the advice of the bank's ingratiating and none-too-competent general manager, Francesco Sassetti, whose family chapel is in the church of Santa Trinita, where Francesco and his four sons, together with Lorenzo and his sons, can all be seen depicted in Ghirlandaio's mural behind the altar.[1]

When warned about Francesco Sassetti's questionable policies Lorenzo would impatiently brush the advice aside, confessing that he 'did not understand such matters'. One after the other the bank's branches got into difficulties through mismanagement or excessive loans, and one after the other they closed. The London branch put up its shutters when King Edward IV failed to repay the money advanced to him during the Wars of the Roses; the Bruges bank also collapsed, having lent large sums of money to Charles the Bold of Burgundy, who was killed in battle at Lyons after the death of Louis XI; so did the Milanese branch where the premises – given to Cosimo de' Medici by Francesco Sforza – were sold to Lodovico il Moro. Within the next few years the whole structure, which Philippe de Commines had described as the greatest commercial house there had ever been anywhere, fell to pieces in the general disintegration of Florentine banking. Yet Lorenzo, as a Ferrarese ambassador commented, had to deal with foreign princes, to entertain them and give them presents as though he were a prince himself, as though the title bestowed upon him, Il Magnifico, though no more than a title of respect in fifteenth-century Florence, betokened the riches and splendour it seemed to imply.

Far more at home with scholars, writers and artists than with men of business, Lorenzo was most happy when, free for the moment from cares of state and wearing the plain, dark clothes he far preferred to robes of splendour, he could entertain his wide circle of clever and amusing friends at the Palazzo Medici or at one or other of his villas outside the city, at Fiesole or Poggio a Caiano, at Cafaggiolo or at Careggi, where every year on 7 November he gave a banquet in honour of Plato's birth.

He had been brought up in the company of humanists. Educated at first by tutors supervised by Gentile Becchi, the Latinist, by Cristoforo Landino,

Lorenzo il Magnifico, a portrait by Giorgio Vasari.

translator of Aristotle and commentator on Dante, and by his grandfather's protégé and friend, Marsilio Ficino, Lorenzo had never tired of the company of such men. He talked with them, read aloud with them, listened to music with them, discussed classical texts and philosophical mysteries with them, supported them in times of need, protected them from ecclesiastical censure. He was, indeed, as one of them said, 'the laurel who sheltered the birds that sang in the Tuscan spring'.

Often to be seen in his company, besides his close friends, the poets Angelo Poliziano and Luigi Pulci, were the bookseller Vespasiano da Bisticci, and the musician Antonio Squarcialupi, the cathedral organist; Giovanni Pico, Count of Mirandola and Concordia, the aristocratic author of *De hominis dignitate oratio*, whose works were so strongly condemned by the Church; Paolo Toscanelli, author of works on mathematics, medicine, astronomy, philosophy and cosmography; and even the now aged Francesco Filelfo, who had fled from Florence after the failure of the Albizzi *coup d'état* against the Medici and who, despite the slanderous abuse he had

Detail from a fresco in Santa Maria Novella by Domenico Ghirlandaio showing a group of humanists, Marsilio Ficino, Cristoforo Landino, Angelo Poliziano and Gentile Becchi.

heaped upon the Medici from Siena, had been allowed in 1481 to return to Florence.

Also to be seen in Lorenzo's company in these contented days were numerous painters and sculptors then working in Florence, amongst them Botticelli and Filippino Lippi, Domenico Ghirlandaio and Antonio Pollaiuolo, whom Lorenzo considered 'the greatest master in the city'. Lorenzo did not himself commission much work from these men, since he had so little money to spare and preferred to spend what he could afford on antique gems and vases, on medals, coins and ancient pottery, believing, no doubt, that these were a safer investment than a big picture, that the thousand florins and more at which many of his gems were valued were more wisely expended than the hundred florins or so paid for a Botticelli or a Ghirlandaio. He was a connoisseur of gem carving, and employed in his household the sculptor, Bertoldo di Giovanni, to produce small bronzes and medals for the Medici collections; and it was probably Lorenzo himself who commissioned from Bertoldo the two fine reliefs, the *Crucifixion* and the *Battle Scene*, now both in the Bargello.

While in no position to be a generous patron in the manner of his grandfather, Lorenzo did take great pains to ensure that Tuscan artists were given commissions in other states, both for their own sakes and for the greater glory and benefit of Florence. Botticelli, Ghirlandaio and Filippino Lippi were all found work in Rome, Antonio Pollaiuolo in Milan, Giuliano da Maiano and Andrea del Verrocchio in Naples; and when Leonardo, an illegitimate boy from the Tuscan village of Vinci, who had come as an apprentice to Verrocchio's workshop in Florence, evinced a desire to spread the wings of his astonishing talent, Lorenzo recommended him to Lodovico il Moro, a generous patron in Milan.

While it is possible that Leonardo lived in the Medici Palace for a time, it is almost certain that another young artist, some twenty years younger, did so. This was Michelangelo Buonarroti, son of an impoverished Tuscan magistrate of aristocratic stock.

Michelangelo's friend, Giorgio Vasari, suggested that the place and time of Michelangelo's birth were no mere accidents, since

> the benign ruler of heaven graciously looked down to earth [and] ... chose to have Michelangelo born a Florentine, so that one of her own citizens might bring to absolute perfection the achievements for which Florence was already justly renowned. So in the year 1474 [1475] in the Casentino, under a fateful and lucky star, the virtuous and noble wife of Lodovico di Leonardo Buonarotti gave birth to a baby son ...
>
> Now when he had served his term of office [as Mayor of Caprese] Lodovico returned to Florence and settled in the village of Settignano, three miles from

the city, where he had a family farm. That part of the country is very rich in stone, especially in quarries of grey stone which are continuously worked by stonecutters and sculptors, mostly local people; and Michelangelo was put out to nurse with the wife of one of the stonecutters... When Michelangelo was old enough he was sent to the grammar school... but he was so obsessed by drawing that he used to spend on it all the time he possibly could. As a result he used to be scolded and sometimes beaten by his father and the older members of the family, who probably considered it unworthy of their ancient house for Michelangelo to give his time to an art that meant nothing to them.

His disinclination to other study, however, and his obvious talent for drawing, persuaded his father to allow Michelangelo to become an apprentice in Domenico Ghirlandaio's workshop and afterwards, perhaps, a pupil of the marble carver, Benedetto da Maiano. In any event, in about 1490, Michelangelo caught the attention of Lorenzo, who arranged with the boy's father to have him given a room of his own at the Palazzo Medici and for him to be found a place in a school which had been founded for such promising boys in a garden near San Marco.[2] 'Michelangelo always ate at Lorenzo's table with the sons of the family and other distinguished and noble persons,' Vasari recorded,

> and Lorenzo always treated him with great respect. During that period, as salary and so that he could help his father, Michelangelo was paid five ducats a month; and to make him happy Lorenzo gave him a violet cloak and appointed his father to a post in the customs. As a matter of fact, all the young men in the garden at San Marco were paid salaries... This place was full of antiques and richly furnished with excellent pictures collected for their beauty, and for study and pleasure. Michelangelo always kept the keys to this garden, as he was more earnest than the others... For example, he spent many months in the church of the Carmine making drawings from the pictures by Masaccio; he copied these with such judgement that the craftsmen and all the others who saw his work were astonished, and he then started to experience envy as well as fame.

It was at this time that Michelangelo, a difficult man, critical, impatient and sardonic, had his celebrated quarrel with the Florentine sculptor, Pietro Torrigiani, who was to make his reputation in England. 'This Buonarroti and I from boyhood used to go to study in Masaccio's chapel in the church of the Carmine,' Pietro Torrigiani told Benvenuto Cellini; 'and because Buonarroti was accustomed to make fun of all those who were drawing there, one day when he was annoying me among the rest, he aroused in me more anger than usual, and clenching my fist I gave him so violent a blow upon the nose that I felt the bone and the cartilage break under the stroke as if it had been a biscuit; and thus marked by me he will remain as long as he lives.'

Lorenzo took great pride in recognizing Michelangelo's genius, as he did in appreciating the virtues of all of Florence's great artists. Indeed, he

Bronze bust of Michelangelo in the Bargello by Daniele da Volterra, his near contemporary (1509–66).

liked to be considered, and came to be considered, the city's foremost arbiter of taste, an expert in architecture as well as in sculpture and painting. It became common practice to consult him when important works, both public and private, were to be undertaken. He was, for instance, asked for his advice by those responsible for the building of the new church of Santa Maria delle Carceri at Prato, recommending Giuliano da Sangallo as architect; and he was invited to become a member of the *opera* of Santo Spirito and again recommended Giuliano da Sangallo as architect for the new sacristy. Even foreign rulers and princes sought his advice. Both King Ferdinand II of Naples and the Duke of Calabria consulted him about new palaces in their domains. And no one would have considered building a palace in Florence in his day without showing him the plans or asking him to suggest the name of an architect who might draw them.

According to Filippo Strozzi's son, his father manipulated Lorenzo when he wanted to build a palace larger and more magnificent than might otherwise have been considered appropriate. The plans for the palace had at first been rejected by Filippo, who protested that they were far too grandiose; but he had had second thoughts when told that Lorenzo would prefer a design that would grace and honour the city. So he consulted Lorenzo, who approved the grand design. Filippo, still feigning modesty, demurred, while praising Lorenzo's taste and discernment, and eventually gave way on the grounds that Lorenzo understood these matters of space and style far better than he did himself. So, without risk of censure from the Palazzo Medici, he got the palace he had always wanted, making provision in his will for his heirs to keep at least fifty workmen employed on the site at all times and, in the event of the palace not being finished within five years of his death, for Lorenzo de' Medici to become supervisor of the work.

Not only was he consulted as a matter of course, Lorenzo was occasionally invited to submit designs himself. He did so, for instance, when a competition was held for the façade of the cathedral of Santa Maria del Fiore, which had long remained without one. Filippino Lippi, Botticelli, Ghirlandaio and Verrocchio were among the several artists who also submitted designs, so that the judges were placed in an embarrassing position, from which they endeavoured to extricate themselves by asking Lorenzo to choose the design himself. Lorenzo in turn escaped by praising all the designs which, he declared, were of such comparable merit that he could not pronounce any one of them to be the best. The problem was, therefore, shelved; and the cathedral was left faceless until a temporary façade was erected in 1515. In the later sixteenth century and the seventeenth century other competitions were held, but these, too, were inconclusive, and the front of the building was covered instead by a canvas curtain. When this was blown down in a gale in the 1690s it was decided to cover the bare stone with frescoes painted by foreign artists brought down for this purpose from Bologna, which would have been inconceivable in Lorenzo's time. These frescoes slowly crumbled away and it was not until the late nineteenth century that the present façade of marble and mosaics was completed.

When the first competition for the cathedral's façade was held in 1491, Lorenzo was forty-two. He had become recognized as one of the greatest of Italian statesmen as well as a patron and collector and a poet of outstanding versatility. He had contributed large sums to the University of Florence, now famed for the lectures given there by his friends, Landino, Ficino and Poliziano, and for its courses in Greek which, supervised by Demetrius Chalcondyles, were attended by students from all over Europe, including Thomas Linacre, who was to be one of the founders of the Royal College of Physicians, and William Grocyn, who was to be one of the first scholars, perhaps the first, to give public lectures in Greek at Oxford University.

Lorenzo had also revived the once renowned but now rather decayed university at Pisa, encouraging the expansion of its faculty of law and thus astutely gaining credit for having the interests of Pisa and Tuscany at heart, while at the same time removing from Florence those interfering legal pundits who were only too ready to question the validity of Medicean policies.

He had become a passionate champion of the Italian language, deriding those humanists who regarded it with disdain and who belittled the Tuscan poets of the immediate past, and arguing strongly against men like the precious Niccolò Niccoli, who had contended that Dante was a poet to be read only by bankers and wool-workers. He had added numerous volumes to the Medici library and had encouraged the printing of books in Florence, where the first printed work had not appeared until 1471 and Bernardo Cennini had not established his press until 1477. This was several years after presses had been set up in Naples, Rome, Venice, Milan and Verona, so strong was the tradition in Florence that printing was rather a vulgar process and that manuscripts should be copied by hand, as they were so beautifully and carefully by the scribes and illustrators in Vespasiano da Bisticci's bookshop.

Much as Lorenzo had achieved, however, there remained much to do and it was feared that he would have little time left in which to do it. He was already ill when he returned from Naples to Florence, suffering from increasingly painful attacks of uricaemia which the waters of the spas at Vigone, Spedaletto, Porretta and Bagno a Morba alleviated for a time but did not cure. At the beginning of 1492 he was taken to the villa of Careggi and was never to return to the Palazzo Medici. From Florence reports of strange portents reached him: a woman in Santa Maria Novella had gone mad during Mass and had rushed about the church, screaming of a raging bull with flaming horns; two of the city's lions had been killed while fighting in their cage in Via dei Leoni; Marsilio Ficino had had visions of giants struggling in his garden; lightning had struck the cathedral lantern and one of its marble balls had crashed down into the Piazza del Duomo. Lorenzo asked on which side it had fallen, and on being told, said, 'I shall die, for that is the side nearest my house.'

His doctor assured him that he would soon recover and, when proved wrong and accused of witchcraft and poisoning, the poor man threw himself down a well at San Gervasio. Another doctor sent from Milan prescribed a concoction of pulverized pearls and precious stones which he noisily banged about in a pestle in a nearby room. Lorenzo seemed to have faith in this remedy and, taking the hands of his old friend Angelo Poliziano into his own, he gazed searchingly into his face. Poliziano looked away and, returning to his own room, burst into tears.

Having lapsed into a kind of coma, Lorenzo de' Medici died on 9 April 1492, speechless, his eyes fixed on a silver crucifix.

★

PIERO DI LORENZO DI PIERO DE MEDICI

Bronzino's portrait of Lorenzo de' Medici's son, Piero (1472–1503).

'The people wouldn't stand for it!' Angelo Poliziano had protested when the dying Lorenzo had told him that he wanted to devote the rest of his life to poetry and study, and to leave the government of Florence to his son, Piero.

Piero was, indeed, although far better looking than most of his family, an unattractive young man, as much disliked in the city as was his haughty Roman wife, an Orsini like his mother. Indulged as a child both by his parents and his grandmother, Piero was impatient, arrogant and spiteful. He was also extremely lazy, content to leave the tiresome details of public affairs in the hands of his secretary and the administration of the rapidly disintegrating family bank to his mother's by-no-means-efficient uncle, Giovanni Tornabuoni. He was far from being capable of dealing with the threat to the Medicean regime precipitated by the accession to the French throne of Charles VIII, an ambitious, restless young man determined to renew the claims of the House of Anjou to the Kingdom of Naples. Nor did he know how to meet the ferocious attacks upon the Medici by a Dominican friar from Ferrara, a man whose fiery, apocalyptic sermons filled the cathedral to overflowing. These sermons greatly impressed Michelangelo, who was to say as an old man that he could still hear the friar's harsh voice ringing in his ears; they alarmed the neurotic Botticelli and so frightened Pico della Mirandola that the philosopher felt his hair standing on end. The name of this unnerving preacher was Girolamo Savonarola.

THE BONFIRE OF
THE VANITIES
1492–8

'Repent, O Florence,
repent while there is still time!'
GIROLAMO SAVONAROLA

Savonarola's father and grandfather had both been physicians at the Ferrarese
court where, although of the strictest moral principles, they had advocated
the consumption of large doses of alcohol in the interests of health and
longevity, a prescription not in the least to the taste of Girolamo, notorious
for his asceticism. He ate as little as he drank; he rarely spoke to women
except to preach at them; he forswore all comfort, wearing coarse cloth
next to his skin and sleeping on a straw mattress thrown over a board.
When leaving home for a Dominican monastery at Bologna he told his
father that he ought to thank God for having given him a son 'deemed
worthy to become His militant Knight', a son who would fight with all his
strength to stop the Devil jumping on to his shoulders.

After several years in Bologna, Savonarola was sent by his Order to preach
elsewhere in Italy, arriving in Florence in 1481 to become *lector* at San
Marco.[1] He was then a small, spare, ugly man of twenty-nine, with sunken
cheeks, an immense hooked nose, thick red lips and intense green eyes that
seemed to flash with fire. His voice was harsh, his gestures violent and
clumsy; but, although at first a far from impressive preacher, not knowing,
as he himself confessed, 'how to move a hen', he gradually acquired so
terrible a power that congregations – who had waited for hours outside for
the doors to open – sat horrified and spellbound by his vivid images, his
imprecations and exhortations, his warnings of the horrors to be faced by
those who did not repent of their sins.

In sermons delivered at San Marco, and afterwards – when that church
could no longer hold the congregations that flocked to hear them – in the
cathedral, Savonarola thundered against the iniquities of the Florentine
people, their dissolute carnivals, their passion for gambling, their extravagant

A portrait of Savonarola in San Marco by his fellow Dominican Fra Bartolommeo (1475–1517).

HIERONYMI·FERRARIENSIS·A·DEO· ·MISSI·PROPHETÆ·EFFIGIES·

clothes, their scent and powder, the sensual pleasures which were destroying their souls and making it impossible for them to reach the Kingdom of God. They must beat virtue into prostitutes, who were nothing but 'pieces of meat with eyes'; they must burn sodomites alive; they must destroy those wanton pictures that made the Blessed Virgin look like a harlot; they must trample underfoot the pagan works of Aristotle and Plato, who were now rotting in hell, and must return to the austere simplicity of the early Christian Church. They must attend to the warnings of the Old Testament prophets if they were to gain eternal life. They must reject the spectacles offered them by the present regime, which were like the bread and circuses offered to the Roman people by the emperors, and they must replace their present tyranny with a true republic.

After long periods of fasting, Savonarola was vouchsafed visions of a terrible future, of plague and famine, tempests, flood and war. 'Repent, O Florence,' he cried, 'repent while there is still time! Clothe thyself in the white garments of purification!' It was not he who spoke, he said. It was God who spoke through him.

'The Lord has placed me here,' he declared, 'and he has said to me, "I have put you here as a watchman in the centre of Italy that you may hear my words and announce them to the people."' The people listened to his words in silent fear, waiting for the fall of the sword of the Lord which hung so threateningly over them, for the foreign armies which, they were told, would soon pour across the Alps, like 'barbers armed with gigantic razors'.

'A Dominican Friar has so terrified all the Florentines that they are wholly given up to.piety,' the Mantuan envoy reported to his master sardonically. 'Three days a week they fast on bread and water, and two more on wine and bread. All the girls and many of the wives have taken refuge in convents, so that only men and youths and old women are now to be seen in the streets.'

Certainly, when the foreign enemies, as forecast by Savonarola, crossed the Alps in the shape of an immense French army under King Charles VIII of France, on the march to claim his Neapolitan inheritance, the Florentines seemed too stunned to offer resistance. Nor, indeed, were the other Italian states prepared to stand in his way.

In Milan, Gian Galeazzo Sforza had come of age, but his uncle, Il Moro, determined not to give up the powers of regent and, concerned that Gian Galeazzo's forthright wife, who was a granddaughter of the King of Naples, might force him to do so, had promised Charles VIII his support. Venice announced her neutrality. The Papal States offered no resistance. Piero de' Medici, who had at first announced his support for the King of Naples, now declared that Florence would, like Venice, remain neutral; and, although he displayed a flurry of unwonted activity when the French, in need of fortresses in Tuscany to give security in their rear while advancing south, attacked and sacked the stronghold of Fivizzano, other leading citizens of Florence made no comparable efforts to prevent the French marching any further south into Tuscany.

'Behold!' declaimed Savonarola in the cathedral. 'The sword has descended. The scourge has fallen. The prophecies are being fulfilled. Behold, it is the Lord God who is leading on these armies... Behold, I shall unloose waters over the earth... It is not I but God who foretold it. Now it is coming! It has come!'

Many in the cathedral's congregation were persuaded that the French troops were, indeed, instruments of God sent to shock Florence and Italy into obedience to his commands. Many more were convinced that resistance was useless. Piero de' Medici's two rich cousins, Lorenzo and Giovanni, sons of Pierfrancesco de' Medici, sent messages to the French headquarters assuring the King of their full support in what he called his 'enterprise', offering money to support it and undertaking to use all their influence in Florence to gain the citizens' sympathy for the invading army. Their message was intercepted and Piero ordered them to be held under house arrest; but they soon escaped and made their way to King Charles at Vigetano to deliver their assurances of support in person.

Deserted by most members of the Medicean party and badgered and anathematized by Savonarola, Piero concluded that he must make his own submission. He rode off to the French camp now at Santo Stefano to do so, dispatching to the Signoria a letter clearly inspired by the one his father had written after his departure for Naples fifteen years before.

The French King received Piero de' Medici with haughty condescension. Charles VIII was a poor figure of a man, small, crooked and ugly, with a nose of monstrous size and loose, thick lips partially concealed by a wispy beard. His features were further distorted by a convulsive tic; his hand also twitched disconcertingly; he was extremely short-sighted; he limped crouchingly on large, misshapen feet. On occasions uneasily affable, he was more usually silent, muttering his words rather than speaking them. Even so he commanded respect, and not only as King of France: there was a force in his personality that made men wary in his presence.

Piero, evidently in awe of him, was only too ready to give way on every point, so the French staff later told Philippe de Commines. He offered to concede to him the right to occupy all the Tuscan strongholds he needed as well as the towns of Pisa and Leghorn.

Hearing of this abject capitulation, and thankful to have a scapegoat for their own helpless inertia, the *priori* ordered the main gate of the Palazzo della Signoria to be shut against him when Piero returned to Florence the next morning to make his report. Later they sent a message telling him they would admit him through a side door provided his guard remained outside; but by now huge crowds had gathered in the Piazza, cursing him and throwing stones. He thought it as well to ride away while he still could for the relative safety of the Medici Palace, from which that night he fled with his wife, his two young children, his younger brother, Giuliano, and his cousin Giulio, then sixteen years old, the illegitimate child of his uncle Giuliano. Piero's other brother, Giovanni, aged eighteen, also fled from Florence, having tried to gather support for the family by riding up and down the streets shouting their rallying cry, '*Palle! Palle! Palle!*'

All these Medici were sentenced by the Signoria to exile in perpetuity, a reward of 4,000 florins being offered for the capture of Piero and 2,000 florins for Giovanni. Their cousins, the sons of Pierfrancesco, were exempted from the ban because of their vaunted opposition to Piero; but they prudently changed their name to Popolano and had the Medici coat of arms removed from the walls of their palace.

Disguised as a Dominican friar, Piero's brother, Giovanni, who, at his father's instigation, had been created a cardinal two years before, managed to convey some of the treasures of the Medici library from the palace to San Marco. Other small treasures had been removed from the palace by Piero himself, who took them with him to Venice; but there was much left to plunder when a mob inevitably broke in, carrying off innumerable pictures and statues. 'The best of the Medici furniture had been conveyed to another house in the city,' Philippe de Commines reported. 'But the mob plundered it. The Signoria got some of Piero's richest jewels, twenty thousand ducats in ready money from his bank in the city, several fine agate vases, as well as an incredible number of cameos admirably well cut, three thousand medals of gold and silver [and much more besides].'

French quartermasters had already entered the city to mark with chalk the buildings considered suitable for the billeting of troops. As one of four delegates sent to Pisa, which the French had occupied and declared to be free of the tyranny of Medici rule, Savonarola assured King Charles that his troops would be welcome in Florence.

'And so at last, O King, thou hast come,' he is reported to have announced sententiously.

> Thou art an instrument in the hands of the Lord who has sent you to cure the ills of Italy as I have long since predicted. I say this to you in the name of the Lord ... Thou hast come as the Minister of God, the Minister of Justice. We receive thee with joyful hearts and a glad countenance ... We hope that, by thee, Jehovah will abase the proud, exalt the humble, crush vice, exalt virtue, make straight all that is crooked and reform all that is deformed. Come then, glad, secure, triumphant, since He that sent you forth triumphed upon the Cross for our redemption.

It was, however, as a military conqueror rather than a 'Minister of God' that King Charles entered Florence on 17 November 1494 by way of the Porta San Frediano. Under a magnificent canopy held over his head by four knights, wearing his crown and a cloth-of-gold cloak over his gilt armour, riding a huge black war-horse and holding his lance at rest, the traditional gesture of conquest, he led a splendid procession of twelve thousand soldiers, Swiss Guards and Gascon infantry, cavalry in engraved armour, cuirassiers and long-bowmen, 'extraordinarily tall men from Scotland and other northern countries, looking more like wild beasts than men'.

True to Savonarola's promise, the citizens greeted the French army warmly, shouting '*Viva Francia!*' as the thousands of troops, regiment after regiment, marched by. In the course of the next eleven days, while the King was entertained in the Medici Palace – to whose looted rooms furniture, tapestry and pictures had been hastily returned – there were far fewer disturbances than might have been expected from the presence of so large a foreign force; and it was not until after the French had gone, declining to pay for most of what their visit had cost, that the Florentines began to feel that their welcome had been more effusive than the circumstances warranted, and that Piero di Gino Capponi had been quite right to make his celebrated protest.

This man had once been Florence's ambassador in France and had known the King as a little boy. He had been present when the terms which the Signoria had made with the French had been read out by a herald. The terms were harsh enough on the Florentines: they were to grant the French possession of Pisa and, for the time being, all the fortresses they had seized; and they were to make a contribution of 150,000 ducats towards the cost of the further advance of the French troops upon Naples. Through some oversight the figure of 125,000 rather than 150,000 had been inserted in the document which the herald read out, and when this lower figure was proclaimed, King Charles stopped the herald in mid-sentence, demanding that the sum of 150,000 be substituted. Otherwise, he threatened, he would order his trumpeters to call out his troops, who would then pillage the city without mercy. Piero di Gino Capponi, as angry as the King, then leapt forward, snatched the document from the herald's hands, tore it up and in a voice which Francesco Guicciardini described as 'quivering with agitation', shouted the words which were to become a Florentine proverb, 'If you sound your trumpets, we shall ring our bells.'

Rather than risk the city being called to arms, and his army being forced to fight at a disadvantage in its narrow, tortuous streets, the King gave way, making light of his objection. He signed the treaty and led his army south for Rome, leaving Florence to be governed in the name of God's servant, Girolamo Savonarola, now Prior of San Marco.

The change of government from Medicean oligarchy to austere theocracy was carried through in a manner respectful to the forms of the Florentine constitution. A *Parlamento* was summoned and a *Balìa* established; the Medicean councils set up by Lorenzo were abolished; and a new republican government on the Venetian model was created, with a *Maggior Consiglio*, a Great Council, of several hundred members, with authority to elect magistrates, about eighty of whom would form a *Minor Consiglio*, or *Ottanta*. The Signoria and the Gonfaloniere were to remain, but neither could act without the authority of both these new councils.

The *Maggior Consiglio* was so large an assembly that no hall of the Palazzo della Signoria was suitable for its deliberations; so, a few months after the departure of the French, Simone del Pollaiuolo, Il Cronaca, assisted by Francesco di Domenico and Antonio da Sangallo, was commissioned to design a new hall, for which both Leonardo da Vinci and Michelangelo were asked to supply paintings.[2]

Inspired by Savonarola, the new government was from the beginning persuaded to believe that its policies would be directed by divine will. 'The wind drives me forward,' the prior announced in a sermon preached shortly before Christmas. 'The Lord forbids my return. I spoke last night with God and I said, "Pity me, O Lord. Lead me back to my haven." "It is impossible," said the Lord. "Do you not see where the wind is forcing you to go?" "I will preach if I must. But why need I interfere with the government of Florence?" "If you would make Florence a holy city, you must establish her on firm foundations and see that her government favours virtue."'

God had called upon him to reform the city and the Church, and he, with crucifix in hand, called upon the government to support him in his mission. He commanded the citizens to fast, to cast aside their showy clothes and ornaments, to sell their jewels and give their money to the poor, to remove silver candlesticks and illuminated books from monasteries and churches. He called upon 'blessed bands' of children to march through the streets, their hair cut short, bearing crosses and olive branches, singing hymns and collecting alms, to enter houses and search out objects of vanity and luxury, to urge their parents to abandon their evil ways and follow the paths of virtue, to report to the authorities all instances of scandalous vice.

The Florentines listened and many obeyed. Courtesans stayed indoors; gamblers concealed their dice boxes; fashionable ladies walked the streets in quiet colours; balladeers closed their books of ribald songs; and bands of children, as Savonarola had urged them to, patrolled the streets singing hymns, keeping wary eyes open for displays of extravagance or ungodliness, seeking admittance to houses and calling upon the inhabitants to deliver up articles of which they had grown unduly fond.

One day in 1497 when Florence was normally given over to the pleasures of the carnival and the streets were full of revellers, a large band of these singing children was seen marching from church to church, carrying a statue of the boy Jesus by Donatello. To some, these children seemed like angels who had 'come down to earth to rejoice with the children of men', to others like dreadful little prigs and informers in need of a sound whipping. 'Some lukewarm people gave trouble,' so the apothecary, Luca Landucci, said, 'throwing dead cats and other rubbish.' But, undeterred, the children helped to carry piles of scent bottles and pomade pots, wigs and jars of rouge, looking-glasses, fans and necklaces to an enormous scaffold in the shape of a pyramid which had been erected in the Piazza della Signoria. They piled them round the base of this scaffold together with heaps of profane books and lewd drawings, stories by Boccaccio and Luigi Pulci, portraits of beautiful women, carnival masks, chessboards, packs of cards, dice boxes and manuals of magic; and on top of the mountainous jumble of vanities there was placed the effigy of a Venetian merchant who had offered 20,000 scudi for the works of art now to be destroyed. As trumpets were blown and choirs sang, as church bells rang all over the city, the flames from this Bonfire of the Vanities leapt towards the sky.

Consumed in the flames, so it was said, were paintings considered lascivious or sensual by the artists themselves. For all the kindness he had received at the hands of the Medici – and Savonarola had declared that any attempt to restore them would be a capital offence – Botticelli was believed to be one of these artists; Lorenzo di Credi was another; so was Fra Bartolommeo. Many others, writers and scholars as well as artists, had been deeply impressed by Savonarola's passionate sermons, his blazing sincerity, his vision of a 'City of God'. 'His efforts to maintain the observance of good behaviour were holy and admirable,' wrote Francesco Guicciardini, a law student in Florence at this time. 'There was never such goodness and religion in Florence as in his day.' Others condemned him as a religious fanatic. Indeed, the silk merchant, Marco Parenti, said in 1497 that opinion in Florence was so mixed that 'it divided fathers and children, husbands and wives, brothers and sisters. Young men between the ages of eighteen and thirty differed greatly about Savonarola.'

Luca Landucci, whose diaries give so vivid a picture of these times, was proud to have children marching in the prior's 'blessed bands'; Giorgio Vespucci, uncle of Amerigo, the navigator, a canon of Santa Maria del Fiore and a learned bibliophile, spoke of Savonarola with respect and admiration; so did the Strozzi brothers, whose vast palace was still under construction. They were far from exceptional: most of his warmest supporters were to be found amongst the poor and middling classes; but his appeal extended also to members of the richest families in the city, who roundly condemned his disdainful critics and the rabble that beat drums to drown his voice. They were proud to be numbered amongst the '*frateschi*' (the friars), the '*capaternostri*' (the prayer mumblers) and the '*piagnoni*' (the snivellers), as the prior's enemies referred to his adherents. These enemies were numerous, but too disparate to be well organized. Among them were men so passionate in their opposition to Savonarola's regime that they were known as '*arrabiati*', as well as hundreds of former Mediceans who, now that they prudently refrained from showing themselves in their true colours, were called '*biggi*' (greys), and scores of rowdy, wild young men, mostly from the families of the *arrabiati*, who became known as '*compagnacci*'.

While these various opponents of Savonarola were making plans to overthrow the government which his preaching had inspired, his apocalyptic pronouncements and accusations were making him enemies far beyond the confines of Florence.

The most influential of these enemies was Roderigo Borgia, the new Pope Alexander VI, a worldly, wily, rich and pleasure-loving Spaniard, as determined to advance the interests of his six sons as he was to drive the French out of Italy. The French army was now in Naples, from which King Alfonso had fled to a Sicilian monastery. King Charles was enjoying himself there with a succession of mistresses, whose portraits he had bound together in a big book.

In order to force the French to withdraw across the Alps, Pope Alexander set about the formation of what he called a Holy League. He persuaded Venice to join the league; he also enlisted the support of Lodovico Sforza of Milan, who was now regretting his earlier encouragement of the French invasion; he won the backing of the Spanish King Ferdinand and of the Emperor Maximilian. The forces were placed under the command of Francesco Gonzaga, the fierce-looking Marquis of Mantua.

Formidable as they seemed, the forces of the Holy League were no match for the large and ruthless French army which now marched north towards the Apennines, a mule loaded with looted treasure to every two men. Gone now were the earlier days of Renaissance warfare when armies manoeuvred around each other in a kind of choreographic parade, when troops were more concerned to pillage than to fight, when such a battle as that at Anghiari in 1440 – in which nine hundred men were killed – was most unusual, when, as Luca Landucci said, the system of Italian soldiers was formulated thus: 'You turn your attention to plundering in that direction, and we will do the same in this. Getting too near each other is not our game.'

The mercenary forces of the Holy League and the outnumbered French army clashed head on by the banks of the River Taro. The battle was short and savage; the iron cannon-balls of the French artillery, which was 'of a sort never seen in Italy before', mowed columns of Italian soldiers down, leaving the wounded to be cut apart by the French camp-followers. The French army, mauled yet still a formidable force, resumed its march to the north.

The Pope had called upon Florence to play her due part in his Holy League; but the Florentines, who had seen for themselves the strength of the French army, and who were anxious not to lose so valuable a customer as France for their manufactured goods, had been deaf to his appeals; while

Savonarola had continued to speak in support of the invader, claiming to be God's mouthpiece in doing so.

The Pope, egged on by a succession of Florentine *arrabiati* who had gone to Rome to spread tales of the iniquities of the detested Prior of San Marco, angrily summoned him to Rome. Savonarola replied that it was not God's will that he should go; the Pope, slowly abandoning hope that the prior's enthusiasm would sooner or later wear itself out, forbade him to preach any more; Savonarola, after allowing one of his disciples to preach in his stead, soon resumed his sermons in the cathedral.

Pope Alexander decreed that the Tuscan Dominicans, who had been granted their independence, should revert to papal control as a preliminary step towards sending the 'pestilential heretic' to another monastery far away from Florence. The Prior of San Marco declared that the Pope had no authority in the matter. In the hope that bribery might succeed where threats had failed, Pope Alexander offered to give Savonarola a cardinal's hat if only he would give up preaching. The prior replied that another kind of hat would suit him better, 'one red with blood'.

In June 1497 Savonarola was excommunicated. For a long time the prior remained silent, praying for guidance as his supporters and opponents struggled for dominance in the *Maggior Consiglio*. Then, evidently encouraged by an election of *priori* favourable to the *frateschi*, he announced that God's word had been vouchsafed to him: on Christmas Day he celebrated High Mass in the cathedral.

'I can no longer place any faith in your Holiness,' Savonarola replied to a threat to place the whole city under an interdict unless the Signoria either sent the prior to Rome or had him thrown into prison in Florence. 'You have not listened to me ... I must trust myself wholly to Him who chooses the weak things of this world to confound the strong. Your Holiness is well advised to make immediate provisions for your own salvation.'

The Signoria, treated with equal high-handedness, had by now come to believe that the quarrel was getting out of hand. Savonarola's opponents were becoming more outspoken every month. Such escapades as those of the *compagnacci* – who desecrated the cathedral pulpit when the prior was about to preach and sent a chest crashing down into the nave when he had reached a particularly alarming passage in his sermon – were not to be taken too seriously. But older, graver men were joining the ranks of the prior's critics, while the clergy were becoming increasingly concerned about his constant insistence that his was the voice of God. The Franciscans, in particular, long antagonized by the Dominicans' claim to a special relationship with the Almighty, were demanding that the Prior of San Marco should offer some proof of God's exceptional favour. Moreover, for a city which was intended to be a model for Italy, Florence was showing few signs of God's approbation. Poor harvests, which had led to food shortages so severe that several poor people had died of starvation in the streets, had been followed by an outbreak of plague; and war had once again broken out with Pisa, which the King of France had not handed back to Florence as he had undertaken to do, but had made over instead to the Pisan people.

Having regard to Florence's plight, and the discord between those who saw the Prior of San Marco as its only hope and those who condemned him as the cause of all their suffering, the Signoria asked him to preach no more. He agreed, on condition that he be allowed to explain himself in a final sermon.

He gave this sermon, so he claimed when permission was granted him, not because he wanted to, but because he was compelled to do so by a raging fire within the very marrow of his bones. 'I feel myself all burning,' he declared, 'all inflamed with the spirit of the Lord. Oh, spirit within! You rouse the waves of the sea as the wind does. You stir the tempest as you pass. I can do no other.' He cited the fulfilment of so many of his prophecies. He had foretold the death of Lorenzo de' Medici and he was dead; he had foretold the deaths of Pope Innocent VIII and King Ferrante of Naples and, soon afterwards, they had both died too; he had issued warnings of the armies of a foreign king which would come pouring across the Alps, and the French had come. It was his bounden duty to continue preaching and prophesying; he had a divine right to resist all unlawful authority, to attack the Church, which was now a mere Satanic institution for the promotion of vice and whoredom.

All this was too much for the Franciscans, one of whom challenged him to walk through fire with him. This would surely show that the Dominican prior was not under divine protection. Savonarola declined the challenge: he was destined for more important work; he had, however, no objection to another Dominican, Fra Domenico da Pescia, taking his place, nor to the Franciscans being represented by Fra Giuliano Rondinelli when their original champion declined to match himself in the ordeal with anyone other than Savonarola himself.

Informed of this proposed revival of the medieval trial by ordeal, the *priori* were horrified. One of them suggested that if these friars wanted to prove that they enjoyed God's protection why did they not try to walk across the Arno without getting wet. Others protested that the people had by now become so excited by the quarrel and its proposed resolution that nothing less than an ordeal by fire would satisfy them. The ordeal was then authorized; and the Piazza della Signoria was prepared for it, a pathway through a pile of firewood being marked out with sticks soaked in oil.

On the appointed day, 17 April 1498, the Franciscans marched into the Piazza followed by the Dominicans, all chanting psalms and walking in pairs behind a crucifix. The champions of their respective orders took up position at either end of the Loggia dei Lanzi, while the *priori* assembled on the *ringhiera* outside the gate of the Palazzo della Signoria. Every window and roof above their heads was crowded with the expectant faces of the citizens of Florence.

As arguments raged as to whether the contestants might take a crucifix or the consecrated host into the flames, storm clouds gathered and a heavy rain began to fall. The arguments continued as the afternoon wore on until the *priori* – who had apparently always intended that the spectacle should be cancelled and the friars blamed for the people's disappointment – announced that it was now too late and too wet for the ordeal to take place that day.

With the dispute thus unresolved the rows between the prior's supporters and their opponents became more frequent and bitter than ever. On Palm Sunday a congregation assembled in the cathedral to hear a sermon by one of Savonarola's Dominican disciples were chased out of the building by shouting *compagnacci* wielding sticks and throwing stones. The congregation ran for safety to the buildings of San Marco, which were soon surrounded by a huge mob.

Savonarola had commanded his fraternity to rely on prayer alone for their protection; but, believing weapons to be of more immediate use, many of the monks had armed themselves with lances and pikes with which they now threatened the mob. They also loosened a pinnacle from the top of the monastery church and sent it crashing down on to the heads of the besiegers who were endeavouring to clamber up the walls.

'The crowd increased all the time,' Luca Landucci recorded in his diary; 'and they brought up three stone-throwing machines by which some people were wounded and others killed. At about [two o'clock in the morning] they set fire to the doors of the church and cloister of San Marco and, penetrating into the church, began to fight.'

The prior ran for safety to Michelozzo's library, where a guard sent by the Signoria to arrest him found him praying at a desk. He was escorted past the jeering crowds to the Palazzo della Signoria and was locked up in the cramped cell known with grim humour as the Alberghettino, the Little Inn. From there, he was taken to be tortured by the city's rack-master in the Bargello, 'being carried there by two men on their crossed hands because his feet and hands were in irons'.

Ambiguously he confessed all that was required of him while suffering the dreadful agonies of the *strappado* but, as soon as the straps had been released, he retracted his confessions. He was tortured again and recanted again. In the end he was found guilty of heresy and condemned to death, together with two of his most devoted disciples. Messengers were sent to Rome for permission to carry out the sentence. The Pope in return sent commissioners to Florence to review the case. The commissioners, in their

turn, 'arriving in Florence with the verdict in their bosom', ordered that the accused should be tortured once more to extract further admissions. Their sentences were then confirmed and orders were given for them to be hanged in chains and burned on a scaffold in the Piazza.

An immense pile of brushwood was prepared; a gallows with three stout arms was erected in its centre; and a high platform built from the gate of the Palazzo to the gallows' ladder so that all who had been disappointed by the cancellation of the ordeal might be compensated by a view of the three friars being conducted to their death. 'They were robed in all their vestments,' Luca Landucci entered in his diary under the heading 22 May.

These were taken off one by one with the appropriate words for the degradation... Then their faces and hands were shaved as is customary in this ceremony... The first to be executed was Fra Silvestro, who was hung to the post and one arm of the cross, and there not being much drop, he suffered for some time, repeating 'Jesu' many times whilst he was hanging, for the rope did not draw tight nor run well. The second was Fra Domenico of Pescia, who also kept saying 'Jesu'; and the third was [the prior] who did not speak aloud, but to himself, and so he was hanged... When all three had been hanged a fire was made on the platform upon which gunpowder was put and set alight, so that the said fire burst out with a noise of rockets and cracking. In a few hours they were burnt, their legs and arms gradually dropping off. Part of their bodies remaining hanging to the chains, a quantity of stones were thrown to make them fall, as there was a fear of the people getting hold of them; and then the hangman and those whose business it was, hacked down the post and burnt it on the ground, bringing a lot of brushwood, and stirring the fire up over the dead bodies, so that the very last piece was consumed. Then they fetched carts, and carried the last bit of dust to the Arno, by the Ponte Vecchio, in order that no remains should be found. Nevertheless, a few good men had so much faith that they gathered some of the floating ashes together, in fear and secrecy, because it was as much as one's life was worth to say a word, so anxious were the authorities to destroy every relic.

The execution of Savonarola in the Piazza della Signoria on 23 May 1498; a painting on the back of a panel of a portrait of Savonarola by an anonymous sixteenth-century Florentine artist.

14

CONSPIRATORS AND CARDINALS
1498–1527

'An appalling spectacle of horrors.'
NICCOLÒ MACHIAVELLI

In the gloomy years following the execution of Savonarola, the bent figure of Sandro Botticelli, 'old and useless, ill and decrepit', as Vasari described him, could be seen hobbling about Florence with the help of crutches. He seemed an incarnation of the sad and weakened state of the city. A long and bitter war with Pisa – during which the *condottiere* paid to conduct it, Paglio Vitelli, was tried and executed for treason – had placed a scarcely supportable strain on the resources of the treasury, while a series of financial crises had brought several of the city's guilds to the verge of bankruptcy. The bitter atmosphere of these sad days is reflected in Luca Landucci's diary entries. A characteristic entry was written on 24 February 1500:

> A Sienese physician was murdered by three men ... who fell upon him from the butcher's shop at the corner of Via Ghibellina next to the Stinche[1] ... They were hanged where they had committed the crime. They went on the executioner's cart, being tortured most cruelly with red-hot pincers all through the city; and here at Tornaquinci the brazier for heating the pincers broke. There not being much fire left, and it not burning properly ... the executioner got out and went for charcoal to the charcoal-burner, and for fire to the baker and used a kettle as a brazier making a hot fire. The *Cavaliere* kept shouting all the time, 'Make it red hot!' And all the people wanted [the murderers] to be tortured without pity. Even young boys were ready to kill the executioner if he did not do his work well. The condemned men shrieked in the most terrible manner. All this I saw at Tornaquinci.

In an attempt to strengthen the government, it had been decided to appoint a Gonfaloniere for life; but the *priore* chosen for this high responsibility, Piero Soderini, was not a man to inspire much confidence. It was generally conceded that he was industrious and honest, a stickler for constitutional propriety, yet as one of his critics said, he had 'no ideas, no imagination and no sparkle'. When faced with any difficult problem he was known to consult one of his government's minor officials, a thin, pale young man of high intelligence, the son of a lawyer from an old Tuscan family, Niccolò Machiavelli.

Deeply interested in the theory and practice of government, Machiavelli was also concerned with the conduct of war, and had long since come to the conclusion that Florence's reliance upon self-seeking mercenaries and *condottieri* was as inept as it was expensive. What was needed, he argued, was a national militia whose soldiers, conscripts and volunteers from Florence's country districts, would fight bravely for causes in which their own honour and interests lay, just as the citizens of ancient Rome had fought to defend their republic. Strongly influenced as always by Machiavelli's ideas, Piero Soderini agreed to the enlistment of a militia and entrusted him with the task of organizing and equipping it. Iron breastplates were ordered as well as lances and arquebuses, and for each man 'a white waistcoat, a pair of stockings, half red and half white, a white cap and a pair of shoes'. In February 1506 a parade of the first recruits, most of them from the farms, villages and small towns of the *contado*, was held in the Piazza della Signoria. 'They were soldiers but lived in their own homes,' wrote Luca Landucci, who was there to watch them march up and down. 'They were obliged to turn out when needed and it was ordered that many should be equipped in this way throughout Tuscany so that we should not need any foreigners. It was thought the finest thing that had ever been arranged for Florence.'

A wooden bust of Niccolò Machiavelli (1469–1527).

It had been arranged none too soon, for Florence was by then under threat from a formidable army raised by the Pope.

The Borgia Pope, Alexander VI, had died three years before; and, after the twenty-six-day papacy of the decrepit Pius III, had been succeeded by the commanding, fearsome and irascible Julius II, the grandson of a Ligurian fisherman and nephew of Sixtus IV, who prided himself on his soldierly qualities. 'I am no schoolman,' he said when asked to suggest a suitable emblem for a statue of him being made by Michelangelo. 'Put a sword in my hand, not a book.'

No sooner had he taken up residence in the Vatican than he was off campaigning in Emilia and the Romagna, determined to compel cities which had rebelled against the papacy in the days of his predecessors to return to their obedience. Having regained Bologna and Perugia, he turned upon Venice – which had presumed to take over Rimini, Faenza and Ravenna – calling upon France and Spain to help him; then, having routed the Venetian army at Agnadello, he demanded that the other Italian states join him in driving the 'foreign barbarians', his recent allies, out of the peninsula.

The Florentines were disinclined to help him. They had no quarrel with Spain; and, although their unfortunate brush with King Charles VIII was a recent and bitter memory, their traditional friendship with the French had not been irreparably damaged. When the Pope heard of their decision to remain neutral he flew into one of his celebrated rages, and was even more angry when almost ten thousand of the men he did eventually manage to assemble, mostly Spaniards, were slaughtered in an exceptionally savage battle with the French by the banks of the River Ronco on Easter Saturday 1512.

Almost as many French soldiers were killed and their young commander, Gaston de Foix, thrown from his saddle by a stray shot, had been hacked to death by Spanish infantrymen. But the Florentines, learning that the Pope's so-called Holy League had been dealt a crushing blow, lit bonfires in celebration, believing that the danger was past.

The danger was not past, however. Their homeland threatened by invasion from both England and Spain, the French withdrew from Italy; and the forces of the Holy League, free from interference and recovered from their recent mauling, now marched upon Florence intent upon replacing the city's government with one more amenable to the Pope's demands.

At the approach of the league's Spanish soldiers, peasant families and the population of entire villages fled to Florence to seek safety behind its massive walls. Within those walls, the citizens remained calm, confident in the ability of their militia to defend them. After all, although supported openly or secretly by Florence's rivals and enemies, the Pisans had been defeated after a struggle lasting fifteen years, mainly by the efforts of the militia; and the militia would surely acquit themselves as well now. There was 'no need to fear', Luca Landucci assured himself. 'On the contrary, it was the enemy who ought to be afraid, because if they came down into these plains they would fare badly. Many battalions of militia had been levied, and all the men-at-arms were eager to encounter the enemy.'

The league's commander, Raymond de Cadorna, was himself not at all confident that his army was strong enough for the task it had been assigned. He had not wanted to advance into Tuscany at all; nor had the Pope's nephew, Francesco Maria della Rovere, Duke of Urbino, who was reluc-tantly accompanying the Spanish army. Also with the army, however, was a young man in the Pope's confidence who had compelling personal reasons to advocate a determined attack upon Florence: Lorenzo de' Medici's second son, Giovanni, now thirty-six years old and a cardinal for the past twenty.

A less likely looking soldier it would be difficult to imagine. Pale, paunchy, extremely short-sighted, with a nose markedly snubbed and a mouth hanging half open as though he were in dazed surprise, Cardinal Giovanni de' Medici had the appearance of a gourmand much given to the pleasures of easy comfort, as, indeed, he was. Yet, when Pope Julius had taken twenty-four grumbling cardinals with him in unwilling attendance on his rampages around the rebellious Papal States, he had been much struck by the young Medici cardinal's good nature, his genial acceptance of the hardships of camp life and his courage. He had noted, too, his sharp intelligence and, behind the carefree manner of the *bon vivant*, a restless ambition.

His elder brother, the unfortunate Piero, with whom he had escaped from Florence during the anti-Medicean uprising of 1494, had been drowned when his boat capsized in the swollen water of the Garigliano, and Giovanni was now head of the Medici family. Determined to claim his inheritance, he urged the Spanish commander forward towards Florence, insisting that no terms should be agreed with the city that did not provide for the restoration of his family to their properties, rights and privileges. He was already in touch with sympathizers in Florence by means of a peasant who carried messages into the city, depositing them in a hole in the wall of a cemetery near Santa Maria Novella; while his cousin, Giulio, had arranged a secret meeting with Antonfrancesco degli Albizzi, a leading member of the proscribed Medicean party, who assured him that the Gonfaloniere would put up only a token resistance.

As it happened, however, Piero Soderini was not a man to give way so readily. Belying his reputation as an efficient but unimaginative administrator, he addressed the assembled crowd in the Piazza della Signoria in an eloquent and moving speech, urging them to fight for their city's liberties and to oppose all efforts to restore the Medici family to their former power. The citizens shouted their support of Soderini's stand; and orders were issued for the imprisonment of all known supporters of the Medici and for the militia to take up positions in all the city's strongholds.

The Spanish troops of the Holy League continued their advance upon Florence, battering their way into Prato, so Francesco Guicciardini recorded, and

> rushing through the town where there was no longer any opposition, but only cries, flight, violence, sack, blood and killing, the terrified Florentine foot soldiers casting away their weapons and surrendering to the invaders ... Nothing would have been spared the avarice, lust and cruelty of the invaders had not the

Cardinal de' Medici placed guards at the main church and saved the women who had taken refuge there. More than two thousand died, not fighting (for no one fought) but fleeing or crying for mercy.

For two days the pillage of Prato continued, as houses, churches and monasteries were ransacked, priests killed at their altars, women raped in the streets, men tortured to reveal the places where their valuable possessions had been hidden and then stripped naked and thrown into wells and ditches already choked with severed limbs.

As news of what Machiavelli called this 'appalling spectacle of horrors' reached Florence, scarcely ten miles from Prato's south-eastern gate, a deputation of Medici supporters went to the Palazzo della Signoria to demand the resignation of the Gonfalionere. Soderini was only too ready now to accede to their request and to escape from the city while he could. Escorted from Florence into exile, he was replaced by a Gonfaloniere sympathetic to the Medici. Cardinal Giovanni's younger brother, Giuliano de' Medici, entered the city on 1 September 1512, a few hours after Soderini left it. Already workmen were busy restoring the Medici *palle* to those buildings from which they had been removed and replacing the Medici emblems on the family palace in Via Larga. Machiavelli's militia was disbanded; and Machiavelli himself, in a purge of officials of the previous regime, was replaced by a Medicean. He left Florence to live in a small house in the country which he had inherited from his father.

Giuliano de' Medici, a well-mannered and good-natured young man, had entered Florence unattended and wearing an inconspicuous *lucco*. His brother, the cardinal, more given to drama and ceremony, rode into the city in state, accompanied by 1,500 troops in the manner of a conqueror. Yet he immediately made it clear to the Florentines that he had no intention of imposing a tyrannical rule. A pro-Medicean demonstration was organized in the Piazza della Signoria; a *Parlamento* was called and a Balìa was appointed, all in the approved constitutional manner. But, although nearly all the members of this Balìa were also members of the Medici party, it was made clear that the government which they were to administer was to be conducted in accordance with the cardinal's motto, '*Jugum enim meum suave est*' ('Truly my yoke is easy'). Florence was to turn her back on the recent past and return to the mood of the happier days of the cardinal's revered father, Lorenzo il Magnifico.

Impressive as was the cardinal's entry into Florence in 1512, it faded into the commonplace when compared with the grand spectacle which the city mounted when, three years later, he returned from Rome as Pope Leo X. His election as Pope Julius II's successor had been greeted in Florence with the wildest excitement. There had been firework displays and processions;

cannon had fired from the forts in the city's wall to be answered by the deep and distant boom of guns from the surrounding hills; crowds had paraded through the streets shouting, '*Palle! Palle! Papa Leone! Palle! Palle!*' Soberer and quieter crowds had followed a procession bearing the miraculous statue of the Blessed Virgin from the church of Santa Maria dell' Impruneta. Banquets had been held in palaces; furniture looted from the houses of the mournful *piagnoni* of Savonarola's day had been thrown upon bonfires in the *piazze*, together with boards and planks from the establishments of the bankers and merchants in the Mercato Nuovo. In Via Larga tables had been piled high with food outside the Palazzo Medici; and on the Palazzo della Signoria's *ringhiera* wine had been liberally dispensed from rows of gilded barrels.

For Pope Leo's ceremonial entrance into the city after his enthronement triumphal arches and obelisks were erected; immense screens were painted with allegorical scenes; statues of classical gods were created, emblems and trophies carved. Whole buildings were demolished to open up vistas; an immense castle, resting on columns, was built in the Piazza Santa Trinita, and an obelisk, fifty feet high, was set up in the Mercato Nuovo. The western front of Santa Maria del Fiore was covered by a splendid façade of wood and plaster designed by Jacopo Sansovino and painted by Andrea del Sarto.

Wearing a jewelled tiara and glittering cape, Pope Leo passed through the Porta Romana accompanied by an immense retinue of guards and prelates. He proceeded slowly down Via Maggio, crossed the Arno by the Ponte Santa Trinita and entered the Piazza della Signoria, raising his hands in benediction as his attendants threw silver coins amongst the crowds. Passing the screen before the church of San Felice,[2] he caught sight of a bust of his father and, through his spyglass, read the inscription beneath it: 'This is my beloved son.' And his eyes momentarily filled with tears. But thereafter he appeared as blissfully content as he had done in Rome during his *Sacro Possesso*, his formal entry into the Vatican, nodding complacently towards the cheering spectators, raising his plump hands in greeting and blessing, smiling amicably. 'God has given us the papacy,' he was reported to have remarked happily to his brother, Giuliano. 'Let us enjoy it.'

There could be no doubt that he did enjoy it. Yet, after his return to Rome, having entrusted Florence to the care of his nephew, Lorenzo, son of Piero, the Florentines soon lost their enthusiasm for his family. Lorenzo was a good-looking young man like his father, energetic and high-spirited. He was also ambitious and, although only twenty years old, determined to be his own master. Impatient of the advice given to him by his secretary, whom the Pope had instructed to report daily upon his nephew's progress, he was equally dismissive of his two other uncles, Jacopo Salviati, husband of his aunt Lucrezia, and Piero Ridolfi, who was married to his aunt Contessina. Authorized by the Pope to assume the title of Captain-General of the Florentine Republic, Lorenzo became increasingly authoritarian, holding quasi-regal court at the Medici Palace, where he required councils to meet, instead of at the Palazzo della Signoria.

The Pope had great plans for Lorenzo. He had visions of the Medici being once again as dominant an influence in Italian politics as they had been in his father's time, and of a central Italian state, encompassing Tuscany and including the cities of Parma, Modena and Piacenza, as well as the duchies of Ferrara and Urbino. He envisaged the young Lorenzo as master of this state; and, at great expense, he did at least succeed in having him proclaimed Duke of Urbino after an arduous campaign in which Lorenzo was wounded by a shot from an arquebus. Thereafter, however, the Pope's plans began to fall apart: Lorenzo, never fully recovering from his wound, died from tuberculosis aggravated by syphilis at the age of twenty-five, soon after marrying a cousin of François I, King of France. Pope Leo's brother, Giuliano, whom King François had created Duke of Nemours, had already died aged thirty-seven at Fiesole, 'utterly shrunken and spent, like an expiring candle', leaving an illegitimate son by a sensuous lady from Pesaro.

Lorenzo's bossy and interfering mother, Alfonsina, had also died; and the Medici heir was now Lorenzo's daughter, a half-French baby girl, Caterina, the only boys on the Pope's side of the family being his nephew, Ippolito – his brother Giuliano's illegitimate son – and Alessandro, presented as the son of Lorenzo, the dead Duke of Urbino, but rumoured to be the natural son of the Pope's cousin, Giulio de' Medici, either by a Moorish slave from Naples or by a peasant woman from the Roman Campagna.

Giulio, appointed Archbishop of Florence by his cousin the Pope in 1513, was a prevaricating man with a cold manner and saturnine appearance. Much disliked in Florence, he was 'morose and disagreeable', Francesco Guicciardini wrote, 'disinclined to grant a favour, reputedly avaricious and very grave and cautious in all his actions. Perfectly self-controlled, he would have been highly capable had not timidity made him shrink from what he should have done.'

It had to be conceded that when he arrived in Florence to supervise the government of the city after Lorenzo's death, Giulio did his best not to offend the citizens' susceptibilities. Retiring and conciliatory, he reorganized the state's finances so successfully that, despite the mismanagement of Lorenzo and his advisers, Florence enjoyed a brief period of prosperity. But when Pope Leo died and Giulio returned to Rome in the hope of being elected Pope himself – a hope realized in 1523 – he made the mistake of leaving Florence in the hands of the bastards, Ippolito and Alessandro de' Medici, as nominal leaders of the Medicean party. These two young men, the unprepossessing, swarthy and fuzzy-haired Alessandro, and the gregarious, extravagant and quarrelsome Ippolito, soon became as much disliked in Florence as Lorenzo, Duke of Urbino, had ever been.

★

When Cardinal Giulio de' Medici became Pope Clement VII at the age of forty-five, after the longest conclave in living memory, he dispatched Cardinal Silvio Passerini to Florence as his representative in the city and adviser to Ippolito and Alessandro. Cardinal Passerini was a grasping, charmless and ill-natured man who immediately aroused the dislike of the citizens. Joined in Florence by two other equally resented strangers foisted upon them by the authorities in Rome, Cardinal Innocenzo Cibò, Archbishop of Turin and Genoa, and Niccolò Ridolfi, he was soon in serious trouble. After an alarming riot in the city a report was sent to Rome by the Pope's confidential adviser, Francesco Guicciardini: 'In the short time I have been here I have seen a thousand things like [this riot], and they all derive from the ignorance of this eunuch [Passerini], who spends the whole day in idle gossip and neglects important matters . . . He does all he can to fill himself and everyone else with suspicion. He makes everyone despair; and has no idea himself what he is up to.'

Passerini's authority was short-lived. For months Pope Clement's vacillating and devious policy had been exasperating the Emperor Charles V, whose viceroy at Naples was eventually instructed to 'teach the Pope a lesson he would never forget'. Even more alarming threats had come from Germany, where the old warrior, Georg von Frundsberg, had assembled an army of *Landsknechte*, mostly Lutherans, fired with a missionary zeal to dispose of the Roman anti-Christ and with a no-less-intense desire to relieve him of his possessions. Swelled by large numbers of Spanish troops from Milan and soon to be joined by men from the estates of the Pope's inveterate enemy, Cardinal Pompeo Colonna, the Emperor's polyglot army of some 30,000 men marched upon Rome. The city came under attack on 6 May 1527 and the next day – after the Pope himself had run for safety to the massive Castel Sant'Angelo – it was sacked and its inhabitants murdered and mutilated with appalling ferocity.

The news of this catastrophe was greeted in Florence with the utmost excitement. The church bells were rung; bonfires blazed; crowds marched through the streets shouting anti-Medicean slogans. An effigy of the Medici Pope was hurled through the door of the church of Santissima Annunziata and torn to pieces in the piazza. Cardinal Passerini and his young charges, Alessandro and Ippolito, fled from the Medici Palace, on which someone had painted a picture of Pope Clement ascending a ladder to the gallows. In the time-honoured way a *Parlamento* was summoned and a Balìa elected; the *Maggior Consiglio* and the militia were re-established; and a respected anti-Medicean, Niccolò Capponi, whose father, Piero, had stood up so bravely to the French King Charles VIII, was appointed Gonfaloniere for a year.

The Pope was powerless to prevent or reverse this *coup d'état* in Florence. After months of incarceration, he had succeeded in escaping from the

Castel Sant'Angelo wearing the clothes of his major-domo. But he was still virtually a prisoner in the remote fastness of the episcopal palace at Orvieto – which could be reached only by a mule track from the valley of the Paglia – where he was endeavouring to rebuild his shattered power and reputation.

After characteristic hesitations and tergiversations, he had come to terms with the Emperor, who, on the understanding that the Pope would recognize imperial authority in Italy and crown him on his arrival there, agreed to return the Medici to Florence, if necessary by force.

SIEGE AND MURDER
1527–37

*'Everyone was beside himself with fright and bewilderment;
no one knew . . . what to do or where to go.'*
BENEDETTO VARCHI

Rather than risk an assault by foreign armies, several of the older citizens of Florence recommended appeasement and compromise. These included the Gonfaloniere, Niccolò Capponi, who, entering into secret negotiations with papal representatives, was summarily dismissed from office when these were discovered. He was replaced by Francesco Carducci, leader of the extreme anti–Medicean party whose members were now known as *arrabiati*, the name formerly given to the rabid opponents of Savonarola's theocracy. The idea of a surrender was, of course, rejected by the *arrabiati* as well as by the majority of the people, who urged the new government to take all necessary means to resist attack. The city's defences were accordingly strengthened and manned; ten thousand militiamen were called out; four thousand young citizens, previously excluded from the militia, were enrolled in sixteen companies. Money was voted for mercenaries; and a Perugian *condottiere*, Malatesta Baglioni, whose father had fought against the Medici, was appointed commander-in-chief. Several villas beyond the city walls which might have offered cover for advancing troops were demolished or turned into blockhouses; new strongpoints were built; and the ingenious Michelangelo, whose gifts were deemed to extend to a mastery of military engineering, was summoned to supervise the works of defence.

Michelangelo, whose statue of David outside the Palazzo della Signoria had been damaged in a recent riot,[1] was then at work in Florence on a Medici family chapel at San Lorenzo.[2] He had also been asked by the Medici to design a library at San Lorenzo.[3] He was, therefore, loth to take up his new duties when appointed procurator-general of the city's fortifications. He did go to Bologna and Ferrara to examine the fortifications there, made several drawings of proposed defences, and advised that the defences of Florence should be extended to circumvallate the hill of San

Miniato and that the belfry on the church should be protected from artillery fire by mattresses. But then, suspecting treachery and pleading that his life was in danger, he ran away to Venice by way of Ferrara, taking a large sum of money with him. Messengers were sent galloping after him and he was induced to return, his conduct being forgiven and attributed to artistic temperament. By the time the imperial forces, mostly Spanish, appeared before the walls of Florence in the early autumn of 1529, the defences of the city were almost complete.

The enemy army, commanded by a young adventurer in the Emperor's service, Philibert, Prince of Orange, was estimated as being 40,000 strong. Confident of a quick victory, some of the soldiers, so it was said, called out derisively, 'Get out your brocades, Florence. We are coming to measure them with our pikestaffs.' But the Prince of Orange held back from a direct assault: scouts reported the city's defences to be exceptionally strong; his soldiers, though numerous, were far from disciplined; the Florentines were clearly determined to resist; patrol after fighting patrol crept out into the *contado* bent upon keeping their supply routes open.

Many of these patrols were led by Francesco Ferrucci, who had sworn to keep the enemy at bay from the city of his birth. He was given the important command of the garrison at Empoli, a small fortified town on the Arno between Florence and Pisa; and from here, with ruthless energy, he directed operations against the besieging forces, hanging a messenger sent to him with a white flag of surrender. For months on end, inspired by Ferrucci's tireless efforts, the Florentines maintained their resistance; but by the summer of 1530 the former high spirits of the citizens had given way to gloom. Many families were on the verge of starvation; mice were sold for high prices in the market; there had been an outbreak of plague. 'Everyone was beside himself with fright and bewilderment,' recorded Benedetto Varchi; 'no one knew what to say any more, what to do or where to go. Some tried to escape, some to hide, some to seek refuge in the Palazzo della Signoria or in churches. Most of them merely entrusted themselves to God and awaited resignedly, from one hour to the next, not just death but death amidst the most horrid cruelties imaginable.'

Crowds marched through the streets shouting for bread, for surrender, for a return of the Medici as the only means of relief from their present miseries. The Perugian commander, Malatesta Baglioni, though he still rode about the streets with the word *Libertas* embroidered on his hat, was already conducting secret negotiations with the enemy. And then, on 3 August 1530, Francesco Ferrucci was captured by Spanish troops in the mountains near Pistoia and hacked to death in the piazza of the village of Gavinana.[4]

A week later a delegation of Florentine citizens agreed to the terms of surrender demanded by the Emperor and the Pope. Although they provided for the payment of a massive indemnity and the handing over of fifty hostages until the money was paid, the terms imposed upon the Florentines were not unduly harsh. Once Medici rule had been re-established under papal authority in Florence, however, those who had opposed it in the past were treated with the greatest severity.

Various leaders of the anti-papal party were executed after torture. Many other opponents of the new regime were imprisoned or banished from Florence for life. Many others went into voluntary exile; and some went into hiding in Florence. One of these was Michelangelo, who, with the help of one of the canons, seems to have concealed himself for two months in the Medici Chapel at San Lorenzo, where drawings attributed to him can still be seen on the walls.[5]

Francesco Guicciardini, who had left the city for Rome on the approach of the imperial army and had now returned as papal representative, considered the punishments inflicted upon the opponents of the Pope and the Medici only just. He found Florence devastated by her people's resistance and all the houses for many miles around Florence, his own villa among many, destroyed. Indeed, 'in many towns of the Florentine dominion the peasant population was immeasurably decreased and the common folk disappeared entirely'. Only a strong government, Guicciardini believed, could restore the damage; and that government must now be exercised by the nineteen-year-old Alessandro de' Medici, to whose service he was assigned as legal adviser.

At first, following his mentors' advice, Alessandro was a firm but not tyrannical ruler. He was created a duke but, in deference to the republican traditions of Florence, he agreed to consult the city's councils and to listen to their advice. After the death of his supposed father, the Pope, however, he abandoned all pretence of constitutional rule, indulging his taste for authoritarian decrees and outraging the citizens not only by his sexual escapades and his constant public quarrels with his cousin, Ippolito, but also by his repeated provocation of republican idealists. He now made a mere show of consulting the councils and committees which had been set up to replace the old government of Gonfaloniere and *priori*. He ordered the construction of an immense new fortress, the Fortezza da Basso, a forbidding symbol of despotism on which three thousand workers from the *contado* were put to work, given their meals and lodging but no wages;[6] and he saw to it that the guns of this fort could be as easily trained upon the citizens of Florence as upon a foreign invader. He had his coat of arms carved prominently over the gateway of the recently enlarged fort at the Porta alla Giustizia. He issued instructions for the impounding of all weapons in private hands, even those which were hung as votive offerings in churches; and he had the great bell of the Palazzo della Signoria, which was sent crashing down into the piazza to symbolize the death of the old republic, melted down and recast as medals glorifying the Medici family.

Reluctant to rise up against him for fear lest another imperial army should be sent against them, the Florentines rested their forlorn hopes in Ippolito, so constantly at odds with Alessandro, and now a cardinal. Before he could intercede on their behalf with the Emperor, however, Ippolito died at Itri of what was said to be malaria, but many naturally believed was poisoning.

There were others, though, only too willing to take Ippolito de' Medici's place in presenting the case against Alessandro at Charles V's court. One of these, an exile from Florence, was Jacopo Nardi, who had been one of Savonarola's leading supporters and whose *Istorie della città di Firenze* was harshly critical of the Medici. His native city, he told the Emperor, had now become a place of terror and repression, in which men went in daily fear of their lives and women were in constant danger of dishonour, a city overawed by a 'great fortress, built with the blood of her unhappy people as a prison and slaughterhouse'.

Francesco Guicciardini, speaking to the Emperor on Alessandro's behalf, strongly rebutted these charges, concluding his address, at once evasive and high-flown, with the totally misleading words, 'One cannot reply in detail to the accusations of rape and similar calumnies uttered in general; but His Excellency's virtue, his fame, the opinion of him held throughout the city, of his prudence, of his virtuous habits, are a sufficient reply.'

Although he had promised 'to do what was just', this was more in line with what the Emperor wished to be told. He declined to accept the exiles' charges and authorized the resumption of preparations for the marriage of his fourteen-year-old natural daughter, Margaret, to the exonerated Duke Alessandro de' Medici. The Duke, however, had not long to live.

The boon companion of his dissipations and frolics in the recent past had been a distant cousin, three years younger than himself, Lorenzino de' Medici. Lorenzino was a strange young man, thin, remote and unpredictable. He had left Rome with a reputation for wild behaviour when drunk, and in Florence he had soon become a familiar and detested figure as he galloped through the streets with Alessandro, often on the same horse, sometimes wearing women's clothes, shouting insults at the passers-by. It was said that the two men occasionally shared a bed; it was certain that they went whoring together and that Lorenzino acted as his cousin's pimp. It was also clear that Lorenzino resented Alessandro's power and rank, and that he longed to achieve fame or, failing that, notoriety himself. He decided to do so by tyrannicide.

Since Alessandro was usually surrounded by guards, the assassination would have to be carefully planned, the victim unprepared, alone and unarmed. Lorenzino arranged this in his familiar role as pimp, offering to bring to his house a Florentine lady of exceptional beauty and virtue who was unaccountably fond of an aged and uninteresting husband. The conquest of such a woman would be a triumph of seduction. Alessandro was accordingly induced to wait in Lorenzino's house for the arrival of this paragon while his guards were left outside. He took off his breastplate, undressed, lay on a bed and was almost asleep when Lorenzino and a hired assassin burst into the room and plunged their daggers into his stomach and neck. Spattered with blood, Lorenzino then galloped away to Venice by way of Bologna, his hand, from which Alessandro had almost bitten off a finger in the attack, encased in a glove.

It was not until the next morning that Alessandro's guard asked how much longer they were expected to wait outside Lorenzino's house, not until that evening that Alessandro's body was found, and not until the following day that the murder became known to the opponents of the regime. By then the *palleschi*, supporters of the Medici, led by Cardinal Cibò and Francesco Guicciardini, were in full control of the city. Alessandro Vitelli, the captain of the Duke's bodyguard, who had been away from the city with several of his men when the murder was committed, had now returned to Florence; and Machiavelli's distinguished friend Francesco Vettori, who might have inspired a successful anti-Medicean revolt had he known of the intended assassination, now accepted that the time for such an uprising had passed. When approached by a party of would-be revolutionaries, he contented himself with expressions of vague support and then left for Guicciardini's house to throw in his lot with the *palleschi*.

A meeting of the *palleschi* was held next morning in the Palazzo della Signoria, now more generally known as the Palazzo Vecchio. Cardinal Cibò proposed that Alessandro's illegitimate four-year-old son, Giulio, should be created Duke with the cardinal himself as regent. This answer to the succession naturally did not recommend itself to others of the *palleschi* present. Guicciardini had another candidate to suggest. This was Cosimo de' Medici, a direct descendant of Giovanni di Bicci. His mother was Maria Salviati, Lorenzo il Magnifico's granddaughter and it was in the Palazzo Salviati in Via del Corso that Cosimo had been born.[7] His father was Giovanni di Giovanni de' Medici, known as Giovanni delle Bande Nere, a courageous warrior who had been mortally wounded while attempting to halt the march of Georg von Frundsberg's *Landsknechte* on Rome. His great-uncle, Pope Leo X, had stood as his godfather and it was at his suggestion that he had been christened Cosimo, 'to revive the memory of the wisest, the bravest and most prudent man yet born to the House of Medici'.

Cosimo was at that time a politically inexperienced seventeen-year-old youth and Guicciardini had selfish reasons for adopting him as his candidate, since he hoped to marry him to one of his daughters and thus rule Florence in his name. But Cosimo had personal qualities that recommended him to leading *palleschi* other than Guicciardini. He was tall, good-looking and athletic, and although patchily educated during a boyhood of constant travelling, knowledgeable and acute.

Even so there were several *palleschi* who opposed his selection. One of these, Palla Rucellai, declared that he 'wanted neither dukes nor lords nor princes in this republic' and, picking up a white bean to throw into the urn on the table, added, 'Here is my vote and here is my head!'

So the argument continued; Guicciardini, who had already taken it upon himself to summon his protégé to Florence from his villa Il Trebbio in the Mugello, angrily protested that he would never again tolerate 'a mob of *ciompi*' getting the upper hand in Florence, while others maintained that a ruler of more experience than the youthful Cosimo ought to be found. Eventually the inconclusive discussions were brought to a sudden end by the intervention of Alessandro Vitelli, captain of the guard, who had been won over to Guicciardini's side by the promise that he would be made lord of Borgo San Sepolcro, once Cosimo had been installed as Duke. Instigating a noisy scuffle beneath the windows of the room where the meeting was taking place, Vitelli induced his soldiers to shout, 'Cosimo! Cosimo! Cosimo! Cosimo, the son of the great Giovanni, for Duke of Florence!' Vitelli himself called out, 'Hurry up! Hurry up! The soldiers can't be controlled any longer.'

The discussion was over; and Cosimo de' Medici entered upon his family's great inheritance.

THE GRAND DUKE
COSIMO I
1537–74

*'It was said of him in Florence that
he doffs and dons the Duke whenever he pleases.'*
THE VENETIAN ENVOY

'They have mounted a man on a splendid horse – then told him he must not ride beyond certain boundaries,' commented Benvenuto Cellini, that most versatile, most quarrelsome and boastful of Florentines, who, having fulfilled several commissions for Pope Clement VII and others for Alessandro de' Medici, was now living in Rome. 'Just tell me who is going to restrain him when he wants to ride beyond them? You can't impose laws on a man who is your master.' At first, though, Cosimo de' Medici was far from being master. While recognized as Alessandro's heir, he was not yet given the title of duke and was required to act in association with what were referred to as certain 'magnificent counsellors'. Moreover, the military commander, Alessandro Vitelli, had occupied the Fortezza da Basso, taking there with him both Cardinal Cibò and his little charge, Alessandro de' Medici's illegitimate son, Giulio, together with Alessandro's widow and most of the treasures which Vitelli's soldiers had looted from the Medici Palace.

Cosimo's 'magnificent counsellors', Francesco Guicciardini and Francesco Vettori and the other leading *palleschi*, soon discovered how masterful Duke Cosimo could be, how vain were their hopes of ruling Florence in his name, how unlikely it was that he would, as Benedetto Varchi put it, 'devote himself to enjoyment and employ himself in hunting, fowling and fishing (sports wherein he greatly delighted) whilst Guicciardini and a few others would govern and, as the saying goes, suck the state dry'.

Secretive and cold in manner, brusque to the point of asperity, often so ungracious as to appear gratuitously insulting, the young Duke trusted no one. He permitted the various councils of the state to remain in existence but, convinced that 'no two Florentines ever contrive to agree about anything', he allowed them little real authority. He listened quietly to the advice his mother and his gifted secretary, Francesco Campana, gave him, but he made up his own mind and kept his feelings hidden even from them. Francesco Vettori eventually faded into the background; Guicciardini retired to his villa to revise his monumental *Storia d'Italia*; Vitelli was dismissed and went off sulkily to Rome; while Cardinal Cibò, having spread rumours in Florence that Cosimo had employed a poisoner to murder the little boy Giulio, was also sent packing from the city.

Cosimo dispatched his other enemies with a ruthlessness which apparently left him quite unmoved. In July 1537 at Montemurlo, near Prato, he routed an army raised by *fuorusciti*, exiles from Florence plotting his overthrow, then had sixteen leaders of the captured rebels, several of them young men from Florence's leading families, paraded before him. They were beheaded one after the other in the Piazza della Signoria on four consecutive days. Other defeated rebels died in prison; yet others were tracked down and murdered in foreign cities. Lorenzino de' Medici, Alessandro's murderer, who had published his *Apologia*, a justification of tyrannicide, was stabbed to death with a poisoned dagger on a bridge in Venice.

In Florence, opposition to Cosimo's regime was savagely punished. Troublemakers were removed from the city to the fearful dungeons of Volterra or quickly assassinated. Even the Dominicans, accused of making 'public professions of dissent', were expelled from San Marco on political grounds.

To their sad objections, the Duke protested, 'Tell me, fathers, who built this monastery? Was it you?'

'No.'

'Who put you in this monastery then?'

'Our ancient Florentines, and Cosimo the Elder of blessed memory.'

'Right. Well, it's the modern Florentines and Cosimo the Duke who are kicking you out.'

Celebrations were held in Florence after Cosimo's victory over the *fuorusciti* at Montemurlo – loaves of bread were thrown to the crowds from the windows of the Palazzo Medici and wine poured out from fountains. There were similar festivities when, after a lengthy and enormously expensive war, the loss of many lives and the devastation of its *contado*, the Duke was at last acknowledged as master of Siena. The bells were rung once again, cannon roared and bonfires were lit when in 1569 Cosimo became Grand Duke of Tuscany. Yet, as an observer noticed, there was 'little real joy to be discerned in the faces of the people'.

In the early months of the Duke's reign he had enjoyed the support of large numbers of the lower classes, who had hoped for more prosperous days under a new regime. He had been supported, too, by the members of a reconstituted militia and by several of Florence's most patrician families;

but, as the years passed, much of this support withered away. He was certainly not a man to cultivate it. Increasingly withdrawn as he grew older, and often sunk in impenetrable gloom, he was rarely seen to smile or to take any evident pleasure in life except when hunting. On occasion he seemed to welcome overtures of friendliness, even familiarity; but then, as a Venetian envoy noticed, he would suddenly turn away with 'his accustomed severity, so much so that it was said of him in Florence that he doffs and dons the Duke whenever he pleases'. Only with his wife, and with his daughters when they were young, did he seem to be at ease. Indeed he appeared to be devoted to his wife, Eleonora di Toledo, the extremely rich daughter of the Spanish viceroy at Naples, though she was as demanding as he was himself, capricious, arrogant and extravagant.

He lived in constant fear of assassination, marching about the city surrounded by his Swiss bodyguard, with a sword and dagger hanging from his belt, wearing a coat of mail under his jerkin and 'with numerous small *stiletti*, with very sharp points, almost as fine as needles, stuck into the lining of his scabbard'. His precautions were justified: several attempts were made upon his life, despite the punishments inflicted upon the would-be assassins, one of whom was tortured with red-hot pincers, dragged round the streets by his ankles, disembowelled and then hurled into the Arno.

Yet towards the end of Duke Cosimo's life it was grudgingly conceded that he had earned a high reputation in Italy, that he had won the people's respect, if not their love, that he had not ignored the interests of the lower classes, and that his rule, tyrannical though it was, had not been altogether unjust and had certainly been efficient. It was also acknowledged that Florence's finances were sound and her government stable, and that – although taxes were heavy and ducal monopolies were used unscrupulously in private trading – farming and irrigation in Tuscany had been much improved, canals had been built, silver mines and olive plantations promoted. The state, under the Duke's careful and industrious guidance, had acquired a creditable fleet, whose galleys had not only protected the shores of Tuscany from Turkish marauders and Barbary pirates but had also played a prominent part in sweeping the Turkish navy from the eastern Mediterranean in the battle of Lepanto in 1571.

Expecting nothing from the 'despicable' Archbishop of Florence, Andrea Buondelmonti – who had paid himself back for the price of his office by selling pardons for breaches of the Lenten fast and was generally regarded as absurd as well as corrupt after preaching a sermon in which he heatedly complained that a pair of his stockings had been stolen – Cosimo set himself the task of trying to make the Church as efficient as the state and cleansing it of such offensive accretions as the canons of San Lorenzo, dirty and lazy, who had allowed Michelangelo's statues to be discoloured by smoke from the fires of charcoal burners.

Duke Cosimo was also given credit in Florence for having encouraged and patronized the traditional popular entertainments of the citizens – their feasts and pageants, their horse-races and their games of football – and for having added to their number by inaugurating chariot races in the Piazza Santa Maria Novella where obelisks still mark the turning-points of their course.[1]

The Duke was, moreover, known to take a far more than passing interest in music and science, in archaeology and agriculture, in horticulture and botany. He was largely responsible for the improvement and enlargement of Florence's herb gardens and for the introduction into Tuscany of medicinal plants from America and of farm crops from the Orient. He was an active member of the fraternity of San Martino – an organization pledged to give help to the deserving poor – as well as a generous benefactor of the Confraternity of the Misericordia,[2] of the Studio Fiorentino and of Pisa University. He was also a connoisseur and collector of medals and artefacts of Etruscan workmanship. He regularly visited the workshops of Florence's painters and sculptors to see their work in progress and to assure them of his interest in it. He also called upon writers and scholars to assure them of his support and to encourage them to advise their friends to come to work in Florence, as the aged historian Paolo Giovio did, after much persuasion by Cosimo himself.

While never a friend of artists in the manner of Cosimo il Vecchio, he was undoubtedly an open-handed and discerning patron. He tried to get the Venetian painter, Titian, to come to work in Florence and Michelangelo to return there; he commissioned work from Niccolò Pericoli, Il Tribolo, from the grumpy, grasping Baccio Bandinelli,[3] and from the lonely and withdrawn Jacopo Pontormo, one of the earliest of Florentine Mannerists, who may have been apprenticed to Leonardo da Vinci and who had certainly been employed in the workshop of Andrea del Sarto. He commissioned both portraits and allegorical pictures from the 'sweet, courteous' Agnolo Tori di Cosimo di Mariano, known as Il Bronzino, whose portrait of the Duke's wife, Eleonora, with their son, Giovanni, is one of the finest examples of Mannerist portraiture and whose portrait of the wary-looking, mournful Duke himself hangs in the Uffizi.

The Duke also encouraged Benvenuto Cellini, who returned to Florence in 1545, and commissioned from him Cellini's two best-known sculptures, the bronze *Perseus* in the Loggia dei Lanzi and the huge bust of Cosimo in the Bargello.[4] The Duke also commissioned work from Giambologna, the Mannerist sculptor who settled in Florence in 1557 and remained there for the rest of his life, executing numerous works for the Medici family, including the fine equestrian bronze of Duke Cosimo in the Piazza della Signoria, several delightful pieces of garden sculpture, and the colossal *Appennino* for the Medici villa at Pratolino.[5] Giambologna was responsible,

Eleonora of Toledo (1522 – 62), wife of the Grand Duke Cosimo I, and their son, Giovanni; a portrait by Bronzino in the Uffizi.

too, for some of the bronzes in the Neptune Fountain which was commissioned for the Piazza della Signoria from Bartolommeo Ammannati, yet another sculptor drawn to Florence by the work to be had there in Duke Cosimo's time.[6]

Architect as well as sculptor, Ammannati was asked by Duke Cosimo to rebuild the Ponte Santa Trinita after the devastating floods of 1557 as well as the Ponte alla Carraia, and, having reconstructed the Palazzo Giugni[7] on the corner of Via dei Cerchi,[8] to enlarge the already immense Pitti Palace for the ducal family.

The Duke and Duchess lived at first in the Medici Palace, which they then made over to their daughter, Isabella, whose husband, the violent and vindictive Paolo Giordano Orsini, having fallen in love with someone else, later strangled her with a rope which accomplices let down to him through a hole in the ceiling as he made a pretence of kissing her passionately. After leaving the Palazzo Medici her parents lived for a time in the Palazzo della Signoria, which they transformed into a ducal palace with apartments for the Duchess on the upper floors, for the Duke on the lower, and for the by then irritatingly fussy and untidy Duke's mother, Maria, on the floor

A bronze relief by Giambologna believed to have been presented by Prince Francesco de' Medici to his prospective brother-in-law, the Emperor Maximilian II, in 1565. The iconography is complex and obscure, but it is supposed that it refers to the plans for the marriage of Prince Francesco into the imperial household.

between.[9] The Duchess was not happy, however, in the Palazzo della Signoria, where, in place of a garden, she had to be content with a small enclosed terrace for her flowers and rare plants. In 1549, therefore, she bought the Pitti Palace and moved into it some years later, though builders were still at work in the courtyard and on the new windows on the ground floor of the façade, while the extensive gardens behind the palace resembled a building site.

These gardens, which stretched south to the heights of San Giorgio and almost as far west as the Porta Romana, had been bought from several families, including the Bogoli, and it was by a corrupt form of their name, Boboli, that the gardens were henceforth to be known. Within a few months of the Duchess's purchase of the Pitti Palace, Tribolo was employed as landscape architect and, after his death in 1550, the work was carried on by Ammannati, Giulio and Alfonso Parigi, and by Baccio Bandinelli, who designed an elaborate rustic grotto here, the Grotticina di Madama, at the Duchess's suggestion.[10]

By the time this grotto was finished, the Duchess was in failing health, losing her interest in splendid clothes and jewellery in which she had formerly delighted, suffering, so the Venetian ambassador reported, from a chronic cough, 'and every morning bringing up her food'. She died in her husband's arms, 'grieving and despairing, refusing to be guided by physicians as was her wont'.

The Duke, already deeply distressed by the death of two young sons and of his favourite daughter, was inconsolable. He tried to overcome his grief by hunting more vigorously than ever and by eating huge meals, his plate piled high with onions and garlic. He shut himself away, refusing to be comforted, eventually taking a young mistress, by whom he had a son, then marrying another young woman whom he soon found to be as ill-tempered as she was demanding. He escaped from her company as often as he could, to spend evenings with his one surviving daughter at the Medici Palace. One evening he had an apoplectic fit there, and died, worn out at fifty-five, on 21 April 1574, having long since delegated most of his duties to his eldest son and heir, Francesco.

PAGEANTS
AND PLEASURES
1560–1765

'I live in Florence in an excellent coole terrene,
eate good melons, drink wholsome wines, look upon
excellent devout pictures, heer choyse musique.'
SIR TOBIE MATTHEW

Soon after his arrival in Florence, Duke Cosimo had begun to consider the possibility of housing the city's scattered judicial and administrative offices, as well as the headquarters of its leading guilds, under one roof close to the Palazzo della Signoria where he could keep a close watch on their activities.

He had it in mind to erect a magnificent building. The Palazzo had already been remodelled and the piazza, now known as the Piazza del Granduca, repaved; the Mercato Nuovo, popularly known as the Porcellino, had been completed to the design of Giovanni Battista del Tasso in 1551;[1] and much new building had been carried out in the suburbs and along the river front. Encouraged by Cosimo, several richer families, the Strozzi, the Uguccioni[2] and the Ricasoli among them, had improved or reconstructed their palaces; and several new palaces had appeared on the Oltrarno in Via Maggio.[3]

For his new offices, Duke Cosimo considered the most suitable site to be a long strip of land which ran down to the Arno from the Palazzo. It was, of course, covered with buildings already: the city's old mint stood on part of the site;[4] so did the church of San Pier Scheraggio, then one of the largest churches in Florence;[5] also here were several houses belonging to the Arte della Seta and many smaller dwellings in private hands. But nothing was to be allowed to stand in the way of the Duke's new offices. Objections that the sandy nature of the soil would present intractable problems in the construction of so large a building were brushed aside: iron would have to be used extensively as a reinforcement. The architect chosen to design the Uffizi, as the long U-shaped building came to be known, was Giorgio Vasari, the first edition of whose celebrated work, *Le vite dei più eccellenti*

1 self-portrait by Giorgio Vasari (1511–74), biographer and architect of the Uffizi, where this picture hangs.

pittori, scultori ed architetti italiani, had been published ten years before in 1550.[6]

A native of the Tuscan town of Arezzo, where his father was in a modest way of business, Giorgio had been sent as a boy to Florence to study with Michelangelo and later with Andrea del Sarto and Baccio Bandinelli. He had found a patron in Duke Alessandro de' Medici, and, after the Duke's assassination, he had left Florence to work successfully for other patrons elsewhere. Returning to Florence in 1555 he had soon established himself as Duke Cosimo's artistic adviser, the busy impresario of ducal ceremonies

and entertainments, director of a large school of assistants, one of the
founders of the Accademia del Disegno,[7] and creator or supervisor of a
large body of work in Florence, much of it uninspired. He was responsible
for the remodelling of the interiors of the church of Ognissanti and of
Santa Croce, where he designed the tomb of his hero, Michelangelo.[8] He
worked on the decoration of the dome of Santa Maria del Fiore and on
several of the enormous fresco cycles in the Palazzo della Signoria, where
he designed the Studiolo di Francesco I for Duke Cosimo's son and heir.[9]
And it was for Francesco's bride, the Archduchess Joanna of Austria, sister
of the Emperor Maximilian II, that he supervised the decoration of the
cortile of the Palazzo della Signoria, himself painting some of the views of
Austrian cities in the lunettes. He also designed the fountain in the centre
of the courtyard, and made the copy of Verrocchio's delightful putto
holding a dolphin, the original of which was brought down to the palace
from the Medici villa at Careggi.

Anxious as her father-in-law had been to make her feel at home, and
spectacular as were the pageants and entertainments given to celebrate her
marriage to Francesco, Joanna, longing for Austria and feeling unwell,
never settled down in Florence, where the people condemned her for what
they took to be her gloomy hauteur and her husband virtually ignored her,
spending as much time as he could with his mistress, Bianca Cappello, a
most attractive Venetian woman for whom he built the charming Villa
Pratolino which so impressed Montaigne,[10] and to whose complaisant
husband he gave a lucrative court appointment as well as a *palazzo* in
Via Maggio.[11] 'According to the Italians [Bianca Cappello] is beautiful,'
commented Montaigne, who was invited to dinner in November 1580.
'She has an agreeable and imposing face, and large breasts, the way they
like them here. She certainly seems capable of having bewitched [the Grand
Duke] and of being able to maintain his devotion.'

Francesco was a taciturn man, graceless and parsimonious, as withdrawn
as his father, though with none of his father's commanding presence.
He was of 'low stature,' the Venetian ambassador reported, 'thin, dark-
complexioned and of a melancholy disposition'.

Florentines, however, had cause to be grateful to him. Their Duke since
the death of Cosimo in 1574 – and Grand Duke since 1576 by imperial
proclamation – he succeeded in keeping Tuscany out of the wars then
raging in Europe and, while spending lavishly upon his own interests and
pleasures, was generous in his benefactions to the state. He founded the
Accademia della Crusca which, dedicated to the study of the Italian language and to the compilation of a Tuscan dictionary, still occupies premises
in the Medici Villa di Castello.[12] On the third floor of the Uffizi – which
had been completed by Bernardo Buontalenti and Alfonso Parigi after

Vasari's death – he created an art gallery, established studios for young artists and workshops for craftsmen, and commissioned from Buontalenti the splendid octagonal Tribuna for the display of treasures from the Medici collections, among them later the Medici Venus, formerly in the Villa Medici in Rome,[13] and a magnificent table in *pietre dure*, a craft in which Francesco took exceptional interest.[14]

Indeed, the Grand Duke Francesco appeared to take more interest in gem-setting and crystal-cutting, in chemistry and alchemy, in glass-blowing and the manufacture of fireworks, in imitation jewellery and porcelain, in feeding his pet reindeer and potting his exotic plants than he did in the process of government. Towards the end of his life he held meetings of his ministers in the laboratory which Vasari had built for him in the Palazzo della Signoria, rather than interrupt his experiments.

His brother, Ferdinando I, who succeeded him in 1587, was far more affable and gregarious than Francesco, more deeply concerned with affairs of state and the well-being of the Florentine citizens, with whom he became the most popular of the later Medici. He promoted commerce and agriculture; he founded hospitals; in an annual and enjoyable ceremony at San Lorenzo he distributed dowries to poor girls who might otherwise have had difficulty in finding husbands; and, after a disastrous flood in 1589, he personally presented baskets of food to the victims of the catastrophe, making a dangerous journey in a small boat to riverside villages to bring promises of help to the stricken inhabitants.

Appointed a cardinal at the age of fourteen, he had renounced the purple in order to succeed to the grand dukedom, and in 1589 had married Catherine de' Medici's plain though agreeable granddaughter, Christine of Lorraine, welcoming her to Florence with a splendour of pageantry to emphasize the reversal of the pro-Spanish policies of a brother whom he had much disliked.

For days on end architects and sculptors, painters and carpenters had been at work on the construction and decoration of a series of magnificent triumphal arches through which the French bride was to pass. Hundreds of other artists and craftsmen, mechanics, rope-makers and pyrotechnists had been busy preparing all manner of scenic devices for the performances to be held in the Pitti Palace and the Boboli Gardens: exploding volcanoes and streams of devils emerging from hell, dragons breathing fire and clouds carrying flights of angels to heaven. Cooks had been planning banquets, musicians, dancers and actors rehearsing ballets, plays and productions of the new *dramma per musica*. Niccolò Gaddi had been placed in charge of *le invenzioni*, Piero Angelio de Barga appointed to write appropriate verses. Alessandro Allori was one of many painters whose talents had been employed upon the creation of huge canvases.

The first triumphal arch was adorned with statuary and with immense paintings celebrating the heroic and largely fanciful early history of Florence; the second paid homage to the greatness of the Medici and of the French royal family, a vast picture of Catherine de' Medici presiding over all like a goddess of fertility. Other arches proclaimed the virtues of various members of the House of Medici and of the Houses of Lorraine and Valois, paid tribute to Florentine victories on land and sea, and to the triumph of Lepanto, glorified Tuscany and the Grand Dukes who had restored her to the ancient purity of monarchical rule, and, above all, glorified the Florence of the Medici, 'its coming to honour and greatness,' in the words of Niccolò Gaddi, 'its coming to its supreme height, and to a royal state'.

'In this way,' Sir Roy Strong commented,

> by means of allegorical tableaux and subtle juxtaposition of historical personages, the Medici family, who less than a hundred years before had been one of many rich mercantile families within Florence, was presented as the heirs of ancient kings, as the equals of the house of Valois, as the preordained saviours of Florence, whose republican period was now viewed as an imperfection and prelude to the perfect rule of Medici autocracy.

For three weeks the celebrations continued. There were fêtes and *intermezzi*, concerts by musicians of the grand-ducal chapel, firework displays, river pageants and exhibitions of animal baiting. There were games of football in the courtyard of the Pitti Palace, which was afterwards flooded to a depth of five feet for representations of naval battles; and there were astonishing spectacles in the Boboli Gardens where, for one production alone, over fifty tailors were employed in the making of 286 elaborate costumes.

Celebrations as lavish and exotic as these also attended the wedding of the Grand Duke Ferdinand's niece, Maria, to Henry of Navarre, whose triumph over the Catholic League, and accession to the French throne as Henry IV, owed much to Medici money. Again there were processions and pageants, firework displays and water fêtes. Bonfires burned in the piazzas; the bells rang; cannon thundered from the fortresses; and in the square before the Palazzo Pitti fountains spurted wine. There were performances at the theatre in the Uffizi where there were marvellously inventive productions of Giulio Caccini's *Il rapimento di Cefalo*, with settings by Buontalenti, and of *L'Euridice* by Jacopo Peri, whose now lost *Daphne* has been called the first opera. On the day of the marriage, 5 October 1600, a stupendous banquet was given in the Palazzo Vecchio, where each extravagantly decorated dish formed part of a fantastic allegory on the martial brilliance of the French King and the outstanding virtues of the Medici family into which he had so wisely and auspiciously married.

The Grand Duke Ferdinando also lavished money on less ephemeral delights. He made many improvements at the Pitti Palace and in the Boboli Gardens, enlarged the Uffizi and augmented its collection; he brought many of the classical statues he had collected in Rome to Florence, six of them (of Roman women) being placed inside the Loggia dei Lanzi. He bought numerous manuscripts for the Medici library; he continued his father's patronage of Giambologna, whose last work was the equestrian statue in the Piazza Santissima Annunziata;[15] and installed the sculptor in the Palazzo Bellini in Borgo Pinti, where the Grand Duke's bust was placed over the door.[16] He commissioned Buontalenti to construct the Forte di Belvedere, the great fortress overlooking the city on the heights of San Giorgio,[17] and he spent an enormous sum on a huge and highly intricate gilded sphere which is now in the Palazzo dei Giudici with several other globes, astrolabes and clocks, Michelangelo's compasses and Galileo's instruments.[18]

At the time of the Grand Duke Ferdinando's marriage to Christine of Lorraine, Galileo Galilei was twenty-five years old. He had been born in Pisa in 1564, the son of a musician, the descendant of a noble Florentine family. Entering the University of Pisa as a medical student after an early education at the monastery of Vallombrosa near Florence, he had soon abandoned medicine for mathematics and physics, but had been withdrawn from the university before taking a degree because his father could no longer afford the fees. For a time he supported himself by giving lectures in Florence; but he had so exasperated his colleagues and superiors by his constant questioning of their assertions, his irritating presumption, his sarcasm and quick temper, that he was not expected to rise far in the academic world. Even so he became a professor at Pisa, and in 1592, by then well known for various revolutionary scientific treatises, he was given a chair at Padua. Some years later he demonstrated his telescope at Rome. By then, however, he had offended and alarmed the ecclesiastical authorities, as well as his less enlightened colleagues, by his defence of Copernican theory in contradiction of the Scriptures and by his ability to expound his theories in clear, concise Italian understandable by all intelligent men. It was at this stage in his career that he was invited by Ferdinando's son, Cosimo, who had once been a pupil of his at Padua, to come to Florence as 'First Philosopher and Mathematician' to the Grand Duke of Tuscany. Grateful for this opportunity to continue his studies and experiments under the Grand Duke's protection, Galileo moved, as the Medici's guest, to a house in Bellosguardo near Florence and, having discovered the satellites of Jupiter, repaid his patron's kindness by naming them Sidera Medicea. Intermittently in trouble with the Church thereafter, he was summoned to Rome to answer charges formulated by the Inquisition, the Jesuits having insisted that his theories would have worse consequences for the Church than 'Luther and Calvin put together'. Found guilty, his sentence was commuted by the Pope and in 1633 he was allowed to return under house arrest to Tuscany. Here he spent the last eight years of his life on a small estate at Arcetri, where he may have received a visit from John Milton, who spent two months in Florence in 1638. On his death, the Church forbade any memorial being erected to Galileo's memory; but the Medici arranged for him to be buried in the Novices' Chapel at Santa Croce, the church which is the burying place of so many of Florence's most distinguished citizens, Ghiberti, Michelangelo and Machiavelli among them.[19]

The Grand Duke Ferdinando I had long since died when Galileo was buried. So too had his son, Cosimo II, whose short reign was marked by little of importance or interest other than his kindness to Galileo, his final closure of the Medici bank as a commercial enterprise no longer appropriate to grand-ducal rank, and the celebrations held to mark his marriage to the Archduchess Maria Maddalena, the highlight of which was an astonishing performance of the *Argonautica* given on the Arno and involving galleys, giant dolphins, fire-spitting hydra and tempestuous seas.

Cosimo's son, Ferdinando II, who entered upon his inheritance in 1621, was as indolent and placatory as his father, anxious to please everyone and to offend no one, declining, for example, to advance his claim to Urbino on the abdication of the childless Duke Francesco Maria II, and allowing the duchy to become part of the Papal States. His portrait by the Flemish-born court painter, Justus Sustermans, shows him in an unconvincingly commanding pose, gazing from the canvas through soft and heavy-lidded eyes, with full Habsburg red lips beneath a bulbous nose and a theatrical black moustache, waxed and curled. He was rather fat and most good-natured, fond of hunting, fishing and playing bowls – provided he was allowed to win – and more attracted to the young men about his court than to his wife, Vittoria della Rovere, a prim and interfering woman, who, having come upon him fondling a page, precipitated a quarrel that was to last intermittently for years.

Her portrait by Carlo Dolci is of an exceptionally plain woman, at once disdainful and wary, a cross on her breast, a prayer-book between plump fingers. One of the main disagreements between them was about the education of their eldest son, who was to succeed his father as Cosimo III in 1670. The father would have liked him to be given a modern education with due attention paid to the scientific discoveries of which the Medici were now traditional patrons; his mother insisted that he be taught by priests in the old-fashioned way. As was to be expected, the Grand Duchess's views prevailed, with sad results for Florence.

The Grand Duchess, regarded as a busybody and an interloper with an unseemly reverence for the Holy See, was never liked in Florence; but her husband was too easy-going and good-humoured to be unpopular. The people approved of the unpretentious way he had wicker-covered bottles

A bust in pietre dure *of Vittoria della Rovere, wife of the Grand Duke Ferdinando II; she died in 1693 at the age of seventy-two. This work, now in the Conservatorio della Quiete, is by Giuseppe Antonio Torricelli, who described it as 'the first life-sized hardstone portrait ever made'.*

hung over the gate of the Pitti Palace, indicating that wine could be bought there in the same way as from other lesser palaces in the city; and they remembered with gratitude that, as a young man of twenty, he had remained in Florence in 1630 during an outbreak of plague when others who could afford it had fled.

This plague had been a terrifying calamity. Victims had developed a sudden high fever and racking headaches followed by the eruption of immense, evil-smelling boils, and then delirium. The dead were carried away in carts, with tinkling bells warning the people not to approach. The corpses were then tipped into common graves round which fences were erected to protect the gravediggers from ravenous dogs. All manner of precautions were taken to prevent the spread of the pestilence: coins were rinsed in tubs of vinegar; streets were regularly swept and washed; houses fumigated, floors scrubbed; the mattresses of the dead and their very beds were thrown on to bonfires. People starved themselves, purged themselves, washed themselves in water boiled with herbs, rubbed their skins with the venom of trapped snakes. Masses were said in the piazzas for those who dared not venture into the churches. Sacred relics were paraded through the streets and prayers were offered up for deliverance. Yet, month after month, the pestilence persisted, and before it was over in 1633 at least seven thousand Florentines had perished.

Commending his behaviour during this plague, the Florentines also recognized that while not much of a connoisseur himself and readier no doubt to spend money on plays at the theatre in Via della Pergola[20] – and on masques, *tableaux vivants*, costume parades, ballets on horseback and musical pageants in the Boboli Gardens – the Grand Duke Ferdinando II, encouraged by his brothers, Gian Carlo and Leopoldo, both cardinals, was prepared to act the part of patron of scientists, artists and craftsmen as a good Medici should.

He took an interest in the scientific academy, the Accademia del Cimento, founded by Leopoldo, which began to meet at the Pitti Palace in 1657;[21] he also interested himself in Leopoldo's collection of self-portraits, now housed in the corridor that links the Uffizi to the Palazzo Pitti,[22] and in the remarkable collection of ivory ornaments assembled by another brother, Mattias.[23] And he went out of his way to encourage the artistic activities of his brother, the handsome, dashing reprobate Gian Carlo, who lived in a lovely villa in a delightful garden off Via della Scala, where he made love to a succession of mistresses, often, so it was said, to several at once, and had at least one tiresome rival drowned in a carp pond. It was Gian Carlo who invited the artist Salvator Rosa to come to Florence; and it was he who, having given money for the building of the theatre in Via della Pergola, rented a *palazzo* for another company in Via del Cocomero, for which Ferdinando Tacca was asked to design sets and scenery.[24]

The Grand Duke himself promoted the Florentine craft of *pietre dure* and, to provide space for the family's ever-increasing collection of paintings and sculptures – including the works brought to Florence as a dowry by his wife – he made extensive alterations to the Pitti Palace, providing it with new galleries decorated by some of the most accomplished artists of his time, among them Pietro da Cortona, who painted the Baroque murals in the Sala della Stufa, and Giovanni di San Giovanni, who worked in the Museo degli Argenti sitting in a tub suspended from the ceiling, his gouty legs swathed in bandages.

Foreign visitors to Florence in these years were much taken with the city, and several decided to settle here. There was a contented colony of English Roman Catholics which included Tobie Matthew, the wayward, witty son of the Archbishop of York, who had written complacently in 1608, 'I live in Florence in an excellent coole terrene, eate good melons, drink wholsome wines, look upon excellent devout pictures, heer choyse musique.' He and his companions inspected the treasures and curiosities of the Medici then on display in the Pitti Palace, strolled down the bay and myrtle terraces and past the statues and fountains in the Boboli Gardens, marvelled at the mosaics of polychrome marble, lapis lazuli and mother-of-pearl in the Cappella dei Principi in San Lorenzo, took riding lessons from the cel-

A view of Florence from the Pignone by Gaspare Vanvitelli (1653–1736) in the Galleria Palatina.

ebrated Rustico Piccardini, made the rounds of the sights which were
already becoming traditional – paying more attention to curiosities, *objets
d'art* and objects of virtue than to the works of the early Florentine artists,
which were not then much admired – and threw themselves wholeheartedly
into the pleasures of the city's festivals, the procession of black-faced
puppets around the lantern-lit streets on Twelfth Night, the costume parades
and the balls and receptions of the Carnival, the festivities of Corpus Christi
and St John's Day when the squares were filled with flowers, and candles

glittered in palace windows and when, in the Piazza della Signoria, stalls were set up for the sale of cakes and wine, and meat and vegetables were cooked in huge pots set upon open fires.

'The beauty and security of the place, and purity of the language' were good reasons for travellers to visit Florence, Sir Henry Wotton, sometime English ambassador in Venice, observed. Other travellers praised the city's inns. Fynes Moryson, whose *Itinerary Containing his Ten Yeeres Travell* was published in 1617, described them as 'most neate', their tables invitingly spread from morning to night with white cloths, glasses of 'divers coloured wines' and dishes of fruit, all gaily decorated with flowers and fig leaves:

> At the table they touch no meate with the hand, but with a forke of silver or other metall, each man being served with his forke and spoone, and glass to drinke... And as they serve small peeces of flesh (not whole joints as with us) so these peeces are cut into small bits, to be taken up with the forke... In Summer time they set a broad earthern vessel full of water upon the Table, wherein little glasses filled with wine doe swimme for coolnesse.

These were the years when, as Sir Harold Acton has observed,

> the characteristics of Florentine life were an extensive gaiety and Bohemianism; and these gave birth to the best literature of the age, to that burlesque poetry and prose which is still so kicking, so alive. Everywhere you looked there was evidence of this gaiety: on the steps of Santa Maria del Fiore, before Santa Croce or on the bridge of Santa Trinita, when the *improvvisatori* sweated verses from every pore... One might go so far as to say that no serious matter was dealt with, no problem solved without a reaction of rollicking repartee. The general feeling was... 'Eat, drink and play at leisure; for after death's no pleasure.' There was an epidemic of *bisboccia*, a term whose syllables express the sense: gross feeding, heavy drinking and a prompt answer to the calls of lust.
>
> The result, instead of an abatement of vigour, was a fermentation in every field, fanned by science into general fecundity. Sweet music was now composed for every instrument; painters frescoed the interiors and exteriors of whole churches and palaces with their riotous visions: complicated perspectives swarming with foreshortened and elongated figures in ecstatic attitudes – deceptive tricks of chiaroscuro, bituminous shadows and sudden shafts of light. The most esteemed painters and architects were those who could work fastest.

Some foreign students, caught up in this excitement, remained for long periods in Florence. Nicholas Stone the Younger, the mason and sculptor, was one of these. In his diary for August 1638 he made entries on successive days: 'I drew after the head of Antonino Pio... I drew after a great head of Cicero; the great Duke [Ferdinando II] came in the gallery; looked on my drawing; told me I was a gallant huomo... I drew after the same head; the great Duke came thaire with his brother, who overlooked all my drawings... I drew after a piece of Carace... I drew a folliage for memory.'

A few years later that indefatigable sightseer, John Evelyn, came to Florence and was much taken by the city's 'fowre most sumptuous bridges', by the Column of Justice in the Piazza Santa Trinita and the 'most remarkable' porphyry statue adorning it, the Church of Santo Spirito 'where the Altar and Reliquary is most rich and full of precious stones', the Strozzi Palace, 'a Princly piece of Architecture if any in the World be', the Pitti Palace, 'of late infinitely beautified', the Boboli Gardens, 'full of all Variety, hills, dales, rocks, Groves, aviaries, vivaries, fountaines... and what ever may render such a paradise delightful'.

Delightful as Florence may have appeared to John Evelyn, the Grand Duke Ferdinando II's son, Cosimo, did not seem to find it so. Plump, priggish and gloomy, with large and heavy features and drooping eyelids, he was 'dominated by melancholy to an extraordinary degree', the Lucchese ambassador reported. 'The Grand Duke is affable with everyone, as ready with a laugh as with a joke, whereas the Prince is never seen to smile.' He exhibited 'symptoms of a singular piety'.

His father, hoping to enliven him, considered that he should be married as soon as possible and that there could be no more suitable bride than the King of France's young cousin, Marguerite-Louise d'Orléans, a healthy girl, sprightly and energetic. The girl herself had other ideas. She was in love with another of her French cousins, Prince Charles of Lorraine, and dreaded the idea of leaving France for marriage to a fat and mournful Italian, heir to a now impoverished duchy.

In Paris, however, the marriage was as much favoured as it was in Florence, since King Louis XIV's powerful minister, Cardinal Mazarin, had hopes of becoming Pope and was anxious to obtain the support of the Medici. Marguerite-Louise, then fifteen years old, knelt before her cousin the King of France, and begged him to save her from her impending fate. Her passionate pleas were in vain: Cardinal Mazarin had his way. In the spring of 1661, having been married by proxy to Cosimo in Paris, she left for Florence, 'crying aloud for everyone to hear'.

She was as miserable in Florence as she had feared she would be, thoroughly disliking her unresponsive, inappetent husband, finding fault with everything Tuscan because it was not French, rarely going out in public and then always masked, affecting to believe that the Florentines, notoriously skilled in such mysteries, were concocting poisons to kill her and insisting that all her food be tasted first by her steward. Homesick, bored and sulky, she was asked how she liked Florence. She grumpily replied she would have liked it much better had it been nearer Paris.

Extravagant as well as pert, spending huge sums of money on her clothes, on her table and her French attendants, she was 'deaf to protests', the Venetian ambassador reported. 'It is her usual conceit to say that she has

The Grand Duke Cosimo III (1642–1723) as a Canon of the Lateran. A portrait by an unknown artist in the Museo Mediceo.

married beneath her, into a family vastly inferior to her proper merit; and this pricks the family at the most delicate point of their sensibilities.' By the end of their first month together her husband, to whom she rarely spoke, had 'couched with her only three times', another observer, the Bishop of Béziers, reported. 'Every time he does not go, he sends a valet to tell her not to wait up for him.'

Refusing to mend her ways, and having, in her own words, 'tried in vain for twelve long years to change her feelings', she was at last permitted to go home to France. There she took to wearing thick rouge and a yellow wig, indulged herself with several lovers, including a renegade monk and a groom who cracked nuts for her between his teeth, chased an abbess who criticized her conduct down the corridors of her convent with a hatchet in one hand and a pistol in the other, and wrote repeated letters to Florence demanding money, though she had taken an immense sum with her when she left, as well as wall hangings, beds and numerous valuable articles from the Medici villa at Poggio a Caiano, where she had lived with an extremely large household numbering over 150 servants and attendants.

At the time of her departure her husband was thirty-two, excessively fat, since he was an inveterate trencherman, consuming gargantuan platefuls of the richest delicacies. More than ever given to pious interjections, he was, however, not quite as priggish as he had been in the past, capable even, when troubling himself to exercise it, of a certain charm of manner. His father had died in 1670, and had been buried near his father and grandfather in the great baroque Cappella dei Principi at San Lorenzo;[25] and, as Grand Duke, Cosimo III had immediately shown himself determined to stamp out immorality in Florence as well as the prevalent heresies.

In obedience to the wishes of the Inquisition, scientists and philosophers were no longer afforded the protection they had been accustomed to receive from his predecessors; and a strict watch was kept upon the instruction given at the University of Pisa to Florentine students, who were expressly forbidden to attend any academic institutions beyond the borders of Tuscany. Whereas his great-grandfather Ferdinando I had promised religious toleration to Jews and encouraged them to settle in Leghorn – which consequently even today has a higher proportion of Jews than any other Italian city – Cosimo persecuted them severely, imposing fines on Christians who employed them. Jews who consorted with Christian prostitutes were also heavily fined, while the prostitutes themselves – compelled to identify themselves by wearing yellow ribbons in their hats or hair and to buy licences to walk abroad at night – were whipped through the streets with a placard reading 'For Whoredom' hung over their breasts. Constantly badgered by officials of the Office of Public Decency, who hid in door-ways to catch them out in some infringement of the law such as not carrying a lighted torch, prostitutes were in perpetual danger of being thrown into the fearful prison, the Stinche, where many ended their days.

Innocent girls caught singing the traditional songs of the May Day festival were also liable to be whipped, and the *Calendimaggio* itself was banned as a pagan celebration. The traditional ceremonies of Lent were observed with exceptional diligence. The seven thorns from Christ's crown were borne in procession through the streets from the church of San Piero

Maggiore;[26] and in another procession were borne all the many objects connected with the Crucifixion, each carried separately in the hands of a long line of mourners – nails and hammers, vinegar and sponge, spear, purple robe and dice – followed by an image of Christ under a black canopy and of the Blessed Virgin, also in black, holding a white handkerchief. There were also processions of chanting flagellants as in the days following the Black Death. A solemn sermon against blasphemy was preached in Santo Spirito, and the city's prostitutes were summoned, under threat of grave penalties, to attend a Holy Week sermon in Santa Maria del Fiore. After the Matins of Darkness clergy and congregation alike beat the floor of the church with willow rods, creating that unearthly noise intended to represent nature's protest at Christ's sacrifice. On Good Friday, as the people were leaving the churches at three o'clock, vergers followed them with wooden clappers, signalling to all in the streets to kneel and pray. The Grand Duke himself, as custom and duty dictated, worshipped in seven churches, going from one to the other on foot. Punishments for the disobedient were severe. In the Grand Duke Cosimo's day, indeed, men could be and sometimes were stretched on the rack for illicit sexual intercourse and beheaded for buggery: the severed heads of sodomites were occasionally displayed on the wall of the Bargello. Public executions became commonplace. Murderers were not merely executed but afterwards quartered; and Cosimo would have had one particular murderer tortured with red-hot pincers had not the magistrates advised against it 'because of the disgust that it would give the city'.

The city was, in fact, already disgusted with Cosimo's rule. All over Tuscany trade was declining, and the population of the whole area was being constantly decreased by malaria, plague and food shortages due to a backward agriculture. There had been repeated crop failures since 1619, which had seen the worst harvests 'in the history and memory of past times'; wool production, which had fallen by half in the first half of the seventeenth century, was still declining; the families which had been proud to run merchant houses in the past now considered commerce beneath them. 'Florence is much sunk from what it was,' wrote Gilbert Burnet, whose account of his travels in Italy was published in 1686. 'They do not reckon there are above fifty thousand souls in it [plague and malaria had both taken heavy toll and, in one particularly virulent epidemic of influenza, some 8,000 people had died in Florence in a single week]... As one goes over Tuscany, it appears so dispeopled that one cannot but wonder to find a country that hath been a scene of so much action now so forsaken and so poor.' A French visitor, François Maximilien Misson, agreed:

> Although Florence is certainly one of the finest cities in the world, and has the advantage of a most delicious situation, yet it must appear a very sad and

melancholy place to those who are accustomed to enjoy the pleasures of society. Sir D., who, you know, has resided here for several years, is not able to express his uneasiness under the intolerable constraint and eternal ceremonies of this place, and particularly exclaims against the invisibility of the beautiful sex.

There were but two reasonable hotels in the 1670s and only one *pensione*; and visitors invited to stay in a private house or palace might well regret accepting the invitation: in the house of Lorenzo Magalotti, secretary of the Academy of the Cimento, a family goat wandered about from room to room until it died after drinking the contents of a chamber-pot − not Lorenzo's pot, he was careful to point out, since drinking the contents of that could have done the goat nothing but good.

Scarcely a month passed without the imposition of some new tax, while the existing rates, from which the clergy were largely exempt, were perpetually being increased. Cosimo also raised money by selling merchants exclusive rights to deal in certain essential commodities such as flour or salt, and then, for a fee, issuing tradesmen with special licences enabling them to evade the monopoly. Severe punishments were imposed upon those who tried to find ways round the regulations. Extracting salt from fish brine, for instance, was declared a capital offence. Occasionally the money raised by taxes was used to buy a work of art to add to the Medici collections; but more often than not it was spent on some expensive present for a distinguished foreign visitor, on a holy relic of dubious provenance or on the expensive delicacies served at the grand-ducal table, where capons, weighed in front of him, were sent back to the kitchens by Cosimo if they did not turn the scales at twenty pounds.

The older he grew the more fanatically religious he became, astonishing Edward Wright by going to 'five or six churches every day'. 'I was told he had a machine in his own apartment, whereon were fix'd little images in silver, of every saint in the calendar,' Wright wrote. 'The machine was made to turn so as to present in front the saint of the day, before which the Duke continually performed his office . . . His zeal was great for gaining proselytes to the Roman Church.'

When Cosimo died, at the age of eighty-one in 1723, his elder son Ferdinando had already been dead for ten years, not greatly mourned by his father. He had been a good-looking young man, intelligent and amusing, resembling his high-spirited mother rather than the lugubrious Grand Duke. A gifted musician himself, he was a generous patron of composers and performers as well as a master impresario, producing operas by Alessandro Scarlatti at Pratolino and corresponding with Jacopo Peri, Bartolomeo Cristofori, Bernardo Pasquini and George Frideric Handel, all of whom he invited to Florence. He assembled a large collection of musical instruments, bought pictures by Raphael and Andrea del Sarto, purchased Parmigiano's unfinished *Madonna dal Collo Lungo*, employed both Sebastiano Ricci and Giuseppe Maria Crespi at the Pitti Palace, and in 1701, in the cloisters of Santissima Annunziata, organized the first formal exhibition of paintings to be held in Florence.

Yet Ferdinando was a grave disappointment to his father. For one thing he was far too attached to his uncle, Francesco Maria, a wildly extravagant man with an infinite capacity for self-indulgence who filled his villa of Lapeggi with young men who waited upon him at table dressed as girls. For another thing, Ferdinando was overfond of young men himself, particularly of a Venetian *castrato* who exercised great influence over him. Grumbling about these unsuitable attachments, the Grand Duke eventually prevailed upon his son to agree to marry Princess Violante Beatrice of Bavaria, a sixteen-year-old girl, plain and shy, who, of course, interested Ferdinando not in the least, though she fell deeply in love with him. The day they were married was so cold that two soldiers on guard at the Porta San Gallo froze to death; and on her return to the Pitti Palace after her wedding in the cathedral the Princess buried her face in her muff, almost in tears, complaining that she had never been so cold in all her life. Not long afterwards her husband left for Venice where he contracted syphilis from a lady of noble family. He returned to Florence with a young mistress, already a dying man, soon lapsing into epilepsy and dementia, nursed by his devoted wife, his memory gone.

His brother, Gian Gastone, now the Grand Duke's heir, was an introspective, unhappy man who passed a lonely existence away from the court, devoting himself to archaeological and botanical studies and to learning foreign languages. At the behest of his father he married the daughter of the Duke of Saxe-Lauenburg, a stupid and argumentative woman of remarkable ugliness who spent most of her time 'holding conversations in the stables' and who refused to leave her dank and gloomy castle near Prague for Florence, where, her confessor told her, she would be sure to be murdered as all the wives of the Medici were, sooner or later.

Having spent most of his time in Bohemia drinking and gambling with his Italian attendants, in gazing mournfully out of his window across a slough of hovels and sedge beds, or in the arms of a pretty, crafty groom, Gian Gastone left his wife in her grim valley and, taking the groom with him, returned to Florence, where he succeeded his father as Grand Duke at the age of fifty-two. For a time it seemed that he might prove to be a competent ruler. Taxation was reduced; the government was freed from the stranglehold of the Church; scientists and scholars were released from the restrictions formerly imposed upon them; anti-Semitic legislation was rescinded; public executions were discontinued. But it was not long before Gian Gastone lost interest in the affairs of Florence and disappeared from public view into a private life of alcoholism and slovenly lubricity.

Prince Ferdinando (1663– 1713) and his sister, Princess Anna Maria Luisa (1667– 1743), with their governess. A portrait by Justus Sustermans in the Museo Stibbert.

Frequently and incapably drunk, swearing and belching his way through meals which he usually ate in bed, he surrounded himself with hordes of handsome youths – known as *ruspanti* after the coins which were paid for their services – who romped and rioted about the Pitti Palace and, when required, coupled in his presence. Rarely was the Grand Duke seen outside the palace walls and, when he was, he was usually as drunk as he was on St John the Baptist's Day 1729, a festival he celebrated by being drawn through the streets in a carriage, poking his head through the window from time to time to be sick, clambering out at the Porta al Prato to watch the horse-races, and shouting obscenities at his pages and the ladies around him before being conveyed back to the palace fast asleep in a litter.

Gian Gastone's dissolute behaviour, which contrasted so strongly with the propriety of his father, seems to have infected Florentine society in general. A slight though momentarily alarming earthquake in the summer of 1729 was interpreted as a warning from on high. Thirty foreign women whose morals were notorious were banished from the city; but a contemporary diarist considered that Florentine women were just as much at fault. So, according to a German who visited the city soon afterwards, were many Florentine men: 'They are, even to a proverb, addicted to that atrocious and unnatural vice which brought down divine vengeance on Sodom and Gomorrah. Thus it is not at all strange that, with such lascivious inclinations, the Florentines should not have the best eyes: immoderate and frequent sexual acts being very pernicious to the sight.'

Without troubling to consult the Grand Duke or the Florentine people, representatives of the European powers met to discuss what had become known as the Tuscan Succession. The House of Medici now being all but extinct, the House of Este had come forward as claimants; so had the Emperor Charles VI; so had Philip V of Spain, who was dominated by his wife, Isabella Farnese, niece and stepdaughter of the Duke of Parma, an ambitious woman determined to find territories in Italy for her sons. Eventually the succession was settled in favour of the Empress of Austria's husband, Francis, Duke of Lorraine, whose representative, the Prince de Craon, formerly the Duke's tutor, arrived in Florence – closely followed by six thousand troops and various glum, pedantic foreigners assigned to take the place of Florentine *funzionarii* in government offices – even before the death of Gian Gastone, the last of the Medici Grand Dukes of Tuscany, in 1737.

Gian Gastone's sister, Anna Maria, a tall, proud, stiff-backed old lady with a deep, masculine voice, was allowed to live out the few remaining years of her life in the Pitti Palace. The widow of the Elector Palatine, who had infected her with a venereal disease which was held responsible for the miscarriages that marred her early life, she received her visitors beneath a black canopy in a comfortless room full of silver furniture. Having, to her eternal credit, made a will leaving the entire property of her family, their palaces and villas and all the treasures which they contained to the new Grand Duke and his successors, on condition that nothing was ever removed from these incalculably valuable collections or taken beyond the borders of Tuscany, she died on 18 February 1743. She was buried in a tomb in the Cappella dei Principi engraved with the words, *Ultima Della Stirpe Reale Dei Medici*, the 'Last of the Royal Medici Line'.

The Florence now occupied by foreigners was a sad place, poor and disconsolate, full of vagabonds and beggars and of monks passing in dreary procession beneath dark buildings with windows of torn oiled paper. The state was almost bankrupt. So were many of the noble families whose ill-paid servants hung gloomily about their palace doorways. Guests were now rarely invited to anything other than a card party or *conversazione*, and rarely offered refreshment other than lemonade or coffee, or, perhaps, ice cream. 'The declining state of this city is very visible,' reported one visitor, 'a great deal of the ground within the walls being unbuilt, so that it is not very populous. Nor are the inhabitants useful, the clergy making up the bulk of the people ... I counted above four thousand monks and friars in one procession.'

The citizens, resentful of being once again ruled by foreigners – and of being curtly informed that all holidays associated with the Medici were to be abolished – watched in silence as the occupying forces took down the Medici balls from public buildings and replaced them with shields bearing Austrian eagles and crosses of Lorraine. Disillusioning as their recent experiences of the family had been, they would have given two thirds of all they possessed to have the Medici back, Charles de Brosses, the French scholar and future president of the Parliament of Burgundy, decided after a visit to Tuscany at this time, 'and they would give the other third to get rid of the Lorrainers ... They hate them.' They showed their resentment by sullen looks and muttered grumbles, occasionally erupting into violence, as they did in a riot in 1738 when two foreign soldiers were attacked and beaten after a rag collector's nose had been cut off in a scuffle.

Soon after this riot, in January 1739, the Grand Duke Francis himself arrived in Florence. Although he had aroused much resentment by authorizing the removal to Austria of such works of art as were deemed to belong to him – and the auctioning of the contents of various Medici properties, extending even to pots and pans – it was agreed, after prompting by an influential senator, founder of the celebrated porcelain business, Carlo Ginori,[27] that the Grand Duke's formal entry should be celebrated in the traditional Florentine manner with parades and processions, balls and pageants, firework displays, the decoration of buildings and the erection of a monumental triumphal arch.[28]

The design of this arch was entrusted to an obscure architect from Lorraine, J. N. Joadot, and four hundred men were set to work upon the monument, labouring day and night to get it finished in time. It was not finished in time. Indeed, when the Grand Duke and Duchess arrived outside Florence at the Villa Corsi, the by-no-means-imposing edifice had had to be given at least an appearance of completion by means of plaster and painted canvas. Fortunately they had been delayed at the Villa Corsi, where they had been entertained to luncheon; and it was dark by the time they arrived in the Piazza San Gallo, now the Piazza della Libertà. It was also very cold; and many of the spectators, tired of waiting, had gone home.

The guns in the Belvedere obediently boomed in the bitter night air; fireworks flashed in the sky above the Arno; fountains poured forth wine; pergolas of lanterns, flares and torches lit the way along which the procession passed down the Via Maggio to the Pitti Palace after a *Te Deum* in the Duomo. But the reception was far from being the triumph which Carlo Ginori had planned.

The Grand Duke Francis and Maria Theresa nevertheless appeared to enjoy their three months' stay in Florence. Holding court in the Pitti Palace, they went on sightseeing expeditions, visiting churches and chapels, museums and galleries and showing particular interest in the Opificio delle Pietre Dure and the workshops of the Uffizi that produced the kind of *objets d'art* of which Francis was later to become a connoisseur and collector as Emperor in Vienna. They remained in Florence for the Carnival, during which they gave three masked balls in the Palazzo Vecchio, once dashing off to change their costumes when, disguised as bats, they were recognized too soon. They attended an exciting game of football, which was still played each year by teams representing the four quarters of the city. And when they left at the end of April, accompanied by an immense convoy of wagons, each drawn by several pairs of oxen and piled high with goods and valuables appropriated from Medici houses in Florence, they promised to return.

They never did return. Thereafter for twenty-seven years, Florence was governed by Regents, first by Count Emmanuel de Richecourt, a vain, authoritarian Bavarian already an elderly man at the time of his appointment, and then by General Antonio Botta-Adorno, a hard-headed Lombard who, although an Italian, had been so oppressively severe as commander of Austrian troops in Genoa that he had provoked a violent insurrection in the city and had been obliged to withdraw his soldiers from it.

Under both these Regents, Florence was persistently and relentlessly plundered for the sake of Vienna and for the Austrian armies kept so long in the field by Maria Theresa and her husband. Cart after cart and line upon line of pack-animals rattled and clattered through the Porta San Gallo on their way north, laden with treasure and goods to support the imperial economy. From time to time there were public protests and demonstrations in the city; but the government in Vienna continued to make their demands upon the resources of Tuscany and encouraged the Regents in the further-ance of their policies.

Taxation was steadily increased; the number of bankruptcies soared; aristocratic families, withdrawing from commercial enterprises most of what remained of their capital thus invested, put their money into land, into the redecoration of their palaces, into the most extravagant enter-tainments for others of their kind and the purchase of ornate carriages 'like portable sitting-rooms'.

Occasionally an imperial decree, usually prompted by the Regents' Florentine advisers, would offer some relief: in 1764, for example, during a serious food shortage in Florence, the Grand Duke supplied funds for the purchase of grain. Indeed, even the most antagonistic of his government's critics had to concede that not all the policies of the *Reggenza* were deleterious, for in its time the powers of the Inquisition were curbed and its prison closed down; the civil and criminal jurisdictions of the feudal landlords were abrogated; ecclesiastical institutions were deprived of certain archaic tax advantages; and the civil service was reformed by new policies of recruitment.

In 1765 the Emperor Francis I, Francis III of Lorraine, died suddenly after a night at the opera. He was succeeded as Emperor by his eldest son, Joseph, and, as Grand Duke of Tuscany, by his younger son, Peter Leopold, who was married at the age of seventeen to the Spanish Infanta, Maria Luisa. The Florentines had grounds for hope that, now the regency was at long last ended, the young Grand Duke and Duchess, who were to come and live amongst them, would pay attention to the people's needs.

18

TOURISTS
AND TUFT-HUNTERS
1740–88

'A scene of enchantment,
a city planted in a garden.'
WILLIAM HAZLITT

A few days before the accession of Peter Leopold as Grand Duke of Tuscany, James Boswell arrived in Florence on his Grand Tour. He found the city had more English and Scottish residents than any other he had yet visited. Travellers from other countries came in by every coach; but few settled here for long, and many rushed off after the briefest visits, though not many so hurriedly as Mozart, who stayed only long enough to give a concert at the Villa Poggio Imperiale[1] – and to make friends with another musical prodigy, the English boy, Thomas Linley, who was in Florence receiving violin lessons from Pietro Nardini – before moving on to Rome.[2]

British visitors, however, as Boswell found, were more inclined to remain in Florence, as though reluctant to leave a city in which they felt so much at home. Among the residents at this time was Boswell's cousin, Earl Cowper, who had come out long before and, having fallen in love with a married *marchesa*, had never gone home again. He confessed to Boswell that the *marchesa* no longer held charms for him, but he had decided to stay on anyway at the Villa Palmieri, since he had made many friends in Italy and had none in England.[3] He later married an attractive young Englishwoman and was made a Count of the Holy Roman Empire purely because, so it was said, the Grand Duke was so very fond of his wife. He became the Grand Duke's musical adviser and 'lived in a very grand way'.

Also living in Florence at this time were the extremely rich Earl Tilney of Castlemaine who followed Cowper's example by entertaining on a most lavish scale; the Marquess of Hertford's son, Lord Beauchamp; Johann Ludwig, Baron von Wallmoden, reputedly the son of King George II by his German mistress, the Countess of Yarmouth; the tall and swarthy Colonel Isaac Barré, who had fought beside General Wolfe at Quebec and

The Piazza Santa Trinita by Giuseppe Zocchi (1711–67).

had subsequently become a fiery orator in the House of Commons; the amiable and impractical poet, Robert Merry, whose affair with Lady Cowper greatly annoyed the Grand Duke; and, among many others – several of whom are to be seen in Zoffany's picture of the Tribuna[4] – two young naval officers, the Hon. Keith Stewart, son of the Earl of Galloway, and the Hon. Peregrine Bertie, son of the Earl of Abingdon.

Also to be seen in this group portrait by Zoffany is Sir Horace Mann, who had been appointed British Resident in Florence in 1740 and was to remain there, becoming increasingly Italian in his manners, for over forty years. Considered by the poet, Thomas Gray, as 'the best and most obliging person in the world', and described by the historian, Edward Gibbon, as 'an agreeable man, quiet and polished but somewhat wrapped up in a round of important trifles', Mann was sixty-four years old at the time of Boswell's arrival in Florence, vain, affected and excessively well groomed.

The son of a prosperous London merchant, he had, as a young man, become an intimate friend of Horace Walpole, son of the Prime Minister; and it was through this friendship that Mann had obtained his appointment in Florence. He had originally come out as assistant to Charles Fane, England's 'Envoy Extraordinary and Minister Plenipotentiary at the Court of Florence'; but he had soon been entrusted with most of the envoy's work, since Fane was a remarkably lazy man who was also extremely touchy, once taking to his bed for six weeks, so Walpole related, because the Duke of Newcastle forgot to put 'very' before 'humble servant' at the end of a letter. Mann succeeded Fane in 1740 and thereafter at his house, the Palazzo Manetti in Via Santo Spirito (known also as the 'King's Arms'),[5] he entertained a constant stream of English visitors, putting several of them up in a smaller guest-house he maintained, the Casa Ambrogi[6] opposite the Pitti Palace. He provided them with excellent dinners, as well as a 'sixpenny pharo table' on Monday evenings, allowed them to fish in the Arno from the windows of the Palazzo Manetti, invited them to his box at the opera and arranged for them to witness various ceremonies at the Pitti Palace, such as the washing of the feet of poor old women by agitated ladies of the court, who scoured away 'with a fervour and devotion according to the extent of their own crimes'. He ensured that they got the best seats at horse-races and games of *palio*, and introduced them to his friend, the painter and caricaturist, Thomas Patch, who had had to leave Rome hurriedly in 1755 when his homosexuality had landed him in trouble. In addition Mann found time to write letters, not only on official business, but also more intimately to his friend Walpole, on a scale, so Walpole said, 'not to be paralleled in the history of the post office'.

These letters, replete with detailed accounts of court ceremonial, masquerades, Florentine customs and characters, were described by Lord Dover, who published Walpole's brilliant replies, as being 'particularly devoid of interest, being written in a dry, heavy style and consisting almost entirely of trifling details of forgotten Florentine society'. Yet since Mann acted as host for almost half a century to virtually every distinguished English person who visited Florence in his days as minister there, from the Dukes of York and Gloucester to Lord Bute, David Garrick, John Wilkes, Tobias Smollett and Samuel Johnson's former friend, Mrs Piozzi, the letters cannot fail, for all the tedium of their style, to contain much of more than passing interest.

To cater for the ever-increasing number of foreign visitors to Florence in Mann's time, new inns were built and existing ones enlarged or moved into more commodious premises. The Aquila Nera was provided with a large annexe in Via Ognissanti; the Albergo di Monsù Massè was also extended; the Locanda dello Scudo di Francia moved from Via Maggio into a much larger building near the Badia; both the Locanda di Giacomo Megit in Santo Spirito and the Albergo della Gran Bretagna on the Lungarno Guicciardini were opened specifically for English guests, some of whom preferred, however, the rather more expensive Locanda della Rossa. All these inns catered for the tastes of English visitors, offering such familiar dishes as *budino di riso all'inglese* as well as *brodo bianco* and *crostini*.

A notably inexpensive inn, warmly recommended by Horace Mann, was Carlo's, on the left bank of the Arno opposite the Palazzo Corsini. This was kept by Charles Hadfield, a man of Irish descent from Manchester, father of several children, four of whom were murdered by an insane nurse, and one of whom, Maria, survived to marry the miniaturist, Richard Cosway, and to become a gifted painter herself.

Carlo's was a very well-run inn. 'Almost all the English live in this house,' Sir Lucas Pepys told his brother in 1767, 'and considering all things we do not pay very extravagantly. Everybody pays 2s.6d. a day for his apartment, not quite 4s. for his dinner, 8d. his breakfast or tea, 1s. fire, and if any choose supper 1s.6d. This is very reasonable considering noblemen and all live in the same manner.' A few years later, the twenty-one-year-old Angelica Kauffman stayed here with her father, 'a painter of very mediocre talent', going day after day for seven months to copy paintings in the Uffizi and, for small fees, undertaking portraits of Hadfield's guests and other people staying or living in Florence.

Hadfield's was generally full, another guest recorded; and the dinner parties held there, 'very lively occasions', were frequently attended by Thomas Patch, who once painted himself holding aloft a punch bowl in a picture of a party commissioned by Lord Grey.[7] Also to be seen from time to time at Hadfield's was Ignazio Enrico Hugford whose house became as hospitable a meeting place for foreign guests as was Horace Mann's. Sir

Thomas Patch's impression of a coffee-house c. 1770.

Joshua Reynolds stayed there; so did the art dealer Gavin Hamilton, the architects Robert Adam and Charles-Louis Clérisseau, and that most sociable of sculptors, Joseph Wilton, who, during his visit, worked on his fine bust of Mann's friend, Antonio Cocchi, the Anglophile Professor of Surgery at the hospital of Santa Maria Nuova.

Ignazio Hugford's father was a Roman Catholic exile who had been appointed watchmaker to the Grand Duke of Tuscany; his elder brother, Ferdinando Enrico, born in Florence, who became abbot of Vallombrosa, was a master craftsman in the working of *scagliola*, a material used since classical times to imitate marble, passing on the secrets of his craft to Lamberto Cristiano Gori.[8] Ignazio himself was an artist of sorts, but, although he spent nine years studying under Antonio Domenico Gabbiani – whose work can be seen in the gallery of the Medici Palace[9] and the Galleria Corsini[10] as well as at San Frediano in Cestello[11] – he never became as successful as a painter as he was stimulating and kindly as a teacher, discerning as a connoisseur and skilful, if rather unscrupulous, as a dealer.[12]

Tobias Smollett, 'a surly Scotchman' in the opinion of one of his contemporaries, chose not to join the gregarious company at Hadfield's when he arrived in Florence a few weeks before Boswell, but put up instead at Vanini's. Although always prepared for the worst and usually finding it – and having already condemned most of the inns where he stayed in Italy as 'abominably nasty' – Smollett discovered Vanini's to be 'an English house delightfully situated', the landlady, herself an Englishwoman, 'very obliging' and the 'entertainment good and reasonable'.

From Vanini's, Smollett set about his sightseeing and, still in uncharacteristically complimentary vein, he told a friend, 'Florence is a noble city that still retains all the marks of a majestic capital, such as piazzas, palaces, fountains, bridges, statues and arcades. I need not tell you that the churches here are magnificent, and adorned not only with pillars of oriental granite, porphyry, jasper, *verde antico* and other precious stones; but also with capital pieces of painting by the most eminent masters.'

He went to all the usual sights, to the Duomo, the Baptistery and San Lorenzo, to the gallery of the Uffizi, the Pitti Palace, the Ponte Vecchio and 'every thing which is commonly visited in this metropolis'. But he sensibly refrained from troubling his correspondent with 'trite observations', since 'all these objects' had been 'circumstantially described by twenty different authors of travels', notably by the indefatigable German author, Johann Georg Keysler, whose *Travels* had just appeared in an English translation and whose laborious descriptions, Smollett complained, he could never read without 'suffering the headache'.

Instead Smollett chose to dwell upon such curiosities as the city's *improvvisatori*, who had 'the surprising talent of reciting verses extempore on any subject you propose', on the chattering audiences at the opera who 'did not seem very attentive to the music' and on the scene on summer evenings on the Cascine,[13] where ladies sat in their carriages talking to their *cicisbei*, their recognized male attendants, who were, infrequently, their lovers, and who, in taking over the social obligations of a husband, allowed the actual husband to act as a *cicisbeo* himself, once he had secured the future of his estate by fathering an heir:

> Every carriage stops, and forms a little separate *conversazione*. The ladies sit within, and the *cicisbei* stand on the foot-boards, on each side of the coach, entertaining them with their discourse. Every married lady in this country has her *cicisbeo*, or *servente*, who attends her everywhere, and on all occasions; and upon whose privileges the husband dares not encroach, without incurring the censure and ridicule of the whole community. For my part, I would rather be condemned for life to the galleys, than exercise the office of a *cicisbeo*, exposed to the intolerable caprices and dangerous resentment of an Italian virago. I pretend not to judge of the national character, from my own observation: but, if the portraits drawn by Goldoni in his Comedies are taken from nature, I would not hesitate to pronounce Italian women the most haughty, insolent, capricious and revengeful females on the face of the earth.

Smollett was also intrigued by the

> undoubted fact that in every palace or great house in this city, there is a little window fronting the street, provided with an iron knocker, and over it hangs an empty flask, by way of signpost. Thither you send your servant to buy a bottle of wine. He knocks at the little wicket, which is opened immediately by a domestic, who supplies him with what he wants, and receives the money like the waiter of any other cabaret. It is pretty extraordinary, that it should not be deemed a disparagement in a nobleman to sell half a pound of figs or a palm of ribbon or tape, or to take money for a flask of sour wine; and yet be counted infamous to match his daughter in the family of a person who has distinguished himself in any one of the learned professions.

Smollett was equally fascinated by the 'exhibitions of church pageantry'. One procession in particular, 'attended by all the noblesse of the city in their coaches, filled the whole length of the street called the Corso'.

> It was the anniversary of a charitable institution in favour of poor maidens, a certain number of whom are portioned every year. About two hundred of these virgins walked in procession, two and two together, clothed in violet-coloured wide gowns, with white veils on their heads and made a very classical appearance. They were preceded and followed by an irregular mob of penitents in sackcloth, with lighted tapers, and monks carrying crucifixes, bawling and bellowing the litanies: but the great object was a figure of the Virgin Mary, as big as life, standing within a gilt frame, dressed in a gold stuff, with a large hoop, a great quantity of false jewels, her face painted and patched, and her hair frizzled and curled in the very extremity of the fashion. Very little regard had been paid to

the image of our Saviour on the cross; but when his lady-mother appeared on the shoulders of three or four lusty friars, the whole populace fell upon their knees in the dirt...

[I have never yet] discovered the least signs of fanaticism. The very disciplinants, who scourge themselves in the Holy-week, take care to secure their backs from the smart, by means of secret armour, either women's bodices or quilted jackets.

Smollett does not mention Sir Horace Mann in his account; but Boswell, the great tuft-hunter, does so, of course. He found him agreeable, hospitable and 'neat-talking', and was much taken by an anecdote which Mann related about a Florentine witch who could say the Lord's Prayer 'not only forwards and backward but sideways'. In the company of the Marchese Venturi, to whom he had been given a letter of introduction, Boswell visited all the usual sights, particularly enjoying the Boboli Gardens and the lions and tigers in the Grand Duke's menagerie.[14] Afterwards he took flute lessons from Nicolas Dothel, whom he described as 'one of the best teachers of the flute in Europe'; and attended a meeting of the Accademia della Crusca but, unable to concentrate on the lecture given there, left after half an hour, restless and lustful.

Not long before, in Venice, he had visited a courtesan, taking with him a fellow tourist, four years younger than himself, the Prime Minister's son, Lord Mount Stuart, upon whom he was meant to be keeping a watchful eye and over whom he was supposed to be exercising a steadying influence. They both 'catched a tartar'. After this 'fine piece of witless behaviour', as he admitted it to be, Boswell resolved not to risk further infection and 'to maintain strict behaviour'.

But, like so many of his similar resolutions, this one was soon broken. 'Quite furious' with lust, he rushed from the lecture hall to the Ponte Vecchio and picked up two girls, 'poor craiturs' as they were described by the doctor whom he was subsequently obliged to consult, Dr Tyrrell, an elderly Irishman long settled in Florence, where he was consulted by numerous tourists afflicted with venereal complaints. He confirmed that Boswell had caught gonorrhoea again and told him he could not engage in any further gallantries for the moment. Annoyed by this unwelcome counsel, Boswell aloofly informed Dr Tyrrell that he had wanted only 'a little advice' and decided to dismiss him. He did, however, also conclude that he had better take the opportunity of asking for condoms before moving on to Siena, where he found the ladies far more amenable and complacent than those in Florentine society, who, so he told Rousseau, were 'very proud and very mercenary'.

Charles James Fox, who arrived in Florence two years later aged eighteen, was at first also disappointed by the responses to his overtures in what he took to be a rather repressive society. 'There was a woman of fashion put in prison lately for fucking (I suppose rather too publickly),' he reported, 'a piece of unexampled tyranny! and such as could happen in no place but this.' Fox himself, as he told a friend the following year, had been a long time before he 'could get a fuck'. 'But in recompense for my sufferings,' he added,

> I have now got the most excellent piece that can be allowed . . . There is a Mrs Holmes here, an Irishwoman more beautiful than words can express, and very agreeable into the bargain. Now it so happens that tho' this woman is exquisite entertainment for Charles, yet, as she is as chaste as she is fair, she does not altogether do for Carlino so well. There is also . . . a silver-smith's wife who is almost as fair as Mrs Holmes, but not near as chaste and she attracts me thither as regularly in the evening as the other does in the morning . . . This has led me to make verses and you shall soon have a poem of my composing upon the pox in Latin.

For those with more aesthetic tastes than the young Fox, and less indulged by a rich father, Florence had much to offer. For a start, living there was quite cheap. 'Noble houses unfurnished,' wrote Mariana Starke, who was in the city in the 1790s, 'may be hired by the year for, comparatively speaking, nothing.' Besides, there was so much to enjoy that cost literally nothing. William Hazlitt never forgot his days in the city, his first sight of it in its circle of surrounding heights on which white villas, olive groves and vineyards sparkled in the sunlight. It was 'a scene of enchantment, a city planted in a garden . . . Everything was on the noblest scale, yet finished in the minutest part.'

Others wrote of the delights of driving along the Arno valley beside rows of mulberry bushes, cypresses and umbrella pines, walking with friends in the Cascine past girls with baskets full of carnations, mignonette, yellow roses and orange blossom, strolling down clean, well-paved streets and across the bridges, listening to street musicians, delighting at night in the brilliance of fireflies, wandering in the Boboli Gardens where the ilex cast shadows in the moonlight across the white statues, and going about without fear of footpads, who infested so many other cities. Here in Florence, one visitor wrote, although there were plenty of poor people in rags and half-starved beggars, as there were everywhere else in Italy, there were 'no assassinations, no robberies and no great crimes'.

Horace Walpole, who considered Florence 'infinitely the most agreeable of all the places [he] had seen since London', remembered how he 'had done nothing but slip out of [his] domino into bed and out of bed into [his] domino. The end of the carnival is frantic, bacchanalian. All the morning one makes parties in masque to the shops and coffee-houses, and all the evenings to the operas and balls. *Then I have danced, good Gods! how have I danced!*'

Robert Adam also much enjoyed the carnival:

You cannot conceive what a scene of madness and distraction among all ranks of people reigns at this place during the carnival . . . Every mortal masked, from a marquis to a shoe-black, traversing the streets from morning to night. Then began the Corso. This is a procession of all the equipages who go to the great square, ride around making a tour through some of the streets of the town, return to the square again – one set going, another coming – by which means those acquainted with the coach they meet, pop their heads out, say a witty thing, then take them in again.

Half a century later, Walpole still recalled those 'delicious nights on the Ponte di Trinita', wearing his 'linen dressing-gown and a straw hat, with *improvvisatori* and music, and the coffee-houses open with ices'. And he remembered, too, the lovely Elizabetta, Marchesa Grifoni, whose *cavaliere servente* and perhaps lover he became.

He had to confess that he had not been over-conscientious in his sightseeing. 'Except pictures and statues, we are not very fond of sights,' he admitted. 'Don't go a-staring after crooked towers, and conundrum staircases . . . have left off screaming Lord this! and Lord that! . . . Instead of being deep in the liberal arts, and being in the Gallery every morning, we are all in idleness and amusements of the town.'

So were many of his friends. Thomas Lyttelton, later 'the wicked' second Lord Lyttelton, took a perverse pride in boasting in his garrulous way that he saw no point in bothering with all this sightseeing and poking about in galleries, the sort of thing done by Edward Gibbon, who was a visitor to the Uffizi gallery on at least fourteen occasions during a single stay in Florence. Men like Lyttelton were quite content just to take a quick look round the Tribuna and stroke the bottom of the Venus de' Medici as all English tourists were expected to do. They would not dream of being as assiduous as Joseph Spence, professor of poetry at Oxford and a travelling tutor to various young Englishmen, who went to the Uffizi about a hundred times. They preferred to spend their days drinking wine at the Porco, coffee at the Caffè Castelmur, Florence's first coffee-house, which had been opened by a Swiss in Via Calzaiuoli, or chocolate at Panoni's in Via Por Santa Maria. Or they might go to one of the city's twenty theatres, as often as not to the Pergola, where Goldoni's plays were especially popular, or to punch parties held in private rooms in the inns, or to eat ice cream, specially made for them from a Neapolitan recipe in Florence's first *gelataria* near the Cocomero theatre. Or they might go to the opera, but probably not to listen to the music, which was no more the thing to do then than it was a hundred years later when, as an American visitor observed, the audience almost drowned the music by their conversation and even turned their backs upon the stage. The Scottish physician, John Moore, travelling tutor to the young Duke of Hamilton, observed that the 'Opera at Florence is a

View of Florence with the Water-mills of San Niccolò. *A print of a drawing by Giuseppe Zocchi, whose work was much favoured by foreigners on the Grand Tour. The bridge is the Ponte alle Grazie.*

place where the people of quality pay and receive visits, and converse as freely as at the Casino... I never was more surprised,' he added, 'than when it was proposed to me to make one of a whist party in a box which seemed to have been made for the purpose, with a little table in the middle. I hinted that it would be just as convenient to have the party somewhere else; but I was told good music added greatly to the pleasure of a whist party.'

There was one great disappointment in Florence for men like Lord Lyttelton: the inhospitality of the upper classes. It was not that they could all plead poverty. Charles de Brosses, who travelled widely in Italy at this time, was struck by the amazing luxury which he observed in Florence in the men's clothes and the women's jewels, in the liveries of their servants and their extravagant carriages.

Yet, while he himself had no cause to complain of inhospitality, later English visitors expressed great dissatisfaction. No one 'ever received guests for dinner', complained Arthur Young, the agriculturist. Marchese Riccardi had forty servants in his palace, Young said, many of whom even had their own servants to wait upon them, but an invitation to dinner there was very rare. The Ranuzzi, Young went on, 'are even richer and even more people live at their expense; but there are no dinners, no parties, no equipages and no comfort'.

Most of those who had hopes of being entertained by Prince Charles Edward Stuart were equally disappointed. The Young Pretender, son of the *soi-disant* King James III of England and VIII of Scotland, had come from Rome to live in Florence in 1775. He was then fifty-five years old; his wife, Louisa, the daughter of Prince Gustav Adolf of Stolberg-Gedern – described by the Duke of Hamilton's tutor as 'a beautiful and agreeable woman, much beloved by those who knew her' – was twenty-two.

For a time they rented the Palazzo Corsini in the Prato;[15] then, with their large household of more than forty attendants and servants, they moved into the Palazzo di San Clemente, a fine palace, designed by Gherardo Silvani in Via Gino Capponi.[16] Ill-matched though they were, the Count and Countess of Albany, as they now styled themselves, had at first seemed tolerably content. While the prince had not abandoned all hope of returning in triumph to London, he was no longer an active participant in Jacobite plots for an invasion of England. He enjoyed listening to music and playing the violin, the bagpipes and the flageolet; he went for strolls in the Cascine attended by servants in livery; he practised fencing; he kept his royal hand in by touching the heads of people suffering from scrofula, the King's Evil.

But as the months passed he started drinking heavily again; and, according to Sir Horace Mann, who had informants in his household, his health began to decline rapidly. He suffered from gout and colic, from diarrhoea, epileptic fits and sores on his legs. He was impotent, moody, dirty and utterly bored by life, 'insupportable in stench and temper'. Yet he insisted on sleeping with his wife, and, between fits of coughing and vomiting, on trying to make love to her, and when unable to do so, treating her in the 'most outrageous manner,' Mann reported, 'by the most abusive language, beating her, committing the greatest indecencies upon her and attempting to choke her'.

Life would have been intolerable for her had she not been comforted by the presence in Florence of Count Vittorio Alfieri, a rich and handsome young poet as passionately devoted to her as she was to him. He was, as he readily admitted himself, self-centred, petulant, neurotic, pedantic and histrionic: he had once cut off his hair and ordered his servants to tie him up so that he could not force his attentions upon a lady who did not welcome them; he had afterwards contracted a venereal disease in Cadiz; and in London had had an affair with the wife of Lord Ligonier, the commander-in-chief. This had resulted in a duel in which, as he unashamedly confessed, he did not kill the field-marshal because he could not, and the field-marshal did not kill him because he chose not to do so. Yet for all his many faults, Alfieri was a tragic poet of remarkable gifts which he determined to use in attacking tyranny and in arousing the national spirit of Italy.

He had come to Florence to improve his Italian since, although born in Piedmont, he was more used to expressing himself in French, still the language of the upper classes in Turin. He had not been long in Florence when he encountered the Countess of Albany, who was to remain dear to him throughout his life; and when she could no longer bear the behaviour of her husband and fled from the Palazzo di San Clemente to the nearby Convento delle Bianchette and thence to Rome, Alfieri followed her.

Left behind in Florence, her husband was lonely and miserable, rarely now seen in public even at the opera, and then so drunk that he was liable to be sick on the floor. He decided to send for his daughter, Charlotte, whom he had not seen for twenty years, the child of his long-discarded Scottish mistress, Clementina Walkinshaw. Charlotte could not come immediately: she had been living in a French convent where she had caught the notice of the Archbishop of Bordeaux, to whose third illegitimate child she had just given birth.

When she did arrive in Florence, aged thirty-one, she was described as 'a tall and robust woman of a very dark complexion and coarse-grained skin with more masculine boldness than feminine modesty or elegance, but with easy and unassuming manners' and a 'voluble tongue'. She was said to have become 'a great favourite in Florentine society'. Certainly she looked after her father dutifully. Created by him Duchess of Albany, she nursed him when he was ill, which he usually was; she tried to help him sort out his financial problems; she accompanied him to the theatre covered in the jewels he had given her; she saw to it that he did not drink more than the specified amount of Cyprus wine which she allowed him. When he decided to move back to Rome, she went with him and was with him when he died there in January 1788, dying herself of what was probably cancer of the liver soon afterwards.

British visitors, while so often disappointed at not receiving invitations to dine at the Palazzo di San Clemente and other palaces in Florence, were at least grateful that the price of meals in most of the city's inns was as reasonable as it was at Hadfield's, so they had plenty of money to spare for the numerous articles they were expected to buy in Florence and to have sent home to friends or family – leatherwork and medals, books and coins, paintings and copies of paintings, melon and broccoli seeds – as well as more expensive items for the family home or the house, in the style of one of the Italian masters, which many of them hoped to build one day for themselves: vases and chimney-pieces, *pietre dure* cabinets, copies of antique statues, *scagliola* table tops, engravings of Florentine views by Giuseppe Zocchi.

Having arranged his purchases the tourist moved on, leaving Florence, so one of them said, 'with a wish, common to nearly all of us, one day to return'.

19

THE GRAND DUKE PETER LEOPOLD
1765–91

'Now at last I see my joy returning;
All my wounds are healed, my wealth's recaptured.
There is he for whom Etruria's long been yearning,
There is he for Flora rules, enraptured;
Behold him: Leopold!'
LORENZO PIGNOTTI

From the day of his arrival in Florence, the Grand Duke Peter Leopold had endeavoured to show the Tuscans that he had their interests rather than those of Austria at heart. Within a short time of his moving into the Pitti Palace, he had been required by his brother, the Emperor, to hand over an enormous sum to the treasury in Vienna as a contribution to the costs of the Seven Years' War, a contribution which Tuscany could ill afford after two disastrous harvests and a winter of the most bitter cold. It had to be partly met, not only by heavy borrowings from Genoese financiers, but also by recourse to the Grand Duchess's dowry, some of which arrived in Florence in the form of gold coins loaded in cases on the backs of a baggage train of fifty mules. The Grand Duke made amends for this early display of his Austrian connections, however, by dismissing the unpopular Botta-Adorno, by pensioning off most of the civil servants from Lorraine and by seeking the advice instead of various Tuscan ministers well known for their reformist views, including Giulio Rucellai. He also earned the citizens' respect by speaking Italian in private as well as in public and by having his baby son baptized Giovanni, after Florence's patron saint. The Florentines were further appeased when a large part of the furniture, pictures and other valuables, which had been removed from Florence in the time of the Grand Duke's father, was returned to the Pitti Palace.

Energetic and inquiring, not to say inquisitive, the Grand Duke Peter Leopold interested himself in every aspect of Florentine life, poking his nose in everywhere, as one of his ministers put it, asking questions, impatiently waiting for answers, sometimes losing his temper but quickly making amends. He concerned himself with agriculture, promoting the draining of the marshes in the Maremma of Grosseto and discussing problems with the recently created Accademia dei Georgofili, which he reorganized as the Royal Academy of Sciences. He took notice of technological developments from ballooning to methods of crystallizing salt. He signified his approval of the discussions held in the Biblioteca Riccardiana where Giovanni Lami, founder of Florence's literary periodical *Novelle letterarie*, met his friends.[1] He busied himself with the problems of education, and supervised the foundation of schools in each of the four quarters of the city for the children of the poor. He authorized the promulgation of a new penal code and took great pride in abolishing torture and the death penalty in Tuscany long before executions had been abolished elsewhere. He proclaimed a wish to see improvements in public health, advocating the beneficial qualities of the waters at Montecatini, urging the building of public baths outside the Porta al Prato, and the enlargement and modernization of the hospital of Santa Maria Nuova, where patients were thoroughly washed, barbered and manicured on admission, given a clean nightshirt, provided with a better diet than most could have afforded at home, and charged only if they could spare the cost of their treatment. Moreover, the Grand Duke took it upon himself to act as what he termed an 'external bishop', studying theological works, issuing lists of suitable books for the clergy and banning contentious texts from convent libraries.

Having a passion for classification and arrangement, he immersed himself in the organization of Florence's archives, supervising the cataloguing of the libraries of the Laurenziana and the Magliabechiana,[2] as well as of the Archivio di Stato, founded in his reign.[3] He also added to the city's collections by buying any private libraries, such as that of the Strozzi family, which happened to come on to the market and reorganized the Crusca and another academy, the Apatisti, in a new Accademia Fiorentina.[4] He created the Accademia di Belle Arti from the old Accademia del Disegno,[5] and encouraged the new director of the Uffizi, Giuseppe Pelli Bencivenni, in his transformation of the gallery – large glass windows were fitted to improve the lighting, the Sala della Niobe was created for the display of the sculpture brought from the Villa Medici in Rome[6] and the public was admitted free of charge. He found much work for the architects Gaspare Maria Paoletti and Francesco Zanobi del Rosso, the first of whom designed the Palazzo Torrigiani for the natural-history museum known as La Specola,[7] the second of whom rebuilt the church of the Carmine after most of it had been destroyed by fire. He provided a scholarship for the Florentine composer, Luigi Cherubini, and encouraged the historian, Riguccio Galluzzi, in the writing of his *History of the Grand Duchy of Tuscany under the House of Medici*.

Turning his attention to politics, the Grand Duke asked one of his principal bureaucrats, Francesco Maria Gianni, to provide the state with a written constitution and, while this had to be shelved for fear of what his brother in Vienna would have to say about such a document, he welcomed the election of a city government which was responsible for improvements in the city's drainage system, for moving the coal and straw market away from its unseemly location in the Piazza San Giovanni, for the building of a large restaurant in the Cascine, and for putting up street signs. With characteristic persistence, he urged the Commune to add to its reforms by improving the city's street lighting, which was then limited to some eighty oil lamps at street corners; and when the Commune baulked at the cost of installing and maintaining the forty-six extra lamps which he proposed, he badgered them until at least twenty-three lamps were authorized.

The Commune were only too well aware of how expensive his reforms and building programmes were proving to be. Having disbanded both the Tuscan navy and the army, as unnecessary extravagances, he sold two naval vessels, disposed of a large amount of military material to the British government and even entered into negotiations with the Russians, then at war with the Turks, for the sale of the island of Elba as a base for the Tsar's fleet in the Mediterranean. This, though, was too much for his mother, who put her imperial foot down and stopped the transaction from proceeding any further. Prevented from raising money in this way, the Grand Duke turned to the Church, greatly increasing the taxation of church benefices, and appropriating much church property. The Jesuit order in Tuscany, like the Inquisition, was suppressed. Ecclesiastical censorship was also abolished; and, while a civil censor remained in office, he was rarely allowed to intervene to suppress publication: book and magazine publishers both flourished.

It had to be admitted that the Grand Duke himself was not very consistent in the matters of freedom of expression and public morality. He liked to present himself as a champion of free speech, yet he closed down more than one theatre and saw to it that critics of his rule were reminded of their obligations to him as their sovereign. He condemned 'the indecent practice' of swimming in the Arno without proper bathing attire, yet he was a notorious womanizer, carelessly exercising a kind of *droit de seigneur* during his regular travels around his domain. 'He constantly portrayed himself as a religious moralist, one who prescribed black dress at court, outlawed prostitution and prohibited dice and card playing,' Eric Cochrane observed.

Indeed, he set an example of civic behaviour by walking to public events at the Uffizi instead of adding to the already chaotic carriage traffic. But every time he made a tour of the country, he left behind a string of violated peasant beds. While in Florence he spent most of his free nights not with his rather homely consort, who was almost always pregnant [and was to give birth to sixteen children] but with Lord Cowper's wife or, after 1786, with a charming young dancer named Livia Raimondi. And Livia gladly repaid him by diligently doing the reading he assigned her in Thomas à Kempis, Fénelon, and a whole shelfful of Jansenist moral theologians.

He had met this pretty girl from Rome when she was performing in the theatre as a ballet dancer. She was a most indifferent dancer and her performances were frequently greeted by catcalls and rude shouts from the university students who filled the upper seats. The girl's father took it upon himself to take her to the Palazzo Pitti where he complained about the audience's behaviour to the Grand Duke in person and asked him to intervene. The father was soon found a post in some government office, while the daughter was taken to the Grand Duke's bed and later installed in the Palazzina Livia[8] on the west side of the Piazza San Marco.

The visit of Livia Raimondi's father to the Pitti Palace was not an exceptional occurrence. Callers were encouraged there and notices were placed on the doors advising them that it was as offensive to offer a tip as to receive one. Occasional parties were given in the Boboli Gardens, where hundreds of guests, irrespective of class, were regaled with food, wine and music. Yet in their own homes the poor still lived sparely. The numerous employees of the government were ill-paid and firmly denied the customary bribes which had formerly supplemented their incomes. The workers in the cloth and silk industries, of whom there were still over 25,000 in a population of about 78,000 when Peter Leopold became Grand Duke, also had good cause to complain of their lot, of low wages and of the prices fixed by the official department known as the *Abbondanza*. These prices were, in any case, largely ignored by the peasants who came in from the *contado* to sell their wares in the market in the Piazza dell'Olio behind the Palazzo Arcivescovile.

Visitors to Florence in the late 1780s, however, were unconscious of any unrest in the city. Even the storming of the Bastille in Paris appears to have had few repercussions here. The theatres in 1789 were packed as usual; the Aquila Nera hotel was fully booked; the Grand Duchess gave a dinner at the Pitti Palace for about forty of the most notable foreign visitors. The police heard rumours of some sort of uprising being planned by two dissidents, one a baker, the other a second-hand-clothes dealer, who were reported as having gone to inspect the Forte di Belvedere, which, since the disbanding of the army and the subsequent dismissal of the militia, was virtually defenceless. But there seemed little danger that the conspiracy would come to anything.

Then, on 20 February 1790, the Emperor Joseph II died in Vienna; and soon afterwards his brother and heir, the Grand Duke Peter Leopold, followed by the Grand Duchess and their numerous children, together with wagonloads of furniture from the Pitti Palace, made their way north for the Alps and Austria.

Within weeks the Regency Council, which had been appointed before the Grand Duke's departure, had a full-scale riot on their hands. A mob armed with sticks and hatchets burst into the market in the Piazza dell'Olio shouting for a reduction in prices and scattering the peasant dealers before rampaging off down the Via de' Cerretani and the Via dei Rondinelli to ransack the houses of two well-known landowners and oil merchants, one of whom narrowly escaped being thrown out of a window of the Palazzo Vernaccia.

Another mob invaded the Mercato del Grano, brandishing axes, pushing aside the peasants there and selling off their stocks of grain, sack by sack, at the first price offered. The rioters then rushed off to the Palazzo Serristori,[9] the home of Antonio Serristori, the elderly president of the Regency Council, who sent them away to the house of a fellow senator, Francesco Maria Gianni, where they immediately made their way to the wine cellar. Sent from there to the house of yet another senator, Marco del Rosso, who, they were assured, would listen understandingly to their requests, they were at length persuaded to disperse.

By then, however, other rioters had decided to attack the Jews in the Ghetto.[10] But, after buying time by sending out delegates with bags full of money to distribute to the mob, the Jews sent for help to the merchants in the Mercato Vecchio; and the merchants, believing that they might well soon be attacked themselves, responded promptly to this request. Seizing such arms as they could lay their hands on, they marched off to the Ghetto, where the more spirited of the Jews were already fighting the invaders. The merchants were soon followed into the Ghetto by a young nobleman, well-liked and persuasive, Alamanno de' Pazzi, who bravely rode through the narrow entrance and succeeded in persuading most of the rioters to follow him back to the Pazzi Palace in the Via del Proconsolo, while an equally public-spirited young citizen, Orso D'Elci, a former officer in the militia, organized squads of *vigilanti* to patrol the streets. So, the uprising collapsed as suddenly as it had begun. Over a hundred men and women were arrested and several were sentenced to imprisonment or exile or to a life in the galleys of Sicily.

The Grand Duke was appalled and characteristically expressed his anger in a stream of letters to the incompetent Regency Council, which, having summoned the officers of Orso D'Elci's hastily formed national guard to a reception, relieved them of their commissions, thus disbanding the force that had helped to save Florence from anarchy.

Approachable, affable and engagingly enthusiastic, the Grand Duke Peter Leopold had been well enough liked in the earlier years of his reign, despite the unpopularity amongst certain interested classes of some of his policies, such as the imposition of free trade and the abolition of the ancient *arti*, which were replaced by a Chamber of Commerce. When he and the Grand Duchess had been carried down the Arno on their frequent visits to the other main cities of Tuscany, they had been loudly cheered by the people crowded along the river banks. Towards the end of his reign in Florence, however, criticisms of his regime had become commonplace. It was pointed out that his much-trumpeted reforms were not as radical as they had seemed: it was all very well to boast, for instance, of an elected Commune but all of the electors were taxpayers and many if not most of them were substantial landowners. Indeed, during the Grand Duke's time, although stripped of various archaic privileges, the aristocracy remained as influential as they had been a generation before, while the discontented clergy had become a significant force in the opposition, and the liberal intelligentsia, once keen supporters of the Grand Duke's reforms, had become increasingly influenced by events in France. The Florentines' new sovereign, Peter Leopold's second son, who became the Grand Duke Ferdinand III in June 1791, had an unenviable inheritance.

NAPOLEONIC INTERLUDE
1796–1827

'Over there, beyond the mountains, are stores,
food, clothes, guns, horses and money to reward us.'
NAPOLEON BONAPARTE

On the last day of June 1796, the Grand Duke Ferdinand III received in Florence an impatient and intense young guest, Napoleon Bonaparte. Less than three months before, the Directory in Paris, well aware that the brilliant and unscrupulous general would not hesitate to replenish their empty coffers with treasure looted from defeated enemies, had appointed him to the command of the French Army of Italy. Their confidence in him was not misplaced. Although they were ill-equipped, some of them without boots and many without pay for months, his soldiers responded eagerly to his call: 'You have had enough of misfortunes and privations. I shall put an end to that. Over there, beyond the mountains, are stores, food, clothes, guns, horses and money to reward us. We shall cast aside everything that keeps us from our enemies. Let us advance and stick our bayonets into their bodies.' Promised 'rich provinces, great cities . . . honour, glory and wealth', the French army – having imposed a separate peace upon the Piedmontese and forced them to cede Savoy and Nice to France – stormed the wooden bridge across the River Adda at Lodi, drove the Austrian defenders from the far bank and took 1,700 prisoners. A few days later Bonaparte entered Milan and occupied the palace from which the Austrian archduke had fled. 'The tricolour flies over Milan, Pavia, Como and all the towns of Lombardy,' he reported to the Directory. It was soon flying also over the castles of the Papal States as far south as Ancona and over Parma and Modena, from whose rulers immense sums of money, supplies of cattle and corn, and numerous works of art had been exacted. Bonaparte had then advanced upon Leghorn in Tuscany to deny the port to British shipping.

From Leghorn he had galloped over to Florence to assure the Grand Duke that Tuscany's declared neutrality would be respected. After making a quick tour of the city, walking briskly round the Boboli Gardens, and momentarily enjoying the splendid view from the windows of Zanobi del Rosso's recently erected Kaffeehaus,[1] he galloped off again, back to his army.

The neutrality he had promised to respect was, however, difficult for the Grand Duke to maintain, since Bonaparte's policy in Italy was to establish vassal republics in conquered territories, and surely Tuscany would soon be forced to become one too. A Cisalpine Republic had been established to govern the former territories of Venice, Lombardy, Mantua, Modena, Ravenna, Bologna and Ferrara; a Ligurian Republic with its capital at Genoa was proclaimed in December 1797, a Roman Republic in February 1798. The creation of this last republic on his northern frontier induced King Ferdinand of Naples to attempt the liberation of Rome from the French and to send six thousand troops to Leghorn to threaten the invaders from the north.

Concerned that this Neapolitan move upon Leghorn would damage his uneasy relations with France, the Grand Duke Ferdinand asked the Neapolitans to withdraw from Leghorn. They agreed to do so; but by then the Directory had seized upon the excuse to march into Tuscany. Their troops, commanded by General Gauthier, did so on Easter Sunday, 24 March 1799, with sprigs of olive fixed to their bayonets as a token of their peaceful intentions.

While his troops arrested the Florentine guards at the Porta San Gallo and imprisoned them in the Fortezza da Basso, General Gauthier established his headquarters, first at Palazzo Medici-Riccardi, then in Palazzo Corsini, and he had a guard, accompanied by a band, mounted at the Pitti Palace. The next day he and the French minister in Florence, Charles Reinhard, called at the Pitti Palace to see the Grand Duke, who received them in the Meridiana pavilion.[2]

They were perfectly polite; but they made it quite clear to him that he would have to leave Florence within twenty-four hours. He left before dawn on 27 March; and on that same day there appeared in Piazza Santa Croce and Piazza Santa Maria Novella those trappings of Jacobinism which were set up in all the newly invaded cities of Italy, the Trees of Liberty. A week or so later, Charles Reinhard, by then styled Civil Governor of Florence, invited the citizens to an official ceremony in which an exceptionally spectacular Tree of Liberty was to be planted in the Piazza della Signoria, now renamed the Piazza della Nazione.

On the appointed day, 9 April, the Palazzo Pitti was festooned with flowers and banners displaying the colours of the French flag; beneath the vault of the arcade entrance there appeared a majestic figure of Liberty wearing a Phrygian cap and carrying a spear in her right hand; and on a pedestal beneath were two paintings of female figures, the one a demure and submissive Etruria, the other a triumphant French Republic. The Palazzo della Signoria was similarly adorned, French flags and tricolours fluttering from the battlements and from every window. Below them the Loggia dei Lanzi was decorated with tapestries and a guard of honour was drawn up on parade around a specially erected amphitheatre in the middle of the piazza.

General Gauthier and his staff marched into the piazza, followed by regiment after regiment of French soldiers, to the obedient cheers of the populace. The French commanders took their seats on a tribune by the palace steps to watch the arrival of the immense Tree of Liberty mounted on a carriage and accompanied by a troop of bridegrooms in formal clothes and brides in white dresses. The brides held doves, the birds' legs attached to long tricolour ribbons which they released into the sky. They then exchanged wedding rings with their grooms, while workmen in their best clothes raised the Tree of Liberty into position beside the amphitheatre.

As night fell the city was illuminated by flambeaux; banquets were given outside in the warm spring air; toasts were offered to 'the bright new life which lay ahead'; and in Piazza Santa Maria Novella and Piazza Santa Croce, where the first Trees of Liberty had been raised, dancing went on far into the night, the French soldiers having no trouble in finding partners.

The friendly relations between citizens and invaders did not, however, last long. The Florentines soon grew exasperated by the number of French edicts and regulations which, headed by the Civil Commissioner's admonitory words, *Nous voulons*, led to the citizens calling their unwelcome visitors *Nuvoloni*, 'Cloud of Locusts'; and they were outraged when it became known that the French were not only requisitioning private property and expropriating church valuables, especially gold and silver altar vessels, but were also packing up treasures for dispatch to the Louvre in Paris, including, eventually, the Medici Venus, a most desirable companion piece, so Bonaparte had decided, for the Belvedere Apollo which had been removed from the Vatican after the French invasion of Rome. There were angry demonstrations against the occupying forces; Trees of Liberty were desecrated and pulled down; French posters and proclamations were defaced and torn from the walls; French soldiers were insulted in the streets.

The upper classes remained aloof. 'The members of high society in Florence live very sad and isolated lives,' commented a French official. 'They get up at midday, usually have lunch at two o'clock, then take a siesta until six when they dress in order to drive out in their carriages to the Cascine Park. Then to the theatre from nine o'clock till eleven and so home to supper and bed. This is what they do invariably from the first day of the year to the last.' Their 'supreme satisfaction' was doing nothing, 'surrounded by fine pictures, sculpture and furniture, attended by numerous servants in livery', and in 'parading the magnificence of their horses, harnesses and carriages in the public promenades'. Their education was 'superficial, without any real knowledge of science or the arts, of agriculture or, indeed, of any useful subjects of study'.

Having approved the construction of a monumental column in Santa Croce and a 'Napoleon Forum' on confiscated land to the north of the city – neither of which was built – Bonaparte returned to Paris where, in November 1799, after his invasion of Egypt, he staged his *coup d'état* which brought the Directory to an end and established himself as the first of a triumvirate of Consuls.

In his absence the French armies in Italy suffered severe reverses and anti-French insurrections broke out on all sides. Among the most violent of these uprisings were those in Tuscany, most particularly that in Arezzo, where a large band of patriots and rebels, mostly peasants, gathered to march upon the French garrisons of Siena and Florence. They were led by Captain Mari, a former officer in the Grand Duke Ferdinand III's dragoon guards, and a limping, hard-swearing Capuchin friar who had appointed himself chaplain to the force. Also with them was the daughter of a butcher from Montevarchi, Cassandra Cini, dressed half as a woman and half as a soldier, who became Captain Mari's wife. This bizarre army of undisciplined insurgents liberated Siena, which they pillaged brutally, and then moved on to Florence as the French forces retreated northwards from the city.

In Florence the French flags and emblems had been torn down from the Palazzo della Signoria and, together with the crumpled-up manifestos and proclamations issued by the Civil Commissioner, had been burned in the Piazza. General Gauthier had thought it as well to gallop out of the city for Leghorn, escorted by a troop of cavalry, taking with him several hostages, who were threatened with execution should anyone in Florence who had displayed French sympathies be killed. None was killed but a number were beaten and imprisoned.

After Gauthier's departure, a provisional government was established, and representatives were sent to negotiate with Captain Mari and the hungry insurgents from Arezzo who had arrived on the outskirts of the city on 7 July. It was agreed that they might pass through the gates, which they did the next day when the Hon. William Frederick Wyndham, the English chargé d'affaires in Florence, offered his services as intermediary.

Wyndham's presence and tact, however, were of little use in dealing with Captain Mari's unruly rabble, which immediately set about plundering Florence as thoroughly as they had recently pillaged Siena, so that the Florentines welcomed with relief the arrival of a force of Austrian and Cossack troops sent to the city by the Austrian commander-in-chief whose army had helped to drive the French from Italy a few months before. They were even prepared to tolerate good-humouredly the sight of Cossacks demonstrating their skill with the lance as they galloped through the Mercato Vecchio spearing the rolls of salami on display on the butchers' stalls.

Having proclaimed the renewed sovereignty of the Grand Duke Ferdinand III, the Austrian and Russian troops left Florence at the end of July 1799 in the care of the city's provisional government, which struggled to restore its finances by vainly appealing for voluntary contributions from the citizens, by attempting to levy a forced loan upon the Jewish community and by imposing fines upon those who had collaborated with the French invaders. Meanwhile, the Grand Duke remained in Vienna, awaiting a more favourable moment to return.

Determined to restore his hold on Italy, Bonaparte marched an army of 40,000 men across the St Bernard Pass in May 1800; and, on 14 June, defeated the Austrians at Marengo in Piedmont. Later that year the French reoccupied Florence; and Tuscany was transformed from a client state of Austria to a client state of France. This Bonaparte achieved by creating a new Kingdom of Etruria and by placing upon its throne the twenty-eight-year-old son of the Bourbon Duke of Parma, who was married to the Infanta Maria Luisa, the lively, proud, ill-educated daughter of King Charles IV of Spain.

Louis of Parma, who thus suddenly found himself King Louis of Etruria, arrived in Florence on 10 August 1801 in a convoy of forty-six Spanish carriages. The citizens were not impressed. He was quite good-looking, tall and very fair, in contrast to his small, dark Spanish wife, but his face bore a vacant look. His dress was untidy; his coat was crumpled; his long hair was tied by a black ribbon into a pigtail; he was said to be frightened of horses and to suffer from epilepsy.

His behaviour in Florence during his brief residence here did nothing to mitigate his unprepossessing appearance. He was ill much of the time and had to leave business to his wife who, bossy, tactless and incompetent, greatly displeased the Florentines by her evident approval of the reintroduction of the Inquisition and of a new atmosphere of religious intolerance. There was, therefore, much apprehension in the city when King Louis died and the Prime Minister announced that his four-year-old son, Carlo Ludovico, would succeed him as King of Etruria, with the child's mother as Regent.

The Regent did her best to ingratiate herself with the Florentine people. She entertained guests lavishly at the Pitti Palace, holding splendid receptions for artists and writers as well as for the aristocracy and government officials. She gave a celebrated party in the Loggia dei Lanzi for two hundred small boys and girls from working-class families, who were allowed to take

*Portrait of Napoleon
Bonaparte by Andrea Appiani
the Elder.*

their plates and glasses, spoons and napkins home after the banquet as the Regent watched complacently from a platform erected outside the Palazzo della Signoria and bands played and cannon boomed from the Forte di Belvedere. But Maria Luisa never gained much liking or respect in Florence and few regretted her departure when, curtly informed by the French ambassador that Tuscany had been annexed to the French Empire, she was sent back to Spain.

Bonaparte had had himself crowned Emperor in Paris in December 1804. He had been proclaimed King of Italy the following year, and, after his brilliant victory over the Austrians and Russians at Austerlitz, had begun dividing Europe up amongst his family. His eldest brother, Joseph, had become King of Spain. A younger brother, Louis, had been placed upon the throne of Holland; another brother, Jérôme, became King of Westphalia. His brother-in-law, Joachim Murat, an innkeeper's son, was proclaimed King of Naples. His sister, Elisa, married to an easy-going Corsican army officer, Felice Bacciochi, was created Princess of Piombino and Lucca; and in March 1809 joint sovereignty of the Grand Duchy of Tuscany was conferred upon her and her husband.

Like her predecessor, the new Grand Duchess went out of her way to establish good relations with the Florentines, in so far as the directives transmitted to her by her imperial brother would allow. She gave grand levees at the Pitti Palace, which was redecorated with money granted to her by Napoleon; she saved various religious houses from extinction and gave valuable aid to a number of charitable institutions. She permitted the general public the use of the Cascine, where, wearing clothes of a distinctly military cut, she took pleasure in reviewing her troops. But, as also with her predecessor, she was never much liked in Florence and her reign there as Grand Duchess came to a sudden end, for in January 1814 yet another army was marching on Florence. This was a Neapolitan force commanded by Joachim Murat who, having lost confidence in Napoleon after the defeat of the Grand Army at Leipzig, had made a treaty with the Austrians by which he undertook to ensure peace in Italy. With their agreement he marched north to occupy Rome and Florence and restore Pope Pius VII and the Grand Duke Ferdinand III to their respective thrones. He entered Florence on 31 January; and the next day, Elisa Bacciochi left it, soon to be followed by the French troops, whose parades and manoeuvres she had taken such pleasure in watching.

A few months later, the Grand Duke Ferdinand returned to the city to the excited acclamations of the people. Elisa Bacciochi settled in Trieste where, calling herself Countess of Campignano, grumpy and embittered, immensely fat and almost bald, she died in 1820, bearing an extraordinary resemblance to Napoleon, who himself by then had but a few months left to live in sad exile on the island of St Helena. Joachim Murat was taken prisoner and shot in Calabria. The Grand Duke Ferdinand III settled down in Florence in apparent contentment, a benign and enlightened ruler enjoying the confidence of his people, guided in his policies by intelligent and experienced politicians, notably Count Vittorio Fossombroni, a highly capable mathematician and hydraulic engineer from Arezzo.

Foreign visitors, so many of whom had abandoned Florence in Napoleon's day, now began to return; and, sooner or later, many of the more distinguished of them found their way to the palace of the Young Pretender's widow, the Countess of Albany. She and her lover, Count Alfieri, had thought it as well to leave Paris – where they had settled after their sojourn in Rome – lest they were forced to follow others of their kind to the guillotine. They had arrived in Florence in 1792, having had to abandon most of their possessions and all their furniture. For a time they had lived in lodgings with their French servants before moving into the Palazzo Masetti on the Lungarno Corsini.[3] Here, in rooms on the top floor which he added, Alfieri read and worked, while in her large, barely furnished *salotto* on the *piano nobile*, the Countess held court, sitting by the fireplace in a simple wooden chair set apart from the others which were arranged as though for a lecture. For thirty years she conducted a *salon* into which her lover, increasingly crotchety, remote and gouty, seldom penetrated, an alarming figure when he did so, frightening the more nervous guests with his persistent scowl, as he looked around the room sucking the golden top of his cane, rarely unbending, although as the Countess's friend, Lady Holland, conceded, he was good company when he condescended to be so. Occasionally he could be seen leaving the palace, a skeletally thin figure with a deeply lined face, to ride about the Cascine like a man possessed.

Driven from Florence by the approach of the French troops, Alfieri and his mistress had gone to live in a villa beyond the Porta San Gallo near the Villa Stibbert.[4] When they had returned to the city he was more difficult than ever, shutting himself up in his room at the top of the house as he struggled to finish his autobiography, grumpy and ill, slamming the door when he returned late at night from one of his regular visits to a woman with whom he was supposed to be conducting an unhappy affair. He died in 1803 and the Countess was desolate. 'I am now alone in the world,' she lamented. 'I have lost all – consolation, support, society, all, all!'

In fact, she was not alone. For some time past she had had another companion, a Frenchman thirteen years younger than herself, a professor of fine arts at the university, who had fled from France to escape the Revolution in 1791. This was François-Xavier Fabre, an intelligent, alert and appealing painter, a former pupil of David, who had first been drawn to the Palazzo Masetti by his admiration for Count Alfieri. He helped the Countess in making arrangements for her dead lover's burial in Santa Croce and for the execution of his memorial by Antonio Canova, then at the height of his fame.[5]

The Countess was fifty at the time of Alfieri's death. She had grown uncommonly fat, and, so Gino Capponi said, 'was not in the least poetical and was dressed like a servant', frequently wearing an apron over her dress and a fichu round her neck. She could no longer be seen walking briskly along the Arno as she so often had in the past, though occasionally she was glimpsed of an evening sitting in her carriage outside the Caffè del Bottegone, from which waiters brought her tea, cake or *pistacchiata* 'which she consumed without getting out of her carriage', James Lees-Milne recorded in his delightful *The Last Stuarts*. 'The beggars from the steps of the Duomo, attracted by the elegant equipage, would congregate round it. Occasionally they would be tossed a coin and told to enter the west door of the Duomo and offer a prayer for their benefactress.'

In the remaining twenty years of her life, she went out but rarely, spending long hours writing letters or reading in her library; but Fabre, who moved into the Palazzo Masetti after his parents and brother had all died, was her constant companion and her *salon* was not abandoned. Madame de Staël came; so did Jean-Charles-Léonard Simonde de Sismondi, the Genevan economist and historian who was Madame de Staël's guide during her journey through Italy. Indeed, Palazzo Masetti had gained so notorious a reputation as a meeting place for opponents of the French regime that the Countess was summoned to Paris in 1809 for an interview with Napoleon.

The Emperor opened the conversation by accusing her of making trouble in Florence where his sister, Elisa, was then Grand Duchess. But it soon became clear to him that the Countess was not much interested in politics, a subject not encouraged in her salon. He asked her if she had ever had a child by Prince Charles, and he seemed disappointed when she said that she had not: a Stuart placed on the throne in London by courtesy of Napoleon would have been a pleasant prospect.

The Countess was permitted to return to Florence, where she resumed her old life, receiving guests at the Palazzo Masetti as in the past, befriending Ugo Foscolo, the poet and novelist, who resembled Alfieri (near whose tomb he was to be buried in Santa Croce),[6] making much of the Comte de Flahaut, Talleyrand's natural son and the lover of both Napoleon's sister, Caroline, and of his stepdaughter, Hortense, Queen of Holland. She intimidated the future statesman, Massimo d'Azeglio – who, in nervously attempting to eat one of those hard, round ice creams known as *mattonelle*, deeply offended her by sending it shooting off his saucer on to the floor at her feet by way of the chest of the Sardinian minister – and exasperated English visitors by her aloof manner and rudely impulsive comments. To one of these English guests, the Duke of Bedford's youngest son, Lord William Russell, she seemed a 'cross, ill-natured old cat, speaking ill of everybody. Her house was crowded with vulgar English.'

It was difficult to believe that this was the woman who not long before had fascinated Alphonse de Lamartine, secretary to the French Consulate in Florence, by her wit and conversation, her sparkling eyes and 'graceful expression', that this was the Countess of Albany whose favour and company had eagerly been sought in these same rooms by Stendhal and Chateaubriand and by almost every person of note who had passed through Florence since the time of the French Revolution. She died on 29 January 1824 and was buried in the Cappella Castellani in Santa Croce, near the tomb of her beloved Alfieri.[7]

In 1823, the year before the Countess of Albany's death, Dorothea de Lieven, wife of the Russian ambassador at the Court of St James and mistress of Prince Metternich, arrived in Florence. She found the Countess a 'source of entertainment', but very few other residents of much interest. She went to 'a great ball' which was given for her by Prince Camillo Borghese. His house was 'beautiful and decorated with taste', but he himself could 'scarcely breathe for fat, diamonds and stupidity'. She went to pay her respects at court where the Grand Duke remembered it was 'exactly a year to the day' since he had seen her for the first time at Verona: 'You have to be a sovereign to possess a memory like that. How ridiculous that he should have nothing better to do.' She went the usual rounds, but 'felt like Madame de Sévigné, who said that what she saw tired her and what she did not see worried her'. At least she walked about a great deal and felt well.

'And I *look* well,' she told Metternich; 'so much so that people laugh when I inform them that I came to Italy for my health. I am growing fat in the very teeth of providence. I cannot understand what has accomplished the miracle. However, as it happened in Florence, I do not see why I should leave such a miraculous spot [even though] what little society exists here is negligible.'

The English society was presided over by Lord Burghersh, the tenth Earl of Westmorland's only son, a talented violinist who had been aide-de-camp

Sir Thomas Lawrence's portrait of the Countess of Blessington (1789–1849), who stayed in Florence, at the Casa Pecori.

to the Duke of Wellington and was to be minister at Berlin. His wife, Priscilla, a daughter of the Earl of Mornington, was a competent artist and accomplished linguist, but 'a woman of severe social principle', who was said to have 'contrived to copy out portions of Byron's memoirs and then, curiosity satisfied, to have destroyed her copy with much public indignation'.

Lady Burghersh was gracious enough to Madame de Lieven, but to another lady of more obviously unconventional morals, who also happened to be in Florence at this time, she was positively hostile. This was Lady Blessington, wife of the rich and extravagant Earl of Blessington, a friend of Lord Byron and of Count d'Orsay, with whom she was to live after her husband's death. On a subsequent visit to Florence in 1826, the Blessingtons found, to their relief, that the prudish Burghershes were away, and ministerial affairs were being attended to by Lord Strangeways and the Earl of Mulgrave's heir, Lord Normanby, one day to be British ambassador in Paris but then a foppish young man with an affected lisp and a passion for theatricals, which were performed in his private theatre in the Palazzo di San Clemente.

Lord and Lady Blessington and Count d'Orsay, who had come to Florence with them, got on extremely well with Lord Normanby, as they also did with Walter Savage Landor. This generous-hearted and explosively quarrelsome author, who had settled in Florence in 1821, was now living with his wife and four young children in rooms at the Palazzo Medici-Riccardi. The Blessingtons and d'Orsay were as often to be seen there as Landor himself was to be found at the house which the Blessingtons had taken, the Casa Pecori.

The Blessingtons' pleasant sojourn in Florence was broken when Lord and Lady Burghersh returned. By then Lord Blessington had eccentrically decided to leave part of his fortune to Count d'Orsay, to whom he was devoted, on condition that the Count married his fifteen-year-old daughter by a former wife. When Blessington, in his usual genial, light-hearted way, apprised Lord Burghersh of this proposal, the minister was naturally horrified, believing as everyone else did that Lady Blessington and d'Orsay were lovers; and, in order to forestall the plan, he insisted that since d'Orsay was a French Roman Catholic, there must be a dual ceremony and that the Anglican ceremony must take precedence over the Catholic one. To this, as expected, the French minister in Florence refused to agree. So Lady Blessington ill-advisedly went to see Lord Burghersh herself, and he was predictably 'very rude' to her. So the whole Blessington ménage moved on to Naples, where the strange marriage took place, after d'Orsay had written to Landor to say he would very much like to cut off Lord Burghersh's nose.

RISORGIMENTO
1814–59

'We have made history.
Now let's have dinner.'
CAMILLO CAVOUR

The ten years that followed the Grand Duke Ferdinand III's return to Florence in 1814 saw numerous reforms and improvements in the government of Tuscany and the administration of Florence, in the police and in prisons, in hospitals and schools, in the judiciary and criminal law, in charities and public works. The grandly imposing Palazzo Borghese appeared in Via Ghibellina;[1] a splendid façade was added to the villa of Poggio Imperiale;[2] and the arcades on either side of Porta alla Croce in what is now Piazza Beccaria were completed, much to the satisfaction of the people attending the market held there every Friday.

The Florentines evinced the greatest pleasure in the return of their agreeable and accommodating Grand Duke, who moved freely and chattily amongst his people, putting aside the strict ceremonial of the court. He entertained guests at the Pitti Palace with conjuring tricks and attended a ball to celebrate the reopening of the Pergola theatre in a plain frock-coat and a top hat from which hung a mask, indicating his approval of the revels without compromising the dignity of his high rank.

The citizens' pleasure in the Grand Duke's return was, however, marred by one slight disappointment: the rather unpromising nature and somewhat unprepossessing appearance of his seventeen-year-old heir, the Archduke Leopold. Tall, thin and stooped, Leopold had been born in Florence and had spent his first years in the Pitti Palace; but he had been educated in Austria and spoke German better than Italian. He was known in Florence as Canapino (and later as Canapone) because of his straw-coloured hair, also as Il Broncio because of his generally lugubrious expression. His high, domed forehead was brushed by a prominent forelock; his dimpled chin, one day to be surrounded by prodigious side-whiskers, was smooth and pale. He was known to be not very intelligent and extremely pious.

When he was twenty he was married in the church of Santissima

Annunziata to the niece of the King of Saxony, Princess Maria Anna Carolina. The ceremony took place a few weeks after the marriage of his sister to the son of Duke Charles Emmanuel of Savoy, Prince Charles Albert, who was to become King of Sardinia-Piedmont in 1831 and the father of King Victor Emmanuel II. But after three years had passed the Archduke Leopold and his wife had failed to have a child; and the arch- duke's father, the Grand Duke Ferdinand III, whose wife had died in 1802, decided that he would have to attempt to secure the succession to the Grand Duchy himself. So he asked his son's father-in-law, Prince Maximilian of Saxony, for the hand of his other daughter. Although this princess was twenty-seven years younger than her ageing suitor, her father readily consented to the marriage, which took place, accompanied by the most elaborate festivities, on 6 May 1821 in the Duomo.

The Grand Duke did not live long to enjoy the company of his pleasant young wife. Having been seriously ill with an acute fever shortly before his marriage, he was struck down again in the summer of 1824 after a visit to the marshlands of the Tuscan Maremma where his chief minister, Count Fossombroni, had instigated an ambitious scheme of land reclamation. Over two thousand of the Grand Duke's subjects called every day at the Pitti Palace to ask after him and to pay their respects; and, after his death on 18 June, for three consecutive days crowds of people lined up in the Piazza Pitti to file past his body, which was laid out on a catafalque in one of the state apartments of the palace.

A proclamation was immediately issued in the name of the new Grand Duke Leopold II announcing his succession and confirming all the existing ministers, as well as magistrates, officials and army officers, in their posts. At the same time Count Fossombroni arranged for the whole grand-ducal family to be moved out of Florence to the villa of Castello to keep them out of reach of the Austrian minister, who was expected to seek a private audience to convey to the Grand Duke advice and instructions from his uncle in Vienna, the Emperor Francis II. As had been feared the Austrian minister did, indeed, attempt to talk to the Grand Duke on behalf of the Emperor; but Count Fossombroni succeeded in keeping him at bay, with the excuse that his master was so overcome by grief at the death of his father that he could see nobody.

The independence of Tuscany was not, however, threatened only by the Austrian Emperor, the embodiment of conservatism in Europe: in Fossombroni's view, its independence was equally threatened by the increas- ingly powerful movement for the unification of Italy. This movement, the Risorgimento, took two forms, the one monarchical, as represented by the Grand Duke's brother-in-law, Charles Albert, King of Sardinia-Piedmont and later by Charles Albert's son, Victor Emmanuel II, the other republican, inspired by the Genoese idealist and conspirator, Giuseppe Mazzini, and

A joust in the Piazza Santa Croce in the sixteenth century by Giovanni Stradano.

A white onyx cameo in the Museo degli Argenti by Antonio De' Rossi (c. 1575) showing the Grand Duke Cosimo I, his wife and children.

A relief in semiprecious stones, enamelled gold, diamonds and sapphires of the Grand Duke Cosimo II (1590–1621) from the centre part of a dismantled altar frontal. Through the window can be seen the Campanile and Duomo in pietre dure with the cathedral's façade as yet unfinished.

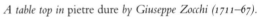

A cassone *panel from the Palazzo Pitti showing the perspective of an ideal city in wood inlay.*

Left: The Festa degli Omaggi *in the Piazza della Signoria, one of numerous festivals held in Florence in the time of the Grand Dukes.*

A table top in pietre dure *by Giuseppe Zocchi (1711–67).*

L'Architettura, *a work in* pietre dure *by Giuseppe Zocchi.*

Visitors to Florence in the early 1760s being introduced to Sir Horace Mann, the British Minister, who stands on the far right. A caricature by Thomas Patch, whose bust is in the corner and whose face is shown in the animal pictures on the wall.

The Tribuna of the Uffizi *by Johann Zoffany, 1772, in the Royal Collection.*
(For the identification of the men in this picture, see note 4, Chapter 18.)

A firework display on the Arno by Giovanni Signorini.

Italian flags paraded through the Piazza della Signoria in 1860, the year in which the people of Tuscany voted for the unification of the Grand Duchy with Italy under King Victor Emmanuel II.

Below: The monument to Dante being erected in the Piazza Santa Croce in 1865, from the painting by V. Giacomelli.

*Above: Annexation of the
Grand Duchy of Tuscany to
the Kingdom of Savoy. Late-
nineteenth-century painting
by Francesco Mochi.*

*Left: The Ponte Vecchio in
1905 by R.C. Goff.*

promoted by Mazzini's movement, Giovane Italia. The policy of the Tuscan government – in the early years of Leopold's reign left largely in the capable hands of Count Fossombroni and his principal colleagues, Neri Corsini and Francesco Cempini – was to assert Tuscan independence against Austrian interference, while at the same time resisting populist pressures for a unified Italy, without outright repression of liberal views.

Indeed, the Florentine authorities were so tolerant of dissent at this time that the city became a haven for moderate liberals and for the literary lions of the Risorgimento. The poet and novelist, Ugo Foscolo, came to Florence from Venice; from Recanati, south of Ancona, came Giacomo Leopardi, some of whose most tragic poetry was inspired by his love for a beautiful Florentine woman, Fanny Targioni-Tozzetti; Leopardi's friend, the scholar, Pietro Giordani, came from Piacenza. The Neapolitan historian, Pietro Colletta, wrote his celebrated *Storia del reame di Napoli* in Florence. Alessandro Manzoni arrived from Milan and rewrote his great novel, *I promessi sposi*, adopting in each successive edition more and more Tuscan language into the text.

These men, and others like them, were in the habit of meeting in the large Gabinetto Scientifico-Letterario in the Palazzo Buondelmonti in the Piazza Santa Trinita. This had been founded by Gian Pietro Vieusseux, a scholar of Swiss descent who was born in Liguria and had settled in Florence in 1819 at the age of forty. Vieusseux had soon made friends with the Marchese Gino Capponi, a cultivated liberal aristocrat and author of a highly regarded history of Florence, and with the Florentine poet, Giuseppe Giusti; and in the large club room of the Gabinetto, where articles for forthcoming issues of Italy's leading review, *Antologia*, were eagerly discussed, Vieusseux welcomed foreigners as well as Italian visitors, among them Chateaubriand, Heine, Byron and Shelley.[3]

The Grand Duke Leopold regarded this intellectual activity with a benign eye. Occasionally, under pressure from Vienna, he was persuaded to take action against some over-zealous reformer or some too-liberal publication: in 1833, for instance, he approved the suppression of Vieusseux's *Antologia*. Yet he seemed for the most part to be on the side of enlightenment, progress and the advancement of scholarship. He welcomed the attachment of several leading Tuscan scientists to the Egyptian expedition led by the great French Egyptologist, François Champollion; and he subsequently founded the Egyptian Museum in the Museo Archeologico.[4] He organized and financed two congresses of Italian scientists; he encouraged the construction of new roads and bridges, and, although Pope Gregory XVI strongly condemned them as likely to 'work harm to religion', he approved the expansion of railway networks throughout Tuscany. In his time tracks were laid between Pisa and Leghorn and soon afterwards the line was completed, joining Prato to Florence, where a railway station was erected near Santa

Maria Novella. Moreover, for the first time in Italy, telegraph wires were suspended beside the railway tracks.

Gas lamps appeared in the streets and, on the night of their introduction, the Grand Duke himself joined the crowds of citizens who went out into Via Maggio and unfolded their newspapers to assure themselves that the light, as they were promised it would do, enabled them to read the *Gazetto di Firenze* at a distance of seventeen arms' lengths from the lanterns. By then the dreaded and unsavoury prison, the Stinche, had been demolished and the site purchased by Girolamo Pagliano, an enterprising entrepreneur, who, having failed as a singer and a banker, and having been for a time a fashionable tailor, made a fortune as the manufacturer of a popular emetic. On the site of the Stinche he constructed houses, shops and a riding ring, which, with money made from a syrup for sore throats and hoarseness, he later converted into the Teatro Pagliano.

Like his father, the Grand Duke Leopold took a close interest in the draining of the marshlands of the Tuscan Maremma, on which some five thousand labourers were employed; and, as a token of his appreciation of the value of this reclamation of so extensive an area of waste land, he imported a stock of prize merino sheep from Saxony to graze there, thus giving a valuable impulse to the Tuscan wool industry.

In Florence itself he encouraged the development of areas outside the city centre and the improvement of existing streets and buildings. Via Calzaiuoli was widened; the Lungarno Amerigo Vespucci was completed, and the Piazza del Duomo enlarged. Housing for over three hundred poor families was built in the area between San Marco and the Fortezza da Basso. Statues of numerous Tuscan notabilities, from Giotto and Dante to Michelangelo, Alberti, Cellini and Petrarch, were installed in the ground-floor arcades of the Uffizi.

By the summer of 1830 – when he presided over a splendid fiesta in the Boboli Gardens, walking through the large assembly and talking amicably to his guests – the Grand Duke Leopold had become almost as popular as his father, though he did not create so favourable an impression upon foreign visitors to Florence. James Fenimore Cooper found him agreeable enough when he was granted an audience at the Pitti Palace. 'He gave me a very civil reception,' Fenimore Cooper recorded. 'I paid my compliments and made an offering of a book which I had caused to be printed in Florence. This he accepted with great politeness... At length he rose and I took my leave of him... When we separated, he went quietly to his maps; and, as I turned at the door to make a parting salute, I found his eyes on the paper, as if he expected no such ceremony.'

Other foreign visitors, however, were far from being so taken with him. Fenimore Cooper's fellow American, Sophie Hawthorne, later described him as looking 'like a monkey, most ugly and mean [with] that frightful, coarse, protruding underlip, peculiar to the court of Austria'; while Thomas Adolphus Trollope considered his manner 'about as bad and unprincely as can well be conceived. His clothes never fitted him and he always appeared to be struggling painfully with the consciousness that he had nothing to say. When strangers would venture some word of compliment on the prosperity and contentment of the Tuscans, his reply invariably was, "*Sono tranquilli* (they are quiet)."' Besides, his guests at the Pitti Palace were allowed to 'behave abominably':

> The English would seize the plates of *bonbons* and empty the contents into their coat pockets. The ladies would do the same with their pocket handkerchiefs. But the Duke's liege subjects carried on their depredations on a far bolder scale. I have seen large portions of fish, sauce, and all, packed up in a newspaper and deposited in a pocket. I have seen fowls and ham share the same fate, without any newspaper at all. I have seen jelly carefully wrapped in an Italian countess's laced *mouchoir*!

Tranquil as the Florentines may have seemed to the Grand Duke in the summer of 1830, they were not long to remain so; for, little more than a fortnight after that grand fiesta in the Boboli Gardens, there were demonstrations and uprisings in Paris, Brussels and Warsaw which were eventually to lead the way to his downfall. At first it seemed that he might weather the gathering storm. Although he appeared to listen more attentively to the pro-Austrian faction at court than to the moderate Count Fossombroni, when he was advised that it might be necessary to call for Austrian troops to suppress outbreaks of violence in the Grand Duchy, he decided against such a provocative step, following instead Fossombroni's advice and recreating the *Guardia Urbana* to defend the government and keep the peace. The *Guardia* was accordingly paraded in the Boboli Gardens on 17 April 1831, the Grand Duke himself taking the salute amidst a great display of public enthusiasm.

Scarcely had the new force been formed, however, than the Grand Duke, under pressure from Austria and in the first of several sudden changes of policy, dissolved it, to the great satisfaction of the officers of Tuscany's small army, who considered their authority to be under threat, but to the chagrin of Fossombroni, who wrote from his home town of Arezzo to a friend in Florence expressing his wish to retire from his thankless office.

There was a brief resurgence of the Grand Duke's popularity with the people of Florence the following year, when the Grand Duchess, who had given birth to three daughters, died after a painful illness; and Leopold, following a period of sincere mourning in which his subjects shared, married for the second time at the age of thirty-five. His eighteen-year-old bride was the Neapolitan Princess Maria Antonia, the short, plump, ill-educated sister of King Francis I. She spoke with a pronounced southern accent, and was later said to be bossy and rather mean; but for the moment the Florentines were captivated by her youthful prettiness and apparent good nature. The welcome given to her in the city was as enthusiastic as that given to her predecessor as Grand Duchess fifteen years before. The church bells rang, cannon were fired from the forts, regimental bands paraded through the splendidly decorated streets with drums beating and trumpets blaring as crowds of spectators cheered and clapped their hands.

The Grand Duke used the occasion of his marriage to increase the goodwill which it had evoked. To the surprise of his bride – whose parsimonious brother would never have been so open-handed in Naples – he announced his intention of making a distribution of gifts among his subjects, of redeeming many pawned goods and returning them to their owners, and of distributing charity to the needy, as well as providing dowries for poor girls whose parents could not afford them. The birth of a daughter and then of an heir to the Grand Duchy, both events being celebrated with characteristic exuberance in Florence, added to the parents' popularity. So did the dismissal of the widely disliked Presidente del Buon Governo, the resolutely pro-Austrian minister responsible for the police and prisons.

Yet disturbances and unrest elsewhere in Italy helped to persuade the Grand Duke that he could not afford to allow the liberals too much freedom to express their views; and soon after the dismissal of the Presidente del Buon Governo – which was noisily welcomed by hundreds of demonstrators shouting abuse outside his house – a number of prominent liberals or republicans were detained or imprisoned. Francesco Guerrazzi, the historical novelist, colleague of Mazzini and founder of the suppressed political journal, *Indicatore livornese*, was exiled to the island of Elba; Vincenzo Salvagnoli, a Florentine anticlerical lawyer living in Leghorn, was incarcerated in the fortress there; other outspoken critics of Austria were imprisoned in Florence itself. In protest at these arrests, Count Fossombroni at last retired from political life, as did his fellow liberal, Neri Corsini, the minister for foreign affairs, both of whom died soon afterwards.

The situation was transformed in 1846 by the election as Pope of the kindly, polite, good-looking and, until then, little-known Cardinal Mastai Ferretti. A man of sensitivity and generosity, virtuous and simple with a charming self-deprecating humour, it seemed at first that Pius IX, as he chose to be known, would prove to be what Metternich, the Austrian state chancellor, condemned as a contradiction in terms, a reforming Pope. Immediately after his election he formed a council to watch over all branches of the administration and to investigate proposals for modernization and change. He promised to support scientific congresses, appointed a commission on railways and on the civil and penal codes, and granted an amnesty for political offences. Metternich was horrified. 'We

Homage paid at the tomb of the Florentine hero, Francesco Ferrucci, during a street demonstration in 1847.

were prepared for everything but a liberal Pope,' he said, appalled at what was happening, 'and now that we have one, who can tell what may happen?' It was 'the greatest misfortune of the age'. 'A new era' was approaching.

Devoutly Catholic as he was, the Grand Duke could not fail to be influenced by the Pope's actions, nor to ignore his lead. He conceded a limited freedom of the press in Florence, where the newspaper *L'Alba* ('Dawn') soon appeared, edited by the Sicilian revolutionary, Giuseppe La Farina, later secretary of the influential nationalist movement, the Società Nazionale Italiana. The Grand Duke also reinstated the *Guardia Civica*, and appointed a well-known liberal, who had once been his tutor, as head of a new council of ministers.

The next year, 1848, revolutions broke out all over Europe; and Tuscany did not escape the general agitation. There were insurrections in Pisa and Leghorn, followed by rumours of an imminent uprising in Florence; and the Grand Duke decided he must grant a constitution to Tuscany as the King of Naples had already done and as the Pope had promised to do in Rome and King Charles Albert in Turin. Leopold also placated the liberals by the appointment as Gonfaloniere in Florence of Baron Bettino Ricasoli, the proud, austere, patrician advocate of moderate reform, later to be the earnest promoter of the union of Tuscany with Piedmont.

In March, news reached Florence of astonishing events in Milan: insurgents had driven the Austrian garrison out of the city and forced the withdrawal of the formidable Marshal Radetzky, who had brought in troops to restore order. Emboldened by this success, Charles Albert, the self-tormenting and indecisive King of Sardinia-Piedmont, at last made up his mind to set out with his army to try to drive the Austrians out of Italy once and for all. In Florence the response to what became known as the Five Days of Milan was immediate. Excited students, members of the *Guardia Civica*, soldiers of the Tuscan army and numerous civilian volunteers, including Carlo Lorenzini (Carlo Collodi, the future author of *Le avventure di Pinocchio*), all flocked to the colours to enrol themselves under the aged General D'Arco Ferrari. Over six thousand men were soon enlisted in two corps to fight alongside the Piedmontese army and were marched off to face the Austrians. Most of the volunteers enrolled in Tuscany fought bravely; but they were no match for the well-trained professional troops of Marshal Radetzky. Sustaining heavy casualties, they were overwhelmed at Curtatone, then at Montanara; while at Custoza, near Verona, the army of King Charles Albert was also defeated, as it was again, this time decisively, at Novara in March 1849.

Baron Bettino Ricasoli (1809–80), appointed Gonfaloniere of Florence in 1848; he succeeded Cavour as premier in 1861.

These disasters, and the consequent abdication of King Charles Albert in favour of his son, Victor Emmanuel, greatly heartened the pro-Austrian faction at court in Florence. At the same time the radicals, determined that the many lives lost in the cause of Italian unity should not have been given in vain, called for the dismissal of the Grand Duke's ineffective government and the appointment as his chief minister of Francesco Guerrazzi, the Mazzinian firebrand, who had been exiled to Elba. The Grand Duke countered by appointing a man whom he hoped would be an acceptable compromise candidate, the sensible and much-respected Florentine, Marchese Gino Capponi. Capponi, however, in failing health and all but blind, was not acceptable to the radicals; so, yielding to pressure, Leopold called upon Giuseppe Montanelli, a professor of law at Pisa University and a known activist in progressive politics, to head a new administration. Montanelli in turn asked the extremist, Guerrazzi, to collaborate with him in government; and, between them, these two radicals persuaded the Grand Duke to allow a number of deputies from the Tuscan assembly to attend a constituent assembly in Rome in accordance with a plan formulated by Mazzini and his followers.

But by now the Pope, alarmed by the consequences of his early example, had become a very bulwark of conservatism. He threatened to excommunicate the members and supporters of any constituent assembly which might meet in Rome, so alarming the Grand Duke Leopold – who was already convinced that the political situation was slipping beyond his control – that he decided to send his family from Florence to Siena where, in early January 1849, he joined them. A few weeks later he left Siena in secret for the coast and then, disguised as a woman, sailed south for Gaeta in the Kingdom of Naples where the Pope had also sought a haven from the violence in Rome.

In Florence a provisional government was established by the triumvirate of Guerrazzi, Montanelli and Giuseppe Mazzini; but, unable to offer the people any protection against the Austrians, this government soon collapsed and the Commune, fearing a complete breakdown of order, formally invited the Grand Duke Leopold to return to Florence. He did so at the end of July 1849, having first arranged to have the city occupied by an Austrian army of occupation, mostly Hungarians and Croatians, who took to stamping through the streets in high black boots and shakos, while their officers in tight white uniforms with bright yellow-tasselled waistbands lounged outside the Caffè Doney in Via Tornabuoni or in the Casino dei Nobili almost opposite.[5]

These were miserable months for Florence, only recently recovered from one of the worst floods in her history, when the waters of the Arno, 'extending in one turbid, yellow, swirling mass', poured across a third of the city. 'The streets, once thronged with gay groups intent on pleasure or hastening from gallery to gallery, are now filled with beggars,' wrote a foreign resident of Florence in 1845. 'Burglaries and street robberies take place in open day ... Thrice within one week the diligence from Bologna was stopped and the passengers robbed of everything, and in one instance, for some imprudent expression of anger, severely beaten.'

The Grand Duke, by turning his back on his moderate past and behaving as though perfectly content with Austrian occupation, had by now lost all the esteem he had ever possessed with the people. On the Emperor Franz Josef's birthday he reviewed a ceremonial parade of Austrian troops in the Cascine park; and, on the occasion of an imperial visit to Italy, he not only travelled to Milan to welcome the Emperor but also accepted the honorary command of a newly raised Austrian regiment known as the Grand Duke of Tuscany's Dragoons. He approved the appointment of an Austrian general to the supreme command of the Tuscan army, withdrew the constitution he had granted earlier, reimposed press censorship, and imprisoned several leading Tuscan patriots.

Yet despite many setbacks and defeats, the general progress of the Risorgimento was inexorable; and in July 1858 it received a new and forceful impetus when Count Camillo Cavour, the great Piedmontese statesman who was to be largely responsible for uniting Italy under the House of Savoy, crossed the French frontier, wearing dark glasses and carrying a passport in the name of Giuseppe Benso, to meet the Emperor Napoleon III at Plombières. As the two men drove about in a phaeton in the hot sun they decided the fate of Italy.

Some excuse for war should be found and then 200,000 French and 100,000 Piedmontese troops would invade Lombardy and drive the Austrians across the Alps. Italy would then become a federation of allied states under the apparent leadership of the Pope and the actual protection of France. The Kingdom of North Italy would include Piedmont, Lombardy, Venetia and the Papal States east of the Apennines; Central Italy would be formed out of Tuscany and Umbria; the Pope would retain Rome; and the Kingdom of Naples would be reformed or else handed over to Lucien Murat, the son of Napoleon I's sister Caroline. King Victor Emmanuel would be asked to give his daughter, Clothilde, in marriage to the French Emperor's cousin Prince Jérôme. Savoy and Nice would be ceded to France.

The matter-of-fact, calculated simplicity of it all made it seem not merely practicable but almost ordained. There were serious difficulties in its execution, though, as Cavour well knew, not least the difficulty of persuading the fifteen-year-old Princess Clothilde to agree to marry Prince Jérôme, the unattractive 'Plon-Plon', a fat and pompous satyr who was rumoured to horse-whip his mistresses and who was older than her father. She would surely not welcome the suggestion; and, indeed, when it was made to the poor girl she burst into tears.

This marriage was an important part of the secret pact, for the French Emperor was not only concerned to link his family with the old and venerated royal House of Savoy, but he also envisaged a day when his cousin, with such a wife, might occupy the throne of the projected state of Central Italy with its capital in Florence. The reluctance of the princess to oblige him and her father made him inclined to suggest that without a marriage there would be no war, while Victor Emmanuel shrank from compelling his daughter to marry a man she found so repulsive. But, her father reminded her, she had not met him yet, and perhaps when she did she would not find him so impossible after all. At length, to Cavour's intense relief, the princess gave way. She told her father that she would agree to meet Prince Jérôme and that if she did not find him actually repellent she would marry him. The marriage took place at Turin Cathedral on 30 January 1859.

A few weeks before the marriage, Napoleon III had said to the Austrian ambassador in the hearing of all the other ambassadors in Paris, 'I regret that our relations are not so good as in the past.' And ten days later Victor Emmanuel had opened parliament in Turin with a speech in which he referred to the *grido di dolore* – a phrase suggested by the French Emperor himself – 'the cry of pain' that came to him 'from so many parts of Italy'.

These two statements were taken as bearing only one interpretation: France and Piedmont were plotting a war against Austria. On 4 February an inspired pamphlet bearing the title *Napoléon III et l'Italie* appeared in the Paris bookshops and mentioned this war as a distinct possibility, thus increasing the growing concern with which the prospect of such a war was viewed all over Europe, and in particular by the English Conservative government.

In England, Lord Malmesbury, the Foreign Secretary, referred privately to Piedmont as a 'mischievous, conceited little state' and professed that he thought it intolerable that 'Europe should be deluged with blood for the personal ambition of an Italian attorney and a tambour major, like Cavour and his master'. The distasteful marriage that had seemed to be a prelude to this coming war, together with the fear that the war would, in its turn, be a prelude to a new era of Napoleonic conquest, had led to a cooling of enthusiasm for Italian nationalism throughout the country.

Elsewhere in Europe the fear that the war would endanger the Pope had roused the Catholics to determined protest; and with such powerful opposition raised against him, Napoleon began to back away from the undertakings he had given at Plombières.

But Cavour had gone too far to retreat. Helped by the Società Nazionale Italiana, he had done all he could to rouse his country to a fervour of patriotism. Italians from all over the peninsula had been encouraged to come to Piedmont to enlist in the forces he was assembling for a war that was presented as a crusade. He could scarcely hope now to dampen the enthusiasm that he had created without destroying his reputation and career. There was, also, an additional complication: he had been warned by Odo Russell, the British diplomatic agent in Rome, that feelings in Europe were running high against him and that if he declared war on Austria, he would lose all the sympathy of his former supporters.

This was a matter which had been discussed at Plombières. Napoleon III had insisted that the war must not appear to be a war of aggression, nor revolutionary in character. Austria must be provoked into the attack. Cavour was confident that she could be provoked. 'I shall force Austria to declare war on us,' he told Odo Russell confidently, 'in about the first week of May.'

By the middle of April, however, it appeared that Cavour's dangerous gamble had failed. Napoleon III, retreating in the face of opinion in England and France, recommended Piedmont to agree to a suggestion made by the English government that there should be an agreed policy of simultaneous disarmament by all the countries involved. Cavour knew that to accept such a solution would mean the collapse of all he had been working for. In despair he locked himself in his room and contemplated suicide. Knowing that Piedmont could not flout the combined will of Europe, he eventually came to the view that he must agree to disarm. Before this was known in Vienna, however, the Austrian government had made up their mind to act.

On 23 April 1859 Cavour was stopped on the steps of the Chamber of Deputies by two Austrian officers who handed him a note from their Emperor. Austria peremptorily demanded the demobilization of the Piedmontese forces; and if a satisfactory answer was not received within three days the Emperor Franz Josef would, 'with great regret, be compelled to have recourse to arms in order to secure it'.

'It is half-past six,' Cavour replied, hiding the gleam of triumph in his eyes by looking down at his watch. 'Come back at this time on 26 April and you shall have your answer.'

When the officers had gone, he turned to a friend, rubbing his hands together as was his habit when he was excited. 'We have made history,' he said. 'Now let's have dinner'.

From the first the war went well for the French and Piedmontese allies. On 4 June 1859, supported by volunteers from many parts of Italy, including Tuscany, they defeated the Austrians at Magenta; immediately afterwards they occupied Milan; and on 24 June, at Solferino, the Austrians were even more decisively beaten in a battle in which uncounted thousands of men on both sides lost their lives. For ever afterwards Napoleon III was to be haunted by their screams as they died. He decided that it was time for peace.

In Florence it had already been decided that the time had come to get rid of the Grand Duke Leopold. Towards the end of April 1859 street demonstrations of several thousand people, many of them wearing the nationalist symbol of the tricolour in their buttonholes, had been organized by members of the Società Nazionale, including Marchese Ferdinando Bartolommei and a revolutionary baker, Giuseppe Dolfi. There were loud shouts of '*Viva l'Italia!*' of '*Guerra all'Austria!*' '*Viva Vittorio Emanuele Re d'Italia!*'

The government ministers handed in their resignations at Pitti Palace on the evening of 25 April. There were further demonstrations the next day when the ministers were advised to stay at home; and on 27 April another huge demonstration was mounted in the Piazza Maria Antonia where tricolour cockades were distributed among the crowds. From many windows tricolour banners were already flying; and the demonstrators were encouraged and comforted by the appearance of an immense tricolour flag on a pole on the Forte di Belvedere. Rapturous applause and cheers greeted the arrival in several carriages of the actors and actresses of a French company then appearing at the Cocomero Theatre.

From the Piazza Maria Antonia the crowd began to march, column after seemingly endless column, to the Piazza della Signoria. At the Palazzo Pitti the Grand Duke had been advised to abdicate by his old tutor, Marchese Cosimo Ridolfi. But he had refused to do so, preferring to leave the city without surrendering his rights. So at about six o'clock in the evening, the Grand Duke and his son Ferdinand joined the rest of their family in the carriages which had been provided for them. They passed through the Porta San Gallo and into Via Bolognese. The people standing by the roadside watched them depart in silence. When his escorts rode back to Florence he parted from them with the word '*Arrivederli*', as though expecting to return once more. But this time there was to be no return. His heir, to whom he abdicated his rights, was never to reign as the Grand Duke Ferdinand IV. The quiet city they left behind had achieved a bloodless revolution. 'Amazing!' the French minister declared. 'Not even a window broken.'

22

THE CAPITAL
OF ITALY

*'Frightful in his person, a great, strong,
burly athletic man, brusque in his manners,
unrefined in his conversation, very loose
in his conduct, very eccentric in his habits.'*
CHARLES GREVILLE

In the middle of the night of 15 March 1860, the minister of justice in the provisional government which had been established in Florence appeared at a window of the Pitti Palace to make an announcement to the crowds standing expectantly in the piazza below. It was just after twelve o'clock but orders had been given to the bell-ringer not to sound his midnight bell until the announcement for which the crowds were waiting could be made, since it might be taken to be a bad omen were the news to be released on a Friday. So, at a time later to be officially given as a quarter to twelve on Thursday night but in fact at five past on Friday morning, the minister began to speak. By an overwhelming majority, he declared, the people of Tuscany had voted for the unification of the former Grand Duchy with the constitutional monarchy of Victor Emmanuel II, King of Piedmont.

Five years later Victor Emmanuel arrived in Florence to take up residence at the Pitti Palace in the Stanze della Meridiana, which had been specially redecorated for him. A squat man with immensely strong, thick legs and an enormous moustache which swept up towards his little grey eyes in a ferociously intimidating crescent, he was described by the English diarist, Charles Greville, who met him on a visit to London, as 'frightful in his person, a great, strong, burly athletic man, brusque in his manners, unrefined in his conversation, very loose in his conduct, very eccentric in his habits'. Untidy in his dress, with the hard, rough handshake of a giant and the suspicions of a brigand, he detested official banquets and preferred to eat huge peasant dishes of steaming ragout smothered in garlic and hot onions. His appetite for women was equally voracious and expressed in the bluntest language. His patient and popular wife had had to grow accustomed to his numerous affairs and his passion for his favourite mistress, the luscious, wanton daughter of a sergeant-major in the Piedmontese army whom he had created Contessa di Mirafiori and for whom he had the Medici villa of Petraia restored and redecorated.[1]

By the time he arrived in Florence in February 1865 the city had become the capital of the new Kingdom of Italy in accordance with the so-called Convention of September, much to the anger of the Piedmontese, who protested in riots which left almost two hundred people dead in the streets of Turin, and much to the annoyance of the King, who expressed his dismay at having to leave Piedmont, where he could so readily indulge his passion for hunting in the forests and mountains. Nor was Victor Emmanuel too sure that he would get on very well with the members of Florence's older families, most of whom were inclined to look down upon the House of Savoy as interloping parvenus and many of whom had recently been tactless enough to attend a funeral mass celebrated at the church of Santa Felicita on the occasion of the death in Germany of the widow of the Grand Duke Ferdinand II. Nor, indeed, was the King too confident of gaining the respect of ordinary Florentine people who, he was told by one of his officials, were very jealous of their old traditions as firm enemies of tyranny and champions of liberty, as exemplified by their most cherished statues, Michelangelo's *David*, Donatello's *Judith Slaying Holofernes* and Cellini's bronze of Perseus trampling on Medusa and holding aloft her severed head. Nor had the King much ground for hope that he would be welcomed by the numerous foreigners living in Florence, so many of whom had been such enthusiastic supporters of Mazzini and Garibaldi. Indeed, one of these, Jessie White, the red-haired daughter of a Hampshire ship-builder, who, with her revolutionary husband, Alberto Mario, had served in Sicily with the Garibaldini, actually shouted an imprecation at the King from the door of the Caffè Doney on his formal entry into the city on 3 February 1865.

This, however, was an unusual outburst. The King was warmly greeted at the railway station by a delegation of senators and deputies of the Italian Parliament and of such distinguished citizens as the blind old Marchese Gino Capponi, doyen of the Florentine patriarchy. He was loudly cheered on his drive through the streets to the Palazzo Pitti; and, on his arrival there, he was called to the balcony time and time again by an immense and enthusiastic crowd, which did not disperse until midnight.

He soon settled down in the palace to an established though eccentric routine, waking at four o'clock in the morning, being out and about by five, and seeing ministers on Thursdays and Sundays before eight. A meal at noon was followed by a siesta, then by work on his correspondence with a secretary and on appeals to his charity, which were often scribbled on bits of paper and lobbed into his carriage when he went out driving. He paid particular attention to these appeals as well as to the newspapers, which were marked for him by a special press secretary. The rest of the afternoon was spent driving about in his carriage. In the evenings, when not in the strong and comforting arms of his mistress, Rosa di Mirafiori, at the Villa della Petraia, he was often to be seen at the theatre or going through a postern gate in the Boboli Gardens to take his dogs for a walk in Via del Campuccio. Occasionally he was host at a ball in the palace, and three times a year he gave a gala dinner. He was a regular visitor to the horse-races in the Hippodrome in the Cascine and was to institute a race for three-year-olds trained in Italy, the Derby Reale, which did not, however, survive his departure from Florence for Rome.

Just as the King had regarded his move from Piedmont with annoyance and apprehension, so had the Florentine people accepted the promotion of their city to capital of the kingdom with mixed feelings. As officials and functionaries took trains from Turin for Italy's new capital, shopkeepers and *rentiers*, hoteliers and lodging-house keepers looked forward to making profits from increased sales, inflated prices and higher rents. But those who could not depend upon a rise in their standard of living looked askance upon the new arrivals, deriding their strange Torinese accents, disliking their women, who showed off their dresses and jewels as they drove through the Cascine in their cabriolets, and complaining of their ability to pay rents which rendered numbers of native Florentines homeless. And why, it was asked, did there have to be so many of them? The Grand Dukes had managed with a mere handful by comparison. Besides, largely for their benefit, the appearance of Florence was to be changed for ever. The plans for new buildings, piazzas and roads, which were considered essential for the city's new status, entailed the destruction of much that was loved or at least pleasantly familiar. Existing buildings were to be put to fresh purposes; transport was to be transformed; Florence was to become, as one enthusiastic developer put it, 'worthy of her great destiny'.

The population of the city had grown from about 60,000 during the Napoleonic occupation to over 114,000 at the time of the 1861 census; and with the arrival of some 20,000 to 30,000 bureaucrats and office workers with their families from the north, the opening up of the city and the construction of new housing became matters of extreme importance. Two commissions were accordingly appointed, one to study proposals for changes within the old city, the other, under the chairmanship of an experienced and imaginative architect, Giuseppe Poggi, to draw up a comprehensive plan for the development of the area around and beyond the old city walls.

So now and in the years that followed there took place a wholesale transformation of the city by various contractors, under the general direction of the Società Anglo-Italiana, which soon handed over operations to the Florence Land and Public Works Company, an affiliate of the Anglo-

Michelangelo's David being transferred from the Piazza della Signoria to the Accademia in 1874.

Italian Bank, of which the principal directors, and chairmen by turns, were Baron Bettino Ricasoli, twice Prime Minister in the 1860s; Sir James Lacaita, a Dante scholar and politician, a naturalized Englishman with an English wife; and Sir James Hudson, former British minister in Turin and, according to Lord Malmesbury, 'more Italian than the Italians themselves'.

Under the direction of the Florence Land and Public Works Company, ring roads and *viali* were built encircling the city; new squares appeared like the Piazza d'Azeglio[2] and the Piazza della Repubblica,[3] together with sweeping avenues such as that which climbs up from the river and passes below San Miniato al Monte to Piazzale Michelangelo. Residential areas were built over the old city walls; open spaces were cleared for markets, notably that around the east and north of San Lorenzo; old houses were demolished for parks and gardens: the Giardino dei Semplici, for example, near San Marco[4] and the Giardino dell'Orticoltura off Via Bolognese.[5]

The Chamber of Deputies conducted their debates in the Palazzo Vecchio, in the Sala del Maggior Consiglio, which had once accommodated Savonarola's Grand Council; senators met in the Sala dei Dugento or in a large room at the top of ninety-seven steps in the Uffizi, which prompted one of them to comment breathlessly, 'It is not for nothing that they call us the Upper Chamber.' Officials, secretaries and clerks moved into a variety of palaces and convents, into the Palazzo Medici and Santa Croce, into Palazzo Frescobaldi, Palazzo del Cepparello and San Firenze, into parts of the convents of Santa Maria Novella and the Badia, settling down to work in rooms all over the city on both sides of the Arno.

Receptions were held in the house of the mayor, Ubaldino Peruzzi, in Borgo de' Greci, where Emilio Visconti-Venosta, a friend of Cavour and several times minister of foreign affairs, could be seen talking to General Count Raffaele Cadorna, the minister for war; there, too, the historian Pasquale Villari, biographer of Savonarola and Machiavelli, encountered the novelist, poet and short-story writer, Edmondo De Amicis.

De Amicis was also to be seen at the Thursday evening soirées at Casa Rattazzi in Palazzo Guadagni,[6] which were presided over by the dashing wife of Urbano Rattazzi, twice Prime Minister in the 1860s. The daughter of the Irish politician and diplomat, Sir Thomas Wyse, and of Laetitia Bonaparte, Napoleon I's niece, she was the author of rather scandalous novels published in Paris and had achieved a lasting reputation for *outré* behaviour by appearing as a scantily clad bacchante at one of the first balls she attended in Florence. The entertainments she provided at the Palazzo Guadagni were a mixture of review sketches, which she wrote and performed with friends in a small theatre installed in the palace, and a succession of athletic cotillions which lasted all night. The Prime Minister and his friends usually withdrew after supper, before these high jinks began.

Receptions were frequently held also by the Principessa Eleonora Corsini Rinuccini at the Palazzo Corsini sul Prato, by the Marchesa Ginori in her palace in Via Ginori, by Cavour's granddaughter, the Marchese Giuseppina Alfieri in Casa Alfieri in Via della Dogana, and in the houses of the diplomatic corps, notably in those of Sir Augustus and Lady Paget, of the American George Perkins Marsh, President Lincoln's first minister to Italy, author of *Man and Nature* and master of twenty languages, of the Russian Count Kisselev, renowned for the expertise of his chef, and of the Turkish minister, always readily recognized by the fez which he seemed never to remove. At the Belgian legation the extremely rich Baron Adrian van der Linden Hoogvorst and his Florentine wife gave the most lavish parties, at one of which a large table collapsed, scattering dishes of food, candelabra, porcelain and silver in all directions, but it was so quickly replaced by another table piled high with a fresh burden of delicacies, plates and ornaments that Florentine guests told each other that the disaster had been engineered to display the wealth of their hosts.

Clubs and cafés were crowded. Senior bureaucrats favoured the Club dell'Unione in Via Tornabuoni; more raffish people chose the Casino

Borghese in the Palazzo Borghese for dancing and gambling; customers of all kinds flocked to the Caffè Doney where the greatest Italian poet since Leopardi, Giosuè Carducci, son of an old Florentine family, could frequently be seen on his visits from Bologna. Also often to be seen in Doney's were the writers Raffaele Lambruschini, Francesco Dall'Ongaro, professor of dramatic literature at the university, and Niccolò Tommaseo, compiler of a seven-volume dictionary of the Italian language, as well as two well-known and very rich foreign residents, Frederick Stibbert, collector, traveller and adventurer, who had fought with Garibaldi and lived in a villa beyond the Porta San Gallo, and Gladstone's friend, John Temple Leader, former member of parliament for Westminster, who bought and restored at great expense several old buildings in and around Florence, including the vast medieval castle of Vincigliata[7] and a house in the Piazza dei Petti where he was to die at the age of ninety-two in 1903.

A favourite haunt of artists was the Caffè Michelangiolo in Via Cavour. Here gathered the group of painters known as the Macchiaioli who, in reaction against hidebound academicians, turned to nature for instruction and often worked out of doors in the manner of the French Impressionists, contending that colour patches (*macchie*) in chiaroscuro were a highly significant aspect of painting. Most successful of the Macchiaioli were

The Mercato Vecchio by Telemaco Signorini, one of the group of Florentine artists known as Macchiaioli.

Giovanni Fattori, Telemaco Signorini, Silvestro Lega and, in the group's early years, Giovanni Boldini, who went on to become one of the most renowned portrait painters of his time.

While Boldini was still painting in Florence, in September 1866, the great hero of the Risorgimento, Giuseppe Garibaldi, arrived in the city. Although the Prussian defeat of the Austrians at Königgrätz in July was to allow Venice to fall into the hands of King Victor Emmanuel, it had otherwise been a sad year for the armies of the Kingdom of Italy in their struggle to wrest the remaining territories in the peninsula from alien hands. The victories of Garibaldi's 'thousand heroes', which had led to the liberation of Sicily and the accession of King Victor Emmanuel to the throne of Naples, had been followed by the defeats of Italian forces by the Austrians at Custoza and Novara and by the destruction of an Italian fleet off the island of Lissa, a sad humiliation, which was to be compounded by the trial in Florence of the Italian admiral, Count Pellion di Persano, and his condemnation to demotion and the loss of his pension. The tragedy of Lissa was followed the very next day by the battle of Bezzecca in which Garibaldi's forces suffered terrible casualties at the hands of the Austrian army.

Garibaldi himself was greeted in Florence that September as a conquering hero, one of the very few Italian leaders to have emerged from the recent fighting with any credit. He was driven through the streets of the city in a carriage accompanied by the voluble revolutionary baker, Giuseppe Dolfi, acknowledging the cheers of the crowd with grave dignity. His deeply set brown eyes, divided by the high bridge of a long and aquiline nose, gazed upon the faces around him without apparent emotion.

Garibaldi was never to achieve his ambition of taking Rome, 'the symbol of united Italy', and handing it over to Victor Emmanuel as he had handed over Naples and Sicily, for, in November 1867, having paid another visit to Florence – where, having recruited a large number of volunteers, he had declared in a rousing speech, 'We have the right to have Rome! Rome is ours!' – he was overwhelmingly defeated by papal troops and their French allies at Mentana. Yet the incorporation of Rome into the Italian Kingdom was not now to be long delayed. In 1870 France declared war on Prussia; and by the time of the French surrender at Sedan on 1 September that year, nearly all the French troops had been withdrawn from Rome in a vain attempt to avert the catastrophe. King Victor Emmanuel's soldiers, commanded by General Cadorna, entered the Holy City after a token resistance by the troops of Pope Pius IX; and the whole of Italy was unified at last.

The next year Italy transferred her capital to Rome and the King left the Pitti Palace to establish his court at the Quirinal, while the Pope withdrew into the Vatican, where he died, a self-styled prisoner, in 1878. The King also died that year, still homesick for Turin and much disliking the gloomy

Quirinal, where, for a long time, foreign royalty, Catholic and Protestant alike, were unwilling to spend the night for fear of offending the Pope. For many years to come, indeed, the papacy and the new regime were to remain unreconciled and Roman society was to be torn by conflicting loyalties.

Florentine society was, in general, thankful to see the government of the country, the officials and the foreign legations, depart for the south; and in the weeks before their departure, the city seemed to be celebrating in a kind of perpetual carnival. One gala ball followed another; parties were given night after night; the city's eleven theatres were all fully booked; and one evening at the Pergola, during a performance of *Tosca*, when Verdi was recognized in the audience, his fellow theatre-goers rose from their seats to give him a standing ovation.

The Florentines' feelings about the departure of the court and government to Rome were well expressed in a popular epigram:

> *Torino piange quando il Prence parte*
> *E Roma esulta quando il Prence arriva.*
> *Firenze, culla della poesia e dell'arte,*
> *Se ne infischia quando giunge e quando parte.*
>
> Turin sheds tears when the King departs
> And Rome's exultant when the King arrives.
> Florence, fount of poetry and the arts,
> Cares not one whit in either case – and thrives.

The attitude of the Florentines towards the government's departure was understandable. The King had been popular enough; but, despite the new building which his government's residence here had made necessary, the city was still overcrowded, the streets often blocked and resounding with the shouts of drivers, the cries of omnibus conductors and the persistent ringing of bicycle bells. It had to be conceded that the years during which Florence had been Italy's capital had brought benefits to the city: the Biblioteca Nazionale, for example, had become a copyright library for books published in Italy, with the right to receive a copy of every book printed in the country; newspapers had proliferated; several new theatres had opened; the university had prospered. But it was quite a relief, as a journalist put it, for the Florentines to be left alone to watch the world go by from the tables of the Caffè Michelangiolo, the Antico Fattori and the Giubbe Rosse,[8] to go to the races at the Hippodrome, to have their photographs taken by the Alinari or at Giacomo Brogi's studio in Corso dei Tintori,[9] to enjoy their own Tuscan way of life which, indeed, many Piedmontese bureaucrats who had reached retirement age had grown so much to enjoy that they decided to settle down in the city to spend the rest of their days there.

The Mercato Vecchio with the Tabernacle of Santa Maria della Tromba and the Column of Abundance *by Guiseppe Moricci. The column, now in the Piazza della Repubblica, bears a copy of Donatello's original statue of Abundance, the* Dovizia.

The redevelopment of the city, accelerated by its brief reign as the capital of Italy, was still proceeding apace. Streets were being widened, *lungarni* being built, houses and towers demolished. The Via de' Panzani was built as an extension of the Via de' Cerretani to the Piazza Stazione; the Mercato Vecchio was transformed; so were Via Tornabuoni and Via Porta Rossa. The city in which Walter Savage Landor spent his last days was, indeed, as he said, scarcely to be recognized as that in which he had come to live nearly half a century before.

After the transfer of the capital of Italy to Rome, Florence fell deeper and deeper into recession. The population dropped from some 200,000 to 167,000; and those who left in large numbers were the higher-paid members of the community, not only government officials, members of parliament, diplomats and courtiers, but also capitalists, many of them in the construction industry, who supposed they would be able to make more money in Rome. For the poor the outlook in Florence was bleak; and the municipality, close to financial collapse, could do little about it, while the government would not help. The crime rate soared; there were more thefts, bankruptcies and suicides per head of the population than in any of the other principal towns in Italy. The rate of deaths from tuberculosis was the highest in the country because of the enormously high mortality in the poor quarters such as Santo Spirito and Santo Croce. In 1884 an epidemic of cholera claimed 8,000 victims. By then the Commune had been forced to declare itself bankrupt.

Soon after this the government of Agostino Depretis was obliged to turn its attention to Florence's plight and a gradual recovery followed. New industries were founded and old ones expanded; banks and insurance companies were established. The railway was extended to Rome and to the Po valley by way of Pistoia and Bologna. In Florence steam-propelled tramways took the place of horse-drawn transport on some routes; and in August 1890 the first electric lights were switched on in the Vie Calzaiuoli, Cerretani and Tornabuoni. By the last years of the century, when the population had reached 200,000 again and was steadily rising, Florence seemed to the increasing number of tourists who went there as prosperous a city as any in Italy.

'VILLE TOUTE ANGLAISE'

'Florence is all that I have dreamed and more.'
CONSTANCE FENIMORE WOOLSON

To the brothers Goncourt, who were there in 1855, it seemed that Florence. was a *'ville toute Anglaise'*. There were English shops in which English tweeds were sold and English mackintoshes, packets of tea imported from England, tins of digestive biscuits, tennis racquets and boxes of cards for playing bridge. In the bookshops there were English novels, in the tearooms muffins and seed cake, on the menus in restaurants English dishes. Visitors could have their ailments treated by English doctors, their teeth extracted by English dentists, their medicines supplied by English chemists, their money exchanged by English bankers.

Walter Savage Landor, characterized by one of his biographers as being 'for nearly ninety years a typical English public schoolboy', moved, after his wife's death, to lodgings in Via Nunziatina, where he shocked various members of the English colony by his intimate relationship with an attractive, young American writer, Kate Field. Among Landor's numerous visitors were William Hazlitt and Leigh Hunt; Keats's friend, Charles Armitage Brown; Algernon Charles Swinburne, who, like Longfellow, stayed at the Grand Hotel Royal in the Borgo Santi Apostoli; Francis Hare, 'a monster of learning', whose delight it was to admit to sins of such appalling depravity that he sent priests fleeing from the confessional box; Charles James Lever, the cheerful, generous though generally impoverished Irish novelist, whose favourite amongst his own books, *The Dodd Family Abroad*, was written in Florence in the 1850s; Lever's friend, W. M. Thackeray, who was often to be seen in the Ristorante Laura in the Via dei Cerchi, where the fish soup so delighted his palate that he wrote a poem about it; Seymour Stocker Kirkup, an indifferent painter and most kindly man who was British consul in Florence and was to live till the age of ninety-two, having married a bride of twenty-two when he was eighty-seven. Charles Dickens, whose *Pictures from Italy* was soon to be published, came to Florence after Landor had returned for a time to England. 'What would Landor like as a remembrance of Italy?' Dickens had asked him before his departure. 'An ivy leaf

Opposite above: The Piazza della Signoria looking towards the Neptune Fountain and the Via dei Cerchi behind Giambologna's equestrian statue of the Grand Duke Cosimo I.

Opposite below: Promenaders in the Cascine.

from Fiesole,' Landor had replied and this Dickens had picked and sent to him.

Frequently in Landor's company also were Robert and Elizabeth Barrett Browning, who had come to live in Florence soon after the arrival of another English writer, Frances Trollope.

Frances Trollope had settled in Florence with her eldest son, Thomas Adolphus, in 1843. She was then aged sixty-three, and by the indefatigable writing of numerous travel books and novels had restored the fortunes of the family, which had been dissipated by the wildly impractical schemes of her late husband, an irascible lawyer and failed farmer, salesman, property developer and encyclopedist. Thomas Adolphus, large, ugly and short-tempered, had also become a writer and was to become even more prolific than his mother, producing some sixty volumes in fifty years, most of them books on Italian history or novels with an Italian setting.

The Trollopes lived at first on the second floor of the Casa Berti in the Via di San Giuseppe, next to the church of Santa Croce. In 1848 they moved to what became known as the Villino Trollope[1] in Piazza Maria Antonia,[2] a famously hospitable meeting place for English and other foreign authors then living in Italy, for various leaders of the Italian nationalist movement and for those numerous friends of the Trollopes who, like Mrs Browning, shared their interest in spiritualism and in the seances conducted by the celebrated medium, Daniel Dunglas Home. Thomas Adolphus's brother, Anthony, was to be seen here occasionally; and in 1860 George Eliot, who, for a time, had put up at the Pension Suisse[3] opposite the Palazzo Strozzi, came to stay with them and began work on her novel about Savonarola's Florence, *Romola*, which was published in the *Cornhill Magazine* in 1862–3. To these and her many other guests, Thomas Adolphus's wife, Theodosia, also a writer and a translator of Italian verse, was a charming and attentive though nervous hostess, whose kindly nature was celebrated in Walter Savage Landor's *To Theodosia*.

Soon after Theodosia's death in 1865, Trollope, whose mother had also died two years before, moved out of the Villino Trollope – where the memories of his past happy life so deeply distressed him – and bought a house beyond the Porta San Niccolò, the Villa Ricorboli. It was already a large house with plenty of room for his extensive library and his collection of antiquities and curios; but Trollope had plans to make it bigger still, to build on a tower for his books and to tame the wild garden. When a young friend of the family came to act as governess to his daughter, Beatrice, then in her early teens, she found the house in confusion with half its roof missing and the builders actually living on the premises.

This friend was Fanny Ternan, sister of the actress Nelly Ternan, whose relationship with Charles Dickens has been so well described by Claire Tomalin in *The Invisible Woman*. Fanny had been to Florence before. She

The Via degli Strozzi looking towards the Piazza della Repubblica, with the Hotel (formerly Pensione) Suisse on the left and the corner of the Strozzi Palace on the extreme right.

had come with her mother, at Dickens's expense, to study singing for a year under Pietro Romani, leaving Nelly in London with their sister Maria. On that occasion Fanny had stayed at the Villino Trollope, where Nelly had joined her for a holiday. At the Villa Ricorboli in 1865 she found that Alfred Austin was also in residence. Then thirty years old, he had abandoned the law for literature on inheriting a fortune from an uncle, and had already conceived so high an opinion of his gifts as a poet that his appointment as poet laureate in 1896 was to strike him as being quite as justly merited as his contemporaries found it ludicrous. Blind to his own faults, he dismissed the virtues of other poets from Tennyson to Browning with contempt. But Thomas Adolphus Trollope was fond of Austin and so was Fanny; while Trollope and Fanny themselves grew sufficiently fond of each other to marry; and, despite the differences in their ages, they settled down happily at the Villa Ricorboli, where guests were entertained as hospitably as they had been at the Villino Trollope in Piazza Maria Antonia.

In the year that the Trollopes had moved to Piazza Maria Antonia, the Brownings moved back into a house in Piazza San Felice. They had left

The Brownings' drawing-room at the Casa Guidi by George Mignaty, July 1861.

Pisa for Florence the year before, largely for a more active social life, though Robert was warned that Florence was 'English-ridden'.

They had stayed at first in the Hôtel du Nord, then moved to rooms in a house in Via delle Belle Donne near the Piazza Santa Maria Novella. Eventually, after an unsuccessful excursion to the Benedictine monastery at Vallombrosa – to which Mrs Browning and her maid were dragged in wine baskets by white bullocks and from which they were soon dispatched by the abbot, who did not like women in the vicinity, even in the guest-house beyond the monastery walls – they rented six high-ceilinged rooms on the *piano nobile* of the Casa Guidi.[4] The house, once the property of the Ridolfi, before being sold at the beginning of the seventeenth century to Camillo Guidi, secretary of state to the Grand Duke, stood not far from the Pitti Palace and close to the church of San Felice in Piazza, whose walls overshadowed the terrace where the new occupants strolled up and down in the evening air. The rent was a guinea a week and this included admission to the Boboli Gardens, though not, unfortunately, for Mrs Browning's beloved dog Flush, which she had carried with her when she had left her father's house in Wimpole Street after her secret marriage. The Brownings' lease ran out after three months, and when Robert tried to renew it he was told that the winter rent was double the summer's. This being beyond their means, they moved out to a much smaller place opposite the Pitti Palace. By the spring of 1848, however, the turmoil in Italy and the fear of what might happen in Florence had driven so many of the English away that rented accommodation was being emptied by the day and landlords were being obliged to accept far lower rents than they would have considered the year before. The Brownings were, therefore, able to move back into a now unfurnished Casa Guidi for no more than twenty-five guineas a year, with permission to sublet whenever they wanted to. They remained there contentedly until 1861, the year of Cavour's death, a loss which profoundly affected Mrs Browning. 'She wept many tears for him,' wrote William Wetmore Story, the American sculptor. 'This agitation undoubtedly weakened her and perhaps was the last feather that broke her down.' She died three weeks later.

Most of her *Casa Guidi Windows*, declaring her enthusiastic support for the cause of Italian liberty, and the blank verse, *Aurora Leigh*, were written in Casa Guidi. So was much of Robert's best work; and their son, Pen, who was later to buy the house, was born here. Their maid, Elizabeth Wilson, an enterprising girl from Northumberland, fell in love with Ferdinando Romagnoli, her employers' dashing manservant, whom she married. Later she established herself as the landlady of a boarding-house in Florence where one of her temporary lodgers, the explosive Walter Savage Landor, having been thrown out of his own lodgings, hurled a dinner, which he pronounced revolting, out of the dining-room window.

Americans were almost as often to be encountered in Florence as the English. James Fenimore Cooper worked here as correspondent for an American newspaper; so also, for a time, did Mark Twain. Harriet Beecher Stowe, author of *Uncle Tom's Cabin*, came in a vain attempt to follow up that great success. The tower of the Villa di Montauto at Bellosguardo was used by Nathaniel Hawthorne as a model for the castle of Monte Beni in *The Marble Faun*. Henry James also lived for a time at Bellosguardo.[5]

When he first arrived in Florence in the early October of 1873, aged thirty, Henry James found the days oppressively hot and the nights a torment because of the mosquitoes. He consequently moved on to Siena; but a few weeks later he was back in Florence, where he was joined by his older brother, William, who described him to their parents as

> wholly unchanged. No balder than when he quit [Massachusetts]; his teeth of a yellowish tinge (from the waters of Homburg, he says); his beard very rich and glossy in consequence he says of the use of a substance called Brilliantine of which he always keeps a large bottle on the table among his papers... He speaks Italian with wonderful fluency and skill as it seems to me, accompanying his words with many stampings of the foot, shakings of the head and rollings of the eye sideways.

He had not yet achieved his great fame but was already a writer of exceptional promise, ponderous in manner, self-regarding, gregarious though emotionally withdrawn, most anxious to be taken for the distinguished master he aspired to be. He spent all morning writing in Florence, then went out walking and sightseeing, looking at pictures, gathering material for a series of articles on the city which were to appear in his *Transatlantic Sketches*.

After a visit to Rome and America, Henry James returned to Florence the following year and rented an apartment at No. 10 Piazza Santa Maria Novella which, although it had two bedrooms and a sitting-room, cost no more than $25 a month. 'Blessed Florence!' he wrote to his sister, Alice. 'My literary labours will certainly show the good effect of my having space to pace about . . . Tell William I find the French restaurant in Via Rondinelli, with the lobsters and the truffles in the window, an excellent place to dine, so that I am altogether most comfortable.'

A portrait of Henry James by John Singer Sargent, who was born in Florence in 1856.

'I am still lingering on here in Florence – one of the few survivors of the winter colony,' he told his mother several weeks later when the hot weather had driven most other visitors away. In the piazza beneath the shuttered windows of his high-ceilinged room the cabmen slept in their boxes, 'while loungers took their siestas half naked, flat on their faces, on the paving-stones'.

'In the morning he took walks and sought the coolness of the churches,' wrote his biographer, Leon Edel. 'He lunched early in a beer-garden, in the shade of a trellis, and spent the long hot hours of the afternoon in his room working when possible, or simply taking a siesta along with the rest of the city. His novel was proceeding "not very rapidly, but very regularly, which is the best way".' This was *Roderick Hudson*, his first important novel, a work soon to be followed by *Daisy Miller* and *Washington Square*, which combined with them to ensure that when he returned to Florence in March 1880 their author had achieved an international renown.

On this occasion James took a room in the Hotel de l'Arno overlooking the river, and here he began to work on the *Portrait of a Lady*, his writing set aside from time to time for social calls, for luncheons and tea parties, and for visits to a fellow American writer, Constance Fenimore Woolson, the thirty-nine-year-old great-niece of James Fenimore Cooper, neat, bright, inquiring and rather deaf.

Miss Woolson, who came to regard Henry James with a kind of devoted reverence, was then living at the Pensione Barbensi, later the Casa Molin on the Lungarno. She had fallen in love with Florence in the manner of so many of her kind. 'Florence is all that I have dreamed and more,' she wrote to a friend.

> Here I have attained the old world feeling I used to dream about, a sort of enthusiasm made up of history, mythology, old churches, pictures, statues, vineyards, the Italian sky, dark-eyed peasants, opera music, Raphael and old Michael, and ever so many more ingredients – the whole, I think, has taken me pretty well off my feet! Perhaps I ought to add Henry James. He has been perfectly charming to me for the last three weeks.

He took her with him on his walks and into churches and galleries and he clearly enjoyed himself displaying his knowledge, his taste and discernment. Mr James was a 'delightful companion,' she thought, 'because he knows all about pictures'. 'He grew didactic and mystic over the round Botticelli of the Uffizi and the one in the Prometheus room at the Pitti. He invented as he went along, and amused himself not a little with his unusual flow of language. He delivered quite an epic upon Giotto's two little frescoes in the second cloister of Santa Maria Novella.'[6] He took her to the Duomo which she had thought 'a great gloomy space' on a previous visit, 'too vast and cold'; but 'H. J. admired it' and so 'tried to make [her]

A view of Florence by Samuel Palmer, who spent two years in Italy in the late 1830s.

admire it too'. He also tried to arouse her enthusiasm for Michelangelo's statues in the New Sacristy at San Lorenzo.

'The Statue of Lorenzo . . . is the finest statue, a thousand times over, I have ever seen,' she wrote in one of her letters. 'But I confess frankly that it is going to take some time for me to appreciate "the nude".' Indeed, the nude statues in the New Sacristry were 'rather beyond' her, she had to confess. She was not 'sufficiently acquainted with torsos, flanks and the lines of anatomy' to judge whether or not they were beautiful; and when James said that he presumed she found them so, she felt constrained to reply that no, she did not: they 'looked so distracted'.

'Ah yes,' he said, '*distracted*. But *then!*' 'Here words failed him and he walked off to look at a fresco, to recover from my horrible ignorance.'

Six years later James and Miss Woolson were in Florence together again. This time Miss Woolson rented rooms in the huge Villa Castellani in Bellosguardo before taking a lease on the nearby Villa Brichieri-Colombi from the kindly novelist Isa Blagden, a friend of the Brownings, who had been born in India and had so dark a complexion it was supposed her mother was a native of that country. Miss Woolson sublet Miss Blagden's villa to James for a month before he moved down into Florence again to stay at the Hôtel du Sud on the Arno. Here he drove his pen steadily, as he put it; but found time as usual for an active social life amongst the 'queer, promiscuous, polyglot (most polyglot in the world) Florentine society', paying calls upon all kinds of people, throwing himself into that 'whirlpool of idiotic card-leaving of which Florentine existence is largely composed'. He called upon the Marchesa Incontri, a mysterious and seemingly 'rather dangerous' literary hostess who wrote novels in English in a lovely villa near the Porta San Gallo; he dined with Dr W. W. Baldwin, an American physician with an extensive practice in Florence, and with Maurice Barrès, then making a name for himself as a writer, whom he found 'of a fearful precocity', a '*poseur* and mystificator'. He went to see Janet Ross, the formidable and talkative Scottish author of *Old Florence and Modern Tuscany*, wife of Henry Ross, a banker in Florence, who lived in the charming villa of Castagnolo[7] where she played on her guitar and struck him as being 'awfully handsome in a utilitarian kind of way – an odd mixture of the British female and the dangerous woman – a Bohemian with rules and accounts'.

James also spent a good deal of his time with Adolf von Hildebrand, the German sculptor and author of the influential *Das Problem der Form in der bildenden Kunst*, who lived in the former convent in the Piazza San Francesco di Paola[8] below the castellated towers and umbrella pines of Bellosguardo; and he saw much, too, of Violet Paget, producer of numerous novels, travel sketches and works on eighteenth-century and Renaissance Italy, who wrote under the name of Vernon Lee.

James, who had first met Miss Lee in London in 1884 when she was twenty-seven, described her then as 'a most astounding young female' – Maurice Baring was later to observe that she was 'by far the cleverest person' he had ever met. She was born in France, the daughter of an English engineer who had been brought up in Warsaw and who, having fled from Poland after the insurrection of 1848, had become tutor to the future poet and novelist, Eugene Lee-Hamilton, whose widowed mother he married. Miss Lee had spent most of her life in Italy and was now living at No. 5 Via Garibaldi, where she presided over a kind of literary salon, receiving visitors in the early afternoons and in the evenings. She was a strange-looking, short-sighted young woman in mannish clothes, with short hair, protruding teeth, gleaming eyes behind little spectacles, an inveterate talker in several languages.

James was most intrigued by her. He described her as 'exceeding ugly, disputatious, contradictious and perverse', able to discuss 'all things in *any* language', 'a really superior talker with a *mind* – almost the only one in Florence'.

Her mother lived with her, a 'grotesque, deformed, invalidical, *posing* woman'. So did her father, the Polish-educated engineer, a man 'in the highest degree unpleasant, mysterious and sinister', who lived quite separately from the rest of the family, with whom he had not sat down to eat for twenty years. Also living in the house in Via Garibaldi was Miss Lee's half-brother, Eugene Lee-Hamilton, by then in his early forties and an invalid, prostrated by a nervous illness which, having cut short a promising career in the diplomatic service, now confined him to a sofa in his room where he received visitors as assiduously as Miss Lee herself and dictated verse to an amanuensis. He was eventually to recover sufficiently from his illness to marry an English novelist, Annie Holdsworth, with whom he went to live in a villa between Florence and Fiesole. When he was nearly sixty his wife gave birth to a daughter, whose death the following year was held responsible for her father's deep depression, which culminated in a stroke. He was buried in the new Protestant cemetery outside the Porta Romana.[9]

It was from Eugene Lee-Hamilton that Henry James heard the story upon which he was to base *The Aspern Papers*. Lee-Hamilton himself had been told the story by John Singer Sargent, who, living with his parents at the Villino Torrigiani, No. 115 Via de' Serragli and later at No. 15 Via Magenta, was a student at the Accademia di Belle Arti.

Sargent was born in Florence at Casa Arretini next to the Palazzo Sperini in the Lungarno Acciaioli. His father was an American doctor, who had brought his wife to Europe on what was intended to be a brief holiday for the sake of her health but turned out to be permanent exile. On the birth of his child he interviewed various Florentine women as prospective wet-nurses, one of whom was so anxious to obtain the appointment that she presented herself twice, the second time with her hair dyed to disguise her appearance, and on both occasions lying brazenly. When he was old enough John was sent to a school kept by a Frenchman, Joseph Domengé, in the former convent I Servi di Maria in the Piazza Santissima Annunziata. He also attended dancing lessons in a house at No. 43 Via Romana, where one day a handsome old lady came into the room to play the piano for the class. This old lady turned out to be Claire Clairmont, the stepsister of Percy Bysshe Shelley's wife Mary, who had been a part of the Shelley ménage in their travels around Italy and was the mother of Byron's daughter, Allegra. She had taken music lessons in Rome, taught music in a Russian family in Moscow and, before coming to live in Florence, worked as a governess.

In the house in Via Romana, which she shared with a middle-aged niece, she had a strange lodger, an American named Edward Augustus Silsbee, who had once been a seaman but had decided to sell his merchant ship and settle in Italy. According to a man who knew him slightly, Silsbee, having spent some time in Venice before coming to live in Florence, 'talked of nothing but Art and Poetry & was christened "Heavy Venice"... He has quite a gift of language, but as he has not been thoroughly educated, he cannot become what his ambition desires, an Essayist, so he frets... Italy is the best place for him.'

He had a consuming interest, verging upon mania, for the poems of Shelley who, upon his first arrival in Florence, had immediately decided that it was 'the most beautiful city' he had ever seen. Silsbee would quote Shelley at length without the least encouragement and endlessly copied out the poet's works. He would sit in an armchair, so Vernon Lee said, 'looking like a deep sea monster on a Bernini fountain, staring at the carpet and quoting his favourite author with a trumpet-like twang quite without relevance to the conversation'.

He knew that Miss Clairmont possessed a collection of Shelley's papers and so anxious was he to acquire these that he never left Florence and, so it was said, rarely left the house in Via Romana in case his old landlady died while he was away. In 1879, however, he was obliged to sail for America and in his absence Miss Clairmont did die. He raced back to Florence, determined to get hold of the papers before they were dispersed. On his return to Via Romana he learned that they had been inherited by Miss Clairmont's niece, by now in her mid-fifties. He asked her about them. Yes, she did have them now. Could he acquire them from her? Yes, he could have them all. Indeed, she would give them to him. But there was one condition: he would have to marry her first. In Lee-Hamilton's version of the story, Captain Silsbee was 'still running'.

Changing the scene of his story from Florence to Venice, Henry James began work on *The Aspern Papers* at the Villa Brichieri-Colombi at Bellos-

A windy day in 1887 on the Lungarno Acciaioli by the Ponte Santa Trinita.

guardo, in the rooms he had taken from Miss Woolson. He worked in the garden there or on the terrace which looked down upon what he described as 'the most beautiful view in the world'. For once he largely shunned 'the vain agitation of particles' which was Florentine society, but occasionally went down into the city, since 1887 was the year in which the façade of the Duomo, for long concealed by scaffolding, was at last to be revealed, and the King and Queen of Italy were to attend some of the city's festivities. James himself went to a fancy-dress ball in the Sala del Maggior Consiglio in the Palazzo della Signoria, 'looking lovely', so he told a friend afterwards, in a red *lucco* and a black velvet cap; and he later watched a marvellous procession of citizens marching through the streets in the costumes of the time of Lorenzo il Magnifico, members of several of Florence's oldest families riding along with them, mounted on horses splendidly caparisoned, indulging that love of splendour and ceremony which the Florentines have never lost.

The next year the Queen of England visited Florence for the first time. Although she travelled incognito, variously describing herself as the Countess of Balmoral, the Countess of Kent or the Countess of Lancaster, no one could doubt that *la Regina d'Inghilterra* had arrived. She was accompanied by scores of attendants and servants, including Scottish Highlanders and Indians, by her dresser, her chef, doctors, secretaries and grooms with their horses and ponies, by innumerable trunks and cases, by various evidently indispensable pieces of furniture in addition to her bed and desk, and by several favourite pictures, hundreds of photographs, mementoes and trinkets. She stayed in Florence at the Villa Palmieri, from which – as soon as she had finished work on the dispatch-boxes that were brought to her with relentless regularity by Queen's messengers – she was escorted, at her own insistence, on protracted rounds of sightseeing, accompanied through the streets by her Indian servants, much to the astonishment of the Florentines who took them for princes from her distant empire. Having spent several hours being wheeled around the Uffizi, she passed sadly by the Casa Gherini where Prince Albert had stayed in 1838. She remembered how he had marvelled at the sculptures of Donatello, which were 'far more beautiful' than he had 'ever imagined', and how he had developed that taste for Italian primitives upon which he was to spend a large part of his then small income.

The Queen also listened sadly to the music of the organ in the Badia which Prince Albert had played. He had played the piano, too; but this had not been a success, since the only instrument he had been able to hire in Florence was old and out of tune.

One day during the Queen's visit in 1888, an English boy, the Hon. George Peel, saw 'policemen clearing the way for a little carriage in the Piazza del Duomo'. 'In it was an old lady with a companion,' Peel told Sir Harold Nicolson over sixty years later. 'It was Queen Victoria. She stopped the carriage, fumbled in her corsage, and drew out a locket which she held up to the [recently completed] façade [of the Duomo].'

> The Lady-in-Waiting afterwards told Peel that it was a miniature of the Prince Consort. She thought it would interest him to see how the Duomo looked after being repaired. Peel had been so impressed by the incident that he wrote a long account of it to Mr Gladstone. He had himself forgotten all about it, but his letter was recently found among Gladstone's papers and returned to him.

Queen Victoria was 'much taken' with Florence and returned to the city in 1893 and again in 1894 when she stayed at the Villa Fabbricotti.[10] Yet before she had personal knowledge of the place herself, the Queen warned Princess Mary Adelaide of Teck against taking her daughter, Princess May, who was to marry the future King George V, to continue her education there. It was, she said disapprovingly, 'a town full of attractions and temptations to expense'. In the event, the sixteen-year-old Princess May at first found Florence, which she was taken to see on excursions from the Hotel Paoli,[11] 'rather a dull place', but after a time, when she had finished trailing round the churches, she decided 'it certainly grows upon one'. Society here was undoubtedly very lively. The great families, like the Corsini and the Torrigiani, rarely gave parties but when they did so they were very grand affairs; and fancy-dress balls went on until breakfast time. The acknowledged leader of the English colony at that time was Lady

The arrival of Queen Victoria in Florence on 16 March 1894.

Orford, who presided over her weekly salon chain-smoking black cigars and was sufficiently tolerant of the easy manners of Florentine society to contemplate an Italian lady playing whist in her drawing-room with her husband, her ex-husband and her lover.

In the year of Queen Victoria's last visit to Florence, Oscar Wilde was also in the city in the company of Lord Alfred Douglas. It was shortly before Wilde's misguided legal action against Lord Alfred's father, the Marquess of Queensberry; and the relationship between the two younger men was already notorious, so notorious, indeed, that when André Gide, whose own homosexuality was suppressed, met them in a café in Florence, he did not at first mention the encounter in the letters he wrote regularly to Paul Valéry. When he did mention Wilde's name, he referred to Douglas merely as '*un autre poète*'.

Wilde had hoped not to be recognized in Florence, but, as his biographer, Richard Ellmann, wrote, 'his attempt to keep his presence a secret was perhaps doomed to fail, since his height and dress and theatrical manner made him conspicuous wherever he went'. He was invited one day to Via

Garibaldi to see the invalid, Eugene Lee-Hamilton. It was evidently 'a great success. Oscar talked like an angel, and they all fell in love with him, even Vernon Lee, who had hated him almost as much as he had hated her. He, for his part, was charmed with her.'

Visitors to Florence in these years of the late nineteenth century were sometimes shocked by the apparent indifference of the inhabitants to the beauties round them, their easy tolerance of what Dickens called 'an irregular kind of market' in the Piazza del Duomo, where 'stores of old iron and other small merchandise were set out on stalls', their ready acceptance of both the principal hackney-coach stand and a busy omnibus station right in front of the door of the Campanile. 'The hackney coaches, with their more or less farmyard-like litter of occasional hay, and smell of variously mixed horse manure,' so John Ruskin complained, rendered it 'impossible to stand for a moment near the Campanile... while the north side [was] enclosed with an iron railing and usually encumbered with lumber as well: not a soul in Florence ever caring now for the sight of any piece of its old artists' work.'

The Ponte Vecchio by William Holman Hunt, who had a studio in Florence. His first wife died there in 1866.

The same sort of thing could be said of the Palazzo della Signoria, where hundreds of men, wrapped in long cloaks, stood for hours 'as if they had

nothing else to do,' Augustus Hare observed, 'talking ceaselessly in deep Tuscan tones'. Near them in the Loggia dei Lanzi prostitutes strolled from side to side, while men shiftily offered objects for sale which were not easily to be found in the markets and were presumed to be stolen.

Earlier, in a sour mood, Walter Savage Landor had complained, 'Florence is, I fear, the filthiest capital in Europe; and I can speak from experience that it is impossible to walk through the market with dry shirts unless you go with a jacket.'

A generation later William Holman Hunt, who had taken a studio in Florence where his wife had died, thought the people 'the filthiest' he had ever known:

> Such stinks meet you on the street and wake you up at night that it seems Pestilence must be on the threshold with destruction for the whole city... What do you think of a boy of fifteen or sixteen in the blazing sunlight at one o'clock on Sunday, in Kensington Gore say, taking his breeches down for a necessary purpose which he performs while he still goes on with his game of pitch and toss with seven or eight companions some two years older who remain in a circle about two or three yards round him. Then again to an old gentleman of the utmost respectability... walking across the road at the Duke of York's column and taking down his black cloth breeches for the same purpose.

In a letter to Holman Hunt, Edward Lear expressed a different opinion of Florence. For him it was all too much of a good thing: 'plum-pudding, treacle, wedding cake, sugar, barley-sugar, sugar-candy, raisins and peppermint drops would not make a more luscious mixture in the culinary world'. It was as well to see the place; but for Lear a month of it was quite enough.

To Nathaniel Hawthorne's wife Sophia, it seemed that the most unprepossessing of all the citizens of Florence were the priests, who always appeared anxious to get through their 'endlessly repeated tasks' in church so that they could 'go and eat and drink'. Doubtless there were many among them truly devout, she conceded. 'But the appearance of the clergy of Florence is almost invariably repulsive and gross, and they are said to be peculiarly depraved. They are mostly fat, with flabby cheeks, chins and throats, of very earthly aspect. There is nothing to compare them to but hogs.'

Sophia Hawthorne's husband was almost as uncomplimentary about Florence's festivals, once so exciting a part of the city's life. The Feast of St John, like the Carnival, had, he thought, degenerated into 'a meagre semblance of festivity, kept alive factitiously, and dying a lingering death'. His fellow American, Fenimore Cooper, was almost as unimpressed by the *corsi dei cocchi* in the Piazza Santa Maria Novella. The setting was pleasant enough, for there was 'much scenic painting, a good parade of guards, both horse and foot, a well-dressed population, and a background of balconies garnished by tapestry and fine women, to say nothing of roofs and chimneys'. But the chariots were small and clumsy, and so constructed that there was little likelihood of their upsetting the charioteers as they turned by the obelisks. Indeed, 'one may witness the same any fine evening in New York, between two drunken Irish cartmen on their way home'.

At least the ceremony of the *Scoppio del Carro* (the Explosion of the Cart) on Easter Day in the Duomo had not lost its charms. Janet Ross described how, during Mass, the attention of the congregation was concentrated upon a cord stretched above their heads and 'a small white speck which, we were informed, was the famous dove', a rocket shaped like a bird.

When the Gloria had been sung, a man went up a ladder with a lighted taper, which he applied to the dove. There was a great spitting and hissing, and all at once she shot forward down the cord, a streak of fire and sparks. There was a stir and hum in the crowd, and a few little screams from some of the women; the dove vanished out of the door, and then there was a series of explosions from outside, while the dove returned as fast as she had gone, and remained still fizzing for a few seconds.

Then all the bells of Florence, which had been silent since twelve o'clock on Thursday, began to ring merry chimes, and the great organ pealed out a triumphal melody. We made our way out of the Duomo as fast as we could, and were in time to see the last of the fireworks on the chariot; they made a tremendous noise . . . When all the squibs and crackers were finished, four magnificent white oxen, gaily decked with ribbons, were harnessed to the cart, which moved off slowly with many creaks and groans round the south side of the cathedral towards the Via del Proconsolo. The crowd was immense . . . The four white oxen were unharnessed and taken away, and a cord being put from the door of the Pazzi Palace to the cart, another dove again flew to the fireworks, and the popping and fizzing was renewed, to the intense delight of the crowd. The dove had flown swiftly and well this year, so the *contadini* returned home joyfully, spreading the glad tidings as they went – '*La colombina è andata bene*' ('the dove has flown well').

RESIDENTS AND VISITORS

*'Iron bedsteads should if possible be selected,
as they are less likely to harbour the enemies of repose.'*
KARL BAEDEKER

Soon after Queen Victoria's first visit to Florence, one of her favourite writers, the novelist who called herself Ouida, was obliged to leave the city, unable to pay her rent, after having lived there for twenty-three years, for most of them in extravagant comfort. Born in Suffolk of a French father and an English mother, Ouida was a small, plain, arrogant woman of affectedly eccentric manners. When in London she stayed at the Langham Hotel, where she gave grand parties, notifying her guests by a prominent notice that morals and umbrellas were to be left in the hall. She and her mother had settled in Florence in 1874, at first staying at the expensive Hôtel d'Italie in the Piazza Ognissanti, then renting the Villa Vagnonville, before moving to the Villa Farinola at Scandicci, where she lived in a most prodigal way, spending large sums on furniture and decorations and wearing clothes designed by Worth which did not suit her. She soon had a wide circle of acquaintances including the imperious, generous-hearted Countess of Orford, and the fastidious Marchese della Stufa, who also lived at Scandicci. But her friendship with Janet Ross was destroyed when she began to harbour the improbable suspicion that Mrs Ross was a rival for the homosexual Marchese della Stufa's affections.

Although she worked assiduously, Ouida's popularity as a novelist gradually declined. Deep in debt, she and her mother were ejected from their villa and forced to return to Florence, where her mother died and was buried in a pauper's grave. Ouida herself lived to hear of the death of Queen Victoria and the accession of King Edward VII, an event she commemorated with the comment, 'At least he is a man of the world and won't publish silly books in bad English.'

English as it seemed to the Goncourts, Florence held a strong appeal for other foreigners, too, as it had done in the eighteenth century, when the Americans John Smibert, John Singleton Copley and Benjamin West had

Ladies in a garden by John Singer Sargent. The gardens of the Torre del Gallo were reconstructed by Stefano Bardini in 1904–6.

come to paint, when Heinrich Heine had written poems here and the art historian Johann Winckelmann had come from Prussia to complain about the city's architecture; when Count Aleksey Grigoryevich, who had played a leading part in the *coup d'état* which brought Catherine the Great to power, rode in from Russia, and when Giacomo Casanova came from Venice, both to enjoy the pleasures of the Carnival.

The immensely rich Anatoly Nikolayevich Demidoff, whose father had lived and died in Florence and whose wife was Napoleon's niece, Princess Mathilde, was considered almost as an honorary Florentine citizen because of his generous benefactions to the city and its people.[1] By the time of his death in 1870, Florence had a large Russian colony for which Demidoff, who had bought himself the Tuscan title of 'Principe di San Donato', built the Russian Church in Via Leone X.[2] Among the most distinguished and richest of the church's congregation was Princess Woronzoff, whose collection of jewellery was so astonishing that people gathered to watch her pass by, wearing her twelve ropes of splendid pearls that reached to her knees. It was a sad day for the Florentines when the Tsar summoned these Russian exiles back to Moscow by ukase in 1885.

There was a large German colony in Florence, too. This centred on the former monastery of San Francesco di Paola, where the sculptor Adolf von Hildebrand entertained a succession of his fellow-countrymen and countrywomen, among them the art theorist, Konrad Fielder, the painter, Hans von Marées, Wagner and Franz Liszt, Clara Schumann and Richard Strauss. 'Liszt played this evening,' Hildebrand recorded in his diary one day in 1876. 'First Chopin, then something Austrussian-Viennese, just to make the women faint.'

An edition of Karl Baedeker's *Italy: Handbook for Travellers*, published when Adolf von Hildebrand was living in the city, estimated the likely 'expenditure of a single visitor to Florence [at] 20–25 francs per day, or at 10–15 francs when a prolonged stay is made', that was to say between 8s. and £1 a day, or $2–5. Gold, silver and copper coins from other countries circulated in Florence, Baedeker continued. But 'the traveller should be on guard against base coin, worn pieces, coins from the papal mint, Swiss silver coins with the seated figure of Helvetia, Roumanian and South American coins. All foreign copper coins (except those of San Marino) should be rejected.' It was advisable to change gold pieces of 10 or 20 francs into paper money at a money-changer's office: 'the French monetary system is now in use throughout the whole of Italy'.

Travellers were also warned to be on guard against giving their nationality away by talking in their native language, for they would be more than likely to be 'made to pay "*all'Inglese*" by hotel-keepers and others, i.e., considerably more than the ordinary charges'.

> Where tariffs and fixed charges exist, they should be carefully consulted. In other cases the traveller must make a distinct bargain... since in Italy the pernicious custom of demanding considerably more than will ultimately be accepted has long been prevalent... The fewest words are best; and travellers will find that calm preparations to go elsewhere will reduce obstinate hagglers to reason much more quickly than a war of words... Prudence is useful at all times; but an exaggerated mistrust is sometimes resented as an insult and sometimes taken to indicate weakness and timidity.

The *Handbook* goes on to warn travellers against the wiles of guides and the importunities of beggars, drivers, porters and donkey attendants who 'invariably expect and often demand as their right a gratuity (*buona mano, mancia, da bere, caffè, sigaro*) in addition to the hire agreed on'. 'The traveller need not scruple to limit his donations to the smallest possible sums'; but since 'there is no other country where one has to give so many gratuities as in Italy, or where such small sums are sufficient', he should always be supplied with an abundant supply of copper coins. The impudent attempts at extortion by railway porters should be firmly resisted.

Under the heading 'Public Safety', Baedeker warned that 'ladies should never undertake expeditions to the more solitary districts without escort;

and even the masculine traveller should arrange his excursions so as to regain the city not much later than sunset . . . Weapons cannot legally be carried without a licence. Concealed weapons (sword-sticks and even knives with spring blades, etc.) are absolutely prohibited, and the bearer is liable to imprisonment without the option of a fine.'

Passports were not required; the examination of luggage at the customs houses was lenient, cigars being the articles chiefly sought for (only six passed free). The *guardie* and *carabinieri* were 'thoroughly respectable and trustworthy'; the railway trains, although often behind time, were very moderate in cost and tolerably comfortable, except for the third class, which was 'chiefly frequented by the lower orders'. The *diligenza*, or ordinary stage-coach, was not so comfortable, and its passengers 'not always select'; but it conveyed travellers 'with tolerable speed'. When travelling either by road or by rail, tourists were urged to place their heavy articles in small packages since 'the enormous weight of the trunks used by some travellers not infrequently causes serious and even lifelong injury to the hotel and other porters who have to handle them. Furthermore, articles of value should not be entrusted to the safekeeping of any trunk or portmanteau, however strong and secure it may seem, as during the last few years an extraordinary number of robberies of passengers' luggage have been perpetrated without detection.'

As for hotels in Florence, those of the first class, such as the Hotel Excelsior, were 'comfortably fitted up' with rooms available from 3s. a night, though rooms with baths cost rather more and guests who did not dine at the *table d'hôte* might also find the prices raised. Luncheon cost about one dollar and dinner about a dollar and fifty cents. The *pensioni* and the second-class hotels, like the Savoy in the Piazza Vittorio Emanuele (now the Piazza della Repubblica), 'though Italian in their arrangements', were 'much more comfortable and more modern in their equipment' than of late. Soap, however, was an extra for which a high price was charged, and, 'if no previous agreement' had been made, an extortionate bill was not uncommon. 'Iron bedsteads should if possible be selected, as they are less likely to harbour the enemies of repose.'

In restaurants it was to be noticed that Florentine customers had no hesitation in sending away at once ill-cooked or stale dishes, nor sometimes on insisting on inspecting the meat or fish before it was cooked. The approved way of attracting the attention of the waiter was by knocking on the table. 'If too importunate in their recommendations waiters may be checked with the word *basta*.' *Osterie* were to be avoided as 'favourite haunts of the lower classes', the rooms being 'generally dirty and uninviting'. Cafés were tolerable for breakfast and luncheon, though not for dinner, since they were often crowded until a very late hour at night and the tobacco smoke was most objectionable. Cigars were 'a monopoly of government, and invariably bad ... Passers-by [were] at liberty to avail themselves of the light burning in every tobacconist's without making any purchase.'

Wherever they were staying visitors to Florence were warned that they were likely to suffer from diarrhoea, which was 'generally occasioned either by the unwonted heat, the injudicious use of fruit and iced drinks or the drinking water'. Insect bites were also only too common: a note added to the listing of even the first-class Grand Hotel in the Piazza Manin (now the Piazza Ognissanti) read, 'On the right bank of the Arno, best situation (mosquitoes troublesome).' Additionally, visitors must always beware of the 'sudden and frequent transitions of temperature, so trying to persons in delicate health'.

Arnold Bennett may well have had this handbook with him when, in 1910, he came to Florence, where much of his novel *Clayhanger* was written. He stayed at the Pensione White, which cost him no more than 8 lire (less than £1) a day inclusive of all meals, and very good meals they were too: the Italian manageress, who had become 'almost English in her very soul', served a 'really A1 dinner' even when her guests came back to the house as late as eleven o'clock at night. Two years later, André Gide did even better at a *pensione* at No. 20 Lungarno Acciaioli where he had 'a very pleasant bedroom and sitting-room (*primo piano* on the quay) at 3 lire a day'.

From the Pensione White, Bennett went on long walks through the city. He did not so much relish such familiar landmarks as the Pitti Palace, which looked like 'a rather expensive barracks', or 'the Uffizi, which gave a general impression of carelessness and poverty in the housing of collections', or the Medici Chapel, where 'a man stood flicking a portable electric light around all the time', or the Accademia, where the guides 'with their broken English and broken French were distressing and a lot of the pictures were in the dark' and 'crowds of people, chiefly young girls' blocked the view and a man 'planted his easel right bang in front of the *Primavera*', but he delighted in the out-of-the-way pleasures and curiosities of the city's life, the excellent second-hand bookshops, the postmen on the *lungarni* ringing doorbells and calling '*La posta! La posta!*' louder and louder as they looked impatiently up at the windows, the crowded buildings in the Borgo Santa Croce, many of them inhabited by a dozen families or more living 'like birds in the side of a precipice', the constant 'movement of bicycles and untidy work-girls on foot' and the never-ending crying of wares. One man he came across was selling combs and 'pretending to bend them with all the force of his muscles. He contorted himself with a whole series of Michel Angelo attitudes, and yet he was a little shapeless man in a shapeless suit. He was also a tremendous orator, with a perfectly smooth flow of impassioned words. Such a man in England would have filled the square and got himself mobbed.'

Bennett was intrigued by the 'shapeless carts' trundling over the Ponte Vecchio, the horses in shafts, 'covered with a red cloth and a pony at either

side', the animals munching as they trotted along, eating out of 'openwork wickerish bags with an ornamentation of bright coloured stuff on the front'. He was fascinated, too, by the astonishingly crowded horse-drawn trams rattling along on both banks of the Arno, and by the little omnibuses going out to villages 'exactly as they must have done for ages', tiny, cream-coloured vehicles with six seats and delicate fringes hanging over the sides of the roof, drawn by 'poor feeble horses', their drivers sitting under large yellow umbrellas.

He was intrigued, too, by housewives letting down baskets by ropes from fourth-floor windows to hawkers in the streets below, by the men working twelve hours a day on the dredging machines in the river wearing 'nothing but a shirt with a scalloped edge that comes down a few inches below the middle', by the 'vast amount of picture-framing and cabinet-work activity (you see it everywhere)', and by the number of 'flittings to be seen every day. Typically there would be a large handcart drawn by one man, with a chain across the shaft chaining him and pressing against the middle of his thighs; pushed behind by one or two others. And perhaps a woman walking alongside with a small chequered bundle, giving a poke now and then to the insecurely balanced goods to keep them safe.'

Left: A photograph by Howard Coster of Arnold Bennett, whose Florentine Journal *provides a vivid picture of the city before the First World War.*

Right: A sketch by Arnold Bennett of the façade of Santa Croce, which was finished to designs by Niccolò Matas in 1863.

There was 'no order whatever in the streets. Pavements are quite inadequate and wayfarers sprawl all over the roadway, so that there is a tremendous confusion, and some danger, and a lot of noise. Very different from Milan, where the difficult crossroads are controlled in an English manner by the most aristocratic-looking policemen to be seen anywhere.' Yet there was 'no hurry and very little ambition in Florence and certainly a great deal more happiness than in England'.

One day he 'couldn't find anything to sketch from any spot which was free from wind and dust [this was in April] until I got to the Piazza Santo Spirito, which is very nice with its fountains and infants and idle gendarmes'. Another day he found himself in the Piazza Peruzzi, which he was told was '*le quartier des filles*'. They appeared to him 'a sinister-looking lot but they suited the architecture'.

Avoiding the 'damned English tea houses', he spent pleasant hours at tables outside cafés 'with a drink and a strange newspaper just out, as fresh as fruit' – preferably the *Nazione*, not as good as the *Corriere della Sera* or the *Secolo* but still 'not at all a bad paper for a continental provincial town' – raising his eyes from time to time to 'glance at women most assuredly got up purposely to be looked at – this experience wants a lot of beating'.

In the evenings there was 'a great deal going on in a cheap, unorganized way', as was indicated by the ubiquitous posters stuck on every wall. There were, for instance, numerous cinemas from whose interiors came the sound of enticing music and outside which bells were rung to inform customers that the performance was about to begin. There were also several large theatres in addition to the famous Pergola where Bennett saw a performance of *Il Re Lear* which his companion pronounced the 'finest Lear [he] had ever seen'. He also went to an opera at the Teatro Verdi where, having paid 2 lire for his seat and counted 120 people in the chorus on the vast stage, he reflected that the performers could not earn very much. The costumes were rich and the scenery elaborate; but 'you could see the theatre had come down in the world'; in the same row as himself he noticed a man 'surreptitiously smoking a cigarette'.

The music-halls were not to be recommended: the Alhambra was 'appallingly tedious', the Apollo only 'slightly better; if there had been a few women in the audience it would have been passable'. Nor did he much enjoy a concert in the Sala del Maggior Consiglio in the Palazzo della Signoria, where cheap chairs of all colours and designs were arranged in rows on a 'dirty tiled floor'. There was, however, no cause for complaint in most of the restaurants. He was particularly taken by Lapi's, which was in a cellar in the Via Tornabuoni:

> Here the cooking is done in full view of the audience. Each dish prepared specially for each client. All by one man. About 35, dark, personable, extraordinarily quick and graceful. If he left his recess for a moment to go upstairs

he would slide down the rail to come back again. Charcoal stove. He blew it up constantly with a fan. Sparks fly. He put on charcoal with his hand. Everything goes through that hand. He would fan with one hand and stir with another. He made an omelette in a moment... Orders called out in a loud voice by the landlord or the boy waiter... Things not in stock, such as ham, sent for and brought down in a paper. When a dish is ready the chef would plant it down on a ledge and whistle, or call out its name... The boy waiter took a pair of loose cuffs from a hat hook and slipped them on, at once giving him an air of *grande toilette*. Later the landlord, evidently bethinking himself, did the same, from another hook. About 15 customers, and all cooked for by this one man. Arched roof all papered with coloured posters of all sorts. Graceful leave-takings from all personnel as we left. Bill and tip $8\frac{1}{2}$ lire for 3 people.

In these years Florence seemed little disturbed by the imminence of war. Doney's was still crowded with customers chattering over their *Gâteau Elena* and their marrons glacés; the Giacosa tearooms opposite were just as popular. There were fancy-dress parties, and tango teas, and balls given by the witty Contessa Rucellai, the tall, orange-haired daughter of a Cossack general. At the Comtesse d'Orsay's, Gabriele D'Annunzio enthralled his hostess and her guests with the flow of his seductive talk. Ronald Firbank could occasionally be seen drifting dandiacally through the streets, his body writhing as he clutched at his hair; and Gordon Craig, having parted from Isadora Duncan and opened a theatre workshop in Via de' Serragli, was a common sight 'with his flowing hair', as Harold Acton, then a schoolboy, described him, 'driving his school, a bevy of Kate Greenaway girls, round the city in a Dickensian stage-coach'.

Italy entered the war on 24 May 1915; but, as Acton recalled, 'the city of Dante remained placid... a city of ivory towers, where art historians could pursue their investigations without disturbance'. Refugees sought shelter here: Prince Alexis Karageorgevitch and his Serbian entourage settled in one of the Acton family villas; in others 'British convalescent officers flirted and danced with those Florentine girls who were not too closely chaperoned.'

In the early months of the war, confirmed Lina Waterfield, who was then living with her aunt, Janet Ross, at Poggio Gherardo, 'life went on as usual for those who had no relations at the front'. Yet by 1917 the mood was one of 'gloom, anxiety and finally of tragedy'. As she wrote to her son in England in January that year, 'It is bitterly cold in Florence, with snow on the ground for several days. The intense cold comes hard on the poor people as fuel is all strictly rationed. People are only allowed enough to cook with day by day, and have to shiver in cold houses. It does not matter how rich you are; money cannot procure for you fuel, petrol, sugar or butter.'

'FIRENZE FASCISTISSIMA'
1919—40

'The military parades were magnificent.
The Germans, who may have been a little sceptical on this
point, will leave with a very different impression.'
COUNT GALEAZZO CIANO

In the second week of October 1919 a large crowd gathered outside Florence railway station to welcome the arrival of the leader of a new political party, a party which had declared war on socialism and had called for supporters 'ruthless and energetic enough to make a clean sweep with the past'. The man the crowd had been waiting for appeared in a dirty flying-suit, wearing also a beret and a pair of goggles pushed towards the crown of his balding head. Squat and strongly built, with intense, rather near-set dark eyes and a massive jaw, Benito Mussolini was then thirty-six years old. The son of a blacksmith and a former editor of a socialist newspaper, he had just returned from Dalmatia where he had flown to congratulate Gabriele D'Annunzio on his seizure, in the name of Italy, of the port of Fiume (now Rijeka) in defiance of the Treaty of Versailles.

In 1919, the number of committed Fascists in Florence was small, and Fascism was not yet a movement to be reckoned with in the city; the first *Fascio* in Florence, formed in April that year, had attracted few members. Mussolini's speech in the Teatro Olimpia in October, interrupted by calls for the death of the Prime Minister, Francesco Saverio Nitti, was well received by his audience; but when he came out into the street his supporters were whistled and hooted at by the crowd.

Yet, as time went by, more and more Florentines, despite the excesses of the black-shirted *squadristi*, came to regard Fascism as the only political organization capable of saving the country from its postwar chaos and from the evils of atheistic Bolshevism. Other *Fasci* were formed; and in June 1920 a former sergeant in the army, Amerigo Dumini, who had joined one of them, was given command of a group of *squadristi* which was to become a powerful and feared force in the city. The Fascists had their headquarters in Piazza Ottaviani, held meetings in the Teatro della Pergola, and – with the support of the Futurists and of Futurism's prophet, the novelist and dramatist Filippo Marinetti, who had welcomed the recent war as 'the most beautiful poem' – orchestrated parades and demonstrations. Fights frequently erupted between the movement's supporters and its enemies; and in the course of one particularly rowdy march in August 1920 a policeman and two workers were murdered. Another policeman was killed and about twenty people were injured when a bomb exploded in February the next year in the midst of a procession through Piazza Antinori; and in revenge for the subsequent death of a young Fascist student, gangs of *squadristi* marched about the city issuing threats, beating up passers-by who refused to give the Fascist salute, closing restaurants and cafés. One squad invaded the head office of the railway workers' union and shot its secretary dead. Immediately the union, followed by other unions, declared a strike, provoking further attacks on the Socialists and their supporters. There were even more violent affrays the next day when barricades were erected, a pitched battle was fought at Porta al Prato, and a young member of the Fascist Party, Giovan Francesco Berta, the son of a businessman, was attacked by strikers as he was cycling across the Ponte Sospeso, beaten to death and flung into the Arno. The army was called in to help the police, but still the violence continued. On several days that year shops and restaurants were closed, trams did not run and electricity and gas supplies were cut off.

In August 1922, to the fury of an exasperated public, a general strike was called; and Mussolini seized his opportunity to take control of the state. By then the acknowledged leader of a party with several seats in the Chamber of Deputies, he declared that if the government did not prevent the strike, the Fascists would. Taking to the streets in the name of law and order, the *squadristi* renewed their attacks on Socialist buildings, Socialist newspapers and all those whom they took to be their enemies. In October, at a party congress held in Naples, Mussolini was so impressed by the obvious determination of 40,000 Fascists that he said more and threatened more than he had ever done before. 'What we have in view,' he declared, 'is the introduction into the liberal state, which has fulfilled its functions... of all the forces of the new generation which has emerged from the war and the victory... Either the government will be given to us or we shall seize it by marching on Rome. It is a matter of days, of hours.'

Responding to the power of Mussolini's oratory, the assembled Fascists took up the cry, shouting in unison, '*Roma! Roma! Roma!*'

Soon afterwards riots broke out in several Italian towns. In Florence, preparations for the *coup d'état* were organized by Italo Balbo, a twenty-six-year-old former student of the university and an officer in the Alpine Corps during the war, and by Tullio Tamburini, also a former army officer, a cunning, daring and duplicitous man of humble origins who had assumed control of a highly active *Fascio* of some two thousand members. Streets were barricaded, buildings, including the post office, the railway station and the telephone exchange, were occupied, telephone wires cut, trains requisitioned, rifles and cars commandeered, legions of Fascists drawn up for the imminent and, in the event, disorderly March on Rome.

The government proclaimed its intention to declare martial law, but the King, fearing that this would mean civil war, and already prepared to countenance a Fascist government, refused to sign the decree and so left the existing administration powerless. In any event, both the army and the police were prepared to stand aside and let the advance of Fascism take its course. In Florence the police retreated into the Palazzo Medici-Riccardi, where several armoured cars were parked without crews in the courtyard.

With Mussolini established as head of the new government in Rome, overt opposition to Fascism began to die down in Florence. In June 1924, however, the murder by Fascist extremists of the brave and respected Giacomo Matteotti, one of Mussolini's most outspoken critics, aroused widespread revulsion in the city. An effigy of the murdered man set up in a private chapel drew crowds of mourners. Tamburini retaliated by bringing out his *squadristi* to intimidate opponents of the regime, while another leading Fascist, Renato Ricci, organized a large and bombastic parade through the city from Piazza Santa Maria Novella to Piazza della Signoria. The offices of the newspaper, *Nuovo Giornale*, were all but destroyed; freemasons' lodges and the chambers of several well-known anti-Fascist lawyers were invaded; while blackshirts ransacked Il Circolo della Cultura, a club which numbered among its members several well-known anti-Fascist intellectuals, including the historians Gaetano Salvemini and Guglielmo Ferrero, and Piero Calamandrei, professor of law at Florence University.

Soon after Matteotti's murder, another anti-Fascist, Giulio Becciolini, was killed, together with a prominent Florentine Fascist, in a rapid exchange of pistol shots; and on the night of their deaths two other opponents of the regime were murdered. By now the Fascist Grand Council was becoming alarmed by the violence in Florence; and Italo Balbo was sent back to bring the local party under control. Tullio Tamburini and some fifty other extremist Fascist leaders were dismissed; efforts were made to establish better relations between the party and conservative and liberal groups, and to gain support from the principal Florentine newspaper, *La Nazione*. The Marchese Luigi Ridolfi, a member of one of Florence's most distinguished families, who had taken part in the March on Rome, was appointed head of the provincial delegation of the Fascist Party; Antonio Garbasso, an outstanding physicist from Turin who had come to Florence in 1913 to work at the Istituto di Studi Superiori, was appointed mayor, or as his office was now to be known, *podestà*; and the highly intelligent Alessandro Pavolini, son of the professor of philology at the Istituto di Studi Superiori – whose days as a pugnacious member of a Florentine *squadra* were largely forgotten – became secretary of the Fascist Federation and founder of their influential journal, *Il Bargello*. Thereafter the membership of the Fascist Party in Florence increased year by year, while its opponents became ever less active and effective.

In the immediate aftermath of Matteotti's murder, various members of the anti-Fascist Circolo della Cultura had founded the clandestine Associazione Italia Libera, which, urging the prosecution of political murderers, the restoration of the freedom of the press and the re-establishment of the Constitution, bravely carried out a number of public demonstrations and published *Non Mollare* ('Don't Let Go'), an underground journal containing reports of Fascist abuses. Such political associations and publications were soon suppressed, however; and several leading opponents of the regime took refuge abroad, as did the brilliant Jew, Carlo Rosselli, a former professor at the Istituto di Studi Superiori, who fled to France, where, after founding the anti-Fascist movement Giustizia e Libertà, he was murdered by extreme right-wing *Cagoulards* at the instigation of Italian agents.

Many of their former colleagues and acquaintances had by now decided to give the new regime the benefit of any doubts. Indeed, while Florentines in general might joke openly about the Duce, 'whose brain was said to be addled by over-indulgence in women', there were thousands who revered him. According to the respected journalist, Luigi Barzini, he was the most popular man in Italy. Among those who attended the parties given by the smart and salacious American-born Marchesa Lulie Torrigiani, whose conversation was so coarse that Max Beerbohm was once sick into a majolica basin at her dinner table, there were those, as Harold Acton said, who 'adored the dictator as a superman'.

Many foreign residents, too, admired the Duce and were prepared to be indulgent towards Fascism. Amongst the members of the British Institute of Florence, which had been founded in 1917 by, amongst others, A. F. Spender and Janet Ross's niece, Lina Waterfield, Mussolini had his ardent supporters.[1] Harold Goad, who had been the honorary director of the Institute since 1922 and lived in the Villa Mirabello, beneath Fiesole, was known to approve of Fascism, while Francis Toye, Goad's successor, who was to spend the coming war in Brazil, seemed to pride himself on his resemblance to Mussolini and used to do a fair imitation of him raising his jaw and rolling his eyes in the accepted manner.

The number of foreign residents had been greatly reduced since 1910, when the British consul in Florence had estimated that there were no fewer than 35,000 people of his nationality living in the region. Since then the rising cost of living in Tuscany had sent thousands of these home; but thousands more remained and many were still coming out. One of those was the Nottinghamshire miner's son, the novelist D. H. Lawrence, who

Above: A crowd estimated at over 100,000 listen to Mussolini speaking in the Piazza della Signoria in 1930.

Right: Mussolini, flanked by army officers and Fascist gerarchi, *addressing the crowd.*

in the 1920s was living at the Villa Mirenda, where he wrote *Lady Chatterley's Lover*, which was first published in Florence in 1928.[2] During his sojourn in Florence, Lawrence compared socialism and Fascism, expressing opinions which were not uncommon at the time:

> By 1920 prices had gone up three times, and socialism was rampant. Now we began to be bullied in every way. Servants were rude, cabmen insulted one and demanded treble fare, railway porters demanded large sums for carrying a bag from the train to the street, and threatened to attack one if the money were not paid. The train would suddenly come to a standstill in the heat of the open country: the drivers had gone on strike for a couple of hours... This was socialism.
>
> Such socialism made itself enemies. In an old civilized country like Italy, it was bound to cave in.
>
> In the summer of 1920 I went north, and Florence was in a state of continual socialistic riot: sudden shots, sudden stones smashing into restaurants where one was drinking coffee, all the shops suddenly barred and closed. When I came back there was a great procession of Fascisti and banners.
>
> This was the beginning of Fascism. It was an anti-socialist movement started by the returned soldiers in the name of Law and Order. And suddenly, it gained possession of Italy. Now the cabs had a fixed charge, a fixed charge for railway porters was placarded in the railway stations and trains began to run punctually.

Two years before making this comparison, D. H. Lawrence wrote *Aaron's Rod*, which is partly set in Florence; in this book he introduced several characters who are clearly based on foreigners living in or near the city at that time. There is Walter Rosen, based on the art critic Bernhard Berenson, who lived at the villa known as I Tatti.[3] There is James Argyle, based on Norman Douglas, that entertaining and unashamedly pagan writer of eclectic sexual tastes, who moved from room to room in Florence as his finances or peccadilloes dictated, settling for a time in an apartment found for him by his friend – and D. H. Lawrence's publisher – G. F. 'Pino' Orioli, before getting into trouble over a young girl and having to leave Florence in a hurry. There is Algie Constable, based on Reginald Turner, an only too justly neglected novelist and extraordinarily gifted mimic who had been a faithful friend of Oscar Wilde and who, so Max Beerbohm said, 'would be eloquent even were he dumb'.

Also living in Florence then was Turner's rival, Reginald Temple, a dainty little former actor. He, too, had known Oscar Wilde and he delighted in telling gruesome stories over the tea table, seeming to live, as Harold Acton put it, 'on buttered toast and nightmares'. There was also Edward Hutton, a prolific writer on Italian subjects, grandly described by himself in *Who's Who* as a 'Man of Letters', who imparted his wide knowledge of matters Italian at Casa Boccaccio, Poggio Gherardo.[4] Occasionally to be seen were Somerset Maugham, who played game after game of bridge while his raffish companion, Gerald Haxton, chose more self-indulgent pursuits; and Aldous Huxley, whose *Time Must Have a Stop* is set in Florence, as is *A Room with a View*, an earlier novel by a fleeting visitor, E. M. Forster, who seems to have based the Pension Bertolini upon either the Simi or the Hotel Jennings-Riccioli.[5] Rebecca West came to stay and so did Hugh Walpole. C. K. Scott Moncrieff, translator of Proust, and Richard Aldington, novelist and biographer, both lived here for a time. Osbert Sitwell came down from the castle his father had bought in his name at Montegufoni,[6] while Osbert Sitwell's mother, Lady Ida, was a frequent visitor when her eccentric husband was away on his travels. The novelist, Ada Leverson, friend of Oscar Wilde, who called her 'the Sphinx', appeared from time to time and always found it hard to leave.

The most celebrated hostess in these years was the charming, discreet, vivacious and Junoesque Hon. Mrs George Keppel, King Edward VII's former mistress, who bought the Villa dell'Ombrellino at Bellosguardo in 1925.[7] Sir Harold Acton, who still lives at La Pietra,[8] well remembers her charm and her amusing talk, free of malice, and the soldier-like appearance of her husband, once a commanding officer of a battalion of the Highland Light Infantry, who 'looked every inch a colonel, with the hearty laugh that denotes a lack of humour'. 'I remember how shocked he was to find my mother reading a book about Oscar Wilde,' Sir Harold wrote in his *More Memoirs of an Aesthete*. '"A frightful bounder. It made me puke to look at him," he muttered. To a certain extent the colonel shared his wife's aura. A guide once pointed him out to a group of inquisitive tourists as *"l'ultimo amante della regina Victoria"*.'

Sir Harold also remembers how at the time of Italy's invasion of Abyssinia – when Anthony Eden, British minister for League of Nations affairs, had successfully rallied support for a policy of sanctions, thus providing Mussolini with an opportunity of uniting his country against the actions and slanders of a hostile world – 'the walls of houses were scrawled all over with slogans which were meant to persuade one that *"La guerra è bella"* . . . My former friends were embittered by the constant reminder that they were among the have-nots – they who possessed Italy, her great culture and her climate – and their appetites were whetted for conquest.'

There was a campaign to expunge foreign words from the Italian language, to rename hotels with English names, the Eden Parks, the Albions, Bristols and Britannias, to purge 'English Tea Rooms' and shops called 'Old England'. 'The world of the Pension Bertolini with its framed portraits of the late Queen and its notice of the English church services, so deftly evoked by E. M. Forster . . . had been attacked in its foundations.'

In the spring of 1938, Mussolini came to Florence with Hitler, his partner in what was to become known as the Rome–Berlin Axis. The Duce had already paraded through Rome with the Führer; and great efforts had been made in Florence to give the city as welcoming an appearance as Rome's had been.

The planning for Hitler's visit had begun six months before. Count Ciano, Mussolini's son-in-law and foreign minister, anxious that nothing should be done in a 'commonplace, countrified sort of way', had paid particular attention to the decoration of the streets; and, while many shopkeepers refused to display portraits of Hitler in their windows, they had been made to look splendidly festive. The Duce had spent hours supervising the arrangements for the military parades, checking the details of every march-past.

The long route of the parade through Florence was lined with soldiers, with *bersaglieri*, *carabinieri*, militiamen and uniformed members of the Fascist Youth, both boys and girls. German and Italian flags flew side by side from the rooftops, specially embroidered swastikas hung from windows next to banners emblazoned with the Florentine lily and the symbol of the Fascist regime, the axe and the lictor's rods of ancient Rome.

The Duce and the Führer were driven along the route in an open car, acknowledging the cheers with their characteristic salutes. They were taken to Santa Croce to pay their respects at the shrine dedicated to the Fascist dead. They were entertained in the Boboli Gardens with a series of tableaux celebrating the glories of Florence's medieval past. They were conducted round the galleries of the Pitti Palace, Hitler appearing to be much more interested in the works of art than the Duce, who looked bored and later complained that looking at pictures tired him. They attended a performance of Verdi's opera *Simon Boccanegra*; they went to the Palazzo della Signoria, where Mussolini wrote gratefully and proudly in the visitors' book, '*Firenze fascistissima*'; and they appeared together on the palace balcony to a tumultuous roar of welcome from the people crowded together in the piazza below.

Not everyone agreed that the reception had been altogether favourable. Lady Una Troubridge, who was then living in Florence with the lesbian novelist, Radclyffe Hall, said that 'such preparations [were] made for Mussolini's reception as the Florentines [were] never likely to forget. From house to house across the narrow streets and across the façades of the ancient palaces were hung great swathes of evergreens studded with brightly coloured fruits... Every house, including our own, was supplied with silken flags, hand-painted and fringed.' Yet, according to Lady Una, the 'angry Florentines refused to applaud Adolf Hitler, an unimpressive-looking little man with a nervous smile. He seemed sheepishly anxious to propitiate the Duce, who appeared to treat him rather cavalierly.'

To most other observers, however, the visit appeared an undoubted success, satisfying the Florentines' well-developed taste for the flamboyant choreographic techniques and the medieval trappings of Fascism. Certainly by the Fascist hierarchy it was deemed a triumph. 'The military parades were magnificent,' Ciano recorded in his diary. 'The Germans, who may have been a little sceptical on this point, will leave with a very different impression.' At the railway station when Hitler said goodbye to Mussolini he was seen to stare at him with an almost dog-like devotion. 'From now on,' the Duce told him, 'no force on earth will be able to separate us.' The Führer's eyes, so Ciano noticed, filled with tears. He returned to Germany satisfied that the Duce would not interfere with his designs on Czechoslovakia. But there were those left behind in Florence who deeply regretted the enthusiasm displayed by so many people during Hitler's visit. The great anti-Fascist poet, Eugenio Montale, lamented, 'No one is guiltless any more.'

In their efforts to emphasize the benefits which the regime had bestowed upon Florence, Fascist sympathizers pointed to the exhibition centre at the Parterre to the north of Piazza della Libertà,[9] the Biblioteca Nazionale at last completed in 1935,[10] the Casa della Gioventù del Littorio (Fascist Youth) in Piazza Beccaria, the Ponte Sospeso, finished in 1932, Raffaello's Accademia Aeronautica at the Cascine, to the splendid Stadio Comunale at Campo di Marte designed by Pier Luigi Nervi and opened in 1932,[11] and to the fine new railway station of 1935, the plans of which, after competing designs had been exhibited in the Palazzo della Signoria, were approved by Mussolini himself.[12]

Presented though he was as a tireless worker who found time to interest himself in all aspects of his country's life and well-being, those who knew the Duce most intimately were well aware of the reality concealed behind the tireless propaganda. They knew that he had no patience with difficult work, a horror of decisions, that he was capable of writing 'approved' on two conflicting memoranda emanating from two different ministries – and then going into another room where one of his mistresses lay waiting to satisfy the urgent demands of a sexual appetite that approached satyriasis. In wild arrogance and wilful misapprehension of Italy's fundamental needs, he had by 1940 made up his mind to go to war again at the side of Germany.

26

WAR AND PEACE
1940–66

'An hour marked by destiny
is striking in the sky of our country.'
BENITO MUSSOLINI

Looking up at the loudspeakers in the squares on 10 June 1940, the Florentine people waited expectantly for the Duce's voice. 'An hour marked by destiny is striking in the sky of our country,' they heard him say. 'We are entering the lists against the plutocratic and reactionary democracies of the West ... People of Italy, to arms!'

Soon afterwards, while Hortense Acton was entertaining a few friends at her villa, La Pietra, a police official called on her and requested her to accompany him to the Questura. 'He explained that it was only a matter of a trifling formality, something to do with her passport,' her son, Sir Harold, has recorded, recounting experiences which other foreign residents in Florence shared.

> He drove her to a prison, where in a flimsy summer dress without even a toothbrush she was immured among prostitutes and others of ill-repute for the next three days and nights. She refused to undress or lie down in that noisome hole, nor would she eat the slops that were handed to her in a tin container ...
>
> No message reached her from outside except an insolent letter from a Fascist female, the wife of an art critic, telling her she had only got what she deserved, she might have been treated much worse, with the slogan '*Il Duce ha sempre ragione*' ('The Leader is always right') appended to her florid signature. When my mother's maid telephoned a powerful friend for help, he snapped back at her: 'Don't you realize that we are at war and that Mrs Acton is an enemy alien?' This distinguished official had been a frequent guest in our house for a quarter of a century ...
>
> My father had a similar experience, in his case aggravated by blackmail. He managed to bribe his way out. Corruption has its advantages and under Fascism it was rife.

Mussolini's declaration of war had long been expected and plans had already been made for the protection of the city's monuments and works of art. Statues were covered and padded; sandbags and blocks of asbestos were piled up against doorways and in windows from which the glass had been removed; yard upon yard of blackout material was tacked to door-posts and shutters; and works of art were removed from walls and packed up for removal to places of safety, to houses and villas beyond the confines of the city, where it was hoped they would be safer in the event of aerial attack.

Many of the principal treasures from the Uffizi and the Pitti Palace, together with pictures from other galleries and from several churches in Tuscany, were taken for safe keeping to the Castello Montegufoni, which in 1940 had been sequestrated by the Italian government. The eccentric antiquarian, Sir George Sitwell, who had gone to live there in 1925, had thereafter, usually unwillingly, entertained guests from Florence invited by his wife. She would, according to their elder son, Osbert, 'forget to tell either my father or the butler or chef; indeed it would pass from her mind altogether. Suddenly, just as my father was having a quiet early luncheon, the guests would arrive, tired and hungry after their long mountain run.'

Sir George had himself once decided to ask several guests. It was to be 'an Artists' Party', he had announced. 'Who would you ask?' Osbert had inquired cautiously. 'I was startled,' Osbert recorded in his memoirs, 'when, as he reeled off for me the list, I comprehended both how thoroughly he had thought it out, and that all of his proposed guests, Whistler, Degas, Renoir, Rodin, Lalique, Sargent, at least possessed one thing in common: they were all dead!'

For the protection of the works of Cimabue, Uccello, Botticelli, Ghirlandaio and other masters in the galleries of Florence, the Italian authorities had decided no better hiding-place could be found for them than the Castello Montegufoni. It was isolated in a remote district and, as Sir Osbert Sitwell said,

> the doors and windows of the chief rooms were big enough to allow the largest pictures to be carried in and out without risk of damage. These treasures were consigned personally to the *contadino* in charge of the castle, Guido Masti, the representative of a family who had occupied the same position of trust under various owners for well over a century ... Among the first arrivals were Uccello's *Battle of San Romano*, the Cimabue *Virgin Enthroned*, the great *Madonna* of Giotto, and Botticelli's *Primavera*. Even my father had never foreseen or thought of a house-party of this fantastic order.

From the first, the war went badly for Italy; and on 25 July 1943 Mussolini was arrested after a meeting of the Fascist Grand Council on the orders of the King. The news was greeted in Florence, as it was elsewhere in Italy, with a kind of stunned relief. Some took to the streets to celebrate, to burn pictures of the Duce, to clamber up the walls of buildings in order to destroy or deface Fascist emblems. Tricolour flags were hung from windows and a bust of Mussolini was shattered in the courtyard of the Conservatorio Luigi Cherubini. But the general mood was one less of excitement than of alarm, an alarm which deepened when Marshal Badoglio, the new head of the government, declared that the war against the Allies would continue.

The anti-Fascists in the city – Socialists, Communists, members of the Popular Party, later the Christian Democrats, and of the recently founded Action Party – had been meeting secretly in the house of Gaetano Pieraccini, a distinguished doctor who was to become the first mayor of Florence after the liberation, and at the convent of San Marco in the room of Giorgio La Pira, a young professor of Roman law at Florence University, who was also to become mayor of Florence in the future. These enemies of the Fascist regime started to meet openly on learning of Mussolini's arrest; and, when Badoglio, in contradiction of his earlier announcement, proclaimed his government's intention of surrendering to the Allies, they began to make arrangements for replacing Fascist officials by men with democratic views and for freeing trade unions from Fascist control. Their plans were soon thwarted, however, as the Germans moved in quickly to take control of Italy, entering Florence on 11 September 1943, arresting Italian soldiers, taking over their barracks and deporting many of them to Germany.

Once again the anti-Fascists were forced underground; Fascists emerged from hiding; and the Tuscan Committee of National Liberation was instituted to conduct an underground war.

The Germans established their headquarters in the Piazza San Marco; but immediately made it clear to the Italian Fascists that they would be permitted to run their own affairs in the city. Florentines were afterwards to remember with gratitude the restraint exercised by the German Consul, Gerhard Wolff, who did his best to resist the depredations of his less humane countrymen, going out of his way to help Italians who had fallen foul of the authorities, blocking Hermann Goering's attempt to acquire several valuable pictures from the Uffizi, and, according to a diary kept by Bernhard Berenson's companion, Nicky Mariano, advising Berenson, a Jew as well as an anti-Fascist American, to leave I Tatti and go into hiding. Indeed, Florentines in general had more to fear from their own people than from the German army. It was, for example, the Florentine 92nd Legion of the Fascist Militia which was responsible for the institution of an office of political investigation, the director of which was Major Mario Carità, whose hundred or so minions were reputed to torture suspects in their headquarters in the Via Benedetto Varchi and later at No. 67 Via Bologna, a large house whose sinister reputation earned it the name of the Villa Triste. Other feared Fascist organizations were the Muti battalion of dedicated blackshirts, some of them criminals from the prisons of the city, and the notorious Decima Mas, an autonomous body of marines commanded by the Roman Prince Valerio Borghese.

While relying upon corps such as these to repress anti-Fascist elements, the authorities endeavoured to maintain the illusion of a city untroubled by strife. To be sure, a committed Fascist was brought in as editor of *La Nazione*; but when the Italian Academy was transferred from Rome to Florence, its president, the Hegelian philosopher Giovanni Gentile, a shining star of the Fascist intellectual firmament, saw to it that contributors to the Academy's publications were not necessarily Fascist supporters. Theatres and the opera were kept open; no fewer than twenty-eight cinemas showed mostly Italian films; art galleries were crowded; the concert season opened as usual; restaurants offered an abundance of food for those who could afford black-market prices; and while there was little meat for the poor, vegetables were in good supply in the markets.

The illusion of a city at peace was also maintained by the infrequency of air raids, a mercy which the Florentines attributed to the Anglo-Saxons' predilection for their ancient city. A raid did take place on 9 September, aimed at destroying the city's rail communications; and, since the railway lines passed close to the city centre, as much damage was done to surrounding buildings as to the Allies' intended target and there were a number of civilian casualties. And in a later raid part of the Teatro Comunale[1] was destroyed. But in the few other raids damage was slight and casualties very few.

Meanwhile the Resistance, largely organized by the Communist Gruppi di Azione Patriottica and the less experienced and generally younger members of the Action Party, kept up their fight against Germans and Fascists alike. They carried out sabotage and terrorist attacks; distributed clandestine newspapers such as the Action Party's *La Libertà*; stole weapons; clashed with the blackshirt militia in the woodlands of Pratolino and Monte Morello; set up commissions to help Jews and Allied prisoners on the run. They attacked the offices of Fascist trade unions and strove to foster strikes; they bombed places of entertainment frequented by German soldiers; and transmitted information about enemy troop movements and positions to the Allied army. They shot an Italian colonel who was active in the recruitment of men for the Fascist army, and this resulted in the execution of five hostages by the Fascist authorities; later, they killed Giovanni Gentile as he was driving home from the Italian Academy's offices in Palazzo Serristori, an assassination which was widely regretted, since Gentile openly disapproved of Major Carità's savage behaviour and was known also to have helped colleagues in difficulties with the regime.

As the Allied army advanced north, the activities of the partisans around Florence – now increasingly supported by the Liberal and Socialist Parties and by the Christian Democrats – increased in intensity, while the Fascist authorities maintained a pretence of defiant normality. Exhibitions were still held in the city's galleries; cinemas and theatres continued their shows; lectures on Dante were given at the Palazzo dell'Arte della Lana; and at the Teatro Verdi the opera was in full swing with *The Barber of Seville*.

By the middle of July, however, as the Allied advance relentlessly continued, the cigarette ration had to be severely restricted; gas and electricity were cut off for long periods, and warnings were given of an imminent restriction of the water supply. On 23 July about fifteen members of the Resistance were shot in the Cascine after one of their number had divulged their names under torture at the hands of Major Carità's vicious henchmen.

By then most of the leading Fascists had fled north, including Major Carità himself, Alessandro Pavolini, and the head of the province of Florence, who disappeared with four million lire of public funds. On their departure the Tuscan Committee of National Liberation issued a manifesto proclaiming itself the sole political authority in Florence.

On 29 July the German high command issued their own order to 'the inhabitants of the area along the Arno within the confines of the streets listed below . . . ' These people, some 150,000 in number, including patients in the hospital of San Giovanni di Dio, were to leave their premises by noon the next day. It would 'not be necessary to move furniture'. 'People who are temporarily obliged to leave their houses and who cannot find accommodation at friends' houses [outside the area to be evacuated] should go to the areas of Campo di Marte and the Cure.'

Taking no notice of the assurance that it would not be necessary to move furniture, families in the designated areas moved out of their houses immediately, pushing as much as they could manage on wheelbarrows and handcarts, leaving piles of their possessions in areas supposed to be safe and going back to their homes to collect more, even after darkness had fallen over a city from which all electricity had now been cut off.

'The Allied forces are advancing on Florence,' warned thousands of leaflets dropped by American planes. 'The city's liberation is at hand. Citizens of Florence, you must unite to preserve your city and to defeat our common enemies . . . Prevent the enemy from detonating mines which they may have placed under the bridges . . . ' Similar pleas were issued by the Committee of National Liberation. There was nothing the Florentines could do, however, to save their bridges. The whole area was cordoned off. German paratroops manned a series of guard posts; a decree issued by the German command forbade the people to leave their houses for any purpose; they were to close all windows and see that they remained closed night and day; they were advised to seek shelter in their cellars or, failing that, in churches or '*in altri grandi edifici*'; German patrols had orders to fire on anyone seen in the streets or at windows. The Swiss Consul, Karl Stein-hauslin, asked the German command to spare the statues on the Ponte Santa Trinita. He was told that the statues were too heavy to move with the equipment and men at their disposal. But at least Steinhauslin could comfort himself with the thought that the greatest treasures of the Uffizi and the Pitti Palace would be spared the effects of the imminent explosions.

On the afternoon of the day on which the Germans ordered the evacuation of houses along Florence's river bank, Wynford Vaughan-Thomas, the war correspondent for the BBC, and Eric Linklater, the novelist, then serving in the War Office's directorate of public relations, arrived at Castello Montegufoni to find it occupied by a battalion of the Mahratta Light Infantry of the 8th Indian Division. Although the German forward positions were scarcely more than a mile to the north, it was a quiet afternoon broken only by the intermittent shelling of the Allied and enemy batteries.

Having driven through Siena – where until recently the presence of Moroccan *goums* of the French army had kept the inhabitants behind locked doors and shuttered windows – Montegufoni's two visitors made their way into the castle, where they found numerous paintings stacked against the walls.

'By this time we had gathered a few spectators,' Linklater recorded.

> Some refugees had been sleeping in the castello ... and now, cheerfully per-ceiving our excitement, they were making sounds of lively approval, and a couple of men began noisily to open the shutters ... Vaughan Thomas shouted, 'Uccello!'
>
> I, in the same instant cried, 'Giotto!' For a moment we stood there, quite still, held in the double grip of amazement and delight ... We went nearer, and the refugees came round us and proudly exclaimed, '*E vero, è vero! Uccello! Giotto! Molto bello, molto antico!*' ... Then I heard a sudden clamour of voices, a yell of shrill delight, and Vaughan Thomas shouting 'Botticelli!' as if he were a fox-hunter view-hallooing on a hill. I ran to see what they had found, and came to a halt before the *Primavera*.

At this dramatic moment a small man with gleaming spectacles wearing a grey tweed knickerbocker suit made his appearance and was proudly intro-duced by the Italians: '*Il Professore, il Professore.*' He turned out to be a curator from the Uffizi who had been placed in charge of the treasures at Montegufoni and at nearby villas at Montagnana and Poppiano. He told the British visitors that the pictures had been removed from their galleries in Florence on the orders of the Fascists after the city's railway station had been bombed in March 1944; and, as the fighting approached nearer Florence, they had been taken out of the city altogether. The Germans had been generous in lending transport; but the Allies, the curator said, had not so far been as sympathetic as their enemies.

So Linklater and Vaughan-Thomas went to see the English commanding officer of the Mahrattas who, although roused from sleep after an exhausting advance, was 'very patient'. He admitted that he knew little about art, wistfully adding that if his wife were there 'she would be more impressed'. She took a great interest in pictures, he said. He put on his shoes and came down to look at the *Primavera*.

> He stood silent for some time and, still without comment, walked slowly past the other pictures, into the adjoining rooms and back again, as though he were making his rounds of a Sunday morning after church parade ... To the north we could hear the sounds of war, and so much concern for a few yards of paint may have seemed excessive to him whose care was men ... But he was evidently pleased with what he saw, and now permitted himself, with a decent restraint, to be infected by our enthusiasm. He would do everything in his power to keep the pictures safe, he promised.

So almost the whole of the great collection was preserved, both at Montegufoni and at the other places where works of art had been stored. At Poppiano some Allied soldiers had broken into the villa, stolen the housekeeper's blankets and her frying-pan, slashed two canvases and smashed a bust of Dante; and at Montegufoni a circular Ghirlandaio, which had been used as a table top, was stained with wine and coffee and scored by table knives. But the rest of the pictures, largely undamaged, were to be returned to Florence when the fighting was over.

At about four o'clock in the morning of 4 August, a few hours after the demolition of the Ponte alle Grazie, a tremendous roar heralded the destruction of the Ponte Santa Trinita, whose statues were sent hurtling into the river. Florence's other bridges were also blown up, with the exception of the Ponte Vecchio, the approaches to which were blocked by piles of debris from the mining of buildings, including numerous looted shops, in Via Por Santa Maria, Via Guicciardini and along the *lungarni*. The shops on the bridge itself were mined and booby-trapped.

As the reverberations of the last thunderous explosion died away, Ugo Procacci of the *Soprintendenza* of Fine Arts, who had been sheltering with his family in the Pitti Palace, climbed to the top storey:

> In the early light I looked from a window overlooking the Piazza. There was no one about, but in a moment from behind the wing of the palace came two partisans. I opened the window and called out, 'Where are the Germans?'
>   'There are none here any more. They are all across the Arno.'
>   'And the bridges?'
>   'All blown up, except Ponte Vecchio.'
>   '*Viva l'Italia!*' cried one of the partisans.
>   '*Viva l'Italia!*' I called back, but Italy no longer had the Ponte Santa Trinita ...

Buildings on the approaches to the Ponte Vecchio destroyed by German mines in 1944.

It was not possible to leave the palace by the front entrances; all the doors had been barred. I ran therefore into the Boboli Gardens, up, up, all the way to the Kaffeehaus. I climbed the stairs in haste. 'Don't look out!' cried a woman. 'The Germans are firing!' I looked out all the same and in the still feeble light of the early morning I saw the massacre of my Florence. The ruins of Oltrarno were there at a few paces. That marvellous panorama which for generations had been admired by the whole world showed a tremendous gash in a tragic foreground along the Arno around Ponte Vecchio, and the dust and smoke were still rising from the rubble . . .

I had hardly returned to the palace when suddenly came the rumour, 'The Allies are here!' The crowd rushed forward – the grand staircase of the palace was blocked with people. While I was trying to get through, suddenly on the landing of the staircase appeared an English soldier and an English officer. They were embraced on every side by the crowd.

Eric Linklater was one of the first of the Allies to reach the city:

We went into that part of Florence which lies south of the Arno. The South African Armoured Division, the New Zealanders, the 24th Guards Brigade, and the 4th Infantry Division had made a race for the city, and the South Africans, I think, had won by a head.

The Florentines of the South Bank, poor people for the most part, gave us a warmer welcome than the Romans. Tears streaked their faces while they cheered, and for an hour or two their affection had almost the peril of a cannibal's. At one moment my companion of the day – Vaughan-Thomas was no longer with me – was mercilessly embraced by a bristle-bearded labourer while I, with my left arm clutched to an unseen but young and palpitating bosom, was being heartily kissed by a pair of the plainest old trouts in Tuscany. But then the crowd broke and scattered as snipers opened fire from a window or a roof, and our partisans replied.

Linklater went through the Boboli Gardens to the Pitti Palace, which was full of refugees and countless children, 'a crawling mass of unfortunate humanity,' as another observer, Frederick Hartt, put it, looking like 'the most crowded slum in Naples'. Linklater met a curator of the gallery who took him through the press of 'amicable and voluble' people to a concrete shelter where, in large crates and packing-cases, were numerous pieces of statuary, much of it dismembered, and Ghiberti's bronze doors from the Baptistery.

The smoke of ruined buildings was still rising by the banks of the Arno and the rattle of machine-gun fire could still be heard echoing along the *lungarni*. 'The Germans and the Fascists still held the northern part of the city and no one knew what its fate would be . . . Florence was divided again as if between more savage Guelphs and Ghibellines . . . In the late afternoon rain drove the people indoors, and all the flowers they had thrown lay wetly trampled on empty streets.'

Another British officer, the Hon. Hubert Howard, serving with the Psychological Warfare Branch at Allied Force Headquarters, was also in the Oltrarno that afternoon. He, too, was overwhelmed by the crowds of people who poured out into the streets, cheering and waving and throwing flowers at the tanks and jeeps.

Making his way towards the Piazza Santo Spirito, Howard came across one of the leading partisan commanders, Aligi Barducci, a former customs officer, whose *nom de guerre* was Potente. Commander of the Garibaldi Arno Division, Barducci was killed soon afterwards when a mortar bomb exploded in the piazza as he was making plans for an attack upon the positions of the German parachutists and Fascist snipers who had been left behind on this side of the Arno as a rearguard when the rest of the army withdrew across the river.

The partisans had hoped the Allies would join them in these operations; but the British commander, General Alexander, determined to spare Florence the damage done to other cities such as Pisa, where heavy fighting had taken place, had given orders for the withdrawal of the advancing troops from the Oltrarno and for an advance on either side of the city towards a point to the north of it where the two arms of the northward thrust could meet.

When the men of Barducci's division decided to go through the city without Allied support to the help of another group of partisans surrounded by the Germans to the north of Florence on Monte Morello, Howard and some other officers decided to go across the river with them and make their way to the Palazzo della Signoria, the tower of which had been occupied by members of the Committee of National Liberation passing themselves off as Fascists. 'A sinister silence dwelled over the city,' Howard recorded.

> We walked silently keeping careful watch on the narrow, deserted, shadowy streets of the medieval city, moving by way of the Via Perione to Piazza Santa Trinita and from there along the Via delle Terme to Por Santa Maria. The great doors of the palaces were barred and the shutters were closed over the windows. Nevertheless as we moved on I noticed that the lower parts of these shutters were slightly open and I felt hundreds of eyes fixed upon us with intense concentration. What impression must have been made by this small group of Englishmen who entered Florence without a military escort and almost unarmed? Then there reached our ears a strange and wonderful sound which we shall surely never hear again. Behind the shutters we were made aware of the gentle, muffled applause of hundreds of hands and the sound of voices whispering welcome.

The night before, the Germans had withdrawn north of the city centre to the line of the Mugnone canal; and later on that morning, their departure having been noticed by a partisan outpost, a woman messenger was sent racing across to the Palazzo della Signoria to tell the men of the Committee of National Liberation to ring the big bell and run up the tricolour at the top of the tower.

As the bells of the Bargello echoed the tolling of La Martinella, and another observation post was established in the cupola of the Duomo, copies of a manifesto were posted up in the streets informing the people that the Committee of National Liberation had taken over as the provisional government. At the same time *La Nazione*, which had been purveying Fascist propaganda for decades, was taken over by a commission which appointed as editor of a new newspaper, *La Nazione del Popolo*, a leading member of the Action Party, Carlo Levi, painter, physician and soon to become internationally renowned as the author of the masterly *Cristo si è fermato a Eboli*.

The first assault by the partisans on the Germans north of Florence on 11 August was repulsed with heavy losses; and, while the Allies were preparing to launch their own attack, the threat of German incursions into the city remained. On the night of 15 August a German patrol, headed by a tank, pushed its way into Piazza San Marco; and as late as 21 August a German shell hit the Campanile, while a fragment of another struck the Madonna outside the Bigallo and took off her head. On that same day the actor Derek Bond, then an officer in the Grenadier Guards, and two other British officers, were taken prisoner, having entered the city on a sightseeing visit on the assurance that the Germans had evacuated it. Fascist snipers, supposed to have been organized by Alessandro Pavolini before his departure from his suite in the Excelsior Hotel, were still firing from rooftops and attics on unwary pedestrians below them. When caught by partisans, these snipers were dragged down into the streets and almost invariably executed after summary trials. One day eleven of them were lined up after a brief trial by a tribunal set up in the Hotel Baglioni, and shot in front of the church of Santa Maria Novella.

When the Allies launched their attack, the German army prepared to retreat. Its commander, Field-Marshal Kesselring, had never intended stopping the Allies along the line of the Arno, but merely planned to delay them while withdrawing his forces to the far stronger Gothic Line which was to stretch across the peninsula from north of Pisa to Pesaro. He abandoned Fiesole on 7 September.

By then the Allied Military Government, established in the Villa Torrigiani,[2] had taken over direct control of Florence, much to the annoyance of the Committee of National Liberation, who considered themselves quite capable of undertaking the responsibility. However, the Allied Military Government did not rescind the orders already given by the Committee and made use of most of the personnel whom they recommended.

There was much for them all to do. Food was in alarmingly short supply for those who could not afford the prices charged on the black market, the Germans having driven off with them large numbers of cattle; housing was also difficult to come by, not only for the thousands of refugees who came into the city from the *contado*, but also for those tens of thousands whose homes had been demolished by the retreating army.

Yet, gradually Florence began to recover from its ordeal and to regain its former appearance. The scaffolding and sandbags were removed from its treasured monuments; shops reopened their doors; works of art, brought from their hiding-places or recovered by the Allies as they were being transported to Germany, were returned to churches and galleries; and, as government rapidly succeeded Italian government and mayor followed mayor, war damage was made good and new buildings appeared. The Ponte alla Vittoria was opened in 1946, the Ponte San Niccolò in 1949, the Ponte alla Carraia in 1951, the Ponte Amerigo Vespucci in 1957. The Ponte Santa Trinita, meticulously rebuilt by masons using copies of sixteenth-century tools and stone from the reopened Boboli quarries, was completed in 1958 but without the head of Pietro Francavilla's statue of *Primavera*, which was missing when the rest of her body was recovered from the river bed. However, it was brought up by a dredger three years later and was replaced with fitting ceremony on the statue's long neck.[3]

FLOOD AND RESTORATION
1966 – 92

'At 9.45 a.m. the flood burst into the Piazza del Duomo.'
FRANCO NENCINI

In the middle of the night of 3 November 1966 the colonel commanding the *carabinieri* in Florence was woken by the ringing of his telephone. He was told that from Figlini and from other places in the valley of the Arno, urgent pleas for help had been made: water in the river was rising fast; farmers were driving their cattle to higher ground; a few people had already clambered to the roofs of their houses.

As the night wore on Florence itself received the first warnings of catastrophe. To the north the Mugnone burst its banks and water cascaded down towards the Cascine, where frantic efforts were made to save the horses in the stables by the racecourse, seventy of which were drowned; water began pouring into cellars of buildings by the Arno; jets of water suddenly began gushing out of manholes, throwing the iron covers high into the air; supplies of electricity and gas were both abruptly cut off; above the Ponte alle Grazie and between the Ponte Santa Trinita and the Ponte Vecchio the rapidly rising waters poured across the *lungarni*, sweeping cars before them in the flood. The arches of the Ponte Vecchio were all but submerged and the bridge itself seemed in danger of collapse.

The night watchman on duty telephoned several of the jewellers who had shops on the bridge to warn them of the danger to their premises. 'We grabbed five or six suitcases,' recalled Signora Albertina Piccini-Risalti, the wife of one goldsmith thus alerted,

> and tore off in the car. It was a dangerous ride, for there were plenty of other cars speeding about. It was pouring with rain when we got to the bridge ... About fifteen rough-looking youths started prancing about behind us, laughing and shouting abuse.
>
> It must have been just on two when we entered the shop. The floor was shaking terribly under our feet, and outside I could see tree trunks charging

along and looking as if they were going to crash in through the window. Our first inclination was to run away. We could hear awful thuds and bangs going on, and the floor was shaking and shaking. The water could not have been more than a metre below us. We spent ten minutes or so in the first room, grabbing the first things that came to hand and articles belonging to our clients. When I think now of all the things we left behind, all the things we lost, I could weep ... Then two *carabinieri* came, and they banged at the door, too. 'Come away! The bridge is in danger!' The boys were still outside, and a friend saw me home. I picked up some more suitcases and went back to the bridge. The lights had gone out and it was pitch dark and pouring with rain ... We collected up some more things but then the bridge started shaking so violently that we thought it was going to collapse at any moment, and we ran for it. The last thing I remember is a huge tree trunk and a Fiat 1100 butting at the window of the shop; I thought for a moment I had gone mad. Some people were still on the bridge, and the *carabinieri* were shouting: 'At your own risk and peril!' And we shouted at the *carabinieri:* 'Why don't you get in your cars and go and give the alarm?' And they replied – and you could see they were embarrassed – 'We have no orders'.

Most of the people of Florence were still in bed, quite unaware of the scale of the disaster, oblivious to the fact that shopkeepers in the lower parts of the city, in Piazza Sante Croce, by San Frediano and in Via Guicciardini, were furiously trying to save their wares, bailing mud and water from their lower floors. But when morning came, there could no longer be doubt that Florence was in the grip of the worst flood since 1844. 'The spray off the yellow, ever spreading river brought visibility down to a minimum,' wrote Franco Nencini, whose *Firenze: I giorni del diluvio*, gives a vivid first-hand account of these days.

> The river had completely burst its banks, sweeping away the parapets and trees and tearing the very stones out of the roads ... The rising waters carried away hundreds of motor-cars, flinging them violently against the walls, doors and street signs ... The mournful sound [of short-circuited car horns] was the day-long accompaniment to the flood – together with the shouts of those who were trapped, the barking of dogs, the pounding of the water against the walls of buildings as high as nine or ten feet above the ground ... Thousands of houses were flooded and the first victims already lay beneath the mud ... From the roofs of low houses in the poorer parts of the city people were crying in vain for help ... At 9.45 a.m. the flood burst into the Piazza del Duomo.

Waters of the Arno rushing through the arches of the Ponte Santa Trinita in November 1966.

From his room in the newly completed offices of Florence's newspaper, the *Nazione*, Franco Nencini saw people on the roofs of houses waving sheets to attract attention. Later, a helicopter rescued some of them; but its operations were hampered by wires and television aerials. An officer lowered himself from the machine and threw bread and milk to the stranded people, together with tins of food, which they had no means of opening. From

time to time Nencini heard loud reports as tanks of carbide were flung together, stores of paraffin blew up and boilers exploded.

'At 9.45 a.m. the flood burst into the Piazza del Duomo.'

In the hospital of San Giovanni di Dio patients in the lower wards were being carried to upper storeys while thousands of gallons of muddy water poured through the ground floor destroying the hospital's stocks of food. At the same time in the Uffizi and the Museo della Scienza treasures were being hurriedly carried upwards out of danger. In the flooded church and cloister of Santa Croce big bundles of manuscripts from the nearby Biblioteca Nazionale were floating about, while monks, using tables as rafts, were endeavouring to salvage what they could. In the Piazza San Giovanni panels from Ghiberti's and Pisano's doors were wrenched loose by the swirling waters which, now thick with oil as well as mud, were sweeping along at nearly forty miles an hour, carrying uprooted trees, vehicles, furniture, doors and window frames in their tumultuous path. From the Santa Teresa prison, where the inmates had been escorted to the top floor, came sounds of firing. The warders had been overpowered, and the prisoners began diving down into the surging waters below to cling to tree trunks and bits of wreckage. One young prisoner hesitated. 'Where do you think you're going?' a woman called to him. 'To take the waters at Montecatini,' he shouted back, before jumping to his death.

A car carried away by the flood outside the Biblioteca Nazionale.

Some of those who escaped made their way later across the rooftops to a house in the Via Manzoni. 'They were shivering with cold and soaked to the skin,' the owner of the house recalled. 'Some of them looked pretty tough customers ... But the odd thing was they all seemed shy and embarrassed ... They were all on their best behaviour, exchanging polite remarks, offering cigarettes – and never failing to use the ashtrays.' They politely accepted food, then swam away down the street. 'I drove up to the Piazzale Michelangelo', wrote Carlo Coccioli in *Il Giorno*.

> Night had fallen by now, and there were no lights to be seen; it rained incessantly, and Florence lay at the mercy of her enraged river. There was no voice offering counsel, not a searchlight, no bells ringing, no help being given – only silence. Talkative, argumentative and sarcastic though they normally are, the people of Florence were playing out their drama in silence. The river alone was heard; there was nothing but the river, with its swirling mixture of oil and mud.

The next morning, as the water level slowly sank, leaving a thick and noisome deposit of mud and oil in the streets, the citizens came out with buckets, brooms and shovels, and, with makeshift implements made out of broken doors and pieces of furniture, set about the Herculean task of clearing away the detritus, a threat to health as well as a barrier to traffic and an affront to the eye. Later there was to be much criticism of the authorities, national and local, for their failure to respond adequately to the crisis; but there could be no doubt about the good-natured determination of the citizens as they worked to make Florence clean again.

It was estimated that over 15,000 cars had been wrecked, 6,000 shops put out of business, and that almost 14,000 families were homeless. The lists of damaged works of art, books and archives made tragic reading. Florence's plight aroused worldwide compassion: offers of help came from all over Europe and from America. In London the Italian Art and Archives Rescue Fund was established under the chairmanship of Sir Ashley Clarke, who had retired as ambassador in Rome four years before; and this organization immediately sent out to Italy Professor Nicolai Rubinstein, author of *The Government of Florence under the Medici*, and John Pope-Hennessy, at that time Keeper of the Department of Architecture and Sculpture at the Victoria and Albert Museum.

In his memoirs Pope-Hennessy describes the devastating consequences of the flood for works of art in Florence. He was 'reminded of the images of supernatural disasters that punctuate Florentine Quattrocento painting':

> The first indications of disaster appeared on the road from Bologna ... Lorry after lorry loaded with rusty cars was climbing slowly northward ... scarcely did we leave the highway than in the western suburbs of the town, far from the river, oil stains started to appear along the streets at shoulder height and piles of rotting woodwork could be seen standing outside each door. Inside the town,

Altogether fifteen thousand cars were wrecked in the floods of 1966, like this one in Piazza Mentana.

parties of soldiers were at work clearing the slime, but more than two weeks after the flood the mud in the Piazza Santa Croce was still ankle deep, and the Via de' Bardi at the south end of the Ponte Vecchio was a morass of mud and oil.

Treasures in the refectory of Santa Croce had been blackened by the mud; on the right wall of the nave of the church Donatello's *Cavalcanti Annunciation* was 'soaked with oil to the level of the Virgin's knees'; inside the Pazzi Chapel the water had risen to about two thirds of the height of the *pietra serena* arcading; the flood waters had submerged the cloisters of Santa Maria Novella and the Ognissanti and cascaded down the Via Ghibellina, smashing the windows of the Casa Buonarroti. The Museo Horne, the Museo di Storia della Scienza and the Museo Archeologico had all been flooded and their contents badly damaged. Marble sculptures in the courtyard of the Bargello had been impregnated with dense patches of oil. Indeed, in the centre of the town, scarcely a monument or a church had survived unscathed.

But, encouraged by an energetic mayor, Piero Bargellini, and the highly capable Superintendent of Fine Arts, Ugo Procacci, groups of restorers were already at work; and others, their expenses paid by Sir Ashley Clarke's Rescue Fund and similar committees in Italy and other countries, were soon to join them. A restoration studio was established in the Palazzo Davanzati and here Kenneth Hempel, 'the most accomplished restorer of Italian sculpture in the world', and Joyce Plesters, head of the research laboratory at the National Gallery in London, jointly discovered, as Pope-Hennessy recorded, 'the first traces of gilding in the hair of Donatello's wooden Magdalen'.[1]

By the end of the decade there was little to show how devastating the flood had been, apart from the marks on walls indicating the height the waters had reached. Florence's four hundred hotels and *pensioni* were filled with tourists, almost five million of whom arrived in 1971, over ten times as many as the resident population. They found a city which appeared to be as prosperous as it had been in the Middle Ages, with a thriving textile trade and numerous fashion houses and manufacturers of leather goods that had made such names as Gucci, Pucci and Ferragamo familiar the world over.

Yet for all the modernity of the city centre, in which speeding mopeds made crossing streets a hazardous experience, the ancient stones of Florence remain solid and immutable; and no visitor can fail to be haunted by the ghosts and moved by remembrances of the past that linger around them. At every corner a figure seems to emerge momentarily from the shadows – Dante angrily throwing the tools out of a workshop where he has heard a smith singing one of his poems so badly; Michelangelo striving to release imprisoned bodies from the blocks of marble in his *bottega* in the shadow of the Duomo; the apothecary, Luca Landucci, exasperated by the huge piles of stones which blocked the street outside his shop when the builders were at work on the vast Palazzo Strozzi; Lorenzo il Magnifico gorgeously arrayed for his victory in the *giostra* at Santa Croce; Fra Angelico, with tears in his eyes, painting Christ on the Cross in San Marco; Alessandro and Lorenzino de' Medici galloping through the streets on the same horse, dressed in women's clothes and shouting insults at the passers-by; Savonarola foretelling doom with such passion and conviction in his apocalyptic sermons that Pico della Mirandola feels his hair stand on end; Anna Maria, the last of the Medici, tall, proud and stiff-backed, living out her remaining years in the Pitti Palace in a comfortless room surrounded by silver furniture; James Boswell, 'quite furious with lust', picking up two girls on the Ponte Vecchio, and Horace Walpole, entranced by the music of the Carnival, strolling across the Ponte Santa Trinita in straw hat and linen dressing-gown; officers of the occupying Austrian army lounging in their white

Florence by night from the Boboli Gardens.

uniforms at the tables outside the Caffè Doney, and Cossacks spearing salami as they gallop headlong through the Mercato Nuovo; W. M. Thackeray writing a poem about the delicious fish soup at the Ristorante Laura, and Walter Savage Landor so disgusted by a meal in his *pensione* that he throws it out of a window; Mrs Browning welcoming guests to tea at the Casa Guidi and taking them for walks in the Boboli Gardens, and Henry James at Bellosguardo, looking up from his work on *The Aspern Papers* to gaze upon 'the most beautiful view in the world'; Queen Victoria in her carriage holding up a miniature of Prince Albert towards the recently completed façade of Santa Maria del Fiore; the monks of Santa Croce, using tables as rafts, struggling to save their precious manuscripts from the swirling waters of the flood; and Timoteo Lucaroni dredging from the mud of the Arno's bed Francavilla's long-lost statue of *Primavera*, a resurrected symbol of the resilient city's long and glorious past.

NOTES ON BUILDINGS
AND WORKS OF ART

In the following notes, buildings printed in capitals have a separate note to themselves.

Since they are so capricious, no attempt has been made to indicate opening times. The latest (the fifth) edition of the *Blue Guide: Florence* by Alta Macadam provides as reliable an indication of these as can be found. This book, Eve Borsook's *Companion Guide to Florence* (now also in its fifth edition), and the Italian Touring Club's guide, *Firenze e dintorni*, give more details about buildings and works of art than room can be found for in these brief notes.

CHAPTER 1 *(pages 1–4)*

1. The façade of **San Miniato al Monte** is, like that of the BAPTISTERY, of white and greenish marble. Some of its architectural features were adapted by Brunelleschi for his own designs, as for instance the marble door surrounds. The large interior has, unusually for Tuscany, a raised chancel over the crypt. The marbles covering the columns and walls are nineteenth-century additions, but the restored open-frame roof dates from 1322. The nave pavement of marble inlay was carved in 1207 with the signs of the zodiac.

   The Chapel of the Cardinal of Portugal was added on to the north wall in the fifteenth century. Designed by Antonio Manetti, Brunelleschi's pupil and biographer, in honour of Cardinal Jacopo di Lusitania, who died in Florence in 1459 aged twenty-five, the chapel contains an *Annunciation* by Alesso Baldovinetti above a throne left empty by the young cardinal's

death. The tomb of the cardinal was carved by Antonio and Bernardo Rossellino (the marble effigy was modelled after a death-mask); the five terracotta tondi on the ceiling are by Luca della Robbia.

   The Cappella del Crocifisso was executed by Michelozzo to house a miraculous crucifix, which was later moved to SANTA TRINITA. Its terracotta coffering is by Luca della Robbia and the late-fourteenth-century altarpiece-cum-cupboard is by Agnolo Gaddi. The chapel is decorated with the family emblems of Piero di Cosimo de' Medici, who commissioned it. Spinello Aretino painted the walls of the sacristy, built in 1387, with scenes from the life of St Benedict. The campanile was built in 1523 to Baccio d'Agnolo's design after the collapse of the original. Michelangelo saved it when Florence was besieged by covering it up with mattresses. A Benedictine foundation, San Miniato al Monte was taken over in 1373 by Olivetans, an independent branch of the order, who are still here in the adjacent convent. The nearby church of San Salvatore al Monte was completed in 1504 to the designs of Simone del Pollaiuolo, Il Cronaca.

2. The name Florentia is also said to be derived from Florinus, a Roman general who died in the assault upon the Etruscan town of Fiesole; from *Fluentia*, confluence of the rivers Arno and Mugnone; or from *florens*, rich in flowers. The lily, the emblem of the commune of Florence, is the Christian symbol of purity. The Guelph city's coat of arms featured a red lily on a white

ground, the Ghibelline's a white lily on a red ground. Both these coats of arms can be seen below the gallery on the west façade of the PALAZZO DELLA SIGNORIA.

3. **Via Porta Rossa** extends from the PIAZZA SANTA TRINITA to the PIAZZA DELLA SIGNORIA. It has borne this name since the early thirteenth century. The Porta Rossa, 'the Red Gate', long since demolished, gave on to what is now the Via del Parione by the church of SANTA TRINITA. On the south side is the PALAZZO BARTOLINI-SALIMBENI. The PALAZZO DAVANZATI is at No. 9, the MERCATO NUOVO at the eastern end. The Hotel Porta Rossa, which occupies a sixteenth-century palace once owned by the Bartolini-Salimbeni, opened as the Albergo Porta Rossa in the middle of the nineteenth century.

4. **Via de' Condotta**, an extension of VIA PORTA ROSSA, north of the PIAZZA DELLA SIGNORIA, was formerly known as Via dei Librai because of the stationers and booksellers who were in business here. One or two such businesses remain.

5. **Via de' Cerretani** takes its name from an influential family which settled in Florence in the twelfth century. The family died out in the eighteenth century.

6. Now one of Florence's smartest shopping streets, **Via Tornabuoni** extends northward from the PONTE SANTA TRINITA to Piazza Antinori. The palaces in the street include the immense PALAZZO STROZZI, PALAZZO BUONDELMONTI and PALAZZO BARTOLINI-SALIMBENI. The well-preserved **Palazzo Spini-Feroni**, at the southern end, was built for Geri degli Spini in the 1280s. The **Palazzo Minerbetti** at No. 3 is of the late fourteenth century; the **Palazzo Strozzi del Poeta** (Giaconi) at No. 5 was rebuilt in the 1620s by Gherardo Silvani; the **Palazzo del Circolo dell'Unione** (No. 7), with a bust of the Grand Duke Francesco I by Giambologna over the doorway, has been attributed to Giorgio Vasari, the **Palazzo Giacomini-Larderel** (No. 19) to Giovanni Antonio Dosio, the handsome **Palazzo Antinori** at the northern end to Giuliano da Maiano. This was built in the 1460s and has been owned by the Antinori since 1506. The Antinori, who seem to have come to Florence

San Miniato al Monte

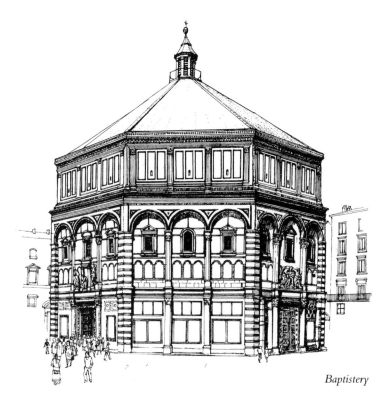

Baptistery

from Lucca, were rich silk merchants and bankers.

The Antinori family chapel, which contains reliefs by the school of Filippo Lippi, is in the nearby seventeenth-century church of **San Gaetano** (Santi Michele e Gaetano). One of the most important churches in seventeenth-century Florence, it was built between 1604 and 1649. The late-seventeenth-century façade is by Pier Francesco Silvani and his son, Gherardo, who, with Matteo Nigetti, created the Baroque interior. Giovanni Battista Foggini carved the marble statues. In the first chapel on the south side is a terracotta *Virgin* by Andrea della Robbia. The bronze crucifix on the east wall of the choir chapel is by Giovanni Francesco Susini. In the north transept are works by Giovanni Biliverti.

7. **Via del Proconsolo**, formerly Via dei Cartolai, is, like VIA CONDOTTA, in an area for long occupied by stationers, illustrators and book-sellers. It links the Piazza San Firenze and the Piazza del Duomo. The BADIA FIORENTINA and the BARGELLO are at the southern end, the PALAZZO NONFINITO and the PALAZZO PAZZI-QUARATESI opposite each other on the corner of BORGO DEGLI ALBIZZI.

8. The medieval buildings in the **Piazza Peruzzi** and Via dei Bentaccordi, some of which bear the Peruzzi family emblem of *pere* ('pears', a pun on their name), still follow the curve of the Roman amphitheatre. The fourteenth-century **Palazzo Peruzzi** has been reconstructed. The Peruzzi Chapel in SANTA CROCE has murals by Giotto and his assistants. The family, extremely successful bankers who came to Florence from Rome, also paid for the Sacristy in Santa Croce. From time to time they let the underground chambers of the amphitheatre to the Commune for use as a prison.

9. The **Baptistery**, dedicated to the Florentines' patron saint, John the Baptist, is perhaps their most cherished building. The Arte della Calimala was responsible for its upkeep and provided white and green marble for its facing from the

eleventh to the thirteenth centuries. Donatello and Michelozzo ingeniously employed the massive granite columns which run right round the interior to their advantage: carved curtains are gathered to the sides of two columns to reveal the marble and bronze TOMB OF BALDASSARRE COSSA. The pavement and vault are decorated with thirteenth-century mosaics; so is the great eight-ribbed dome, which is divided into four circles illustrating stories from the Book of Genesis and from the lives of St John the Baptist, Christ and Joseph and his brothers. Over the apse is a Last Judgement with a Christ over twenty-five feet tall.

For the DOORS see Chapter 7, notes 1 and 2, and Chapter 5, note 16.

10. **Via delle Terme** extends from the PIAZZA SANTA TRINITA to VIA POR SANTA MARIA. The PALAZZO BARTOLINI-SALIMBENI and PALAZZO BUONDELMONTI are at the western end, the PALAZZO DI PARTE GUELFA at the eastern end. Between them, on the north side, is the fifteenth-century **Palazzo Canacci** with grisaille decoration beneath a splendid loggia and the family emblem of chains, a visual pun on their name.

11. **Via del Campidoglio** is north of the PIAZZA DELLA REPUBBLICA, extending westwards from Via dei Pescioni to Via Brunelleschi.

12. At No. 3 Via Capaccio is the **Palazzo dell'Arte della Seta**. The guild has had its headquarters on this site since the end of the fourteenth century. The guild's emblems can be seen on the façade surrounded by cherubs.

13. **Via Calimala** extends from the MERCATO NUOVO to the PIAZZA DELLA REPUBBLICA. The PALAZZO DELL'ARTE DELLA LANA is opposite the back of ORSANMICHELE. **Via del Corso** is also an old Roman way. It runs from **Via de' Calzaiuoli** to VIA DEL PROCONSOLO. SANTA MARGHERITA IN SANTA MARIA DE' RICCI and the PALAZZO SALVIATI are on the north side.

CHAPTER 2 *(pages 5–12)*

1. This early church which stood on the site of the present SAN LORENZO is believed to have been consecrated in 393. Probably the next oldest church in Florence is **Santa Felicita** between the PONTE VECCHIO and the PITTI PALACE. The first church on this site dates back to the late fourth or early fifth century. It was reconstructed in the eleventh century and again in 1739 by Ferdinando Ruggieri. The church is notable chiefly for the Capponi Chapel, which Ruggieri left largely intact. The Barbadori family commissioned the chapel, probably from Brunelleschi. After the exile of the Barbadori, their rights were assigned to the Capponi, for whom Pontormo executed his *Annunciation* fresco, *Entombment* altarpiece, and, with Bronzino, the *Four Evangelists* in the roundels. In the sacristy is a *Sacra Conversazione* by Taddeo Gaddi. From the Piazza Santa Felicita, where a granite column was erected in 1381 to mark the site of Florence's first Christian cemetery, the Costa San Giorgio leads to the church of **San Giorgio sulla Costa**. This little Vallombrosan church has a fine Baroque interior by Foggini, completed in 1705. Giotto's *Madonna and Child with Saints*, now in the UFFIZI, came from here.

2. The **Column of St Zenobius** was erected in Piazza San Giovanni in 1384.

3. Remnants of **Santa Reparata** were uncovered in the 1960s beneath the DUOMO. The excavations, revealing architectural fragments and pieces of mosaic pavements, can be approached by steps inside the Porta del Campanile.

4. A Benedictine foundation, the **Badia Fiorentina**, was one of the richest monasteries in medieval Florence. Little now remains of the original building, which was rebuilt in the late thirteenth century, and again in 1627–31 by Matteo Segaloni. The campanile is, perhaps, the most delicate in the city, and, according to Dante (who, so tradition has it, first saw Beatrice here), life was organized around the ringing of its bell. It is entered from VIA DEL PROCONSOLO through a portal by Benedetto da Rovezzano, who also

designed the portal in Via Dante Alighieri. Apart from his marble tomb of Ugo, Mino da Fiesole also sculpted the tomb of Bernardo Giugni, a Florentine statesman who died in 1466, and the altarpiece of the *Virgin with Saints*. Filippino Lippi painted the panel of *St Bernard Appearing to the Virgin*. In the chapel are the remains of four frescoes of the *Passion of Christ*, possibly by Nardo di Cione, Orcagna's brother.

To the right of the choir, a door leads to the Chiostro degli Aranci, so-called after the orange trees which were grown here. The loggia has been attributed to Bernardo Rossellino. The frescoes of the 1430s represent scenes from the life of St Benedict, who is also depicted in a lunette by the young Bronzino.

5. The **Palazzo Arcivescovile**, rebuilt in 1895, incorporates the church of San Salvatore al Vescovo, the interior of which was frescoed in the 1730s.

6. The church of **Santa Trinita** underwent a remodelling in the second half of the thirteenth century, and Neri di Fioravanti made further additions and alterations in the fourteenth century. Buontalenti designed the façade in 1593-4. The church contains several depictions of its founder, San Giovanni Gualberto, as well as remnants of his robes in the chapel to the left of the high altar. In the third chapel in the right-hand aisle (NB, the altar is at the west end in this church) is a *Madonna Enthroned* by Neri di Bicci and a *Marriage of St Catherine* by a follower of Spinello Aretino. The fourth chapel, the **Bartolini-Salimbeni Chapel**, was decorated by the Sienese Lorenzo Monaco in the early fifteenth century with frescoes and an *Annunciation* altarpiece, and is probably just as he left it. The ONOFRIO STROZZI CHAPEL is in the sacristy. Adjoining it, to the right of the choir, is the SASSETTI CHAPEL.

Behind the high altar are remains of frescoed scenes of Old Testament figures by Alesso Baldovinetti. Cimabue's *Maestà*, now in the UFFIZI, was the altarpiece here. In the first chapel to the left of the altar is Empoli's *Christ Giving St Peter the Keys* and Allori's *St Peter on the Waters*. In the second chapel, the Scali Chapel, is Luca della

Robbia's tomb of Benozzo Federighi. The austere marble effigy of the Bishop of Fiesole, who died in 1450, contrasts with the cheerful glazed terracotta bouquets of flowers around him.

Continuing round the church, the second chapel in the nave aisle contains an *Annunciation* by Neri di Bicci, and in the third chapel is the *Mystic Marriage of St Catherine* by Antonio del Ceraiuolo. The last chapel in the aisle, the Strozzi Chapel, with a vault painted by Bernardino Poccetti, was undergoing restoration in 1992. Steps in the nave lead to the eleventh-century crypt.

In the **Piazza Santa Trinita** stands the Column of Justice, a granite monolith from the Baths of Caracalla in Rome. It was presented to the Grand Duke Cosimo I by Pope Pius IV. The porphyry figure of Justice is by Francesco del Tadda (1581). The bronze cloak is a later addition.

7. The two factions are commemorated in **Via Guelfa**, which extends from Piazza del Crocifisso to Via Cavour, and **Via Ghibellina**, which runs from north of the BARGELLO, past the PALAZZO BORGHESE, the Teatro Verdi and CASA BUONARROTI, to the ARCHIVIO DI STATO. On the south side of Via Guelfa, on the corner of Via Panicale, is the church of **San Barnaba** with a Della Robbia lunette of the Madonna and Child above the fourteenth-century portal. The name Ghibelline is said to have been derived from Weiblingen, a town in Württemberg belonging to the Hohenstaufen Emperor Conrad III, the name of which was used as a battle-cry by the Emperor's followers. Guelph is believed to be the Italian form of Welf, also a battle-cry, and the name of the leader of the Emperor's opponents, Welf VI of Bavaria.

CHAPTER 3 *(pages 13-26)*

1. Other twelfth- and thirteenth-century towers still to be seen in Florence, some of them showing the holes into which the ends of the beams that supported the wooden balconies were inserted, are:

Torre degli Alberti di Catenaia on the corner of the Via de' Benci and Borgo Santa Croce.

The original tower was destroyed by a Ghibelline mob in 1260, the Alberti being notable Guelphs. Their family emblem, crossed chains (*catene*), can be seen on the capitals of the columns of the *loggetta* which was added to the tower in the fifteenth century.

Torre della Castagna, Piazza San Martino, the meeting place of the *priori* before they moved to the PALAZZO DELLA SIGNORIA.

Torre Cerchi, Via dei Cerchi.

Torre Greci (Galigai), Via dei Tavolini.

Torre Baldovinetti on the corner of Borgo Santi Apostoli and Via Por Santa Maria.

Torre Compiobbesi, Via Calimala. This is incorporated into the late-fourteenth-century oratory of Santa Maria della Tromba.

Torre La Pagliazza, Piazza Sant'Elisabetta, a prison in the thirteenth and fourteenth centuries, now converted for use as a hotel, which opened as the Brunelleschi in 1988.

Torre dei Donati (Cocchi), Piazza San Pier Maggiore. The Donati also built the tower which rises above the nearby No. 11 Borgo degli Albizzi.

Torre dei Mannelli, on the south side of the PONTE VECCHIO, built to defend the bridge.

Torre Marsili di Borgo, on the corner of Via Toscanella and Borgo San Jacopo, with an *Annunciation* by the Della Robbia above the door.

2. **Santa Margherita in Santa Maria de' Ricci** was built in the early seventeenth century. The portico is by Gherardo Silvani; the interior was restored by Zanobi del Rosso in 1769.

3. The **Ponte Vecchio** is very close to the site of the first Roman bridge which carried the road from Paris to Rome across the Arno. The only bridge across the river in Florence until 1218, it was rebuilt in 1345 after the disastrous floods of 1333, which also swept away an equestrian statue of Mars at its northern end. There have always been shops on the Ponte Vecchio since the early twelfth century. All sorts of craftsmen and tradesmen displayed their wares here until 1593, when Ferdinando I complained about the squalor and decreed that only goldsmiths and jewellers could conduct business here. Jewellers' shops still line the bridge today. In honour of the goldsmiths, Benvenuto Cellini is commemorated with a

Ponte Vecchio

1900 bust by Raffaelo Romanelli in the middle of the bridge – the only bridge not destroyed in the Second World War. The raised corridor, the **Corridoio Vasariano**, whose line of windows can be seen above the roofs of the shops, was built by Vasari in 1565–6 to link the PALAZZO DELLA SIGNORIA and the UFFIZI with the PITTI PALACE. In the 1970s the river bed beneath the Ponte Vecchio was deepened to reduce water pressure on its foundations; but in 1992 fears were expressed for its safety after bits of masonry fell off the façade at the north end, the result, it was suggested, of the re-routeing of bus services along the north bank of the Arno.

4. Of the three thirteenth-century bridges built after the PONTE VECCHIO, the first, originally called the Ponte Nuovo, became known as the **Ponte alla Carraia** because the road from it led to the Porta Carraia, which took its name from the *carri*, or carts, that passed through the gate. The bridge was rebuilt in 1269 and again in 1333. Repaired in 1559, it was enlarged in 1867.

The second, the **Ponte alle Grazie**, was so-called because a chapel dedicated to the Madonna alle Grazie was built on it.

The third, the **Ponte Santa Trinita**, has been described as the most beautiful bridge in the world. After it was destroyed by floods, the Grand Duke Cosimo I conceived the new bridge as a triumphal route and asked Vasari to supervise its reconstruction. Vasari in turn consulted Michelangelo in Rome. The plans were turned over to Ammannati, who had just rebuilt the Ponte alla Carraia, in 1567. The statues of the Seasons are by Pietro Francavilla (see also Chapter 26, note 3).

5. The **Palazzo Frescobaldi** (Palazzo dei Padri delle Missioni) in the Piazza dei Frescobaldi at the Oltrarno end of the PONTE SANTA TRINITA was almost entirely rebuilt in the seventeenth century and its façade adorned by busts of Medici Grand Dukes. The Palazzo Frescobaldi in Via Santo Spirito has a long façade at Nos. 5–13 and a shorter one in Via dei Coverelli. Behind the Palazzo Frescobaldi in the Oltrarno, in Borgo San Jacopo, is the church of SAN JACOPO SOPR'ARNO.

6. **Fiesole Cathedral**, *il Duomo di Fiesole*, is dedicated to San Romolo, who, according to tra-

Ponte Santa Trinita

Piazza Santo Spirito

dition, was appointed the first pastor of Fiesole by St Peter, and was martyred under Domitian. Giovanni della Robbia carved his statue in the niche above the main portal. The building, begun in 1028, was enlarged in 1256. It was again enlarged in the fourteenth century, and heavily restored in the nineteenth. The crenellated campanile was built in 1213. The two rows of pillars inside the cathedral are surmounted by Roman capitals taken from ancient monuments. To the right of the presbytery is the Salutati Chapel. The tomb of Leonardo Salutati is by Mino da Fiesole, who also executed the altar frontal. The frescoes of the *Evangelists and Saints* are by Cosimo Rosselli.

7. The façade of **Santo Spirito** overlooks the Piazza Santo Spirito. In 1434 Brunelleschi was asked to design a new building to replace the late-thirteenth-century church adjoining the Augustinian monastery. Work began two years before Brunelleschi's death, and was not completed until forty years later amid controversy

over the architect's intentions. The plan is a simple Latin cross, and the interior is defined by the forest of Corinthian columns which form a continuous arcade. There are forty semicircular chapels right round the church. The chapels are marked on the walls, inside and out, by the emblem of the families who endowed them, for example, the Corbinelli stag, the black and white device of the Capponi family, who paid for five chapels, and the emblem of the Frescobaldi, on whose land part of the church was built. The flamboyant Baroque high altar, with its ciborium and *baldacchino*, is by Caccini. The Nerli Chapel, the third from the right in the south crossing, has a *Sacra Conversazione* altarpiece by Filippino Lippi. The altarpiece of St Monica and Augustinian nuns in the east corner of the north crossing is attributed to Verrocchio. Next to it the *Sacra Conversazione* altarpiece is by Cosimo Rosselli. Its painted wooden frontal, possibly by Neri di Bicci, is one of the very few to survive intact in Italy. The adjoining chapel contains a sculpted altarpiece by Sansovino. A door in the north aisle leads to a vestibule by Cronaca, beyond which is the octagonal sacristy by Giuliano da Sangallo. The refectory at No. 29 Piazza Santo Spirito is all that remains of the fourteenth-century monastery which was destroyed by fire in 1471. It contains an emotional Crucifixion attributed to Orcagna and his brother, Nardo di Cione, as well as the Fondazione Salvatore Romano which includes works by Tino da Camaino, and sculptures attributed to Donatello, Jacopo della Quercia and Ammannati. A plaque on the wall outside the church records that the sculptor, Raffaelo Romanelli, had his studio in the piazza from 1894 to 1928. The statue of Cosimo Ridolfi here is his work. For the attractive, early-sixteenth-century PALAZZO GUADAGNI which rises up to its left at No. 10, see Chapter 22, note 6.

8. Rebuilt and greatly enlarged in 1294 (possibly by Arnolfo di Cambio), **Santa Croce** became one of the most important Franciscan monasteries in Tuscany, rivalling the great Dominican church of SANTA MARIA NOVELLA. Construction was slow, chiefly because of arguments

between the austere Franciscans and their more relaxed brothers, but was helped by contributions to the order from Florentine families, many of whom built chapels here. Vasari remodelled the interior in 1560 by building the side-altars. The neo-Gothic façade is a nineteenth-century addition, paid for in large part by an Englishman, Francis Sloane. The interior, with its open timber roof, is one of the most richly decorated in Florence. The narrative nature of the frescoes – many of them by Giotto – is typical of a preaching order. On the first pillar on the south aisle is a relief of the *Madonna* by Antonio Rossellino. The altarpiece at the second altar depicts the *Way to Calvary* by Vasari. On the third pillar is a pulpit by Benedetto da Maiano carved with scenes from the life of St Francis. Opposite the fifth pillar is Donatello's *Cavalcanti Annunciation* tabernacle. All along the south transept are family chapels. The first, on the west side, is the Castellani Chapel. The second is the Baroncelli Chapel, in which the fresco decoration is by Agnolo Gaddi's son, Taddeo. The altarpiece of the *Coronation of the Virgin* is by Giotto and his workshop. Beyond the sacristy

Santa Croce

is the Rinuccini Chapel, entirely covered with frescoes by Giovanni da Milano. At the east end of the church are the family chapels of the Velluti (with very early frescoes by a follower of Cimabue), the Calderini, the Giugni, the Peruzzi and the Bardi. The last two are notable for their frescoes by Giotto and his pupils. The sanctuary was decorated by Agnolo Gaddi, who also designed the stained-glass Gothic windows. Continuing along the east end are more chapels. The first two are the Tosinghi and the Capponi. The third is undedicated. The fourth is the Bardi di Libertà, with an altarpiece by Giovanni della Robbia and frescoes of scenes from the lives of St Stephen and St Lawrence by Bernardo Daddi. The last, the Bardi di Vernio, has frescoes by Maso di Banco of scenes from the life of St Sylvester. In the north transept is the Niccolini Chapel, remodelled in 1580 in an early Baroque style. The fresco decoration is by Allori, Bronzino's pupil, and the statues by Francavilla. The Bardi Chapel contains Donatello's wooden crucifix. In the Salviati Chapel is the tomb of Sofia Zamoyska Czartoryska by Lorenzo Bartolini, who also executed the monument to Leon Battista Alberti at the seventh pillar in the north side of the nave. Outside the chapel is the tomb of the composer, Cherubini. Opposite the sixth pillar in the north aisle is the tomb of Carlo Marsuppini by Desiderio da Settignano, opposite that of Bruni, another humanist scholar. At the altar between the fourth and fifth pillars is a *Deposition* by Bronzino. Ghiberti and his son were buried here at the foot of the fourth pillar.

The statue of God the Father in the cloister is by Baccio Bandinelli, that of a warrior by Henry Moore. At the east end of the cloister is the PAZZI CHAPEL. To the south is the **Museo dell'Opera di Santa Croce**, the contents of which were nearly ruined in the floods of 1966, including its most precious possession, Cimabue's crucifix, now in the former refectory. In the Museo are Taddeo Gaddi's *Last Supper*, a detached fourteenth-century fresco, possibly by Giovanni del Biondo, Domenico Veneziano's *Saints John the Baptist and Francis*, and Donatello's gilded bronze *St Louis of Toulouse* commissioned by the Parte Guelfa for a niche at ORSAN-MICHELE. In other rooms of the museum are works from the Della Robbia workshop, and works by or attributed to Uccello and Donatello. Beyond the Museo is the second cloister, attributed variously to Brunelleschi, Giuliano da Maiano and Bernardo Rossellino.

9. **Santa Maria Novella** was completed in the mid fourteenth century by the monk, Jacopo Talenti. The façade is by Alberti, who had to leave its lower half intact, because the Baldesi family had paid for some of its tomb niches, the *avelli*, which gave their name to the street on the south flank of the church. Alberti's patrons, the Rucellai family, are commemorated in the Latin name of Giovanni Rucellai, which is emblazoned across a frieze below the tympanum, and, less prominently, by their emblem, a ship's sail, in the main frieze entablature. The Medici family, into which Bernardo Rucellai married, is also commemorated by three ostrich feathers in a ring on the frieze over the main portal. The two astronomical instruments which hang on the façade were made by Fra Ignazio Danti, Cosimo I's versatile court astronomer.

The interior is notable for its attractive green-and-white-patterned arches. Many of the chapels were built by survivors of the 1348 plague. To the right of the main portal is a *Nativity* attributed to the youthful Botticelli; to the left, an *Annunciation* by Santi di Tito. The founder of the convent, Giovanni da Salerno, is commemorated in a monument by Vincenzo Danti in the eastern corner of the second bay. In the sixth bay, a door leads to the Cappella della Pura. It has a fresco of the *Virgin and Child with St Catherine of Siena* (removed from one of the tomb niches). The RUCELLAI CHAPEL is at the end of the south transept; the BARDI CHAPEL and the FILIPPO STROZZI CHAPEL are next to each other at the east end.

Behind the main altar, with its bronze crucifix by Giambologna, is the sanctuary, or CAPPELLA MAGGIORE. Next to this is the GONDI CHAPEL. The ceiling of the next chapel, the **Gaddi Chapel**, is decorated by Allori. This chapel contains Bronzino's last work, an altarpiece of *Christ Raising the Daughter of Jairus*. The last chapel at the east end is the CAPPELLA STROZZI. In the sacristy is a terracotta lavabo by Giovanni della Robbia and an immense cupboard designed by Buontalenti. In the third bay of the north aisle is Masaccio's *Trinity with Two Donors*, a perfectly executed example of the newly discovered laws of perspective. It has been suggested that Brunelleschi designed the triumphal arch which frames the crucifix. The donor, dressed in the red robes of a Gonfaloniere, kneels modestly with his wife outside the arch. On the second column from the west end is a pulpit designed by Brunelleschi and carved by his adopted son, Buggiano.

The entrance to the Chiostro Verde, or Green Cloister, is to the left of the church. Badly deteriorated frescoes decorate the walls. The scenes from Genesis, on the south wall, notably a nightmarish *Flood*, are by Uccello. Through a window can be seen the Chiostro Grande which now belongs to the *carabinieri*; and, through a passage in the south-eastern corner, is the Chiostrino dei Morti, the Little Cloister of the Dead. Here are damaged frescoes from the fourteenth

Santa Maria Novella

century, and a *Noli Me Tangere* terracotta tabernacle from the Della Robbia workshop. Above this cloister were the apartments built for Pope Martin V's visit to Florence.

To the north of the Chiostro Verde is the Spanish Chapel, so-called because the entourage of Eleonora of Toledo worshipped here. It was originally the chapter house – St Catherine faced her tribunal here – and was designed by Jacopo Talenti with a massive groin vault. The fresco cycle, which covers the entire chapel, is by Andrea di Bonaiuto (also known as da Firenze). On the right wall is the *History of the Dominican Order* (or the *Way to Salvation*). Here, Andrea has imagined that SANTA MARIA DEL FIORE is complete with cupola. The Pope points his flock (including Dante, Petrarch, Boccaccio, Giotto and Cimabue) to the Heavenly Gates, guarded by St Peter. He is helped by Dominicans and a pack of 'Dogs of the Lord', *Domini Canes* (a pun on the name of the order), who sniff out heresy. Above the Gate, Christ is enthroned, adored by angels. On the opposite wall, St Thomas Aquinas presides over personifications of Christian learning. Over the entrance wall are scenes from the life of St Peter Martyr. The apse chapel was decorated by Allessandro Allori and Bernardino Poccetti. The polyptych is by Bernardo Daddi.

At the south-western corner of the Spanish Chapel is the Cappella degli Ubriachi, now a museum of relics of the church. Here are also displayed the *sinopie* of Uccello's Chiostro Verde paintings. Beyond the museum is the refectory with a *Last Supper* by Allori and a *Sacra Conversazione* by a follower of Agnolo Gaddi.

10. The original of Donatello's **Marzocco** is now in the BARGELLO. A copy is in the PIAZZA DELLA SIGNORIA. It was commissioned in 1418 for the apartments in SANTA MARIA NOVELLA which were specially built for the visit of Pope Martin V, although Donatello probably did not finish it in time. This life-size sandstone lion is the best-known example of all Florence's Marzoccos, the heraldic symbol of justice and the Republic's protector. The name probably derives from a diminutive of Mars, and it has been suggested that the lion in turn derives from a time-worn

Bargello, courtyard

Roman equestrian statue of Mars that used to guard the PONTE VECCHIO until it was washed away in the 1333 flood.

11. The **Palazzo del Bargello**. This and the PALAZZO DELLA SIGNORIA are the oldest surviving seats of Florentine government. The building of the Bargello, which was also a court of justice and a prison, began in 1255, perhaps to a design by Arnolfo di Cambio's master. Having been known as the Palazzo del Popolo, then the Palazzo del Podestà, from 1574 it was the residence of the chief of police, and therefore called the Bargello, meaning police station. Like the Palazzo della Signoria it was designed to withstand attack. The outside ground-floor windows are consequently small and high up. Inside, light comes from the Gothic courtyard, where there is a well. In 1332 Neri di Fioravanti started building the staircase whose walls are decorated with coats of arms of former residents. The Bargello is now the Museo Nazionale del Bargello, its doors first opening to the public in 1865. It contains an outstanding collection of Renaissance sculpture formerly in the UFFIZI and partly the bequest of Anna Maria de' Medici.

There are works by, among many others, Donatello, Verrocchio, Michelangelo, Cellini, the Della Robbia family, Pollaiuolo and Giambologna.

12. The **Palazzo di Parte Guelfa** stands in the tiny Piazza di Parte Guelfa between its church, Santa Maria Sovraporta, now deconsecrated, and the PALAZZO CANACCI. The Guelphs held meetings in the church until the late thirteenth century. Their headquarters are divided by two clear styles: the medieval part of the palace and the Renaissance extension, which was commissioned from Brunelleschi in 1430. There are also the remains of a small part of an extension which was almost completely demolished to make way for Brunelleschi's work. At ground-floor level, on the medieval side, there were shops, probably rented out to members of the Silk Guild, whose offices were also in the square. A covered staircase leads to the *piano nobile*. Over the door are the Guelph coats of arms and beyond the door the Guelph council hall with its mullioned windows.

Brunelleschi's extension is unfinished, since Guelph power rapidly diminished, and funds ran out. Over the huge round-arched windows the *oculi* are bricked in. It is not clear whether Brunelleschi intended to place terracotta tondi here, or windows.

By 1558, the party had lost all authority, and the building was turned over to the Monte, the governing body of pawnbroking and bonds, whose emblem, six little hills, a pun on the name, is over a door next to Brunelleschi's extension, above an inscription bearing Cosimo I's name. Inside Vasari's balcony over this door are the Medici *palle*.

13. For example in the 1490s, Amerigo Vespucci, the Florentine merchant and navigator who gave his name to America, worked in the Medici branch in Seville, which was mainly occupied in the outfitting of ships. Niccolò Acciaiuoli worked in Naples; Niccolò di Jacopo degli Alberti in Avignon; the historian, Giovanni Villani, in Bruges; and the Medici's Geneva branch was opened by Francesco Sassetti, who commissioned the frescoes of the life of St Francis by Ghirlandaio in the SASSETTI CHAPEL in SANTA TRINITA and appears, with Lorenzo il Magnifico, in the lunette above the altar. It was Tommaso Portinari, a member of the family of Dante's Beatrice, who, while working in Bruges, commissioned from Hugo van der Goes the immense, magnificent and influential triptych of the *Adoration of the Shepherds*, now in the UFFIZI, in which various members of the Portinari family are depicted on the side pieces.

CHAPTER 4 *(pages 27–34)*

1. The **Palazzo dell'Arte della Lana** was built at the end of the thirteenth century, bought by the guild at the beginning of the fourteenth and heavily restored in 1905. The Tabernacolo della Tromba inside is by Jacopo del Casentino (*c.* 1335). The heraldic devices on the façade include the Arte's *Agnus Dei*. At the base of the tower is the fourteenth-century oratory of Santa Maria della Tromba, which was brought here from the MERCATO VECCHIO.

2. The medieval buildings in **Via Por Santa Maria** were destroyed in 1944 before the Allies entered the city. The church of **Santo Stefano al Ponte**, in a little piazza off the southern end of the street, was originally built in the tenth century. The decoration of the façade was finished in 1233. The interior, which is now used for concerts, was remodelled by Ferdinando Tacca in the seventeenth century; it incorporates altar steps by Buontalenti, which came from SANTA TRINITA, and a high altar by Giambologna from SANTA MARIA NUOVA. In the nearby Casa dell' Orafo ('House of the Goldsmith') are several jewellers' workshops.

3. The **Palazzo dell'Arte dei Beccai** in Via Orsanmichele was the headquarters of the guild until 1534. Their emblem, a goat, is on the façade together with other medallions of three interlocking circles and the Florentine lily. The building is now occupied by the ACCADEMIA DEL DISEGNO.

CHAPTER 5 *(pages 35–60)*

1. Dante is said to have been born either in the Casa di Dante in Via Dante Alighieri or in a house in Via Alighieri. He is also said to have been married to Gemma Donati in the church of **Santa Margherita de' Cerchi**, a twelfth-century foundation which contains a fine altarpiece by Neri di Bicci. The parish church of Dante's family and that of the Donati was on the site of the chapel of **San Martino del Vescovo.** This was originally built in the tenth century and rebuilt in the fifteenth. It was the headquarters of the charitable brotherhood, the Compagnia dei Buonuomini di San Martino, founded in 1442 by St Antonio, Archbishop of Florence, whose bust, attributed to Verrocchio, is in the chapel. The frescoes of the life of St Martin in San Martino del Vescovo are from the workshop of Ghirlandaio. There is also a painting of the Madonna by Niccolò Soggi, a follower of Perugino.

The monument to Dante outside the church of SANTA CROCE is by Enrico Pazzi (1865). The

Orsanmichele

cenotaph inside the church is by Stefano Ricci (1829). A column from the tomb of Dante's teacher, Brunetto Latini, survives in the church of **Santa Maria Maggiore,** an eighth- or ninth-century foundation on the corner of Via de' Cerretani and Piazza Santa Maria Maggiore, rebuilt in the late thirteenth century.

The thirteenth-century Palazzo Cerchi is at No. 52 Vicolo dei Cerchi. The TORRE CERCHI is on the corner of Via dei Cerchi and Canto alla Quarconia. The Torre dei Donati stands almost opposite SANTA MARGHERITA IN SANTA MARIA DE' RICCI. The Palazzo Donati, formerly the Palazzo Neroni, is at No. 7 Via de' Ginori. The coats of arms of both families are on the porch of Santa Margherita de' Cerchi.

2. The Vallombrosan abbey buildings at **San Salvi** house a collection of sixteenth-century altarpieces and reliefs by Benedetto da Rovezzano from the tomb of San Giovanni Gualberto. Andrea del Sarto's masterly *Last Supper* is in the refectory.

3. The existing church of **Orsanmichele** was built as a market in 1337 by Francesco Talenti, Benci di Cione and Neri di Fioravante. The windows enclosing the arcades, soon after bricked up, were finished in 1380 to the designs of Simone Talenti. The upper storey, the granary, was completed in 1404. For the statues see Chapter 7, note 26; for the tabernacle, see below, note 5.

4. The **Confraternity of the Laudesi** was founded in *c.* 1245 by St Peter Martyr, who is depicted in a celebrated painting by Fra Angelico in SAN MARCO with a wounded head and a finger to his lips. The Cappella dei Bardi Ilarioni in SANTA MARIA NOVELLA was formerly theirs. For it, in 1285, they commissioned from Duccio the *Madonna Enthroned* which was moved to the CAPPELLA RUCELLAI before being taken to the UFFIZI in 1948.

5. **Orcagna's tabernacle** at ORSANMICHELE was finished in 1359. Made of marble, lapis lazuli, gold and stained glass, it cost 86,000 florins. The

money had been left to the church by victims of the plague and by the plague's grateful survivors, who had prayed to the miraculous Virgin for salvation. The iconography is obscure and has been much debated, but it seems generally to concern the path to salvation through the intercession of the Virgin.

6. **Sant'Ambrogio**, in the Piazza Sant'Ambrogio, is one of the earliest Christian foundations in the city, probably dating from the fifth century. Rebuilt in the late thirteenth century, it has undergone a few modifications. The present façade is a nineteenth-century addition. On the south side is a *Sacra Conversazione* by a follower of Orcagna. In the chapel to the left of the high altar is a tabernacle by Mino da Fiesole which contains a miraculous relic. A fresco by Cosimo Rosselli depicts the people of Florence marvelling at this relic in the piazza. On the north side, at the fourth altar, is Verrocchio's tomb. Cronaca and members of the Del Tasso family are also buried in this church, as well as Mino da Fiesole. Alesso Baldovinetti and his pupil, Graffione, painted the *Nativity*; and Agnolo Gaddi probably painted the *Martyrdom of St Sebastian* on the west wall.

7. The Acciaiuoli palace on the Arno was destroyed in 1944. The family had other palaces in BORGO SANTI APOSTOLI (Nos. 3–10). These were rebuilt in the fifteenth century. The family came from Brescia, settling in Florence in the middle of the twelfth century. Before going into banking and the wool trade, they dealt in metal, hence their name (*acciaio*, steel). Niccolò di Acciaiuolo Acciaiuoli, who died in 1365, was an official at the Angevin court in Naples. He founded the Certosa (charterhouse) of Galluzzo, south of Florence, the emblem of which can be seen on the tower of No. 8 Borgo Santi Apostoli.

8. The basilican design of the **Duomo (Santa Maria del Fiore)**, with its three polygonal tribunes, is traditionally attributed to Arnolfo di Cambio. The building was enlarged in the mid fourteenth century by Francesco Talenti and others; and Brunelleschi's dome was completed in 1436. After Brunelleschi's death, Michelozzo crowned the dome with its lantern and Verrocchio added the bronze ball and cross. Between 1857 and 1887 the façade was almost completely replaced by Emilio de Fabris and Augustino Conti, except for the lower register of the south flank.

On the south side, next to the tribune, is the Porta dei Canonici, which was decorated in the late fourteenth century by Lorenzo d'Ambrogio and Piero di Giovanni Tedesco. Opposite it on the north side is the Porta della Mandorla, called after the almond-shaped aureole which frames Nanni di Banco's *Assumption of the Virgin*. The young Donatello, then Ghiberti's assistant on the BAPTISTERY doors, carved the prophet and sybil on either side of the gable. The *Annunciation* in the lunette is by Domenico and Davide Ghirlandaio. Inside, Baccio d'Agnolo and Francesco da Sangallo, among others, designed the marble pavement, Ghiberti the stained-glass roundels in the west wall, on which there is a mosaic of the *Coronation of the Virgin* attributed to Gaddo Gaddi. The fresco of angels with four musicians is by Santi di Santo. Uccello painted the great twenty-four-hour clock. The statue of the melancholic Antonio d'Orso is by Tino da Camaino. In a tondo in the south aisle is a bust of Brunelleschi by his adopted son, Buggiano, and close by it a bust of Giotto by Benedetto da Maiano. Brunelleschi's tomb was discovered here in 1972 when excavations of the older SANTA REPARATA were taking place.

The stained-glass windows between the Porta del Campanile and the Porta dei Canonici are by Agnolo Gaddi, the bust of Marsilio Ficino just to the west of the Porta dei Canonici by Andrea Ferrucci. The dome is covered with a fresco by Vasari and Federico Zuccari of the *Last Judgement* (concealed for restoration at the time of writing). The stained-glass windows in the drum are, starting from the east window, by Donatello (*Coronation of the Virgin*); by Ghiberti (*Ascension, Agony in the Garden* and *Presentation in the Temple*); by Uccello (*Nativity*); by Castagno (*Pietà*); and by Uccello (*Resurrection*). In the last of these the skewed tomb is the first known example of perspective in stained glass.

Duomo (Santa Maria del Fiore)

At the piers below are sixteenth-century statues of eight apostles, including works by Jacopo Sansovino, Benedetto da Rovezzano, Bandinelli, Bandini, Andrea Ferrucci and Vicenzo de' Rossi. The marble sanctuary is by Bandinelli and has a wooden crucifix by Benedetto da Maiano. The stained-glass windows in the chapels of the three tribunes were designed by Ghiberti.

A lunette of the *Ascension* in the South Sacristy, between the south and east tribunes, is by Luca della Robbia, who also executed the angels on the altar of the third chapel of the east tribune. In this chapel is a bronze urn by Ghiberti, containing relics of St Zenobius. Here once stood Donatello's choir loft, or singing gallery, now in the MUSEO DELL'OPERA. Luca, with Michel-ozzo's help, also designed the bronze doors of the North Sacristy, as well as the *Resurrection* lunette over them. This was the original location of Luca's choir loft, also now in the Museo dell'Opera. It was to this sacristy that Lorenzo il Magnifico escaped on the day of his brother's murder. The intarsia cupboards here were made under the supervision of Giuliano da Maiano in the 1460s.

In the north aisle are two stained-glass windows by Agnolo Gaddi, and beyond these the two famous EQUESTRIAN MURALS OF SIR JOHN HAWKWOOD and NICCOLÒ DA TOLENTINO. At the last altar before the west door is a statue of Joshua, by either Donatello or Nanni di Bartolo, which is said to be a likeness of the humanist scholar, Poggio Bracciolini.

Campanile

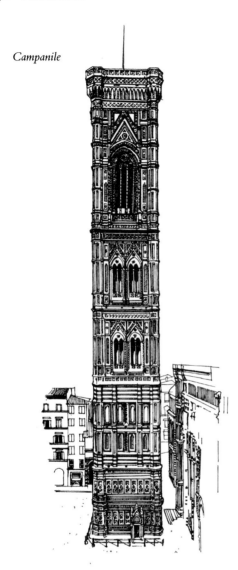

Planets, the mythological inventors, the Platonic Virtues, the arts, industries and sciences; and Alberto Arnoldi or Maso di Banco carved the Seven Sacraments. In the next century Luca della Robbia carved the Liberal Arts. In the niches of the second storey are statues of prophets and sybils, notably three by Donatello.

Originals of the reliefs and statuary are in the **Museo dell'Opera del Duomo**, No. 9 Piazza del Duomo, where the body responsible for the fabric of the Duomo has been housed since the early fifteenth century. The museum was opened to the public in 1891. It contains works of art brought here from the Campanile and the BAP-TISTERY, as well as from the cathedral. Exhibits include work by Arnolfo di Cambio, Baccio Bandinelli, Buontalenti, Giambologna, Andrea Pisano, Antonio del Pollaiuolo, Verrocchio and Nanni di Banco. The *Pietà* on the landing is by Michelangelo, the wooden statue of *St Mary Magdalen* by Donatello, who was also responsible for the organ loft with a frieze of putti on the right wall of the first room on the first floor. The organ loft on the left wall opposite is by Luca della Robbia. The statues standing against the walls of this room are by, amongst others, Donatello, Nanni di Bartolo and Andrea Pisano. The reliefs in the smaller room next door are mostly by Andrea Pisano and Luca della Robbia. They were originally made for the lower storeys of the Campanile. In Room 11 are displayed four of Ghiberti's restored gilded bronze panels from the EAST DOORS of the Baptistery (one of these was removed for exhibition in Seville in 1992) and a silver-gilt altar, also from the Baptistery, begun in the 1360s by Florentine gold-smiths and including work by Michelozzo and Antonio del Pollaiuolo. The bust of the Grand Duke Cosimo I over the entrance to the museum is by Giovanni Bandini, who may also have been responsible for the bust of Brunelleschi in the entrance hall. Michelangelo worked on his *David* in the courtyard (see Chapter 15, note 1).

9. Work on the **Campanile** began in 1334. Upon Giotto's death in 1337, Andrea Pisano assumed the role of *capomaestro*, and, when he died in 1352, Francesco Talenti was appointed to the office, which he held until the free-standing bell-tower was completed in 1359. At 280 feet, it was a lofty exception to the law of 1324 which limited the height of towers, long a symbol of secular power in Florence. Apart from the Seven Sacraments and the scenes from Genesis, the reliefs on the four faces of the tower use non-Christian images. Pisano himself and his work-shop carved the Genesis reliefs, the Seven

10. The **Piazza della Signoria** had more or less assumed its present dimensions by the end of the fourteenth century, when it was paved and heavy traffic was prohibited. This pedestrian area has

always been the centre of Florentine political and ceremonial life. Here the *popolo* met, summoned by the bell in the PALAZZO DELLA SIGNORIA which juts into the eastern side of the piazza. The LOGGIA DEI LANZI stands on the south side; and, in the corner between them, is the UFFIZI. At No. 7 is the PALAZZO UGUCCIONI, and at No. 10 the Tribunale di Mercanzia, which was founded in 1308 and first occupied these premises in 1359. It commissioned the famous Seven Virtues (now in the Uffizi) from Piero del Pollaiuolo for cupboards which contained the records of its affairs. One of the Virtues was, in the event, painted by Botticelli. Like so many regulatory bodies in Florence, the Mercanzia was responsible for the upkeep of various buildings, including, jointly, the ORSANMICHELE.

A fourteenth-century MARZOCCO was the first piece of public sculpture in the piazza. Now a copy of Donatello's *Marzocco* stands here outside the Palazzo, as does a copy of his JUDITH SLAYING HOLOFERNES, confiscated from the PALAZZO MEDICI in 1494, and a copy of MICHELANGELO'S DAVID, commissioned by the Commune in 1501. Judith and David both served as symbols of Liberty triumphing

over oppression. Giambologna made the bronze equestrian statue of Cosimo I in 1595. Cosimo himself ordered the vast FOUNTAIN OF NEPTUNE. Baccio Bandinelli, whose HERCULES AND CACUS stands in front of the *palazzo*, entered the competition for the fountain and spitefully damaged the block of marble, still in its quarry, to make the carving difficult.

11. The original **Palazzo della Signoria**, probably designed by Arnolfo di Cambio, was completed in 1302, its tower, the tallest in the city, in 1310. It has had many names. First known as the Palazzo dei Priori, it was later called the Palazzo

Palazzo della Signoria

del Popolo, then, in the fifteenth century, the Palazzo della Signoria. When it became the Grand Duke Cosimo I's residence, it became the Palazzo Ducale, and when the Medici took over the Palazzo Pitti in 1549, the Palazzo Vecchio. In 1848 and again in 1859, it was the seat of the provisional Italian government, and between 1865 and 1871, it housed the Italian Foreign Ministry and Chamber of Deputies. It is now the town hall as well as a museum. The west façade is adorned with twenty coats of arms under the machicolation.

The entrance to the palace is on this side. The armless statues on either side of it are by Bandinelli and Vincenzo de' Rossi. Above the portal, two lions guard Christ's monogram. The courtyard was remodelled by Michelozzo in the mid fifteenth century. To the left is the Sala d'Arme; the main portal would originally have opened into this groin-vaulted early-fourteenth-century hall.

Vasari's ceremonial double staircase leads to the first floor and the vast SALA DEL MAGGIOR CONSIGLIO, also known as the Salone del Cinquecento. In the south-east corner of the hall is the STUDIOLO OF FRANCESCO I. Opposite this is a door leading to the Quartiere di Leone X, rebuilt by Vasari. Here are seven rooms all decorated with scenes from the life of the Medici family. In the Sala di Clement VII there is a panoramic view of Florence by Vasari. In the north-western corner of the palace is the Sala dei Dugento, named after the two hundred members of the government who met here. It was remodelled in 1477 by Benedetto and Giuliano da Maiano, who also designed the fine wooden ceiling decorated with rosettes surrounded by fleurs-de-lis.

From the Quartiere di Leone X, a staircase leads to the second floor. The rooms of the Quartiere degli Elementi in the south-eastern corner of the palace on this floor are decorated with representations of the elements. In the Terrazzo di Giunone is displayed Verrocchio's *Putto with Dolphin*.

Across the other side of the palace, on the south flank, are the QUARTIERE DI ELEONORA DI TOLEDO.

The Sala d'Udienza also has a fine ceiling by Giuliano da Maiano. Salviati painted the frescoes with scenes from the life of the Roman Marcus Camillus. Above the door is Benedetto and Giuliano da Maiano's statue of *Justice*. On the other side of the wooden door are the intarsia figures of *Dante* and *Petrarch*, crowned by the marble *St John the Baptist*, all by Benedetto da Maiano. The door leads to the Sala degli Gigli, called after the predominant lily motif on the ceiling by Benedetto and Giuliano da Maiano. Domenico Ghirlandaio frescoed *St Zenobius Enthroned with Saints Stephen and Lawrence*. On either side of the triumphal arch are figures of Roman heroes. Here also is the original of Donatello's JUDITH SLAYING HOLOFERNES.

In the Cancelleria, which was Machiavelli's office, is a portrait of Machiavelli by Santi di Tito, and a bust of him by an unknown sculptor.

In the Sala delle Carte Geografiche, maps by Cosimo I's astronomer, Fra Ignazio Danti, are displayed. He painted the entire known world, and also constructed the globe.

Outside the Sala degli Gigli are steps to the Quartiere del Mezzanino. This contains the collection, left to Florence by the art historian Charles Loeser, of works by Pontormo, Giovanni Rustici, Pietro Lorenzetti, Tino da Camaino, Piero di Cosimo, amongst others, and the portrait of Bartolommeo Ammannati's wife, Laura Battiferri, by Bronzino.

12. The **Loggia dei Lanzi** on the south side of the PIAZZA DELLA SIGNORIA was built between 1376 and 1382, and was then known as the Loggia della Signoria. Its architects were Benci di Cione and Simone Talenti. The Virtues in the spandrels were designed (1384–9) by Agnolo Gaddi and the best, which were executed by Giovanni d'Ambrogio, are some of the finest of the late fourteenth century. It has been suggested that the head of *Faith* was taken from Donatello's *Dovizia*, formerly in the MERCATO VECCHIO. Towards the end of the eighteenth century, the loggia became a sculpture gallery. Here are exhibited, amongst others, Cellini's outstanding *Perseus Trampling Medusa* (he was forced to melt down his household pans and plates for the

Loggia dei Lanzi

casting), and Giambologna's masterpiece, the *Rape of the Sabine Woman* (which the sculptor was as happy to identify as 'Phineas and Andromeda', or 'Pluto and Proserpine', or 'Paris and Helen'), as well as Ferdinando I's Roman statues. The loggia was being restored in 1993.

13. The façade of the church of **Ognissanti** overlooks the Piazza Ognissanti. The Umiliati, a Benedictine order, founded the church in 1256, having moved into the adjacent convent. Expert in manufacturing woollen cloth, they introduced important techniques from their native Lombardy, and built workshops by the Arno. This area of the city became the centre of the cloth trade. Ognissanti was turned over to the Franciscan order in the sixteenth century after the Medici expelled the Umiliati; and in the following century the church was rebuilt with a façade by Matteo Nigetti. The campanile sur-

vived the reconstruction, as did the columns in the cloisters. The church was, and is, rich in decoration. (Giotto's magnificent *Ognissanti Madonna* panel, now in the UFFIZI, came from here.) Ghirlandaio's altarpiece, the *Madonna della Misericordia*, was painted for the Vespucci family, the artist's patrons. They lived near by in Borgo Ognissanti, and their tombstone, dated 1471, is to the left of the second altar on the right. They also commissioned the *St Augustine* from Botticelli, who is buried here in a chapel in the south transept. Opposite *St Augustine*, on the north side, is Ghirlandaio's *St Jerome*.

In the refectory of the convent is another Ghirlandaio fresco, *The Last Supper*; little, apart from a patient cat in the foreground, distinguishes it from his *Last Supper* in SAN MARCO. The frescoes in the sacristy are by Taddeo Gaddi. The *Resurrection* here has been attributed to Agnolo Gaddi.

14. The first church of **Santissima Annunziata**, overlooking what is now the PIAZZA SANTISSIMA ANNUNZIATA, was a mid-thirteenth-century Gothic building, dedicated by the Servites to the Virgin of the Annunciation. It became an important shrine after 1314, when a fresco of the Annunciation, started by a monk, was said to have been completed by an angel. Pilgrims would hang wax effigies, or *voti*, of themselves from rafters.

Piero de' Medici commissioned Michelozzo, whose brother was prior, to rebuild the church. Work began in 1444. Michelozzo planned a circular tribune, serving as a choir, at the east end of the nave, influenced no doubt by Brunelleschi's then unfinished Santa Maria degli Angeli, and by the philosophy of the humanists, who considered the circle to be the perfect geometric form, as it represented the universe and eternity.

The loggia, designed by Caccini in 1600, is an imitation of the loggias on the east and west sides of the piazza. The portal leads into the Chiostrino dei Voti, notable for its frescoes by many of the most renowned painters of the early sixteenth century, including Pontormo, Andrea del Sarto, Alesso Baldovinetti and Cosimo Rosselli.

In the second chapel on the south side is a wooden crucifix by Antonio da Sangallo; in the fifth is Bernardo Rossellino's monument to Orlando de' Medici. In the east transept chapel is a *Pietà*. The sculptor, Baccio Bandinelli, who is buried here, carved his own portrait in the face of Nicodemus, who supports Christ; and Bandinelli and his wife are portrayed in the relief behind the group.

In the tribune, Volterrano painted the dome with a *Coronation of the Virgin*. The high altar frontal is by Giovanni Battista Foggini, and the ciborium by Alfonso Parigi. Andrea del Sarto is buried at the left of the entrance to the triumphal arch, just outside which is Francesco da Sangallo's tomb of Bishop Angelo Marzi Medici. There are nine chapels radiating from the tribune. The ninth, at the east end, contains Giambologna's tomb and was designed by him. His pupils, Francavilla and Tacca, carved the statues. Tacca is also buried here. In other chapels

in the tribune there are works by Allori, Bronzino and Perugino.

The sacristy is also by Michelozzo. Beyond the large chapel in the north transept, which contains a terracotta *St John the Baptist* by him, is the Chiostro dei Morti. Over the portal is Andrea del Sarto's *Flight into Egypt*, known as the *Madonna del Sacco* after the sack which Joseph leans on.

At the east end of the cloister is the Chapel of St Luke, the patron saint of artists. This appropriately belongs to the ACCADEMIA DEL DISEGNO. Many artists are buried here, including Francabigio, Cellini and Pontormo. The altarpiece of *St Luke Painting the Virgin* is by Vasari and is a self-portrait.

In the north side, from east to west, the first chapel has an *Assumption* by Perugino; the third, a *Trinity with St Jerome*; the fourth a *Christ with St Julian*, both by Andrea del Castagno.

At the west end is the Shrine of the Virgin, housed in a vast tabernacle by Michelozzo, which Piero de' Medici commissioned. The OPIFICIO DELLE PIETRE DURE executed the panels for the adjoining Medici chapel.

15. The façade of **Santa Maria del Carmine** overlooks the Piazza del Carmine in the Oltrarno. The present Baroque church, built at the end of the eighteenth century, replaced the original church of 1268, which, except for the sacristy and chapels, was destroyed by fire.

One of Florence's most precious treasures is the recently restored fresco cycle of scenes from the life of St Peter in the Brancacci Chapel in the south transept. They were commissioned by the Brancacci family in the early 1420s from Masolino, but it is the work of the young Masaccio, who collaborated with him on the frescoes, which so influenced the history of Western art. It has been suggested that *The Tribute Money*, an unusual subject, was a comment on the recently introduced tax, the *catasto*. Sixty or so years later, Filippino Lippi completed the cycle, skilfully adapting his style to suit the earlier work.

In the north transept is the Chapel of Sant' Andrea Corsini, Bishop of Fiesole, who died in 1373. This was designed by Pier Francesco Silvani, with a frescoed ceiling by Giordano. In the sacristy, built in 1394, are early-fifteenth-century frescoes of scenes from the life of St Cecilia.

16. The bronze **South Doors** of the BAPTISTERY facing the LOGGIA DI BIGALLO were cast from wax models made by Andrea Pisano and erected in 1336; they were moved to their present position in 1424, having originally been on the east side. The twenty-eight gilt-bronze reliefs, set in quadrilobe frames, include scenes from the life of St John the Baptist. The portal surrounds are by Vittorio Ghiberti, the bronze figures over the doorway (1570–71) by Vincenzo Danti.

17. The gates which have survived at least in part are: **Porta al Prato**, at the junction of Viale Fratelli Rosselli and Il Prato, completed in 1284. The **Palazzo Corsini sul Prato** near by to the south was designed by Buontalenti and begun in the 1590s. It was finished in the 1620s by Gherardo Silvani for Filippo di Lorenzo Corsini, who bought it in 1621. The Young Pretender stayed here in 1774–7.

Porta San Gallo, the old city's northern gate, now stands isolated in the busy Piazza della Libertà. The Via del Ponte Rosso leads north out of the piazza to the Ponte Rosso, spanning the Mugnone, and the Via Bolognese, the old road to Bologna, the GIARDINO DELL'ORTI-COLTURA, the horticultural garden opened in 1859, and to Sir Harold Acton's villa, LA PIETRA.

Porta San Niccolò, built in the first half of the fourteenth century and restored in 1979, stands below the PIAZZALE MICHELANGELO. A steep road leads up to the fourteenth-century **Porta San Miniato** and, by way of the Via di Belvedere, to the **Porta San Giorgio** of 1260, the city's oldest surviving gate. The stone relief of St George is a copy of an original of 1284, now in the PALAZZO DELLA SIGNORIA.

Porta Romana, at the west end of the BOBOLI GARDENS, was built in 1327 to a design by Andrea Orcagna.

Porta San Frediano, also known as the Porta Pisano, may have been designed by Andrea Pisano. Its tall tower was built in the first half of the fourteenth century. The church of **San Frediano in Cestello** to the east, its large dome dominating this part of the Oltrarno, was reconstructed by the Roman architect, Cerruti, known as Il Colonnello, in the 1680s and 1690s. The cupola and bell tower were added by Antonio Maria Ferri in 1698. The **Granaio di Cosimo III** in the adjacent Piazza Cestello, now a barracks, was built in 1695 to the designs of Giovanni Battista Foggini.

VIA PORTA ROSSA and VIA POR SANTA MARIA commemorate gates which have disappeared. The site of the Porta di Giustizia, where gallows once stood, is now the Piazza Piave.

18. **Palazzo Davanzati**, Via Porta Rossa, is also known as the **Museo della Casa Fiorentina Antica**.

Palazzo Davanzati, interior courtyard

19. The **Mercato Vecchio** was not only the geographical centre of Florence, it was also, by the Middle Ages, the commercial centre of the whole region. All kinds of comestibles were sold here, and there was a lively trade in wool as well as in the wares of the local artisans.

Before their execution, criminals passed through the market, being compelled to pray before one of the largest tabernacles in the city, that of Santa Maria della Tromba, which was moved later to the ORSANMICHELE. In the early 1430s, the Commune commissioned Donatello to sculpt the market's symbol: Dovizia, or Abundance. Holding a cornucopia and a basket of fruit, she stood on an ancient Roman column which towered over the market. A fresco from Vasari's workshop in the Salone della Gualdrada, in the PALAZZO DELLA SIGNORIA, shows her *in situ*.

The Mercato Vecchio, the church of San Tommaso, and the neighbouring GHETTO were all demolished in the nineteenth century to make way for the PIAZZA DELLA REPUBBLICA. Architectural fragments salvaged can be seen in the museum of SAN MARCO.

20. The figure on the top of the **Colonna dell'Abbondanza**, which replaced Donatello's, is a copy of a statue by Giovanni Battista Foggini. There is another column of Abundance in the BOBOLI GARDENS above the Neptune Pond. It was intended that this should be erected in the Piazza San Marco with a statue of the Grand Duchess Giovanna of Austria on the top. The column broke and the statue, which had been started by Giambologna, was transformed into Dovizia by Pietro Tacca.

CHAPTER 6 *(pages 61–73)*

1. The **equestrian mural of Sir John Hawkwood** in the DUOMO is by Paolo Uccello (1436).

2. The number of *palle* on the Medici emblem was never fixed. Originally there were twelve; but there were usually seven in Cosimo il Vecchio's time, though there are only six at the corners of Verrocchio's roundel in the chancel of SAN LORENZO. There are eight on the ceiling of the Old Sacristy at San Lorenzo, five on Duke Cosimo's tomb in the CAPPELLA DEI PRINCIPI and six on the Grand Duke Ferdinando's arms on the entrance to the FORTE DI BELVEDERE.

3. The palace now known as **Palazzo Capponi delle Rovinate**, No. 36 Via de' Bardi, was built for Niccolò da Uzzano about 1420. It was afterwards acquired by the Capponi family, still its owners. It houses their private art collection, which includes works by Pontormo, Andrea del Sarto and Sustermans. **Palazzo Capponi**, No. 26 Via Gino Capponi, was the home of the nineteenth-century statesman after whom the street in which it stands was named. This *palazzo* was built in 1698–1713 by Carlo Fontana. **Palazzo Capponi**, No. 1 Lungarno Guicciardini, has a *salone* frescoed by Bernardino Poccetti in 1583. Neri Capponi's sarcophagus in SANTA SPIRITO is by Bernardo Rossellino.

The Capponi family chapel, attributed to Brunelleschi, is in SANTA FELICITA.

4. **Borgo degli Albizzi** extends from VIA DEL PROCONSOLO to Piazza San Pier Maggiore. The graffiti on Palazzo Matteucci Ramirez di Montalvo (No. 26), few bits of which now remain, have been attributed to Bernardino Poccetti. The fifteenth-century Palazzo Altoviti (dei Visacci) at No. 18 was enlarged towards the end of the next century. The fifteen figures of famous Florentines on the façade are by Giambattista Caccini. Canova had his studio at Palazzo degli Alessandri, No. 15. PALAZZO NONFINITO is on the corner of Via del Proconsolo opposite PALAZZO PAZZI-QUARATESI. PALAZZO DEGLI ALBIZZI is at No. 12.

CHAPTER 7 *(pages 74–91)*

1. The **North Doors** of the BAPTISTERY, with scenes from the life of Christ, the Four Evangelists and Four Fathers of the Church, have twenty-eight panels, like the South Doors. A self-portrait of the artist, with a turban-like cloth wrapped round his head, can be seen on the left

San Lorenzo

door, the fifth head from the top in the middle band. The bronze figures over the doorway are by Giovan Francesco Rustici, who may have been assisted by Leonardo da Vinci.

2. The panels of the **East Doors** of the BAP-TISTERY are copies erected here in 1990. Four of the originals, having been restored, are now in the MUSEO DELL'OPERA. The surround is also by Ghiberti. The Paradise referred to by Michelangelo was probably not the place of Dante's *Divina Commedia* but the name of the courtyard which once led from the Baptistery to SANTA REPARATA. Ghiberti's self-portrait is on the left door, the fourth from the top in the second row from the left. The porphyry columns on either side of the east doors commemorate Florence's former friendship with Pisa. They were presented to the Florentines by the Pisans in 1117 in acknowledgement of help given against piratical raiders from the Balearic Islands.

3. The **Old Sacristy** at SAN LORENZO was built by Brunelleschi in 1421–9. The roundels in the pendentives of the cupola, the bronze doors on either side of the chapel and the stucco reliefs over the doors are all by Donatello. The astrological mural in the cupola depicts the stellar configuration on 6 July 1439, the day upon which the successful outcome of the Council of Florence was announced in the DUOMO.

In the middle of the sacristy is the table-like tomb slab of Giovanni di Bicci de' Medici and his wife. For the tomb of his grandsons, Piero and Giovanni, Verrocchio conceived a monument that would also be visible from the transept by placing a bronze grille in the form of rope-work over the marble tomb inlaid with porphyry and serpentine. At the time of writing the chapel was closed '*per atti vandilici*'.

4. The church of **San Lorenzo** overlooks the Piazza San Lorenzo with its busy street market and Baccio Bandinelli's seated statue of Giovanni delle Bande Nere. It was rebuilt in the second half of the eleventh century, and the present church was one of the very first to be built in the new Renaissance style. Its harmony derives from Brunelleschi's use of simple geometric forms.

The OLD SACRISTY was the first part of the church to be completed. After Brunelleschi's death in 1446 the rest of the church was finished by his biographer, Antonio Manetti, and Michelozzo. The NEW SACRISTY was added by Michelangelo to Brunelleschi's designs; while the CAPPELLA DEI PRINCIPI was begun in 1604 by Matteo Nigetti. The rough brick façade remains unfinished: Pope Leo X's invitation to Michelangelo to decorate it did not bear fruit, but his model survives in the CASA BUON-ARROTI. The first chapel in the south transept contains a Roman sarcophagus and a wooden crucifix by Antonio Pollaiuolo. The high altar is in *pietre dure* of the late eighteenth century. Under the dome Cosimo de' Medici's grave is marked by his family's emblem.

The first chapel of the left transept contains a mid-fourteenth-century statue of the *Virgin and Child*, possibly by Alberto Arnoldi. In the chapel next to it is an altarpiece of *Saints Anthony Abbot, Leonard and Julian* by a follower of Domenico Ghirlandaio. In the second chapel in the right aisle is an altarpiece of the *Marriage of the Virgin* by Rosso Fiorentino. Just before the right transept is an outstanding marble tabernacle carved perspectively to give an illusion of deep recession by Desiderio da Settignano. Opposite are DONATELLO'S BRONZE PULPITS. The last chapel in the left transept is the Martelli Chapel with an *Annunciation* altarpiece by Fra Filippo Lippi. The predella depicts scenes from the life of St Nicholas of Bari, the name-saint of the donor, Niccolò Martelli, whose sarcophagus is here. There is also a monument to Donatello. In the left aisle, opposite Desiderio's tabernacle, is a fresco by Bronzino of the *Martyrdom of St Lawrence*. In the first chapel beyond this is a painting of Christ as a child in the carpenter's shop by Pietro Annigoni.

In the left aisle is the entrance to Antonio Manetti's cloister, in the style of Brunelleschi. In the corner of the cloister, a staircase in a vestibule leads to Michelangelo's BIBLIOTECA LAU-RENZIANA.

5. The **Ospedale degli Innocenti**, properly known as the Ospedale di Santa Maria degli Innocenti, overlooks the PIAZZA SANTISSIMA ANNUNZIATA. In 1294 the care of foundlings

Courtyard of the Ospedale degli Innocenti

was entrusted to the Silk Guild, which, in 1419, bought a piece of land from the Albizzi and commissioned Brunelleschi to build a hospital. It is believed to be the first hospital for foundlings in the world. Sometimes a baby would be brought with a note to identify it should a parent ever be in a position to recover it. The hospital always kept a meticulous record, which can still be seen. As the numbers of children increased – 1,320 in 1513 – wet-nurses were often hard to find because their remuneration was so small. In the late sixteenth century this problem was largely overcome, so it is said, when extra-ordinary news came from abroad: Spanish babies were being successfully fed on cow's milk.

By 1427 the loggia, which has been described as the first truly Renaissance work, had been completed. Brunelleschi intended that the spandrels of the arcade should be left empty; but they were filled with terracotta roundels of swaddled babies by Andrea della Robbia. It seems that the delegates also tinkered with Brunelleschi's plans for the rest of the hospital, which was completed after his death.

At the left end of the arcade behind the present grille was a wheel upon which babies could be deposited without the persons bringing them being seen. A plaque above informs the passer-by that for four centuries until 1875 the '*Ruota degli Innocenti*' was a '*segreto rifugio di miserie e di colpe*'.

There are two cloisters. The larger, the Chiostro degli Uomini, is decorated with the emblems of the Silk Guild, and of two hospitals which were united with the Innocenti in the course of the fifteenth century. In the north-west corner is the entrance to the church, which was remodelled in 1786. Over the door is a lunette of the *Annunciation* by Andrea della Robbia.

Steps in the cloister lead to galleries containing works by Botticelli, Piero di Cosimo, Luca della Robbia, Bernardino Poccetti, Domenico Ghirlandaio and others. In the background of Ghirlandaio's *Adoration of the Magi*, the Massacre of the Innocents is depicted. The priest in the middle ground is probably the donor, the hospital's prior, Francesco Tesori. In the corner

diagonally opposite the entrance to the church a passage leads to the Chiostro delle Donne, reserved for the female members of the staff. The hospital still functions as an orphanage.

6. The portico of the hospital of **Santa Maria Nuova** is by Bernardo Buontalenti. As well as the monastery of Santa Maria degli Angeli, the much-enlarged hospital has absorbed the church of **Sant'Egidio**, which was completed about 1420 and consecrated by Pope Martin V. Bernardo Rossellino carved the marble tabernacle. The bronze door is a copy of one executed for the church by Ghiberti. A *Madonna and Child* by Andrea della Robbia is now in the office of the Presidenza. This also contains the original of Dello Delli's terracotta *Coronation of the Virgin*, a cast of which is on Buontalenti's portico. The hospital's numerous benefactors have included Filippino Lippi and Leonardo da Vinci. From the fifteenth to the seventeenth centuries it was admired throughout Europe; Henry VII requested a copy of its *regolamento* when planning the Savoy hospital in London.

7. The main building of the **Studio Fiorentino**, now called the Università degli Studi, is in the south-east corner of the Piazza San Marco. After a strike at the University of Bologna, Bolognese professors were offered posts in Florence, and the university was founded in 1321. It never became as reputable a university as Bologna or Padua, and from time to time it was closed down altogether. It did, however, develop a good reputation as a centre for humanist studies in the course of the fifteenth century.

8. The **Tomb of Baldassarre Cossa**, Pope John XXIII, who died in Florence in 1419 was designed by Donatello and executed by Michelozzo *c.* 1424–7. The bronze effigy of the Pope is attributed to Donatello.

9. As well as the family chapel in SANTA CROCE, there is a **Bardi Chapel** in SANTA MARIA NOVELLA. The family took it over in 1334. It was once used by St Peter Martyr's Laudesi brotherhood, who commissioned Duccio's

Rucellai Madonna, which was later moved to the CAPPELLA RUCELLAI and is now in the UFFIZI. The lunettes of the *Virgin Enthroned* have been attributed to Cimabue. The altarpiece is by Vasari. The **Palazzo Bardi alle Grazie**, No. 5 Via dei Benci, built about 1430, has been attributed to Brunelleschi.

10. The **Via de' Bardi** runs parallel with the Arno from the south end of the PONTE VECCHIO to the Piazza dei Mozzi at the end of the PONTE ALLE GRAZIE. The CASA AMBROGI was at the eastern end. The PALAZZO CAPPONI DELLE ROVINATE is at No. 36; the Palazzo Canigiani, with a courtyard ascribed to Michelozzo, at No. 30. The church of Santa Lucia dei Magnoli (Santa Lucia fra le Rovinate) at No. 24 was first built in the early eleventh century. The lunette of Santa Lucia over the entrance door is by Benedetto Buglioni, the picture of her on the first altar on the left is by Pietro Lorenzetti. Domenico Veneziano's *St Lucy* altarpiece, which once hung over the third altar on the right, is now in the UFFIZI. It has been replaced by a copy of Andrea del Sarto's *Disputà*, the original of which is in the PITTI PALACE. The Palazzi dei Mozzi beyond the church were built in the thirteenth and fourteenth centuries for the Mozzi, a rich Guelph family of papal bankers who entertained Pope Gregory X here in 1273. Andrea de' Mozzi was Bishop of Florence before being moved to Padua because of the scandalous escapades which caused Dante to include him among the sodomites.

At No. 1 Piazza dei Mosti is the **Museo Bardini** in the Palazzo Bardini, which was built by Stefano Bardini in 1883 to house his varied collection of paintings, sculpture, furniture, ceramics, musical instruments, swords, drums, shields, armour and numerous architectural fragments including well-heads, fountains, fireplaces, tomb effigies, and various emblems of the Parte Guelfa and the city's guilds. There are early works by the Della Robbia, frescoes by Giovanni di San Giovanni from the Palazzo dei Pucci, and a painting of St Michael by Antonio Pollaiuolo. The collection was presented to Florence by Bardini in 1923.

Beyond the Palazzo Bardini, in Via di San Niccolò, are the fifteenth-century Palazzo Alemanni (No. 68) with copies of Giambologna demons on its façade, and the church of **San Niccolò sopr'Arno**, an eleventh-century foundation rebuilt in the fourteenth century, which contains, in the sacristy, a fifteenth-century fresco attributed to Baldovinetti within a *pietra serena* tabernacle from Michelozzo's workshop.

11. The **Piazzale Michelangelo** affords a spectacular vista of Florence. It is reached by the tortuous Viale Giuseppe Poggi from the PORTA SAN NICCOLÒ. Copies of Michelangelo's works, including his *David*, have been placed here. Above the Piazzale stands the church of **San Salvatore al Monte**, much admired by Michelangelo. When Castello Quaratesi's offer to provide funds to face SANTA CROCE was turned down, he put his money towards this new Franciscan church. A monk provided the initial design, and it was completed by Cronaca. In the second chapel on the north side is a terracotta *Deposition*, probably by Giovanni della Robbia. The *Pietà* in the chancel is attributed to Neri di Bicci.

12. Pier Francesco Silvani rebuilt the **Palazzo degli Albizzi**, No. 12 BORGO DEGLI ALBIZZI, in the seventeenth century. Only a small part, on the left with the medieval tower, now remains of the fourteenth-century palace. The Albizzi owned other palaces in the street.

13. The **equestrian mural of Niccolò da Tolentino** in the DUOMO is by Andrea del Castagno (1456).

14. As well as the PALAZZO ACCIAIUOLI, there are several other palaces or parts of palaces in the **Borgo Santi Apostoli** and the **Piazza del Limbo**. The Palazzo Altoviti is on the corner of Via delle Bombarde, the early-sixteenth-century Palazzo di Oddo Altoviti by Benedetto da Rovezzano at No. 1 Piazza del Limbo. The **Palazzo Rosselli del Turco**, with a relief of the *Madonna* by Benedetto da Maiano, has a façade on to the

View of Florence from the Piazzale Michelangelo

Borgo Santi Apostoli by Baccio d'Agnolo. The thirteenth-century **Palazzo Usimbardi**, or what was spared of it by the bombing in the Second World War, at No. 19, has its principal façade overlooking the Arno. It used to be the Grand Hotel Royal, where Charles Dickens stayed in 1845. Ruskin, Henry James, Swinburne and Longfellow also stayed here. Beyond the eastern end of the Borgo is the church of **Santo Stefano al Ponte** with a façade of 1233 and an interior altered by Ferdinando Tacca in 1649. The church of SANTI APOSTOLI is in Piazza del Limbo.

15. **Palazzo Guicciardini**, No. 15 Via Guicciardini, stands on the site of an earlier family palace burned down in the Ciompi riots of 1378. Francesco Guicciardini, the statesman and historian, was born here in 1483. The Machiavelli houses on the other side of the street no longer exist. There are two other palaces of the same name in Florence: Palazzo Guicciardini, No. 14 Via Santo Spirito, and Palazzo Guicciardini, No. 7 Lungarno Guicciardini. Next door to the latter at No. 9 is Palazzo Lanfredini by Baccio d'Agnolo.

16. **San Giovannino degli Scolopi** was begun in 1579 by Bartolommeo Ammannati, who designed the second chapel on the left as his burial place. His wife, the poet, Laura Battiferi, is also buried here. The altarpiece is by Alessandro Allori and Giulio and Alfonso Parigi.

17. The **Chapel of Onofrio Strozzi** is the sacristy of SANTA TRINITA. The altarpiece by Gentile da Fabriano, in which are portraits of various members of the Strozzi family, has been removed to the UFFIZI; but his decoration of the chapel arch can still be seen. The altar steps are inlaid with Strozzi emblems.

18. The church of **Santa Maria dell'Impruneta** is the parish church of Impruneta, south of Florence. It was consecrated in 1054. According to tradition, the site was chosen by two bullocks bearing the foundation stones. It was rebuilt in the mid fifteenth century through the generosity of its parish priest, and reconstructed after its near destruction in the Second World War. The Romanesque thirteenth-century crenellated campanile survives. Michelozzo built the two chapels on either side of the high altar. The

Chapel of the Madonna, on the left, contains the Virgin's miraculous image, and on the right is the Chapel of the Cross, with a terracotta *Crucifixion* from the Della Robbia workshop.

19. The **Noviziata**, or Novices' Chapel, in SANTA CROCE, is also known as the Medici Chapel. The glazed terracotta altarpiece is by the Della Robbia.

20. **Cafaggiolo** was more like a fortress than a villa. Vasari described it as having 'all the requisites of a distinguished country house' with a pleasant garden, groves and fountains. But its high towers and battlemented arches were surrounded by a moat crossed by a drawbridge. It was bought, together with Il Trebbio, by Prince Borghese, who had the central tower pulled down and the moat filled in. The *Sacra Conversazione*, which Alesso Baldovinetti painted for the chapel dedicated to SS. Cosmas and Damian is now in the UFFIZI.

21. **Belcanto**, later known as the **Villa Medici**. The reconstruction carried out for Giovanni de' Medici was finished in 1461. Vasari describes the high cost of building foundations on a steep slope. The villa was intended to accommodate great cellars for storing produce from the estate as well as wine and oil presses. Sold by the Grand Duke Cosimo III in 1671, it was renovated in the 1770s for Robert Walpole's widow, the Countess of Orford: and in the nineteenth century was bought by the English painter and collector, William Blundell Spence, when it became known as the Villa Spence. More recently it belonged to Lady Sybil Cutting, whose daughter, Marchesa Iris Origo, was brought up there. The Marchesa bought it in 1959.

22. From the courtyard of the **Palazzo Medici** (now the **Palazzo Medici-Riccardi**), in which Donatello's *David* used to stand, one staircase leads to the Medici Chapel. Benozzo Gozzoli's fresco has been cut to accommodate the staircase which was added in the seventeenth century. The iconography was doubtless chosen by the

Medici because of their close association with the Compagnia dei Magi, a confraternity dedicated to the cult of the Magi. The other staircase off the courtyard leads to the MEDICI GALLERY. The Medici Museum on the ground floor, in the former private apartments, is devoted to the history of the family.

23. **Niccolò Grosso's lamps** hung outside several Florentine palaces. Permission to display spiked lamps of this sort had to be obtained by special decree. Of the very few that now survive, an example can be seen in Piazza dei Davanzati as well as on the Medici Palace. The lamps Grosso made for the PALAZZO STROZZI were designed by Benedetto da Maiano. Grosso was nicknamed 'il Caparra' (advance payment) since he never gave credit.

24. Constantly increased by Cosimo and his heirs, the **Medici Library**, the **Biblioteca Laurenziana**, was eventually to contain no fewer than 10,000 *codices* of Latin and Greek authors

Palazzo Medici-Riccardi

Michelangelo's staircase, Biblioteca Laurenziana

and hundreds of manuscripts from the time of Dante and Petrarch, as well as others from Florence's remote past. Cosimo kept the library first at the VILLA MEDICEA DI CAREGGI, and later at the PALAZZO MEDICI. Confiscated by the Signoria in 1494, when fines of as much as fifty florins were imposed on borrowers who did not return books immediately, it was transferred to SAN MARCO at the suggestion of Savonarola. The library was bought back in 1508 by Pope Leo X, who removed it to Rome. Returned to Florence by Clement VII it was – in 1532 – placed in the building in the cloisters of SAN LORENZO, where it remains.

25. The **Badia Fiesolana** was Fiesole's cathedral until 1028. Reconstruction and enlargement began in 1467. The façade of the earlier Tuscan Romanesque church, reminiscent of SAN MINIATO and the BAPTISTERY, was preserved, enclosed by the later enlargement. The monastery itself now houses the European University Institute, a postgraduate college founded by the EC.

26. The **Orsanmichele statues** are, from left to right:

Via dei Calzaiuoli
(1) *St John the Baptist* by Lorenzo Ghiberti for the Calimala (importers of cloth) – removed for restoration in 1993.

(2) *Doubting Thomas* by Verrocchio for the Tribunale di Mercanzia (the niche was originally made for the Parte Guelfa by Donatello and Michelozzo) – newly restored and on exhibition in the Palazzo Vecchio in 1993. The glazed terracotta emblem of the Mercanzia above is by Luca della Robbia. Donatello's *St Louis of Toulouse*, originally made for this niche, is now in the museum of SANTA CROCE.

(3) *St Luke* by Giambologna for the Arte dei Giudici e Notai (magistrates) (an earlier statue by Niccolò di Piero Lamberti which stood here is now in the BARGELLO).

Via Orsanmichele
(1) *St Peter* attributed to Bernardo Ciuffagni for the Beccai (butchers) – removed for restoration in 1993.

(2) *St Philip* by Nanni di Banco for the Conciapelli (tanners) – removed for restoration in 1993.

(3) The *Quattro Coronati* (the four Christian sculptors who were killed for refusing to make a heathen statue of the Emperor Diocletian) by Nanni di Banco for the Maestri di Pietra e Legname (workers in stone and wood). The relief illustrating the work of the guild is also by Nanni di Banco. The terracotta emblem above is by Luca della Robbia.

(4) Copies of *St George* and the relief of *St George and the Dragon* by Donatello for the Armauoli (armourers). The originals are in the BARGELLO.

Via dell'Arte della Lana
(1) *St Matthew* by Lorenzo Ghiberti for the Cambio (bankers).

(2) *St Stephen* by Ghiberti for the Lanaiuoli (wool merchants).

(3) *St Eligius* by Nanni di Banco for the Maniscalchi (smiths and farriers) – removed for restoration in 1992.

Via Lamberti
(1) *St Mark* by Donatello for the Linaiuoli e Riggatieri (linen drapers and used-clothes dealers).

(2) *St James the Great* attributed to Niccolò di Piero Lamberti for the Pellicciai (furriers) – removed for restoration in 1993.

(3) *Madonna della Rosa* variously attributed to Giovanni Tedesco, Niccolò di Piero Lamberti and Simone Ferrucci for the Medici e Speziali. The *Madonna Enthroned* above is by Luca della Robbia.

(4) *St John the Evangelist* by Baccio da Mondelupo for the Setaiuoli e Orafi (silk weavers and goldsmiths). The terracotta above is by Andrea della Robbia.

CHAPTER 8 *(pages 92–6)*

1. The **Villa Medicea di Careggi** was purchased in 1417 by Giovanni di Bicci de' Medici. Michelozzo enlarged it for Cosimo, and Giuliano da Sangallo added the loggias on the south side for Lorenzo il Magnifico. It was looted and damaged by fire after the flight from Florence of Lorenzo's son Piero. Verrocchio's *David*, his terracotta *Resurrection* (both now at the BARGELLO) and his fountain of a little boy holding a spouting fish (now at the PALAZZO DELLA SIGNORIA) were all commissioned by the Medici for this villa. Restored by the Grand Duke Cosimo I, it subsequently fell into disrepair and was sold by the Medici's successors to Count Vincenzo Orsi. It is now used as offices for the hospital here.

2. **Donatello's bronze pulpits** in SAN LORENZO were his last works. They were finished by his pupils Bartolommeo Bellano and Bertoldo di Giovanni, and were placed on columns in the seventeenth century.

3. **Donatello's David** (*c.* 1430) is now in the BARGELLO. On its confiscation by the Grand Council after the expulsion of Piero de' Medici in 1494 orders were given for it to be erected on a column in the courtyard of the PALAZZO DELLA SIGNORIA.

4. **Donatello's Judith Slaying Holofernes** (*c.* 1460) was removed from the Medici Palace by order of the Signoria after the flight of the Medici in 1494 and set up on the *ringhiera* at the PALAZZO DELLA SIGNORIA with an inscription on its base to the effect that it had been placed there as a warning to all tyrants: '*Exemplum. Sal[utis]. Pub-[licae]. Cives. Pos[uere].* MCCCCXCV.' A copy now stands in front of the Palazzo. The original is on display inside, in the Sala dei Gigli.

5. For a description of this cycle of murals see Chapter 5, note 15.

6. Among the works Filippo Lippi painted while living at the PALAZZO MEDICI were the *Coronation of the Virgin* for the church of SANT' AMBROGIO and, perhaps, the *Annunciation* altarpiece in the Martelli Chapel at SAN LORENZO. His later *Virgin and Child with Saints Cosmas, Damian, Francis and Anthony of Padua*, commissioned by the Medici and painted for the Noviziata at SANTA CROCE, is, now, together with several others of his works, in the UFFIZI, though the *Nativity* altarpiece, which used to be in the chapel of the Palazzo Medici, is now in Berlin and has been replaced by a copy. His *Annunciation*, now in the National Gallery in London (in which can be seen Cosimo's device of three feathers within a ring) and his *Seven Saints* (two of whom are once again Cosmas and Damian), also in the National Gallery, were commissioned by Cosimo in 1448 and probably served as bed heads in the Medici Palace.

7. Other frescoes at SAN MARCO have been attributed to Zanobi Strozzi and Benozzo Gozzoli. The portrait of Savonarola in the prior's rooms is by Fra Bartolommeo.

CHAPTER 9 *(pages 97–108)*

1. The **Palazzo Strozzi** is bounded on three of its massive sides by the Via Tornabuoni, Via Strozzi and the little Piazza Strozzi. Its portals, one in each façade, are placed directly under the middle of the nine windows on the first and second floors. Originally, it was planned as a free-standing block with gardens laid out to Via Porta Rossa. It was more or less complete by 1536; but lack of funds left Cronaca's great overhanging cornice unfinished. The spacious rectangular courtyard, with its open ground-floor

Palazzo Strozzi

loggia, is one of the finest in the city. The palace now houses Giuliano da Maiano's original model for the building in a small museum. A lending library, the Gabinetto Viesseux, is housed on the ground floor. There are two Strozzi Chapels in SANTA MARIA NOVELLA. The **Cappella di Filippo Strozzi**, next to the sanctuary, has frescoes by Filippino Lippi, who also designed the stained-glass window. Filippo Strozzi's tomb was carved by Benedetto da Maiano. A party of young people meet here during the Black Death in Boccaccio's *Decameron*. The **Cappella Strozzi** is at the end of the north transept. It has frescoes by Nardo di Cione. The altarpiece of *Christ Giving the Keys to St Peter* is by Nardo di Cione's brother, Andrea di Cione, known as Orcagna. Together they designed the stained-glass windows.

2. The **Palazzo Grifoni**, now the **Palazzo Riccardi-Mannelli**, is in the PIAZZA SANTISSIMA ANNUNZIATA. Ammannati, Giuliano di Baccio d'Agnolo, Buontalenti and Giambologna all seem to have had a hand in its design. It was built in 1557–63 for Ugolino Grifoni, one of the Grand Duke Cosimo I's secretaries. It is now occupied by the Presidente della Regione Toscana.

3. The **Palazzo Ricasoli**, No. 2 Piazza Goldoni, has been doubtfully attributed to Michelozzo. Begun in about 1480, it was finished much later.

The statue of Goldoni in the piazza opposite is by Ulisse Cambi (1873). The sixteenth-century Palazzo Ricasoli-Firidolfi is at No. 7 VIA MAGGIO.

4. The **Palazzo Rucellai**, on the corner of Via del Palchetti and Via della Vigna Nuova, was begun some time after 1446, and finished by Bernardo Rossellino for Giovanni Rucellai, author of *Zibaldone*. It was the first palace in Florence to apply the revived classical orders to a façade, but, although the superimposed pilasters and capitals became a commonplace in church architecture, the novelty did not catch on in other palaces.

5. The late-fourteenth-century **Palazzo Alberti** is in Corso dei Tintori, which takes its name from the dyers' workshops which were established here from the thirteenth century. Further down the street is the **Palazzo Spinelli**, with graffiti decoration on the façade, which was built in the 1460s. Giorgio Vasari lived in the nearby Casa Morra.

6. **Palazzo Bartolini-Salimbeni (Palazzo Torrigiani)**, No. 1 Via delle Terme, was built in the 1520s by Giuliano di Baccio d'Agnolo for Giovanni Salimbeni. It was the first palace in the centre of Florence to be built entirely in High Renaissance style. It became the Hôtel du Nord in 1839 and was a favourite haunt of Americans: Herman Melville, James Russell Lowell and Ralph Waldo Emerson all stayed here. It is now mostly used as offices. The Bartolini-Salimbeni Chapel is in SANTA TRINITA.

7. The statue of the *Madonna and Child* in the **Cappella Rucellai** in SANTA MARIA NOVELLA is by Nino Pisano, the bronze tomb plate of Francesco Lionardo Dati by Ghiberti. Duccio's *Madonna*, which used to be here, is now in the UFFIZI.

8. The **Cappella Rucellai (the Cappella di San Sepolcro)** was built in 1467 by Alberti. The model of the Sanctuary of the Holy Sepulchre was based on measurements which Giovanni

Rucellai had specially taken for him in Jerusalem. Bernardo Rucellai, who was married to Nannina de' Medici, Lorenzo il Magnifico's sister, arranged a sculpture gallery in the Orti Oricellari, Via Bernardo Rucellai. The Palazzo degli Orti Oricellari, formerly the Palazzo Ginori-Venturi, was sold to Bianca Cappello in 1573.

9. The church of **San Pancrazio**, founded in the tenth century, was deconsecrated in 1809; and, having been used as a cigarette factory, is now a museum of sculptures by Marino Marini, who left them to Florence.

10. No documentary evidence has come to light to support the traditional and generally undisputed attribution of the **Pazzi Chapel** to Brunelleschi. In exchange for burial rights, Andrea de' Pazzi commissioned the chapel as the chapter house for the Franciscan monks of SANTA CROCE – although no family members are buried here – and construction, based on designs of a simple square and circles, began in the 1430s. The interior is, for the period, uncharacteristically plain: twelve terracotta roundels, perhaps from Luca della Robbia's workshop, representing the Apostles, decorate the walls between the superimposed pilasters. The roundels in the frieze are probably by Desiderio da Settignano; while the four tondi of the Evangelists in the pendentives are attributed to Brunelleschi himself by some scholars, to Donatello by others. The ornate entrance door was carved by Giuliano da Maiano

Pazzi Chapel, Santa Croce

after Brunelleschi's death. It is highly unlikely that its appearance is as the architect would have wished, being somewhat out of keeping with the reticent interior. The portico, with enamelled terracotta decoration by Luca della Robbia, is probably also by Giuliano da Maiano.

11. Work on the **Palazzo Pazzi-Quaratesi**, No. 10 VIA DEL PROCONSOLO, may have begun as early as 1458 but it seems that the family did not move into the palace until 1478. The architect was evidently charged with designing the monumental façade deliberately to rival the PALAZZO MEDICI. There were small high windows in the heavily rusticated ground floor, all giving the traditional impression of fortress-like strength. The larger lower windows are a later addition. This suggestion of impregnability was emphasized by the fact that there was only one door on Via del Proconsolo which opened into the courtyard. The courtyard columns are without precedent in medieval or Renaissance Tuscany. According to Professor Andres, 'they refer to late Roman examples, when traditional Greek and Hellenistic prototypes were abandoned in favour of inventive combinations of figures and vegetation'. The palace was once attributed to Brunelleschi; and certainly the architect must have had the PALAZZO DI PARTE GUELFA in mind when he placed *oculi* above the high round-arched windows in the smooth stucco of the upper floors. Giuliano da Maiano worked on the building, helped by his brother, Benedetto, as well, it seems, as Giuliano da Sangallo. Grand shields bearing dolphins, the Pazzi emblem, can be seen both in the vestibule and on the façade on the corner of Via del Proconsolo and Via degli Albizzi.

The Convent of **Santa Maria Maddalena dei Pazzi** is dedicated to a member of the family, a Florentine Carmelite nun who was canonized in 1669. A Cistercian foundation, it was taken over by the Carmelites and is now occupied by French Augustinians. The early-sixteenth-century Cappella del Giglio was frescoed by Bernardino Poccetti and his workshop. The cloister, completed in 1492, is by Giuliano da Sangallo. The Baroque choir chapel in the church (1675) is by Cirro Ferri and Pier Francesco Silvani. The well-preserved fresco, the *Crucifixion and Saints*, in the chapter house is by Perugino.

12. The **Palazzo Gondi**, No. 2 Piazza San Firenze, was begun about 1490 by Giuliano da Sangallo. The first occupants moved in eight years later, although the building as it exists now was not completed until the nineteenth century, when the street between it and the PALAZZO VECCHIO, the Via dei Gondi, was widened, entailing the demolition of part of the palace. The façade on the Via dei Gondi was designed by Guiseppe Poggi in the late nineteenth century.

The **Gondi Chapel** is in SANTA MARIA NOVELLA. It contains a wooden crucifix by Brunelleschi, which traditionally is the one described by Vasari, who said that Donatello had challenged the architect to make it, having been ridiculed for his version in the Bardi Chapel of SANTA CROCE. Vasari describes how Brunelleschi then invited Donatello to supper and showed him his crucifix. So impressed was Donatello that he dropped the eggs he was carrying in his apron. The chapel was decorated in marble by Giuliano da Sangallo.

Opposite the Palazzo Gondi, the buildings known as **San Firenze**, one of the best examples of Florentine Baroque, were erected in the seventeenth and eighteenth centuries by the Oratorian Fathers as their headquarters in the city.

On the left is the church of **San Filippo Neri**, which stands on the site of an old oratory dedicated to San Fiorenzo. This was designed by Gherardo and Pier Francesco Silvani, with a façade of 1715 by Ferdinando Ruggieri. The church on the right, **Sant'Apollinare** (now suppressed), was designed by Francesco Zanobi del Rosso; this, too, has a façade by Ruggieri. The building in the centre (now the law courts, which extend into the former Sant'Apollinare), 1772–5, is also by Francesco Zanobi del Rosso.

13. The **Villa of Poggio a Caiano** was rebuilt by Giuliano da Sangallo for Lorenzo de' Medici, who had bought it from the Strozzi in 1479. The

remains of Filippino Lippi's fresco on the façade can still be seen inside the loggia. The enamelled terracotta frieze, attributed to Andrea del Sansovino, which also once decorated the façade, is now inside, in the theatre. This was built for Cosimo III's wife, Marguerite-Louise. The frescoes in the *salone* on the first floor by Franciabigio and Andrea del Sarto were completed by Alessandro Allori. The lunette of the Etruscan god Vertumnus and his lover, Pomona, goddess of gardens, is by Pontormo. The villa was the favourite country retreat of several of the Medici family and their successors, and was also used for receptions. The Emperor Charles V was entertained here in 1536; Montaigne in 1581; Bianca Cappello died here in 1587. The house and its surrounding garden and park were presented to the nation by Victor Emmanuel III in 1912. After restoration the villa was reopened to the public in 1986.

14. The long façade of the **Pitti Palace** overlooks the sloping Piazza dei Pitti. Some historians, taking their lead from Vasari, believe that it was Brunelleschi's plan for the PALAZZO MEDICI, rejected by Cosimo de' Medici, which the arrogant Luca Pitti used for his own palace, on which construction began in 1458. Originally it consisted only of the seven heavily rusticated central bays. The palace was unfinished by 1472, Luca having fallen out with the Medici and into penury. Eleonora di Toledo bought the palace in 1549 and charged Ammannati with enlarging it, making it one of the biggest palaces in Europe. Ammannati also designed the splendid Mannerist courtyard which overlooks the gardens. Vasari connected the palace to the UFFIZI by means of the CORRIDOIO VASARIANO, which now houses the Medici's famous collection of self-portraits. The curving wings which partially enclose the piazza were added to the south side in the late eighteenth century, and to the north in the early nineteenth. The royal family used the palace until 1919, when Victor Emmanuel gave it to the state.

The palace now houses a vast collection of works of art, largely those acquired by the seventeenth-century Medici Grand Dukes. It was

Pitti Palace, garden front

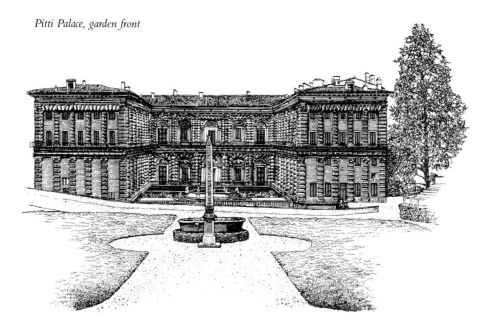

opened to the public in 1833, and the state acquired it in 1911. There are six museums: the MUSEO DEGLI ARGENTI, the Galleria Palatina, the Galleria d'Arte Moderna, the Collezione Contini-Bonacossi, the Museo delle Carrozze (the coach museum), and the Appartamenti Monumentali (the Royal Apartments). The last is closed indefinitely. The Galleria Palatina contains works by Titian, Rubens, Raphael, Botticelli, Fra Filippo Lippi, Caravaggio and many Flemish artists, among others. The Contini-Bonacossi Collection contains earlier Italian works, and works by Goya, El Greco, and Velasquez. The Galleria d'Arte Moderna is devoted almost exclusively to nineteenth- and twentieth-century Italian painters, but there are two landscapes by Pisarro.

15. Since SAN LORENZO is the basilica of St Ambrose and contains many martyrs' relics beneath the altar, the Church's rules did not allow the body to be buried in the nave immediately below the memorial. So it was placed in the vault; but, so as to join the tomb to the porphyry and serpentine memorial, a massive stone pillar, eight feet square, was placed between them. On this pillar are the words: 'Piero has placed this here to the memory of his father.'

CHAPTER 10 *(pages 109–30)*

1. Diotisalvi Neroni lived at **Palazzo Neroni** (now **Donati**), No. 7 Via de' Ginori. Other palaces in this street include Palazzo Barbalani di Montauto, No. 9, with windows on the ground floor attributed to Ammannati; Palazzo Ginori, No. 11, attributed to Baccio d'Agnolo, the architect of No. 15, Palazzo Taddei, which was built for the merchant of that name who commissioned the Royal Academy's tondo from Michelangelo. Raphael stayed here in 1505.

2. This bust is in the BARGELLO. Mino da Fiesole lived at No. 7 Via Pietrapiana.

3. Giovanni Tornabuoni, Lucrezia's brother, acquired the patronage of the **Cappella Maggiore** at SANTA MARIA NOVELLA from the Ricci and Tornaquinci. It was he who commissioned the murals here from Ghirlandaio. Lucrezia is represented as the third female figure on the right in the *Birth of the Baptist*. Portraits of her brother and sister-in-law, Francesca Pitti, the donors, are on the altar wall. The murals present a vivid picture of contemporary Florentine life. Ghirlandaio also designed the stained glass in the lancet windows. The choir stalls are by Vasari.

4. Some of Luca della Robbia's glazed terracotta decorations made for Piero de' Medici's study are now in the Victoria and Albert Museum.

5. One of the panels of Uccello's *Rout of San Romano* is in the UFFIZI, another in the Louvre, the third in the National Gallery.

6. Although the pretty young man in blue near the front of the procession riding a prancing horse on which a leopard also sits is usually identified as Giuliano de' Medici, it has been suggested that Gozzoli may have intended by way of a pleasant joke to represent the fearsome and cruel Castruccio Castracani degli Antelminelli, lord of Lucca, one of Florence's most powerful enemies in the fourteenth century. The leopard was the symbol of the Castracani.

7. Both Botticelli's *Primavera* and his *Birth of Venus* are now in the UFFIZI.

8. This portrait of a lady in a brown dress, now in the PITTI PALACE, was formerly believed to represent either Clarice Orsini or Simonetta Vespucci, but is now thought more likely to be Fioretta Gorini, mistress of Giuliano de' Medici and mother of Giulio, later Pope Clement VII.

9. Botticelli appears to have introduced both Piero de' Medici's sons, Lorenzo and Giuliano, in the *Madonna of the Magnificat*, as angels kneeling before the Madonna, Giuliano in the saffron dress with the curl falling over his brow. The picture is now in the UFFIZI.

10. The man on his knees in the foreground has been identified as Piero de' Medici; the king holding out his hands to the child as Cosimo il Vecchio; the arrogant figure on the left as Lorenzo; and the man in the red hat talking to him as Giovanni Pico della Mirandola. Between these last two is Angelo Poliziano and behind them Gaspare di Zanobi del Lama, who commissioned the picture. Among the figures on the right are Giovanni and Giuliano de' Medici, Filippo Strozzi and Lorenzo Tornabuoni.

11. The portrait, now in the UFFIZI, is conceivably of Botticelli's brother, Antonio, who was known to cast medals for the Medici.

12. **Piazza Santa Croce** had been used for such spectacles as this since the fourteenth century. The Palazzo dell'Antella, at No. 2, was built by Giulio Parigi. The Palazzo Serristori (now Cocchi) opposite the church has been attributed to Giuliano da Sangallo.

13. The portraits of Federigo da Montefeltro and his wife, Battista Sforza, are in the UFFIZI.

14. The tabernacle commissioned by Piero at SAN MINIATO AL MONTE is in the Cappella del Crocifisso; the one at SANTISSIMA ANNUNZIATA was designed by Pagno di Lapo Portigiani.

15. The treasures which so delighted Piero formed the basis of the collection called the **Museo degli Argenti**, now housed in the former state rooms of the Grand Dukes in the PITTI PALACE. Piero's descendants added to the collection. Here can be seen works in *pietre dure*, crystal, ivory and many other materials, as well as Lorenzo de' Medici's collection of vases, some classical. On the walls in the first room are seventeenth-century allegorical paintings of the Medici dynasty, notably by Giovanni da San Giovanni.

CHAPTER 11 *(pages 131–5)*

1. **Santi Apostoli** stands in the tiny PIAZZA DEL LIMBO, which was named after the former burial ground of unbaptized babies. Although legend ascribes the church's foundation to Charlemagne, it was probably built in the eleventh century. It has been restored many times, most recently in 1938; but its façade largely retains its original Romanesque features, apart from the sixteenth-century portal, which is possibly by Benedetto da Rovezzano. Nor has the interior, which follows the early Christian basilican plan, been greatly altered. It has a painted wooden ceiling and green marble columns and capitals, two of which are thought to come from Roman baths. Works of

San Marco, cloister of St Antonino

art include an *Immaculate Conception* altarpiece by Vasari in the third altar of the south aisle. In the first chapel of the north aisle is the *sinopia* of a *Virgin and Child* by Paolo Schiavo; and at the end of this aisle is the tomb of Oddo Altoviti by Benedetto da Rovezzano, who also built the palace for the Altoviti family at No. 1 Piazza del Limbo. The tabernacles are by Andrea della Robbia.

2. This ceremony is described at the end of Chapter 23.

CHAPTER 12 *(pages 136–49)*

1. Ghirlandaio was commissioned to fresco the **Sassetti Chapel** in SANTA TRINITA in 1483. In the scene taking place in the PIAZZA DELLA SIGNORIA above the altar, the *Confirmation of Franciscan Rule*, Luigi Pulci and Angelo Poliziano, the Medici boys' tutors, can be seen, as well as members of the Sassetti and Medici families. The miracle of the boy being brought back to life by St Francis is shown happening in the Piazza Santa

Trinita. Francesco Sassetti, standing beside his wife, Nera Corsi, is also shown in the altarpiece, Ghirlandaio's *Adoration of the Shepherds*. His tomb is attributed to Giuliano da Sangallo.

2. According to Vasari, the site of Lorenzo's school was a garden in the Piazza San Marco. Caroline Elam has been able to document it there as belonging to Lorenzo from 1475.

CHAPTER 13 *(pages 150–63)*

1. The church and priory of **San Marco** were founded in 1299, but by 1436 the Sylvestrine Order had so badly neglected the buildings that Pope Eugenius IV gave them to the austere Observant branch of the Dominicans of Fiesole, for whom, through the patronage of Cosimo de' Medici, Michelozzo provided new designs. In the corners of the first cloister, the Cloister of St

Antonino, are frescoes by Fra Angelico, several of whose other works, many of them from Florentine churches, are in the Pilgrims' Hospice on the south side. On the east side is the Great Refectory, the end wall of which was frescoed by Sogliani depicting St Dominic being fed by angels. To the north is the chapter house containing Fra Angelico's *Crucifixion with Saints*; and north of this, in the corner of the second cloister, the Cloister of St Dominic, is the Small Refectory with a fresco by Domenico Ghirlandaio of the *Last Supper*.

Along the east side of the cloister were the guest quarters, which now house fragments of buildings salvaged from the MERCATO VECCHIO and the GHETTO. The extensive renovation of the ground floor of the priory followed traditional patterns, but the upper floor incorporates two innovations: first, the Dominicans took advantage of the 1419 papal concession allowing monks to be accommodated in individual cells rather than communal dormitories; secondly, over the guest-rooms, Michelozzo's light, airy library breaks away from gloomy, windowless medieval tradition. At the top of the stairs to the cells is Fra Angelico's fresco of the *Annunciation*. The Virgin's loggia with its groin vaulting and Ionic capitals echoes Michelozzo's cloister below. The Observants held that their cells could only be decorated with images of the Virgin, the Crucifixion and St Dominic. Fra Angelico and his assistants, however, gave themselves some freedom from this rule. The church was rebuilt again in 1588 to the designs of Giambologna, who built the Chapel of St Antonino, which contains the saint's body. The church also has an eighth-century mosaic of the Virgin from Constantinople, and a *Sacra Conversazione* by Fra Bartolommeo, who painted the portrait of his mentor, Savonarola, in the prior's cell in the priory. This was closed for restoration at the time of writing. The tribune by Pier Francesco Silvani was added in 1678. The façade was completed in 1780.

The statue in the garden of Piazza San Marco is of General Manfredo Fanti, a hero of the Risorgimento, who died in Florence in 1865. It is by Pio Fedi, whose studio was at No. 99 Via de' Serragli. Fedi was also responsible for the monuments to those other patriots, Gino Capponi and Giovanni Battista Niccolini, in SANTA CROCE, and for the *Rape of Polyxena* (1866) in the LOGGIA DEI LANZI.

2. Leonardo had finished only a fragment of his mural of the battle of Anghiari before he left Florence for Milan in 1506. This fragment, of which no trace remains, can be seen in a painting of 1557 in the Sala di Ester on the second floor of the PALAZZO DELLA SIGNORIA. Michelangelo's cartoon for a mural of the battle of Cascina between Florence and Pisa was also incomplete when he was summoned to Rome. It, too, has been lost.

The **Sala del Maggior Consiglio**, also known as the **Salone dei Cinquecento**, was completed in 1496. The room was transformed for the Grand Duke by Bandinelli and Ammannati, and redecorated under the direction of Vasari. On the ceiling is the *Apotheosis of Cosimo I*, surrounded by depictions of the history of Florence and her victories by Vasari, who also painted the monumental panels. At the north end is the Udienza, or Audience Gallery, with frescoes by Francesco Salviati, designed by Baccio Bandinelli and Giuliano di Baccio d'Agnolo. In the niches there are statues of the Medici family. Opposite the Udienza are antique Roman statues. By the east wall, left of centre, is Michelangelo's *Victory*. Directly opposite is Giambologna's *Victory Triumphing over Vice*. The other statues around the walls of the *Labours of Hercules* are by Vincenzo De' Rossi and were placed here in the 1590s.

CHAPTER 14 *(pages 164–72)*

1. In 1303 the first prisoners incarcerated in the **Stinche**, which stood on the site of the present Teatro Verdi in Via Ghibellina, were members of the Cavalcanti family. Ironically, the building had once been the Cavalcanti palace. Later the inmates were largely debtors. Over the door was an inscription, *Oportet misereri*, 'We should be merciful'. But no mercy was shown to common criminals, who were frequently tortured through the streets of Florence before being publicly

hanged outside the prison. In the 1780s an English visitor noted the humane 'machine for decollation', which severed the head at a stroke.

2. The façade of **San Felice**, completed in 1458, has been attributed to Michelozzo and Antonio Manetti. The *Madonna and Saints* on the south side (sixth altar) is by Ridolfo and Michele Ghirlandaio. On the north side there are frescoes by Giovanni da San Giovanni (seventh altar) and a triptych by Neri di Bicci (sixth altar).

CHAPTER 15 *(pages 173–8)*

1. **Michelangelo's David**, completed by the twenty-nine-year-old sculptor in 1504, had been commissioned soon after Piero Soderini became Gonfaloniere in 1501. In his diary, Luca Landucci described how the wall of the Opera del Duomo had to be broken down so that it could be got out into the street. 'It went very slowly, being bound in an erect position and suspended so that it did not touch the ground with its feet ... It took four days to reach the piazza ... It was moved along by more than forty men.' Although Botticelli wanted it placed in the LOGGIA DEI LANZI, and others proposed the steps of the Duomo as a more suitable position, it was eventually placed in front of the PALAZZO DELLA SIGNORIA, where one of the arms was broken in a riot in 1527. The statue continued to stand there until 1873, when it was replaced by the copy which stands there now. The original – the gilding of the hair and the band across the chest still faintly visible – is in the GALLERIA DELL'ACCADEMIA, in the specially built tribune designed by Emilio de Fabris in 1882.

2. The **New Sacristy** at SAN LORENZO, known as the **Medici Chapel**, was completed by Michelangelo in 1543. Lorenzo and Giuliano are buried by the *Madonna and Child*, near the entrance door. The sarcophagus of Giuliano, Duke of Nemours, is on the right. The Duke is portrayed as an officer in the service of the Church with a male statue of *Day* and a sleeping female *Night* reclining at his feet. On the left is the tomb of Lorenzo, Duke of

Urbino, the dedicatee of Machiavelli's *The Prince*, portrayed as a soldier, his eyes cast down in thought. Below him are statues of *Dawn* and *Dusk*. The decoration of the chapel was not finished when Michelangelo left Florence in 1534. Plans for tombs for Lorenzo il Magnifico and Giuliano, as well as for Pope Leo X, were never realized.

3. Michelangelo's entrance and staircase to the BIBLIOTECA LAURENZIANA were largely finished by the time the artist left Florence. They were completed by Bartolommeo Ammannati and Giorgio Vasari in accordance with plans and instructions which Michelangelo left behind.

4. The little town of Gavinana, surrounded by chestnut groves, is now a holiday resort. In the piazza is an equestrian monument to Francesco Ferrucci. There is also a small museum here dedicated to him and the battle he lost.

5. These charcoal drawings, one of them a study for a Resurrection, were discovered in 1975. Some of them are attributed to Michelangelo's pupils, among them Tribolo.

6. The massive **Fortezza da Basso** was designed by Antonio da Sangallo the Younger. The entrance in Viale Filippo Strozzi incorporates a medieval tower. When no longer needed for its original purpose, the fortress was used as a prison, then as a barracks and arsenal. It opened as an exhibition centre in 1967.

7. The fifteenth-century **Palazzo Salviati** is at No. 6 Via del Corso. In the little Courtyard of the Emperors, whose vaults were decorated by Allori with frescoes of stories from the *Odyssey*, stands a sixteenth-century statue of Cosimo I. The palace, which was built by the Portinari family, was bought in 1546 and enlarged by Jacopo Salviati. It is now the head office of the Banca Toscana. The Palazzo Salviati, No. 76 Borgo Pinti, was formerly celebrated for its garden. The well-preserved fourteenth-century Palazzo Salviati-Quaratesi is on the corner of Via dell'Isola delle Stinche and Via della Vigna Vecchia.

CHAPTER 16 *(pages 179–85)*

1. These obelisks of Serravezza marble in **Piazza Santa Maria Novella** rest on turtles by Giambologna. On the south side of the piazza opposite the church is the late-fifteenth-century Loggia di San Paolo, based upon the loggia of the OSPEDALE DEGLI INNOCENTI. The terracottas are by Giovanni della Robbia and the lunette of St Francis meeting St Dominic by Andrea della Robbia. Beyond the loggia, at No. 16 Via della Scala, where it has been since 1612, is the Officina Profumo-Farmaceutica di Santa Maria Novella, which occupies a fourteenth-century chapel decorated in the 1840s by Enrico Romoli.

2. The **Misericordia**, the Venerabile Arciconfraternita della Misericordia di Firenze, founded by St Peter Martyr in 1244, moved to its present site on the corner of Via de' Calzaiuoli and Piazza del Duomo in 1576. It had previously been housed in the building opposite, the LOGGIA DEL BIGALLO – attributed to Alberto Arnoldi – which was built for them in the 1350s. On the wall of the Oratory of the Misericordia there is a painting of a member of the institution carrying an invalid by Pietro Annigoni. Inside the Oratory, the enamelled altarpiece is by Andrea della Robbia. The unfinished statue of St Sebastian is by Benedetto da Maiano, to whom are also attributed the wooden crucifix in the sacristy, and the *Madonna and Child* in the Sala di Campagnia. The museum above contains many paintings and other works of art acquired by the institution over the centuries. At the time of writing the museum was closed. The brotherhood now numbers several thousand volunteers, 300 of whom are on duty daily. 'Our institution,' the archivist writes, 'accepts men and women from every social class, who wish to relieve those

Piazza Santa Maria Novella

who need spiritual and material help... The Misericordia is considered to be the busiest and most famous charitable institution in the world.' Its members can still be seen in Florence going about their missions of mercy in black capes and hoods.

The **Compagnia di Santa Maria del Bigallo** was founded in 1245 and amalgamated with the Misericordia in 1425. Before moving to the Piazza San Giovanni in that year, the Compagnia's headquarters were near ORSAN-MICHELE. The three fourteenth-century statues on the loggia's façade were brought here from that building.

The small **Museo del Bigallo** (closed at the time of writing) contains works by, amongst others, Bernardo Daddi and Domenico di Michelino. The fresco in the Sala dei Capitani contains the earliest known view of Florence, showing the CAMPANILE unfinished. There is also a fresco by Niccolò di Pietro Gerini and Ambrogio di Baldese depicting lost and abandoned children being handed over to foster-mothers after having been exhibited in the loggia for three days. The Bigallo is now independent of the Misericordia.

3. Bandinelli's most prominent work in Florence is the huge statue of **Hercules and Cacus** (1533–4) to the right of MICHELANGELO'S DAVID. It was derided in the Grand Duke Cosimo's presence by Cellini, who called Bandinelli 'the filthiest ruffian ever born in this world'.

4. Cellini's *Perseus*, commissioned by Cosimo I, was set up in the LOGGIA DEI LANZI in 1554.

5. Giambologna's huge statue of *Appennino* was restored in 1988.

6. The **Neptune Fountain** was finished in 1575, the equestrian statue of the Grand Duke in 1595. Restoration of this statue was completed in 1993. A porphyry plaque in the pavement in front of the fountain marks the place where Savonarola and his fellow Dominicans were burned in 1498.

7. Ammannati began work on the **Palazzo Giugni**, No. 48 Via Algani, in the early 1570s for the banker Simone da Firenzuola. Characteristically, he employed smooth stucco rather than rustication. Decoration is reserved for the portal and the coat of arms on the first floor.

8. The Cerchi, a rich mercantile family which died out in the nineteenth century, came from Acone in the Sieve valley. The **Palazzo Cerchi**, now **Palazzo dell'Antella**, is at Nos. 21–2 PIAZZA SANTA CROCE. There is another Palazzo Cerchi dating from the thirteenth century on the corner of Vicolo dei Cerchi. The family's chapel was in what is now the MUSEO DELL'OPERA DI SANTA CROCE. It contains a glazed terracotta altarpiece by Andrea della Robbia.

9. The **Quartiere di Eleonora di Toledo**, on the second floor of the PALAZZO DELLA SIGNORIA, were decorated for the Grand Duchess in the 1540s. The chapel is the work of Bronzino; the vault of the Camera Verde is by Ridolfo del Ghirlandaio, the ceiling of the small study by Francesco Salviati. Other artists who worked here include Vasari, Giovanni Stradano and Bernardo del Tasso. The fifteenth-century lavabo in the Sala di Ester came from the PALAZZO DI PARTE GUELFA.

10. The **Boboli Gardens** were opened to the public in 1766. Just inside the arch entrance is the so-called Fountain of Bacchus, featuring Cosimo I's favourite dwarf astride a tortoise, sculpted by Valerio Cioli (1560). To the left, in the north-eastern corner of the gardens is the eccentric Grotta Grande of Buontalenti (attributed also to Ammannati). Baccio Bandinelli carved the statues of *Apollo* and *Ceres* on the façade for Vasari's niches. Copies of Michelangelo's *Slaves*, struggling out of their marble, stand in the corner (the originals are in the GALLERIA DELL'ACCADEMIA). Vincenzo de' Rossi carved *Paris Abducting Helen* in the second chamber, and beyond that, in the third, is *Venus* by Giambologna.

A path continues southwards to Eleonora di Toledo's Grotticina di Madama. Further south still, before FORTE DI BELVEDERE is reached, is Zanobi del Rosso's KAFFEEHAUS.

Immediately behind the palace is the amphitheatre by Giulio and Alfonso Parigi, in the middle of which is a granite bath from the Baths of Caracalla in Rome and, supported on little turtles, the obelisk of Rameses II plundered by the Romans from Heliopolis.

Further up the terrace is the Fountain of Neptune (1565–8) by Stoldo Lorenzi, which stands in a large pond. Beyond this, towards the southern limit of the gardens, is a large *Abundance*, started by Giambologna and completed by his pupil, Pietro Tacca. Above *Abundance* is the Museo delle Porcelane, formerly a defensive bastion built by Michelangelo and closed at the time of writing.

Alfonso Parigi laid out the beautiful cypress avenue, the Viottolone, north-west of the museum, past the row of greenhouses. It is lined with statues by Roman sculptors and with others by Giovanni Battista Caccini. Parigi also laid out the Isolotto, or Little Island, at the end of this avenue. This is really two little islands surrounded by moats. In the middle is a copy of Giambologna's Fountain of Oceanus (the original is in the BARGELLO), and statuary by Parigi and from the school of Giambologna. To the right of the Viottolone, at the northern limits of the

gardens by the Annalena Gate, is a late-eighteenth-century orangery by Zanobi del Rosso. At the northern end, outside the Porta Romana, is the **Istituto d'Arte**, which has a celebrated collection of casts of classical and Renaissance sculpture.

CHAPTER 17 *(pages 186–207)*

1. There has been a market on the site of the **Mercato Nuovo** since the early eleventh century. It is popularly known as Il Porcellino, the Piglet, after the bronze boar which stands here. Pietro Tacca copied it from Ferdinando II's Roman marble boar, which is in the UFFIZI. Sellers of gold and silk plied their trade here under the new loggia which Cosimo I commissioned, as did money-changers, for this had long been the neighbourhood of the banks – seventy-two of them were counted in 1421. The market now sells such things as bags and belts and cheap souvenirs.

2. The **Palazzo Uguccioni** stands at No. 7 PIAZZA DELLA SIGNORIA. When Cosimo I moved his family out of the PALAZZO MEDICI into the PALAZZO DELLA SIGNORIA in 1540, he conceived grand plans to renovate his new home

Boboli Gardens, showing amphitheatre

and the square. Various plans were rejected, including Michelangelo's to continue the arcade of the LOGGIA DEI LANZI round the piazza; and it seems that Cosimo channelled his interest in the square into the Palazzo Uguccioni. A Roman architect, Mariotto di Zanobi Folfi, was commissioned to build the new palace for Giovanni Uguccioni, one of Cosimo's courtiers. The influence of the architect's fellow-countryman, Bramante, is clear. Uguccioni was allowed to bring the façade of the palace forward on to the common pavement of the piazza, despite the objections of his neighbours. In gratitude, the bust of Francesco I by Giovanni Bandini was placed over the door. In 1993 the palace was awaiting restoration.

3. The **Via Maggio**'s name is abbreviated from Maggiore which indicates its original importance as a main thoroughfare. On the Oltrarno, it joins the PONTE SANTA TRINITA to the Piazza San Felice, close by the PITTI PALACE. There had long stood palaces on this street; but when Eleonora di Toledo moved into the Pitti, it became especially fashionable. As well as the PALAZZO RICASOLI and PALAZZO DI BIANCA CAPPELLO, the principal palaces in the street are the Palazzo Peruzzi de' Medici (formerly Delci), recently restored; No. 42, Palazzo Corsini Suarez, which was rebuilt by Gherardo Silvani and is now partially occupied by the Gabinetto G. P. Vieusseux's Servizio Conservazione. Palazzo Ridolfi, No. 13, is attributed to Santi di Tito. Next door is the early-fifteenth-century Palazzo di Cosimo Ridolfi.

4. The **Mint**, or Zecca, stood behind the LOGGIA DEI LANZI. Vasari demolished most of it to make way for the UFFIZI, but left parts of the walls, which he fused with the new building. The first florins were minted here in 1252.

5. The large Romanesque church of **San Pier Scheraggio** was founded in a flurry of church building between 1050 and 1070. The *priori* used to meet here before the PALAZZO DELLA SIGNORIA was built. The church was situated at the south end of what was to become the PIAZZA DELLA SIGNORIA. The Via della Ninna, which runs eastwards out of the piazza, takes its name from the *Madonna della Ninna* (meaning sleeping child) which Cimabue painted for the church. On this street can still be seen some of the columns which Vasari incorporated into the fabric of the UFFIZI.

6. The ground plan of the **Uffizi** is a long rectangle open at one end with rooms and galleries of assorted shapes and sizes projecting outwards. In the enclosed regular space, variously described as a piazza or a courtyard, nineteenth-century statues of eminent Tuscans, mostly writers and artists, are set in the niches cut out of the loggia pilasters.

On the outside of the Uffizi, which now houses one of the world's greatest art collections, can be seen the remains of SAN PIER SCHERAGGIO and the MINT. Bernardo Buontalenti designed the bizarre Porta delle Suppliche at the end of the Via Lambertesca. The broken pediment with the two halves placed back to back was his invention. Florentines could post

The Uffizi

petitions through a slot in this Door of Supplications; and Francesco I would secretly watch the petitioners through the peephole in the space provided between the two wings of the pediment. Bandini sculpted the bust of Francesco set in between the two halves.

A door towards the southern end of the west loggia opens into the CORRIDOIO VASARIANO. The gallery was temporarily closed after a bomb attack in May 1993.

7. The **Accademia del Disegno**, the first academy of art in Europe, is housed in the PALAZZO DELL'ARTE DEI BECCAI, No. 4 Via Orsanmichele. Its founding is indicative of the transformation in the social status of the artist: the previous centuries had regarded the artist as a tradesman whose shop was expected to execute works to order, but by the time this Accademia was founded, in 1563, the artist was capable of being described as 'divine', as Michelangelo was. He and Cosimo I were the first Academicians elected by the Academy's founding members.

8. After his death in Rome in 1564, Michelangelo's body was brought to Florence for burial in SANTA CROCE. His tomb, designed by Vasari, is at the west end of the south aisle opposite a relief by Antonio Rossellino of the *Madonna del Latte* on the first pillar. Below this relief is the tomb of Lorenzo de' Medici's friend, Francesco Nori, who was killed in the DUOMO by Giuliano de' Medici's murderer in the Pazzi Conspiracy. Three houses on the site of **Casa Buonarroti**, No. 70 Via Ghibellina, were bought by Michelangelo in 1508. They were converted into one house by Michelangelo's nephew, Leonardo, to whom they were bequeathed. Leonardo's son, also named Michelangelo, converted them into a gallery. This was opened to the public in 1858 by his descendant, the last of his line. As well as drawings and sculptures by Michelangelo, including his earliest known work, *The Madonna of the Steps*, the museum contains works of art collected by the later members of his family.

9. The windowless **Studiolo di Francesco I** is approached from the SALA DEL MAGGIOR CON-SIGLIO. It was created by Vasari to a scheme suggested by Vincenzo Borghini. The walls are covered with Mannerist paintings. Among the many artists whose work can be seen here are Alessandro Allori, Ammannati, Giambologna and Vasari. The portraits of Cosimo I and Eleonora of Toledo on the barrel vault are by Bronzino. A staircase leads up to Cosimo I's study, the Tesoretto.

10. The **Villa Pratolino**, designed by Buontalenti in 1569, was fifteen years in the making. Galileo stayed here in 1605–6 when tutor in the Grand Duke's family. It was demolished in 1822.

11. The **Palazzo di Bianca Cappello**, No. 26 VIA MAGGIO, was restored in 1987. The graffiti decoration is attributed to Bernardino Poccetti.

12. The **Villa di Castello** was bought by Lorenzo de' Medici's cousins, Giovanni and Lorenzo di Pierfrancesco de' Medici, in the late 1470s. Botticelli's *Primavera, Birth of Venus* and *Pallas and the Centaur* all hung here until 1761. Inherited by Giovanni delle Bande Nere, the villa was restored by Cosimo I, who employed Bronzino and Pontormo here. The gardens were laid out by Niccolò Tribolo (who created the Grand Fountain) and his successor, Bernardo Buontalenti. The bronze figures of Hercules and Antaeus made for this fountain are by Ammannati, who also created the figure of Appennino. Giambologna's bronze birds from the Grotto are now in the BARGELLO. The villa, which was remodelled and redecorated for the House of Savoy, is now the headquarters of the **Accademia della Crusca**, founded in 1582 for the study of the Italian language and the compilation of a dictionary. *Crusca* means bran and is probably a reference to the separation of the good and bad in language. The Academy's seats were made in the shape of panniers used for carrying bread. Also to be seen here are plaques bearing the mottoes of old *cruscanti*.

13. The Medici Venus is exhibited in the **Tribuna** created by Buontalenti in 1585–9. The walls are covered with portraits of various members of the

Medici family, including Pontormo's celebrated posthumous portrait of Cosimo il Vecchio and many of later Medici by Bronzino. The *pietre dure* table in the middle of the room was made in the mid seventeenth century in the OPIFICIO DELLE PIETRE DURE.

14. Ferdinando I, like his brother, Francesco, had a passion for *pietre dure* and founded the **Opificio delle Pietre Dure** in 1588. It occupies premises at No. 78 Via degli Alfani. There is a little museum here (closed for reconstruction at the time of writing), as well as a workshop where craftsmen restore works of art in *pietre dure* as well as other materials.

15. Giambologna's statue of the Grand Duke Ferdinando I was finished in 1608 by his pupil, Tacca, who designed the plinth with its fantastic sea creatures. The **Piazza Santissima Annunziata** in which it stands is probably the first example of town planning in Florence. When the OSPEDALE DEGLI INNOCENTI was completed on the east side of the square in 1444, Antonio da Sangallo the Elder copied the arcade in his Loggia dei Serviti opposite. At the north end of the square, the delicate arcade was used again by Giambattista Caccini in 1600 as a model for the façade of SANTISSIMA ANNUNZIATA. At the south end stands the PALAZZO GRIFONI. Just outside the piazza is the **Chiostro di San Pierino**. The glazed terracotta lunette above the entrance depicting the Annunciation and two

members of the Compagnia della Santissima Annunziata is by Santi Buglioni. The frescoes in the cloister are by Bernardino Poccetti among others.

16. The **Palazzo Bellini** is at No. 26. After Giambologna's death, his pupil Tacca lived here. **Borgo Pinti** extends from the eastern end of the Via dell' Oriuolo to Piazza Donatello. Existing palaces in the street are Palazzo Roffia at No. 13 and Palazzo Caccini (also known as Geddes di Filicaia) at No. 33. Both are of the seventeenth century. Palazzo Ximenes at No. 68 belonged to the Sangallo family in the fifteenth century. **Palazzo della Gherardesca** opposite PALAZZO SALVIATI at the Piazza Donatello end was built by Giuliano da Sangallo for Bartolomeo Scala and enlarged in the eighteenth century by Antonio Ferri. The large garden extends to the Kunthistorisches Institut at No. 44 Via Giuseppe Giusti. The institute has recently acquired the nearby **Casa di Andrea del Sarto** (No. 22 Via Gino Capponi) where the artist died in 1530. After his death the house was bought by the Roman artist, Federigo Zuccari, who had a studio in the strange building with odd reliefs at No. 43 Via Giuseppe Giusti.

17. The **Forte di Belvedere**, also known as the Forte di San Giorgio, was designed by Buontalenti. Approached either by way of the Via di Belvedere and the PORTA SAN GIORGIO, or through the BOBOLI GARDENS, its grounds were

Piazza Santissima Annunziata,
façade of the Ospedale degli Innocenti

Forte di Belvedere, Palazzetto

opened to the public in 1958. They provided a magnificent setting for an exhibition of the work of Henry Moore who, a frequent visitor to the white marble quarries at Carrara, gave to Florence – which he said he had loved since his first visit in 1925 – the statue of a warrior in the first cloister of SANTA CROCE. The Via di San Leonardo which winds up from the Belvedere towards Arcetri leads to the church of **San Leonardo in Arcetri**, which has an early-thirteenth-century pulpit from the demolished SAN PIER SCHERAGGIO and paintings by Neri di Bicci. Tchaikovsky stayed at No. 64 Via di San Leonardo in 1878, a year for him of prolific composition.

18. **Palazzo dei Giudici** (formerly Palazzo Castellani) in Piazza dei Giudici now houses the **Museo di Storia della Scienza**. Among the many scientific instruments on display are those used or designed by Galileo. The library of the Istituto di Storia della Scienza is on the ground floor.

19. Galileo's body was removed from the Novices' Chapel in SANTA CROCE in 1737 and reburied on the north side of the west door. The monument then erected is by Giovanni Battista Foggini. Lorenzo Ghiberti and his son, Vittorio, are buried between the fourth and fifth altars in the north aisle. Machiavelli's monument in Santa Croce is by Innocenzo Spinazzi (1787). It is in the south aisle between Alessandro del Barbiere's *Flagellation of Christ* on the fourth altar, and Andrea del Minga's *Agony in the Garden* on the fifth. Dante was buried in Ravenna. His cenotaph in Santa Croce by Stefano Ricci (1829) is in the south aisle between Vasari's *Way to Calvary* on the second altar and Jacopo Coppi di Meglio's *Ecce Homo* on the third. The monument outside the Salviati Chapel to the composer Luigi Cherubini (who was born at No. 22 Via Fiesolana) is by Odoardo Fantacchiotti. Leon Battista Alberti's monument, also in the north aisle, is by Lorenzo Bartolini, Carlo Marsuppini's by Desiderio da Settignano.

20. The original wooden **Teatro della Pergola**, No. 12 Via della Pergola, was built to the designs of Ferdinando Tacca in 1656. It was reconstructed by Bartolomeo Silvestri in the 1820s. One of Eleonora Duse's finest performances, as Rebecca West in Ibsen's *Rosmersholm*, was given here in 1906. At No. 59 Via della Pergola is the house where Cellini lived and died, and where he cast his *Perseus*.

21. There had long existed a tradition of informal *accademie* in Florence, but the **Accademia del Cimento** was the first devoted to science. With

its emphasis on practical research, experimentation (*cimento* means experiment) and recording of data, it was perhaps the first modern scientific institution in Europe and an important influence on the Royal Society. It published its journal, possibly the first scientific society to do so, in 1667, the year it was dissolved.

22. The collection of self-portraits includes works by Andrea del Sarto, Bernini, Bronzino, Batoni, Rubens, Rembrandt, Zoffany, Hogarth, Romney, Reynolds, Kneller, Lely, David, Corot and Ingres. The collection is not now open to the public.

23. The Medici collection of ivories is now in the MUSEO DEGLI ARGENTI.

24. Via del Cocomero is now **Via Ricasoli**, between PIAZZA DEL DUOMO and Piazza San Marco. In the small piazza where the street crosses the Via degli Alfani is the **Conservatorio Luigi Cherubini**, which houses a museum of musical instruments, including violins and cellos by Stradivari, and a music library. At the time of writing the building was being restored and the musical instruments were in store. **Palazzo dei Pucci**, with façades also on Via dei Pucci and Via dei Servi, is one of the biggest palaces in Florence. It is mostly of the sixteenth century with seventeenth-century additions. The family came to prominence in the days of Puccio di Antonio, a pro-Medicean Gonfaloniere. The most recent head of the family was a leading fashion designer. The nearby church of **San Michele Visdomini** was originally built further south and was demolished in the fourteenth century to make way for the east end of the DUOMO. It was reconstructed here in the 1370s by Giovanni di Lapo Ghini. The façade is by Ammannati. The altarpiece in the second chapel on the right is by Pontormo. The *Vices Domini* stood in for the Bishops of Florence when they were absent from the city or when the office was vacant. Their office was hereditary and Visdomini had become a family name by the eleventh century, when they enlarged the original church. The **Palazzo Incontri** opposite was owned by Piero di Cosimo de' Medici. It was rebuilt in the seventeenth century.

25. Although work began in 1605, under the direction of Ferdinando I, to realize Cosimo I's conception of a huge **Cappella dei Principi**, the

Cappella dei Principi

structure was not finished until 1737, and the decoration of the cupola not completed until 1836. The marble pavement, begun in 1882, was not finished until 1962. Until ready to receive them in the reign of Cosimo III, the bodies of the Grand Dukes and their wives and sons were temporarily buried in the NEW and OLD SACRISTIES. Generations of craftsmen in *pietre dure* were kept intermittently at work on the elaborate tombs of the three Cosimos, the two Ferdinandos and the Grand Duke Francesco which surround the walls. The two huge gilt bronze statues of Cosimo II and Ferdinando I are by Pietro Tacca and his son, Ferdinando.

The sixteen coats of arms inlaid in the floor in marble, coral, jasper, agate, mother-of-pearl and lapis lazuli are of the cities subject to the Grand Duchy. All the Grand Dukes were buried in the crypt below the mausoleum with their jewelled crowns still upon their heads and their sceptres in their hands. All the Grand Duchesses were also buried here, with the one exception of Francesco I's widow, Bianca Cappello. When Buontalenti asked Ferdinando I where his sister-in-law should be buried, the Grand Duke, who had detested her, replied, 'Wherever you like, we will not have her amongst *us*.' The site of her grave is unknown.

26. All that remains of the Benedictine convent of **San Piero Maggiore**, destroyed in the eighteenth century, is a portico by Matteo Nigetti in BORGO DEGLI ALBIZZI. One of Florence's largest fourteenth-century altarpieces, Jacopo di Cione's *Coronation of the Virgin*, now in the National Gallery, London, was commissioned for the church. Every new Bishop of Florence would traditionally celebrate his election with the abbess of the adjoining convent, giving her a ring to symbolize the religious unity of the city.

27. Carlo Ginori founded his porcelain factory in 1735. The firm, now known as Richard-Ginori, is still in existence at Sesto Fiorentino. The **Museo della Porcellane di Doccia** is next to the factory in a building built in 1965 to the designs of Piero Berardi.

28. This unfortunate arch still stands in the **Piazza della Libertà** (formerly Piazza San Gallo and also known as Piazza Cavour). The sculpture on it is by Marcello Tommasi.

CHAPTER 18 *(pages 208–19)*

1. The **Villa of Poggio Imperiale**, beyond the PORTA ROMANA in the Viale del Poggio Imperiale, was confiscated by Cosimo I from the Salviati family, who had acquired it from the Baroncelli. Remaining in the hands of the Grand Dukes of Tuscany, it was enlarged and redecorated in the seventeenth, eighteenth and early nineteenth centuries. Napoleon's sister, Elisa Bacciochi, lived here as Grand Duchess of Tuscany. It is now used as a girls' school and for educational and administrative purposes.

2. Mozart stayed at the **Albergo Aquila Nera**, then at No. 8 Borgo Ognissanti, which is now the Hotel Goldoni.

3. The **Villa Palmieri** is at No. 126 Via Giovanni Boccaccio. Its garden, now celebrated for its lemon trees, is said to be the scene of one of the stories in the *Decameron*. In the second half of the fifteenth century the villa belonged to Marco Palmieri. It was owned in the nineteenth century by James Ludovic Lindsay, 26th Earl of Crawford.

4. In Zoffany's picture of the Tribuna – on the walls of which are shown various works brought from elsewhere – James Bruce, the African traveller, is seen with his hands behind his back beside the Medici Venus. In front of him, his hand on his sword, wearing a star, is Sir Horace Mann. Talking to him with his right hand on Titian's *Venus of Urbino* – in Mark Twain's opinion 'the foulest, the vilest, the obscenest picture the world possesses' – is Thomas Patch. Sitting down in front of Patch is the Hon. Felton Hervey. The figure on the far left, beside *Cupid and Psyche*, is George, 3rd Earl Cowper; next to him, wearing a star, is Sir John Dick, British Consul in Leghorn; to his left is the 6th Earl of Plymouth. The man talking to Plymouth, beside

Raphael's *Madonna*, is Zoffany himself. The picture was painted under the patronage of Queen Charlotte.

5. **Palazzo Manetti** is at No. 23 Via Santo Spirito. Lord and Lady Holland lived next door at **Palazzo Feroni**, where G. F. Watts stayed as their guest in 1844–7.

6. The **Casa Ambrogi** was one of the houses near the south end of PONTE VECCHIO destroyed in 1944. It was here that Horace Walpole and Thomas Gray stayed in 1740.

7. Thomas Patch became an authority on Masaccio and early Florentine art. This picture, commissioned by Lord Grey, is now in the Royal Academy. The man proposing the toast is Sir Charles Bunbury. Sitting at the other end of the table is Sir Henry Mainwaring.

8. Examples of Gori's work can be seen in the MUSEO DELL'OPIFICIO DELLE PIETRE DURE at No. 78 Via degli Alfani.

9. The best work in the **Medici Gallery** in the PALAZZO MEDICI-RICCARDI is a *Virgin and Child* by Filippo Lippi. The fresco of the apotheosis of the Medici is by Luca Giordano.

10. The **Galleria Corsini**, No. 11 Via Parione, is the best private art collection in Florence. It was largely formed by Marchese Bartolommeo Corsini and his son, Filippo, in the seventeenth century. As well as the frescoes by Gabbiani there are works by, amongst others, Maratta, Luca Giordano, Giovanni Bellini, Pontormo, Ridolfo del Ghirlandaio and Sustermans.

11. The frescoes in the dome at **San Frediano in Cestello** are by Gabbiani.

12. Ignazio Hugford's *Tobias Visiting His Father* is in **Santa Felicita**, the ancient church off the Via Guicciardini rebuilt by Ferdinando Ruggieri in the 1730s. His *Death of St Andrea Avellina* is in **San Gaetano** (the seventeenth-century church in Via Tornabuoni with a façade by Gherardo Silvani) and his altarpiece of the *Annunciation* in **San Jacopo sopr'Arno**, Borgo San Jacopo, whose Baroque interior was painted at the beginning of the eighteenth century. The rare thirteenth-century portico here was removed in 1529 from the now demolished church of San Donato a Scopeto which once stood beyond the PORTA ROMANA. There is also a painting by Hugford in **San Paolino**, in Via Palazzuolo, a tenth-century foundation rebuilt in 1669. Over three thousand items from his collections were purchased by the Uffizi from his executor.

13. The **Cascine**, the long, narrow, unenclosed park beyond the PORTA AL PRATO, was opened to the public by the Grand Duke Pietro Leopoldo. For generations the land had belonged to the Medici, who had farms and hunted here. (*Cascina* means dairy farm.) Shelley conceived his 'Ode to the West Wind' in the park. The Monumento dell'Indiano at the western end was erected in memory of the Maharaja of Kolhapur who died in Florence in 1870. There are two racecourses here as well as sports grounds, tennis-courts and a swimming-pool.

14. Lions, heraldic symbols of the city, had been kept in Florence since the thirteenth century, at first in a cage opposite the BAPTISTERY, then in pens near the PALAZZO DELLA SIGNORIA, where the smell of them proved too offensive for Cosimo I, who had them removed. The Via dei Leoni commemorates their presence here.

15. **Palazzo Corsini sul Prato** was designed by Buontalenti in the 1590s and completed and enlarged in the 1620s for the Corsini family, who still live here. There are two other Florentine *palazzi* bearing the same name: the immense Baroque **Palazzo Corsini** on the Lungarno Corsini (which was built over a period of eighty years from the 1640s to the designs of a variety of architects including Ferdinando Tacca, Pier Francesco Silvani and Antonio Ferri) and **Palazzo Corsini**, No. 6 Borgo Santa Croce, an early-sixteenth-century building now occupied by the Istituto Araldico.

16. **Palazzo di San Clemente** is at No. 15 Via Gino Capponi on the corner of Via Micheli. It is now partially used by the university and awaits restoration. There is no indication that the Young Pretender lived here. The large **Palazzo Capponi** opposite was built in 1698–1713 by Carlo Fontana.

CHAPTER 19 *(pages 220–25)*

1. The **Biblioteca Riccardiana**, No. 14 Via de' Ginori, is in the seventeenth-century extension of the PALAZZO MEDICI-RICCARDI. It was founded by Riccardo Riccardi at the beginning of the seventeenth century, opened to the public in 1718 and sold to the Commune in 1812. The reading-room has frescoes by Luca Giordano. The library contains the Villani chronicles of Florence, a copy of Dante's *Divina Commedia* with notes by Cristoforo Landino, and the books of the Peruzzi bank. At the time of writing the library was 'temporarily' closed.

2. Antonio Magliabechi, Cosimo III's librarian, a clever, sardonic little hunchback, assembled an immense collection of codices and manuscripts which are now in the Biblioteca Nazionale. He was said to have been able to recall every word in almost every line he had ever read. He lived in an airless, unswept house opposite Santa Maria Novella where visitors, so Eric Cochrane wrote, 'had to avoid tripping over the disorderly pile of books that filled every corner of every room, slipping on the breadcrusts and apple peels scattered about the floor, sitting on the "miserable bed" littered with paper and garbage, and looking at the deformed face, frozen between a smile and a sneer, which nature had given the proprietor in order "to make the beauty of his intellect shine forth more clearly". They also had to suffer the stench of clothes never washed and never taken off.' The Biblioteca Magliabechiana was first opened to the public in 1747.

The **Biblioteca Nazionale** overlooks the Arno next to SANTA CROCE. The main building was begun in 1911. As well as those of Magliabechi, the collections include the Biblioteca Palatina-Medicea and the library of the Grand Duke Ferdinando III. Stored here are some three hundred volumes of Galileo's papers and the letters of numerous great Florentines, including Michelangelo and Machiavelli.

3. The **Archivio di Stato**, founded in 1582 and containing archives from before the days of Bishop Hildebrand, has been housed since 1989 in the new building on the south side of Piazza Beccaria.

4. The former **Accademia Fiorentina** had been founded in 1541 by the Grand Duke Cosimo I. The new academy was established in 1784.

5. The **Accademia di Belle Arti** was founded by the Grand Duke in 1765. Its loggia, the Loggia dell'Ospedale di San Matteo, is one of the oldest in Florence. The lunettes over the doors are by the Della Robbia. The adjoining building is the **Galleria dell'Accademia**, No. 60 Via Ricasoli. It contains works brought here for study by students at the Accademia. Among the paintings are works by Filippino Lippi, Taddeo Gaddi, Perugino, Baldovinetti, Fra Bartolommeo, Botticelli, Lorenzo di Credi, Bronzino, Pontormo and Andrea Orcagna. The gallery's most prized exhibits are MICHELANGELO'S DAVID, the slaves from his unfinished tomb for Pope Julius II in Rome and his *St Matthew* from the DUOMO.

6. The **Sala della Niobe** is Room 42 of the UFFIZI. It was designed by Gaspare Maria Paoletti. The frescoes are by Tommaso Gherardini. Among the antiquities exhibited here is the Medici Vase, which was acquired by Lorenzo de' Medici. The group, *Niobe and Her Children*, was found in a vineyard near the Lateran and brought here from the Villa Medici in 1775.

7. **La Specola**, No. 17 Via Romana, takes its name from the astronomical observatory which was established here in the Palazzo Torrigiani by the Grand Duke Pietro Leopoldo and was visited by Humphry Davy and Michael Faraday in 1814.

The exhibits in the Museo Zoologico include a collection of anatomical models in wax by Clemente Sisini made between 1775 and 1814. The Palazzo Torrigiani at No. 1 Via delle Terme was formerly the PALAZZO BARTOLINI-SAL-IMBENI. The façade (*c.* 1530) of **Palazzo Buon-delmonti** opposite is also attributed to Baccio d'Agnolo. It was here in 1819 that the Swiss bibliophile, Gian Pietro Vieusseux, founded his literary and scientific association (now in the PALAZZO STROZZI). There is another Palazzo Torrigiani, a sixteenth-century building, on the Lungarno Torrigiani. The **Giardino Tor-rigiani** west of the Via de' Serragli between the Pitti Palace and Bellosguardo was created by Pietro Torrigiani in the early nineteenth century. It is the largest private garden in Florence.

8. The small **Palazzina Livia** in PIAZZA SAN MARCO was designed by Bernardo Fallani. The drawing-room was painted in blue and white *trompe-l'oeil* on the Grand Duke's orders.

9. **Palazzo Serristori**, on the Lungarno Ser-ristori, was built at the beginning of the sixteenth century. The façade overlooking the Arno opposite the BIBLIOTECA NAZIONALE was added in 1873. It is now the headquarters of the Soprintendenza Archeologica della Toscana. Palazzo Serristori of *c.* 1475, also known as Palazzo Cocchi, No. 1 PIAZZA SANTA CROCE, formerly attributed to Baccio d'Agnolo, is now believed to be by Giuliano da Sangallo.

10. The **Ghetto** was created in 1571 on the orders of Cosimo I. It extended northwards from the middle of the present PIAZZA DELLA REPUB-BLICA to Via dei Pecori and westwards from the Via Roma to the Via Brunelleschi. Architectural fragments from the Ghetto, which was demol-ished in the nineteenth century, can now be seen in the Museo di Firenze Antica, which is approached from the Chiostro delle Spese at SAN MARCO. The Ghetto could be entered only by way of two narrow entrances on the north and south sides. The large synagogue in Via Farini was built in 1874–82 to the designs of Mariano Falcini, Vincenzo Michele and Marco Treves.

CHAPTER 20 *(pages 226–36)*

1. The **Kaffeehaus** below the FORTE DI BELVEDERE is still a café, open in the summer.

2. The **Palazzina della Meridiana** was begun in 1776 by Gaspare Maria Paoletti. At the east end of the PITTI PALACE, it was opened in 1983 as the Galleria del Costume. The Collezione Contini-Bonacossi, including works by Veronese, Bernini, Tintoretto, Goya, Velasquez and El Greco, is on the upper floor.

3. **Palazzo Masetti (Castelbarco)**, No. 2 Lung-arno Corsini, is now the British Consulate. The **Palazzo Gianfigliazzi**, next door at No. 4, a reconstructed fifteenth-century building, was a hotel in the early nineteenth century. Alessandro Manzoni stayed here in 1827; and Louis Bon-aparte, who had been made King of Holland by his brother, died here, a querulous old man confined to a wheelchair, in 1846. The palace now houses the Ristorante Corsini as well as the Pensione Bretagna and three shops.

4. Frederick Stibbert was born in Florence in 1838. His mother was Italian, his father English. Artist and traveller, he fought under Garibaldi in 1866. He was extremely rich and formed an extra-ordinarily diverse collection of paintings, fur-niture, porcelain, *cassoni*, tapestries, firearms, malachite and glass. His splendid collection of armour includes that of Giovanni delle Bande Nere and some of the best examples of Japanese armour to be found anywhere in the world. The costumes include the clothes worn by Napoleon during his coronation as King of Italy in 1805. To house his treasures, Stibbert built a huge villa beyond the PORTA SAN GALLO designed for him by Cesare Fortini. On his death in 1906 he be-queathed it to the British government, who made it over to Florence. The entrance to the **Museo Stibbert** is at No. 26 Via Frederico Stibbert. The large park is also open to the public. It adjoins the park of the VILLA FABBRICOTTI.

5. **Canova's monument to Alfieri,** completed in 1810, is in the south aisle of SANta croce, facing

the pulpit by Benedetto da Maiano by the nave pillar. There were delays in its erection because the friars were uneasy about Alfieri's relationship with the Countess of Albany.

6. **Ugo Foscolo's sepulchral statue** by Antonio Berti (1939) is at the eastern end of the south aisle of SANTA CROCE next to Cigoli's *Entry into Jerusalem* on the sixth altar, on the other side of which are Giuseppe Cassioli's monument to Rossini and Bernardo Rossellino's tomb of Leonardo Bruni of *c.* 1446.

7. The **monument to the Countess of Albany** by Emilio Santarelli is in the **Castellani Chapel** at SANTA CROCE, which has frescoes by followers of Agnolo Gaddi and terracotta statues of saints by the Della Robbia.

CHAPTER 21 *(pages 237–49)*

1. The **Palazzo Borghese**, No. 110 VIA GHI-BELLINA, was built (1821–2) on the site of a palace belonging to the Salviati family for Pauline Bonaparte's husband, Camillo Borghese. It took less than a year to complete. The neoclassical façade, with its heavily rusticated ground floor, was designed by Gaetano Baccani.

2. The neoclassical façade (1814–23) of the **Villa of Poggio Imperiale** is by Pasquale Poccianti and Giuseppe Cacialli.

3. Shelley took 'pleasant apartments for six months' in 1819 at Palazzo Marino in the Via Valfonda, where what is left of the once large and celebrated Gualfonda garden, laid out at the beginning of the sixteenth century, can still be seen. Shelley's 'Ode to the West Wind' was written in Florence at this time; and his son, Percy Florence Shelley, who succeeded to the baronetcy, was born here.

4. Since 1879 the **Museo Archeologico** has been housed in the Palazzo della Crocetta, which was built in the 1620s for the Grand Duchess Maria Maddalena, probably to the designs of Giulio Parigi. It contains one of the world's best collections of Etruscan antiquities. The Etruscan Topographical Museum on the ground floor was established by Luigi Adriano Milani in 1897, the Egyptian Museum and the Etrusco-Greco-Roman Museum on the upper floors after an expedition to Egypt directed by François Champollion and Ippolito Rosellini in 1828–9. Among the exhibits are the Etruscan *Chimera* discovered in Arezzo and brought to Florence by Vasari; a bronze of an orator, the *Arringatore*, of the third century BC; the Greek *Idolino* of the fifth century BC; a Hittite chariot in wood and bone from a Theban tomb; and the Attic *François Vase* acquired by the Grand Duke Leopoldo II in 1845.

Other museums in Florence not mentioned in the text are:

The **Museo di Firenze com'era**, Via dell' Oriuolo. In the former Convento delle Oblate, this is a topographical and historical museum. It contains maps, engravings, photographs and views of Florence by, amongst others, Thomas Patch, Giuseppe Maria Terreni and Giuseppe Zocchi, as well as a series of lunettes of Medici villas by Giusto Utens.

The **Museo Horne**, established by Herbert Percy Horne, an English art historian – and author of a pioneering monograph on Botticelli – who died in 1916. His collection of painting, sculpture, furniture, medals, coins, ceramics and miscellaneous works of art is housed in the **Palazzo Corsi**, No. 6 Via de' Benci, which has been attributed to Simone del Pollaiuolo, Il Cronaca. Artists whose works can be seen here include Jacopo Sansovino, Filippino Lippi, Lorenzo di Credi, Dosso Dossi, Bernardo Daddi, Benozzo Gozzoli, Giambologna and Ammannati. The *St Stephen*, part of a polyptych, is by Giotto, the tondo of the Holy Family by Beccafumi.

The **Museo Nazionale di Antropologia ed Etnologia** on the corner of Via del Proconsolo and Borgo degli Albizzi. Containing exhibits from Asia, Africa, South America and Mexico, it was founded in 1869 by Paolo Mantegazza and is housed in **Palazzo Nonfinito** which, begun by Buontalenti in 1593, was continued by Vincenzo Scamozzi, G. B. Caccini and Dionigi Nigetti. As its name suggests it was never finished. The courtyard is by Ludovico Cardi da Cigoli, and the stairway by Santi di Tito.

The **Museo Fiorentino di Preistoria**, No. 21 Via Sant'Egidio, founded in 1946.

5. **Doney's**, founded by Gasparo Doney in the 1820s, remained one of Florence's most popular cafés and pastry-shops for generations. Stendhal, the Brownings, the brothers Goncourt, Herman Melville, Ralph Waldo Emerson and Jessie White Mario were all more or less regular customers. Théophile Gautier praised it highly in his *Voyage en Italie* (1851). It was still a favourite rendezvous in the 1980s, but has now closed. The **Gambrinus** still survives, however, in Via Brunelleschi. It was at the old Gambrinus that André Gide met Gabriele D'Annunzio and watched him indulging 'with obvious greediness in little vanilla ices served in small cardboard boxes'.

CHAPTER 22 (*pages 250–59*)

1. The **Villa della Petraia** was bought by the Medici from the widow of Filippo Salutati in 1595 and rebuilt by Buontalenti. The fountain of *Venus Drying Her Hair* in the garden is by Giambologna. The courtyard is decorated with frescoes celebrating the history of the Medici family by Baldassare Franceschini, Il Volterrano, who painted them for the Grand Duke Ferdinando I's son, Lorenzo de' Medici. The villa was given to the state by King Victor Emmanuel III in 1919.

2. One of the largest of the city's squares, the **Piazza d'Azeglio**, with its fine plane trees, is at the far end of the Via della Colonna.

3. The construction of the **Piazza della Repubblica**, formerly known as the Piazza Vittorio Emanuele, in the late nineteenth and early twentieth centuries entailed the demolition of several medieval buildings as well as the MERCATO VECCHIO and much of the GHETTO. The granite Roman Colonna dell'Abbondanza was erected on its present site in 1428. The figure on the top of the column is a copy of the original by Giovanni

Battista Foggini. Among much other work in Florence, Foggini was responsible for the fine Baroque interior of **San Giorgio sulla Costa**, the tribune and side chapels in SANT'AMBROGIO, and the huge marble statues of the Apostles and Evangelists in the church of SAN GAETANO. Talking to 'elderly persons' in 1911, E. V. Lucas discovered that nothing so distressed them as 'the loss of the old quarter for making this new spacious piazza'. 'And,' he added, 'nothing can so delight the younger Florentines as its possession, for having nothing to do in the evenings, they do it chiefly in the Piazza Vittorio Emanuele.'

4. The botanical gardens to the north of the university, known as the **Giardino dei Semplici**, Via Micheli, are on the site of a botanical garden created for the Grand Duke Cosimo I by Niccolò Tribolo in 1545. In this area are the Botanical Museum, the Museum of Minerals and the Palaeontological Museum.

5. The **Giardino dell'Orticoltura** was laid out in 1859. The greenhouse of 1880 is by Giacomo Roster.

6. The **Palazzo Guadagni** is at No. 10 Piazza Santo Spirito. It was probably designed by Simone del Pollaiuolo, Il Cronaca, and built about 1505. The *sgraffito* work is by Andrea del Sarto; the wrought-iron lamps have been attributed to Niccolò Grosso. The façade with its loggia on the top floor shaded by wide eaves was much copied in sixteenth-century Florence. Built for Rinieri Dei, whose family commissioned the *Madonna del Baldacchino* for their chapel in the church of SANTO SPIRITO, it was left in 1683 to the Compagnia dei Buonuomini di San Martino, a charitable organization for *poveri vergognosi*, poor people too ashamed to beg (see also Chapter 5, note 1).

7. The **Castello di Vincigliata** near Settignano was built in 1855–65 around an old early-eleventh-century tower.

8. The **Giubbe Rosse** in PIAZZA DELLA REPUBBLICA is so called because the waiters used to wear red jackets.

9. The **Museo di Storia della Fotograffia Fratelli Alinari**, which contains material illustrating the history of the firm, is in the PALAZZO RUCELLAI.

CHAPTER 23 *(pages 260–76)*

1. The **Villino Trollope** later became a *pensione*. Thomas Hardy stayed here in 1887, later moving to No. 1 Via del Podere.

2. The Piazza Maria Antonia laid out in 1869 was the first of Florence's nineteenth-century squares. It is now the **Piazza dell'Indipendenza**. The statues here are of Baron Bettino Ricasoli, the statesman, who had been elected Gonfaloniere of Florence in 1848, and Ubaldino Peruzzi, Mayor of Florence in 1870. The former is by A. R. Valta (1893), the latter by Raffaello Romanelli (1897).

3. The **Pension Suisse**, an inexpensive establishment, was much favoured by foreigners. Dostoevsky stayed here in 1861 before moving to No. 8 (now 22) Via Guicciardini, where he worked on *The Idiot*.

4. The **Casa Guidi**, Piazza San Felice, was built in the late fifteenth century. It was bought by Count Camillo Guidi, the Grand Duke's Secretary of State, in 1619. The Brownings' rooms have been occupied by the Browning Institute since 1971. A painting by George Mignaty shows how they appeared in the Brownings' time. The façade of the house bears an inscription to the effect that Elizabeth Barrett Browning wrote here, and died here in 1861.

5. The villas at **Bellosguardo** are on the high ground to the west of the PITTI PALACE above the late-sixteenth-century church of SAN FRANCESCO DI PAOLA. The view over Florence from the Villa Brichieri-Colombi is described by Elizabeth Barrett Browning in the seventh book of *Aurora Leigh*. Florence Nightingale was born in 1820 at the Villa La Colombaia, now a school. The names of other celebrated people who have lived at Bellosguardo are shown on a plaque on the wall of VILLA DELL'OMBRELLINO. They include, in addition to those mentioned above, Ugo Foscolo, James Fenimore Cooper, Henry James, Franz Brentano, Hans von Bülow, Ouida, Jessie White Mario and Galileo.

6. Henry James was talking about the fourteenth-century frescoes in the **Chiostrino dei Morti** at SANTA MARIA NOVELLA. These were then attributed not to Giotto di Bondoni but to Giotto di Stefano, known as Giottino.

7. The villa of **Castagnolo** belonged to the Marchese Lottaringa della Stufa, who came occasionally to stay while the Rosses were living there. From here they moved to Poggio Gherardo, formerly known as Il Palagio del Poggio, the Palace on the Hill. It had come into possession of the Gherardi family in the fifteenth century. The Rosses bought it in 1888 from three old sisters, the Contesse Gherardi, the last of their line.

8. Hildebrand bought the convent and its surrounding garden in 1874. He added an upper storey for his friend, Hans von Marées, the reticent German painter who lived in Italy for twenty years from 1864. The nearby church of **San Francesco di Paola** was built in 1589. Its fresco of the Madonna del Parto is by Taddeo Gaddi. The large Villa Pagani with a tower opposite the church was built in 1896.

9. The **Cimitero degli Inglesi** is on a large mound in the middle of the Piazza Donatello. Opened in 1827, it was closed fifty years later when the Cimitero degli Allori in the Via Senese took its place. It is Swiss property and is officially known as the Cimitero Protestante rather than the English Cemetery, but when it was in use all foreigners were commonly known as '*Inglesi*', whatever their nationality. Among those buried here were Arthur Hugh Clough (d. 1861); Gian Pietro Vieusseux (d. 1863); Isa Blagden (d. 1873); Frances Trollope (d. 1863); Walter Savage Landor (d. 1864); William Holman Hunt's wife, Fanny, who died at Fiesole in 1866 while her husband

was at work on his *Isabella and the Pot of Basil*; and, as recorded on a plaque on the wall, 'the great American preacher, Theodore Parker' (d. 1860). Robert Davidsohn, the German historian of Florence, who lived in the city for many years, was buried here in 1937. Elizabeth Barrett Browning's tomb was designed by her husband and sculpted by Lord Leighton and Luigi Giovanozzi.

10. The **Villa Fabbricotti** is at No. 48 Via Vittorio Emanuele. It is now the Università per gli Stranieri.

11. Princess May and her parents had a suite of rooms at Paoli's Hotel, where 'English comfort & tastes' were considered. The proprietor had been courier to Sir James Hudson. After the Duke suffered a stroke here he was taken to the Villa Stibbert (see Chapter 20, note 4). He later joined his wife and daughter at the Villa I Cedri, which is about four miles from the Porta San Niccolò near Bagno a Ripoli. This villa was built in the fifteenth century for the Laroni family and was later owned by Miss Bianca Light, whose family had bought it in the 1840s.

CHAPTER 24 *(pages 277–84)*

1. The park of the VILLA PRATOLINO was bought in 1872 by the Demidoff, who built what is now known as the **Villa Demidoff**.

2. The **Russian Church**, designed by Russian architects, was consecrated in 1904. The majolica decoration on the façade was made by the Ulisse Cantagalli workshop. Other non-Roman Catholic churches in Florence are the American Episcopalian **St James's** at No. 9 Via Bernardo Rucellai, a neo-Gothic building of 1911; the **Lutheran Church**, No. 11 Lungarno Torrigiani, built in 1899; the **Greek Orthodox Church**, No. 76 Viale Mattioli; and the neo-Gothic **Waldensian Church**, No. 26 Via Micheli, built as Holy Trinity in 1903 by G. A. Bodley and Cecil Hare on the site of an earlier Anglican church. At a Sunday service at the Anglican church in 1837

Edward Lear once found a congregation of '300 English, besides servants!!!!!' The Anglican church of St Mark's is at No. 16 Via Maggio. For the synagogue, *see* GHETTO.

CHAPTER 25 *(pages 285–93)*

1. Lina Waterfield found premises for the British Institute's library in the **Loggia dei Rucellai**, which she leased from her friends Conte and Contessa Rucellai. It is attributed to Alberti. The British Institute's library, the largest English-language library in Italy, is now in the Palazzo Lanfredini on the Lungarno Guicciardini.

2. The **Villa Mirenda** is next to the church of San Paolo a Mosciano.

3. The **Villa I Tatti**, Via Vincigliata, probably takes its name from its sometime owners, the Zati family. It was bought in 1905 by Bernhard Berenson, the American art historian of Lithuanian descent and author of *Italian Painters of the Renaissance* (1930). He lived here for the rest of his long life, receiving innumerable visitors, who have left accounts of his remarkable scholarship, his astonishing memory and fascinating talk. Although, according to Sir Harold Nicolson, 'he debauched his talent to make money', he was an inspiration to younger men. He 'resembled an Old Master, whether a Titian or an El Greco depended upon his mood,' Sir Harold Acton has written. 'Most art critics are limited by the exigencies of their profession, but Berenson's mind ranged far beyond it.' Sir John Pope-Hennessy felt 'permeated by his personality. One felt protective and affectionate and uncritical.' However, Pope-Hennessy found the inside of I Tatti, 'despite the presence of great works of art, a little daunting... The most unnerving feature of the house in those days [the 1930s] was its quietness. It was a temple where the prevailing silence was never, save at mealtimes, broken by a human voice.' Berenson left the house, with its library and art collection, to Harvard University as a centre for Italian Renaissance studies. The garden was laid out by Cecil Pinsent in 1908–15.

4. **Casa Boccaccio** near Poggio Gherardo was owned by Giovanni Boccaccio's father. Boccaccio himself lived there until his stepmother persuaded her husband to move down into Florence.

5. The **Jennings-Riccioli** still stands at No. 2 Lungarno delle Grazie near the BIBLIOTECA NAZIONALE.

6. The **Castello Montegufoni** was bought by Sir George Sitwell in 1909, when it was occupied by almost 300 peasants. It had formerly belonged to the Acciaiuoli. 'The roof is in splendid order,' Sir George told his elder son in whose name he purchased it, 'and the drains can't be wrong, as there aren't any.' He came to live here permanently in 1925.

7. The **Villa dell'Ombrellino** at BELLOSGUARDO was once rented by Galileo. Mrs Keppel's daughter, Violet Trefusis, lived there until her death in 1973. Restored in 1988, it is now a conference centre, and partly occupied as the consulate of the Grand Duchy of Luxemburg (see also Chapter 23, note 5).

8. The **Villa of La Pietra** off the Via Bolognese in the middle of Montughi Hill takes its name from a stone pillar indicating the distance of one mile from the old city gate, PORTA SAN GALLO. In the fourteenth century the villa belonged to the Macinghi. It was subsequently acquired by the Sassetti, then by the Capponi. The gardens were created at the beginning of this century by Sir Harold's father, Arthur Acton, who collected the statues and the early Tuscan paintings. Many of these were acquired from the American painter, Francis Alexander, who had settled in Florence for the sake of the health of his daughter Francesca, whose illustrations to Italian folk stories were so much admired by John Ruskin.

9. The **Parterre** was laid out as a park in the eighteenth century on the site of the Convent of San Gallo. The exhibition halls have been largely demolished.

10. The architect of the final and principal buildings of the **Biblioteca Nazionale** was Cesare Bazzani.

11. The **Stadio Comunale** was renovated for the World Cup Soccer Championship in 1990.

12. The group of Tuscan architects and engineers responsible for the **Stazione Centrale Santa Maria Novella** included Giovanni Michelucci, Piero Berardi, Nello Baroni and Italo Gamberini.

CHAPTER 26 *(pages 294–304)*

1. The interior of the **Teatro Comunale**, which is on the corner of Via Magenta and Corso Italia, was reconstructed in 1961. Florence's annual musical festival, the Maggio Musicale Fiorentino, is usually held here and in the TEATRO DELLA PERGOLA. The nearby American Consulate, facing the Lungarno Amerigo Vespucci, was designed by Giuseppe Poggi, who also built the Villa Favard on the other side of the Via Palestro.

2. The **Villa Torrigiani** is in Via Fratelli Rosselli. Alfred Lord Tennyson stayed here in 1851 when his brother Frederick was living in the house with his Italian wife.

3. *Primavera* and her sister seasons had been carved to celebrate Cosimo III's wedding. Since her head was found, *Primavera*'s right arm has been broken off.

CHAPTER 27 *(pages 305–13)*

1. Donatello's wooden *St Mary Magdalen*, formerly in the BAPTISTERY, is now in the MUSEO DELL'OPERA DEL DUOMO.

TABLE OF PRINCIPAL EVENTS

1st CENTURY BC Foundation of Florentia

AD 405 Ostrogoths besieging the city are defeated by Flavius Stilicho

476 German warlord, Odoacer, becomes King of Italy, establishing capital at Ravenna

751 Lombard King, Aistulf, captures Ravenna

978 La Badia founded

1013 Work begins on San Miniato al Monte

1018 Mercato Nuovo built

1076 Matilda becomes Countess of Tuscany

1078 New circle of walls begun

1125 Florentines capture Fiesole

1216 Murder of Buondelmonte de' Buondelmonti seen as inaugurating quarrel between Guelphs and Ghibellines

1228 Santa Croce begun

1246 Santa Maria Novella begun

1252 Gold florin first minted

1255 Guelph government of Florence orders construction of Palazzo del Popolo

1260 Florentines and their allies defeated by Sienese at Montaperti

1265 Dante born in Florence

1289 Florentines defeat Ghibellines of Arezzo at Campaldino

1293 Ordinances of Justice institute office of Gonfaloniere

1296 Foundation stone laid of new cathedral

1299 Work begins on Palazzo della Signoria

1302 Dante exiled and Cimabue dies

1308 Giovanni Villani begins his *Storia fiorentina* Corso Donati killed

1315 Florentines defeated at Montecatini

1328 Death of Castruccio Castracani

1333 Florence flooded

1334 Gotto appointed *Capomaestro* of cathedral Foundations of Campanile laid

1337 Orsanmichele built as a market

1339 King Edward III of England repudiates his debts with the Bardi and Peruzzi banks

1342 The Duke of Athens elected Lord of Florence

1345 New Ponte Vecchio completed

1348 Black Death

1350 Boccaccio at work on the *Decameron*

1374 Death of Petrarch

1378 Riots of the *ciompi*

1393 Maso degli Albizzi becomes Gonfaloniere

1406 Pisa surrenders to Florence

1419 Work begins on Brunelleschi's Ospedale degli Innocenti

1421 Florence buys Leghorn Giovanni de' Medici becomes Gonfaloniere

1420s Masolino and Masaccio at work on frescoes in Santa Maria del Carmine

1432 Florence forces under Niccolò da Tolentino defeat Sienese at San Romano

1434 Cosimo de' Medici returns from exile Fra Angelico enters monastry of San Marco

1436 Brunelleschi's dome completed Uccello completes monochrome fresco of Sir John Hawkwood in the cathedral

1437 Fra Filippo Lippi returns to Florence from Padua

1439 General Council of Greek and Roman Catholic churches held in Florence

1440 Defeat of the Visconti at Anghiari

c. **1440** Donatello completes his *David*

1444 Michelozzo's new buildings at San Marco consecrated

1452 Ghiberti's east doors of the Baptistery finished

1457 Pitti Palace begun

1464 Death of Cosimo de' Medici

1469 Lorenzo de' Medici succeeds his father, Piero

1472 Benedetto Dei's *Cronaca fiorentina*
Sack of Volterra

1478 Pazzi conspiracy

1481 Savonarola arrives in Florence

c. **1482** Domenico Ghirlandaio starts work on
Sassetti Chapel in Santa Trinita

c. **1485** Botticelli's *Birth of Venus*

1489 Foundation stone of Strozzi Palace laid

1492 Death of Lorenzo de' Medici

1494 Medici driven from the city
King Charles VIII's troops enter the city

1497 The Bonfire of the Vanities

1498 Trial and execution of Savonarola

1504 Michelangelo's *David* finished

1505 Machiavelli organizes Florentine militia

1512 The return of the Medici

1515 Giovanni de' Medici enters Florence as Pope
Leo X

1520 Michelangelo begins work on the New
Sacristy at San Lorenzo

c. **1524** Michelangelo's staircase to Biblioteca
Laurenziana begun

1527 Alessandro and Ippolito de' Medici flee from
Florence after the sack of Rome

1529 Florence under siege

1530 Florence surrenders

1531 Alessandro de' Medici becomes Duke of
Florence

1537 Alessandro murdered by Lorenzino de' Medici
Cosimo de' Medici is chosen as Alessandro's
successor
Cosimo's enemies defeated at Montemurlo

1545 Benvenuto Cellini returns to Florence

1555 Siena surrenders

1557 Giambologna settles in Florence

1559 Ammannati reconstructs the Ponte alla Carraia

1560 Uffizi begun to the designs of Vasari

1567 Ponte Santa Trinita rebuilt by Ammannati

1569 Cosimo proclaimed Grand Duke of Tuscany

1574 Francesco I succeeds father as Grand Duke

1584 Buontalenti builds Tribuna

1587 Ferdinando I succeeds his brother, Francesco I

1590 Work begins on Forte di Belvedere

1604 Cappella dei Principi begun at San Lorenzo

1609 Cosimo II succeeds his father, Ferdinando I

1621–70 Reign of Cosimo II's son, Ferdinando II

1670–1723 Reign of Ferdinando II's son, Cosimo III

1723–37 Reign of Cosimo III's son, Gian Gastone

1737 Francis, Duke of Lorraine installed as Grand
Duke

1740–86 Sir Horace Mann British envoy in
Florence

1743 Death of the last Medici, Gian Gastone's sister,
Anna Maria, who bequeaths Medici treasures
to the House of Lorraine on condition that
none is removed from Tuscany

1743–65 Florence ruled by foreign regents after
Grand Duke Francis's return to Austria

1765 The Grand Duke Francis dies and is succeeded
by his younger son, Peter Leopold

1775 La Specola built

1784 Accademia delle Belle Arte opened

1790 The Grand Duke Peter Leopold becomes
Emperor of Austria and appoints his second
son Grand Duke Ferdinand III

1799 French troops enter Florence

1801 Tuscany becomes part of Napoleon
Bonaparte's Kingdom of Etruria

1809 Napoleon's sister, Elisa Bacciochi, created
Grand Duchess of Tuscany

1814 The Grand Duke Ferdinand III welcomed
back to Florence

1824 Death of Ferdinand III and succession of his
son, Leopold II

1840 Florence flooded

1848 The Grand Duke Leopold II grants a
constitution

1849 The Grand Duke joins the Pope at Gaeta
Republican government established
The Grand Duke invited to return

1859 Demonstrations in Florence in support of a
united Italy force the Grand Duke to leave
the city

1860 The people of Tuscany vote for the unification
of the former Grand Duchy with the constitutional monarchy of Victor Emmanuel II,
King of Piedmont

1865 Florence becomes capital of Italy

1871 Capital of Italy removed to Rome

1915 Italy enters the war

1922 Fascists march on Rome

1940 Mussolini declares war

1943 Germans enter Florence after the Italian
surrender

1944 Allies enter Florence

1966 The year of the flood

THE MEDICI FAMILY

1. DESCENDANTS OF COSIMO DI GIOVANNI DI BICCI DE' MEDICI

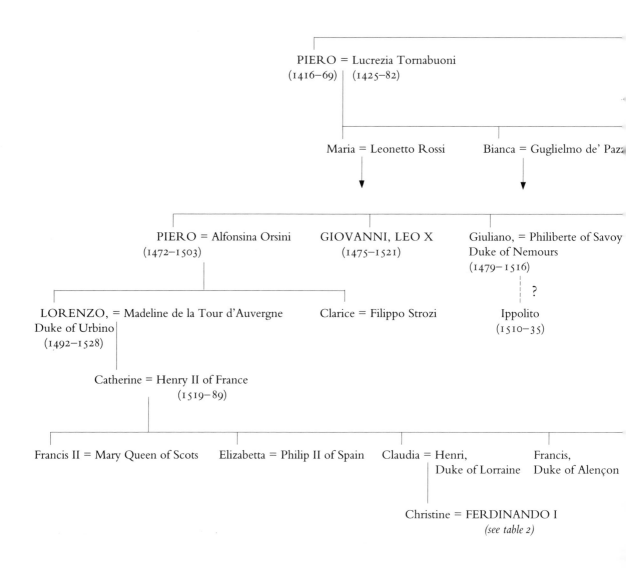

PIERO = Lucrezia Tornabuoni
(1416–69) | (1425–82)

Maria = Leonetto Rossi

Bianca = Guglielmo de' Pazzi

PIERO = Alfonsina Orsini
(1472–1503)

GIOVANNI, LEO X
(1475–1521)

Giuliano, = Philiberte of Savoy
Duke of Nemours
(1479–1516)

LORENZO, = Madeline de la Tour d'Auvergne
Duke of Urbino
(1492–1528)

Clarice = Filippo Strozi

Ippolito
(1510–35)

?

Catherine = Henry II of France
(1519–89)

Francis II = Mary Queen of Scots

Elizabetta = Philip II of Spain

Claudia = Henri,
Duke of Lorraine

Francis,
Duke of Alençon

Christine = FERDINANDO I
(see table 2)

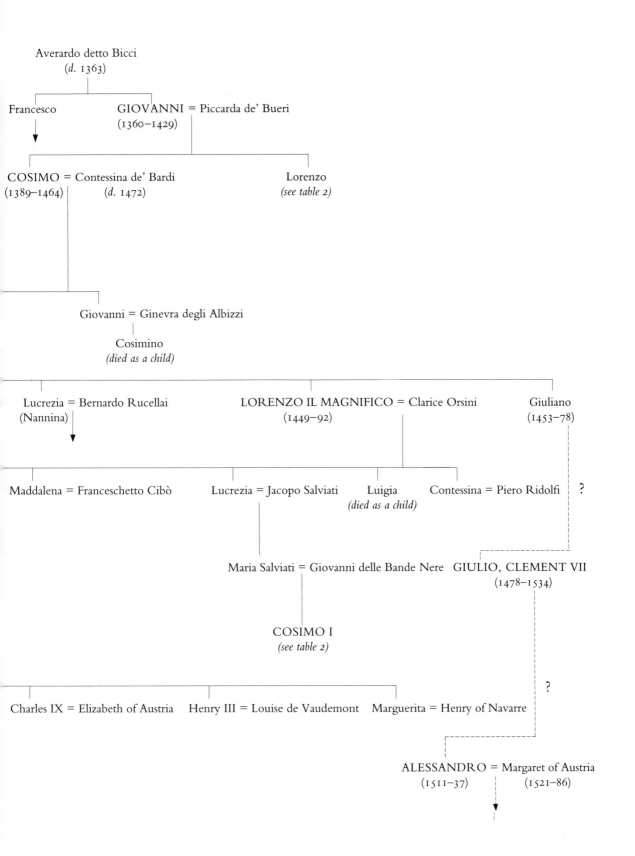

2. DESCENDANTS OF LORENZO DI GIOVANNI DI BICCI DE' MEDICI

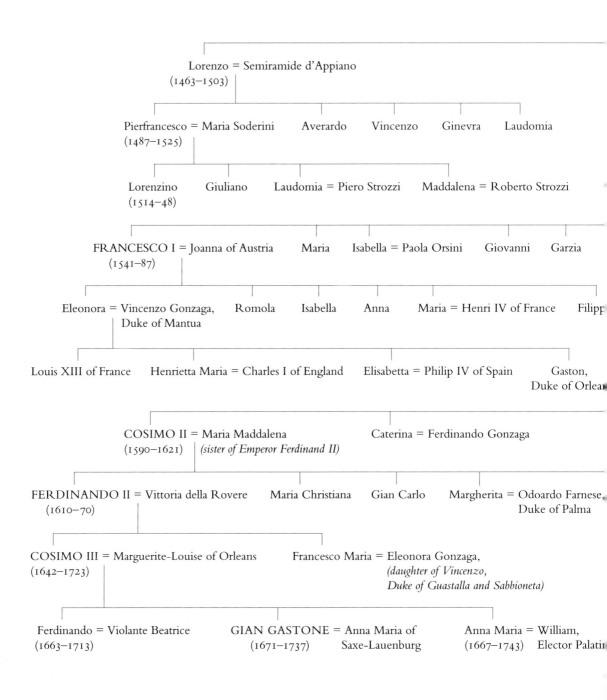

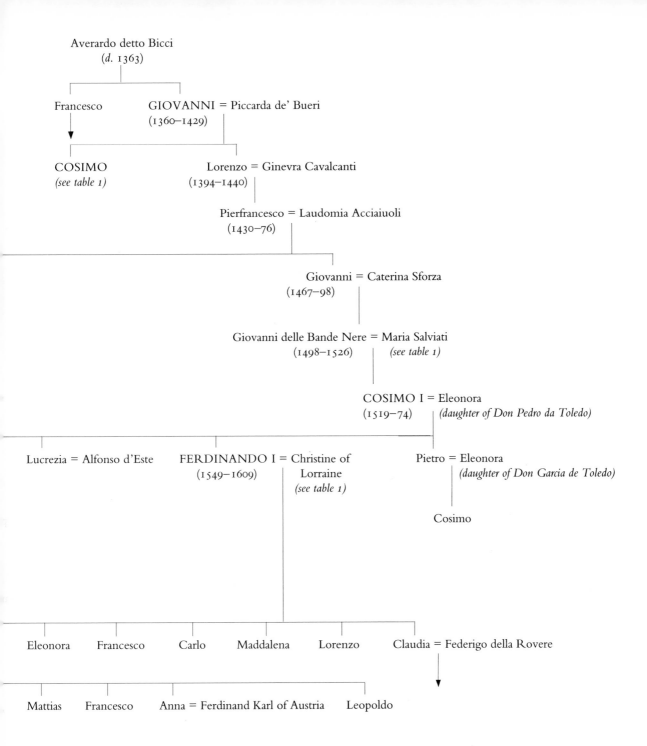

Averardo detto Bicci
(d. 1363)

Francesco   GIOVANNI = Piccarda de' Bueri
(1360–1429)

COSIMO   Lorenzo = Ginevra Cavalcanti
(see table 1)   *(1394–1440)*

Pierfrancesco = Laudomia Acciaiuoli
(1430–76)

Giovanni = Caterina Sforza
(1467–98)

Giovanni delle Bande Nere = Maria Salviati
(1498–1526)   *(see table 1)*

COSIMO I = Eleonora
(1519–74)   *(daughter of Don Pedro da Toledo)*

Lucrezia = Alfonso d'Este   FERDINANDO I = Christine of   Pietro = Eleonora
(1549–1609)   Lorraine   *(daughter of Don Garcia de Toledo)*
(see table 1)

Cosimo

Eleonora   Francesco   Carlo   Maddalena   Lorenzo   Claudia = Federigo della Rovere

Mattias   Francesco   Anna = Ferdinand Karl of Austria   Leopoldo

BIBLIOGRAPHY

Ackerman, J. S., *The Architecture of Michelango*, London, 1961

Acton, Harold, *The Last Medici*, rev. edn, London, 1958; illustrated edn, 1980

—— *Memoirs of an Aesthete*, London, 1948

—— *More Memoirs of an Aesthete*, London, 1970

—— *The Pazzi Conspiracy: The Plot against the Medici*, London, 1979

—— *Tuscan Villas*, London, 1973

Acton, Harold, and Edward Chaney, *Florence: A Travellers' Companion*, London, 1986

Acton, Harold, with photographs by Martin Hürlimann, *Florence*, London, 1960

Ady, Cecilia M., *Lorenzo dei Medici and Renaissance Italy*, London, 1955

Alberti, Leon Battista, *Della famiglia, 1434–43* (trans. Renée Watkins, *The Family in Renaissance Florence*), University of South Carolina Press, 1969

Albertini, R. von, *Firenze dalla repubblica al principato*, Turin, 1970

Allodoli, Ettore, *I Medici*, Florence, 1928

Ammirato, Scipione, *Istorie fiorentine*, Florence, 1647

Amor, Anne Clark, *William Holman Hunt: The True Pre-Raphaelite*, London, 1989

Andres, Glenn, John M. Hunisak and A. Richard Turner, *The Art of Florence*, New York, 1988

Antal, Friedrich, *Florentine Painting and its Social Background*, London, 1948

Arditi, Bastiano, *Diario di Firenze e di altre parti della Cristianità (1574–1579)*, ed. Roberto Cantagalli, Florence, 1970

Armstrong, Antonio Edward, *Lorenzo de' Medici and Florence in the Fifteenth Century*, London, 1911

Baedeker, Karl, *Handbook for Travellers: Northern Italy*, London, 1872

—— *Northern Italy*, London, 1913

Baldaccini, R., *Il Ponte Vecchio*, Florence, 1947

Barfucci, Enrico, *Lorenzo de' Medici e la società artistica del suo tempo*, Florence, 1945

Bargellini, Pietro, *La splendida storia di Firenze*, Florence, 1964

Bargellini, Simone, and Alice Scott, *Reflections on Florence*, Florence, 1984

Baron, Hans, *The Crisis of the Early Italian Renaissance*, rev. edn, Princeton, 1966

Bayley, C. C., *War and Society in Renaissance Florence*, Toronto, 1961

Becker, Marvin B., *Florence in Transition*, 2 vols., Baltimore, 1967

—— 'The Republican City State in Florence', *Speculum*, Jan. 1960, pp. 39–50

Bennett, Arnold, *Florentine Journal*, London, 1967

Berenson, Bernhard, *Italian Painters of the Renaissance*, London, 1930

—— *Rumour and Reflection: 1941–1944*, London, 1952

Bertelli, S., *Il potere oligarchico nello stata – città medievale*, Florence, 1978

Berti, Luciano, *Palazzo Davanzati*, Florence, 1958

Biagi, Guido, *The Private Life of the Renaissance Florentines*, Florence, 1896

Bini, G., and P. Bigazzi, eds., *Vita di Filippo Strozzi il vecchio scritta da Lorenzo suo figlio con documenti*, Florence, 1851

Black, Jeremy, *The British Abroad: the Grand Tour in the 18th Century*, London, 1992

Bocca, Giorgio, *Storia dell'Italia partigiano*, Bari, 1966

Bond, Derek, *Steady, Old Man*, London, 1990

Booth, Cecily, *Cosimo I, Duke of Florence*, Cambridge, 1921

Borsook, Eve, *The Companion Guide to Florence*, rev. edn, London, 1988

—— *The Mural Painters of Tuscany from Cimabue to Andrea del Sarto*, 2nd edn, Oxford, 1980

Boyer, Ferdinand, *Le Monde des arts en Italie*, Turin, 1969

Boyle, John, 5th Earl of Cork and Orrery, *Letters from Italy in the years 1754 and 1755*, London, 1773

Brandi, Karl, trans. C. V. Wedgwood, *The Emperor Charles V*, London, 1965

Braudel, Fernand, trans. Siân Reynolds, *Civilization and Capitalism: 15th–18th Century*, vol. 2, *The Wheels of Commerce*, London, 1982

Brion, Marcel, trans. Giles and Heather Cremonesi, *The Medici: A Great Florentine Family*, London, 1969

Brown, The Revd J. Wood, *Florence Past and Present*, London, 1911

Brucker, Gene, ed., *The Civic World of Early Renaissance Florence*, Princeton, 1977

—— *Firenze, 1138–1743. L'Impero del Fiorino*, Milan, 1983

—— *Florentine Politics and Society, 1348–1378*, Princeton, 1962

—— *Renaissance Florence*, Berkeley, Calif., 1983

—— *The Society of Renaissance Florence: A Documentary Study*, New York, 1971

—— *Two Memoirs of Renaissance Florence: The Diaries of Buonaccorso Pitti and Gregorio Dati*, New York, 1967

—— 'The Medici in the Fourteenth Century', *Speculum*, Jan. 1957

Bryant, William Cullen, *Letters of a Traveller, or Notes on Things Seen in Europe and America*, New York, 1850

Burckhardt, Jacob, *The Civilization of the Renaissance in Italy*, new edn, 2 vols., New York, 1958

Burke, Peter, *Culture and Society in Renaissance Italy*, London, 1972

Burnet, Gilbert, *Some Letters Containing an Account of what Seemed Most Remarkable in Travelling through Switzerland, Italy, etc.*, London, 1689

Butters, H. C., *Governors and Government in Early Renaissance Florence*, Oxford, 1985

Caggese, Romolo, *Firenze dalla decadenza di Roma al Risorgimento d'Italia*, 3 vols., Florence, 1912–21

Calamandrei, Piero, *Uomini e Città della Resistenza*, Bari, 1955

—— 'Il Ponte S. Trinita', *Il Ponte*, x, 9, September 1954

Camugliano, G. Nicolini di, *The Chronicles of a Florentine Family 1200–1400*, 1933

Cantagalli, Roberto, *La guerra di Siena*, Siena, 1962

Capodigrassi, Antonio, *Gli Inglesi in Italia*, Bari, 1949

Capponi, Gino, *Storia della Repubblica di Firenze*, 2 vols., Florence, 1875

Carden, R.W., *The Life of Giorgio Vasari*, London, 1910

Castellan, Antoine Laurent, *Letters on Italy*, London, 1820

Cavalcanti, Giovanni, *Istorie fiorentine*, 2 vols., Florence, 1839

Cavallucci, C. J., *S. Maria del Fiore*, Florence, 1881

Cellini, Benvenuto, trans. George Bull, *Autobiography*, Harmondsworth, 1956

Chabod, Federico, trans. David Moore, *Machiavelli and the Renaissance*, 1958

Chamberlin, E. R., *Everyday Life in Renaissance Times*, London, 1965

—— *The World of the Italian Renaissance*, London, 1982

Chaney, Edward, *The Grand Tour and the Great Rebellion: Richard Lassels and 'The Voyage of Italy in the Seventeenth Century'*, Geneva–Turin, 1985

—— 'Robert Dallington's *Survey of Tuscany*: A British View of Medician Florence', *Apollo*, August 1992

—— 'The Visit to Vallombrosa: A Literary Tradition', in *Milton in Italy*, ed. M. di Cesare *et al.*, Binghamton, New York, 1991

Chastel, André, *Art et humanisme à Florence au temps de Laurent le Magnifique*, Paris, 1961

Clark, Kenneth, *Another Part of the Wood: A Self-portrait*, London, 1974

Cleugh, James, *The Medici*, London, 1989

Cobbett, James P., *Journal of a Tour in Italy*, London, 1830

Cochrane, Eric, *Florence in the Forgotten Centuries*, 1527–1800, Chicago, 1973

—— 'The Florentine Background of Galileo's Work', in *Galileo Man of Science*, ed. Ernan McMullin, New York, 1967

—— *The Late Italian Renaissance*, New York, 1970

Cohn, Samuel Kline, *The Labouring Classes in Renaissance Florence*, New York, 1980

Collier, William, 'Wyndham versus Bonaparte: the Tuscan crisis of 1796–7', *Journal of Anglo-Italian Studies*, vol. II, Malta, 1992

Commines, Philip de, *The Memoirs of Philip de Commines, Lord of Argenton*, ed. Andrew R. Scobie, 2 vols., 1906

Compagni, Dino, *Cronica Fiorentina di Dino Compagni delle cose occurrenti ne' tempi suoi*, Milan, 1880

Conti, Giuseppe, *Firenze vecchia*, Florence, 1899

Cook's Handbook to Florence, London, 1924

Cooper, James Fenimore, *Gleanings in Europe*, Italy, 1838

Cordero, Franco, *Savonarola*, 4 vols., 1986–8

Cronin, Vincent, *The Florentine Renaissance*, London, 1967

Crosland, Margaret, *Louise of Stalberg: Countess of Albany*, 1962

Crutwell, Maud, *Verrocchio*, London, 1904
—— *Antonio Pollaiuolo*, London, 1907

Dallington, Sir Robert, *A Survey of the Great Duke's State of Tuscany. In the Year of Our Lorde 1596*, London, 1605
Dalzell, Charles F., *Mussolini's Enemies*, Princeton, 1961
Dami, Brunetto, *Giovanni Bicci dei Medici*, Florence, 1899
Dati, Gregorio, *Istoria di Firenze dal 1380 al 1450*, Florence, 1735
Davidsohn, Robert, *Storia di Firenze*, 8 vols., Florence, 1956–65
Davidson, Angus, *Edward Lear*, London, 1938
De Felice, Renzo, *Autobiografia del Fascismo*, Bergamo, 1978
De' Giorgi, Elsa, 'Un partigiano arriva a Firenze', *Il Ponte*, x, 9, September 1954
Deiss, Joseph Jay, *Captains of Fortune: Profiles of Six Italian Condottieri*, London, 1966
Del Lungo, Isodoro, *Florentina: Uomini e cose del Quattrocento*, Florence, 1897
—— ed., *Dino Campagni e la sua cronica*, 3 vols., Florence, 1879–80
Dentler, C. L., *Famous Foreigners in Florence*, London, 1964
Diaz, F., *Il Granducato di Toscana. I Medici*, Turin, 1976
Dickens, Charles, *Pictures from Italy*, London, 1846
Doran, John, *'Mann' and Manners at the Court of Florence*, 2 vols., 1876
Doren, Alfred, *Le arti fiorentine*, 2 vols., Florence, 1940
Dupaty, Charles Marguerite Jean Baptiste Mercier, *Travels through Italy in a series of letters written in the year 1785 by President Dupaty. Translated from the French by an Englishman*, London, 1781

Edel, Leon, *The Life of Henry James*, 3 vols., London, 1953, 1962, 1963
Einem, Herbert von, trans. Ronald Taylor, *Michelangelo*, London, 1973
Elam, Caroline, 'Lorenzo the Magnificent and the Florentine Building Boom', *Art History*, 1, 1978, pp. 43–66
—— 'Lorenzo de' Medici's Sculpture Garden', in *Mitteilungen des Kunsthistorischen Institutes in Florenz*, 1992
Ellmann, Richard, *Oscar Wilde*, London, 1987
Erickson, Carolly, *Bonnie Prince Charlie: A Biography*, New York, 1989
Eustace, John Chetwode, *A Classical Tour through Italy*, 3rd edn, London, 1815

Evans, Joan, *John Ruskin*, London, 1987
Evelyn, John, *The Diary of John Evelyn*, ed. E. S. Beer, 6 vols., Oxford, 1955

Fabroni, A., *Laurentii Medicis Vita*, 2 vols., Pisa, 1784
Fanelli, Giovanni, *Firenze: architettura e città*, Florence, 1973
Favaro, Antonio, *Galileo Galilei*, Milan, 1939
Felice, Berta, *Donne Medicee avanti il Principato*, Florence, 1904
Ferrai, Luigi Alberto, *Cosimo I de' Medici, Duca di Firenze*, 1882
Ferrara, Mario, ed., *Savonarola: prediche e scritti*, Florence, 1952
Ferrero, Guglielmo, trans. Bertha Pritchard and Lily C. Freeman, *The Gamble: Bonaparte in Italy 1796–1797*, London, 1939
Firenze e dintorni, Touring Club Italiano, Milan, 1974
Fleming, John, *Robert Adam and his Circle in Edinburgh and Rome*, 2nd edn, London, 1978
Forster, E. M., *Selected Letters of E. M. Forster*, ed. Mary Lago and P. N. Furbank, London, 1983
Forster, Margaret, *Elizabeth Barrett Browning*, London, 1988
Francovich, Carlo, *La Resistenza a Firenze*, Florence, 1961
Freedberg, Sidney, *Painting of the High Renaissance in Rome and Florence*, Cambridge, Mass., 1961
Fugier, André, *Napoléon et l'Italie*, Paris, 1947

Gadol, Joan, *Leon Battista Alberti*, Chicago, 1969
Gage, John, *Life in Italy at the Time of the Medici*, London, 1968
Gallenga, A., *Italy Revisited*, 2nd edn, 2 vols., London, 1876
Galluzzi, Riguccio, *Istoria del Granducato di Toscana sotto il governo della Casa Medici*, 7 vols., Florence, 1820–21
Gilbert, Felix, *Machiavelli and Guicciardini: Politics and History in Sixteenth-Century Florence*, Princeton, 1965
Gill, Joseph, *The Council of Florence*, Cambridge, 1959
Ginori-Conti, Piero, *La Basilica di S. Lorenzo di Firenze*, Florence, 1940
Giusti, Giuseppe, *Tutti gli scritti e cure di F. Martini*, Florence, 1943
Glendinning, Victoria, *Trollope*, London, 1992
Goethe, J. W. von, trans. W. H. Auden and E. Mayer, *Italian Journey, 1786–1788*, Harmondsworth, 1970
Goldthwaite, Richard A., *The Building of Renaissance*

Florence: An Economic and Social History, Baltimore, 1980

—— 'The Building of the Strozzi Palace: The Construction Industry in Renaissance Florence', *Studies in Medieval and Renaissance History*, 10, 1973, pp. 157–9

—— 'The Florentine Palace as Domestic Architecture', *American Historical Review*, 1972, pp. 977–1012

—— *Private Wealth in Renaissance Florence: A Study of Four Families*, Baltimore, 1968

Gombrich, E. H., 'The Early Medici as Patrons of Art: A Survey of Primary Sources', in *Italian Renaissance Studies*, ed. E. F. Jacob, New York, 1960

Guicciardini, Francesco, *Storia d'Italia*, ed. Constantino Panigada, 5 vols., Bari, 1929; English edn ed. Sidney Alexander, New York, 1969

Guidi, G., *Il governo della città–repubblica di Firenze del primo Quattrocento*, 3 vols., Florence, 1981

Gutkind, Curt S., *Cosimo de' Medici: Pater Patriae 1389–1464*, Oxford, 1938

Hale, J. R., *England and the Italian Renaissance*, London, 1954; 2nd edn, 1963

—— *Florence and the Medici: The Pattern of Control*, London, 1977

—— *Machiavelli and Renaissance Italy*, London, 1961

—— *Renaissance Fortification: Art or Engineering*, London, 1977

Hall, Michael, 'Lorenzo in his Landscape', *Country Life*, 27 August 1992

Hamilton, Olive, *The Divine Country: The British in Tuscany, 1372–1980*, London, 1982

—— *Paradise of Exiles*, London, 1974

Handbook for Travellers in Northern Italy, London, 1877

Hartt, Frederick, *Florentine Art under Fire*, Princeton, 1949

Haskell, Francis, *Patrons and Painters: A Study in the Relations between Italian Art and Society in the Age of the Baroque*, new edn, London, 1980

Hawthorne, Sophia, *Notes in England and Italy*, New York, 1869

Hay, Denys, *The Italian Renaissance in its Historical Background*, 2nd edn, London, 1977

Heriot, Angus, *The French in Italy 1796–1799*, London, 1957

Hibbard, Howard, *Michelangelo*, London, 1975

Higgins, John R., *A Historical Guide to Florence*, London, 1973

Hoby, Sir Thomas, *The Travels and Life of Sir Thomas Hoby, Knight of Bisham Abbey, written by himself, 1547–1564*, ed. Edgar Powell (Campden Society, *Miscellany*, vol. x), London, 1902

Hodgkin, Thomas, *Italy and Her Invaders*, 11 vols., Oxford, 1880

Holmes, George, 'How the Medici became the Pope's Bankers', *Renaissance Studies*, London, 1968

—— *The Florentine Enlightenment 1400–50*, London, 1969

Hook, Judith, *Lorenzo de' Medici*, London, 1984

Horner, Susan and Joanna, *Walks in Florence*, 2 vols., London, 1873

Howard, Hubert, 'Entrata a Firenze', in *Il Ponte*, x, 9, September 1954

Hutton, Edward, *Florence*, new edn, London, 1966

Hyett, Francis A., *Florence: Her History and Art to the Fall of the Republic*, London, 1903

Hyman, Isabelle, ed., *Brunelleschi in Perspective*, New Jersey, 1974

Imbert, G., *La vita fiorentina nel Seicento*, Florence, 1906

Jackson, W. G. F., *The Battle for Italy*, London, 1967

Jacob, E. F., ed., *Italian Renaissance Studies*, London, 1960

James, Henry, *Italian Hours*, London, 1909

—— *William Wetmore Story and His Friends*, 2 vols., London, 1903

Janson, H. W., *The Sculpture of Donatello*, 2 vols., Princeton, 1957

Jarvis, James Jackson, *Italian Sights and Papal Principles*, London, 1865

Jemolo, Arturo Carlo, *Chiesa e Stato in Italia negli ultimi cento anni*, Turin, 1948

Kauffman, Georg, *Florence: Art Treasures and Buildings*, London, 1971

Kent, Dale, *The Rise of the Medici: Factions in Florence, 1426–1434*, Oxford, 1978

Kent, Francis William, *Household and Lineage in Renaissance Florence: The Family Life of the Capponi, Ginori and Rucellai*, Princeton, 1977

Keysler, Johann Georg, *Travels through Germany, Bohemia, Hungary, Switzerland, Italy, etc.*, 4 vols., London, 1760

King, Francis, *Florence: A Literary Companion*, London, 1991

Kirby, P. F., *The Grand Tour 1700–1800*, New York, 1952

Knight, Cornelia, *Autobiography*, London, 1861

Krautheimer, Richard, and Trude Krautheimer-Hess, *Lorenzo Ghiberti*, Princeton, 1956

Labande, Edmond René, *Florence*, London, 1949

Landucci, Luca, *Diario fiorentino dal 1450 al 1516 di Luca Landucci continuato da un anonimo fino al 1542*, Florence, 1883; trans. Alice de Rosen Jervis, London, 1927

Lapini, Agostino, *Diario fiorentino*, Florence, 1900

Lassels, Richard, *The Voyage of Italy, etc.*, Paris, 1670

Lawrence, D. H., *Letters* (The Cambridge Edition, vol. v), London, 1991

Lees-Milne, James, *The Last Stuarts*, London, 1983

Levi, Carlo, 'Palazzo Pitti', *Il Ponte*, x, 9, September 1954

Lightbown, Ronald, *Sandro Botticelli*, London, 1978

Linklater, Eric, *The Art of Adventure*, London, 1947

—— *The Campaign in Italy*, London, 1951

Links, J. G., *Travellers in Europe*, London, 1980

Lisci, Leonardo Ginori, trans. J. Grillo, *The Palazzi of Florence: Their History and Art*, 2 vols., Florence, 1985

Lloyd, Stephen, 'The "accomplished" Maria Cosway: Anglo-Italian Artist, Musician, Salon Hostess and Educationalist (1759–1838), *Journal of Anglo-Italian Studies*, vol. II, Malta, 1992

Lopes Pegna, Mario, *Firenze dalle origini al medioevo*, Florence, 1962

Lopez, R. S., and W. R. Irving, *Medieval Trade in the Mediterranean World*, New York, 1955

Lucas, E. V., *A Wanderer in Florence*, London, 1912

Lucas-Dubreton, J., trans. A. Lytton Sells, *Daily Life in Florence in the Time of the Medici*, London, 1960

Macadam, Alta, *Blue Guide: Florence*, 5th edn, London, 1991

McCarthy, Mary, *The Stones of Florence*, New York, 1959

Machiavelli, Niccolò, trans. George Bull, *The Prince*, Harmondsworth, 1961

—— *Istorie fiorentine*, ed. Plinio Carli, 2 vols., Florence, 1927

Mack Smith, Denis, *Italy*, Ann Arbor, 1959

—— *Italy and Its Monarchy*, New Haven, 1989

—— *The Making of Italy*, New York, 1968

MacLeod, Joseph, *People of Florence: A Study in Locality*, London, 1968

Maguire, Yvonne, *The Women of the Medici*, London, 1927

Manetti, Antonio di Tuccio, trans. Catherine Enggass, *The Life of Brunelleschi*, ed. Howard Saalman, 1970

Marquand, Allan, *Andrea della Robbia and His Atelier*, Princeton, 1922

Martin, George, *Red Shirt and the Cross of Savoy*, London, 1970

Martinelli, Giuseppe, *Tutto su Firenze rinascimentale*, 1968; English trans., *The World of Renaissance Florence*, 1968

Martines, Lauro, ed., *Lawyers and Statecraft in Renaissance Florence*, Princeton, 1968

—— *The Social World of the Florentine Humanists*, Princeton, 1963

—— *Violence and Disorder in Italian Cities*, Berkeley, Calif., 1972

Matthews, Herbert L., *The Fruits of Fascism*, New York, 1943

Mattingly, Garrett, *Renaissance Diplomacy*, London, 1955

Mead, William Edward, *The Grand Tour in the Eighteenth Century*, New York, 1914

Medici, Lorenzo de', *Lettere*, ed. Riccardo Fubini, Nicolai Rubinstein and Michael Mallett, 6 vols., Florence, 1980–91

Mendelssohn-Bartholdy, Felix, trans. Lady Wallace, *Letters from Italy and Switzerland*, London, 1865

Michelangelo, *Le lettere di Michelangelo*, ed. Gaetano Milanesi, Florence, 1875

Miller, Betty, *Robert Browning: A Portrait*, London, 1952

Minor, Andrew C., and Bonner Mitchell, *A Renaissance Entertainment: Festivities for the Marriage of Cosimo I*, University of Missouri Press, 1968

Mobili, Vitelleschi, Marchesa, *A Court in Exile*, 2 vols., 1903

Moloney, Brian, *Florence and England: Essays on Cultural Relations in the Second Half of the Eighteenth Century*, Florence, 1969

Moore, John, *A View of Society and Manners in Italy*, 6th edn, 2 vols., London, 1795

Morassi, Antonio, *Il tesoro dei Medici*, Milan, 1963

Morgan, Lady Sydney, *Italy*, 2 vols., London, 1821

Moryson, Fynes, *An Itinerary Containing his Ten Yeeres Travell*, London, 1617

Murray, Linda, *Michelangelo*, London, 1980

Murray, Peter, *The Architecture of the Italian Renaissance*, London, 1969

Murray, Peter and Linda, *The Art of the Renaissance*, London, 1963

Napier, Henry Edward, *Florentine History from the Earliest Authentic Records to the Accession of Ferdinand the Third, Grand Duke of Tuscany*, 6 vols., London, 1846–7

Nardi, Jacopo, *Istorie della città di Firenze dall'anno 1494 fino al 1531*, 2 vols., Florence, 1858

Nencini, Franco, *Firenze: I giorni del diluvio*, Florence, 1966; English trans., *Florence: The Days of the Flood*, London, 1967

Noakes, Vivien, *Edward Lear: The Life of a Wanderer*, new edn, London, 1985

Nugent, Mr (Sir Thomas), *The Grand Tour, Containing an Exact Description of Most of the Cities, Towns and Remarkable Places of Europe*, 4 vols., London, 1749

Olson, Stanley, *John Singer Sargent: His Portrait*, London, 1986

Origo, Iris, *The Merchant of Prato*, London, 1957

—— 'The Domestic Enemy: The Eastern Slaves in Tuscany in the 14th and 15th centuries', *Speculum*, 1955, pp. 21–66

Ottokar, N., *Il Comune di Firenze alla fine del Dugento*, Florence, 1926

—— *Studi comunale e fiorentini*, Florence, 1948

Pampaloni, Guido, *Firenze al tempo di Dante: Documenti sull'urbanistica fiorentina*, Rome, 1973

—— *Palazzo Strozzi*, Rome, 1963

Panella, Antonio, *Storia di Firenze*, Florence, 1949

Pater, Walter, *Studies in the History of the Renaissance*, London, 1873

Patrizi, P., *Giambologna*, Milan, 1905

Paul, Jürgen, *Der Palazzo Vecchio*, Florence, 1969

Pellegrini, Carlo, *La Contessa d'Albany e il salotto del Lungarno*, 1951

Perrens, F. T., *Histoire de Florence*, 6 vols., Paris, 1877–83

Pesci, Ugo, *Firenze capitale*, Milan, 1904

Phillips, Mark, *The Memoir of Marco Parenti: A Life in Medici Florence*, London, 1989

Piozzi, Hester Lynch, *Observations and Reflections Made in the Course of a Journey through France, Italy and Germany*, 2 vols., London, 1789

Plumb, J. H., ed., *The Horizon Book of the Renaissance*, London, 1961

Polidori Calamandrei, E., *Le vesti delle donne fiorentine nel Quattrocento*, Florence, 1924

Pope-Hennessy, John, *Fra Angelico*, rev. edn, London, 1974

—— *Italian Gothic Sculpture*, rev. edn, London, 1972

—— *Italian High Renaissance and Baroque Sculpture*, rev. edn, London, 1970

—— *Italian Renaissance Sculpture*, revised edn, London, 1971

—— *Learning to Look*, London, 1991

—— *Luca della Robbia*, London, 1980

—— *Paolo Uccello*, revised edn, London, 1972

Pottinger, George, *The Court of the Medici*, London, 1978

Pottle, Frederick, *James Boswell: The Earlier Years, 1740–1769*, London, 1966

Pottle, Frederick A., and Frank Brady, eds., *Boswell on the Grand Tour: Italy, Corsica and France*, London, 1955

Prescott, Orville, *Princes of the Renaissance*, New York, 1970

Pucci, Eugenio, *Il diluvio su Firenze*, Firenze, 1966

Querci, Giorgio, 'Firenze alla guerra', *Il Ponte*, x, 9, September 1954

Randolph, G., *Florentine Merchants in the Age of the Medici*, London, 1932

Reresby, Sir John, *Travels and Memoirs*, London, 1813

Richards, Gertrude R. B., *Florentine Merchants in the Age of the Medici*, Cambridge, Mass., 1932

Ridolfi, Roberto, trans. Cecil Grayson, *The Life of Francesco Guicciardini*, London, 1967

—— *The Life of Girolamo Savonarola*, London, 1959

—— *The Life of Niccolò Machiavelli*, London, 1959

Rodolico, N., *I Ciompi*, Florence, 1945

Rogers, Samuel, *The Italian Journal*, ed. J. R. Hale, London, 1956

Roover, Raymond de, *The Rise and Decline of the Medici Bank 1397–1494*, Cambridge, Mass., 1963

Roscoe, William, *The Life of Lorenzo de' Medici Called the Magnificent*, London, 1851

Rosi, Michele, *L'Italia odierna*, 4 vols., Turin, 1942

Ross, Janet, *Florentine Palaces and Their Stories*, London, 1905

—— *Italian Sketches*, London, 1887

—— *Old Florence and Modern Tuscany*, London, 1904

—— ed. and trans., *Lives of the Early Medici as Told in their Correspondence*, London, 1910

Roth, Cecil, *The Last Florentine Republic (1527–1530)*, London, 1925

Rubinstein, Nicolai, *The Government of Florence under the Medici 1434–1494*, Oxford, 1968

—— 'Cradle of the Renaissance: The Beginnings of Humanism in Florence', in *Age of the Renaissance*, ed. Denys Hay, London, 1986

—— ed., *Florentine Studies: Politics and Society in Renaissance Florence*, London, 1968

Ruskin, John, *The Diaries of John Ruskin*, ed. Joan Evans and J. H. Whitehouse, 3 vols., London, 1956–9

—— *Mornings in Florence: Being Simple Studies of Christian Art for English Travellers*, Orpington, 1875–7

Salvatorelli, Luigi, and Giovanni Mira, *Storia d'Italia nel periodo fascisto*, 2 vols., Milan, 1972

Salvemini, Gaetano, *Magnati e popolani in Firenze dal 1280 al 1292*, Turin, 1960

Sandberg-Vavalà, Evelyn, *Studies in the Florentine Churches*, Florence, 1959

Santi, Bruno, *Botticelli*, Florence, 1991

Sapori, Armando, *Le Marchand italien au moyen âge*, Paris, 1952

Scaife, Walter, *Florentine Life during the Renaissance*, Baltimore, 1893

Schevill, Ferdinand, *History of Florence from the Founding of the City through the Renaissance*, London, 1937

—— *The Medici*, New York, 1949

Segni, Bernardo, *Istorie fiorentine dell'anno 1527 al 1555*, Florence, 1857

Shapiro, Harold I., *Ruskin in Italy*, London, 1972

Sharp, Samuel, *Letters from Italy*, London, 1766

Sharp, William, *The Life and Letters of Joseph Severn*, London, 1892

Sinibaldi, Giulia, *Il Palazzo Vecchio di Firenze*, Rome, 1950

Sismondi, J. C. L. Simonde de, *Histoire des républiques Italiens du moyen âge*, 16 vols., Paris, 1809–18

Sitwell, Osbert, *Great Morning*, London, 1948

Smollett, Tobias, *Travels through France and Italy*, 2 vols., London, 1766

Spadolini, Giovanni, *Firenze mille anni*, Florence, 1984

—— *Firenze capitale*, Florence, 1979

Spence, Joseph, *Letters from the Grand Tour*, ed. Slava Klima, London, 1975

Spini, Giorgio, *Architettura e politica da Cosimo I e Ferdinando I*, Florence, 1976

—— *Cosimo I de' Medici e la indipendenza del Principato Mediceo*, Florence, 1945

Spini, Giorgio, and Antonio Casali, *Firenze*, Bari, 1986

Sprigge, Cecil, 'Agosto 1944', *Il Ponte*, x, 9, September 1954

Sprigge, Sylvia, *Berenson*, London, 1960

Stace, Christopher, *Florence: City of the Lily*, London, 1989

Stendhal (Henri Beyle), ed. and trans. Robert Sage, *The Private Diaries of Stendhal*, London, 1955

Strong, Roy, *Splendour at Court: Renaissance Spectacle and Illusion*, London, 1973

Strozzi, Lorenzo, *Vita di Filippo di Matteo Strozzi*, ed. G. Bini and P. Bigazzi, Florence, 1851

Symonds, John Addington, *The Renaissance in Italy 1875–86*, 6 vols., London, 1875–86

Sznura, Franek, *L'espansione urbana di Firenze nel Dugento*, Florence, 1975

Taine, Hippolyte, trans. J. Durand, *Italy*, 4th edn, New York, 1875

—— *Voyage en Italie*, Paris, 1874

Taylor, K. K., *Ordeal by Water*, London, 1967

Thomas, Donald, *Robert Browning: A Life within a Life*, London, 1982

Thomas, Dylan, *Collected Letters*, ed. Paul Ferris, London, 1985

Tolnay, Charles de, *Michelangelo*, Princeton, 1943–60

Tomalin, Claire, *The Invisible Woman: The Story of Nelly Ternan and Charles Dickens*, London, 1990

Treves, Giuliana Artom, *Anglo-Fiorentini di cento anni fa*, Florence, 1953

Trexler, R., *Public Life in Renaissance Florence*, New York, 1980

Trollope, Thomas Adolphus, *A History of the Commonwealth of Florence*, 4 vols., London, 1865

—— *What I Remember*, London, 1887

Troubridge, Lady Una, *The Life and Death of Radclyffe Hall*, London, 1961

Turner, A. Richard, *see* Andres

Tutaev, David, *Consul of Florence*, London, 1966

Twain, Mark, *Innocents Abroad*, Hartford, Connecticut, 1870

Twilight of the Medici: Late Baroque Art in Florence, 1640–1743, Detroit, 1974

Vannucci, Marcello, trans. Charles Lambert, *Storia di Firenze*, Rome, 1988

Varchi, Benedetto, *Storia fiorentina*, new edn, Florence, 1963

Vasari, Giorgio, *Le vite dei più eccellenti pittori, scultori ed architetti*, 9 vols., Florence, 1906; trans. George Bull, *The Lives of the Artists*, Harmondsworth, 1965 (first edition 1550)

Vaussard, Maurice, *La Vie quotidienne en Italie au XVIIIe siècle*, Paris, 1959; trans. Michael Heron, London, 1962

Vavala, Evelyn Sandberg, *Uffizi Studies: The Development of the Florentine School of Painting*, London, 1948

Vespasiano da Bisticci, *Vite di uomini illustri*, ed. P. D'Ancona and E. Aeschlimann, Milan, 1959

Villani, Giovanni, *Cronica fiorentina*, 8 vols., Florence, 1823

—— trans. Rose E. Selfe, *Villani's Chronicle, being selections from the first nine books of the Cronica fiorentina*, 1906

Villani, Matteo, *Cronica di Matteo Villani*, ed. Dragomanni, 2 vols., Florence, 1846

Villari, Pasquale, *I primi due secoli della storia di Firenze*, 2 vols., Florence, 1893–4

—— trans. Linda Villari, *Life and Times of Girolamo Savonarola*, 2 vols., London, 1888

Waley, Daniel, *Italian City Republics*, London, 1988

Walpole, Horace, *Correspondence*, ed. W. S. Lewis (Yale Edition), 34 vols., London, 1937–65

Waterfield, Lina, *Castle in Italy*, London, 1961

Weinstein, Donald, *Savonarola and Florence: Prophecy and Patriotism in the Renaissance*, Princeton, 1971

—— 'Savonarola: Preacher and Patriot?', *History Today*, November 1989, pp. 30–36

Weiss, Roberto, *The Renaissance Discovery of Classical Antiquity*, Oxford, 1969

Weissman, Ronald F. E., *Ritual Brotherhood in Renaissance Florence*, New York, 1982

Wilde, Oscar, *The Letters of Oscar Wilde*, ed. Rupert Hart-Davis, London, 1962

Wotton, Sir Henry, *The Life and Letters of Sir Henry Wotton*, ed. Logan Pearsall Smith, 2 vols., Oxford, 1907

Wright, Edward, *Some Observations Made in Travelling through France and Italy, etc., in the Years 1720, 1721 and 1722*, 2nd edn, London, 1764

Young, Arthur, *Travels in France and Italy during the Years 1787, 1788 and 1789*, ed. T. Okey, London, 1915

Young, G. F., *The Medici*, 2 vols., London, 1911

Casino Mediceo, Via Cavour, the site of the Medici Garden

INDEX

Page numbers in italic refer to illustrations.
Page numbers in bold type refer to Notes on Buildings and Works of Art.

Accademie:
di Belle Arti, 221, 269, **363**; del Cimento, 194, **359–60**; della Crusca, 188, 214, 221, 354, **357**; del Disegno, 188, 221, **357**; Fiorentina, 221, **363**; Galleria dell'Accademia, 253, 281, 352; dei Georgofili, 221
Acciaiuoli, Agnolo, 83, 99, 110
Acciaiuoli family, 42, 61, 328, 369
Acton, Arthur, 369
Acton, Sir Harold (b. 1904), 284, 290, 291, 294, 335
Acton, Hortense, 294
Adam, Robert (1791–1875), 212, 216
Aistulf, King of the Lombards (d. 756), 6
Albany, Louisa, Countess of (1753–1824), 218, 219, 232, 233–4; monument, **365**
Albergo Aquila Nera, **361**
Albert, Prince Consort (1819–61), 272
Alberti, Leon Battista (1404–72): Cappella Rucellai, 345; and Fancelli, 107; Loggia dei Rucellai, 368; monument, 323, 359; Palazzo Rucellai, 106; polymath, 105–6; S. Maria Novella, 105, 323; and his wife, 111
Alberti family, 14, 80; emblem, 105
Albizzi, Antonfrancesco degli, 167
Albizzi, Maso degli (1347–1417), 72, 73
Albizzi, Rinaldo di Messer Maso degli (1370–1442), 73, 83, 84
Albizzi family: banking, 25; and Cosimo *Pater Patriae*, 83; exiled, 84; government, 73; Ospedale degli Innocenti, 339; palaces, 340; *priori*, 42, 72–3
Aldington, Richard (1892–1962), 291
Alexander, Francesca, 369
Alexander, Francis (1800–1881), 369
Alexander III, Pope (r. 1159–81), 16, *16*
Alexander V, Pope (r. 1409–10), 82
Alexander VI, Pope (r. 1492–1503), 158, 159, 165
Alexander of Tunis, 1st Earl (1891–1969), 302

Alfieri, Vittorio (1749–1803), 218–19, 232–3, **364–5**
Alfonso I, King of Naples (1385–1458), 98, 99
Alfonso II, King of Naples (1448–95), 158
Allori, Alessandro (1535–1607), 189; altarpiece, 341; frescoes, 347, 352; *St Peter on the Waters*, 318; work in S. Maria Novella, 323, 324 *bis*
Altoviti, Oddo, 350
Ambrogio, Giovanni, 332
Ambrogio, Lorenzo d', 328
Ambrogio di Baldese (1352–1429), 354
Ambrose, St (*c.* 339–97), 6
Amicis, Edmondo de (1846–1908), 254
Ammannati, Bartolommeo (1511–92): Biblioteca Laurenziana, 352; Grotta Grande, 354; Neptune Fountain, 184; Pitti Palace, 347; Ponte S. Trinita, 320; S. Giovannino degli Scolopi, 341; S. Michele Visdomini, 360; windows, 348
Andrea di Bonaiuto (*fl.* 1343–77), 324
Andrea del Sarto (1486–1530): *Disputà*, 340; *Flight into Egypt*, 334; frescoes, 334, 347; Grand Prince Ferdinando and, 201; *Last Supper*, 327; *sgraffito* work, 366; tomb, 334; Vasari and, 187, west front of Duomo, 169
Angelico, Fra (1387–1455), 74, 95–6, 327, 351
Anna Maria, Electress Palatine (1667–1743), *203*, 204–5, 325
Anna Maria, Grand Duchess, 202
Annigoni, Pietro (1910–88), 338, 353
Antinori family, 315–16
Appiani, Andrea the Elder (1754–1817): portrait of Napoleon, *231*
Archivio di Stato, 221, 363
Aretino, Spinello (*fl.* 1373–1410), 16, 314
Arezzo, 73, 229
Arno, River: *Argonautica*, 192; bridged, 3; bridges repaired, 49; in flood, 43, 245, 305; naumachias, 127; Pazzi's corpse, 135;

Peter Leopold travels on, 225; representation of hell, 46
Arnoldi, Alberto (d. 1377), 330, 338, 353
Arnolfo di Cambio (*c.* 1245–1302), 48, 322, 328, 331
Arte della Lana, 62, 74, 79, 343
Arte di Calimala, 43, 49, 316, 343
Arte del Cambio, 74, 89, 343
Arte della Seta, 186, 317, 339
arti: ciompi riots, 68–9; government, 28, 30, 41, 64; guilds for labouring classes, 62; history, 42; membership, 27–8, 42; merchants and nobles, 14; militia, 28, 30; oligarchy, 28; Ordinances of Justice, 30, 31; Orsanmichele statues, 343; situation of, 27; statutes and penalties, 62–3
Athens, Duke of, *see* Brienne, Count Gaultiero di
Attila, King of the Huns (*fl.* 5th century AD), 5
Austin, Alfred (1835–1913), 263
Austria: and Florence, 220, 238, 241; Florentine works of art removed to, 205, 206–7; Leopold II and, 245; Risorgimento, 244, 245, 246, 256; war with France and Piedmont, 248
Azeglio, Massimo d' (1798–1866), 234

Baccani, Gaetano (1792–1867), 365
Baccio d'Agnolo (1462–1543): campanile, 314; *palazzi*, 341, 348, 364 *bis*; palazzo façade, 340–41; pavement, 328
Badoglio, Pietro (1871–1956), 296
Baedeker, Karl (1801–59), *Italy: Handbook for Travellers*, 279–81
Baglioni, Malatesta, 173, 174
Balbo, Italo (1896–1940), 286, 287
Baldesi family, 323
Baldovinetti, Alesso (1425–99): *Annunciation*, 314; frescoes, 318, 334, 340; *Nativity*, 328; *Sacra Conversazione*, 342
Bandinelli, Baccio (1493–1560): Cellini and, 354; Grotta Grande, 354; *Hercules*

and Cacus, 331, **354**; *Pietà*, 334; statues, 323, 332, 337; Vasari and, 187; works in Duomo, 329

Bandini, Giovanni (1540–99), 329, 330, 356, 357

banking, 24–5; Anglo-Italian Bank, 253; general disintegration, 141; Medici, 74, 80, 82, 139, 141, 149; Mercato Nuovo, 355; Pazzi, 131; Peruzzi, 42, 363; training in, 25

Baptistery, **316–17**; Dante baptized, 35; East Doors, 76, *77*, *78*, 78, **337**; effigy of John XXIII, 94; mosaics, 49; North Doors, 76, **336–7**; St John the Baptist's Day, 127; South Doors, 335

Barbadori, Niccolò, 84

Barbieri, Alessandro del, 359

Bardi family, 25, 61, 82, 83

Bardini, Stefano, 278, 340

Barducci, Aligi (d. 1944), 302

Barga, Piero Angelio de, 189

Bargellini, Piero, 312

Bargello, 20 *bis*, **325**; Bertoldo's reliefs, 143; Botticelli's murals, 135; bust of Niccolò da Uzzano, 71, *72*; Cellini's bust of Cosimo I, 182; Donatello's *David*, *94*; executions in courtyard, 135; flood, 311; *Hercules and Antaeus*, 118; painting on chest, *52*; detail from *Paradise*, *37*; Savonarola tortured, *161*; severed heads, 200; World War II, 303

Baroncelli, Bernardo Bandini (d. 1478), 133, 135

Baroni, Nero, 369

Barré, Isaac (1726–1802), 208

Barrès, Maurice (1862–1923), 268

Bartolini, Lorenzo (1777–1850), 323, 359

Bartolommeo, Ferdinando, 248

Bartolommeo, Fra (1475–1517), 157, 344, 351 *bis*

Battiferri, Laura, 341

battles:
  Agnadello (1510), 166; Altopascio (1325), 41; Anghiari (1440), 71, 158; Austerlitz (1805), 231; Campaldino (1289), 30, 31, 36; Legnano (1176), 16; Leipzig (1813), 231; Lepanto (1571), 181; Marengo (1800), 230; Montaperti (1260), 21–2, 41; Montecatini (1315), 40; Montemurlo (1537), 180; Novara (1849), 244; of the Risorgimento, 166; River Ronco (1512), 166; River Taro (1495), 158

Bazzani, Cesare, 369

Beatrice Portari (d. 1290), 36, 79

Beauchamp, Viscount, *later* 2nd Marquess of Hertford (1743–1822), 208

Beccafumi, Domenico (1485–1551), 365

Becchi, Gentile, 141, *142*

Becciolini, Giulio (d. 1924), 287

Beerbohm, Sir Max (1872–1956), 288

Bella, Giano della (d. *c.* 1305), 28, 30, 31

Bellano, Bartolommeo (*c.* 1440–96), 344

Bellosguardo, 265, 268, 270–71, 291, **367**

Bencivenni, Giuseppe Pelli, 221

Benedetto da Maiano (1442–97): *Madonna* relief, 340; Michelangelo and, 144; Palazzo Pazzi, 346; Palazzo Strozzi lamps, 342; pulpits, 322, 365; Strozzi tomb, 345; works in Duomo, 328, 329; works in Misericordia, 353; works in Signoria, 332

Bennett, Arnold (1867–1931), 281–4, *282*

Bentivoglio, Giovanni II, Lord of Bologna (1443–1508), 137

Berardi, Piero, 361, 369

Berenson, Bernhard (1865–1959), 290, 296, 368

Bernardino of Siena, St (1380–1444), 112

Berta, Giovan Francesco (d. 1920), 286

Berti, Antonio, 365

Bertie, Hon. Peregrine, 209

Bertoldo di Giovanni (*c.* 1440–91), 143, 344

Biblioteche:
  Laurenziana, 173, 221, **342–3**, 352, 363; Magliabechiana, 221, 363; Nazionale, 257, 293, 308, *309*, **363**, **369**; Riccardiana, 221, **363**

Biliverti, Giovanni (1576–1644), 316

Bisticci, Vespasiano da: bookshop, 79, 147; Duomo celebrations, 91; and Lorenzo the Magnificent, 142; and Luca Pitti, 84; on women's duty, 111

Blagden, Isa (d. 1873), 268, 367

Blessington, Countess of (1789–1849), 234, *235*, 236

Blessington, 1st Earl of (1782–1829), 236

Boboli Gardens, **354–5**; Boswell, 214; Brownings, 264; Eleonora di Toledo and, 185; entertainments, 194; Evelyn on, 197; Ferdinand I's wedding celebrations, 189, 190; Florence by night from, *312*; foreign visitors, 194, 215; *Guardia* parades, 241; improvements, 190; Leopold II's fiesta, 240; Mussolini and Hitler, 292; Napoleon, 227; Peter Leopold's parties, 223; stone quarry, 104, 107, 304; Victor Emmanuel II, 252

Boccaccio, Giovanni (1313–75), 59, 102, 369; on Dante, 35; *Decameron*, 345; petits bourgeois and government, 64; on plague, 59

Bodley, G.A., 368

Boldini, Giovanni, 256

Bonaiuto, Andrea di (*fl. c.* 1337–77), 45

Bonaparte, Caroline, Queen of Naples (1782–1839), 234

Bonaparte, Jérôme, King of Westphalia (1784–1860), 231

Bonaparte, Joseph, King of Spain (1768–1844), 231

Bonaparte, Louis, King of Holland (1778–1846), 231, 364

Bonaparte, Napoleon, *see* Napoleon

Bond, Derek, 303–4

Boniface VIII, Pope (r. 1294–1303), 33, 34

Borghese, Prince Camillo (1775–1832), 234, 365

Borghese, Prince Valerio, 297

Borghi:
  degli Albizzi, 316, **336**; Pinti, 191, 193, **358**; S. Croce, 281; SS. Apostoli, 260, **340**

Borghini, Vincenzo (1515–80), 357

Boswell, James (1740–95), 208, 214

Botta-Adorno, Antonio, Marquis (1688–1774), 206, 220

Botticelli, Sandro (1444–1510): brother Antonio, 349; Cathedral façade, 146; history, 118, 164; Lorenzo the Magnificent, 143; Pazzi conspiracy, 135; Piero de' Medici and, 120; Pollaiuolo brothers influence, 118; Savonarola and, 149, 157; standard, 125; tomb, 333
  Adoration of the Magi, 111, *111*, 118, 119, *119*; *Birth of Venus*, 119, 349, 357; *Fortitude*, 118; *Lady in a Brown Dress*, 119, 349; *Madonna of the Magnificat*, 119, 349; *Nativity*, 323; *Pallas and the Centaur*, 357; *Primavera*, 119, 349, 357; *St Augustine*, 118, 333; *Young Man with a Medal*, 119

Braccio da Montone (1368–1424), 70

Bracciolini, Poggio, 79–80, 329

Brancacci family, 334

Brandini, Ciuto, 63

Brentano, Franz (1838–1917), 367

Brienne, Count Gaultiero di, Duke of Athens (d. 1356), 61

British Institute of Florence, 288, 368

Bronzino, Il (1503–72): altarpiece, 323; *Deposition*, 323; Eleonora di Toledo's chapel, 354; fresco, 338; Medici portraits, 358; portrait of Cosimo I, 357; portrait of Eleonora di Toledo, *183*, 357; portrait of Giovanni di Bicci de' Medici, 74, *75*; portrait of Laura Battiferri, 332; portrait of Piero di Lorenzo de' Medici, *148*; S. Felicita roundels, **317**

Brosses, Charles de (1709–77), 205, 217

Brown, Charles Armitage (1786–1842), 260

Browning, Elizabeth Barrett (1806–61), 262, 263–5, 366, 367, 368

Browning, Pen (b. 1849), 265

Browning, Robert (1812–89), 262, 263–5, 366, 368; drawing-room, *264*

Brunelleschi, Betto de', 43

Brunelleschi, Filippo (1377–1446), *90*; Baptistery north doors, 76; bust of, 328; Capponi Chapel, 317; Cathedral dome, 89–91, 328; crucifix, 347; Donatello and, 347; and Ghiberti, 90–91; influenced by architecture of S. Miniato, 314; Old Sacristy, 337; Ospedale degli Innocenti,

79, 339; Palazzo di Parte Guelfa, 325, 326; Pazzi chapel, 106, 132, 133, 346; *pietra serena*, 104; pulpit, 324; S. Lorenzo, 79, 84, 86, 337; S. Spirito, 321; temperament, 76, 86; tomb of, 328

Bruni, Leonardo (1369–1444), 79, 323, 365

Buggiano (1412–62), 78, *90*, 324, 328

Buglioni, Benedetto (1461–1521), 340

Buglioni, Santi, 358

building: city walls and watch-towers, 17; in Florence after unification, 252; inns built and enlarged, 210; palaces, 102–7 *passim*; redevelopment of city, 258; stone towers, 13–14

Bülow, Hans von (1830–94), 367

Buondelmonti, Andrea, Archbishop of Florence, 181

Buondelmonti family, 18–19

Buontalenti, Bernardo (1531–1608): altar steps, 326; Castelo garden, 357; cupboard, 324; Forte di Belvedere, 191, 358; Grotta Grande, 354; *palazzi*, 335, 362, 365; Porta delle Suppliche, 356; S. Maria Nuova hospital, 339; S. Trinita façade, 318; theatrical settings, 190; Tribuna, 189; Uffizi, 188; villas, 357, 366

Burghersh, Lady Priscilla, *later* Countess of Westmorland (1793–1879), 236

Burghersh, Lord, *later* 11th Earl of Westmorland (1784–1859), 234, 236

Burnet, Gilbert (1643–1715), 200

Bute, 3rd Earl of (1713–92), 210

Buti, Lucrezia, 95

Butteri, Giovanni Maria (*c.* 1540–1606), *The Return from the Palio*, *126*

Byron, 6th Baron (1788–1824), 236, 239

Caccini, Giovanni Battista (1559/62–1613), 355, 358, 365

Caccini, Giulio (1550–1618), 190, 321, 334, 336

Cacialli, Giuseppe (1770–1828), 365

Cadorna, Raffaele, 254, 256

Cadorna, Raymond de, 166

cafés
    Antico Fattori, 257; del Bottegone, 233; Casino dei Nobili, 245; Castelmur, 216; Doney's, 245, 251, 255, 284, **366**; Gambrinus, **366**; Giubbe Rosse, 257, **366**; Kaffeehaus, 227, 301, 355, 364; Michelangiolo, 255, 257; Paroni's, 216

Calabria, Duchess of, *neé* Ippolita Sforza, 138

Calabria, Duke of (d. 1328), 41

Calabria, Duke of, *later* Alfonso II, King of Naples, *q.v.* (1448–95), 136, 137, 139, 145

Calamandrei, Piero, 287

Cambi, Ulisse (1807–95), 345

Campagnia di Santa Maria del Bigallo, **354**

Campana, Francesca, 180

Campanile, 274, 303, **330**; Giotto, 48; Pisano's bas-reliefs, 28, *29*

Campo di Marte, Stadio Comunale, 293, **369**

Canova, Antonio (1757–1822), 233, 336; monument to Alfieri, **364–5**

Cappella Rucellai, **345**

Cappella di S. Sepolcro, **345**

Cappello, Bianca, 188, 346, 347, 361

Capponi, Gino (early 15th century), 72, 73

Capponi, Gino, Marchese (1792–1876), 239, 251

Capponi, Neri, 99, 336

Capponi, Niccolò, 171, 173

Capponi, Piero de Gino (1447–96), 155, 171

Capponi family, 317, 321, 336, 369

Carafa, Diomede, 138

Cardona, Raymond of, 41

Carducci, Francesco, 173

Carducci, Giosuè (1835–1907), 255

Carità, Mario, 296, 297

Carlo Ludovico (Louis II), King of Etruria (1799–1849), 230

Casanova, Giacomo (1725–98), 278

Cascine, the, 215, 261, **362**; Accademia Aeronautica, 293; Alfieri, 232; Austrians' ceremonial parade, 245; executions of Resistance, 298; Grand Duchess Elisa, 231; flood, 305; Hippodrome, 252; restaurant, 222; Smollett, 212–13; Young Pretender, 218

Case:
    Ambrogi, 210, **362**; di Andrea del Sarto, **358**; Boccaccio, 290, **369**; Buonarroti, 311, **357**; Ghenini, 272; Guidi, 264, **367**

Casentino, Jacopo del (*c.* 1300–1349), 326

Cassidi, Giuseppe (1865–1942), 365

Castagno, Andrea del (*c.* 1419–57), 59, 328, 334, 340

Castello Montegufoni, 295, 299–300, **369**

Castello di Vincigliata, 255, **366**

Castruccio Castracani degli Antelminelli, Duke of Lucca, (1281–1328), 40, 41

Cattaneo, Simonetta, 119

Cavalcanti, Guido (*c.* 1250–1300), 32, 36

Cavalcanti family, 83, 351

Cavour, Count Camillo (1810–61), 244, 246, 247–8

Cellini, Benvenuto (1500–1571): and Bandinelli, 354; bust of, 319–20; bust of Cosimo I, 182; home, 359; *Perseus*, 182, 332, 359; personality, 179; tomb of, 334

Cempini, Francesco, 239

Cennini, Bernardo (1415–*c.* 1498), 147

Ceraiuolo, Antonio del, 318

Cerchi, Ricoverino de', 33

Cerchi, Vieri de' (*fl.* 1300), 31–2, 33

Cerchi family: Boniface VIII and, 33; and Donati, 31, 32, 33; mercantile house, 43; provenance, 354; Whites, 33, 34, 36

ceremonies: consecration of dome, 92; Lent, 199–200; *Scoppio del Carro*, 132

Chalcondyles, Demetrius (1424–1511), 146

Champollion, Jean François (1790–1832), 239, 365

Charlemagne, Emperor (*c.* 742–814), 6, 67

Charles V, Holy Roman Emperor (Charles I, King of Spain; 1500–1558), 171, 172, 176, 347

Charles VI, Holy Roman Emperor (1685–1740), 204

Charles VIII, King of France (1470–98), 149, 152–5 *passim*, 160

Charles of Anjou, King of Sicily (1226–85), 22, 23, 26

Charles of Lorraine, Prince, 197

Charles of Valois (1270–1325), 33, 34, 36

Charles Albert, King of Sardinia-Piedmont (1798–1849), 236, 243, 244

Charles Edward Stuart, Prince, the Young Pretender (1720–88), 218, 219

Chateaubriand, Vicomte de (1768–1848), 234, 239

Cherubini, Luigi (1760–1842), 221, 323, 359

children, 25 *bis*; Bonfire of the Vanities, 156–7

Chiostro di San Pierino, **358**

Christine of Lorraine, *see* Medici, Christine de'

Church, the, 7, 9, 92–3, 94, 181

churches (*see also* S. Croce, S. Lorenzo, S. Marco, S. Maria Novella, S. Miniato al Monte, S. Spirito, S. Trinita, convents): Badia Fiesolana, **343**; Badia Fiorentina, 7, 49, 254, 272, **317–18**; Greek Orthodox Church, **368**; Lutheran Church, **368**; Ognissanti, 118, 188, 311, **333**; Russian Church, 278, **368**; S. Ambrogio, 47, **328**; SS. Annunziata, 49, 87, 171, 202, **334**; S. Apollinare, **347**; SS. Apostoli, 132, **349**; S. Barnaba, **318**; S. Bartolommeo, 89; S. Egidio, **339**; S. Felice in Piazza, 169, 264, **352**; S. Felicita, 251, **317**, **362**; S. Filippo Neri, **347**; S. Francesco di Paola, 279, **367**; S. Frediano in Cestello, 212, 307, **335**, **362**; S. Gaetano, 316, **362**; S. Giorgio sulla Costa, **317**, **366**; S. Giovanni, 4, 7; S. Giovannino degli Scolopi, 86, *87*, **341**; S. Jacopo sopr'Arno, **362**; St James's, **368**; S. Leonardo in Arcetri, **359**; S. Lucia dei Magnoli, 340; S. Margherita in Santa Maria de' Ricci, 14; S. Maria del Carmine, 144, 221, **334–5**; S. Maria de' Cerchi, **326**; S. Maria del Fiore, *see* Duomo; S. Maria dell'Impruneta, 87, 169, **341**; S. Maria Maggiore, **327**;

St Mark's, 368; S. Martino del Vescovo, **326**; S. Michele Visdomini, **360**; S. Niccolò sopr'Arno, **340**; S. Pancrazio, 105, **346**; S. Pier Scheraggio, 186, **356**; S. Piero Maggiore, 110, 199–200, **361**; S. Reparata, 14, **317**; S. Salvatore al Monte, 314, **340**; S. Stefano al Ponte, **326**, **341**; Waldensian Church, **368**

Ciano, Galeazzo (1903–44), 292, 293

Cibò, Innocenzo, 171, 177, 179

cicisbei, 213

Cigoli (1559–1613), 365

Cimabue (*fl.* 1272–1302), 48, 318, 323, 340, 356

Cimitero degli Inglesi, **367–8**

Cini, Cassandra, 229

Cioli, Valerio (1529–99), 354

ciompi riots, 67–9

Cione, Andrea di, *see* Orcagna

Cione, Benci di (1337–1404), 327, 332

Cione, Jacopo di, 361

Cione, Nando di (d. 1365), 318, 322, 345 *bis*

Circolo della Cultura, 287, 288

Ciuffagni, Bernardo (1381–1458), 343

Clairmont, Claire (1798–1879), 270

Clarke, Sir H. Ashley (b. 1903), 310, 312

Clement IV, Pope (r. 1265–8), 22

Clement V, Pope (r. 1305–14), 38–9

Clement VII (r. 1523–34), 111, 171–2, 175, 343

Clérisseau, Charles-Louis (1722–80), 212

Clothilde, Princess, 246

Clough, Arthur Hugh (1819–61), 367

Cocchi, Antoine (1695–1758), 212

Coccioli, Carlo, 310

coinage, 57

Colleoni, Bartolomeo (1400–1475), 115

Colletta, Pietro, 239

Colonna dell'Abbondanza, **336**

Colonna, Pompeio, 171

commerce (*see also* banking), 4; *arti*, 14–15; dyes, 24; exports, 24; foreign policy and customs duties, 20; prosperity, 57; textile industry, 129; wool, 24, 57, 62, 200, 240

Compagni, Dino (*c.* 1250–1323), 36, 38

Conradin, King of the Romans (1252–68), 23

Conservatorio Luigi Cherubini, **360**

Conservatorio della Quiete, **193**

Constantine the Great, Roman Emperor (d. 337), 5, 6

Conti, Augustino, 328

convents (*see also* churches): delle Bianchetti, 219; Ognissanti, 48–9; SS. Annunziata, 49, 89; S. Antonino, 128; S. Lorenzo, 86; S. Marco, 86, 87, 296, 350; S. Maria degli Angeli, 79; S. Maria del Carmine, 49, 94–5; S. Maria

Maddalena dei Pazzi, **346–7**; S. Miniato al Monte, 1, 7; S. Piero Maggiore, **361**; S. Salvi, 40, **327**; S. Spirito, 17

Cooper, James Fenimore (1789–1851), 240, 265, 367

Copley, John Singleton (1737–1815), 277

Corridoio Vasariano, **320**

Corsini, Bartolommeo, 362

Corsini, Filippo, 362

Corsini, Neri, 239, 242

Cosimo I, Grand Duke (1519–74), 177–82 *passim*; *accademie*, 357, 363; building works, 184; Cappella dei Principi, 360; Column of Justice, 318; death, 185; equestrian bronze, 182, 354; Ghetto, 364; Mercato Nuovo, 355; Palazzo Uguccioni, 356; Ponte S. Trinita, 320; statue, 352; Vasari and, 187; villas, 344, 357, 361

Cosimo II, Grand Duke (1590–1620), 191, 192, 361

Cosimo III, Grand Duke (1642–1723), 192, 197–201 *passim*, *198*, 342

Cossa, Baldassare, *see* John XXIII, Pope

Cosway, Maria, *née* Hadfield (*fl.* 1820), 211

Cosway, Richard (1740–1821), 211

Cowper, Countess, 208, 209

Cowper, Earl, 208

Craig, Gordon (1872–1966), 284

Craon, Prince de, 204

Crespi, Giuseppe Maria (1557–1633), 202

Cristofori, Bartolomeo (1655–1731), 201

Cronaca, *see* Pollaiuolo, Simone del

Daddi, Bernardo (*c.* 1312–48), 47, 323, 324, 354

Dall'Ongaro, Francesco (1808–73), 255

Daniele da Volterra (1509–66): bust of Michelangelo, *145*

D'Annunzio, Gabriele (1863–1938), 284, 285, 366

Dante Alighieri (1265–1321), *37, 39*; Beatrice, 36, 79; birth and marriage, 326; and the blacksmith, 36, 38; cavalryman, 36; cenotaph, 359; condemns ostentation, 53; exiled, 36; family background, 35; guild membership, 28, 36; home, 102; influences on, 35, 36; monument, 326; White *priore*, 34; works, 35–6, 38 *bis*, 363

Danti, Fra Egnazio (1536–86), 323, 332

Danti, Vincenzo (1530–76), 76, 335

Davanzati, Bernardo di Antonfrancesco, 25

Davidsohn, Robert (d. 1937), 368

Davy, Sir Humphry (1778–1829), 363

Dei, Benedetto, *Cronica fiorentina*, 100–102

Dei, Rinieri, 366

Dei family, 366

D'Elci, Orso, 224

della Robbia, Andrea (1435–1525): altarpieces, 353, 354; Loggia di S. Paolo, 353; *Madonna and Child*, 339; Ospedale

degli Innocenti, 339; tabernacles, 350; terracotta *Virgin*, 316; terracottas in Loggia di S. Paolo, 353

della Robbia, Giovanni (1469–1529), 321, 323, 340, 353

della Robbia, Luca (1399/1400–1482): *Arte de Lana* emblem, 62; Campanile, 330 *bis*; Cappella del Crocifisso, 314; choir loft, 134, 329; lavabo, 324; *Madonna Enthroned*, 344; Pazzi Chapel roundels, 133; Piero de' Medici and, 115; terracotta emblems, 343; tomb of Federighi, 318; works in Duomo, 329 *bis*; work in Pazzi Chapel, 346

Delli, Dello (1403–post 1466), 339

Demidoff, Anatoly Nikolayevich (d. 1870), 278

de' Rossi, Vincenzo (1525–87), 329, 332, 354

Desiderio da Settignano (1429–64), 323, 338, 346, 359

Dickens, Charles (1812–70), 260, 262, 263, 341

Diocletian, Roman Emperor (245–316), 5

Dolci, Carlo (1616–86), 192

Dolfi, Giuseppe, 248, 256

Domingo de Guzmán (St Dominic; 1170–1221), 18

Dominicans: Alexander VI and Tuscan, 159; assemble for ordeal by fire, 160–61; S. Marco, 180, 350, 351; S. Maria Novella, 18, 49; support papacy against Emperor, 18

Donatello (*c.* 1386–1466), 115; Baptistery, 317; and Brunelleschi, 347; bust of Niccolò da Uzzano, 71, *72*; Campanile, 330 *bis*; choir loft, 329; monument to, 338; Orsanmichele niche and statues, 343; Pazzi chapel tondi, 346; pulpits, 344; reliefs in Old Sacristy, 74; statue of boy Jesus, 156; tomb of John XXIII, 82, 86, 339; and Uccello, 116; works, 94; works in Duomo, 328 *bis*, 329; works in Old Sacristy, S. Lorenzo, 337; works in S. Croce, 322, 323 *bis* *Cavalcanti Annunciation*, 311; *David*, 342, **344**; *Dovizia*, 336; *Judith Slaying Holofernes*, 110, 332, **344**; *Marzocco*, **324**; *St Mary Magdalen*, 312, 330, 369

Donati, Corso (d. 1308), 30–31, 32, 33

Donati, Lucrezia, 120, 123, 125

Donati family, 30; Blacks, 33–4; Boniface VIII and, 33; and Brunelleschi, 43; and Corso Donati, 32, 33; Torre dei Donati, 319

Dosio, Giovanni Antonio (1533–1609), 315

Dostoevsky, Fyodor Mikhailovich (1820–81), 367

Dothel, Nicolas, 214

Douglas, Lord Alfred (1870–1945), 273

Douglas, Norman (1868–1952), 290
dress: Charles VIII, 154; Clarice Orsini, 123; Countess of Albany, 233; Eugenius IV, 91; fourteenth and fifteenth century, 53; Gonfaloniere, 42; Grand Duchess Elisa, 231; Leo X, 169; Lorenzo the Magnificent, 123, 125; *lucco*, 52, 168; militia, 163; Misericordia, 354; *priori*, 42, prostitutes, 57; slaves, 113; sumptuary laws, 112, 122; trousseaux, 112; upper-class wives, 111–12; Villani on, 52–3; Walpole, 216; young men in Renaissance, 127
Drogo, Abbot, 1
Duccio di Buoninsegna (1260–1319), 327, 339–40
Dumini, Amerigo, 285
Duomo, 7, 48, **328–9**; beggars, 233; cenotaph of Hawkwood, 66; *compagnacci* in, 159, 161; dome, 89–91; façade, 125, 146, 169, 271; Ferdinando III's second marriage, 238; Filelfo lectures in, 79; Michelino's painting of Dante, *38*; Pazzi conspiracy, 133–4; prostitutes summoned to, 200; Queen Victoria, 272; relics, 127; Savonarola, 149, 150, 153, 159; *Scoppio del Carro*, 132, 276; *Te Deum*, 206; Uccello's work, 115; Vasari, 188; work begins on, 48; World War II, 303
Duse, Eleonora (1859–1924), 359

Edward III, King (1312–77), 61, 82
Edward IV, King (1442–83), 141
Eleonora di Toledo, Grand Duchess (1522–62), *183*; apartments in Signoria, 184, 354; death, 185; Grotticina di Madama, 354; Palazzo Pitti, 185, 347; personality, 181; Spanish Chapel, 324
Eliot, George (1819–80), 262
Elisa Bacciochi, Grand Duchess (1777–1820), 231–2, 361
emblems:
    Alberti, 105; Austrian eagle, 205; Bartolini, 105; Canacci, 317; Cross of Lorraine, 205; Florentine badge, 20; German imperial eagle, 39; lily, 314–15; Marzocco, 20, **324**; Medici, 67, 88, 89, 105, 110, 205, **336**; Pazzi, *105*, 132; Peruzzi, 316; Ricasoli, 105; Rucellai, 105; Strozzi, 105
Emerson, Ralph Waldo (1803–82), 345, 366
Empoli, 174
Empoli, Jacopo Chimenti da (1551–1640), 111, 318; still life, 55
Este, Borso d', Duke of Ferrara (1413–71), 113
Este, Ercole d', Duke of Ferrara (1433–1505), 137
Este, House of, 204
Etruria, Kingdom of, 230

Etruscans, 2
Eugenius IV, Pope (r. 1431–47), 91–4 *passim*, 350
Evelyn, John (1620–1706), 197

Fabre, François-Xavier (1766–1837), 233
Fabris, Emilio de (1808–83), 125, 328, 352
Faggiuola, Ugoccione della (d. 1319), 40
Falcini, Mariano, 364
Fallani, Bernardo (*fl.* 1771–8), 364
Fancelli, Luca (1430–95), 107
Fane, Charles, 209–10
Fantacchiotti, Odoardo (1809–77), 359
Fanti, Manfredo (1805–65), 351
Faraday, Michael (1791–1867), 363
Fascism, 285–7, 288, 293, 296–7, 298
Fattori, Giovanni, 256
Federigo, Prince of Naples, 138
Fedi, Pio (1816–92), 351
Felice, Bacciochi, Grand Duke (1762–1841), 231
Ferdinand, King, V of Castile, II of Aragon and Sicily, and III of Naples (1452–1516), 158
Ferdinand II, King of Naples (1469–96), 145
Ferdinand IV, King of Naples, later Ferdinand I, King of the Two Sicilies (1751–1825), 227
Ferdinand III, Grand Duke (1769–1824): benign and enlightened ruler, 232; and Bonaparte, 226; death, 238; leaves Florence, 227; library, 363; neutrality of Florence, 227; popularity, 237; reforms and improvements under, 236; renewed sovereignty proclaimed, 230; restored to throne, 231; succeeds, 225
Ferdinando I, Grand Duke (1549–1609): Cappella dei Principi, 360; equestrian bronze, 358; expenditure on building and works of art, 190–91; Opificio delle Pietre Dure, 358; Ponte Vecchio, 319; Roman statues, 191, 333; Taccas' gilt bronze statues, 361; wedding celebrations, 189–90; well-being of citizens, 189
Ferdinando II, Grand Duke (1610–70), 192–4, 197, 199
Ferrante, King of Naples (1423–94), 138
Ferrante, Don, 99
Ferrari, D'Arco, 244
Ferrero, Guglielmo (1871–1942), 287
Ferri, Antonio Maria (1651–1716), 335, 358, 362
Ferri, Ciro (1634–89), 347
Ferrucci, Andrea (1465–1526), 328, 329
Ferrucci, Francesco, 174, *243*, 352
festivities: banquets, 121–2, 123, 141; *Calendimaggio*, 199; Carnival, 206, 215, 216; *corsi dei cocchi*, 275; Cosimo I encourages, 182; on election of Pope Leo

X, 168–9; entry of Grand Duke Francis into Florence, 205–6; Florentine, 125, 127; foreigners enjoy festivals, 195–6; French Jacobin, 227–8; Leopold II's fiesta, 240; May Day, 127; pageant of General Council (1439), 92, 93; St John the Baptist's Day, 127, 275; *Scoppio del Carro*, 276; tournaments, 120, 123, 125; for uncovering of façade of Duomo, 271; for victories, 180; wedding celebrations, 122, 189, 190, 242
Ficino, Marsilio (1433–99), 94, *142*, 146, 147, 328
Field, Kate, 260
Fielder, Konrad, 279
Fiesole, 2, 5, 15; Cathedral, **320–21**
Filelfo, Francesco (1398–1481), 79, 142–3
Firbank, Ronald (1886–1926), 284
Firmin, Piero, 364
Flahaut de la Billarderie, August (1785–1870), 234
floods, 42–3, 245; wrecked cars (1966), *309*, 311
Foggini, Giovanni Battista (1652–1735): altar frontal, 334; Colonna dell'Abbondanza, 366; Galileo's monument, 359; Granaio di Cosimo III, 335; S. Giorgio sulla Costa, 317, 366; statues, 316
Foix, Gaston de (1489–1512), 166
Folfi, Mariotto di Zanobi (1521–1600), 356
Fontana, Carlo (1634–1714), 336, 363
food, 55, 56, 63, 64, 122, 123
Forster, E.M. (1879–1970), 291
Forte di Belvedere, 206, 223, 231, 248, **358–9**; Buontalenti, 191
Fortezza da Basso, 40, 175, 179, 227, **352**
Fortini, Cesare, 364
Foscolo, Ugo (1778–1827), 233, 239, 367; sepulchral statue, **365**
Fossombroni, Vittorio (1754–1844), 232, 238, 239, 241, 242
Fox, Charles James (1749–1806), 214–16
Francavilla, Pietro (1548–1615), 304, 320, 323, 334, 369
France: army in Florence, 155; army in Naples, 158; battle of River Ronco, 106; battle of River Taro, 158; Florence and, 166; invasion of Italy, 138; and Risorgimento, 246; war with Austria, 248; war with Prussia, 256; withdraws forces from Italy, 166
Francesco I, Grand Duke (1541–87), 185, 188–9, 356, 357
Francesco Maria II, Duke of Urbino, 192
Franciabigio, 347
Francis of Assisi, St (1181/2–1226), 17, 18
Francis II, Holy Roman Emperor (1768–1835), 238
Francis I, King of Naples and Sicily (1777–1830), 242

Francis, Grand Duke, *later* Francis I, Holy Roman Emperor (1708–65), 204, 205–6, 207

Franz Josef I, Emperor of Austria (1830–1916), 245, 248

Frederick II, Holy Roman Emperor (1194–1250), 18, 20

Frederick of Antioch, Viceroy of Tuscany, 18, 19, 20

Frederick I Barbarossa, Holy Roman Emperor (c. 1123–90), 16, *16*, 17

Frescobaldi family, 14, 321

Frundsberg, Georg von (1473–1528), 171

furniture, 52–3, 55

Gabbiani, Antonio Domenico (1652–1726), 212, 362

Gaddi, Agnolo (c. 1333–96): altarpiece, 314; attribution, 333; Loggia dei Lanza spandrels, 332; *Martyrdom of San Sebastian*, 328; sanctuary decoration, 323; stained-glass windows, 323, 328, 329

Gaddi, Gaddo (c. 1260–1332), 328

Gaddi, Niccolò, 189

Gaddi, Taddeo (fl. 1332–63), 322, 323, 333, 367

Galilei, Galileo (1564–1642), 191–2, 357, 359, 363

Galleria dell'Accademia, **363**

Galleria Corsini, 212, **362**

Galluzzi, Riguccio, 221

Gamberini, Italo, 369

Garbasso, Antonio, 287

gardens, *see* GIARDINI

Garibaldi, Giuseppe (1807–82), 256

Garrick, David (1717–79), 210

Gauthier, General, 227, 228, 229

Gautier, Théophile (1811–72), 366

Gentile, Giovanni, 297

Gentile da Fabriano (1370–1427), 93, 341

Gerini, Niccolò di Pietro (fl. 1368–1415), 354

Gherardini, Tommaso (1715–97), 363

Ghetto, 224, **364**

Ghibellines: Clement IV and, 22; Emperor's supporters, 12; excluded from government, 64–5; Faggiuola, 39; and Guelphs, 18–20, 23, 26; return to Florence, 22; Siena welcomes, 20; Whites (Cerchi), 34

Ghiberti, Lorenzo (c. 1378–1455): Baptistery doors, 76, *77*, *78*, 78, 93, 302, 308, 337; bronze foundry, 118; Brunelleschi and, 90–91; burial place, 192, 323, 359; Orsanmichele statues, 343; self-portraits, 337; statue of St Matthew, 89; works in Duomo, 328 *bis*, 329 *bis*

Ghiberti, Vittorio (1419–96), 335, 359

Ghini, Giovanni di Lapo (fl. 1355–71), 360

Ghirlandaio, Davide (1451–1525), 328

Ghirlandaio, Domenico (1449–94): altarpieces, 333, 350; Cathedral façade, 146; frescoes, 141, *142*, 332, 333, 348, 350, 351; Lorenzo the Magnificent and, 143; stained glass, 348

  Adoration of the Magi, 339; *Annunciation*, 328; *Last Suppers*, 333, 351

Ghirlandaio, Michele di Ridolfo (1503–77), 352

Giambologna (1529–1608): bronze birds, 357; bronze relief, *184*; bust of Francesco I, 315; crucifix, 323; equestrian bronzes, 331, 358; Ferdinando I and, *191*; high altar, 326; S. Marco, 351; tomb of, 334; turtles, 353; works, 182, 184

  Abundance, 355; *Appennino*, 182, 354; *Rape of the Sabines*, 333; *St Luke*, 343; *Venus*, 354; *Venus Drying her Hair*, 366

Gian Gastone, Grand Duke (1671–1737), 194, 202, 204

Gianni, Francesco Maria, 222, 224

giardini (*see also* Boboli Gardens): Gualfonda, 365; dell'Orticoltura 253, **366**; dei Semplici, 253, **366**; Torrigiani, **364**

Gibbon, Edward (1737–94), 209, 216

Gide, André (1869–1951), 273, 291, 366

Ginori, Carlo (1702–57), 205, 206, 361

Giordani, Pietro (1774–1848), 239

Giordano, Luca (1632–1705), 335, 362, 363

Giotto di Bondone (1267–1337): altarpiece, 322; bust of, 328; Campanile, 28, 48; *capomaestro*, 48; frescoes, 316, 322, 323; personality, 48; style, 47–8

  Ognissanti Madonna, 333; *Paradise*, 36, *37*; *St Stephen*, 365

Giovanni del Biondo (fl. 1356–92), 323

Giovanni Gualberto, St (c. 990–1073), 8–9

Giovanni da Milano, 323

Giovanni da Salerno, 323

Giovanni di San Giovanni (1592–1636), 194, 340, 349, 352

Giovanozzi, Luigi, 368

Giovio, Paolo (1483–1552), 182

Giuliano di Baccio d'Agnolo (1491–1555), 345

Giuliano da Maiano (1432–90): cupboards, 329; Lorenzo the Magnificent and, 143; *palazzi*, 315, 345, 346; Pazzi Chapel door and portico, 346; works in Signoria, 332

Giusti, Giuseppe (1809–50), 239

Gloucester, Duke of (1743–1805), 210

Goad, Harold, 288

Goering, Hermann (1893–1946), 296

Goes, Hugo van der (d. 1482), 326

Goldoni, Carlo (1707–93), 216, 345

Goncourt, Edmond de (1822–96), 260, 366

Goncourt, Jules de (1830–70), 260, 366

Gondi, Giuliano, 106

Gonzaga, Francesco, Marquis of Mantua (1466–1519), 158

Gori, Lamberto Cristiano, 212, 362

Gorini, Fioretta, 349

government of Florence: Albizzi, 73, 83; Alessandro de' Medici, 175; appoints *Capitano di Guerra*, 41; attempt to strengthen, 164; Balìa, 42, 84; bankruptcy, 259; changes from oligarchy to theocracy, 155; commune, 15; consuls, 14; Council of Seventy, 138; election of Signoria, 42; foreign policy, 20, 60; Guelphs, 20, 23; guilds, 28; Lorenzo the Magnificent, 128, 129; *Maggior Consilio*, 155–6; Medicean Signoria, 114; minor modifications, 98; oligarchy, 42; Ordinances of Justice, 30, 31, 32; Parte Guelfa and Ghibellines, 64; Podestà, 17; *Primo Popolo*, 20; provisional late-eighteenth-century, 229, 230; Risorgimento, 253–4; Savonarola, 156, 160; Signoria, 84, 129, 154; triumvirate, 245; Tuscan policy, 239

Gozzoli, Benozzo (1420–97): *Procession of the Magi*, 93, 116, *117*, 342, 349; S. Marco frescoes, 344

Graffione (1455–c. 1527), 328

Granaio di Cosimo III, **335**

Gray, Thomas (1716–71), 362

Gregory VIII, Pope and St (r. 1073–85), 9–12

Gregory IX, Pope (1227–41), 18

Gregory X, Pope (r. 1271–6), 26, 33

Gregory XVI, Pope (r. 1831–46), 239

Greville, Charles (1794–1865), 250

Grey, 1st Earl (1729–1807), 212

Grifoni, Elizabetta, Marchesa, 216

Grifoni, Ugolino, 345

Grigoryevich, Aleksey, 278

Grocyn, William (c. 1446–1519), 146

Grosso, Niccolò, lamps, 88, **342**, 366

Guarinus, Abbot, 8

Guelphs: and Count of Luxembourg, 38; Dante, 36, 38; defeat at Montecatini, 40; and Ghibellines, 18–20, 22, 23, 26; government in Florence, 20, 25; Latini, 35; Papal supporters, 12; Parte Guelfa, 23, 28, 32, 64, 67–8; Pisa and Siena accept supremacy of, 23

Guerrazzi, Francesco (1804–73), 242, 244, 245

Guicciardini, Francesco (1483–1540): birthplace, 341; and Cosimo di Giovanni, 177, 178; Florence after surrender, 175; Grand Duke's counsellor, 179; *palleschi*, 177; Pope's confidential adviser, 171; quoted, 97, 123, 157, 167–8, 170, 171; retires to his villa, 180

Guicciardini, Giovanni, 84

Guicciardini, Luigi, 68

Guidi, Camillo, 264, 367

guilds, *see* arti

Hadfield, Charles, 210–11
Hadrian, Roman Emperor (76–138), 4
Hall, Radclyffe (1886–1943), 292
Hamilton, Gavin (1723–98), 212
Handel, George Frideric (1685–1759), 201
Hardy, Thomas (1840–1928), 367
Hare, Cecil, 368
Hare, Francis, 260
Hawkwood, Sir John (c. 1320–94), 65, 66, **336**
Hawthorne, Nathaniel (1804–64), 265, 275
Hawthorne, Sophie, 240–41, 275
Hazlitt, William (1778–1830), 215, 260
Heine, Heinrich (1797–1856), 239, 278
Hempel, Kenneth, 312
Henri, duc de Valois, later Henri II, King of France (1519–59), 111
Henry IV, Holy Roman Emperor (1050–1106), 10, 10, 12
Henry V, Holy Roman Emperor (1086–1125), 15
Henry VII, Holy Roman Emperor (1275–1313), 38–40
Henry IV, King of France (1553–1610), 190
Hildebrand, Bishop of Florence, 1, 8
Hildebrand, Adolf von (1847–1921), 268, 279, 367
Hitler, Adolf (1889–1945), 291–3
Holdsworth, Annie, 269
Holland, 3rd Baron (1773–1840), 362
Holland, Lady (1770–1845), 232, 362
Holy League, 158, 166
Home, Daniel Dunglas (1833–86), 262
Hoogvorst, Adrian van der Linden, Baron, 254
Horne, Herbert Percy (d. 1916), 365
Hortense, Queen of Holland (1778–1846), 234
Hotel Jennings-Riccioli, 291, **369**
houses, fourteenth-century, 53, 55
Howard, Hon. Hubert, 302, 303
Hudson, Sir James (1810–85), 253
Hugford, Ferdinando Enrico (1696–1771), 212
Hugford, Ignazio Enrico (1703–78), 211, 362
humanists, 79–80, 83, 141–2, 142
Hunt, Fanny (d. 1866), 367
Hunt, James Henry Leigh (1784–1859), 260
Hunt, William Holman (1827–1910), 275, 367; Ponte Vecchio, 274
Hutton, Edward (1875–1969), 290
Huxley, Aldous (1894–1963), 291

Imola, 131, 133
Innocent IV, Pope (r. 1243–54), 18
Innocent VIII, Pope (r. 1484–92), 139
inns, 210–11, 212
Inquisition, 199, 207, 222, 230
Isabella Farnese, Queen of Spain (1692–1766), 204

Istituto Araldico, 362
Istituto d'Arte, 355
Italy, Kingdom of, 251, 256

James, Henry (1843–1916), 265–9, 266, 271, 341, 367 bis
James, William, 265
Jérôme, Prince (1784–1860), 246
Jews, 199, 224, 230
Joadet, J.N., 206
Joanna of Austria, Archduchess, 188
John XXIII, Pope (r. 1410–15): deposed, 82; Donatello's effigy of, 94; and Giovanni di Bicci de' Medici, 80; tomb, 82, 86, 317, 339
John VIII Palaeologus, Byzantine Emperor (1390–1448), 92–3
Joseph II, Holy Roman Emperor (1741–90), 207, 220, 223
Julius II, Pope (r. 1503–13), 131, 165–6, 167, 169–70
Justinian I, Byzantine Emperor (1483–1565), 5

Karageorgevitch, Prince Alexis, 284
Kauffman, Angelica (1741–1807), 211
Keppel, Hon. George, 291
Keppel, Hon. Mrs George, 291
Kesselring, Albert (1885–1960), 304
Kirkup, Seymour Stocker (1788–1880), 260
Kolhapur, Maharaja of (d. 1870), 362

La Farina, Giuseppe (1815–63), 243
La Pira, Giorgio, 296
Lacaita, Sir James, 253
Lama, Gaspare di Zanobi del, 119, 349
Lamartine, Alphonse de (1790–1869), 234
Lamberti, Niccolò di Piero (c. 1370–1451), 343, 344
Lambruschini, Raffaele (1788–1873), 255
Lami, Giovanni (1697–1770), 221
Landino, Cristoforo (1424–1504), 141, 142, 146, 363
Lando, Michele de, 68, 69
Landor, Walter Savage (1775–1864): burial place, 367; on dirt of Florence, 275; lodgings, 260, 265; personality, 236; and Theodosia Trollope, 262; visitors, 260
Landucci, Luca: on execution of Savonarola's disciples, 163; on executions at Tornaquinci, 164; on Michelangelo's David, 352; on militia, 165; quoted, 103–4, 156–7, 166
Latini, Brunetto (c. 1220–c. 1294), 35, 38
Lawrence, D.H. (1885–1930), 288, 290
Lawrence, Sir Thomas (1769–1830): portrait of the Countess of Blessington, 235
Leader, John Temple (1811–1903), 255
Lear, Edward (1812–88), 275, 368

Lee, Vernon (prop. Violet Paget; 1856–1935), 268–9, 270, 274
Lee-Hamilton, Eugene (1845–1907), 269, 274
Lega, Silvestro, 256
Leghorn, see Livorno
Leighton, Baron (1830–96), 368
Leo X, Pope (r. 1513–21), 168–9, 170, 177, 343
Leonardo da Vinci (1452–1519), 143, 156, 337, 351
Leopardi, Giacomo (1798–1837), 239
Leopold II, Grand Duke (1797–1870): appearance, 237, 241; attitude to current intellectual activity, 239; and Austria, 245; François Vase, 365; industrial and social reforms, 239–40; leaves Florence, 249; limited liberalism, 243–4; marriages, 237–8, 241–2; popularity, 240, 242; Risorgimento, 244–5; succeeds, 238
Lever, Charles James (1806–72), 260
Leverson, Ada, 291
Levi, Carlo (1902–75), 303
libraries, see Biblioteche
Lieven, Dorothea, Princess de (1784–1857), 234, 236
Ligonier, Earl (d. 1782), 218
Linacre, Thomas (c. 1460–1524), 146
Linklater, Eric (1899–1974), 299–300, 301–2
Linley, Thomas, the Younger (1756–78), 208
Lippi, Filippino (1457–1504): altarpiece, 321; apprentice, 118; Cathedral façade, 146; frescoes, 334, 345, 347; Lorenzo the Magnificent and, 143; parentage, 95; St Bernard, 318
Lippi, Filippo (c. 1406–69): altarpieces, 338, 344; Botticelli and, 118; history and personality, 94–5; Piero de' Medici and, 115; various works, 344; Virgin and Child, 362
Liszt, Franz (1811–86), 279
Livorno (Leghorn), 69, 73, 227
Loeser, Charles, 332
Loggia dei Lanzi, **332–3**; Cellini's Perseus, 182, 354; Fedi's Rape of Polyxena, 351; Ferdinando I's statues, 191; former uses, 49; French Jacobin celebrations, 228; Queen Regent gives a party, 230–31; prostitutes and crooks, 275
Loggia dei Rucellai, **368**
Longfellow, Henry Wadsworth (1807–82), 260, 341
Lorenzetti, Pietro (c. 1280–1348), 340
Lorenzi, Stoldo (1534–83), 355
Lorenzini, Carlo, 244
Lorenzo de Credi (1439–1537), 157
Lorraine, Francis II, Duke of, see Francis, Grand Duke

Lothar III, Holy Roman Emperor (1075–1137), 15

Louis I, King of Etruria (1773–1803), 230

Louis II (Carlo Ludovico), King of Etruria (1799–1849), 230

Louis XI, King of France (1423–83), 110, 115

Louis XIV, King of France (1638–1715), 197

Louisa, Countess of Albany (1753–1824), 218, 219, 232

Lowell, James Russell (1819–91), 345

Lucaroni, Timoteo, 313

Lucca: Faggiuola, 40; Florence and, 17, 71, 136; Margraves of Tuscany, 7, 11, 12

Lungarni:
    Acciaioli, 269, 271, 281; Amerigo Vespucci, 240; Corsini, 232; delle Grazie, 369

Lyttelton, 2nd Baron (1744–79), 216, 217

Lusitania, Jacopo di (1434–59), 314

Luxembourg, Henry IV, Count of, *see* Henry VII, Holy Roman Emperor

Macchiaioli, the, 255–6

Machiavelli, Niccolò (1469–1527): burial place, 192; busts, *165*, 332; *Istorie fiorentine*, 108; leaves Florence, 168; letters, 363; militia, 165; monument, 359; pillage of Prato, 168; portrait, 332

Magalotti, Lorenzo, 201

Magliabechi, Antonio (1633–1714), 363

Malmesbury, 3rd Earl of (1807–89), 247

Manetti, Antonio (1423–97), 314, 337, 338, 352

Manetti, Gianozzo (1396–1459), 99

Manfred, King of Sicily (1232–66), 21, 22

Mann, Sir Horace (1701–86), 209, 210, 214, 218

Manzoni, Alessandro (1785–1873), 239, 364

Marées, Hans von (1837–87), 279, 367

Marguerite-Louise, Grand Duchess, *née* Marguerite-Louise d'Orléans (1645–1721), 197–9, 347

Mari, Captain, 229

Maria Anna Carolina of Saxony, Grand Duchess, 238, 241

Maria Antonia, Grand Duchess, 241–2

Maria Luisa, Queen of Etruria (1782–1824), 230–31

Maria Luisa, Grand Duchess, 207, 220

Maria Maddalena, Grand Duchess, *formerly* Archduchess of Austria, 192, 365

Maria Theresa, Empress of Austria (1717–80), 206, 222

Marie de Medicis, Queen of France, (1573–1642), 190

Marinetti, Filippo (1876–1944), 286

Marini, Marino (1901–66), 346

Mario, Alberto, 251

Mario, Jessie White, 251, 366, 367

Marsh, George Perkins (1801–82), 254

Marsuppini, Carlo, 79, 323, 359

Martelli, Niccolò, 338

Martin V, Pope (r. 1417–31), 33, 82

Masaccio (1401–c. 1428), 95, 324, 334

Maso di Banco (*fl.* 1341–6), 323, 330

Masolino da Panicale (1383–c. 1440), 334

Matas, Niccolò, 282

Matilda, Countess of Tuscany (1046–1115), 11, 11–12, 13

Matteotti, Giacomo (*d.* 1924), 287

Matthew, Sir Tobie (1577–1655), 194

Maugham, William Somerset (1874–1965), 290

Maximilian I, Holy Roman Emperor (1459–1519), 158

Maximilian II, Holy Roman Emperor (1527–76), 184

May of Teck, Princess, *later* Queen Mary (1867–1953), 272, 368

Mazarin, Jules (1602–61), 197

Mazzini, Giuseppe (1805–72), 245

Medici, Alessandro de', Duke of Penne (1511–37): appearance, 170; despot, 175–6; doubtful parentage, 170; flees, 171; murdered, 176–7; Passerini and, 171; and Vasari, 187

Medici, Alfonsina de' (*d.* 1519), 170

Medici, Anna Maria di Cosimo de', Princess, *see* Anna Maria, Electress Palatine

Medici, Averardo de', 67

Medici, Averardo detto Bicci de' (*d.* 1363), 74

Medici, Carlo de', illegitimate son of Cosimo *Pater Patriae*, 82

Medici, Caterina di Lorenzo de', Duchess of Urbino and later Queen of France (1519–89), 111, 170, 190

Medici, Christine de', Grand Duchess (1565–1636), 189

Medici, Cosimino di Giovanni de', 107

Medici, Cosimo di Ferdinando de' (1590–1620), *see* Cosimo II, Grand Duke

Medici, Cosimo di Ferdinando de' (1642–1723), *see* Cosimo III, Grand Duke

Medici, Cosimo di Giovanni de', *Pater Patriae* (1389–1464): advice from his father, 86; art patron, 94–6; banker, 141; benefactions, 86, 89; bibliophile, 80, 89; Biblioteca Laurenziana, 342, 343; birth, 74; Botticelli's *Adoration of the Magi*, 118, 349; criticized, 88–9; education, 79; foreign affairs, 99; Gonfaloniere, 94; Gozzoli's *Procession of the Magi*, 116, 118; and Greek scholars, 93–4; imprisoned, 83; 'master of the country', 97; in old age, 107–8; *palazzo*, 86, 87, 88–9, 105; posthumous portrait, *81*, 358; returns to Florence, 84; and Sforza, 98–9; title *Pater Patriae*, 108; tomb, 108, 338, 348; in Venice, 83; wife, 82, 107, 111

Medici, Cosimo di Giovanni de' (1519–74), *see* Cosimo I, Grand Duke

Medici, Ferdinando di Cosimo de' (1549–1609), *see* Ferdinando I, Grand Duke

Medici, Ferdinando di Cosimo de' (1610–70), *see* Ferdinando II, Grand Duke

Medici, Ferdinando di Cosimo de', Grand Prince (1663–1713), 201–2, *203*

Medici, Filigno de', 67

Medici, Francesco di Cosimo de', *see* Francesco I, Grand Duke

Medici, Francesco Maria di Ferdinando de' (1660–1710), 202

Medici, Gian Carlo di Cosimo de', Cardinal (1611–63), 194

Medici, Gian Gastone di Cosimo de', *see* Gian Gastone, Grand Duke

Medici, Giovanni di Bicci de' (1360–1429), 75; advice to his sons, 75–6, 86; appearance, 74; banker, 80, 82; Baptistery north doors, 76; benefactions, 78–9; death, 82; history, 74; personality, 75; sons' education, 79; tomb, 78, 337; Villa Careggi, 344

Medici, Giovanni di Cosimo de' (1421–63), 82, 107, 118, 128, 337

Medici, Giovanni di Cosimo de' (1543–62), *183*

Medici, Giovanni di Giovanni de', called Giovanni delle Bande Nere (1498–1526), 177, 357, 364

Medici, Giovanni di Lorenzo de', later Pope Leo X, *q.v.* (1475–1521), 154, 167, 168, 349

Medici, Giovanni di Pierfrancesco de', 153, 357

Medici, Giuliano di Lorenzo de', later Duke of Nemours (1479–1516), 153, 168, 170, 349, 352

Medici, Giuliano di Piero de' (1453–78): burial place, 352; *giostra*, 125; Pazzi conspiracy, 133–4; portrayed by Botticelli, 118, 119; portrayed by Gozzoli, 349

Medici, Giulio de', illegitimate son of Alessandro de' Medici, 177, 179

Medici, Giulio de', illegitimate son of Giuliano di Piero, later Pope Clement VII, *q.v.* (1478–1534), 154, 167, 170

Medici, Ippolito de', illegitimate son of Giuliano di Lorenzo (d. 1535), 170, 171, 175, 176

Medici, Isabella di Cosimo de', 185

Medici, Joanna de', Grand Duchess, 188

Medici, Leopoldo di Cosimo de', Cardinal (1617–75), 194

Medici, Lorenzino (Lorenzaccio) di

Pierfrancesco de' (1514–47), 176–7, 180
Medici, Lorenzo di Giovanni de' (1395–1440), 79, 82
Medici, Lorenzo di Pierfrancesco de' (1463–1503), 118–19, 153, 357
Medici, Lorenzo di Piero de', later Duke of Urbino (1492–1528), 169–70, 352
Medici, Lorenzo di Piero de', 'Il Magnifico', (1449–92), *111*, *140*; his advice on architecture sought, 145–6; appearance, 121; and artists, 143, 144, 350; assumes leadership of Medicean party, 128–9; betrothal celebrations, 120; Botticelli and, 118, 349; burial place, 252; Cathedral façade, 146; collector, 143; death, 147; encourages printing, 147; and his father, 113; financial obligations, 141; and humanists, 141–2; and Innocent VIII, 139; and Italian language, 147; and Medici bank, 139, 141; Medici Vase, 363; and Michelangelo, 144; negotiations in Naples, 137–8; *Parlamento*, 114; Pazzi conspiracy, 133–5; personality, 121, 123, 129, 139; Poggio a Caiano, 347; in *Procession of the Magi*, 118; and Salviati, 133; and Sixtus IV, 131; Uccello's works, 115; universities, 146–7; untitled head of state, 138–9; Volterra, 129, 130; wedding banquets, 121–2, 123; and his wife, 123
Medici, Lucrezia di Piero de', 122
Medici, Maddalena di Lorenzo de', 139
Medici, Maria de', *née* Salviati, 177, 185
Medici, Maria di Francesco de', *see* Marie de Medicis, Queen of France
Medici, Maria Maddalena de', *see* Maria Maddalena, Grand Duchess
Medici, Mattias di Cosimo de' (1613–67), 194
Medici, Pierfrancesco de', 113
Medici, Piero di Cosimo de', 'Il Gottoso' (1414–69): art patron, 115, 116, 118, 120; attempted usurpation of, 113–14; birth, 82; Cappella di Crocifisso, 314; collector, 128; death, 128; gout, 107; health and ability, 110; and Luca Pitti, 114; Milanese alliance, 110; Palazzo Incontri, 360; represented in paintings, 118, 349; SS. Annunziata, 334, 349; tomb, 128, 337; works commissioned by, 128, 349
Medici, Piero di Lorenzo de' (1471–1503), *148*; and Charles VIII, 153; death, 167; flees Florence, 153–4; and French invasion, 152; Medici treasures, 154; personality, 149; Savonarola and, 153
Medici, Salvestro de', 67–8, 74
Medici family, 73; Cascine, 362; *coup d'état* against, 171; demonstration in favour of, 168; insignia, 67; library, 147, 154, 191; medals, 176; Medici bank, 80, 82, 131, 149, 192; Medici collections, 143, 360;

Medici holidays abolished, 205; Medici rule re-established, 175; *palazzi*, 67; Palazzo Pitti, 107; patron saints, 74; patrons of scientific discovery, 192; Pazzi conspiracy, 134; property bequeathed to Grand Duke, 205; Rucellai and, 106; S. Lorenzo, 84; S. Maria Novella, 323; Savonarola and, 157; sentence of exile revoked, 84; Signoria exiles, 154; tombs, 352; villas, 87, 94, 106, 108, 121, 141, 182, 188, 199, 202
Medici Library, *see* Biblioteca Laurenziana
Meglio, Jacopo Coppi di' (1523–91), 359
Melville, Herman (1819–91), 345, 366
Mercato del Grano, 224
Mercato Nuovo, 169, 186, **355**
Mercato Vecchio, 56, *255*, *258*, **336**; banking, 80; Colonna dell'Abbondanza, *56*, 57; Cossacks, 230; fancy-dress parties, 125; Jews send for help, 224; Pucci's poem, 57–8; St John the Baptist's Day, 127; transformed, 258
mercenaries, 41
merchants (*see also* commerce), 24; aid Jews during riots, 224; *catasto*, 70; and *ciompi* riots, 68, 69; consuls, 14; government, 23, 31, 42; *Primo Popolo*, 20; reluctance to take up arms, 41
Merry, Robert (1755–98), 209
Metternich, Prince von (1773–1859), 234, 242
Mezzabarba, Peter, Bishop of Florence, 9
Michelangelo Buonarroti (1475–1564), *145*, 156; Accademia del Disegno, 357; Biblioteca Laurenziana, 352; Casa Buonarotti, 357; charcoal drawings, 352; compasses, 191; Cosimo I and, 182; defence works, 173–4, 314, 355; in hiding, 175; letters, 363; lost work, 351; New Sacristy, 352; Palazzo Medici, 88; personality, 144; quarrel with Torrigiani, 144; S. Lorenzo, 173, 337, 338, 352; and Savonarola, 149; statue of Julius II, 165; tomb, 188, 357; tondo, 348; Vasari and, 143–4, 187
    David, 253, **352**, 363; *Madonna of the Steps*, 357; *Pietà*, 330; *St Matthew*, 363; *Slaves*, 354, 363
Michele, Vincenzo, 364
Michele di Lando, 68–9
Michelino, Domenico di, 39, 354
Michelozzo, Michelozzi (1396–1472): Baptistery columns, 317; Cappella del Crocifisso, 314; churches, 334, 337, 341, 350, 352; courtyards, 332, 340; niche, 343; Palazzo Medici, 86, 87; Palazzo Ricasoli, 345; Piero de' Medici and, 115; S. Marco library, 351; on stone quarries, 104; tomb of John XXIII, 82, 86, 339; Villa Careggi,

344; work in Duomo, 328, 329; works, 86–7
Michelucci, Giovanni, 369
Mignaty, George, 367; Brownings' drawing-room, *264*
Milan, 98, 99, 100, 110, 244
Milan, Dukes of, *see* Sforza, Visconti
Milani, Luigi Adriano, 365
militia, 165, 166, 168, 171, 173
Milton, John (1608–74), 192
Minga, Andrea del (*c.* 1540–96), 359
Miniato, St (*fl.* 3rd century AD), 1
Mino da Fiesole (1430–84): bust of Piero de' Medici, 110; dwelling, 348; tabernacle, 328; tomb of, 328; tomb of Salutati, 321; work in La Badia, 7, 318
Mint, 186, **356**
Mirafiori, Rosa, 251
Mirandola, Giovanni Pico della (1463–94), 349
Misericordia, Confraternity of, 182, **353–4**
Misson, François Maximilien, 200–201
Monaco, Lorenzo (*c.* 1370–1425), 318
monasteries, *see* convents
Montaigne, Michel Eyquem de (1533–92), 188, 347
Montale, Eugenio, 293
Montanelli, Giuseppe (1813–62), 244, 245
Montefeltro, Federigo da, Duke of Urbino (*c.* 1410–82), 120, 131, 136, 349
Montefeltro, Guido da (d. 1298), 28
Montesecco, Gian Battista (d. 1478), 133, 135
Moore, Henry (1898–1986), 323, 359
Moore, John, 216–17
Moricci, Giuseppe, 258
Moryson, Fynes (1566–1630), 196
Mount Stuart, Viscount, *later* 1st Marquess of Bute (1744–1814), 214
Mozart, Wolfgang Amadeus (1756–91), 208, 361
Mozzi, Andrea del, 340
Mozzi family, 340
Murat, Joachim, King of Naples (1767–1815), 231, 232
Musei (*see also* Museo dell'Opera del Duomo):
    Archeologico, 239, 311, **365**; degli Argenti, 194, **349**; Bardini, **340**; del Bigallo, 110, 303, **354**; della Casa Fiorentina Antica, **335**; Fiorentina di Preistoria, **366**; di Firenze com'era, **365**; Horne, 311, **365**; Nazionale di Antropologia ed Etnologia, **365**; dell'Opera di S. Croce, **323**; della Porcelane, 355; della Porcelane di Doccia, **361**; Stibbert, 202, **364**; di Storia della Fotografia Fratelli Alinari, **367**; di Storia della Scienza, 308, 311, **359**
Museo dell'Opera del Duomo, **330**; emblem of Arte della Lana, *62*; Pisano's bas-reliefs,

28, 29; silver altar frontal, 86–7, 118
Mussolini, Benito, 289; arrested, 295; bust
  shattered, 296; declaration of war, 294;
  Fascism, 285, 286; Florence railway
  station, 293; head of new government,
  287; and Hitler in Florence, 291–3;
  personality, 293; popularity, 288

Nanni di Banco (c. 1380–1421), 328, 343
Nanni di Bartolo (fl. 1419–51), 329
Naples: Charles VIII and, 149, 152, 158;
  Florence at war with, 69–70; Garibaldi,
  256; Lorenzo the Magnificent negotiates
  in, 138–9; Murat, 231; Risorgimento,
  246
Napoleon Bonaparte, later Emperor of the
  French (1769–1821), 231; conquests in
  Europe, 226; coronation robes, 364; and
  Countess of Albany, 233; establishes vassal
  republics in Italy, 227; crowned Emperor,
  231; returns to Paris, 229; on St Helena,
  232
Napoleon III, Emperor of the French
  (1808–73), 246–8
Nardi, Jacopo, 176
Nardini, Pietro (1722–93), 208
Nencini, Franco, 307–8
Neri di Bicci (1418–91): altarpieces, 318,
  326; Pietà, 340; triptych, 352; works in S.
  Leonardo in Arcetri, 359; works in S.
  Trinita, 318 bis
Neri di Fioravante (fl. 1340–84), 318, 325, 327
Neroni, Diotisalvi, 110, 348
Niccoli, Niccolò, 80, 89, 147
Niccolini, Giovanni Battista (1785–1861),
  351
Niccolò da Tolentino, 83, 340
Niccolò da Uzzano, 71–3, 72, 83, 84, 336
Nicholas III, Pope (r. 1277–80), 26, 33
Nigetti, Dionigi (fl. 1565–70), 365
Nigetti, Matteo (1560–1649), 316, 333, 337,
  361
Nightingale, Florence (1820–1910), 367
Nitti, Francesco Saverio (1868–1953), 285
Nori, Francesco, 357
Normanby, 1st Marquess of (1797–1863),
  236
Novello, Guido, 22

Odoacer, King of Italy (c. 433–93), 5
Ongaro, Francesco dall', 255
Opificio delle Pietre Dure, 206, 358
Orange, Philibert, Prince of (r. 1502–30),
  174
Orcagna (Andrea di Cione; c. 1308–68):
  altarpiece, 345; Crucifixion, 322;
  Orsanmichele tabernacle, 47, 327–8;
  Porta Romana, 335; stained-glass
  windows, 345
Orford, Countess of, 272–3, 277, 342

Orioli, G.F., 290
Orsanmichele, 327; Cosimo Pater Patriae,
  89; grain market, 46; statues, 89, 94, 343–
  4; tabernacle, 47, 327–8
Orsay, Comte d' (1801–52), 236
Orsay, Comtesse d', 284
Orsini, Clarice, 120–21, 123, 349
Orsini, Isabella, née Isabella di Cosimo de'
  Medici, 184
Orsini, Paolo Giordano, 184
Ospedale degli Innocenti, 79, 102, 120,
  338–9
Ouida (1819–1908), 277, 367

pageants, see festivities
Paget, Sir Augustus, 254
Palazzi (see also Palazzo Medici, Palazzo
  Pitti, Palazzo della Signoria and Palazzo
  Strozzi):
  degli Acciaiuoli, 48, 328; Alberti, 345;
  degli Albizzi, 340; dell'Antella, 349, 354;
  Arcivescovile, 318; dell'Arte della Lana,
  48, 63, 68, 326; dell'Arte dei Beccai, 326;
  dell'Arte della Seta, 317; Bardi alle Grazie,
  340; Bartolini-Salimbeni, 345; Bellini,
  191, 358; di Bianca Cappello, 357;
  Borghese, 237, 255, 365; Buondelmonti,
  239, 364; Canacci, 317; Capponi (later
  Capponi delle Rovinate), 71, 336;
  Capponi (Lungarno Guicciardini), 336;
  Capponi (Via Gino Capponi), 336, 363;
  Cerchi, 354; Corsi, 365; Corsini (Borgo
  S. Croce), 362; Corsini (Lungarno
  Corsini), 362; Corsini sul Prato, 218, 335,
  362; Corsini Suarez, 356; della Crocetta,
  365; Davanzati, 51–2, 53, 312, 335;
  Donati, 348; Ducale, 41; Feroni, 362;
  Ferranti, 92–3; Frescobaldi, 254, 320;
  Gagliano, 63; della Gherardesca, 358;
  Gianfigliazzi, 364; dei Giudici, 191, 359;
  Giugni, 184, 354; Gondi, 106–7, 347;
  Grifoni, 104, 345; Guadagni, 254, 366;
  Guicciardini, 341; Incontri, 360;
  Manetti, 210, 362; Masetti, 232, 233, 364;
  Neroni, 348; Nonfinito, 365; di Parte
  Guelfa, 48, 325; Pazzi (later Pazzi-
  Quaratesi), 106, 132, 346; Peruzzi, 316;
  del Podestà, 31, 41, 45; del Popolo, see
  Palazzo della Signoria; dei Pucci, 360;
  Rosselli del Turco, 340–41; Riccardi-
  Manelli, 345; Rucellai, 105, 106, 345;
  Salviati (Borgo Pinti), 352; Salviati (Via
  del Corso), 177, 352; Salviati-Quaratesi,
  352; di S. Clemente, 218, 363; Serristori
  (Lungarno Serristori), 224, 297, 364;
  Serristori (Piazza S. Croce), 364; Spinelli,
  345; Tornabuoni, 111; Torrigiani, 221,
  363, 364; Uguccioni, 186, 355;
  Usimbardi, 341; Vecchio, see Palazzo
  della Signoria

palazzine: Livia, 223, 364; della Meridiana,
  364
Palazzo Medici (later Medici-Riccardi), 87,
  342; Bennett on Chapel, 281; Captain-
  General holds court, 170; celebrations,
  180; Charles VIII, 155; construction, 87–
  8; Cosimo I, 184; Cosimo Pater Patriae,
  82, 87; demolition of houses for, 102;
  Donatello's works, 94; Gabbiani's work,
  212; Gauthier's headquarters, 227;
  Gozzoli's Procession of the Magi, 118, 119,
  120; Landor, 236; Filippo Lippi, 95;
  Medici Gallery, 362; Medici Library, 342;
  Michelangelo, 143, 144; ornamentation,
  88–9; Piero di Lorenzo, 153; Piero il
  Gottoso fortifies, 114; plundered, 154,
  179; police retreat into, 287;
  Risorgimento, 254; Sforza on, 88;
  wedding banquets, 123; works of art, 118
Palazzo Pitti (see also Boboli Gardens), 347–
  8; Accademia del Cimento, 194;
  Ammannati, 184; Baroque murals, 194;
  behaviour of guests, 241; callers
  encouraged, 223; ceremonies, 210;
  Cooper on, 240; Cosimo Pater Patriae
  and, 197; dinner for notable foreign
  visitors, 223; Eleonora di Toledo buys,
  185; Evelyn on, 197; Ferdinand III, 237,
  238; Ferdinando I's wedding
  celebrations, 189, 190; Ferdinando II,
  194; fountains of wine, 190; French
  Jacobin celebrations, 227–8; furniture,
  etc., returned to, 220; Gauthier and
  Reinhard, 227; Grand Duke Francis, 206;
  Grand Duke Gian Gastone, 204; Grand
  Duke Peter Leopold, 220; Grand Prince
  Ferdinando, 202; grandiosity, 107;
  improvements, 190; Medici treasures,
  194; museums, 348; Mussolini and
  Hitler, 292; Princess Anna Maria, 204;
  Princess Violante Beatrice, 202; Queen
  Regent entertains, 230; Risorgimento,
  250; sale of wine, 193; treasures in safe
  keeping, 295; Victor Emmanuel, 251;
  World War II, 300–301, 302
Palazzo della Signoria (Palazzo Vecchio),
  331–2; Augustus Hare on, 274–5; bell, 84,
  175–6; celebration for Pope Leo X, 169;
  Cosimo I lives in, 184; Cosimo Pater
  Patriae imprisoned, 83; Donatello's
  David, 94, 94; executions, 180;
  government, 253; Maria de' Medici's
  wedding banquet, 190; Mussolini and
  Hitler, 292; Palazzo del Popolo, 20, 22;
  palleschi meet after murder of Alessandro,
  177; Pazzi conspiracy, 134; and Piero di
  Lorenzo, 153; popolo minuto demonstrate,
  67–8; Quartiere di Eleonora di Toledo,
  354; riot against Gauthier, 61–2;
  rustication, 104; Sala del Maggior

Consiglio, 253, 283, **351**; Salone dei Cinquecento, 3, **351**; Savonarola imprisoned, 161; Stradano's fresco, 56; Studiolo di Francesco I, 188, **357**; Vasari's work, 188; works of art, 120, 173; World War II, 303

Palazzo Strozzi, 103, 263, **344–5**; building of, 102, 104, 157; emblems and insignia, 105; Evelyn on, 197; improved, 186; Lorenzo the Magnificent and, 145–6; stonework, 106

Palmer, Samuel (1805–81), *View of Florence*, 267

Palmieri, Matteo (1406–75), 105

Paoletti, Gaspare Maria (1727–1813), 221, 363, 364

Paolo da Certaldo, 46

Paolo Schiavo (1397–1478), 350

Papacy: disreputable pontiffs, 9; Florentine war against, 65, 67; and Medici bank, 80, 82

Papal States: Duchy of Urbino, 192; Gregory X and, 33; Hawkwood's White Company, 65; join Most Holy League, 100; Napoleon, 226; Risorgimento, 246; Sixtus IV and, 131; territory, 6

Parenti, Marco: on government of Cosimo *Pater Patriae*, 109; and Luca Pitti, 114; on support for Piero de' Medici, 113; Savonarola, 157; wife's trousseau, 53, 111–12; young men's dress, 127

Parigi, Alfonso the Elder (*fl.* 1590), 188, 334, 341, 355 *bis*

Parigi, Giulio (*d.* 1635), 341, 349, 355, 365

Parker, Theodore (1810–60), 368

Parmigiano (1503–40), 201

Parterre, Il, 293, **369**

Pasquini, Bernardo (1637–1710), 201

Passerini, Silvio, 171

Patch, Thomas (*d.* 1782), 210, 211

Pavolini, Alessandro, 287, 298, 304

Pazzi, Alamanno de', 224

Pazzi, Andrea de', 346

Pazzi, Enrico (1819–99), 326

Pazzi, Francesco de' (*d.* 1478), 131–2, 133–4, 135

Pazzi, Jacopo de' (*d.* 1478), 106, 133, 135

Pazzi, Renato de' (*d.* 1478), 135

Pazzi family, 105, 131–2, 133–5

Pazzo di Ranieri, 132

Peel, Hon. George, 272

Pension Suisse, 262, 263, **367**

Pepin III, the Short, King of the Franks (*d.* 768), 6

Peri, Jacopo (1561–1633), 190, 201

Persano, Pellion di, 256

Perugino (1446–1523), 334

Peruzzi, Ridolfo, 84

Peruzzi, Ubaldino, 254, 367

Peruzzi family, 25, 43, 61, 84

Peter Leopold, Grand Duke, later Leopold II, Holy Roman Emperor (1747–92): Cascine, 362; contribution to cost of Seven Years' War, 220; and Lady Cowper, 208, 209, 223; cultural activities, 221; leaves for Austria, 222–3; marriage, 207; politics, 222; popularity wanes, 224–5; and Raimondi, 223; social reform, 221, 222; La Specola, 363; succeeds, 207; in sympathy with Florence, 220

Peter Martyr, St (1205–52), 18, 353

Philibert, Prince of Orange (r. 1502–30), 174

Philip IV, the Fair, King of France (1268–1314), 33

Philip V, King of Spain (1683–1746), 204

Piazza S. Maria Novella, **353**; chariot races, 182, 275–6; *ciompi* riots, 68; Fascist parade, 287; Henry James, 266; Tree of Liberty, 227

Piazza S. Trinita, 209; Blacks and Whites fight, 33; celebration for Pope Leo X, 169; Column of Justice, 197, **318**; May Day, 127; Palazzo Buondelmonti, 239

Piazza della Signoria, 261, **330**; Bonfire of the Vanities, 157; cakes and wine, 196; *ciompi* demonstrate, 68; circuses, 127; conversion into piazza, 48; crowd listening to Mussolini, *289*; equestrian bronze of Cosimo I, 182, 354; execution of Savonarola, *162*, *163*; Fascist parade, 287; French flags, etc., burned, 229; French Jacobin celebrations, 228; Leo X, 169; masked balls, 206; Michelangelo's *David*, 253; Neptune Fountain, 184, 354; ordeal by fire, 160–61; *Parlamenti*, 61, 98; pro-Medici demonstration, 168; renamed, 186; Risorgimento march, 249; St John the Baptist's Day, 127; Tree of Liberty, 227, 228

Piazzale Michelangelo, **340**

Piazze (*see also* Piazza S. Maria Novella, Piazza S. Trinita *and* Piazza della Signoria): Antinori, 286; d'Azeglio, 253, 366; Beccaria, 237, 293, 363; del Duomo, 75, 127, 240, 274, *308*; dell'Indipendenza, **367**; della Libertà, 206, 293, **361**; del Limbo, **340**; Maria Antonia, 248, 262, 263; Ognissanti, 277; dell'Olio, 223, 224; Ottaviani, 285; Peruzzi, 3, 283, **316**; Pitti, 17, 238; della Repubblica, 2, 4, 56, 253, 258, **366**; SS. Annunziata, 79, 191, **358**; S. Croce, 120, 125, 127, 227, 307, **349**; S. Felice, 263; S. Gallo, 206; S. Giovanni, 7, *125*, 222, 308; S. Marco, 296, 303; S. Spirito, 17, 283

Piccardini, Rustico, 195

Piccini-Risalti, Albertina, 305, 307

Piccinino, Niccolò (1386–1444), 70

Pico della Mirandola, Giovanni (1463–94), 142, 149

Piedmont, 65, 246, 247, 248, 251

Pieraccini, Gaetano, 296

Piero della Francesca (1416–92), 120

pietre dure, 194

Pietro da Cortona (1596–1669), 194

Pinsent, Cecil, 368

Piozzi, Hester Lynch (1741–1821), 210

Pisa: Faggiuola, 40; Florence and, 17, 20, 21, 160, 164; Florence takes, 69, 73; French occupation, 154; Galileo, 191; and Guelphs, 23; University, 147, 182, 191, 199; World War II, 302

Pisano, Andrea (*c.* 1270–1349): Baptistery doors, 49, 308, 335; bas-relief panels, *29*; *capomaestro*, 49, 330; Porta San Frediano, 335

Pissaro, Camille (1830–1903), 348

Pitti, Luca: calls for *Parlamento*, 98; Cosimo *Pater Patriae* and, 84; in isolation, 114–15; makes fortune, 97; and Milanese alliance, 110; Palazzo Pitti, 107, 347, personality, 107; and Piero de' Medici, 114

Pitti family, 129

Pius II, Pope (r. 1458–64), 97, 100, 108

Pius III, Pope (r. September–October 1503), 165

Pius IV, Pope (r. 1559–65), 318

Pius VII, Pope (r. 1800–1823), 231

Pius IX, Pope (r. 1846–78), 242, 245, 256

plague: Baptistery north doors, 76; Black Death, 58–60; depletes servant population, 51; Ferdinand II, 193; fifteenth-century outbreaks, 137, 160; outbreak in 1630s, 193; Villani on, 47

Plasters, Joyce, 312

Plethon, Giorgios Gemistos (*c.* 1355–1450), 93

Poccetti, Bernardino (1548–1612), 318, 324, 336 *bis*, 346

Poccianti, Pasquale (1774–1858), 365

Poggi, Giuseppe (1811–1901), 252, 347, 369

Poliziano, Angelo (1454–94), 142; Botticelli's *Adoration of the Magi*, 349; in Ghirlandaio's fresco, 350; lecturer, 146; Lorenzo the Magnificent and, 147, 149; poet, 125

Pollaiuolo, Antonio (*c.* 1432–98), 116, 118 *bis*, 143, 338, 340

Pollaiuolo, Piero (1443–96), 118, 331

Pollaiuolo, Simone del, *called* Cronaca (1457–1508): *palazzi*, 103, 344, 365, 366; S. Salvatore al Monte, 314, 340; S. Spirito vestibule, 322; tomb, 328

Ponte S. Trinita, 49, *306*, **320**; Ammannati, 184; demolished, 300; flood, 305; Frescobaldi, 14; Leo X, 169; rebuilt, 304; statues, 299

Ponte Vecchio, 49, 274, 301, **319–20**;

Boswell, 214; date, 14; fire, 45; flood, 305; horse-drawn traffic, 281; rebuilt, 50; World War II, 300

Ponti (*see also* Ponte Santa Trinita *and* Ponte Vecchio):
alla Carraia, 14, 46, *49*, 184, **320**; alle Grazie, 14, *49*, 217, 300, 305, **320**; Rubaconte, 14; S. Niccolò, 304; Sospeso, 286, 293; alla Vittoria, 304

Pontormo, Jacopo Carucci da (1494–1556): altarpiece, 360; frescoes, 317, 334; lunette, 347; portrait of Cosimo *Pater Patriae*, *81*, 358; tomb of, 334; works in S. Felicita, 317

Pope-Hennessy, Sir John (b. 1913), 310–11

population: after transfer of capital to Rome, 258–9; after unification, 252; Britons in Tuscany, 288; by 1170s, 17; by end of thirteenth century, 23; decline, 4; fifteenth-century, 100; increases, 13, 63; late-nineteenth-century, 259; plague reduces, 59; Villani's account, 50

Porcellino, Il, 186, 355

Porte:
alla Croce, 127, 237; alla Giustizia, 175; al Prato, 127, 204, 221, 286, **335**; Romana, 40, 169, 269, **335**; Rossa, 2, 74, 258, **315**; S. Frediano, 154, **335**; S. Gallo, 114, 202, 206, 227, 249, **335**; S. Giorgio, **335**; S. Miniato, **335**; di S. Pier Gattolini, 82; di S. Piero, 36; delle Suppliche, 356–7

Portigiani, Pagno di Lapo (1407–60), 349

Portinari, Beatrice (d. 1290), 36, 79

Portinari, Folco, 79

Portinari family, 83, 352

Porto Pisano, 69, 73, 91

power: electricity, 259; gas, 240; steam, 259

prisons: S. Teresa, 309; Stinche, 199, 240, **351–2**

Procacci, Ugo, 300–301, 312

prostitutes, 57, 199, 200

Pucci, Antonio (*fl.* 14th century), 57–8

Pucci, Puccio, 57, 97

Pucci family, 360

Pulci, Luigi (1432–84), 125, 142, 157, 350

Quercia, Jacopo della (*c.* 1378–1442), 76

Radetzky, Joseph (1766–1858), 244

railway, 239–40, 259, 289, **369**

Raimondi, Livia, 223

Raphael (1483–1520), 201, 348

Rattazzi, Urbano (1808–73), 254

Reinhard, Charles, 227

religious orders (*see also* Dominicans): Benedictines, 314; Camaldolese, 79; Carmelites, 49, 94; Franciscans, 17, 18, 159, 160–61, 333; Jesuits, 191, 222; Laudesi, 47, **327**; Servites, 49;

Sylvestrines, 350; Umiliati, 49, 333

Resistance, 297, 298

Return from the Palio, 126

Reynolds, Sir Joshua (1723–92), 212

Riario, Girolamo (d. 1488), 131, 139

Ricasoli, Bettino (1809–80), 243–4, *244*, 253, 367

Riccardi, Riccardo, 363

Riccardi family, 87, 217

Ricci, Renato, 287

Ricci, Sebastiano (1659–1734), 202

Ricci, Stefano (1765–1837), 327, 359

Richecourt, Emmanuel de, 206

Ridolfi, Cosimo, 249, 322

Ridolfi, Luigi, 287

Ridolfi, Niccolò, 171

Ridolfi, Piero, 169

Rinascimento, 83, 102

Rinuccini, Eleonora Corsina, 254

riots, 68, 224

Risorgimento, 238, 244, 246

Robbia, *see* della Robbia

Robert I, King of Naples (1277–1343), 41

Romagnoli, Ferdinando, 265

Roman Empire, 4, 5, 6

Roman Republic, 2–4

Romanelli, Raffaelo, 320, 322, 367

Rome: capital city, 256; Fascist march on, 287; Galileo, 191; Murat, 231; Mussolini heads new government, 287; Quirinal, 256, 257; Risorgimento, 246; sack of, 171

Romuald, St (*c.*950–1027), 7, 9

Romulus Augustulus, Roman Emperor (5th century AD), 5

Rosa, Salvator (1615–73), 194

Rosellini, Ippolito (1800–1843), 365

Ross, Henry, 268, 367

Ross, Janet, 268, 276, 277, 284, 367

Rosselli, Carlo, 288

Rosselli, Cosimo (1439–1507), 321 *bis*, 328, 334

Rossellino, Antonio (1427–79), 314, 322, 357

Rossellino, Bernardo (1409–64): Cardinal Lusitania's tomb, 314; loggia, 318; Medici monument, 334; Palazzo Rucellai, 345; sarcophagus, 336; tabernacle, 339; tomb of Bruni, 365

Rossi, Roberto de', 37

Rossini, Gioacchino (1792–1868), 365

Rosso, Francesco Zanobi del (1724–98), 221, 227, 347, 355 *bis*

Rosso, Marco del, 224

Roster, Giacomo, 366

Rovere, Francesco Maria I della, Duke of Urbino (1490–1538), 166

Rovezzano, Benedetto da (1474–*c.* 1554): altarpieces and reliefs, 327; apostle statue, 329; Palazzo di Oddo Altoviti, 340;

portals, 317–18, 349; tomb of Oddo Altoviti, 350

Rubaconte da Mandello, 23

Rubinstein, Nicolai, 310

Rucellai, Bernardo (1449–1514), 122, 323, 346

Rucellai, Giovanni, 105, 106 *bis*, 323, 345, 346

Rucellai, Giulio, 220

Rucellai family, 105, 323

Rudolf I of Habsburg, German King (1218–91), 33

Ruggieri, Ferdinando (*c.* 1691–1741), 317, 347, 362

Ruskin, John (1819–1900), 274, 341

Russell, Odo, *later* 1st Baron Ampthill (1829–84), 247

Russell, Lord William, 234

Rustici, Giovan Francesco (1475–1554), 337

Salvemini, Gaetano, 287

Salviati, Francesco, Archbishop of Pisa (d. 1478), 133, 134–5

Salviati, Francesco, painter (1510–63), 354

Salviati, Jacopo, 169, 332, 352

Salviati, Maria, *later* Maria de' Medici, 177, 185

S. Croce, church of, **322–3**; Alfieri's memorial, 233; *borse*, 41; Castellani Chapel, **365**; Cosimo *Pater Patriae*, 89; Countess of Albany, 234; date, 17; drawing of façade, *282*; flood, 308, 311; Foscolo's burial place, 234; Galileo's tomb, 192; Michelangelo's tomb, 188, 192; Noviziata, 87, **342**; Pazzi Chapel, 106, 132, 311, **346**; Pazzi Chapel roundels, *133*; Peruzzi Chapel, 316; rebuilt, 48; shrine to Fascist dead, 292

S. Firenze, **347**

S. Giovanni di Dio, hospital of, 308

S. Lorenzo, church of; 17, 78–9, *85*, **337**; Biblioteca Laurenziana, 173, 221, **342–3**, 352, 363; Cappella dei Principi, 194, 199, 205, **360–61**; Donatello's pulpits, 94; Medici and, 78–9, 84, 86; Medici tombs, 108, 128; Michelangelo in hiding, 175; Michelangelo's statues, 181; New Sacristy (Medici Chapel), 173, 175, **352**; Old Sacristy, 74, 78, 79, 128, **337**; reconstruction, 78–9; St Ambrose, 6

S. Marco, church and convent of, **350–51**; Cosimo *Pater Patriae*, 86, 89, 96; Dominicans expelled, 180; *Dream of Emperor Justinian*, 74; fighting, 161; Fra Angelico, 96; Medici library treasures, 154; Michelozzo, 87; Savonarola, 150, 155, 161

S. Maria del Fiore, *see* Duomo

S. Maria Novella, church of, 18, 49, **323–5**;

Albizzi summoned to, 84; Bardi Chapel, **339–40**; Botticelli's *Adoration of the Magi*, 118, 119, *119*; Cappella di Filippo Strozzi, **345**; Cappella Maggiore, **348**; Cappella Rucellai, 105, **345–6**; Cappella Strozzi, **345**; Chiostrino dei Morti, **367**; Dominicans, 18; executions in front of, 304; façade, 105; flood, 311; frescoes, *44*, *45*, *142*; Gaddi Chapel, **323–4**; Gondi Chapel, **347**; papal apartments, 82, 91, 93; rebuilt, 48; Uccello's work in Chiostre Verde, 115

S. Maria Nuova, hospital of, 79, 221, 339

S. Miniato al Monte, church of, *xviii*, **314**; capitals, 1, 4; Giovanni Gualberto, 8–9; position, 1; protection of belfry, 174; tabernacle, 128, 349

S. Spirito, church of, 17, **321–2**; Dei Chapel, 366; dinner for stonecutters, 63; Evelyn impressed, 197; Lorenzo the Magnificent and, 145; payments in kind, 102; sermon against blasphemy, 200

S. Trinita, church of, **318**; Bartolini-Salimbeni Chapel, **318**; Fra Angelico's *Deposition*, 96; Giovanni Gualberto founds, 9, 318; miraculous crucifix, 314; Sassetti Chapel, 141, **350**; Strozzi Chapel, 87, 93, **341**

Sangallo, Antonio da, the Elder (1455–1537), 14, 15, 334, 358

Sangallo, Antonio da, the Younger (1483–1546), 352

Sangallo, Francesco da (1494–1576), 328, 334

Sangallo, Giuliano da (1445?–1516): cloister, 346; *palazzi*, 103, 106, 346, 347, 349, 358, 364; Poggio a Caiano, 347; Villa Careggi, 344

sanitation, 47, 52

Sansovino, Andrea (*c.*1460–1529), 76, 321, 347; *Baptism of Christ*, 77

Sansovino, Jacopo (1486–1570), 169, 329

Santarelli, Emilio, 365

Santi di Tito (1538–1603), 323, 356, 366

Santo, Santi di, 328

Sargent, John Singer (1856–1925), 269–70; *Ladies in a Garden*, *278*; portrait of Henry James, *266*

Sassetti, Francesco, 114, 141, 326, 350

Savonarola, Girolamo (1452–98), *151*; Alexander VI and, 159; asceticism, 150; challenged to ordeal by fire, 160; condemned to death, 161; execution, *162*, *163*, 354; fanatical preacher, 149, 150–52, 156, 160; opponents, 157–8; and Piero di Lorenzo, 153; portrait, 344, 351; supporters, 157; supports Charles VIII, 154, 159

Scamozzi, Vincenzo (1552–1616), 365

Scarlatti, Alessandro (1660–1725), 201

Schumann, Clara (1819–96), 279

Scott Moncrieff, C.K. (1889–1930), 291

Segaloni, Matteo (*fl.* 1627), 317

Serristori, Antonio, 224

Sforza, Battista, 349

Sforza, Francesco, Duke of Milan (1401–6): Cosimo *Pater Patriae* and, 98–9, 141; death, 110; and Duchy of Milan, 98, 100; history, 70; unusual behaviour, 122–3; at war with Florence, 71

Sforza, Galeazzo Maria, later Duke of Milan (1444–76), 88, 110, 137

Sforza, Gian Galeazzo (1469–94), 88, 152

Sforza, Ludovico, 'il Moro' (1451–1508), 137, 141, 152, 158

Shelley, Percy Bysshe (1792–1822), 239, 270, 362, 365

Siena: battle of Montaperti, 21–2; Boswell, 214; Cosimo I master of, 180; Florence and, 15, 20, 136; and Florentine/Luccan war, 71; and Guelphs, 23; liberated and pillaged, 229; Palazzo Pubblico frescoes, 16; Visconti gains control, 69

Signorini, Telemaco, 256; Mercato Vecchio, *255*

Silsbee, Edward Augustus, 270

Silvani, Gherardo (1579–*c.* 1675): *palazzi*, 218, 315, 356; S. Filippo Neri, 347; S. Gaetano façade, 316, 362

Silvani, Pier Francesco (1620–85), 316, 335, 347, 351, 362

Silvestri, Bartolomeo, 359

Simonde de Sismondi, Jean-Charles-Léonard (1773–1843), 233

Sisini, Clemente, 364

Sitwell, Sir George (1860–1943), 295, 369

Sitwell, Lady Ida, 291, 295

Sitwell, Sir Osbert (1892–1969), 291, 295

Sixtus IV, Pope (r. 1471–84), 129, 131, 133, 136, 139

slavery, 51, 112

Sloane, Francis, 322

Smibert, John (1684–1751), 277

Smollett, Tobias (1721–71), 210, 212–14

Soderini, Niccolò, 109–10, 114

Soderini, Piero (*c.* 1450–1513), 164–5, 167, 168

Soderini family, 42, 109, 129

Soggi, Niccolò (*c.* 1480–1552), 326

Sogliani, Giovanni Antonio (1491–1544), 351

Specola, La, 221, **363–4**

Spence, Joseph (1699–1768), 216

Spence, William Blundell, 342

Spender, A.F., 288

Spinazzi, Innocenzo (d. 1798), 359

Spini, Geri degli, 315

Spini family, 80, 82

Squarcialupi, Antonio (d. *c.* 1475), 142

Stadio Comunale, 293, **369**

Staël, Madame de (1766–1817), 233

Starke, Mariana (1762?–1838), 215

Stazione Centrale S. Maria Novella, 239–40, **369**

Steinhauslin, Karl, 299

Stendhal (1783–1842), 234, 366

Stephen II (III), Pope (r. 752–7), 6

Stewart, Hon. Keith (1739–95), 209

Stibbert, Frederick (1838–1906), 255, 364

Stilicho, Flavius (*c.*365–408), 5

Stinche, 199, 240, **351–2**

Stone, Nicholas the Younger (d. 1647), 196

Stowe, Harriet Beecher (1811–96), 265

Strangeways, Lord, 236

Strauss, Richard (1864–1949), 279

Strozzi, Caterina, 53

Strozzi, Filippo the Elder (1428–91), 104; and Lorenzo the Magnificent, 146; Palazzo Strozzi, 103, 105, 145–6; tomb, 345; wealth, 104; wife, 122

Strozzi, Marietta, 127

Strozzi, Palla (1372–1462), 84

Strozzi, Zanobi (1412–68), 344

Strozzi family: banished, 84; banking, 25; library, 221; palace, 186; Poggio a Caiano, 347; *priori*, 42; Rucellai and, 106

Stuart, Charlotte, Duchess of Albany (1753–90), 219

Studio Fiorentino, 79, 86, 182, **339**

Stufa, Marchese della, 277, 367

Susini, Giovanni Francesco (d. 1646), 316

Sustermans, Justus (1597–1681), 192; portrait of Prince Ferdinando, *203*

Swinburne, Algernon Charles (1837–1909), 260, 341

Tacca, Ferdinando (1616/19–86): gilt bronzes of Grand Dukes, 361; Palazzo Corsini, 362; S. Stefano al Ponte, 326, 341; Teatro della Pergola, 359; theatre sets and scenery, 194

Tacca, Pietro (1577–1640): *Abundance*, 355; burial place, 334; *Dovizia*, 336; dwelling place, 358; gilt bronzes of Grand Dukes, 361; plinth, 358

Tadda, Francesco del (1497–1585), 318

Talenti, Francesco (14th century), 327, 328, 330

Talenti, Jacopo (d. 1362), 323, 324

Talenti, Simone (14th century), 327, 332

Tamburini, Tullio, 286, 287

Targioni-Tozzetti, Fanny, 239

Tasso, Giovanni Battista del (1500–after 1556), 186

taxation: *catasto*, 70; *Cento*, 98; and critics of Medici party, 97; *gabella*, 60, 102; under Gauthier, 61; under Grand Duke Francesco, 207; increasing, 201; reduced under Gian Gastone, 202

Tchaikovsky, Piotr Ilyich (1840–93), 359

Tedesco, Piero di Giovanni (*fl.* 1386–1402), 328

Temple, Reginald, 290

Tennyson, Alfred Tennyson, 1st Baron (1809–92), 369

Ternan, Fanny, 262–3

Ternan, Nelly, 262, 263

Thackeray, William Makepeace (1811–63), 260

Theatres
Cocomero, 216, 249; Comunale, 297, **369**; Pagliano, 240; Pergola, 216, 237, 257, 283, 285, **359**; Verdi, 283, 298, 351

Theodoric the Great, Ostrogoth King of Italy (*c.* 454–526), 5

Tilney of Castlemaine, 2nd Earl, 208

Tino di Camaino (*c.* 1285–1338), 322, 328

Titian (d. 1576), 182

Tommaseo, Niccolò, 255

Tommasi, Marcello, 361

Tornabuoni, Giovanni di Francesco, 114, 149, 348

Tornabuoni, Lucrezia (wife of Piero de' Medici), 111, 113, 348

Torri:
degli Alberti di Catenaia, **318–19**; Baldovinetti, **319**; della Castagna, **319**; Cerchi, **319**; Compiobbesi, **319**; dei Donati, 14, **319**; del Gallo, 278; Greci, **319**; *il Guardamorto*, 20; Marsili di Borgo, **319**

Torricelli, Antonio, bust of Vittoria della Rovere, *193*

Torrigiani, Lulie, 288

Torrigiani, Pietro (1472–1528), 144

Toscanelli, Paolo (1397–1482), 142

Toye, Francis, 288

Traversi, Ambrogio, 79, 83

Trefusis, Violet (d. 1973), 369

Treves, Marco, 364

Tribolo, Niccolò (1500–1550), 352, 357, 366

Trivulzio, Gian Giacomo (*c.* 1441–1518), 137

Trollope, Anthony (1815–82), 262, 263

Trollope, Frances (1780–1863), 262, 367

Trollope, Theodosia (1825–65), 262

Trollope, Thomas Adolphus (1810–92), 241, 262

Troubridge, Lady Una, 292

Turner, Reginald, 290

Tuscany: anti-French uprisings, 229; client state of France, 230; constitution granted, 243; France invades, 227; Hawkwood's White Company, 65; Risorgimento, 246, 250; threats to independence, 238–9

Twain, Mark (1835–1910), 265

Uberti, Farinata degli, 20, 21

Uberti family, 18–19, 49

Ubertini, Francesco (1494–1557), 55; Florentine street scene, *54*

Uccello (1397–1475): cenotaph of Hawkwood, *66*, 336; frescoes, 324; history and personality, 115–16; *Rout of San Romano*, 349; works in Duomo, 328 *tre*

Uffizi, **356–7**; architect, 186; church demolished for, 49; collection augmented, 190; flood, 308; Gibbon, 216; Grand Duke Francis, 206; paintings in, *54*, *55*, *81*, *119*, *183*; under Peter Leopold, 221; Queen Victoria, 272; Sala della Niobe, **363**; senators, 253–4; statues, 240; theatre, 190; treasures in safe keeping, 295; Tribuna, 189, 209, **357–8**, 361–2; Vasari, 186

Ugo, Margrave of Tuscany, 7–8

Uguccioni, Giovanni, 356

University of Florence, 146

Utens, Giusto, 81, 365

Uzzano, Niccolò da, 83, 84, 336

Valta, A.R., 367

Vannini, Ottavio: portrait of Lorenzo il Magnifico, *111*

Vanvitelli, Gaspare (1653–1736), *View of Florence, 194–5*

Varchi, Benedetto, 174

Vasari, Giorgio (1511–74): altarpieces, 322, 334, 340, 350; balcony, 326; Biblioteca Laurenziana, 352; Casa Mori, 345; Cathedral dome, 91; choir stalls, 348; Corridoio Vasariano, 320, 347; Etruscan *Chimera*, 365; *Foundation of Florence, 3*; fresco, 328; history and works, 187–8; niches, 354; Palazzo del Circolo dell'Unione, 315; portrait of Lorenzo il Magnifico, *140*; quoted on artists, 48, 89–90, 94, 115, 116, 143–4, 164, 357; S. Croce, 322 *bis*; self-portrait, *187*, 334; Studiolo di Francesco I, 357; Uffizi, 186, 356; *Way to Calvary*, 359; works in Signoria, 332 *bis*

Vatican, 169, 256

Vaughan-Thomas, Wynford (1908–87), 299–300, 302

Veneziano, Domenico (d. 1461), 115, 323, 340

Venice: Cosimo *Peter Patriae* in, 83; and Duchy of Milan, 98; and Florence, 70, 99; Holy League, 100, 158; Julius II and, 166; Victor Emmanuel acquires, 256

Verdi, Giuseppe (1813–1901), 257

Verrocchio, Andrea del (1435–88): altarpiece, 321; bust of St Antonio, 326; Cathedral façade, 146; commissions for Villa Careggi, 344; *Doubting Thomas*, 343; Duomo ball and cross, 328; helmet, 125; Medici tombs, 108, 128, 337; *Putto with

Dolphin, 332; tomb of, 328; wax figures of Lorenzo the Magnificent, 135

Vespucci, Amerigo (1451–1512), 326

Vespucci, Giorgio, 157

Vespucci, Marco, 119

Vespucci, Simonetta, 349

Vespucci family, 118, 333

Vettori, Francesco, 179, 180

Victor Emmanuel II of Piedmont, first King of Italy (1820–78): appearance and personality, 250–51; daily routine, 251–2; Quirinal, 256–7; Risorgimento, 238, 246, 247, 250; succeeds, 244; throne of Naples, 256

Victor Emmanuel III, King of Italy (1869–1947), 247 *bis*, 366

Victoria, Queen, (1819–1910), 271–2, *273*

Vie:
de' Bardi, 71, 82; Benedetto Varchi, 296; Bologna, 296; Bolognese, 249; Bufalini, 76; Calimala, 4, 27, **317**; Calzaiuoli, 216, 240, 259, 367; del Campidoglio, 4, **317**; del Campuccio, 252; Capaccio, 4; Cassia, 3; Cavour, *see* Larga; dei Cerchi, 184, 260; de' Cerretani, 2, 258, 259, **315**; del Cocomero, 194; della Colonna, 366; della Condotta, 2, **315**; del Corso, 127, 177, 213; della Fornace, 105; Garibaldi, 269; Ghibellina, 237, 311, **318**; Gino Capponi, 218; de' Gori, 86, 88; Guelfa, **318**; Guicciardini, 84, 300, 307; Larga (Cavour), 75, 86, 88, *124*, 168, 169, 255; Leone X, 278; Magenta, 269; Maggio, 169, 186, 206, 240, **356**; Manzoni, 310; Nunziatina, 260; de' Panzani, 258; del Parione, 315; della Pergola, 194; Por S. Maria, 27, 216, 300, **326**; del Proconsolo, 2, 106, 132, **316**; Ricasoli, **360**; Romana, 270; di S. Giuseppe, 262; S. Spirito, 210; de' Serragli, 269, 284; Strozzi, 103, *263*; delle Terme, 4, **317**; del Tornabuoni, 2, 103, 245, 258, 259, 283–4, **315**; della Vigna Nuova, 105, 127

Vieusseux, Gian Pietro (d. 1863), 239, 364, 367

Villani, Giovanni (1275–1348): battle of Montaperti, 21, 22; city walls, 50; chronicles of Florence, 18, 43, 45–6, 47, 48, 61–2, 363; death, 58; dress, 53; history, 43; hospitals, churches, houses, 50; meat, 55; survey of Florence, 50–51

Villani, Matteo (d. 1363), 60, 64

Villari, Pasquale (1826–1917), 254

Villas:
Belcanto (Medici), 87, **342**; Brichieri-Colombi, 367; Cafaggiolo, 67, *81*, 87, 141, **342**; Careggi, 108, 113, 121, 128, 141, 188, 343, **344**; Castagnolo, 268, **367**; di Castello, 188, 238, **357**; La Colombaia, 367; Corsi, 206; Demidoff, **368**;

Fabricotti, 272, **368**; Favard, 369; at Fiesole, 141; Le Fontanelle, 94; Lapeggi, 202; Mirenda, **368**; Medici, *see* Belcanto *above*; dell'Ombrellino, 291, **369**; Pagani, 367; Palmieri, 208, 272, **361**; della Petraia, 251, **366**; La Pietra, 291, **369**; Poggio a Caiano, 106, 121, 141, 199, **347**; Poggio Imperiale, 208, 237, **361**, **365**; Pratolino, 182, 188, 201, **357**; Ricorboli, 262, 263; I Tatti, 290, **368**; Torrigiani, 304, **369**; Il Trebbio, 342
Villino Trollope, 262, 263, **367**
Violante Beatrice of Bavaria, Princess, 202
Visconti, Bianca, 70
Visconti, Filippo Maria, 3rd Duke of Milan (1391–1447), 70–71, 98
Visconti, Gabriele Maria, Lord of Milan (d. 1408), 69
Visconti, Gian Galeazzo, 1st Duke of Milan and Count of Pavia (1347–1402), 69
Visconti-Venosta, Emilio (1829–1914), 254
Vitelli, Alessandro, 177, 178

Vitelli, Paglio, 164
Vittoria, Grand Duchess, *née* Vittoria della Rovere, 192, *193*
Volterrano (1611–89), 334, 366

wages, 59, 63
Wagner, Richard (1818–83), 279
Wallmoden, Johann Ludwig, Baron von, 208
Walpole, Horace (*later* 4th Earl of Orford; 1717–97), 209, 210, 215, 362
Walpole, Hugh (1884–1941), 291
Waterfield, Lina, 284, 288
West, Benjamin (1738–1820), 277
West, Dame Rebecca (1892–1983), 291
White, Jessie, 251, 366, 367
Wilde, Oscar (1854–1900), 273–4
Wilkes, John (1727–97), 210
Wilson, Elizabeth, 265
Wilton, Joseph (1722–1803), 212
Wincklemann, Johann (1717–68), 278
Wolff, Gerhard, 296
women in Middle Ages, 111–13
Woolson, Constance Fenimore (1840–94),

266–8
World War II: Allied advance, 298; Allies in Florence, 301–4; bridges, 298, 300, 304; Germans in Florence, 296, 298; Hortense Acton interned, 294; illusion of normality, 297, 298; protection of city's treasures, 294–5, 299–300; recovery, 304; rejoicing as Germans withdraw, 303; Resistance, 297, 298
Woronzoff, Princess, 278
Wotton, Sir Henry (1568–1639), 196
Wyndham, Hon. William Frederick, 229

York and Albany, Duke of (1763–1827), 210
Young, Arthur (1741–1820), 217

Zenobius, St (d. 433), 6–7
Zenobius, St, Column of, **317**
Zocchi, Giuseppe, 219; Palazzo Medici, *87*; Piazza S. Trinita, *209*; *View of Florence*, 217
Zoffany, John (1733–1810), 209, 361–2
Zuccari, Federigo (1542–1609), 328, 358